HUMAN
RIGHTS
WATCH
WORLD
REPORT
1997

■ Featured in World Report 1997

■ Featured in World Report 1997

HUMAN RIGHTS WATCH WORLD REPORT 1997

Events of 1996

New York • Washington • London • Brussels

ISBN 1-56432-207-6
ISSN 1054-948X

Human Rights Watch
485 Fifth Avenue
New York, NY 10017-6104
Tel: (212) 972-8400
Fax: (212) 972-0905
E-mail: hrwnyc@hrw.org

Human Rights Watch
1522 K Street, NW, #910
Washington, DC 20005-1202
Tel: (202) 371-6592
Fax: (202) 371-0124
E-mail: hrwdc@hrw.org

Human Rights Watch
33 Islington High Street
N1 9LH London
United Kingdom
Tel: (44171) 713-1995
Fax: (44171) 713-1800
E-mail: hrwatchuk@gn.apc.org

Human Rights Watch
15 Rue Van Campenhout
1000 Brussels, Belgium
Tel: (322) 732-2009
Fax: (322) 732-0471
E-mail: hrwatcheu@gn.apc.org

Website Address: http://www.hrw.org
Gopher Address: gopher://gopher.humanrights.org:5000/11/int/hrw
Listserv address: To subscribe to the list, send an e-mail message to
majordomo@igc.apc.org with "subscribe hrw-news" in the body of the
message (leave the subject line blank).

HUMAN RIGHTS WATCH

Human Rights Watch conducts regular, systematic investigations of human rights abuses in some seventy countries around the world. Our reputation for timely, reliable disclosures has made us an essential source of information for those concerned with human rights. We address the human rights practices of governments of all political stripes, of all geopolitical alignments, and of all ethnic and religious persuasions. Human Rights Watch defends freedom of thought and expression, due process and equal protection of the law, and a vigorous civil society; we document and denounce murders, disappearances, torture, arbitrary imprisonment, discrimination, and other abuses of internationally recognized human rights. Our goal is to hold governments accountable if they transgress the rights of their people.

Human Rights Watch began in 1978 with the founding of its Helsinki division. Today, it includes five divisions covering Africa, the Americas, Asia, the Middle East, as well as the signatories of the Helsinki accords. It also includes three collaborative projects on arms transfers, children's rights, and women's rights. It maintains offices in New York, Washington, Los Angeles, London, Brussels, Moscow, Dushanbe, Rio de Janeiro, and Hong Kong. Human Rights Watch is an independent, nongovernmental organization, supported by contributions from private individuals and foundations worldwide. It accepts no government funds, directly or indirectly.

The staff includes Kenneth Roth, executive director; Michele Alexander, development director; Cynthia Brown, program director; Holly J. Burkhalter, advocacy director; Barbara Guglielmo, finance and administration director; Robert Kimzey, publications director; Jeri Laber, special advisor; Lotte Leicht, Brussels office director; Susan Osnos, communications director; Dinah PoKempner, acting general counsel; Jemera Rone, counsel; and Joanna Weschler, United Nations representative.

The regional directors of Human Rights Watch are Peter Takirambudde, Africa; José Miguel Vivanco, Americas; Sidney Jones, Asia; Holly Cartner, Helsinki; and Eric Goldstein, Middle East (acting). The project directors are Joost R. Hiltermann, Arms Project; Lois Whitman, Children's Rights Project; and Dorothy Q. Thomas, Women's Rights Project.

The members of the board of directors are Robert L. Bernstein, chair; Adrian W. DeWind, vice chair; Roland Algrant, Lisa Anderson, William Carmichael, Dorothy Cullman, Gina Despres, Irene Diamond, Edith Everett, Jonathan Fanton, James C. Goodale, Jack Greenberg, Vartan Gregorian, Alice H. Henkin, Stephen L. Kass, Marina Pinto Kaufman, Bruce Klatsky, Harold Hongju Koh, Alexander MacGregor, Josh Mailman, Samuel K. Murumba, Andrew Nathan, Jane Olson, Peter Osnos, Kathleen Peratis, Bruce Rabb, Sigrid Rausing, Anita Roddick, Orville Schell, Sid Sheinberg, Gary G. Sick, Malcolm Smith, Domna Stanton, Nahid Toubia, Maureen White, Rosalind C. Whitehead, and Maya Wiley.

ACKNOWLEDGMENTS

A compilation of this magnitude requires contribution from a large number of people, including most of the Human Rights staff. The contributors were:

Gamal Abouali, Fred Abrahams, Donna Arzt, Marcia Allina, Suliman Baldo, Jennifer Bailey, Luis Jesus Bello, Vince Beiser, Roya Boroumand, Sebastian Brett, Cynthia Brown, Samya Burney, Bruni Bures, Holly Cartner, Sheila Carapico, Jim Cavallaro, Allyson Collins, Erika Dailey, Sarah DeCosse, Rachel Denber, Alison DesForges, Richard Dicker, Panayote Dimitros, Jamie Fellner, Janet Fleischman, Gustavo Gallón, Beatriz Galli, Arvind Ganesan, Eric Goldstein, Stephen Goose, Patricia Gossman, Rachel Guglielmo, Jeanine Guthrie, Malcolm Hawkes, Julia Hall, Steve Hernández, Sinsi Hernández-Cancio, Elahé Hicks, Joost Hiltermann, Ernst Jan Hogendoorn, LaShawn Jefferson, Mike Jendrzejczyk, Sidney Jones, Robin Kirk, Jeri Laber, Paul Lall, Robin Levi, Zunetta Liddel, Timothy Longman, Ivan Lupis, Bronwen Manby, Anne Manuel, Joanne Mariner, Maxine Marcus, Kerry McArthur, Michael McClintock, Evelyn Miah, Anna Monteiro, Lynette Munez, Robin Munro, Binaifer Nowrojee, Martin O'Brien, Laura Palmer, Heather Patton, Diane Paul, Paul Paz y Miño, Christopher Panico, Susan Peacock, Ariana Pearlroth, Ann Peters, Alexander Petrov, Dinah PoKemper, Regan Ralph, Shira Robinson, Alina Rocha Menocal, Jemera Rone, Ken Roth, Steven Rothman, Houeida Saad, Awali Samara, Mina Samuels, Karen Sorensen, Sara Scalenghe, Emily Shaw, Jennifer Schense, Virginia N. Sherry, Milbert Shin, Joel Solomon, Mickey Spiegel, Joe Stork, Peter Takirambudde, Dorothy Thomas, Yodon Thonden, Lee Tucker, Alex Vines, José Miguel Vivanco, Tim Waters, Marti Weithman, Lois Whitman, Joyce Wan, and Fatemeh Ziai.

Cynthia Brown, Michael McClintock, and Jeri Laber edited the report, with editing and production assistance by Sahr MuhammedAlly. Various sections were reviewed by Holly Burkhalter, Lotte Leicht, Dinah Pokempner, and Joanna Weschler. Robert Kimzey, Sahr MuhammedAlly, Susan Osnos and Elizabeth Reynoso proofread the report.

CONTENTS

HUMAN RIGHTS WATCH

INTRODUCTION

While the major global powers wavered in their commitment to human rights, 1996 saw the emergence of new and powerful sources of support for the human rights cause. The major powers repeatedly deferred the immediate promotion of human rights in the name of often dubious long-term strategies. They allowed their quest for trade and investment opportunities to weaken their opposition to human rights abuse. And by failing to arrest serious human rights abusers for trial, they risked squandering the first opportunity in nearly fifty years to promote an international system of justice.

Yet pressure to counter these disturbing trends built from various quarters. A wide variety of governments worked at the national level to hold abusive officials to account for serious human rights offenses and at the international level to overcome the reluctance of the major powers to establish a permanent International Criminal Court for the worst human rights offenders. The continued expansion of a global economy, by linking consumers and manufacturers across wide distances, spawned a growing interest in labor rights and the human rights practices of multinational corporations. And while a burgeoning human rights movement faced repression in many countries, this was an unfortunate testament to its effectiveness in exerting pressure on governments to respect international human rights standards.

What follows is Human Rights Watch's review of human rights practices in seventy-four countries. This report, released in advance of Human Rights Day, December 10, covers events from December 1995 through mid-November 1996. Most chapters examine significant human rights developments in a particular country and the response of global actors, such as the United States, Japan, the European Union, the United Nations and the World Bank, as well as restrictions on human rights monitoring. Other chapters address thematic issues. This introduction describes certain patterns and trends that Human Rights Watch has witnessed in

the course of its work over the past year.

This volume is Human Rights Watch's seventh World Report on global human rights practices. It does not include a chapter on every country where we work, nor does it discuss every issue of importance. The countries and issues treated reflect the main focus of our work in 1996, which in turn was determined by the severity of abuses, our access to information about them, our ability to influence abusive practices, and our desire to balance our work across various political and regional divides and to address certain key concerns, such as women's rights, children's rights, and arms transfers to abusive governments.

The Facade of a Human Rights Policy

Although few governments dared to jettison human rights explicitly, the major powers settled far too often in 1996 for the facade of a human rights policy rather than a genuine effort to promote human rights. Rare would be the explicit claim that trade with China is more important than the rights of Chinese citizens, that safeguarding troops of the NATO-led Implementation Force (IFOR) must take precedence over protecting Bosnians from genocidal killers, or that halting another round of slaughter in Chechnya must take a back seat to ensuring the reelection of Russian President Boris Yeltsin. Instead, the subordination of human rights was itself dressed up as a human rights policy. The language of human rights became a cover for their abandonment.

The major powers regularly argued that immediate defense of human rights must give way to the task of creating conditions which, over the long term, would guarantee respect for human rights. The noble ends, we were assured, will justify the distasteful means.

In China, we were told, too much criticism of the arbitrary detention of dissidents, religious activists or Tibetan nationalists must not be allowed to jeopardize security and trade concerns. In any case, it was said, "constructive engagement" and continued economic reform were exposing the Chinese people to new ideas and loosening the control of the Communist Party. Never mind that this reluctance to criticize emboldened Chinese authorities to new heights of audacity. From the eleven-year prison sentence handed down for Tiananmen Square student leader Wang Dan to the imprisonment of International Monetary Fund executive Hong Yang, there was no sign of progress on human rights. On the contrary, Chinese leaders were given every reason to conclude that, for the rest of the world, access to Chinese markets far outweighs the rights of Chinese citizens.

In Bosnia, we were cautioned, the arrest of indicted war criminals, the safe return of refugees and the displaced, and even the free press and open campaigning needed for meaningful elections must await the creation of national institutions that supposedly will assure basic rights. This approach had the virtue of excusing IFOR from the tasks of arresting the killers or protecting the victims. It also allowed U.S. President Bill Clinton, in the midst of a reelection campaign, to maintain a veneer of progress in Bosnia. But in the process, the U.S. government, taking profound liberties with the truth, forced through the certification of severely compromised elections. The elections, in turn, provided a cover of respectability to rabid nationalists who, while lending only token endorsement to national institutions, are working closely with the indicted war criminals who remain at large to pursue their vision of ethnic partition, deny rights to minorities, and continue the forced displacement of hundreds of thousands.

In Russia, the official wisdom went, public protest over new atrocities in Chechnya could not be allowed to jeopardize the Yeltsin candidacy or risk the emergence of an openly repressive government. Instead, at the height of Russia's renewed slaughter of civilians in Chechnya, the Council of Europe ignored its own human rights standards to admit Russia as a member, and the International Monetary Fund awarded Russia a US$10 billion loan. Yet this same kid-glove approach to Russia's last round of slaughter in Chechnya in 1994-95 only encouraged the killing by suggesting international acquiescence in whatever ghastly steps Moscow takes to rein in the breakaway republic.

In the Middle East, the delicacy of the peace process was cited as justification for silence in the face of abuses on all sides: the Palestinian Authority's arbitrary arrest and torture of suspected militants and "opponents of peace," Syria's continuing ruthless suppression of dissenting voices, and Israel's punitive "closure" of all Palestinian territory and indiscriminate attacks on the civilian population of Lebanon. Indeed, as Israel responded to terrorist attacks with arbitrary arrests, U.S. Secretary of State Warren Christopher spoke approvingly of Israel's "firm action." Both Israel and the U.S. government successfully pressed for a similar "anti-terrorist" crackdown by the Palestinian Authority. Meanwhile, the tension and distrust bred by continuing human rights abuses posed a serious threat to the peace process.

This past year was not the first in which the major powers embraced human rights justifications to excuse the abandonment of human rights. During the Cold War in the 1980s, the U.S. government often trumpeted voting as a human rights panacea and then cited the mere holding of elections to excuse persistent human rights abuses by elected governments. Today's stratagem is no less a sophism. It presumes that respect for human rights can be bought on the cheap, that the inconvenience of upholding rights today can be dispensed with in the name of a pain-free deliverance tomorrow. It cannot. Until human rights become an integral and immediate part of the quest for peace, trade, and democracy, the world will remain plagued with the intolerance, repression and violence that underlie many of today's crises.

The Global Clamor for Truth and Justice

Fortunately, a more genuine commitment to promoting human rights could be found in many parts of the world, illustrated most dramatically by a growing clamor that human rights offenders be brought to justice and their crimes revealed. In increasing numbers, victims of serious human rights abuse insisted that their ordeal not be forgotten and that their persecutors not escape with impunity. Out of respect for these victims and to prevent a repetition of past horrors, a remarkable array of governments took steps to expose past atrocities and subject their perpetrators to the rule of law.

For example, South Africa's National Commission on Truth and Reconciliation in December 1995 began a highly publicized effort to reveal abuses committed by the apartheid regime. With the power to subpoena testimony and amnesty those who fully confessed their crimes, the commission was the most powerful of its kind ever established, offering the prospect of a detailed and verifiable accounting of apartheid's violence. General Johann van der Merwe, the former chief of police, offered a tantalizing sample of what the commission might achieve by alleging complicity in violent abuse by cabinet-level officials of the apartheid government.

Facing parallel prosecution, Eugene de Kock, commander of the once-secret Vlakplaas security police unit of the apartheid era, was found guilty in August of six murders. In arguing for a reduced sentence, he implicated senior members of the former government, including former Presidents P.W. Botha and F.W. de Klerk, in "dirty tricks" against anti-apartheid activists. Although the high-profile but poorly conducted murder prosecution of former Defense Minister Magnus Malan and nineteen others ended in acquittals in October, it offered detailed proof of the previous government's covert training of the Inkatha "cultural movement" in similar "offensive activities."

India took several important steps toward addressing its periodic communal violence. It produced the first murder conviction stemming from the 1984 anti-Sikh pogroms in Delhi, which left 3,000 dead following the assassination of then-premier Indira Ghandi; eighty-nine men also were sentenced on lesser charges to five years of imprisonment for their role in the pogroms. India reinstated an investigation into the 1992-93 Bombay riots in which more than 1,000 people, the majority of them Muslim, were hunted down and killed by police and organized Hindu extremists. The government also issued a report citing *prima facie* evidence that the Punjab police had secretly disposed of 984 bodies between 1990 and 1995, a period in which hundreds of Sikh men "disappeared" in police custody. And it arraigned nine police officials responsible for the 1995 abduction and forced disappearance of human rights lawyer Jaswant Singh Khalra in Punjab.

In Guatemala, after decades of violent abuse, President Alvaro Arzú acknowledged that gross violations of human rights had been carried out with impunity. Several bold actions, including the purging of corrupt and abusive members of the army and police, the launching of prosecutions against those engaged in organized crime, and the announced dissolution of the highly abusive civil patrols, contributed to a reduction in forced disappearances and political assassinations.

In South Korea, former Presidents Chun Doo-hwan and Roh Tae-woo were convicted on charges of mutiny, treason, and corruption, in part for their role in the 1980 Kwangju massacre in which the army killed hundreds. Chun was sentenced to death (Human Rights Watch opposes the death penalty), and Roh was sentenced to twenty-two-and-a-half years in prison.

In Indonesia, twenty soldiers suspected of human rights abuses, including murder and excessive use of force, were convicted for the minor charge of violating military procedures. While the charges were unduly light, the number of prosecutions was greater than in any previous year.

In Honduras, nineteen military officers, all fugitives from justice, have been indicted for violent abuses committed in the 1980s. The Honduran Supreme Court affirmed that amnesty laws passed in 1987 and 1991 do not preclude the judicial investigation of soldiers charged with human rights violations.

In Malawi, former President Hastings Banda and his leading henchmen were tried, though acquitted, for the 1984 murder of three ministers and a member of parliament.

In Mozambique, while officials of both the current government and the former rebel group continued to insist that merely to expose the abuses committed during the 1977-92 civil war would undermine national reconciliation, many local communities disagreed, holding traditional healing ceremonies at which those responsible for past abuses publicly confessed their crimes.

Some countries are actively struggling with bringing security forces under the rule of law. For example, following governmental consultation with domestic and international human rights organizations, Brazil's President Fernando Henrique Cardoso released a National Human Rights Plan in May. It would, among other things, grant civilian courts jurisdiction over human rights abuses committed by uniformed police officers.

Yet the Brazilian Senate continues to block passage of the necessary legislation. As a result, some parts of Brazil's decentralized federal system continue to reflect appalling rates of official murder, often of common criminal suspects, with impunity. To make matters worse, Rio de Janeiro instituted a bravery bonus and promotion program, which rewards police officers for neutralizing criminals, dead or alive. By contrast, a new program in São Paulo to track police officers involved in fatal shootings and to remove them at least temporarily from active duty contributed to a dramatic decrease in the rate of killings by police to 15 percent of the 1992 figure.

In several cases, governments recognized the need to seek justice, but progress was slow.

Extensive delays continue to plague Ethiopia's prosecution of some 1,700 leading members of the former Derg regime. The trial of forty-six is proceeding, but the remainder have been in custody since 1991 without the filing of charges against them.

Rwanda's judiciary, which had been decimated by the 1994 genocide, is now, with the help of foreign donors, almost fully staffed. A law has also been passed to facilitate plea-bargaining for those accused of participating in the genocide. Yet no trials have begun for the 83,000 detainees held in inhumane conditions.

Haiti's slow progress in prosecuting military and paramilitary forces responsible for violent abuses under the 1991-94 military government—in part because of obstruction by the U.S. government—encouraged continued violence both by the new police force and by apparent armed sympathizers of the former military government. It also took nearly a year after the report's completion for the Haitian government to publish the Commission for Truth and Justice's 1,200-page report on abuses under the military regime.

Setbacks

The year was also marked by some clear setbacks in the effort to establish accountability for serious human rights abuse.

Cambodia agreed to amnesty Ieng Sary, one of the masterminds of the Khmer Rouge 1975-79 reign of terror—the most egregious step yet in the pattern of impunity that continues to plague the country.

Armed infiltrators from Rwandan refugee camps in Zaire targeted and killed nearly 300 people in Rwanda, including scores of Tutsi survivors of the genocide, in an apparent effort to silence witnesses to the slaughter.

Ignoring the role of impunity in fueling further abuse and conflict, Angola passed yet another amnesty law for human rights violators, its sixth since 1981. Disappointingly, the amnesty was welcomed by Alioune Blondin Beye, the special representative of the U.N. secretary-general and a member of the African Commission on Human and People's Rights.

Russia did nothing to punish members of its military who were responsible for indiscriminate and deadly attacks in

Chechnya—except to publish falsehoods and exaggerations concerning its efforts to bring them to justice. Russia also adopted a new criminal code and code of criminal procedure, which increased the difficulty of achieving justice for women victims of sexual violence. These laws add to the obstacles that deter all but a tiny minority of victims from reporting sex crimes.

Japan remains unwilling even to acknowledge culpability for its mistreatment of 200,000 "comfort women" from China, Indonesia, Korea, and the Philippines, who were forced to serve as sex slaves for the Japanese army during World War II. Although limited compensation has been offered to survivors, many victims have rejected the offer because of both its small amount and its origins in a private rather than official fund.

The Prison Litigation Reform Act, passed in April in the United States, severely restricts prisoners' ability to enforce their rights.

The U.S. government, though at times a proponent of justice, is not always principled when the process of accountability might implicate its own officials. In the face of allegations that the Central Intelligence Agency (CIA) helped to create and promote the murderous FRAPH (Front for the Advancement and Progress of Haiti) organization, a paramilitary ally of the brutal 1991-94 military regime in Haiti, Washington has agreed not to deport FRAPH leader Emmanuel Constant, allowing him to take refuge in the United States on the apparent condition that he not speak publicly about his alleged CIA sponsors. Washington is also refusing to return to the Haitian government some 160,000 documents, including "trophy photos," that it seized from FRAPH and Haitian army headquarters in 1994—unless it first blacks out the names of all U.S. citizens and, thereby, any CIA connections. These actions raised a serious obstacle to Haitian efforts to prosecute those responsible for violent abuses under the military regime.

The CIA and the Pentagon also refused to declassify information about Honduras's murderous Battalion 3-16, which the CIA reportedly supported, trained, and worked closely with in the 1980s. Nor have all U.S. documents been released about CIA asset and confirmed killer Colonel Alpírez in Guatemala; while the State Department has declassified nearly 5,000 documents, the Pentagon and U.S. intelligence agencies have refused to follow suit and have reportedly blocked the State Department from releasing other incriminating documents. New CIA guidelines issued in February "generally bar" formal relationships with human rights abusers. However, despite the likelihood that abusive foreign officials will understand the CIA's maintenance of such a relationship as a license to continue human rights violations, a gaping loophole still permits CIA relationships with abusive officials "in special cases when national security interests so warrant."

An International System of Justice: A Diminishing Opportunity
In contrast to significant national advances in the quest for justice, a historic opportunity to create an international system of justice for the most culpable human rights offenders was largely squandered over the past year. A half-century after the trials in Nuremberg and Tokyo, the international community has taken tentative steps toward ending the impunity that lies behind the most horrendous atrocities of our time by establishing the International Criminal Tribunals for Rwanda and the Former Yugoslavia. The tribunals hold out the promise that even the victorious in war, such as Serb forces in Bosnia, cannot escape accountability for atrocities they commit. Indeed, in 1996 the Yugoslav tribunal held its first trial, of Dusko Tadic, a low-level Bosnian Serb accused of murder and torture at the infamous Omarska detention camp.

While the 1995 Dayton peace accord demonstrated that permitting justice for genocide and mass murder need not stand in the way of a peace agreement, Western governments, obsessed with minimizing risks to

IFOR troops, betrayed that commitment in 1996 and allowed the masterminds of the Bosnian genocide to remain at large. The massive IFOR presence in Bosnia succeeded in largely stopping the slaughter for the moment, but the failure to arrest the architects of "ethnic cleansing" makes it likely that the halt will be only temporary, and that, in the end, revenge will triumph over reconciliation. Bearing greatest responsibility for this short-sighted policy of expedience was U.S. President Bill Clinton. When it came to providing funding and political support, Washington was a friend of the Yugoslav tribunal. But when it came to actually bringing indicted war criminals to justice, President Clinton's support vanished.

Without question there is some risk in arresting war criminals, although with nearly 55,000 NATO troops in Bosnia backed by over $500 billion in annual Pentagon resources, the risk should be containable. But President Clinton, preoccupied with his re-election, lacked the leadership and courage to make the case for assuming that risk. He would not hesitate to ask a big-city cop to risk his or her life to apprehend a murder suspect, since that is the price to be paid for upholding the rule of law at home. But when it came to deploying law enforcement officials abroad—in this case, IFOR—to arrest suspects in genocide and mass murder and uphold the most basic international law, he balked. Sadly, he was willing to accept the chance of encouraging more slaughter tomorrow to avoid the political risks of leadership today.

President Jacques Chirac of France and Prime Minister John Major of Britain also bear particular blame for this failure. Despite a history of accepting some casualties among their many troops in Bosnia as a price for securing a peace, they contented themselves in 1996 with hiding behind President Clinton's timorous lead.

Particularly at a time when the international community is reluctant to deploy troops to stop, let alone prevent, mass killing, a functioning international system of justice would be a powerful deterrent to those contemplating atrocities. Indeed, when abusive leaders are all too willing to sacrifice countless lives in their quest for power, the targeted thrust of justice can be far more effective than the less discriminate tool of military intervention. Yet in their fixation on avoiding casualties among IFOR troops, international leaders only increase the likelihood of far more costly and dangerous interventions in the future.

The International Criminal Tribunal for Rwanda has had more success in gaining custody of some of the leaders of the Rwandan genocide, despite funding and personnel shortages and problems of local leadership. Zambia, Kenya, Belgium, Switzerland, and the United States have arrested indicted killers and agreed to deliver them to the tribunal. Cameroon has arrested several of the most important genocide participants, including a key leader, Colonel Théoneste Bagosora, although it has delayed surrendering them to the tribunal. But Zaire, with international acquiescence, allowed its territory to become a haven for participants in the genocide who, until military setbacks at the hands of rebel troops in November, continued to control the million or more Rwandan refugees in the country. In addition, the tribunal has blatantly neglected the widespread rape and sexual abuse of women that occurred during the genocide.

However, given the symbolic importance of Bosnia as the second genocide of this century in Europe, the success of the Nuremberg legacy is likely to be judged far more by the Yugoslav tribunal. If that tribunal can show no more for its labors than the trial of a handful of low-level thugs, it will be deemed a failure. The cause of international justice risks being set back for decades more.

There is little time for salvaging this effort. With plans for a reduction of international troops in Bosnia at the end of 1996, the window of opportunity for arresting war criminals is closing. Popular pressure on President Clinton and other Western leaders is urgently needed, lest the remaining chance also be squandered.

An International Criminal Court

Given the slow progress of the Yugoslav and Rwandan tribunals, perhaps the most promising development at the international level has been the growing support for a permanent International Criminal Court (ICC)—a court which, unlike tribunals set up on a case-by-case basis by the U.N. Security Council, would be available to try the most serious human rights offenders wherever national courts are ineffective or unable to do the job. Momentum for an ICC picked up dramatically during 1996, as traditional northern supporters of international justice, mainly in Europe, were joined by a contingent of states from Africa, Latin America, the Caribbean, the Middle East, and the Pacific.

A growing number of governments embrace the ICC as insurance against abusive forces within their own countries who might be tempted to assume power and commit atrocities with the intention of avoiding prosecution by crippling the national judiciary or insisting on amnesty as a condition for stepping down. They understand that an international tribunal, by effectively removing amnesty from the bargaining table, can help avoid the slaughter that this strategy of impunity might breed. These ICC proponents seek to finalize the treaty establishing the court by mid-1998.

Unfortunately, the most outspoken opponents of an effective ICC are the permanent members of the Security Council, particularly the United States, Britain, France, and China. They are joined by the Japanese government which, worried about its record of atrocities in World War II, is unwilling to embrace even a mechanism of justice that, under all proposed versions, would not apply retroactively. While nominally endorsing the court, these governments persist in using delaying tactics to halt momentum and in promoting a weak court that would be subordinate to the Security Council and hence to the permanent members' veto power.

The ICC could provide a bulwark for international security by dissuading would-be tyrants from resorting to the violent abuse that underlies many of today's armed conflicts and humanitarian emergencies. Yet the permanent members of the Security Council are willing to sacrifice this powerful tool to their desire to maintain a monopoly of power within the U.N. to maintain international peace and security. They also seek to avoid even the possibility that a strong and independent ICC might try to hold their own soldiers or officials to account, as if the rule of law can apply exclusively to others, not to themselves. Given this parochial exercise of their duty to safeguard global security, it is little wonder that calls for reform of the Security Council are gaining in force and number.

Profits Before Human Rights Principles

In recent years, an important tool in promoting human rights has been the linkage of international assistance to the recipient's respect for international human rights standards. However, with a rapidly expanding global economy, many abusive governments now see international trade and investment as more important than bilateral or even multilateral assistance. Many industrialized countries have been reluctant to use this new form of economic leverage for human rights purposes. Fearing a loss of trade and investment opportunities in "big emerging markets" or resource-rich economies, the industrialized powers continue regularly to choose profit over principle when asked to apply human rights standards universally. While quite willing to exert economic pressure in the name of human rights on poor states like Burundi, Cuba, Libya, or Sudan, they acquiesced in abuses by economically attractive countries like China, Indonesia, Mexico, Nigeria, and Saudi Arabia.

This trend was particularly apparent in Asia. In March, the European Union (E.U.) held its first summit with Asian nations with barely a mention of human rights; indeed, the main human rights topic was a French and German effort to find a way to drop an E.U.-sponsored resolution criticizing China's human rights record at the U.N. Commission on Human Rights. The Association of South

East Asian Nations (ASEAN), for its part, pronounced a convenient faith in "constructive engagement" with Burma—where Singapore, Malaysia, Thailand, and Indonesia have growing investments—despite mass arrests of over 1,000 opposition activists in 1996 and the ongoing use of forced labor. In June, the European Commission issued its first official position paper on E.U.-India relations. Describing an "enhanced partnership," the paper stressed European desire for access to India's "enormous market" while deliberately downplaying human rights.

Despite demands from around the world to cancel his visit to Indonesia to protest assaults on the pro-democracy movement, German Chancellor Helmut Kohl proceeded to Jakarta in October with a delegation of over fifty business leaders. Any concern over the impending subversion trials of labor and pro-democracy activists was muted to ensure that contracts were signed for the purchase of some $395 million from German industries. Australian Prime Minister John Howard also failed to make any public mention of human rights during a September visit to Indonesia.

In the case of China, governments around the world downplayed human rights in their quest for warm relations with Chinese leaders and lucrative business deals in the world's largest market. Indeed, China actively sought to buy this silence by threatening to grant or deny contracts on the basis of the prominence that its trading partners gave to its human rights practices.

Nigeria, with its substantial oil reserves, escaped with only modest sanctions after its shocking execution of Ken Saro-Wiwa and eight other Ogoni activists in November 1995. The U.S. government's response was limited to denying visas to Nigerian leaders, banning military assistance and training, and prohibiting the sale and repair of military goods. Yet Washington studiously avoided seizing assets of military leaders or banning new investments in the oil industry, let alone imposing an oil embargo, which would immediately have been felt by the Nigerian military and might have hastened the seemingly endless transition to elected government.

The E.U. denied visas to leaders of the military regime, prohibited future arms sales, and insisted that development assistance pass through nongovernmental organizations (NGOs), but further steps were opposed by Britain, Germany, Italy, and the Netherlands, all of which have significant commercial interests in Nigeria. The Commonwealth suspended Nigeria and threatened to expel it if a democratically elected government were not in place within two years, but it stalled on proposed further sanctions, including freezing financial assets, denying visas, ceasing military training, or banning the export of arms.

Meanwhile, Chief Moshood K.O. Abiola, the presumed winner of the military-annulled 1993 elections in Nigeria, passed his second year in detention, while in June his senior wife and the most prominent campaigner for his release, Kudirat Abiola, was assassinated in Lagos by unidentified gunmen assumed by most to be acting on behalf of the government. Severe persecution of the Ogoni people, including killings and detentions, also continued.

In the case of oil-rich Saudi Arabia, there was not even the pretense of a dialogue to improve human rights. Rather, the U.S. government in its annual human rights report sought to excuse Saudi repression by asserting without any evidence that Saudi Arabia's "rigorously conservative form of Islam"—a euphemism for severe restrictions on women and intolerance of political dissent—"enjoys near-consensus support among Saudi citizens." By contrast, dissidents and opposition movements were labeled "rigidly fundamentalist," tacitly justifying their harsh treatment. For its part, Britain sought to expel an outspoken Saudi asylum seeker for fear of losing lucrative defense contracts with Saudi Arabia, until its efforts were stymied by a court.

Both the United States and Britain likewise declined numerous opportunities to criticize the government of Bahrain for a host of abuses ranging from torture and arbitrary detention to the wholesale denial of basic civil rights, including freedom of speech and assembly.

Labor Rights and the Global Economy

While the industrialized powers were ready to forsake human rights where market opportunities beckoned, the global economy produced a surprising new source of support for the human rights cause. One of the great challenges for the international human rights movement is convincing people outside of an abusive country to care for the fate of remote victims. Although the international press plays a key role in this process, it is too easy to turn away from disturbing articles, to close one's eyes to ghastly pictures, and to retreat in comfortable isolation. Surprisingly, the global economy is helping to cut through this indifference by establishing new and immediate connections among distant people. Because the goods purchased in one country may be produced by victims of repression in another, the very act of consumption can be seen as complicity in that repression unless steps are taken to ensure that manufacturing is free of labor rights abuse. The result has been a burgeoning of consumer and press interest in labor rights in parts of the world that have been ignored.

Multinational corporations have been linked to human rights abuse in ever more public ways. In a few cases, they have changed their conduct rather than risk further tarnishing of their valuable brand names and corporate images. For example, during the past year campaigns in Europe and the United States led Heineken, Carlsberg, British Home Stores, and Liz Claiborne to leave Burma because of the extreme difficulty of operating there without becoming an accomplice to human rights abuse. Other companies faced strong consumer and public pressure over their human rights records, including Royal Dutch/Shell for its role in Nigeria, Total and Unocal for their presence in Burma, Freeport McMoRan and Nike over their actions in Indonesia, Disney for its activities in Haiti, and Zenith and General Motors for gender discrimination in Mexico.

Governments have also had to respond to this new interest in labor rights:

During a trip to India in January, Canadian Prime Minister Jean Chrétien, a strong proponent of Canadian corporate activity abroad, was compelled to mention publicly the possibility of Canadian restrictions on the import of goods made with child labor after his initial refusal to meet with a thirteen-year-old Canadian child-labor activist led to scathing press coverage.

The U.S. government also responded to revelations that American companies were using abusive labor practices with a high-profile Rose Garden ceremony to launch the Fair Labor Coalition. The coalition is supposed to report its nonbinding recommendations to President Clinton next year. Its impact remains uncertain.

South Korea was admitted in October to the Organization for Economic Cooperation and Development (OECD), the exclusive club of twenty-seven developed nations, but only after the OECD had set up an unprecedented committee to monitor Korea's labor practices for rights violations. The European Union played a helpful role in keeping Korea's labor rights record on the OECD agenda.

UNICEF announced that it would henceforth not purchase material made with child labor. The World Bank responded to a Human Rights Watch report on bonded child labor in India by working out an agreement with the Indian government to initiate pilot projects aimed at eradicating this form of slavery. The release of the report for the annual donors meeting on India prompted a number of governments to make useful interventions with the Indian government.

The U.S. Labor Department's National Administrative Office (NAO), established under the labor-rights side agreement of the North American Free Trade Agreement (NAFTA), issued a report finding serious fault with Mexico's labor adjudication system. The NAO is also working on two new labor rights cases, including one filed by Human Rights Watch.

Pakistan, responding to international criticism and threats of trade sanctions for its labor practices, improved implementation of its child labor laws, including 2,500 prosecutions and 395 convictions of employers.

Some of the growing interest in labor rights practices is based on straightforward self-interest. For example, labor unions increasingly call attention to repression in distant countries for fear that jobs will be lost because of lower labor costs abroad made possible when workers are prevented from speaking out and organizing around workplace issues. Some businesses favor a strong and independent press as the best antidote to corruption. Many business executives have an obvious interest in the rule of law to help avoid arrest or violence in countries where they travel, such as occurred in 1996 when China detained officials from Royal Dutch/ Shell and the International Monetary Fund and Saudi Arabia detained and mistreated a foreign engineer on the pretext that he had information about the political opposition. Even Peru's President Alberto Fujimori recognized the importance of the rule of law in a global economy when he lamented in his July state of the nation address that Peru lacked a "system of justice on which citizens and businesspeople, nationals and foreigners can rely."

Perhaps the most potent force in support of labor rights is the desire of many consumers to avoid personal complicity in human rights abuse. With growing frequency, consumers are insisting on guarantees that they are not buying the products of abusive labor conditions. While consumers currently lack adequate information on every product, Human Rights Watch and other organizations are devoting increasing resources to monitoring workers' rights worldwide. The press has performed a service by conveying this information to the consuming public. And a growing number of multinational corporations, deeply concerned about protecting their image, have adopted codes of conduct embracing human rights principles. A smaller number are discussing steps to ensure that these codes are implemented conscientiously and transparently.

In this way, just as the end of the Cold War spawned indifference to rights issues around the world, the global economy is providing new reasons for engagement. Few people want to benefit from human rights abuse. The global economy can make that linkage unavoidable—unless consumers take a broader interest in human rights practices. When a trip to the local department store becomes an opportunity for human rights activism, the human rights movement gains important new adherents.

Aid to Abusive Governments

Conditioning international assistance on respect for human rights remains a significant tool for promoting reform. All major donor governments as a matter of either legislation or policy now uphold such conditionality in theory. Indeed, the provision of international assistance to abusive governments is less of a problem today than during the Cold War, when geopolitical interests frequently prevailed.

Yet most major donors continue to provide significant financial assistance to at least some abusive regimes without serious efforts to link that aid to an end to human rights abuses. Typical was Japan, which in 1995 sent $1.4 billion to China, $880 million to Indonesia, and $271 million to Pakistan, but made no apparent effort to use its ensuing leverage to press for human rights improvements. Similarly, the U.S. government made no visible attempt to employ the $3 billion it sends to Israel each year for the purpose of stopping torture, arbitrary detention, and the indiscriminate use of military force, or the more than $2 billion sent to Egypt each year to end torture, severe restrictions on political activities by the moderate Islamist opposition, and the use of military courts to convict civilians for nonviolent political activities. The World Bank gave nearly $3 billion to China and $991 million to Indonesia without using its enormous leverage to challenge those governments when they restrict the freedom of expression needed to rein in pervasive corruption and its toll on economic development.

U.S. arms sales to Colombia were at their highest levels ever during 1996, despite its troubling record of political executions and "disappearances." The United States provides $175 million in military assistance to Turkey, despite torture by Turkish police and a highly abusive war with Kurdish insurgents in southeastern Turkey.

Although President Chirac said that it would be "legitimate" for France to link its $1.2 billion of annual assistance to Algeria to its pace of democratization, there was no evidence that France had in any way conditioned its assistance on an end to extrajudicial executions, forced disappearances, and torture by Algerian security and paramilitary forces. French assistance to Tunisia doubled in 1996 to $220 million despite its continued jailing, torture, or abuse of thousands of Islamists for nonviolent expression and association.

The Abandonment of Refugees

1996 saw a serious erosion in the protection of refugees from persecution. Western countries rolled up the welcome mat and shirked their responsibilities under international law as refugee flows changed direction with the end of the Cold War, with fewer refugees coming from former communist countries in Europe and more originating in developing countries. European countries, particularly Germany, threatened to repatriate Bosnian refugees without ensuring the arrest of their persecutors in Bosnia and the restoration of their personal freedoms. Many refugees fleeing to Western Europe now face a series of entry barriers, accelerated screening procedures, and "safe third country" rules which tend to bounce them back to countries on the periphery of the European Union without any guarantee of protection.

The E.U. has also adopted a narrow definition of refugees that protects only those facing official or officially condoned persecution; those whom governments fail to protect from insurgent groups are left without recourse. The United States adopted a new law which authorizes the use of summary procedures to review asylum claims and imposes arbitrary deadlines for filing asylum claims. The United States also continued large-scale detention of asylum seekers (including children) to deter others from seeking asylum.

Taking their cue from wealthier nations, Ghana, Ivory Coast, Nigeria, and Sierra Leone refused permission for two boatloads of Liberian refugees to dock during the height of renewed fighting in Monrovia. Russia refused to grant asylum to, and frequently extradited, dissidents from other former Soviet republics. To stem the tide of Rohingya Muslims who were fleeing forced labor and other abuse in Burma, Bangladesh jailed new arrivals or barred them from entering the country. In one incident in April, twenty-five asylum seekers, mostly women and children, drowned as Bangladeshi forces towed them back to Burma.

Perhaps the greatest threat to refugees came from a change in the paradigm for how to treat them. While the foremost duty toward refugees has always been the requirement that they not be forcibly returned to face persecution—the rule of non-refoulement—this first principle has increasingly given way to the management of population flows. Even the U.N. High Commissioner for Refugees (UNHCR), Sadako Ogata, has been toying with this new perspective on refugees. For example, to ensure repatriation to Tajikistan of some 7,000 refugees in northwestern Afghanistan, UNHCR cut their food and fuel rations, even though returning refugees faced harassment by neighbors and law enforcement officials who were unwilling to safeguard them. Protective efforts in Tajikistan by UNHCR and the Organization on Security and Cooperation in Europe (OSCE) significantly improved security for many returnees, but UNHCR's and OSCE's resources were inadequate to ensure the safety of all those who returned.

Concern with resources and an eroding willingness to host refugees drive this new commitment to repatriation. Refugee camps are expensive to operate. With resettlement in the west an increasingly remote option, repatriation can appear to be an attractive solution. But UNHCR and the major powers must be vigilant not to allow their desire to repatriate refugees to supersede their obligations under international law to refrain from returning refugees to countries where their lives or freedom would be threatened.

Landmines Progress: Sidestepping the Plague of "Consensus" at the U.N.

One of the quieter but more insidious threats to the enforcement of human rights is the U.N.'s increasing preference to operate in this realm by "consensus." As applied in U.N. circles, the "consensus" rule gives any government license to block action—a universal veto power. The result is that majority rule gives way to rule by the lowest common denominator, as the most abusive or recalcitrant states are permitted to prevent strong action in defense of human rights.

Already, most U.N. negotiations to set or enforce human rights standards are conducted on these terms. For example, progress toward creating a U.N. body to visit detention facilities was blocked in 1996 by China, Cuba, Japan, and Mexico. A campaign was also launched to make "consensus" the preferred tool for decision-making by the U.N. Human Rights Commission. Not surprisingly, its main proponents included such abusive or obstructionist governments as Algeria, Angola, China, Cuba, India, Indonesia, Iran, Iraq, Malaysia, Nigeria, Pakistan, Sri Lanka, and Vietnam. But those who take advantage of this system are not only the traditional opponents of human rights enforcement: the U.S. and British governments have profited from "consensus" traditions to block action on the International Criminal Court.

An important breach in the "consensus" system emerged in 1996 as a result of the campaign to ban the use, production, transfer, and stockpiling of antipersonnel landmines—inherently indiscriminate weapons which kill or maim thousands each year. A review conference settled in May for largely token new restrictions rather than a ban.

Operating under "consensus" negotiating rules, the U.S., Chinese, Russian, Indian, and Pakistani governments, among others, insisted on subordinating the humanitarian imperative for a landmines ban to the preferences of their military establishments.

Yet an international campaign for a definitive ban on landmines—initiated by a small coalition of groups including Human Rights Watch but now joined by more than 700 NGOs and more than fifty governments—has bypassed this lowest common denominator. As a result, Canada, in a heroic move, announced in October that it would sidestep the absurdities of the "consensus" rule and open for signature in December 1997 a treaty that bans all antipersonnel landmines without exception. Belgium has offered to host a drafting conference in June 1997. Those who want to subscribe to a genuine ban will thus be able to do so. Those who choose not to may, of course, refuse to sign, but they will no longer be able to use the "consensus" rule to water down a landmine ban.

The Clinton administration, in particular, will no longer be able to pretend to support a landmines ban while watering down genuine prohibition. As a result, public pressure to join a complete ban is likely to increase. It is thus no surprise that, as this report goes to press, Washington is trying to strong-arm Ottawa into qualifying its courageous stand against landmines. It can only be hoped that Canada will resist, for the benefit not only of tomorrow's potential landmine victims, but also for the prospect of enforcing human rights standards through the U.N. without the curse of "consensus."

Other U.N. Action

The U.N.'s continued marginalization of its human rights bodies remained a concern in 1996. During the Cold War, many governments found it expedient to relegate human rights to Geneva, a convenient distance from U.N. headquarters in New York. Today, as human rights abuses play a central role in many humanitarian and security crises, it is time for better integration. For example,

despite the considerable human rights expertise accumulated by Geneva-based special
rapporteurs on countries such as Burundi,
Iraq, Sudan, and Zaire, not a single rapporteur was asked to address the Security Council. José Ayala Lasso, the U.N. high commissioner for human rights, only compounded the problem by his painfully low-
key approach to defending human rights.
The failure to consider seriously and act
upon the human rights dimension of global
problems hurt not only the cause of human
rights but also the success of many of the
operations launched by the U.N.'s operational bodies in New York.

Other areas of concern at the U.N. include the following:

U.N. Secretary-General Boutros
Boutros-Ghali once more showed his unwillingness to criticize the human rights
records of the major powers. In August, as
Russian troops were indiscriminately bombing Grozny and hundreds of thousands were
fleeing a Russian offensive in Chechnya, his
spokesperson failed to express concern about
this human rights emergency by asserting
that Chechnya was considered an "internal
matter of the Russian Federation."

The budget crisis facing the U.N. provided a ready pretext for inaction on human
rights. Much-needed operations to defend
human rights have been left stillborn or
seriously understaffed on budgetary grounds.
For example, lip service was paid to the need
for human rights monitors in Burundi, but in
April only five were sent. Nor was any
action taken on the call in February by the
special rapporteur for Burundi for the creation of an international tribunal for that
country to deter further slaughter. Adequate
funding for the International Criminal Tribunal for Rwanda became available only in
mid-1996, two years after the Rwandan genocide.

A laudable effort to increase access for
nongovernmental organizations to U.N. bodies was hijacked by abusive governments
intent on stifling human rights criticism.
Human rights NGOs were singled out for
special restrictions.

A low point for the U.N. Human Rights
Commission came when China succeeded in
using commercial threats and blandishments
to block a vote or even discussion regarding
a much-deserved resolution critical of
China's human rights record.

Special praise is due the professional
and effective U.N. human rights verification
mission in Guatemala (MINUGUA), which
virtually guaranteed scrutiny of any abuse
that occurred. The U.N. also moderated the
successful peace talks between the Guatemalan government and guerrillas. In response to a letter from Human Rights Watch
expressing concern over the prospect that
the final agreement might include an amnesty for violent human rights abuses, U.N.
Under-Secretary for Political Affairs Marrack
Goulding pledged in August that the U.N.
would not condone such an agreement. The
U.N. Human Rights Field Operation in
Rwanda also did a much improved job in
difficult circumstances of reporting on accelerating abuse.

Other Noteworthy Developments

Other developments worth highlighting, both
positive and negative, include the following:

The free and competitive elections in
Taiwan helped further to undermine the argument, conveniently advanced by repressive Asian governments, that Asians value
orderly government more than popular participation. So did the massive outpouring of
support for Megawati Soekarnoputri, daughter of Indonesia's first president, as an alternative to President Soeharto.

In a sign of the increasing importance
of women's rights to public perception of a
government's legitimacy, the Taliban in
Afghanistan received a cool international
welcome upon taking Kabul in part because
of severe restrictions it placed on public
activities by women. However, in the case of
Saudi Arabia, which imposes many compa-
rable restrictions, even the increasingly powerful international women's rights movement could not prevent the country's wealth
from purchasing silence on human rights.

The Czech Republic, Greece, the Federal Republic of Yugoslavia, Zaire and Zambia adopted or narrowly interpreted citizenship laws to deny citizenship to native-born or long-term residents on grounds of ethnicity. Evidence suggests that the Czech law was intended to disenfranchise and ultimately expel the Roma community there. A citizenship law in Greece continued to be used to strip citizenship from certain non-ethnic Greeks who leave the country. A new citizenship law in the Federal Republic of Yugoslavia threatened statelessness for ethnic Albanians in Kosovo. A Zambian law called into question the fairness of presidential elections by making the main opposition candidate, former President Kenneth Kuanda, ineligible for the office. The Zairian threat to enforce an earlier withdrawal of citizenship from Tutsi, known as Banyamulenge, and to attack them if they did not leave the country sparked the armed conflict and refugee crisis in November.

Preoccupation with common crime led to official and popular pressure to compromise human rights guarantees in several parts of the world. In Latin America, the problem was most acute in Brazil, Colombia, Mexico, and Venezuela. Frustration with the judicial system also led to the lynching of suspected common criminals in Guatemala, Haiti, and Mexico. Efforts in Bulgaria to control organized crime served as a pretext for beatings and due process violations. Russia's crackdown on organized crime led to the harassment, mistreatment, and arbitrary detention of people from the Caucasus, especially Chechens. Both the police and judiciary in Bangladesh grossly mistreated criminal suspects. Police in India and Bulgaria beat street children and detained them arbitrarily. The "war on drugs" as waged in the United States led to racially discriminatory prosecutions and sentencing.

Subregional groups in Africa, while still embryonic, showed encouraging initiatives on behalf of human rights. The Southern African Development Community began to call on its member states to improve respect for human rights. Similarly, the states of East and Central Africa responded decisively to a coup in Burundi.

After years of defending discriminatory laws as legitimately rooted in local custom, the Botswana legislature finally gave in to domestic and international pressure and granted women equal citizenship rights.

While activists worldwide increasingly used the Internet to exchange human rights information and to organize campaigns against abuse, many governments tried to impose penalties or restrictions on Internet use, including Burma, China, Cuba, Germany, Singapore, South Korea, the United States, and Zambia. Human Rights Watch joined a so-far successful court challenge to a restrictive U.S. law on Internet use and issued a report on the problem worldwide.

Attacks on Human Rights Monitors
It is a sad but useful measure of the effectiveness of the human rights movement in generating pressure against abusive governments that those governments so often retaliate with violence or repression aimed at the monitors of human rights themselves. In the past year, seven human rights monitors were killed or forcibly disappeared. India and Colombia remained two of the most dangerous places for human rights monitoring, with two monitors killed in each country.

In India, Kashmiri human rights lawyer Jalil Andrabi was abducted by Indian security forces and murdered in March. Parag Kumar Das, an editor and human rights activist from Assam, was killed in May.

In Colombia, a gunman in October shot dead Josué Giraldo Cardona, a lawyer with the Civic Committee of Meta, whose members have suffered systematic persecution by the army and paramilitary groups for years. In November, Jafeth Morales, a human rights monitor who had been the subject of frequent death threats, was killed in the city of Ocanha by armed men believed to be members of a local paramilitary group.

Fernando Reyes, a human rights lawyer, was shot in the head at his desk in Zamboanga del Sur in the Philippines by unknown assailants.

Kalpana Chakma, a tribal rights activist

in the Chittagong Hill Tracts of Bangladesh and organizing secretary of the Hill Women's Federation, was abducted by army gunmen on the eve of general elections in June and has not been seen again. Her two brothers also were abducted but managed to escape unhurt. One brother identified Lieutenant Ferdous, an officer from the Ugalchhari army camp, as one of the abductors.

In October, Francisco Gilson Nogueira de Carvalho, a lawyer with the Center for Human Rights and Popular Memory, was killed by machine-gun fire in the northeastern Brazilian state of Rio Grande do Norte. Nogueira had been investigating connections between death squads and local authorities, particularly Deputy Secretary of Public Security Maurilio Pinto de Medeiros.

Human rights monitors in a variety of other countries faced violence and serious threats to their safety:

Two national police officers in the Dominican Republic, in full view of a crowd, fired repeatedly at Danilo de la Cruz, a member of the Dominican Human Rights Committee, just after he held a press conference in El Capotillo in June to denounce the police for a drowning death. An investigation into this case of attempted murder was announced, but no progress has been made. Police in October also threatened to kill Virgilio Almánzar, president of the same organization, shortly after he videotaped them roughing up several youths.

In Mexico, staff members at the Miguel Agustín Pro Juárez Human Rights Center received detailed and persistent death threats, apparently in response to the organization's documentation of human rights violations by the military and the police. In addition, in March, Héctor Gutiérrez Ugalde, an assistant to National Human Rights Commission staff member Julián Andrade Jardí, was abducted, severely beaten, and informed of death threats to Andrade and his mother, human rights activist Teresa Jardí.

In April in the Guatemalan village of Guineales, civil patrollers, former municipal authorities, and a former military commissioner threatened to kill Julio Ixmatá Tziquín

of the human rights group Defensoría Maya. They were about to set him on fire when relatives and neighbors intervened.

In January, three human rights activists in Bangalore, India, who tried to investigate the detention of environmentalists protesting the harmful effects of prawn aquaculture had their tires punctured by unidentified armed men and were threatened with "dire consequences" if they continued their investigation.

The Rwandan government responded to legitimate criticism from local human rights organizations by accusing them of "covering up" for people guilty of genocide and "unwittingly serv[ing] as propaganda channels for genocidal leaders"—charges which in Rwanda's inflamed atmosphere can amount to a death sentence.

Human rights attorney Asma Jehangir of Pakistan received death threats for pursuing a case to establish the right of a woman to marry without her male guardian's consent.

As renewed combat erupted in Monrovia, Liberian human rights activists were targeted by the warring factions, forcing them to take refuge with international peacekeepers.

Peruvian human rights lawyers working to convict human rights abusers suffered death threats and other harassment.

Other human rights monitors faced arbitrary detention and mistreatment for their work:

In September, Turkey indicted the translator and publisher of the Turkish translation of a Human Rights Watch report for "defaming and belittling the state's security and military forces." The report had described the use of foreign-supplied weapons in Turkey's abusive counterinsurgency campaign against Kurdish rebels.

In Burma, twenty-one political prisoners who had attempted to send information about prison conditions to the U.N. special rapporteur were badly beaten and given additional sentences of from five to twelve years.

Employing vague criminal prohibitions

of "illegal association" and "enemy propaganda," Cuba used short-term detention and criminal prosecution to crack down on the Cuban Council, a coalition of 135 Cuban NGOs, which included several human rights organizations.

In the Middle East, human rights activists were imprisoned by Syrian, Tunisian, Israeli, and Palestinian authorities. Activists from the Syrian Committees for the Defense of Democratic Freedoms and Human Rights in Syria were serving the longest prison terms—up to ten years.

The Zairian government detained human rights monitors who tried to draw attention to human rights problems in eastern Zaire prior to the onset of open conflict in the region.

China prohibited human rights monitoring by its citizens, as illustrated by the eleven-year prison sentence imposed on Wang Dan for trying to inform Chinese citizens of the situation within their country by publishing articles abroad.

Turkmenistan has not permitted a single human rights monitor to function since its independence in 1991. Indeed, no member of the opposition is at liberty within the country. At least two are incarcerated without medical reason in a psychiatric hospital.

The Malaysian government brought criminal charges of "false reporting" against human rights activist Irene Fernandez for her reporting on torture, mistreatment, and deaths among migrant workers in Malaysia's immigrant detention centers. Fernandez is free on bail during her prolonged trial.

In Tunisia, parliamentarian and human rights activist Khemais Chammari received a five-year prison term on spurious charges, and the government declined to investigate complaints of torture by imprisoned human rights lawyer Nejib Hosni.

South Korea detained Chin-kwan, a monk who is co-chair of the Buddhist Committee for Human Rights, on suspicion of violating the much-abused National Security Law by exchanging information on the activities of dissident organizations with the chair of the North Korean Buddhist Alliance.

Uzbekistan detained members of the Human Rights Society of Uzbekistan and continued to deny it the right to register. The police also briefly detained and mistreated Human Rights Watch's representative in Tashkent.

Nigeria detained, among others, human rights lawyers Gani Fawehinmi and Femi Falana.

The Cuban government continued to prevent access by the U.N. special rapporteur for Cuba, Carl-Johan Groth. Burma refused access to U.N. Special Rapporteur Rajsoomer Lallah and also barred a delegation from the International Labor Organization sent to investigate Burmese labor rights practices. Iraq continued to refuse permission either for an investigation by Special Rapporteur Max van der Stoel or for deployment of U.N. human rights monitors. Indonesia rejected a request for a visit to East Timor by U.N. Special Rapporteur on Torture Nigel Rodley. China denied UNICEF access to some orphanages it sought to visit to examine the conditions in which children were being kept following publication of a Human Rights Watch report.

Local human rights organizations remained effectively banned in Bahrain, Bhutan, Brunei, Burma, China and Tibet, Libya, North Korea, Saudi Arabia, Singapore, Sudan, Syria, Turkmenistan, and Vietnam. Investigations by Human Rights Watch and other international organizations remained impossible or were rejected by Bahrain, Burma, Cuba, Iraq, and Saudi Arabia.

HUMAN RIGHTS WATCH WORLD REPORT 1997

HUMAN RIGHTS WATCH

AFRICA

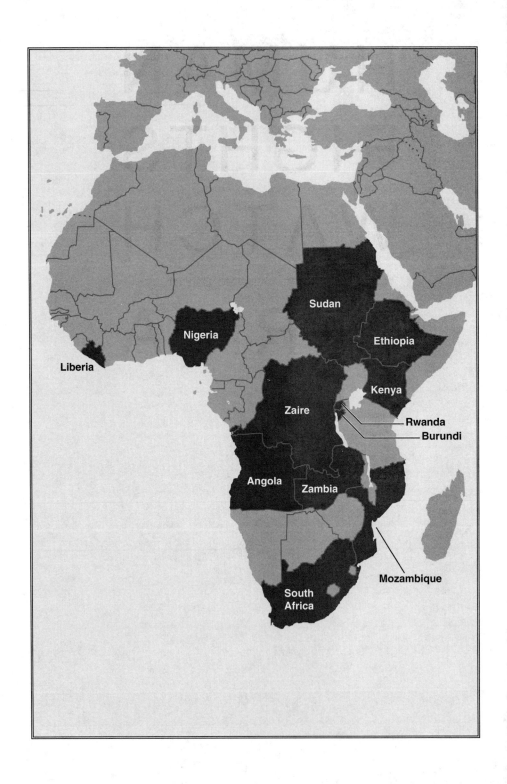

HUMAN RIGHTS WATCH/AFRICA OVERVIEW

Human Rights Developments

Africa in the news headlines was a continent of collapsed states, internal armed conflicts, communal violence and flagging democracies. The grim news often obscured some of the hopeful developments in countries where peace was being restored or where, despite continuing problems, popular mobilization and political reform resulted in greater freedom than in the past to take part in civic life. Furthermore, a resilient group of human rights activists in virtually every country continued to challenge government abuses, often at great personal risk.

The independent media continued to operate notwithstanding numerous government efforts to restrict freedom of expression. In 1996, newspaper editors and journalists in countries such as Nigeria, Kenya, and Zambia continued to suffer arson attacks on their premises or criminal charges brought against them for articles critical of the government.

The efforts of local nongovernmental organizations to exercise their rights and to expand the space for civil society to function were not, however, sufficiently reinforced or reflected at the international level. With the possible exception of Burundi, the international community either watched Africa's major human rights crises silently or stopped short of investing the political and financial commitment necessary to promote a strong human rights policy. This was all the more disheartening given that civilians were the primary casualties of political oppression and upheaval, and Africa accounted for the world's largest refugee and internally displaced population.

Some of the most serious human rights violations occurred as fighting continued or resumed in countries such as Burundi, Liberia, Somalia, and Sudan. These countries reflected the character of war in today's world—internal conflicts exacerbated by ethnic or religious antagonisms—with civilians constituting the bulk of the casualties. Increasingly, the massive refugee populations which flooded into neighboring countries led to tensions with local populations and heightened insecurity within the region due to cross-border raids by combatants. The mobilization of exile armies among the refugee millions was further fueled by increased weapons flows to the area.

No conflict epitomized this phenomenon more than the growing morass in the Great Lakes region, which demonstrated the inextricable links between the struggles for political control in Rwanda, Burundi, and Zaire, violence against civilians, and large numbers of refugees and displaced persons. By the year's end, the chaos in eastern Zaire became the latest humanitarian catastrophe in the region. Two years after the genocide, which killed between 500,000 and one million Rwandans, mostly Tutsis, and the defeat of the Hutu government responsible for the massacres, close to 2 million Rwandan refugees remained exiled for most of the year in Zaire and Tanzania, still controlled—and prevented from returning to Rwanda—by the Hutu extremist authorities.

Attacks by a Zairian armed opposition group on the refugee camps in eastern Zaire in October ended the stalemate and led to a mass repatriation of Rwandan refugees in November.

The reluctance of many refugees to return home was reinforced by the largely Tutsi-led Rwandan government's continued imprisonment of some 83,000 persons accused of genocide and the inordinate delay in the start of trials. Members of the former military and militia used the refugee camps as bases from which to launch a growing number of incursions this year, increasingly targeting survivors or witnesses of the genocide and local officials. Rwandan military authorities responded with operations that killed hundreds of mostly Hutu civilians.

The crisis was worsened by Zaire's attempt, with the support of the regrouped Rwandan forces loyal to the former government, to expel Zairian citizens of Tutsi origin from the Masisi area in North Kivu to Rwanda. In a complex chain of violence, people of Hutu origin attacked Tutsi, and in other places attacked or were attacked by Zairians of different ethnic background, forcing these Zairian Tutsi to flee to Rwanda. By October, another group of Zairian Tutsis in South Kivu, known as Banyamulenge, who were threatened and attacked by Zairian military and civilians, took up arms and, with the apparent support of the Rwandan government, attacked the Zairian military and Rwandan and Burundian refugees and dispersed most of the refugee camps. The insecurity in the area forced international humanitarian agencies to withdraw in October. By mid-November, all the refugee camps in eastern Zaire had been attacked and a flood of Rwandan refugees crossed back into Rwanda. Meanwhile, the conflict in Burundi also continued to intensify, as contenders in what became an open civil war attacked unarmed civilians on ethnic grounds as the Tutsi-led government and the armed Hutu opposition groups fought to consolidate their bases of support. That violence spawned further waves of refugees and internally displaced persons.

While the Great Lakes region received more attention, other major refugee situations elsewhere on the continent also blurred the distinction between refugee populations and encamped armed opposition groups, as well as the spill-over of the conflict in cross-border raids. The thirteen-year-old conflict in Sudan between the Muslim Arabic-speaking north and marginalized Sudanese peoples, led by mostly non-Muslim black African southerners, continued to have an impact on bordering countries. Because Sudan is the largest country, geographically, in Africa and borders on ten countries, its regional armed conflicts have spawned refugee flows to several neighboring countries, often accompanied by Sudanese rebels. Similarly, refugees and preexisting rebel groups in neighboring countries have taken refuge in Sudan. In 1996, governments of Eritrea, Ethiopia, and Uganda accused the Sudan government of supporting rebel movements in these three countries, and the Sudan government in turn accused all three of helping the rebel Sudan People's Liberation Movement/Army. Since countries in the region gained independence, charges that one government used another's rebels as proxies to destabilize another were made by governments of all stripes in the Horn of Africa. The alleged interference was along political lines more often than religious or ethnic lines—for instance, Sudan's Islamic government was alleged to assist non-Muslim groups, such as the nominally Christian Lord's Resistance Army in Uganda. Nevertheless, ethnic animosity was exacerbated since the rebel groups usually had an ethnic origin or appeal.

A booming arms trade continued to profit from and fuel the conflicts in Africa—often supported by governments who sought to advance their geostrategic interests by supplying weapons to certain factions. In the Great Lakes region, military shipments continued to flow to the defeated Rwandan government's forces in eastern Zaire with the complicity of Zairian authorities. In Angola, arms shipments persisted to both the government and the rebel National Union for the Total Independence of Angola (UNITA) forces in clear violation of an international arms embargo.

In countries undergoing the fragile transition from war to peace, the critical need for human rights concerns to be centrally integrated into the peace process was underscored by the setbacks caused to the peace. In Angola, serious violations of the ceasefire continued, and other violations including the restriction on freedom of movement, abduction of civilians and the intimidation of journalists created grave concerns as to whether the peace process would hold. In Liberia, the absence of any mechanism in the peace accord to hold combatants accountable for rights violations was one of the reasons which allowed the factions to renew fighting with impunity in April and May.

In countries that were undergoing democratization, the news was good and bad. South Africa continued to hold out hope for Africa's ability to institute democratic governance. Significant reforms continued to be implemented to address past inequalities and to introduce a culture of respect for human rights. Following the approval of a draft final constitution by the constitutional assembly in May, the constitutional court endorsed the bill of rights but objected to some other provisions of the draft constitution. The constitutional assembly reconvened in September and adopted an amended draft on October 11 subject to further certification by the constitutional court on November 18. Malawi's democratic transition remained on course despite difficulties experienced in coalition-based governance. The breakdown of the coalition between the United Democratic Front (UDF) and the Alliance for Democracy (AFORD) created uncertainty regarding the ability of President Bakili Muluzi to govern for the duration of his five-year term. Nonetheless, Malawi continued to enjoy a vastly improved climate for civil and political rights.

Against the background of setbacks for democratic transition in such countries as Niger, Chad, and Gambia, two countries stood out as beacons of hope for successful democratic change and consolidation: Mali and Benin. Years after the end of the repressive Derg in Ethiopia, political debate and institution building gradually increased under the coalition government, and while grave rights problems remained, there were efforts to develop a high-level human rights commission and ombudsman, and the independent press continued—despite government crackdowns—to be outspoken. In Eritrea, the draft of a permanent constitution providing for guarantees of fundamental human rights was finalized in July. The post-independence period continued, however, to be marked by minimal political progress. High-ranking officials insisted that multipartyism was not to be expected in the country for another decade at least. Conscientious objectors had their citizenship officially revoked, while nonviolent opposition groups could only function in exile.

A number of other governments, which professed to be democratizing following the introduction of multipartyism in the early 1990s, had not introduced the institutional reform essential to effective change and misused state institutions to partisan ends. The governments of Kenya, Zaire, and Zambia, in the run-ups to their next multiparty elections, resorted to harassment of the political opposition, intimidation of the independent press, and blatant manipulation of the electoral process and the judiciary, in order to retain power. In Nigeria, a January 1996 military decree formalizing the country's second "transition program" to civilian rule under the new military leadership showed little promise, particularly since decrees suspending constitutional rights, allowing detention without charge or trial and criminalizing criticism of the government remained in force.

The manipulation of ethnicity to further political ends was an ever-present factor on a continent with hundreds of ethnic groups often randomly divided by national boundaries placed during the colonial period. In many conflicts, such as those in Liberia, Burundi, and Zaire, ethnicity was used by leaders who manipulated and exploited these differences and have erroneously portrayed the ensuing tensions as inevitable and intractable tribal conflicts. This year, the Zairian government capitalized on the Rwandan refugee crisis to "cleanse" the country of certain groups of its citizens by denationalizing them on the basis of their ethnicity. The manipulation of ethnicity was also evident in multiparty states such as Kenya and Zambia, where state-sponsored attacks were directed against ethnic groups perceived to be opposition supporters.

The issue of accountability for past abuses remained a critical issue for the rule of law and lasting reconciliation in countries moving toward restoring peace. In South Africa, the National Commission on Truth and Reconciliation was empowered to investigate and document human rights violations between 1960 and 1993, to recommend reparations for the victims, and to grant amnesty to perpetrators in return for full disclosure of the acts they had committed. It began its hearings in April. In Malawi on December 23, 1995, the high court found ex-President Banda and his leading henchmen not guilty on charges of murders of three Malawi cabinet ministers and a member of parliament in 1984. The trials of seventy-three top-ranking officials of the Derg charged with committing genocide and war crimes continued since their opening in mid-December 1994. Twenty-eight of the defendants were being tried in absentia: Col. Mengistu Haile Mariam, who headed the Derg, was in comfortable asylum in Zimbabwe. Hopes for prosecutions to commence inside Rwanda, where more than 80,000 people were held on suspicion of genocide in grossly overcrowded and inhumane conditions, were frustrated for the second year by a lack of political will to proceed with trials and an impotent judiciary. In September the passage of a genocide law which legislated procedures and penalties for the trial of genocide crimes removed one of the obstacles toward the resumption of the judicial system.

The Right to Monitor

A local human rights movement existed in virtually every African country. Although often nascent, and frequently under attack, this nongovernmental sector was critical to the creation of a broader rights constituency within Africa and a hope for lasting change. While many of these groups needed to further clarify their role and develop their capacity, local human rights organizations had become an important force on the continent, and inter-African links had also begun to develop. In countries such as Kenya, Liberia, Nigeria, South Africa, Zaire, and Zambia, human rights organizations continued to be a growing force in curtailing government abuse and calling for accountability. These organizations, among other things, publicized government abuses; educated the public about their rights; provided legal and other assistance to victims of human rights abuses; and conducted advocacy work within their country and in regional and international fora for greater respect of rights by their governments.

An unfortunate testimony to the effectiveness of these groups were the steps that governments or warring factions often resorted to in order to silence these monitors. Human rights activists on the African continent took enormous risks in order to carry out their work. In 1996, human rights activists continued to face harassment, imprisonment, torture and even death in many countries. Repression also took the form of blocking or rescinding legal registration, banning the maintenance of a bank account or the receipt of foreign donations, and vilification in the official press. The Sudanese Human Rights Organization continued to function outside the country since it was banned after the 1989 coup. When fighting broke out in Monrovia, Liberia in April, many leading human rights activists were targeted by the warring factions and were forced to go into hiding or leave the country. Nigeria's thriving human rights community continued to persevere, despite the execution of nine Ogoni activists at the end of 1995. During 1996, a number of leading activists were detained, others were prevented from traveling abroad to attend meetings of the U.N. Commission on Human Rights or other meetings, and some had their passports confiscated.

The Role of
the International Community

The political will for international involvement in supporting human rights and humanitarian initiatives in Africa continued to diminish, prompted by recollections of failed U.N. peacekeeping operations and diminished geopolitical interests in post-Cold War Africa. This disengagement was coupled with growing calls for greater regional involvement in seeking solutions to Africa's problems. Even where the wider international community remained engaged, international efforts often failed to integrate vigorous observation of human rights practices into its approach. Policy initiatives by the U.N., the OAU, the E.U., and the major powers frequently overlooked or compromised human rights concerns in the hope of hastening an end to a political crisis.

Talk continued about the need to create early warning systems to identify and prevent potential crises on the African continent, recognizing that preventative action was more desirable than massive humanitarian aid following a crisis. Yet, the case of Burundi starkly illustrated the futility of early warning systems if not accompanied by the political will to take meaningful steps to avert a looming disaster. The creation of the mandate of a special rapporteur on human rights in Burundi and the recommendations of the U.N. International Commission on Burundi were not followed by concerted action to influence the human rights emergency they observed.

Other protracted conflicts in Africa received much less international attention generally, and little or no emphasis was placed on human rights. Since the departure of the international intervention force from Somalia, which never made human rights a priority, no international attention focused on the human rights concerns of Somalis, despite continuing violations and low-level conflict. In Sudan, the civil war underway since 1983 against the rebel Sudan People's Liberation Army (SPLA) continued with serious violations of human rights on both sides. However, while the U.N. Commission on Human Rights condemned Sudan's human rights record for the fourth consecutive year and renewed the mandate of the special rapporteur, the government was able to block the distribution of emergency relief to certain locations of strategic value to the SPLA and the deployment of human rights monitors on Sudan's borders was stalled. Even in Liberia, which had a regional peacekeeping force and a U.N. observer team, the peacekeepers did nothing to protect civilians or to stop the fighting when a fresh outbreak of fighting erupted in April.

For many international donors who had previously taken a strong human rights position against autocratic one party states, the introduction of a multiparty system became the benchmark to discontinue pressure for change in a number of transitional democracies. There was a lack of sustained attention to human rights concerns in countries in transition such as Ethiopia, Kenya, Zaire, and Zambia as leaders consolidated power in systems that were multiparty in name, while suppressing the freedoms of expression, association and other fundamental rights without which political participation is a dead letter.

Regional Organizations

The gradual disengagement by the wider international community was accompanied by calls for African organizations to play a greater role in conflict resolution. While there was still a willingness to countenance intervention for humanitarian reasons, the major powers were reluctant to commit their troops. There was a readiness on the part of some African governments to respond to this challenge, although Africa's regional institutions remained weak and attempts to date were disappointing. One such example was the West African peacekeeping force ECOMOG (the Economic Community of West African States Monitoring Group) deployed in Liberia since 1990. When fighting between the factions erupted in Monrovia in April 1996, the regional peacekeepers displayed an astonishing reluctance to intervene to stop the fighting or the looting, or to protect civilians. Some ECOMOG soldiers even participated in the looting and took sides in the fighting.

Nonetheless, an encouraging development during this year was the emergence of new initiatives, however limited, by the Organization of African Unity (OAU) to respond to regional human rights crises. In December 1995, the African Commission on Human and Peoples' Rights, a substructure of the OAU, held its second extraordinary session (the first extraordinary session to consider a country situation), in response to the execution in Nigeria of nine minority rights activists, including internationally known author Ken Saro-Wiwa. The commission expressed its "serious concern on the situation of human rights in Nigeria" and resolved to send a fact-finding mission to Nigeria to meet with Nigerian authorities. The Nigerian military government, however, rejected the proposed dates in February for the mission to take place, and no new dates had been agreed by the end of the year. Disappointingly, the commission did not follow up on the initiative of the extraordinary session to make any detailed statement on Nigeria. Other fact-finding missions the African Commission agreed to send to Rwanda, Chad, Zaire, and Sudan never materialized. At its nineteenth ordinary meeting in Ouagadougou, Burkina Faso, in March, the African Commission adopted a "Plan of Action Against Impunity in Africa," including commitments to strengthening national judicial systems and the establishment of an African court. At its sixty-fourth regular session in Yaounde, Cameroon in July, the OAU Council of Ministers endorsed the plan. The OAU also passed a summit resolution on Liberia on the possible establishment of a war crimes tribunal for Liberia.

Subregional groups on the continent, while still nascent, also showed some initiative this year in addressing issues with human rights implications. In particular, the political developments in South Africa had a positive impact on regional stability and on bids to strengthen the rule of law in the region. In August, the Southern African Development Community (SADC) launched its Organ on politics, defense, and security whose mandate included human rights issues. Furthermore, the Southern African region began as a group to call on their neighbors to improve respect for the rule of law. Following an attempted coup by the king of Lesotho, SADC pushed for the restoration of civilian rule there. The same approach was adopted in Swaziland to pressure the king there to move toward a more constitutional form of government.

A subregional response by Eastern and Central African states to the crisis in Burundi and Zaire also represented possible movement toward a more institutionalized response to regional crises. In June, at a subregional meeting in Arusha, Tanzania, East and Central African leaders resolved to create an African Intervention Force to be deployed in Burundi. The plan was never implemented in part because the authorities in Burundi revoked their prior agreement to the arrangement and later events overtook the plan following the military coup in July. After the coup, East and Central African leaders imposed economic sanctions on Burundi to foster a quick return to civilian rule and a peaceful settlement of its internal crisis, and the OAU endorsed the decision to impose sanctions. Following the outbreak of violence in eastern Zaire, regional leaders met in Nairobi, Kenya, on November 5 to seek regional solutions to the crisis.

Within the Horn of Africa, the heads of member states of the Inter-Governmental Authority on Drought and Development—Sudan, Uganda, Kenya, Ethiopia, Eritrea, and Djibouti—signed amendments to the charter of the organization in March, ten years after its foundation. The new charter brought about changes in the structure of the organization and expanded its mandate from the original concerns over food security and environmental conservation to broader issues, including conflict prevention and resolution in the subregion.

United Nations

Although U.N. involvement on the African continent remained extensive, its initiatives in Africa consistently downplayed the human rights role of its various mandates. Although U.N. reporting and monitoring of human rights abuses improved—through human rights field operations such as the one in Rwanda and the reports of special rapporteurs in Sudan, Burundi, and Zaire—information or recommendations contained in reports submitted to headquarters were frequently not integrated into the wider U.N. policy. The shortsightedness of this approach was revealed in the U.N. peacekeeping operations in Liberia and Angola as the warring factions continued to undermine the peace process with impunity.

The potential for effective U.N. action was highlighted by its positive contributions. The special rapporteurs for Sudan, Burundi, and Zaire acted as vigorous advocates for human rights concerns to be integrated into U.N. work and their reports ensured that timely information was available for policymakers. The U.N. Human Rights Field Operation in Rwanda, which showed more promise under new leadership in late 1995, improved its monitoring of human rights violations in Rwanda and its influence with the Rwandan government. Similarly, in Sudan, the United Nations Children's Fund (UNICEF), won praise for its work in Operation Lifeline Sudan (Southern sector) in conducting field investigations of attacks affecting civilians, and extracting a commitment by the warring factions to commit to ground rules that complied with humanitarian law.

However, these individual successes remained isolated. The rhetoric on human rights was often not followed with the necessary resources to translate the recommendations into reality. This was most apparent in the U.N.'s policy toward Burundi. Despite extensive warnings about the need to take action to prevent further violence in Burundi and vigorous advocacy efforts by the U.N. special rapporteur, the U.N. remained reluctant to take meaningful next steps. In February, the special rapporteur called for the creation of an international tribunal, yet no action was taken to this end. Lip service continued to be paid to the need for human rights monitors to be deployed in Burundi. In April only five monitors were sent, and further funding pledged for more monitors in July did not result in any further appointments.

Important international efforts, which held promise over a year ago, appeared to have run into problems. The performance of the U.N. International Commission on Burundi, established in 1995 to investigate the 1993 assassination of President Ndadaye and the massacres that had ensued, was dis-

appointing. The Security Council's reluctance to make the findings of the International Commission's report public and the commission's failure to insist upon prosecutions and accountability for human rights violations diminished the commission's potential effectiveness. When the report was released in August, after government sources selectively leaked favorable parts of it, its reporting of the situation appeared unbalanced as did its conclusions: these called for the creation of an international tribunal to deal with the "acts of genocide" attributed to the Hutu, while not calling for any similar examination of the ethnic slaughter of Hutus committed by the Tutsi-dominated army.

Similarly, the International Criminal Tribunal for Rwanda, which was set up by the U.N. in 1994 to hold perpetrators of the genocide accountable, faced serious resource, staffing, and logistical constraints. During the year, tribunal investigations continued to compile evidence to bring indictments against those accused of organizing the genocide. By November, the tribunal had indicted twenty-one persons in thirteen indictments, but only three were in the custody of the tribunal in Arusha, Tanzania. Zambia, Kenya, Belgium, Switzerland, and the United States had arrested indicted persons and agreed to hand them over to the tribunal. The Rwanda tribunal continued to receive comparatively less attention than its counterpart for the former Yugoslavia, and adequate funding only became available in mid-1996. In addition to the financial and logistical difficulties, Rwanda tribunal investigations were initially undermined by the appointment of unqualified personnel, limited training, and faulty methodology and investigative procedures. These problems were magnified with regard to the investigation of gender-based crimes such as rape. As trials opened in September in Arusha, Tanzania, it became clear that the Rwanda tribunal had paid inadequate attention to the need for effective witness and victim protection, which is important in light of reported reprisals against those who agreed to testify.

Commonwealth of Nations

The Commonwealth of Nations, to which many African countries belong, including Mozambique as well as former British colonies, suspended Nigeria for a period of two years at its November 1995 heads of government meeting in Auckland, New Zealand, which took place at the time of the execution of Saro-Wiwa and the eight others. This was the first time such action had been taken against a member state. At the same time, the Commonwealth adopted the Millbrook Action Program on the 1991 Harare Commonwealth Declaration, which included a commitment to democratic governance. A Commonwealth Ministerial Action Group (CMAG) was appointed to consider the cases of Nigeria, the Gambia and Sierra Leone, the three African countries which were in violation of the declaration (elections in Sierra Leone later removed it from the list). In April CMAG recommended a series of sanctions against Nigeria, pending the restoration of civilian rule, but the implementation of these sanctions was suspended pending further dialogue with the government. In September, the Nigerian government agreed to allow a CMAG fact-finding mission to visit the country, but refused to give guarantees that the members of the mission would be free to meet with whom they wanted.

European Union

The European Union is one of the most significant donors of humanitarian and development assistance to Africa. The European Development Fund has earmarked US$16.25 billion to Africa for the period 1996 to 2000. Additionally, the E.U. granted $218.71 million for development programs through NGOs and $23.75 million in support of democracy and human rights.

However, the E.U. failed to make full use of it leverage and did not play a comparably strong role in defense of human rights on the continent, often because individual member states opposed to strong positions were able to block E.U. action. In the case of Nigeria, E.U. member states agreed to impose certain legally binding sanctions in the wake of the execution of Ken Saro-Wiwa and eight other Ogoni activists. These sanctions include visa denials, a prospective arms embargo and suspension of all development cooperation with the Nigerian government. The E.U., however, failed to establish sufficient implementation procedures for the arms embargo and major European trading partners appeared opposed to further measures against the abusive regime.

In the Great Lakes region, the E.U. has been the primary contributor of humanitarian assistance—$674.87 million since 1994—adding the contributions of individual member states the amount is $943.56 million. On the diplomatic front, the E.U. has appointed a special envoy to the region, and E.U. officials have on some occasions made strong statements emphasizing the need for respect for human rights. The E.U. also provided funds for projects such as the U.N. Human Rights Operation in Rwanda and an independent radio in Burundi. In general, however, the E.U. only has a lackluster record on the promotion of human rights in the Great Lakes region.

In April 1996, France broke with E.U. policy on Zaire and announced a resumption of its bilateral aid to the Mobutu government, which had been cut off by E.U. member states in 1991. The French decision, which came at the height of the expulsion of Tutsi from Zaire, was apparently not linked to any determination that human rights had improved there, although it indicated that human rights concerns were not high on the French policy agenda in Zaire.

United States

The administration sent a number of high-level delegations to Africa in 1996, including Secretary of State Warren Christopher, U.N. Ambassador Madeline Albright, the late Commerce Secretary Ron Brown, and National Security Advisor Anthony Lake, although Africa was not a high priority for U.S. policy. Even in those countries where the U.S. was more engaged, the administration was unable to forge a consensus and build a strong human rights policy. The main exception to this pattern involved the consistent U.S. attention to Burundi, which stemmed in part from the shame associated with the international failure to respond to the 1994 Rwandan genocide.

The prime example of the lack of a clear policy involved Nigeria, where the U.S. expressed outrage over the execution of Saro-Wiwa and the eight other Ogonis and the continued dismal human rights situation. Yet after taking some steps such as extending pre-existing bans on military links and extending a visa ban, no further concrete measures were adopted, despite the fact that no improvements occurred in Nigeria. In the Great Lakes region, although considerable U.S. diplomatic activity centered on the Burundi crisis, similar attention was not paid to other countries in the region. In Rwanda, the U.S. failed to use its substantial leverage with the government to press for human rights improvements, especially in the area of the judicial system and military attacks on armed civilians. Zaire, too, represented a case where the U.S. muted human rights criticism in the interests of gaining President Mobutu's cooperation in other regional issues. Even in countries that were engaged to some degree in a transition to democracy, like Kenya and Ethiopia, the U.S. refrained from vigorously protesting the narrowing political space in which civil society and dissenting voices could operate. And in Liberia, the closest that the U.S. ever had to a colony in Africa, the U.S. deferred for too long to the West Africans to attempt to resolve the devastating conflict.

In Burundi and Angola, the U.S. demonstrated that it was capable of formulating a more forceful policy. The U.S. invested political capital and played an important role, with varying degrees of success, in efforts at conflict resolution in both countries. In addition, the U.S. involvement in southern Africa provided an indication of the potential impact of sustained U.S. engagement.

Increasingly, the U.S. sought to deal with crises in Africa by encouraging African solutions to African problems. To this end,

in September the U.S. launched an initiative to create an African Crisis Response Force (ACRF). Although the idea had been raised before, the impetus for the force was the Burundi crisis, and the clear indications that no U.N. force would be mounted quickly to deal with an even worse humanitarian disaster. The U.S. proposal envisioned a force of 5,000 to 10,000 troops to be on standby in their respective countries to play a humanitarian, rather then a peacekeeping, role. The administration was actively seeking support among European and African countries. Unfortunately, no human rights component to such a force was contemplated.

The U.S. provided some $717 million in development assistance to sub-Saharan Africa during fiscal year 1996. In addition, it provided approximately $923 million in humanitarian aid, including food aid and refugee and emergency assistance.

The Work of
Human Rights Watch/Africa

Throughout 1996, Human Rights Watch/Africa continued its work of monitoring and documenting human rights abuses in about a dozen countries in Africa. An attempt was made to balance the work on humanitarian disasters—such as Burundi, Liberia and Sudan—without neglecting to address the human rights abuses taking place in countries in which a transition to democracy had been pledged, including Ethiopia, Kenya, Nigeria, Zaire, and Zambia. We also monitored countries emerging from recent conflict such as Angola and Mozambique, and worked in Rwanda in the aftermath of genocide. The reform process underway in South Africa allowed us to contribute in a different way, often commenting on or contributing to proposed legislative reform. Acknowledging the growing refugee and internally displaced populations on the continent, the division created a new researcher position to monitor the human rights issues arising from forced displacement. In 1996, Human Rights Watch/Africa sent missions to Angola, Eritrea, Ethiopia, Kenya, Mozambique, Namibia, Nigeria, Rwanda, South Africa,

Zambia, and Zimbabwe. The division also worked closely with Human Rights Watch's Arms Project, Children's Rights Project, and Women's Rights Project.

Human Rights Watch/Africa provided regular briefings, reports and documentation to governments and U.N. representatives, as well as nongovernmental and humanitarian organizations. We continued to actively monitor and seek to influence the policies of governments, in particular, those of Africa, Europe, and the U.S. government, as well as the international financial institutions. We expanded our advocacy into the impact of multinational corporations operating in Africa, particularly oil companies operating in Nigeria. Similarly, we met with representatives of African governments in order to raise issues of concern in their own countries and elsewhere on the human rights front. We increased attention to the African Commission on Human and Peoples' Rights, attending meetings as observers and raising concerns with the commissioners. Through our reports, articles and frequent media interviews, we sought to sensitize broader public opinion internationally about human rights conditions in Africa.

Significant resources were committed to monitoring and advocacy on the situation in the Great Lakes region. We remained a key source of information on Burundi, among other things, providing information and documentation to the U.N. special rapporteur on Burundi and to the U.N. Commission of Investigation into the assassination of President Ndadaye and subsequent massacres. In support of the special rapporteur, we advocated an arms embargo on all sides to the conflict in February and pressed for the establishment of an international tribunal for Burundi. We wrote several letters to the U.N. Security Council on Burundi calling for an arms embargo, expressing concern over the proposal of a standby force, and urging for the creation of an International Criminal Tribunal for Burundi.

In collaboration with the International Federation of Human Rights Leagues, Human Rights Watch/Africa continued to maintain a field office in Rwanda with a tripartite mission: documenting the genocide, monitoring the current situation in Rwanda and Burundi, and supporting local human rights monitors. The Rwanda-based project located, catalogued, and translated more than a thousand pages of documents from the period of the genocide from prefectural and communal offices. Along with interviews with hundreds of witnesses, the documentary record served as the basis for ongoing analysis and reporting on the mechanics of the genocide, to be published in a forthcoming report. In monitoring the current situation, we published numerous press releases and met with Rwandan and international authorities to protest the abuses investigated. We also provided information and expertise to the International Tribunal for Rwanda and national judiciaries in Europe and North America for prosecution of former Rwandan officials implicated in the genocide and in related civil court cases. In collaboration with the International Federation of Human Rights Leagues and the Human Rights Watch Women's Rights Project, we conducted an in-depth investigation resulting in a book-length report entitled *Shattered Lives: Sexual Violence during the Rwandan Genocide and its Aftermath* in September. The report received extensive press coverage that prompted renewed attention to the lack of rape indictments before the International Criminal Tribunal for Rwanda and the need for assistance to Rwandan women.

In seeking to pressure the U.N. to incorporate a human rights component into its peacekeeping operations, and specifically into the plans for disarmament, demobilization, and repatriation, we continued to monitor peacekeeping operations in Liberia and Angola. In conjunction with the Human Rights Watch Arms Project, we published in February *Between War and Peace: Arms Trade and Human Rights Abuses since the Lusaka Protocol*. The report attracted widespread press coverage and contributed to forcing the U.N. to admit that weapons flows continued unchecked to the country. In April we organized a conference in London on "Southern Africa 2000: New Regional Dynamics" in conjunction with a number of other organizations, the proceedings of which were published as a special edition of the human rights magazine, *African Topics*.

Human Rights Watch/Africa continued to monitor countries undergoing transition. In August and September, Human Rights Watch/Africa visited Kenya and Zambia respectively to examine the human rights record of these governments in the run-up to multiparty elections. We also met with U.S. and European policymakers to raise human rights concerns during the year. We continued to monitor the human rights situation in South Africa, commenting on legislation relating to the new police complaints mechanism and on the proposed review of the Prevention of Family Violence Act. Throughout the year, we protested rights violations to the Nigerian military authorities and pressed the U.K. and U.S. governments as well as the E.U. institutions to take effective action to promote human rights in Nigeria. We assisted the U.N. special rapporteurs on the independence of judges and lawyers and on extrajudicial, summary or arbitrary executions in their preparation for a mission to Nigeria. In September, we published a report *Permanent Transition: Current Violations of Human Rights in Nigeria*. Human Rights Watch called upon the U.N. to appoint a special rapporteur on Nigeria and to agree to a strong resolution condemning human rights developments in Nigeria.

Human Rights Watch/Africa closely monitored the human rights situation in the countries of the Horn of Africa and frequently consulted and exchanged views with local and international groups on the situation of human rights in the region. In June and July, we visited Ethiopia to investigate the progress of the trials of prisoners held for human rights crimes under the former government, as well as reports of continuing abuses in regions affected by insurgencies and harsh government restrictions of the freedoms of association and expression. We engaged in a constructive dialogue with the government on the urgent need for account-ability for current as well as past abuses. We also called for the charging or release of the remaining 1,700 officials of the previous government who passed their fifth year in prison without charges or trial. In a visit to Eritrea in July, we familiarized ourselves with the constitutional developments and government restrictions on civil society. A book-length report on Sudan was published in May entitled *Behind the Red Line: Political Repression in Sudan*, noting that political parties remained banned and freedom of the press, association, assembly and other basic civil rights were not permitted. We frequently commented on the issue of slavery in Sudan, urging the government to prosecute those responsible and to assist families to locate missing relatives. We also denounced the secret military trial of thirty-one persons, including some civilians, for an alleged February coup attempt. We criticized the UNHCR for not taking adequate steps to prevent boys in camps it supports from being conscripted by opposition groups. We also urged the U.N. Commission on Human Rights to establish three U.N. human rights monitors on the borders of Sudan.

Human Rights Watch/Africa closely monitored the situation of refugees and internally displaced populations in the Great Lakes region and in Kenya. In July, we published a report entitled *Zaire—Forced to Flee: Violence Against the Tutsis* on violations against Zairians of pre-colonial Rwandan origin attacked and driven from North Kivu, Zaire. We traveled to Kenya in August in order to monitor the situation of the internally displaced population and to assess the success of a joint U.N. Development Program/Kenyan government resettlement program, which ended in September 1995. We also traveled to the Somali refugee camps in north-eastern Kenya on a follow-up mission to document protection measures that had been put into place to prevent and assist rape victims. In a discussion paper which was distributed at the October UNHCR Executive Committee meeting, Human Rights Watch examined the implications of the UNHCR Guidelines on the Protection of

Women, making recommendations based on the Kenya mission, for better integration of the guidelines into the agency's protection activities worldwide.

In cooperation with the Human Rights Watch Arms Project, we continued to work on the legacy of landmines in Africa, visiting Mozambique, South Africa, Zambia, and Zimbabwe on this issue. Our lobbying contributed to the Angola government's announcement in May that it was committed to work toward a ban on the stockpiling, transfer and use of anti-personnel mines.

ANGOLA

Human Rights Developments

Angola remained in transition between war and peace and human rights conditions of 1996 did not improve over those of 1995. Both the Movement for the Popular Liberation of Angola (MPLA)-led government and the armed opposition group, the Union for the Total Independence of Angola (UNITA), were responsible for abuses, including restrictions on freedom of movement, abduction of civilians and the intimidation of journalists.

Serious violations of the cease-fire continued to decline in 1996, although in December 1995 the government's capture of a string of UNITA-held hamlets in the northwest brought deadlock and delayed the whole peace process. By October 1996 the majority of reported cease-fire violations by the government and UNITA were limited attacks on civilians designed either to control the movement of food aid in contested areas or to stop people from moving into areas controlled by the other side. However, there were also continued violations of the Lusaka cease-fire protocols by the government's Angolan Armed Forces (FAA) taking up forward positions.

On March 1, President Jose Eduardo dos Santos and UNITA leader Jonas Savimbi met in Libreville, Gabon, and agreed to complete confinement to quarters of troops by June, to form a joint senior military command, and to integrate UNITA forces into the national armed forces by June. They also agreed to the formation of a "government of national reconciliation" by July, and an indefinite extension of the legislative and executive term to allow the government of national unity to play a constructive role. At that meeting, one of the two vice presidencies was offered by the government to UNITA, which Savimbi formally rejected in August, claiming his party had decided that he should do so.

In May, the National Assembly formally approved an amnesty law for all human rights abuses committed between May 31, 1991 and May 8, 1996: the sixth Amnesty Law passed by Angola's parliament since 1981. U.N. Special Representative Alioune Blondin Beye immediately afterwards announced that this amnesty law would provide a new impetus for the peace process.

The quartering and reintegration of soldiers under the Lusaka Protocol has been slow. UNITA almost completed its confinement to quarters quota of 62,500 in early October, when most of UNITA's fifteen camps for its disbanded units closed. However, over 12,000 UNITA fighters left the demobilization camps after having registered, and U.N. figures show that 7,600 of those quartered were under the age of eighteen and many of them were civilians that had been forced into the camps by UNITA. U.N. and aid officials stated that as many as half of those quartered were not real soldiers, suggesting that UNITA was filling its demobilization quota, without reducing its troop strength to the extent claimed. UNITA also retained its elite units outside the quartering process and its top generals in their fighting units ready for a resumption of hostilities.

In June, the first fourteen UNITA officers arrived at a designated base outside Luanda. It was not until September 9 that five generals from UNITA's army arrived in Luanda to join the Angolan Armed Forces following strong pressure from the U.S. and the U.N. Under the Lusaka Protocol, UNITA generals were made responsible for deciding with other officers of the armed forces how to incorporate 26,500 UNITA soldiers and officers into the army, with the rest being demobilized. A further five generals arrived in Luanda in October, but the reintegration process was many months behind schedule.

UNITA also failed to confine to quarters its self-proclaimed police force, despite strong demands that it do so. UNITA appeared to have replaced uniformed soldiers in some areas with persons that it claimed were its police, even though the establishment of such a force was contrary to the Lusaka Protocol. Road blocks previously operated by UNITA soldiers were under the control of UNITA "police." Estimates of the strength of this force varied from 5,000 to 15,000. The Lusaka Protocol provided for the incorporation of UNITA members into the National Police so that it would function as a nonpartisan institution. These included arrangements for the participation of 5,500 UNITA members, including 180 officers. This was not implemented. As the year ended, it was increasingly evident that the government's paramilitary Rapid Intervention Police (or "Ninjas") were also being discreetly redeployed rather than confined to barracks.

UNITA did not hand over all weapons in its possession, in particular its heavy weapons and sophisticated ground-to-air missiles. UNITA surrendered heavy weaponry at N'tuco in the north and Muxinde in the north-east but maintained a reserve arsenal. The U.N. claims that the ammunition and 30 to 40 percent of the weapons handed to it were in poor condition or unserviceable. By October UNITA had handed over to the U.N. 28,762 personal arms and 3,969 crew-served weapons systems.

Although arms shipments significantly declined in the past year, new heavy weaponry including multiple rocket launcher systems from Brazil and Hind helicopter gunships from Russia reached the government in the first half of 1996. These purchases were made after the Lusaka Protocol and ignored Security Council Resolution 976 of February 1995, which called on both sides to cease any acquisition of arms and war material.

UNITA continued its crossborder, sanction-busting operations, bringing in new weapons and supplies both overland and on secret flights from Zaire and Congo to airstrips in the two diamond-rich Lunda provinces. In January, an Antonov 32 transport plane which crashed in Kinshasa, Zaire, killing 350 people both aboard and on the ground, was found to be carrying petroleum products into UNITA areas, also contrary to U.N. sanctions imposed in 1993. An aircraft involved in a further crash in Kinshasa in June was believed to have been carrying military equipment from Bulgaria for UNITA.

UNITA appeared determined to maintain its grip on its remaining diamond assets. Sporadic but fierce fighting continued in the diamond areas. UNITA earned around US500 million a year from control of diamond production. UNITA did not reply to a government offer to allow it to retain control of the mines in return for selling the diamonds to the state-owned Endiama company.

Although the Lusaka Protocol demanded the "repatriation of all mercenaries," the South African firm Executive Outcomes (EO) maintained some 400 to 500 men in Angola, mostly under contract to the Angolan Armed Forces. This became a contentious issue, and under pressure from the U.S. and others, the Angolan government finally told EO to withdraw in January. A number of its soldiers were redeployed into companies linked to EO, such as Branch Mining, Shibata Security, and Stuart Mills Associates.

Repatriation of prisoners of war has been slow. The International Committee of the Red Cross (ICRC) supervised the release of 523 prisoners of war. Of these, 361 had been held by the government and 162 by UNITA.

Arbitrary detention and assault on suspects by the government's police force remained widespread, and there continued to be many accounts of police requiring payment in return for release. Following a spate of strikes by government workers, the government embarked on aggressive policing with its Rapid Intervention Police in June. A German priest, Father Konrad Liebsher, was arrested on June 26 for distributing leaflets containing "dissenting" information and released on July 3 after being sentenced to a one month sentence suspended for two years for encouraging discontent. In August, the government launched "Operation Cancer Two," rounding up over 2,000 West Africans and Lebanese and ordering their summary expulsion.

Some 40,000 people remained trapped against their will by UNITA in its former headquarters of Jamba in the south, where conditions were very bad. Although UNITA claimed it had invited the international community to help evacuate them, in effect UNITA refused to allow civilians to move out of UNITA zones. The Namibian authorities exacerbated the situation by keeping its border near Jamba closed, fearful that an open border would permit a mass exodus of Jamba residents onto Namibian soil.

Press freedom remained illusory, although President dos Santos told Human Rights Watch/Africa in December 1995 that in Angola "there is more freedom of the press than anywhere." In 1996 journalists continued to be targeted and intimidated. In March, Pires Ferreira, the sports editor at the government-run *Jornal de Angola* was fired after filing stories in a different newsletter about government abuse of power in his own paper. In June, the news program, "Opiniao" on government television was terminated by the government for being too "controversial" after a feature on freedom of expression. Journalists in the provinces were also intimidated. Joao Borges the correspondent for ANGOP, the Angolan news agency in Bie province, was fired after the governor there, Paulino dos Santos, blamed him for publishing an anonymous letter in a weekly newsletter about the governor's abuses of power. Rafael Marques, a journalist from *Jornal de Angola*, was banned from his newspaper when he returned from study leave abroad in October because he had previously organized a strike and had published in Europe a series of articles about the lack of a free press in Angola.

The government continued to refuse a permit for a U.N. radio station to operate in Angola although this was mandated by Security Council Resolution 976 of February 1995. The government claimed that constitutionally only the state could run a short wave radio station. After months of delay, Voice of America radio opened a temporary office in Luanda in March to work with Angolan journalists for a year with a view to providing them some degree of protection. UNITA continued to tolerate little press freedom and its radio station, Voice of the Resistance of the Black Cockerel (VORGAN), continued to disseminate hostile anti-government propaganda in contravention of the Lusaka Protocols.

On September 23, Angola's foreign minister confirmed to the U.N. General Assembly that Angola supported all efforts aimed at the complete elimination of the production, use and trading of anti-personnel mines in both international and domestic conflicts. The U.N. estimated that Angola had up to fifteen million mines and over 70,000 mine amputees. The National Institute for the Removal of Mines and Explosive Devices (INAROEe) estimated in May that 800,000 had been cleared since the November 1994 Lusaka Protocol. In 1996 some mines continued to be planted along roads in acts of economic banditry and sabotage.

In July a mass grave was discovered by mine-clearing teams near Soyo. Many skulls, including those of children, were found with bullet holes in them, with remnants of the region's typical women's clothing found around many of the bones. Soyo was occupied by UNITA in 1993-94. Both UNITA and the government denied responsibility and the National Assembly called for an inquiry.

The Right to Monitor

The absence of effective publicity or lobbying on human rights issues by any sector of civil society remained noticeable. The Luanda-based Angolan Association of Human Rights (AADH) remained the sole functioning human rights group. It held a seminar on human rights for the police and prison services in Luanda in June and attended various domestic and international meetings on human rights. The National Assembly also maintained a cross-party human rights commission and UNITA reported its human rights concerns through its Lisbon-based Association of Surviving Angolans (ACAS).

The Role of the International Community

United Nations
During 1996 the United Nations Angola Verification Mission (UNAVEM III) was the biggest and most expensive U.N. peacekeeping operation in the world, costing around US$1 million a day. There remained strong pressure, particularly from the U.S., not to allow the operation to drag on indefinitely. Largely for this reason, UNAVEM-III's mandate was renewed by the Security Council repeatedly but for only short periods: on February 8 (three months), May 8 (two months), July 11 (three months), and October 11 (two months).

With the peace process badly delayed, it became a U.N. priority to reduce UNAVEM's 7,264-strong military component. It had been originally planned that UNAVEM III would complete its mission in February 1997. However, due to slippage in the Lusaka Protocol's timetable, the mandate was likely to be extended beyond February 1997 in a reduced form; reduction of UNAVEM's presence was to commence in December.

In late November 1995 UNAVEM held its first human rights seminar in Luanda, focusing on the role of the Lusaka Protocol in the protection of human rights and on UNAVEM's plan of action in this area up to February 1997. In early 1996 the Human Rights Unit of UNAVEM expanded its coverage with a presence in each provincial capital, and a series of human rights regional seminars on human rights were held in government and UNITA controlled zones under

its auspices. In April, the Human Rights Unit produced a report on the human rights situation in Angola, but it was not made widely available. The unit continued to employ skilled personnel but their efforts were frustrated by a lack of political will in UNAVEM to see human rights as an important aspect of its mandate. UNAVEM's human rights unit appeared to exist mainly to fulfill reporting requirements by the U.N. Security Council.

European Union
European Union countries played a less dramatic but still significant role. The E.U. allocated $210 million in aid in June and provided ECU 300,000 for six human rights specialists working for UNAVEM's Human Rights Unit, through a project of the Netherlands-based European Parliamentarians for (Southern) Africa (AWEPA).

United States
The U.S. remained one of the most influential forces in the Angolan peace process and Angola was a key country of interest for the Clinton administration. The first official trip by an Angolan head of state to the White House took place on December 8, 1995. The warm public embrace of President dos Santos by the Clinton administration dramatized the complete reversal of U.S. Cold War policies in Angola, particularly since President Clinton had met very few African heads of state.

In 1996 the U.S. provided $190 million in emergency funding for post-war reconstruction in addition to being one of the main financial contributors to UNAVEM. In 1995 the U.S. provided more than $8 million to nongovernmental organizations carrying out mine clearance and mine awareness programs but the extension of this support was complicated by new congressional restrictions limiting funding to operations with direct U.S. military participation. U.S. military cooperation in Angola was not to begin until the unification of the two armies was completed. It was proposed that a U.S. firm, Military Professional Resources Inc. (MPRI) would then be responsible for assistance to the new unified army.

The central focus of U.S. policy in Angola remained the implementation of the Lusaka Protocol. An extraordinarily high number of senior U.S. officials visited Angola in 1996: U.S. Secretary of State Warren Christopher; U.S. Ambassador to the U.N. Madeline Albright (January); USAID Administrator Brian Atwood (February); Deputy Commander of the European Command General James Jamerson (March); Assistant Secretary of State for African Affairs, George Moose (January and July); and Paul Hare, President Clinton's Special Representative (January and April).

Other countries played a less dramatic but still significant role. The E.U. allocated $210 million in aid to Angola in June and provided $3,740 for six human rights specialists working for UNAVEM's Human Rights Unit, through a project of the Netherlands-based AWEPA.

BURUNDI

Human Rights Developments

Contenders in the undeclared civil war in Burundi killed thousands of unarmed civilians, many of them children, women or the elderly. The battle between the minority Tutsi and the majority Hutu grew in extent during 1996 until it touched most of the fifteen provinces of Burundi. The Hutu armed opposition groups pushed forward aggressively in March and April and again in September, when they bombarded the capital, Bujumbura. Struggling to maintain control in the face of attacks from three Hutu opposition movements, the Tutsi-dominated army killed thousands of noncombatants in the course of its operations. Occasionally it took responsibility for the deaths—although it usually underreported the number killed—but sought to justify the killings by saying that the civilians were actually rebels or had been helping the armed opposition groups. In an apparent change of policy in late October, the army officially acknowledged that

soldiers had murdered some fifty civilians at a military camp in Bururi province on October 13. Declaring that the civilians had been wrongfully killed, the army said the "indisciplined" soldiers would be punished.

By late in the year, the Front for the Defense of Democracy (FDD), a largely Hutu movement, took control of areas of northwestern Burundi. At first it concentrated mostly on military objectives, but it increasingly attacked civilians, particularly displaced Tutsi or Hutu who refused to assist them. The other two armed opposition groups, PALIPEHUTU and FROLINA, also killed noncombatants. Among the worst of the army attacks were those at Buhoro in Gitega province on April 26, where some 230 civilians were killed; at Kivyuka in Bubanza on May 3, where some 375 were slaughtered; at Mutambu where 111 were killed on June 12; and at Nyeshenza, commune Mugina, where some 500 were killed on June 27. Among the raids by Hutu rebels which took the most lives were those on Butezi, in Ruyigi province, on May 28, in which forty-nine people were slaughtered, and on Teza, in Muramvya province, on July 3 where some eighty persons were killed. In one of the most terrible attacks on a Tutsi displaced persons camp, some 340 persons were massacred at Bugendana on July 20. The military blamed that attack on Hutu rebels as well, but other sources report that local, resident Hutu carried out the massacre in retaliation for the part played by the displaced persons in a previous attack on their community by the Burundi army. According to physicians working in Burundi, these attacks generally killed five persons for every one left wounded. Both hospitals and schools were attacked. The U.N. special rapporteur on Burundi concluded in a February 27 report that neither the rebel forces nor the Burundian army observed the principles of international humanitarian law.

Leaders of regular army or armed opposition units sometimes disclaimed responsibility for slaughter of civilians, saying such attacks were unauthorized excesses carried out by undisciplined subordinates. Civilian and military authorities claimed to have investigated some military abuses but in most cases produced unconvincing reports justifying the actions of the soldiers and minimizing the number of civilian casualties. No soldiers were brought to trial for having killed civilians in the course of these operations.

Military units often permitted, encouraged or sometimes participated in attacks executed by supposedly civilian militia units. Many militia were composed of young people, particularly secondary school students. On May 17, for example, Tutsi secondary school students from Kiganda, directed by six soldiers, killed fifty-one people from a near-by community—targeted because they were Hutu. In late July, Tutsi students reportedly killed thirty of their Hutu classmates at an agricultural school in Gitega.

In what may portend a legitimation of violence by civilians, the government in April proposed the creation of a "self-defense force." Such a force helped carry out the genocide in neighboring Rwanda two years ago. In July, young Tutsi recruits were being trained, although the goals of the program had not been defined and safeguards against its misuse had not been implemented. According to the Burundian human rights league, Iteka, the program was being used as an excuse by some radicals to commit abuses against their opponents.

Dozens of persons "disappeared" either after having been seized during military operations or after having been detained for questioning by military or police.

On July 25, Major Pierre Buyoya, a past president of Burundi, was put in power by a military coup. He announced the suspension of the national parliament and banned political parties, declaring that he anticipated a three year period of control before restoring democratic institutions. In the days after the coup, the army killed hundreds of civilians in Muramvya and elsewhere, thus undermining Buyoya's claim to have taken power to end the violence. Subsequent to the coup and the banning of political parties, twenty-five members of the National Assembly in

exile in Tanzania and Kenya called for a united front with the National Council for the Defense of Democracy (CNDD), the parent organization of the FDD guerrilla forces. They were all members of the largely Hutu FRODEBU party. Shortly after, sixteen other FRODEBU deputies living in Zaire also announced their support for the CNDD. Their shift from attempting to work within the government to allying with armed opposition forces attacking it showed the erosion of a middle ground. Moderates without guns appeared increasingly forced to align themselves with armed groups.

Throughout the year, extremists used assassination to eliminate Hutu political leaders, such as the governor of Cibitoke province and his adviser, the director of internal documentation, and the provincial director of agricultural services in Gitega. In addition, two Tutsi officers known to be moderate, Lt. Col. François Fyiritano and Lt. Col. Dieudonné Nzeyimana, were slain by unknown assailants. In early September, Archbishop of Burundi Msgr. Joachim Ruhuna, a Tutsi known also for his moderate views and opposition to violence, was assassinated in early September along with a nun who was traveling in his automobile. On May 3, three Hutu teachers were apparently arrested by soldiers at Gikungu in Bujumbura and taken to the Gasenyi displaced persons' camp where militia killed them.

In a positive measure, perhaps in response to international concern over media incitement to genocide, the government licensed the new, private Radio Umwizero [Radio Hope] financed by the European Union, to broadcast information promoting human rights and reconciliation. Studio Ijambo, funded by the U.S., prepared radio programs along the same lines. The following month, the government banned seven publications, three identified with Tutsi, four with Hutu, for having promoted ethnic hatred. Six of the seven had apparently been guilty of doing so.

A series of attacks and threats on vehicles, offices, and residences of international relief agencies in late 1995 caused them to briefly suspend assistance throughout Burundi. In late April 1996, assailants threw grenades at buildings of the International Committee of the Red Cross (ICRC) in Gitega, forcing the organization to withdraw personnel from this central city. In June, three expatriate ICRC workers, traveling in a clearly marked convoy, were ambushed and killed in northwestern Burundi, leading to the withdrawal of the ICRC from the country. No one had been arrested or tried for these attacks but the assailants were believed to be soldiers. A December 1995 broadcast by the Burundi State Radio was part of a propaganda offensive that charged the relief organizations with excessive help to the Hutu or even with actually providing arms and funds to Hutu rebels. By mid-year, many organizations had withdrawn all their personnel to the capital city, thus restricting services to the needy and reducing opportunities for outsiders to observe human rights developments in the provinces.

Some 350,000 Burundian refugees live abroad, mostly in Tanzania and Zaire, with about 400,000 more displaced within the country. During the past two years, regions where Hutu and Tutsi formerly lived together were subject to ethnic clashes and massive population movements, with Tutsi now largely concentrated in towns or at military camps and Hutu dispersed in the countryside. In addition, at the start of the year, some 90,000 Rwandan Hutu refugees clustered in camps along the northern frontier of Burundi. They had fled their homes in 1994 when the Rwandan Patriotic Army defeated the government responsible for the genocide. In February, the Burundi army made efforts to drive Rwandan refugees away, but stopped in the face of severe international criticism. They resumed again in July with threats and attacks on refugee camps, driving some 15,000 Rwandans back across the border. Again, international protests forced a halt to this refoulement. But, in August, Burundian authorities, in cooperation with the Rwandan government, closed the remaining camps and forced most of the remaining refugees to return home, leaving some 200 Rwandan refugees in Burundi. In several cases, Burundian soldiers killed refugees, such as at Magara camp in mid-August, where they beat three refugees to death and wounded another three.

A small-scale guerrilla movement, led by PALIPEHUTU, existed in Burundi before 1993, but the present large-scale conflict resulted from efforts of a part of the Tutsi elite to recapture power lost in the June 1993 election when their UPRONA party was defeated by FRODEBU, a party that represented mostly Hutu. A group of military officers, posing as the protectors of the Tutsi, murdered the democratically elected president, Melchior Ndadaye and then stood by—or collaborated—as increasingly radical Tutsi groups used violence in the streets to reassert Tutsi predominance in government in the months that followed. In the weeks just after Ndadaye's assassination, between 30,000 and 50,000 Burundians were killed: Hutu massacred Tutsi, often under the direction of local government officials or political leaders, and the army slaughtered thousands of Hutu, supposedly on the pretext of restoring order. A few lower-ranking officers were arrested on charges of having assassinated the president, and some 2,600 others, most of them civilians, were detained for having participated in the 1993 killings. Some 150 of the detainees were soldiers. Criminal courts, blocked by judicial vacancies that the National Assembly failed to fill, held no trials for more than two years. During that time, nearly 3,000 other persons were arrested, many on charges of politically-linked crimes, resulting in a total of some 5,500 persons awaiting trial. The great majority of persons accused were Hutu, while the judiciary was virtually exclusively Tutsi. Judges coped with a number of problems due to limited resources, but the greatest obstacle to fair trials was intimidation of the judges by radical Tutsi. In addition, almost all lawyers were Tutsi and few agreed to take Hutu clients, especially for cases of political importance. After judges were finally named, the courts reopened for sessions in February and June. Of some 150 cases heard, the courts handed down eighty-nine convictions with the death penalty and thirty-six with the penalty of life imprisonment. None of the convicted had access to legal counsel.

The Right to Monitor

Local human rights organizations were permitted to continue operations, including publishing criticisms of all parties to the conflict and monitoring the progress of court cases. Several activists have had their lives threatened by soldiers or Tutsi extremists, which may have influenced the organizations to moderate their criticism of the army. Several activists chose exile, including Tharcisse Nsavyimana, a leader of the most credible human rights group, ITEKA.

Five monitors from the office of U.N. High Commissioner for Human Rights had been investigating the human rights situation in Burundi since April 1996. On at least one occasion, when they sought to travel to the site of the Kivyuka massacre, the army prohibited the mission, giving the insecurity of the region as a reason.

The Role of
the International Community

Highly conscious of the consequences of their failure to act during the genocide in Rwanda, the U.N., the Organization of Africa Unity (OAU), the European Union (E.U.), a group of Burundi's neighbors, and individual donor nations all devoted great attention to resolving the conflict in Burundi and to averting—or at the least preparing for—further disaster. Symbolic of the intense focus on Burundi was the plethora of special envoys charged with facilitating a solution to the crisis in Burundi or in the larger region, including former Tanzanian president Julius Nyerere, former U.S. President Jimmy Carter, E.U. special envoy Aldo Ajello, and U.S. special envoy Howard Wolpe.

United Nations

Despite protestations of the need to be prepared for further violence in Burundi, only three of fifty member states approached in early 1996—Ethiopia, Uganda, and Tanzania—indicated willingness to contribute troops to a multinational force for humanitarian intervention. In January and again in March, the Security Council encouraged contingency planning and recognized the need to combat media that promoted ethnic hatred. In January, it expressed a willingness to consider a ban on arms for Burundi and travel restrictions and other measures against leaders who incited violence, proposals repeated in an August 31 resolution that set a sixty-day deadline, after which the council would move to implement these measures if no progress had been made.

After having established one commission to examine the assassination of President Ndadaye and subsequent massacres and having refused to make public its report, the Security Council sent a second commission to Burundi to repeat the investigation. Inadequately funded and hampered by lack of access to materials and witnesses, the commission produced a truncated report in July. A witness accused of having participated personally in the murder, who had been in custody at the central prison since late 1993, was shot by guards in a so-called attempted escape just before the commission was to begin its work. The council initially tried to keep the second report secret as well, but when politicians in Bujumbura selectively leaked those parts that implicated their rivals, the council decided to publish the document at the end of August. The report relied heavily on evidence already published by an nongovernmental organization investigatory commission sponsored by Human Rights Watch, among others, in 1994, but reached very different conclusions. The U.N. report was, however, more severe toward Hutu political leaders than toward Tutsi military authorities: it labeled Hutu killings of Tutsi "acts of genocide" and proposed that they should be tried before an international tribunal but called military slaughter of Hutu "indiscriminate repression of civilians," which it said fell within the internal jurisdiction of Burundi. It maintained that there was no hope of fair and effective investigation or prosecution of these crimes in Burundi given the current situation, and so concluded that it was "unrealistic" to seek an end to impunity before trying to resolve the overall crisis.

In March, the U.N. Human Rights Commission examined the situation in Burundi and its special rapporteur Paulo Sergio Pinheiro, who conducted two missions to Burundi in 1996, served as an effective and vigorous advocate for international action. In February, he called for an international tribunal to try cases resulting from the killings in Burundi. The five monitors sent by the office of the U.N. High Commissioner for Human Rights published one detailed report in July, reflecting a conscientious effort to document abuses by all parties. Although unable to travel frequently outside the capital, they played an important role in gathering data and in confirming information from other sources, particularly concerning killings by the Burundi army. In July, the high commissioner requested funds to expand the number of monitors to twenty-five in order to staff two provincial sites as well as a central office.

European Union

By the appointment of envoy Aldo Ajello as well as by a series of statements, the E.U. made clear its support for an end to the violence and human rights abuse. European Commissioner for Humanitarian Affairs Emma Bonino visited Burundi together with USAID Administrator J. Brian Atwood in April to express concern over growing insecurity and to emphasize that the two funders, who give about 80 percent of the assistance received by the region, would refuse development aid unless progress were made toward peace and stability. This message was repeated at a donors meeting on Burundi in Geneva in June. Following the coup in July, the E.U. suspended its development aid to Burundi but continued its humanitarian aid program to the country. In September, the European Parliament passed a resolution urging the E.U. not to recognize the authority of the Bujumbura regime. The Parliament also supported the sanctions imposed on Burundi by neighboring African countries and urged them to extend the ban to weapons and ammunition.

Slow to honor its pledge to support U.N. human rights monitors, the E.U. did produce the funds necessary to field five of these observers in April, nearly a year after its original pledge of assistance. In addition, it provided US$1.87 million to fund the OAU monitors.

OAU and Regional Collaboration

The OAU had maintained a sixty-person observer mission in Burundi since 1995. Nearly ended in March for lack of money, it finally received funding from the E.U. Some of the observers monitored the conduct of the Burundian army, but their effectiveness was limited by a regulation that a Burundian military escort accompany them wherever they went. Following the July coup, the OAU withdrew the military part of the observer team but left others who served in civilian, technical assistance capacities.

In late June, the Burundian president and prime minister, representing the two sides of the conflict, agreed to accept a force of Ugandan, Tanzanian, and Ethiopian troops to help restore order. The agreement was reached at a meeting in Arusha of the OAU president and representatives from Tanzania, Uganda, Ethiopia, Zaire, and Rwanda as well as Burundi. Although subsequent objections from Tutsi radicals and the July coup prevented its implementation, the agreement marked a significant step toward local actors taking the initiative to resolve conflicts in themselves internal but with consequences for the whole region.

On July 31, the presidents of Kenya, Rwanda, Tanzania and Uganda and the prime ministers of Ethiopia and Zaire, meeting with other African, U.S., and E.U. authorities, decided to impose a total economic blockade on Burundi to force an end to prohibitions of political party activity and meetings of the National Assembly and to oblige President Buyoya to undertake negotiations with the rebels. The blockade, first relaxed to permit deliveries of essential supplies to infants and the sick, later to permit supplies for displaced persons, did serious damage to the already weak economy. In mid-September, Buyoya lifted the ban on political parties and the National Assembly and a week later agreed to negotiations with the rebels, a concession opposed by other Tutsi leaders.

United States

From the time of a visit to Burundi by U.S. Ambassador to the U.N. Madeleine Albright early in the year, the U.S. insisted that it "will not support a government installed by force or intimidation and reiterates that it will work actively to isolate any such regime." Confronted with the July coup, the U.S. restated this policy but was nonetheless reluctant to condemn Major Buyoya too harshly on the grounds that he was considered far more moderate than the other likely candidate for the post, Major Bagaza. In the last two years, USAID had provided a $145,000 grant to a foundation established by Buyoya. The U.S. nonetheless suspended $1.7 million in development aid to Burundi, as well as $60,000 in self-help development funds, $10,000 in human rights and democracy funds and $50,000 for IMET military training. It continued to provide the $3.6 million in humanitarian aid scheduled for 1996.

President Sylvestre Ntibatunganya, deposed by Buyoya's coup, sought refuge in the U.S. ambassador's residence. The U.S. continued to recognize him as president and held that he should be allowed either to participate in national reconciliation efforts or to leave the country. At this writing, he remained in the residence.

The U.S. supported efforts at mediation by former Presidents Nyerere and Carter and sent a number of high-ranking delegations to Bujumbura. It pressed for contingency planning at the U.N. for possible military intervention and for coordinating humanitarian aid in case of future catastrophe. It offered to provide airlift and other logistical assistance to support an international response to such a crisis.

Lawyers from the U.S. State Depart-

ment found that much of the killing in Burundi constituted "acts of genocide," but the U.S. had not yet shown any determination to suppress or punish such acts.

In September, the U.S. launched the initiative for an African Crisis Response Force described above. Although it was intended to assist in disasters anywhere on the continent, the chief and immediate impulse for its creation was the Burundi crisis.

ETHIOPIA

Human Rights Developments

The ruling Ethiopian People's Revolutionary Democratic Front (EPRDF) marked in mid-1996 the fifth anniversary of the defeat of the former government, the Derg, and of its taking power after almost a decade of a devastating civil war. A transitional period culminated in the May 1995 parliamentary elections and the proclamation of the Federal Democratic Republic of Ethiopia the following August. The EPRDF, a coalition of ethnically-based movements that fought the Derg dominated by the Tigray People's Liberation Front (TPLF), gained control of the legislative and executive bodies of the state while its military wing assumed the responsibilities of national defense and policing. This dominant role of the EPRDF, which was established in the transitional period, continued in the elected parliament and the new federal government.

A fundamental tenet of the public platform of the ruling party during the transitional government and subsequently was that the liberalization of the economy and the introduction of political pluralism would help bring about economic prosperity and political stability in the war-torn and poverty-ridden country. While the economy showed positive responses to the government's internationally-backed restructuring programs, genuine political pluralism and participation remained to be achieved and the EPRDF's commitment to this was increasingly called into question. The EPRDF had in effect sponsored sixteen parties, which it called People's Democratic Organizations, each based on the dominant ethnic groups in the various regions. This strategy ensured a monopoly of power by the EPRDF and its allied or satellite parties in both regional and federal assemblies following a series of elections from 1992 to 1995 that major opposition groups boycotted.

It also underscored the predominant role that ethnicity came to occupy in contemporary Ethiopian politics and society. The new constitution of the federal republic promoted ethnic federalism and gave the nations of Ethiopia the right of self-determination including secession, although the new government acted to suppress low-level insurgencies in a number of regions that were waged in the name of self-determination. The federal system fueled strong opposition to the EPRDF in urban elite circles, such as the All Amhara People's Organization (AAPO), which argued for a restoration of the traditional form of centralized power. The EPRDF claimed for its part that only the constitutional guarantees of equality through ethnic federalism could allay the anxieties of minority groups that had suffered from decades of repression and exploitation under the centralized power structures of imperial and later on military-ruled Ethiopia. However, the commitment to regional autonomy, which translated into formal moves toward the devolution of powers to the regions, was contradicted by the center's control of the political process at the regional level through the network of regional parties allied to the EPRDF.

The new government demobilized thousands of EPRDF fighters, mostly from the TPLF, and said it had achieved the proportional recruitment of soldiers from other groups as a step toward the creation of a representative and apolitical army. Security in rural areas, where more than 85 percent of the population lived on subsistence agriculture and pastoral activities, remained in the hands of local militia who acted in tandem with military detachments but ostensibly under local political control. These, according to government officials, did not come under the direct chain of command of the army, which however assisted in their training and arming. Testimonies of victims of abuse by rural security personnel persistently pointed to the role of security committees, consisting of local officials, political cadres of the EPRDF and its affiliates and army officers, in control of these "peasant militias." The committee system made the militia an integral part of the national political structure and placed them under the control of the central government through the ruling party apparatus. They provided the interface between local authorities, the militia, the army, and the ruling party, in practice subordinating local security structures to the federal authorities.

The federal government maintained its formal commitment to the respect of the rule of law and international human rights standards. However, as the trial of the Derg officials for crimes against humanity stalled, political killings, torture, and arbitrary detention were reported in the context of civil strife, and the government continued to show intolerance toward the manifestations of an increasingly dynamic, independent-minded civil society.

The trial of seventy-three top-ranking officials of the Derg, charged with committing genocide and war crimes, progressed at a slow pace, with twenty-six of the defendants, including Colonel Mengistu, tried in absentia. Meanwhile, authorities continued to hold an estimated 1,700 prisoners without charges for the fifth consecutive year for their alleged crimes under the Derg, a situation which the prime minister admitted was "no longer justifiable." Those not charged were not allowed access to their dossiers and there was no public information on the documentation recovered from the Derg period, which provided the basis for prosecutions.

The army waged counterinsurgency operations against the Oromo Liberation Front (OLF) and the Islamic Front for the Liberation of Oromia and countered sporadic attacks by Al-Ithad Al-Islami (Islamic Unity) and the Ogaden National Liberation

Front in Somali Region and by the Afar Revolutionary Democratic Unity Front in Afar Region.

Local militiamen carried out hundreds of arrests without warrant of people suspected of collaborating with insurgent groups, often in sweeps through rural communities in which virtually all residents were treated as suspects. Many of these security detainees were held for weeks or months in temporary rural camps before being released or turned over to regional authorities. Only after transfer to regional civil or military authorities were such detentions normally acknowledged, although prolonged detention without charge or trial was also widely reported in ad hoc detention centers in administrative buildings, commandeered schools, or police stations under the authority of regional governments. Although in recent years large numbers of suspected members of violent opposition groups were detained in army camps, most such camps were believed to have been closed, although dozens of security detainees were reported held in the army camp at Hegere Mariam as recently as mid-1996. Of the 20,000 detainees officially described as demobilized OLF fighters who were held at the army's camps at Hurso, Dedessa, Agarfa, and Zeway between 1992 and 1995, all but ninety-three were reportedly released. The ninety-three were transferred to civilian prisons, pending trial.

Despite the federal constitution's guarantees of due process, and its barring of the torture or ill-treatment of prisoners—in Articles 18, 19, 20, and 21—Human Rights Watch/Africa documented a number of cases of torture and other cruel, inhuman or degrading treatment of security detainees. Most involved individuals who had been detained by local militia and political cadre. These individuals described having been tortured in brutal field interrogations at the time of their detentions, or punished in repeated beatings in temporary rural detention camps by local authorities, where they also described being deprived of sleep and of food. We interviewed such former detainees who showed injuries consistent with their accounts of having been flogged, burnt with cigarettes, and having been cut with knives and bayonets by their captors. In what appeared to be a routine form of restraint, former detainees described having had their elbows tied behind their backs with plastic cords or wire, leading in some cases we observed both to scarring and to more severe and permanent disabilities. Most were released without having been subject to any formal detention procedure; treatment improved for the small minority who were transferred to a regional government detention facility or were seen by a judge or prosecutor.

The physical torture of rural prisoners according to these testimonies was systematic and prolonged and seemed a form of punishment as well as a means of pressing prisoners to provide information or to confess to collaboration with armed groups. Testimonies also revealed the wide use of threats against and the actual detention of family members, particularly mothers, wives, and daughters, to force fugitive suspects to turn themselves in for interrogation. In one case, the daughter of a suspected OLF activist was detained repeatedly with a view to forcing the father's surrender: she was reportedly raped by the head of the local administration in her community following her short-term detention in early 1996. Her father, himself a torture victim, had fled the town.

Human Rights Watch/Africa interviewed former detainees from Oromia State's Western Shewa, Borana, and Western Harerge zones who described torture or ill-treatment in rural detention camps and in some detention facilities under regional government or military control. Some former detainees who had been held during 1994 in Hegere Mariam military camp number three —on federal, rather than regional authority— also described systematic ill-treatment, including being beaten and forced to do harsh physical exercise.

Appeals by relatives to higher regional police or prosecution authorities, according to testimonies, sometimes led to the release of prisoners detained without charge, but there seemed to be no effective channel for complaints and appeals for judicial review readily available to the majority of detainees, particularly in the regions remotest from the capital, Addis Ababa. Many allegations of abuse came from people in the capital who told Human Rights Watch/Africa they had fled local officials in the countryside where the rule of law was largely absent.

Although some of the individuals interviewed by Human Rights Watch—and by local human rights monitors, notably the Ethiopian Human Rights Council (EHRCO)— made complaints to the courts and to executive authorities about their treatment, no official inquiries were known to have been made into reports of torture and ill-treatment in the past year. In a limited concession to mounting criticism, however, the government announced a series of dismissals and other disciplinary measures against officials implicated in unspecified human rights abuses.

Reports of abuses at the national level related to the federal government's crackdown on the press, civic associations, and trade unions in violations of rights that the federal constitution provide for. The constitution guarantees the rights of peaceful assembly and association and provides for the right to engage in unrestricted peaceful political activity. Sixty-three political parties were registered with the government as of August: fifty-six were regional while the rest were national parties. The government authorized a number of opposition parties and pressure groups to stage demonstrations in the center of Addis Ababa and its representatives received and responded to letters of protests from marchers. However, in other instances the government used laws requiring permits and harassment tactics to restrict the rights of association and peaceful assembly. Opposition groups such as AAPO were the object of closures of their regional offices, harassment, detention, and suspicious killings of activists, and lack of meaningful access to the state-controlled broadcasting media. While the government allowed some

civic groups to operate without interference, its regulatory agencies restricted the freedom of other associations. Some nongovernmental organizations (NGOs) with a mandate to promote human rights education and monitoring and civic education faced obstacles in their attempts to register with the Ministry of Justice and police action—including arrests without warrant—that harassed and intimidated their personnel.

On February 29, security officials closed down the Addis Ababa offices of the Oromo Relief Association (ORA), a leading indigenous relief and rehabilitation NGO. In the preceding months, the Oromia state government had ordered the search and closure of ORA's offices and operations in the region one after the other, accusing it in the media of providing resources and political capital to the insurgent OLF and of blocking other NGOs from access to the region. ORA was, however, never given the opportunity to defend itself before a court of law. Officials detained senior workers from at least three of ORA's regional offices for up to eight months in harsh conditions without charges or trial. The coordinator in Dire Dawa, Ahmed Mohamed, was arrested in mid-February and his whereabouts remained unknown to his family until his release in late September.

The Constitution of Ethiopia guarantees in Article 29 the freedoms of thought, opinion, and expression as essential to the functioning of a democratic order. The government continued, however, to use the vague formulation of the 1992 press proclamation to reign in critical reporting and allowed opposition groups only limited access to the state-owned radio and television. By the end of the year six journalists of the private press were in prison.

The constitution and the 1993 labor proclamation provide for the right of workers to form and join unions and to bargain collectively. This notwithstanding, the government lashed back at the Ethiopian Teachers Association (ETA) and the Confederation of Ethiopian Trade Unions (CETU), the two largest and best established labor organizations in the country, for raising concerns about the impact on their members of new national educational and economic policies, respectively. As the confrontation escalated, the government arrested many activists of ETA and CETU, closed most of ETA's regional offices without a court order, and froze the bank accounts of both unions. Local officials harassed elected ETA officers in a number of regional branches and forced them to flee, leaving behind their families and their jobs as teachers. One survived an attempt on his life when he briefly returned to his home province on family business. Pro-government activists established parallel unions, apparently to validate government challenges to the legitimacy of the refractory ones.

The Right To Monitor

The government continued for the fourth year to deny the registration as an NGO of the Ethiopian Human Rights Council (EHRCO), the only monitoring organization in the country, charging that it was politically motivated. EHRCO managed to function without government recognition, while its bank account remained blocked since April 1995 and security officials closely monitored visitors to its office.

During a three-week mission to Ethiopia in mid-1996 two Human Rights Watch/ Africa researchers were able to discuss the human rights situation in the country in private meetings with groups from different sectors of civil society, interview former prisoners and relatives of victims of human rights abuse, and meet with the minister of justice and other senior officials. The government also authorized other international human rights organizations to send research missions to the country, including Reporters Without Borders, the Committee to Protect Journalists, and the Lawyers Committee for Human Rights. It continued, however, to deny the country researcher of Amnesty International (AI) an entry visa to the country although another AI representative was permitted to observe sessions of the Derg trials in June.

The Role of the International Community

United Nations

In response to complaints about the administrative decision to cancel the registration of the Confederation of Ethiopian Trade Unions (CETU) and to close down its office, the Committee on Freedom Of Association of the International Labour Organisation (ILO) called upon the Ethiopian government in December 1995 to respect its obligations under the 1948 Convention on Freedom of Association and Protection of the Right to Organize and the 1949 Convention on the Right to Organize and Collective Bargaining, both of which Ethiopia ratified. In a related development, the governing body of the ILO, responding to similar complaints, unanimously adopted a resolution supporting the reinstatement by Ethiopia of CETU. An agreement signed in 1993 between Ethiopia, Sudan, and the U.N. High Commissioner for Refugees allowed the voluntary repatriation and reintegration of thousands of Ethiopian refugees to continue, in spite of worsening relations between the two countries.

European Union

During a January visit to Ethiopia, the German president linked aid and respect for human rights, saying that a donor country could at any time withdraw its help from a country whose policy undermined democracy. Coming days after the signature of a US$33 million dollar German aid agreement for the purchase of fertilizers, the statement did not contradict the continued good relations the Ethiopian government enjoyed with bilateral and multilateral donors. In the same month, the Netherlands and Britain joined the World Bank in contributing toward the write-off of $250 million of Ethiopia's estimated $270 million commercial bank debt. In July it was announced that Ethiopia would receive $39 million in development from Germany.

In a resolution on human rights in Ethiopia passed in July, the European Parliament condemned the arrest on May 30 of Taye Woldesemayat, the chair of the Ethiopian Teachers' Association. It urged the Ethiopian authorities to release him and two other prominent political prisoners and to guarantee freedom of expression and action to ETA. In its response, the Ethiopian government stated that it dealt with the three cases in full conformity with the law and dismissed the resolution as indicative of "lack of seriousness and purpose."

Organization of African Unity

Ethiopia held the rotating presidency of the Organization of African Unity (OAU) for most of 1996. Following the July coup in Burundi, it joined Burundi's neighbors and the OAU in imposing economic sanctions on that country to foster a quick return to civilian rule and a peaceful settlement of its internal crisis. Ethiopia seized a former Rwandan official and a leading genocide suspect at Addis Ababa airport, and handed him over to the Rwandan judiciary in late July. Meanwhile, persistent tensions characterized its relations with neighboring Sudan and Somalia, both of which it accused of sheltering violent opposition groups.

United States

United States officials expressed confidence in the steps that the government undertook to democratize and liberalize the country and called on opposition groups to participate in the political process. Ethiopia occupied a pivotal position in the U.S. policy initiatives aimed at consolidating regional stability. It emerged as a close partner in the U.S.-led efforts to counter the Islamist government of Sudan's influence in the region. A measure of this close partnership was the high level of official exchanges between the two countries. U.S. Secretary of State Warren Christopher stopped in Addis Ababa for official talks during his first tour in sub-Sahara Africa in October. In April, the director of the U.S. Central Intelligence Agency visited Addis Ababa and discussed with officials regional security concerns. This followed a visit in February by the deputy assistant secretary of defense for international security affairs, who pledged U.S. assistance to Ethiopia's army and a commitment to contributing to the consolidation of peace in the Horn of Africa. Levels of bilateral economic assistance reflected the prominence of Ethiopia as it ranked, with $109 million, as the third highest recipient of U.S. aid to the continent in Fiscal Year 1996.

Local human rights advocates told Human Rights Watch/Africa that U.S. embassy officials sought to investigate some of the incidents they reported. While this was reflected in a thorough and critical chapter on the human rights situation in Ethiopia in State Department's annual *Country Reports on Human Rights Practices for 1995*, officials of the Clinton administration made no public criticism of the current government's rights record. A welcome departure from this attitude occurred during the secretary of state's visit to Ethiopia in October when he declined an invitation by Ethiopian officials to address a joint press conference in protest, as his aides announced, against the harassment and imprisonment of independent journalists and their exclusion from official press conferences. The secretary of state told reporters later that "Ethiopia has made progress in human rights during the past five years, but the United States wants to see more. One of the areas of our concern is the freedom of the press and the treatment of journalists."

KENYA

Human Rights Developments

As the country's attention began to focus on the run-up to the next election, likely to be called in 1997, the government of President Daniel arap Moi became more blunt in its efforts to consolidate power through the denial of free speech, association, and assembly. The Kenyan constitution required new parliamentary and presidential elections to be held before early 1998, when the government's mandate expires, but as of this writing, the government had not announced a date. The government's measures to restrict the activities of the political opposition and to undermine national voter registration posed grave doubts as to whether a free and fair multiparty election was possible in Kenya.

The National Electoral Commission remained a presidentially-appointed body despite calls by nongovernmental organizations and the political opposition for some input into the selection of members. This year, the commission announced the creation of twenty-two new election constituencies, some of which redrew boundaries in the politically controversial Rift Valley Province and were based on ethnicity. Many Kenyans believed that the redistricting was designed to allow the ruling Kenya National African Union (KANU) to win more parliamentary seats in the next election. Although in May, KANU and opposition parliamentarians agreed to a parliamentary review of the electoral laws, no further action was taken.

Beginning in December 1995, a system for the reissue of national identity cards was instituted throughout the nation. The issue of new national identity cards quickly became another means through which the government could disenfranchise select groups. Without a national identity card, a citizen could not obtain a voter registration card. As of June 30, 1996, only 4.6 million identity cards had been issued to a projected eligible voting population of 13.5 million. The registration process was extremely slow, with reports of delays of up to six months, requests for bribes by issuing officers, and selective registration of KANU supporters in some areas. In the Rift Valley Province, some people from ethnic groups which were generally considered to support the opposition were reportedly told to go to their "ancestral area" to register for their identity cards. Following national pressure, the Electoral Commission announced that voter cards would also be issued on the basis of the old expired national identity cards in order to ensure that eligible voters would be able to cast their ballots. However, in July President

Moi overruled the Electoral Commission, announcing that voter registration cards would be issued solely on the basis of new identity cards and that the old identity cards would not be recognized. Kenyan nongovernmental organizations estimated that some 6.2 million people could be disenfranchised as a result.

The government continued to ignore registration applications from over a dozen political parties, including Safina, a party formed by top members of Kenya's opposition in 1995 and heavily attacked by President Moi at the time. The block on registration prevented new parties from being formed, while exacerbating political struggles between factions in the opposition parties since no one could leave and form a new party. The existing political opposition parties—the Forum for the Restoration of Democracy-Kenya (FORD-K), FORD-Asili, and the Democratic Party—remained divided largely on ethnic lines, and divisions within the parties deepened.

Numerous opposition supporters complained of disruption of their meetings by police or local authorities, as well as the denial of permits to hold meetings without cause or right of appeal. Under Kenyan law, a license had to be obtained in advance from the local district commissioner and opposition members of parliament could not hold a meeting in their constituencies without permission from the government. In March, an assistant minister in the office of the president announced that local government officials could cancel political rallies at any time, even if a license had been granted. Following the announcement, several peaceful rallies were closed down on the grounds that President Moi was being insulted. In June, opposition politicians were prevented by police and members of KANU's youth wing from entering Molo town where they planned to campaign. The "youth wingers" also stabbed *East African Standard* photographer Rapheal Munge in the hand and beat reporter Samuel Mburu. In July, opposition politicians from Safina were arrested while giving out trophies at a volleyball game and detained briefly. Meanwhile, KANU members continued to blatantly use government assets in their campaigns. At one KANU rally in Machakos town, food relief provided by international relief organizations for refugee populations was reportedly distributed to potential voters.

The government continued to curb free speech. Journalists came under attack for writing articles critical of the government. The government refused to relinquish its monopoly on the broadcast media, severely restricting the ability of the political opposition to disseminate information while using the media to promote KANU. Sedition charges were brought in July against *Finance* magazine editor Njehu Gatabaki for an article critical of the government. On August 27, the premises of Fotoform Printers, which published some of the more outspoken publications, were firebombed. In the past, police raided Fotoform, shut down the printers, impounded their equipment, and charged its owner with sedition.

The government unsuccessfully attempted to legislate restrictions against free speech in early 1996. Following an outcry, the government shelved proposed legislation which would have given the Minister of Information and Broadcasting extensive powers over licensing, registration and regulation of all broadcast and print media operations, and which would have allowed journalists to be jailed or barred from practicing for flouting a government-mandated code of conduct.

The government continued to use the judiciary to silence critics and to punish political opponents. No progress was made during 1996 by the legal reform task forces formed by the attorney general in 1993 to amend or repeal repressive legislation. The trial of prominent opposition figure Koigi wa Wamwere, a former member of parliament and founder of a human rights organization, his brother Charles Kuria Wamwere, and G.G. Njuguna Ngengi on charges of armed robbery continued on appeal. The lower court proceeding, which resulted in a sentence of four years and six strokes of the cane in October 1995, was criticized by local and international human rights groups and bar organizations for not conforming to international standards. They remained in custody, having been denied bail.

Thousands of Kenyans, predominantly from the Kikuyu, Luo and Luhya ethnic groups, remained destitute and displaced, driven off their land by state sponsored "ethnic" violence in the early 1990s. The attacks had pitted Kalenjin and Masai, the ethnic groups of the president and his ruling elite, against those ethnic groups associated with the political opposition, particularly in the Rift Valley Province. The government used the violence prior to the 1992 multiparty election to reward and empower the Kalenjin and Masai communities by allowing its members to occupy or buy land illegally in the Rift Valley Province. The redistribution of land in the fertile Rift Valley Province to government supporters strengthened the government's political and economic base. Although the large-scale violence, which characterized the ethnic persecution at the outset has diminished, periodic incidents continued. Moreover, the government did not take adequate steps to investigate reports of incitement of the violence and direct participation by government personnel, to hold the perpetrators of political killing and illegal appropriation of land responsible, to compensate the displaced, or to provide security and protection to the displaced. Many of the displaced were unable to return because of continuing acts of violence or intimidation, illegal occupation of the land by Kalenjin or Masais or fraudulent transfers of land titles.

A joint Kenyan government and United Nations Development Program (UNDP) project to resettle the estimated 300,000 displaced was ended after two years by UNDP in September 1995, despite the fact that thousands had not returned to their land. Throughout the duration of the UNDP program, the government consistently undermined and obstructed genuine resettlement efforts, partly through forced relocation away from the displaced's home areas. While by the end of 1996 people had returned to some areas in Nyanza and Western Provinces, in other areas in Western and Rift Valley Provinces tensions remained high and fears of renewed violence prevented return. Although UNDP claimed to have resettled some 180,000 people by September 1995, local organizations working with the displaced assert that this figure was inflated.

Kenya continued to host thousands of refugees predominantly from Somalia, Sudan, Ethiopia, and Rwanda. Government policy toward refugees, however, remained hostile and Kenyan police periodically conducted sweeps through Nairobi arresting non-Kenyans, including documented aliens and refugees. Some were held without charge for short periods in order to extort money.

The Kenyan government took two positive steps in its foreign policy towards the Great Lakes region. In September, the Kenyan government arrested Obed Ruzindana, a Rwandan national charged with genocide and crimes against humanity by the U.N. International Criminal Tribunal for Rwanda—the first arrest in Kenya in connection with the 1994 massacres in Rwanda. The arrest was all the more significant since a number of prominent genocide perpetrators had sought asylum in Kenya and President Daniel arap Moi had previously stated that he would not cooperate with the International Tribunal. In July, Kenya joined other East and Central African countries in imposing sanctions against Burundi following a military coup in that country and in November hosted a regional meeting in response to the crisis in eastern Zaire.

The Right to Monitor

A wide array of local human rights organizations were engaged in monitoring human rights in Kenya, among others the Catholic Justice and Peace Commission, Centre for Governance and Development, Concerned Citizens for Constitutional Change, International Commission of Jurists (Kenya), the International Federation of Women Lawyers (FIDA-Kenya), the Kenya Anti-Rape Organization, the Kenya Human Rights Commission (KHRC), the Legal Advice Center (LAC), Public Law Institute, and Release Political Prisoners (RPP). The National Council of Churches of Kenya and the Catholic Church continued to assist the displaced population and to monitor ethnic persecution.

Throughout the year, the government criticized the nongovernmental community in public speeches. A number of peaceful meetings were broken up by police during the year, including a civic education seminar convened by the League of Women voters, which was organized by the wife of an opposition leader. Members of RPP were particularly harassed this year. In March, RPP members who attempted to water trees at Nairobi's Uhuru park to mark the fourth anniversary of a violent confrontation to protest against political imprisonment were dispersed. On July 19, twenty-one RPP members were arrested after trying to hold a three-day cultural celebration they had organized in memory of their secretary-general, Karimi Nduthu, who was murdered in March. Under Kenyan law, cultural meetings did not require a license. On July 22, they were charged with holding an illegal meeting and possessing seditious documents that related to the death of Karimi Nduthu—namely the program for the cultural celebration. They were initially denied bail and were held for almost two weeks before being released. The charges were pending, as of November.

In May, the government announced the creation of a nine-member standing Human Rights Committee to investigate violations of human rights. The government gazette mandated the committee to investigate violations of fundamental rights, alleged injustice, abuse of power, and unfair treatment of any person by public officers in the exercise of official duties. This was the second government announcement creating a human rights body. In 1995, shortly before donors met to discuss Kenya, the government announced the creation of a similar committee which never materialized. In April, the government responded for the first time to a human rights report from the Kenya Human

Rights Commission (KHRC), publishing a reply accusing the KHRC of publishing an "unprofessional and mediocre" report. In June, the government restored the registration of the Centre for Law and Research International (CLARION). CLARION had been banned in 1995 following a report it published on government corruption. Another independent organization, Mwangaza Trust, closed at the same time, remained banned.

The Role of the International Community

The international community continued to mute its criticism of the government's human rights record. Since 1991, when aid to Kenya was suspended on economic and human rights grounds, donors had failed to sustain pressure for the respect of human rights and made clear to the Kenyan government that aid would be restored as long as significant steps toward economic reform were maintained. After January 1994, donors increasingly moved to renew their assistance, sending a signal that economic reforms need not be matched by political reforms. The government, in turn, complied with demands for economic reform, but continued to restrict freedom of speech, association and assembly.

In March, bilateral donors pledged US$730 million to Kenya. Some of this aid had been previously pledged in 1995, but not disbursed primarily because of unhappiness over widespread corruption and the lack of economic reforms. Donors continued to pay lip service to human rights concerns, although withholding or renewal of aid remained dependent predominantly on questions of economic reform.

This trend was also reflected by the multilateral lending institutions. In April, the International Monetary Fund (IMF) agreed to release a $316 million loan to Kenya which had been blocked since late 1994. The IMF had expressed dissatisfaction with the government's handling of corruption and economic reform following a visit in September 1995; the release of the

funding followed government steps to address donor complaints about the need for economic reform. In January, a campaign against corruption resulted in the suspension of dozens of senior civil servants and the firing of the head of the Kenya Port Authority and the minister of transport. By approving the loan, the fund signaled an end to the human rights conditions placed by the international lending institutions on the Kenyan government. The resumption of IMF aid in 1996 was expected to lead not only to the release of remaining frozen funds, but to pave the way for the resumption of aid to Kenya in the next year from bilateral donors, the World Bank and multilateral donors such as the European Union. Many bilateral donors had withheld much of the $800 million they pledged in 1994 pending the clean bill of health from the IMF.

United States

Having played a critical role in supporting human rights and the movement toward multiparty democracy during the tenure of Ambassador Smith Hempstone until 1993, U.S. influence in the democratization process diminished significantly under his successor Ambassador Aurelia Brazeal. The U.S. became less outspoken on human rights and appeared unwilling to take the lead to press for multilateral donor action. In 1996, U.S. aid to Kenya totaled $27.19 million, 90 percent of which was directed to nongovernmental sources. In September 1996, a new U.S. Ambassador to Kenya, Prudence Bushnell, was named. In October, Ambassador Bushnell called on the government to relinquish its monopoly of the broadcast media.

LIBERIA

Human Rights Developments

Despite hopes that the 1995 peace accord might finally end Liberia's bloody civil war, the warring factions again plunged the country into a frenzy of looting, lawlessness, and killing throughout April and May. The fighting centered on the capital, Monrovia, creating a devastating humanitarian situation and destroying the city's economy. By mid-October, a new peace agreement was in place—the fourteenth since the war began—and hopes were again raised that the peace process might take hold. Yet despite a new cease-fire and a new timetable for disarmament and elections, fighting between the factions continued sporadically, the humanitarian situation in many places outside of Monrovia was very grave, and progress toward implementation of the peace agreement remained precarious.

The renewed crisis was set in motion in February, when the Council of State, the ruling body created in the prior peace agreement and representing all the warring factions, suspended Roosevelt Johnson as minister for rural development after he was ousted as leader of the United Liberation Movement for Democracy in Liberia, Johnson faction (ULIMO-J). The real crisis was triggered when Charles Taylor's National Patriotic Front of Liberia (NPFL) and Alhadji Kromah's United Liberation Movement for Democracy in Liberia, Kromah faction (ULIMO-K) attempted to arrest Johnson on murder charges. The fighting pitted the factions largely composed of members of the Krahn ethnic group—ULIMO-J, the Armed Forces of Liberia (AFL), and the Liberian Peace Council (LPC)—against the NPFL and ULIMO-K.

The fighting in Monrovia was the worst in three years. The international airport was badly damaged, buildings and homes throughout the city were burned, and some 80,000 civilians were displaced. No reliable death toll was compiled, but it was believed that hundreds of people were killed in the fighting. Virtually all the leading figures in civil society—human rights activists, journalists, lawyers, former politicians, church leaders—immediately went into hiding, and many were pursued by one of the warring factions. Taylor's NPFL burned down the offices of the *New Democrat* and the *Inquirer* newspapers, and reportedly looted the independent shortwave and FM radio transmitters. The AFL and ULIMO-J stormed the prison and freed AFL general Charles Julu and other prisoners who had been involved in an attempted coup in 1994. The looting was clearly sanctioned by the faction leaders, especially Taylor and Kromah.

Fighters from all the factions systematically looted Monrovia's businesses and stores, in addition to the offices and warehouses of the United Nations and all the international aid agencies. The United Nations humanitarian assistance office in Monrovia stated that 489 vehicles valued at US$8.2 million were stolen from the U.N. and various nongovernmental organizations (NGOs). The U.N. also stated that "the majority of those vehicles are now in the hands of factional leaders and fighters who, despite concrete evidence and repeated appeals by the international community, refused to return them so that we can assist Liberians as needed."

Much of the actual fighting took place at the Barclay Training Center, where the Krahn-based factions were under siege by the NPFL/ULIMO-K forces. At the beginning of the crisis, the Krahn factions held civilians, including foreigners, and the Economic Community of West African States Monitoring Group (ECOMOG) soldiers hostage at the training center in a clear violation of international law prohibiting the use of civilians and captured soldiers as human shields. The hostages were eventually released unharmed.

When the crisis erupted, the West African peacekeeping force, ECOMOG, displayed an astonishing reluctance to intervene to stop the fighting or the looting, or to protect civilians. Some ECOMOG soldiers actually participated in the looting, and there were reports of ECOMOG soldiers assisting the NPLF and ULIMO-K in the fighting at the training center. Citing the lack of resources and the refusal of the warring factions to abide by the terms of the 1995 Abuja peace accord, ECOMOG claimed that it could not protect civilians or attempt to end the fighting. It was not until late May that the factions' leaders ordered their forces to withdraw from the center of Monrovia and surrendered their positions to ECOMOG. By late July, ECOMOG was again in control of the city. The poor conduct of ECOMOG forces during the crisis contributed to the decision to assign a new, Nigerian field commander and rotate out many of the troops.

As has been the case throughout the Liberian war, civilians were the main victims. In the April crisis, thousands of civilians were displaced, lost their homes and belongings, and suffered from hunger and disease. In the Graystone compound alone, across from the U.S. embassy, some 15,000 to 20,000 civilians sought refuge. An additional 20,000 civilians sought refuge on the ECOMOG base. Civilians also fled to relief warehouses, hospitals, orphanages, and other sites around the city.

Armed factions have proliferated in the Liberian conflict, and all the factions were responsible for systematic human rights abuses against civilians. Before the fighting erupted in April, civilians suffered abuses, including rape, robberies, and beatings perpetrated by ULIMO-K in Grand Cape Mount County. ULIMO-J fighters were responsible for robbing, beating, raping, torturing, and killing civilians in lower Bomi County. In the southeast, LPC fighters also abused civilians through practices such as robbery, beatings, killings, and forced labor. In January and February, the Council of State took action against Liberia's feisty independent press, harassing and detaining journalists who criticized the NPFL and other warring factions.

The burden felt by regional states from hosting some 750,000 Liberian refugees became increasingly apparent in April and May when thousands of Liberians attempted to flee the country by boat, including one vessel called Bulk Challenge which carried some 2,000 Liberians. The governments of Sierra Leone, Ivory Coast, Nigeria, and Ghana refused to allow the boats to dock, leaving them stranded on the high seas, in an effort to evade their responsibilities under international law. Eventually, the government of Ghana accepted the refugees from the Bulk Challenge.

At the Economic Community of West African States (ECOWAS) Heads of State meeting in Abuja in August, a new chair of Liberia's transitional government was named—Ruth Perry, a former opposition senator under the government of Samuel Doe and a former member of the Transitional Legislative Assembly. The faction leaders remained on the Council of State, as per the 1995 peace accord. A new timetable for disarmament, demobilization, and elections was established: ECOMOG was to deploy to a series of safe havens throughout the country beginning on November 7; disarmament, demobilization, and repatriation was to proceed from November 22 through January 21; and elections were scheduled for May 30, 1997. The member states also committed themselves to observe the arms embargo against Liberia and to take steps to stop the flow of arms.

The most significant new feature of this peace plan was that the ECOWAS countries committed themselves to implement sanctions against any of the Liberian factions if they did not comply with the peace plan. These measures included visa restrictions on recalcitrant faction leaders; freezing business activities and assets; exclusion from participation in the elections; expulsion of family members of faction leaders and their associates from member states; and invoking the Organization of African Unity (OAU) 1996 summit resolution, the possible establishment of a war crimes tribunal for Liberia.

The Right to Monitor

A number of human rights organizations functioned relatively freely in Monrovia in early 1996, including the Catholic Church's Peace and Justice Commission, the Center for Law and Human Rights Education, the Liberian Human Rights Chapter, the Association of Human Rights Promoters, and Liberia Watch for Human Rights. However, access outside Monrovia was difficult for most groups, and virtually all human rights activity ground to a halt when the fighting erupted in April. Many leading human rights activists were targeted by the factions and either took refuge on the ECOMOG base or were evacuated by the U.S. embassy. Samuel Kofi Woods, for example, the director of the Peace and Justice Commission, was evacuated after it was clear that the NPFL was searching for him. Woods returned to Liberia shortly thereafter, and has resumed his work with the commission.

The Role of
the International Community

United Nations
In September 1993, the United Nations Security Council created a U.N. Observer Mission in Liberia (UNOMIL) to help supervise and monitor the Cotonou peace agreement, in conjunction with ECOMOG. UNOMIL had a mandate to report on violations of the cease-fire and violations of humanitarian law. In late 1995 UNOMIL was also entrusted with the mandate "to investigate and report to the Secretary-General on violations of human rights...." and some human rights information was subsequently included in the secretary-general's progress reports on the UNOMIL mission. UNOMIL should also have monitored the ECOMOG mission, since the two were supposed to deploy together and the conduct of ECOMOG contingents required scrutiny. On February 1, UNOMIL's mandate in Liberia was extended until May 31; it was again extended until August 31; and then again through November 30.

Throughout the year, fighting impeded UNOMIL's deployment outside Monrovia. The UNOMIL team withdrew from Tubmanburg on December 30, 1995, due to fighting between ECOMOG and ULIMO-J. The team went back on January 31, but withdrew on March 2, after ECOMOG had withdrawn without notifying UNOMIL. UNOMIL withdrew from Kakata on March 8 because of fighting between the NPFL and ULIMO-J. Soon after fighting broke out in Monrovia in April, the ninety-three UNOMIL observers fled to the U.S. embassy.

UNOMIL's human rights reporting was largely limited because the three human rights officers' posts envisioned were not filled. In his October report to the Security Council, the secretary-general indicated his intention to reactivate these posts and stated that the monitors, among other functions, will also coordinate with local human rights groups. In early October, following the September 28 massacre of civilians in the village of Sinje, in which at least twenty-one people lost their lives, the special representative of the secretary-general sent a large team that included representatives of local human rights groups to investigate the event. Preliminary results of the investigation were included in the October report to the Security Council. Earlier in the year, the U.N. also sent James Jonah, chair of the national electoral commission in Sierra Leone and former U.N. under secretary-general as a special envoy to Liberia. His report on the situation has not been published.

Although the U.N. first imposed an arms embargo on Liberia in 1992, and renewed it in 1995, the embargo was never enforced. In fact, the sanctions committee has never met formally to discuss violations. According to the U.N., this was due to the fact that no embargo violations were reported. Nevertheless, arms apparently continued to enter Liberia in violation of the embargo.

United States
The U.S. remained the largest contributor to humanitarian assistance in Liberia, providing US$65 million in 1996 and approximately $447 million since the start of the war in 1990. In addition, the U.S. provided approximately $70 million for conflict resolution and peacekeeping in Liberia, largely assistance to ECOMOG.

In 1996, the U.S. earmarked $10 million for logistical support for ECOMOG, and an additional $30 million was promised in equipment, training, and other support, provided that ECOMOG demonstrated "a renewed capacity to play a neutral and effective role," according to State Department spokesperson Glyn Davies. In addition, $62 million was pledged for demobilization, reintegration and resettlement, and food aid.

Administration officials described U.S. policy as focusing on the following areas: increased support for ECOMOG, enhanced diplomatic efforts to maintain the cease-fire and restore the peace process, and increased pressure on the faction leaders to cooperate with that process. They also contended that the Abuja Accord, which provides for an interim government, disarmament, demobilization and elections, was the best framework for a permanent solution. However, despite strong rhetoric in April and May, by year's end the Clinton administration had stemmed its early criticism of the faction leaders in order to focus on the need to hold elections in May 1997, in accordance with the new timetable. It remained crucial for the U.S. to maintain a strong human rights policy in the period leading up to the elections so that conditions required to make them meaningful would be met well in advance. These included meaningful disarmament and demobilization, an end to human rights abuses against civilians, safeguards against voter intimidation by the warring factions, and steps to ensure that all parties have equal access to the media and can campaign freely.

In April, the U.S. positioned a naval task force off Liberia with 1,500 marines to assist in the evacuation of foreign nationals and others under threat and to provide security for the U.S. embassy. In his notification to Congress on April 12, President Clinton said that while the U.S. forces were equipped for combat, "the evacuation is being undertaken for the purpose of protecting American citizens and is not intended to alter or preserve the existing political status quo in Liberia." The U.S. military airlifted out more than 2,300 foreign nationals between April 10 and May 27.

Diplomatic efforts included sending a team led by Deputy Assistant Secretary for African Affairs William Twaddell, on April 22, to assist in negotiations and discuss additional assistance to ECOMOG. While in Monrovia, Deputy Assistant Secretary

Twaddell stated: "I reminded members of the Council of State and others that should anyone seize power by force, my government would move to isolate and ostracize that leader and the illegitimate regime that might ensue." This policy was stated even more strongly by Assistant Secretary of State for African Affairs George Moose when he visited Monrovia on April 30 and specifically mentioned Charles Taylor: "We need to make it perfectly clear to the faction leaders, to Mr. Taylor, that the course they are pursuing is a course that will put them beyond the pale, it will lead to the total ostracism, rejection, the total condemnation of their efforts and their actions by the international community." Unfortunately, these strong statements were not accompanied by a clear U.S. policy, but instead the U.S. continued to defer largely to the West African initiatives.

On May 3, the Department of State announced new visa restrictions on faction leaders and others obstructing the peace process and transition to democracy. According to State Department spokesperson Nicholas Burns, "This action results from the refusal of faction leaders to heed the pleas of the Liberian people or to respond to calls from the international community to stop the wanton fighting, looting and killing in Monrovia and to return to the peace process."

MOZAMBIQUE

Human Rights Developments
Human rights practices gradually improved in many parts of the country, two years after Mozambique's first ever multiparty election. However, significant human rights concerns remain, including restrictions on freedom of movement and expression by the former armed opposition group Mozambique National Resistance (RENAMO), heavy-handed policing including torture, and appalling prison conditions.

Accountability for human rights abuses during the 1977-1992 civil war continued to be discussed in the media but both ruling Front for the Liberation of Mozambique (FRELIMO) and RENAMO officials continued to advocate impunity, arguing that any trials or exposure of the past would undermine national reconciliation. However, local communities across the country conducted traditional healing ceremonies at which people made public confessions about human rights abuses. In March Lutero Simango, leader of the opposition National Convention Party (PCN), announced that he would bring the case of the summary execution of his father Uria Simango by the government in the early 1980s before the courts.

RENAMO continued to rule some areas it controlled at the end of the war four years ago, and to exclude government officials. In Maringue, RENAMO's wartime capital in Sofala province, RENAMO expelled five government officials, including the deputy administrator in May. A parliamentary delegation tried the same month to investigate this incident but was intimidated and a meeting in Maringue was abandoned after intense heckling by RENAMO youths. The opposition Democratic Party (PADEMO) had also complained in January that it was unable to work freely in Maringue district because of serious obstructions by RENAMO sympathizers.

The frequency of this type of incident continued to decline elsewhere in Mozambique in 1996 although there were accounts of RENAMO representatives forcing people not to send their children to school because they were government-run. RENAMO also refused to allow freedom of movement in parts of Niassa province and in various locations around the country insisted that those traveling in its administrated areas should carry RENAMO travel permits.

Police behavior remained a serious concern and continued to be the source of the majority of complaints Human Rights Watch/ Africa received from Mozambique in 1996. Arbitrary detention, torture, disappearances, and bribery were common allegations. For example, Luis Franque TChembene died on June 9 from injuries sustained after being tortured for eleven hours on suspicion of steeling a car by police from Maputo's 7th precinct. The police's thirteenth precinct in Maputo's Triunfo Ward also had a particularly bad reputation for torture in 1996.

A paramilitary police unit used to protect highway No.1, Buffalo Battalion, continued to be associated with human rights abuses too. The unit was accused of being responsible for the disappearance of Abdul Mota on May 21 after being arrested on suspicion of being a car thief. Soldiers of the Third Brigade of the Mozambique Defence Force (FADM) stationed in Chimoio in March also detained and tortured six civilians they suspected of trying to steel scrap from their barracks. The six were only freed by the soldiers when each of them paid the soldiers US$13.

The justice minister in June admitted to a parliamentary hearing that there were illegal detentions and seizure of goods from innocent citizens by the police, a growing problem, especially for foreign tourists and truck drivers who faced harassment by police demanding bribes to escape trumped-up charges of minor infractions. Attorney General Sinai Nhatitima also admitted in November 1995 that police used "illegal means of investigation in order to extract the truth," a phrase commonly understood to mean torture: 555 police were expelled for excesses in 1995, around 5 per cent of the police force.

Prison conditions and detention without trial remained a source of grave concern. The Interior Minister Manuel Antonio provoked a public outcry in January when after being asked about deaths of inmates in interior ministry jails, he claimed that they were in police custody "because they committed misdeeds and they have to bear the responsibility." This revealed a gross misunderstanding of the law. People held in interior ministry jails are under preventive detention and should be held under the presumption of innocence.

In September Nampula's main jail housed 317 prisoners although it was built for ninety; only thirty-four of these inmates were serving sentences. Nampula is not unique. In 1996 at least five prisoners died in Quelimane's main prison which had 406 inmates although it was built to house ninety; most of them awaited trial. Chimoio's provincial prison, "cabeca do velho," the scene of appalling conditions and deaths in 1995, attracted public attention again in April when inmates complained that little had improved and that two prison guards were demanding money in return for not beating them up.

A parliamentary delegation found in May that prisoners had not seen the sun in a year, and were forbidden from receiving visitors in Beira's main police station. "BO" prison in Maputo was also reported to refuse inmates daily deliveries of food from their families and prisoners were permitted to receive tinned food once a fortnight only when they paid bribes to prison officials.

The Ministry of the Interior became worried about such negative publicity and in June sent instructions to all districts not to allow unauthorized visits to police or prison installations. Justice Minister Jose Abudo acknowledged in June that there were poor prison conditions and called for an end to the system whereby some prisons were run by the justice ministry and others by the interior ministry. Conditions in interior ministry jails are inferior to those run by the justice ministry.

Mozambicans continued to lack confidence in the legal system and the police. Citizens had a constitutional right of access to the courts but there was a shortage of judges and lawyers and the poor remained unable to afford the fees for defense lawyers. Deputy Attorney General Agostinho Abdul became embroiled in a scandal when in June the newspaper *Domingo* claimed that in 1993 he released three arms traffickers in exchange for $1,500. Drug-trafficking in Mozambique and the failure of the judicial system to bring anyone involved to justice also became an area of international concern. Local human rights groups campaigned for judges to receive a pay increase because judges earned between $50-150 a month, making them financially prone to corrup-

tion.

Throughout 1996 there were incidents of banditry. A shadowy group called the Chimwenje, allegedly made up of Zimbabwean dissidents and ex-RENAMO fighters, was blamed in March for the abduction of fourteen people in Manica province. It was also blamed by both the Mozambican and Zimbabwean governments for numerous armed robberies and theft in the border region but its real origins remained uncertain. There were also occasional riots and violent demonstrations by ex-combatants whose demobilization subsidy ended in March and also incidents where landmines had been used by highwaymen or criminal gangs to ambush vehicles or close roads.

The Right to Monitor

The Mozambique Human Rights League (LDH) campaigned for better prison conditions and police conduct. In early 1996 the LDH signed with the Interior Ministry a memorandum to train police officers in human rights practices but the Ministry later postponed implementation of this project. In July the Criminal Investigation Police Studies Office held a training seminar for its officers in human rights, technical, and legal developments but without the formal help of LDH.

The Association for Defence of Human Rights (ADDH) did not conduct any high profile work in 1996 but the Order of Lawyers of Mozambique (OLM) lobbied for a reorganization of the legal profession and a redefinition of the national standards for accreditation as an attorney. In January UNESCO sponsored a conference "Culture of Peace and Human Rights," which attracted publicity and was well attended.

The Role of
the International Community

The World Bank's Consultative Group on Mozambique (Paris Club) pledged more than $881 million in loans to the government in April. Although donors raised concerns about the growth of corruption and drug-trafficking in Mozambique they remained generally supportive of the post-election government. In June Spain and the Netherlands announced a $9.4 million grant to train or retrain the 9000-strong police force.

United States

Bilateral U.S.-Mozambican relations remained cool although President Clinton signaled a warming in July when he received the credentials of the new Mozambican ambassador to the U.S. and described Mozambique as a "genuine success story [which] has made remarkable progress politically and economically in the transition from war to an enduring peace." The revived Clinton administration interest in Mozambique was also demonstrated by a drop-by meeting in Washington of Secretary of State Warren Christopher on Mozambican Prime Minister Pascoal Mocumbi on September 20.

The tutorial style of U.S. Ambassador to Mozambique Dennis Jett, who ended his posting in July, had contributed to the cool relationship. USAID continued to shift its strategy and resources away from emergency relief toward a longer-term development program. Total U.S. aid to Mozambique in 1996 was estimated at $64.67 million making it one of the main international donors.

U.S. administration visits were kept at deputy assistant level. U.S. Deputy Assistant Secretary of State for African Affairs Bill Twaddell visited Mozambique in April and October and a deputy assistant from the treasury also visited during the year. During July and August a six week program of "Joint Combined Exchange Training" between the Mozambican and U.S. armed forces was conducted. Eleven members from the Third Airborne Group of U.S. Special Forces conducted the training alongside an unspecified number of Mozambican commandos.

A U.S. embassy policy of boosting RENAMO's image, and they hoped therefore confidence in the democratic process, continued with the State Department's *Country Reports on Human Rights Practices for 1995* deliberately down-playing RENAMO

abuses. Human Rights Watch was informed that Ambassador Jett personally edited out references from the original draft.

NIGERIA

Human Rights Developments

Nigeria's human rights record failed to improve during 1996, despite international pressure on the military government of Gen. Sani Abacha following the execution of Ken Saro-Wiwa and eight other Ogoni rights activists on November 10, 1995. Political detentions, restrictions on freedom of expression and association, torture and summary executions, interference in the judicial process, appalling prison conditions, and other human rights violations continued, without noticeable efforts to check such abuses.

In January, military decrees formalized the "transition program" announced by head of state Gen. Sani Abacha on October 1, 1995, and local government elections were held in March 1996 on a "zero party" basis. However, the elections were so compromised by executive interference that they could not be counted as a step forward. Guidelines for the registration of political parties published in June appeared designed to prevent any party from successfully fulfilling the stated criteria. Meanwhile, the presumed winner of the annulled 1993 elections, Chief Moshood K.O. Abiola, passed his second year in detention. On June 4, Kudirat Abiola, Chief Abiola's senior wife and most prominent campaigner on his behalf was assassinated in Lagos by unidentified gunmen presumed by most people to be acting on behalf of the government. Those convicted in 1995 of involvement in an alleged coup plot, including journalists and pro-democracy campaigners who had commented on the allegations, also remained incarcerated.

The decrees promulgated by successive military governments suspending constitutional guarantees of human rights, allowing detention without trial, and criminalizing criticism of the government or its policies, remained in force during 1996. The Transition to Civil Rule (Political Programme) Decree 1 of 1996 made it an offense to "misrepresent, accuse or distort" the transition program. Although the government lifted a controversial 1994 decree that suspended the operation of *habeas corpus* in case of detentions under the notorious Decree 2 of 1984, the courts remained barred from inquiring into the legality of detentions under Decree 2 or examining government actions under numerous other decrees. Other supposed reforms, including the appointment of a national human rights commission, the institution of a review panel to consider detentions on security grounds, and the restoration of a right to appeal in certain cases held before special tribunals appeared to be purely cosmetic and had no effect in practice.

Harassment of opposition activists remained severe, despite the nominal lifting of all restrictions on political activity by a fresh program for the restoration of civilian rule. Threats of violence were made against numerous activists, while other activists in Nigeria and in exile in Europe and the United States suffered attacks on their property, including arson, vandalism, and robbery. Many opposition and human rights activists were detained, for long or short periods, among them Frank Ovie Kokori, secretary-general of the National Union of Petroleum and Natural Gas Workers (NUPENG), held since August 1994 and still in detention in October 1996. Some long-standing detainees were released during the year, including Chima Ubani, secretary-general of Democratic Alternative and a staff member of the Civil Liberties Organisation (CLO), Abdul Oroh, executive director of the CLO, and Tunji Abayomi of Human Rights Africa, all held for one year or more. Family members of opponents of the military regime were also targeted: in several cases children were believed to have been arrested in the hope that their parents would attempt to get them released, and thus expose themselves to arrest. Travel documents were confiscated from a number of human rights and opposition activists. Meetings and rallies were routinely disrupted by the security services.

Other pro-democracy activists and journalists remained in prison, following their convictions in 1995 before a special tribunal of involvement in an alleged—but widely suspected to be invented—coup plot. The arrests followed their publication of information relating to the alleged plot and the trial of the military personnel accused of involvement. They included Beko Ransome-Kuti, chair of the Campaign for Democracy, and journalists Christine Anyanwu, Kunle Ajibade, George Mbah and Ben Charles-Obi. Among the military and former military officers convicted in the trial were former head of state Olusegun Obasanjo and his deputy Musa Shehu Yar'Adua.

Although one of the strongest in Africa, the independent press remained under threat of government interference and harassment. In addition to frequent detentions and other persecution of journalists, newspaper offices suffered a number of arson attempts. In February, Alex Ibru, publisher of the independent newspaper *The Guardian*, survived an assassination attempt. Journalists with the foreign media were also targeted: in January, London *Financial Times* correspondent Paul Adams was detained for a week; in February, BBC World Service correspondent Hilary Anderson was detained overnight; and in July, a reporter for the Middle East News Agency was detained for a week. The broadcast media remained under virtual government monopoly, although an opposition radio station, "Radio Kudirat Nigeria," began broadcasting on short wave from outside the country on June 12, the anniversary of the 1993 elections.

Union activities continued to be restricted, in particular in the oil sector and on university campuses. In May, the federal Ministry of Education announced that the activities at the national level of unions at Nigerian universities, including the Academic Staff Union of Universities (ASUU), were banned, although chapters on individual campuses could continue to function.

In August, ASUU and two other university unions were banned outright, and their assets confiscated. A number of ASUU members were detained at different times and meetings disrupted.

Nigerian citizens not involved in politics also continued to face a consistent pattern of human rights violations. Summary executions and torture by the security forces remained routine, while notoriously bad prison conditions failed to improve. Traders occupying markets constructed (with the permission of the local authorities) under or near highway flyovers in Lagos were removed by the security forces, with excessive force and without due process.

In Ogoniland, home of the Movement for the Survival of the Ogoni People (MOSOP), of which Ken Saro-Wiwa was leader before his execution in November 1995, repression continued during 1996. On January 4, three people were killed by security forces firing on crowds of Ogonis celebrating "Ogoni Day." At least fifty Ogonis were detained following the celebrations. Others were detained around the visit of a fact-finding team appointed by the U.N. secretary-general in April and in other raids during the year. Meetings of MOSOP were disrupted, and activists—including Ledum Mitee, the deputy president of MOSOP, who was acquitted of murder charges in the trial before a special tribunal leading to the execution of Saro-Wiwa and eight others— were harassed. Nineteen Ogonis remained in prison facing charges of murder before a special tribunal in connection with the same facts as those for which the Ogoni Nine were executed. The authorities showed no signs of actually bringing them to trial. The U.N. High Commissioner for Refugees reported in March that around 1,000 Ogonis had crossed the border to Benin; by September 600 Ogonis had been registered as refugees in Benin, and 400 still awaited interviews.

The Right to Monitor

Nigeria's numerous and sophisticated human rights groups continued their activities of monitoring, advocacy, and education throughout the year, despite routine harassment by the authorities. Seminars on human rights sponsored by the CLO, the Committee for the Defence of Human Rights, the Constitutional Rights Project (CRP), the Third World Forum, the Southern Minorities Movement, and other groups were disrupted or prevented during the year by members of the state security services. Human rights activists were detained on numerous occasions; others were prevented from traveling abroad to attend the meetings of the U.N. Commission on Human Rights or other important meetings. Olisa Agbakoba, former president of the CLO, Ayo Obe, current president of the CLO, and Tunde Olugboji, project officer with the CRP, all had their passports confiscated during the year as they tried to leave Lagos to attend U.N. meetings. In November, Human Rights Watch honored Anyakwee Nsirimovu, the executive director of the Institute of Human Rights and Humanitarian Law at their annual human rights monitors ceremony for his work in eastern Nigeria.

The Role of
the International Community

The November 10, 1995 executions of the Ogoni Nine caused a huge outcry from the international community. Sanctions put in place at the time of the annulment of the 1993 elections and the military coup which followed were strengthened and Nigeria was isolated to an unprecedented degree. Nevertheless, international attention on Nigeria lessened during 1996, as Nigeria's major trading partners returned to protecting their short-term economic interests at the expense of human rights issues. The military government's strategy of continuing to promise a "transition" to civilian rule appeared to be successful in fending off serious action against it.

United Nations

The United Nations General Assembly adopted a resolution on Nigeria on December 22, 1995, in which it condemned the executions of Ken Saro-Wiwa and the others, welcomed the steps taken by the Commonwealth, and expressed "the hope that these actions and other possible actions by other States" would encourage Nigeria to restore democratic rule, thus (unusually) encouraging member states to impose their own sanctions even without Security Council action.

The U.N. Commission on Human Rights adopted a resolution on April 22, in which it requested two thematic special rapporteurs (on the independence of judges and lawyers and on extrajudicial, summary or arbitrary executions) to submit a report on Nigeria at the next session of the Commission in 1997 and an interim report to the U.N. General Assembly meeting in late 1996. In October, the Nigerian government agreed to allow the two special rapporteurs to visit Nigeria at the end of November. However, a paragraph calling for the appointment of a special rapporteur on Nigeria, proposed by the member states of the European Union and supported by the U.S., was not adopted, largely because of the failure of African countries to support the measure. In March and April, a fact-finding mission sent by the U.N. secretary-general visited Nigeria and reported on the trial of Ken Saro-Wiwa and the other Ogonis, as well as on progress toward the restoration of civilian rule. The report condemned the violations of due process during the trial, and recommended that compensation be paid to the families of those executed. The team also recommended a series of "confidence building measures" including the release of political detainees.

The U.N. Human Rights Committee, monitoring compliance with the International Covenant on Civil and Political Rights (ICCPR), found severe violations of the ICCPR by Nigeria in April and July, on considering Nigeria's first report submitted to the committee in accordance with the terms of the covenant. The Working Group on Arbitrary Detention considered and denounced a number of cases of detention without trial in Nigeria. Different organs of the International Labour Organization conference also adopted resolutions condemn-

ing Nigeria's violations of the right to freedom of association. No action has been taken against Nigeria at Security Council level.

European Union

All European Union member states recalled their ambassadors for consultation following the executions. By Common Positions of the Council of the European Union dated November 20, 1995 and December 4, 1995, European Union member states agreed to impose visa restrictions on members (including civilians) of the Nigerian Provisional Ruling Council and the Federal Executive Council and their families (in addition to members of the Nigerian military and security forces and their families, on whom restrictions were imposed in 1993); to expel all military personnel attached to the diplomatic missions of Nigeria in member states and to withdraw all military personnel attached to diplomatic missions of E.U. members in Nigeria; to deny visas to official delegations in the field of sports and to national teams; to introduce a prospective embargo on arms, munitions, and military equipment (allowing existing contracts to be fulfilled); and to suspend development cooperation except to projects through non-governmental organizations and local civilian authorities. These sanctions were extended in June, without discussion, and were to be reconsidered and extended or modified in November. Nigeria's major European trading partners, including Britain, were opposed to further measures.

The Commonwealth

The Commonwealth Heads of Government Meeting (CHOGM) that was taking place in Auckland, New Zealand at the time of the executions immediately demonstrated its outrage by suspending Nigeria from the Commonwealth, the first time that this step had been taken. Nigeria was given two years to comply with the terms of the Commonwealth's Harare Declaration, which committed Commonwealth members to democratic governance, failing which it would face expulsion. At the same meeting

CHOGM adopted the Millbrook Commonwealth Action Programme on the Harare Commonwealth Declaration, which included a commitment to take measures in response to violations of the Harare principles. A Commonwealth Ministerial Action Group (CMAG) was appointed to deal with persistent violations, which committed itself to examining, in the first instance, Nigeria, Sierra Leone, and the Gambia, the three Commonwealth countries without democratically elected governments at that time.

On April 23, following its second meeting, CMAG recommended various measures for implementation by Commonwealth members with regard to Nigeria, including visa restrictions on and denial of educational facilities to members of the Nigerian regime and their families, withdrawal of military attachés and cessation of military training, an embargo on the export of arms, a visa-based ban on sporting contacts, and the downgrading of diplomatic and cultural links. At a further meeting on June 24-25, however, the imposition of the sanctions agreed upon in April, which had been delayed to give Nigeria time to engage in dialogue with CMAG about its human rights record, was further postponed, although existing measures consequent on Nigeria's suspension from the Commonwealth remained in place. In September, CMAG met again and announced that a fact-finding mission—which had previously been blocked by the Nigerian government—would travel to Nigeria as soon as possible. No further sanctions would be imposed in the meantime. No guarantees were obtained that the fact-finding mission would be able to visit political detainees.

Organization of African Unity

African countries were in general reluctant to condemn Nigeria's human rights record in strong terms. In December 1995, OAU Secretary-General Salim Ahmed Salim spoke against the response of the international community to the hangings of the Ogoni Nine, stating that, although the OAU would like to see a democratic Nigeria, with greater respect for human rights, "we do not subscribe

to the campaign to isolate Nigeria....We would not want anything to be done which would have the effect of destabilizing Nigeria."

West African states, including Ghana, Niger, Senegal, and the Gambia, indicated their support for Nigeria against "threats to its sovereignty" from the condemnation surrounding the November 10, 1995 executions. Southern African states, meeting at a summit of the Southern African Development Community (SADC) in December 1995, also failed to take measures against Nigeria. The proposal for the appointment of a U.N. special rapporteur on Nigeria, included in the draft resolution submitted by E.U. member states to the 1996 meeting of the U.N. Commission on Human Rights, was not supported by most of the African delegates and had to be deleted before the resolution could be adopted.

At the CHOGM meeting in New Zealand in November 1995, South Africa led the call for strong action against Nigeria. South Africa became less outspoken in 1996, failing, for example, to support the proposal at the 1996 U.N. Commission on Human Rights meeting for the appointment of a special rapporteur on Nigeria. In July, President Nelson Mandela, speaking prior to the OAU summit in Yaounde, Cameroon, acknowledged that "Africa is not speaking with one voice," and indicated that he had "received representations from countries in West Africa as well as from [U.N. Secretary-General] Boutros Boutros-Ghali," who had reminded him that "Nigeria is responsible for law and order in Sierra Leone and Liberia," as it contributes the largest contingent of troops to the West African peacekeeping force the Economic Community of West African States Monitoring Group (ECOMOG) in Liberia.

On December 18 and 19, 1995, at the insistence of Nigerian and international non-governmental organizations, the African Commission on Human and Peoples' Rights (an organ of the OAU) held its second ever extraordinary session at Kampala, Uganda, in order to consider the human rights situation in Nigeria. The commission had been amongst those bodies pleading for clemency in the case of Ken Saro-Wiwa and his code-fendants after the death sentences were passed. The commission also resolved to send a fact-finding mission to Nigeria. Dates for the mission originally agreed upon with the Nigerian government for February fell through and by October no alternative dates had been set.

United States

The United States also responded to the executions by recalling its ambassador, Walter Carrington, for consultation. In addition, it extended pre-existing restrictions on military links (which included the termination in July 1993 of all military assistance and training) by banning the sale and repair of military goods. It extended a pre-existing ban on the issue of visas to senior military officers and senior government officials and their families to cover "all military officers and civilians who actively formulate, implement or benefit from policies that impede Nigeria's transition to democracy"; and introduced a requirement that Nigerian government officials visiting the U.N. or international financial institutions in the U.S. remain within twenty-five miles of those organizations. It also stated it would begin consultations immediately on appropriate U.N. measures. The U.S. government also cut the USAID budget, while reprogramming all USAID assistance exclusively through the nongovernmental sector.

In 1996, however, the U.S. like other countries was stronger on rhetoric than action. While the U.S. issued strong statements condemning military rule and human rights violations, no further concrete measures were adopted. In June, Assistant Secretary John Shattuck visited Nigeria and noted "a steady deterioration in the human rights situation in Nigeria since 1993." Like the E.U., the U.S. publicly stated that all possible measures against Nigeria, without exclusion, were still under consideration; but no steps were announced by the administration to put these statements into effect.

RWANDA

Human Rights Developments

From the start of the year, the Rwandan government fought a growing threat from soldiers (ex-Armed Forces of Rwanda) and militia of the former government, who had been leading incursions from refugee camps in Zaire. The infiltrators, part of the force that carried out a genocide that killed at least half a million Tutsi and slaughtered thousands of Hutu moderates in 1994, remained committed to returning to Rwanda by force and to completing the extermination of the Tutsi. At first the infiltrators used bombs and mines to target electricity pylons, vehicles, and buildings but during the course of the year, they moved to attacking civilians, primarily survivors of or witnesses to the genocide and local government officials. As they grew in confidence, the attackers penetrated further into the country, from the western regions closest to Lake Kivu and Zaire to areas quite close to the capital. By October, the infiltrators had killed at least 278 people.

The current government's Rwandan Patriotic Army (RPA) responded to the incursions by increasing patrols and search and cordon operations, during which some 600 people were killed through the month of October, many of them civilians. Military authorities sought to cover up these killings with unconvincing claims that civilian victims were infiltrators or their accomplices or were accidentally slain in exchanges of gunfire. In many cases, including one investigated by Human Rights Watch in the commune of Ramba, unarmed civilians were shot at close range or when they were in flight. The Ramba massacre, like those at Kanama in September 1995 and at Satinsyi in April 1996 where the slaughter of civilians also followed killings of RPA soldiers, was consistent with a reported government policy of severely punishing the people of any community where soldiers are attacked. A substantial number of the victims in infiltrators' raids and reprisals by government forces have been children, women or elderly people.

In the search and cordon operation in several communes in Ruhengeri prefecture in August 6 to 8, soldiers assembled some 10,000 men on a hilltop and held them there for two days without food or water. Some who failed to respond to the summons and sought to hide or escape were shot when caught. After interrogation, some 300 men were further detained, reportedly in Mukamira military camp. The military penal code was amended in January to permit civilians accused of aiding the enemy to be detained in military facilities and tried under military regulations.

Following an attack, which killed three civilians and wounded a fourth in December 1995, RPA soldiers accused of the crime were tried by a military court before a community gathering. On December 28, 1995, the court found all four guilty and condemned a sergeant, the highest ranking of the four, to death. The sentence was being appealed at the time of this writing. According to military authorities, more than 1,300 RPA soldiers were detained and awaiting trial on a variety of charges, some of which were reportedly related to killings of civilians and other human rights abuses. Apparently none had been brought to trial on charges related to killings done during military operations. Following considerable international protest over the number of persons killed in the July and August operations, Col. Charles Ngoga, commander of the Gisenyi-Ruhengeri sector where the killings had taken place, was relieved of his command, but reportedly was re-assigned in the eastern sector.

Some seventy-five local officials had been killed through the month of October. Some were slain by infiltrators, particularly in areas on the western frontier, but others were apparently killed by RPA soldiers, including the burgomaster, the deputy prosecutor, and a school director in Rushashi commune and the burgomaster of Nyabikenke commune, all murdered in July. Although authorities had investigated some of these cases, no one was brought to trial for

these murders. Two burgomasters who criticized military operation in their communes of Karago and Nyamutera were suspended from office in early September and put under house arrest. The burgomaster of Nyamutera was later imprisoned.

In January, the president and vice-president called on citizens to join soldiers on patrol to combat the incursions. In June, the president renewed this call, as did delegations of high government officials. There were several reports of beatings by civilian patrols, acting either alone or in the company of RPA soldiers. Civilian participation in local security operations was a practice before and during the genocide, one that was clearly abused at that time and that could lead to further abuses.

The judicial and police systems, nearly totally paralyzed since the genocide, received important numbers of new personnel during the year. In September, 280 judges and magistrates, trained in a brief, intensive course in legal procedure, were sworn in. At almost the same time, however, the minister of justice was obliged to resign and was charged with corruption. A number of other officials were removed on charges of corruption, mismanagement, or on belated accusations of involvement in the genocide, including the president of the court of first instance in Kigali, the assistant prosecutor in Kigali, the prosecutor of Butare, and the prosecutor of Kibuye. The latter three were all subsequently arrested. Judicial officials, many of whom expressed concern for their personal safety, experienced frequent problems with administrative officials or military officers who interfered with the execution of their duties. In some areas, unauthorized persons, including soldiers and local officials, made arrests, sometimes without subsequently informing judicial authorities, often during military search and cordon operations. In March, 750 policemen were graduated from a British-run training program.

Tutsi recruits appeared to be far more numerous than Hutu among new judicial and police staff, as was the case with local officials installed last year. Many of these Tutsi returned to Rwanda only after the RPA victory in July 1994. Foreign funders and trainers apparently hesitated to raise the ethnic identity of candidates with authorities, who had made commitments to eliminate the distinctions that formed the basis for the genocide. The large number of Tutsi in official positions as well as in secondary schools and the university caused considerable resentment among the Hutu population.

On September 1, the government officially promulgated a law establishing procedures for punishing genocide and crimes against humanity. It divides perpetrators into four categories: in the first are planners, organizers, instigators, and leaders of the genocide as well as those who killed with particular zeal or malice and those who committed acts of sexual torture; in the second are those who killed or committed assaults resulting in death; in the third are those who committed assaults that resulted in serious injury; and in the fourth are those who committed offenses against property. The accused are to be assigned to categories by prosecutors, whose decision cannot be appealed. Those in category one, if convicted, face death by firing squad. Guilty in other categories will face prison terms and may receive reduced sentences in return for full confessions.

With the adoption of the new law, the appointment of judicial personnel, and the addition of considerable funds from outside donors, the government was well placed to begin trials of those accused of genocide. In October, some 83,000 persons were being held, most of them pending charges of genocide, in a variety of prisons, communal lockups and military places of detention. In virtually all of these locations, inmates were confined in overcrowded, inhumane conditions. In mid-May, ninety-four detainees were confined in a single twenty-meter square room in Kivumu commune. Seventeen of them died of suffocation during one night; six others died under similar conditions in another Kivumu lockup at about the same time. The next week, forty-six detainees died when grenades were thrown into a detention center in Bugarama commune. Local authorities said infiltrators had thrown grenades at the building, but inspection of the site revealed that the grenades had exploded from inside the building outward and showed as well that some of the detainees had been shot. Persons held in central prisons rarely reported mistreatment, while those in communal lockups often complained of being beaten. Several died each month as a result of mistreatment in the communal lockups.

The growing insecurity resulted in large part from the continued presence of large numbers of refugees, approximately 1.7 million, mostly in Zaire and Tanzania. Refugees in Tanzania caused considerable disruption to the local ecology, depleting local supplies of firewood and water, but those in Zaire caused more extensive problems by also attacking locally resident peoples. After making an initial effort to drive out Rwandan refugees in the early part of the year, Burundi finally drove out all but some two hundred in July and August. The majority of the 76,000 Hutu refugees forcibly returned from Burundi encountered relatively few problems in Rwanda and were able to return to their homes and land. Several hundred were arrested, however, and one was reported beaten to death by a crowd. In early October, Rwanda took its turn in driving refugees back across the border when it warned some 4,000 people who had fled violence in Burundi that they had one week to go home. Zaire, which had been trying for some time to send the refugees home, agreed with Rwanda in late July that the camps would be closed. But in October, both Zaire and Tanzania still sheltered a virtually undiminished refugee population and expressed again their determination to send the refugees home.

The violence against Zairians ethnically related to Tutsi and Tutsi of Rwandan origin, first in North Kivu and then in South Kivu, Zaire and the subsequent flight of thousands of them into Rwanda worsened relations between Rwanda and Zaire. Relations between the two countries were already poor because Zaire had tolerated, if not encouraged, the regrouping of the army of the former Rwandan government. In late September and October, the two armies exchanged heavy arms fire across the border of southwestern Rwanda. Zaire accused Rwanda of sending troops into South Kivu to fight civilian and military assailants of the Banyamulenge, Zaire's long-resident Tutsi population.

Following attacks in October by a Banyamulenge opposition group operating with the support of the Rwandan government, the Rwandan refugee camps in Zaire were dispersed and former Rwandan military and militia leaders lost control of them. As of this writing, a mass exodus of Rwandan refugees flooded over the border from Zaire to Rwanda.

The Right to Monitor
Although the government continued to profess its support for human rights and its openness to being monitored, it showed growing impatience at criticism. An April press release from the Ministry of Information stated that human rights organizations sometimes "unwittingly serv[e] as propaganda channels for genocidal leaders" because they collect "slanted" information from informants who were involved in the genocide and "jump at any opportunity to project a negative public image of the government." A subsequent radio broadcast by a high government official accused some Rwandan human rights groups of "covering up" for people guilty of genocide. Local activists have frequently been threatened, usually by unidentified harassers.

In the early part of the year, UNHCR protection officers were denied access or access without official escort to several communes in Butare and Kigali prefectures. Officers conducting an inquiry in Mugesera commune were detained briefly at a military base. Human Rights Watch researchers investigating the Ramba massacre together with Rwandan colleagues were also briefly detained by a military patrol.

After accounts of the Ramba massacre were published by Human Rights Watch and the International Federation of Human Rights Leagues and by the U.N. Human Rights Field Office, Rwandan authorities, including the minister of information and an adviser to the vice-president, criticized their reports as "biased."

The Role of the International Community
The international community continued to contribute far more funds to provide for the basic needs of Rwandans in exile in neighboring countries than to those within the country. Since July 1994, donor nations had spent approximately US$2.5 billion on the refugee camps, while devoting about $572 million to programs in Rwanda itself. At a roundtable conference in Geneva in June, however, donors pledged some $617 million toward a three-year development program in Rwanda that would require $800 million for its complete implementation. Sustaining the refugee camps became a financial burden that donor nations were no longer willing to shoulder. For many months, the refugees had been supported at a cost of approximately a million dollars a day. In June, an appeal for $288 million to fund refugee support for 1996 had raised only $95 million. At Geneva, the United States suggested a new initiative to close the current camps by relocating some further from the frontier and encouraging the rest to return to Rwanda. It pushed harder for this plan in October, when Secretary of State Warren Christopher emphasized the need to close the camps at the Arusha meeting of a number of African heads of state. In September, the UNHCR announced that the twenty persons indicted by the International Tribunal could no longer be considered refugees and it was exploring ways to draw up a longer list of persons who could be excluded on the basis of participation in the genocide.

United Nations
In March, UNAMIR, the peacekeeping force that had been in place before the genocide, reduced and paralyzed at the start of the killing, and then strengthened again at its end, completed its assignment. Although

infiltrations and government reactions to them increased after that time, the gradual increase in violence actually dated back to late 1995, before the end of the U.N. military presence.

In September, the Security Council ended an embargo on arms transfers to the current government, which had been imposed on the previous government of Rwanda during the genocide, but failed to link the decision to demands for progress in halting serious violations, such as the killings of civilians by government soldiers. The council retained the embargo against forces of the former government based in Zaire.

While the genocide was still in progress, the U.N. Human Rights Commission named a special rapporteur for Rwanda and also created a field office of monitors to assist him. In January, the special rapporteur, René Degni-Ségui, published a report dealing with events through the end of 1995 and drawing particular attention to crimes against women and children during the genocide. In February, the Field Office experienced serious financial problems because donor nations had failed to pay their pledges and had to temporarily reduce the number of its investigators. Throughout the year, its staff documented the growing violence of RPA soldiers against civilians and sought discreetly to have authorities correct these abuses. In July and again in August, the Field Office marked its concern by making its data about military killings of civilians publicly available. The International Criminal Tribunal for Rwanda (ICTR), established by the U.N. Security Council subsequent to a finding by its Commission of Experts that genocide had been committed in Rwanda, at first received little more than rhetorical support from the international community. In March, the tribunal had available only twenty-eight investigators and a skeletal legal staff. But in the next few months, various donor nations were persuaded of the need for adequate funding and a budget of $36 million was provided for its operation. By October, the tribunal had indicted twenty persons, including several of major importance in the genocide. Zam-

bia, Kenya, Belgium, Switzerland, and the United States had arrested indicted persons and agreed to hand them over to the tribunal. The Cameroon government, which had arrested several of the most important of the accused, including Col. Théoneste Bagasora, who took charge of military and militia activities from the start of the genocide, delayed delivering them over to the tribunal. Even after all judicial formalities had been completed, President Paul Biya still refused to sign the documents necessary for their transfer to custody of the tribunal.

Because of early financial and staffing difficulties, the tribunal had failed to deal adequately with such issues as witness protection and the prompt provision of necessary materials to defense lawyers. But by October it appeared that these problems had been resolved and the first trial was scheduled to begin at the end of October.

European Union

In April, E.U. special envoy to Rwanda, Achim Kratz, summed up E.U. policy by saying "We have no other solution but to support this government. It may not have a democratic basis but it ended the genocide." The Africa-Caribbean-Pacific European Union Joint Assembly, the parliamentary body of the E.U. and its associated partners in Africa, Caribbean, and Pacific countries, reaffirmed this position in late September when it passed a resolution calling for aid to Rwanda to boost reconstruction and the return of refugees, for prompt implementation of the new Rwandan law on the genocide, and for international assistance in preventing the reorganization and arming of those responsible for the genocide. There was no mention of human rights violations by the current government.

United States

The U.S., like the E.U., had apparently decided to back the current government of Rwanda strongly. A speech given by Richard McCall of the U.S. Agency for International Development gave virtually unqualified support to the government and raised few concerns about its human rights record. While acknowledging that the government needed to address the problems of justice "more effectively," he went on to say that the issue was very complex in ways that the international community might never be able to appreciate.

In July the United States sent nine U.S. soldiers to Rwanda to provide training to RPA soldiers in small-scale operations. Although Ambassador Robert Gribbin acknowledged serious concerns about the killing of civilians by the RPA, he indicated that he believed such concerns were best addressed privately with the appropriate authorities.

In August, Vice-President Paul Kagame, the minister of defense and leading military authority, visited the U.S. and met with such high-level administration officials as National Security Advisor Anthony Lake and Defense Secretary Perry. According to the State Department, they discussed refugee repatriation, rebuilding the justice system, prison conditions and regional peace efforts.

The U.S. was a key supporter of the ICTR, both politically and financially. In addition to $1,683,000 in assessed U.N. contributions for 1994-1995, the U.S. has made voluntary contributions of cash, personnel and equipment at a cost estimated at $3,900,000. The U.S. insisted on the importance of prosecuting those accused of genocide. As of this writing, it had contributed $5,650,000 to the tribunal, $650,000 of which was earmarked for prosecution of mass rape and sexual crimes.

The U.S. cooperated in the arrest of one person, Elsephane Ntakirutimana, indicted by the ICTR. There was no provision in U.S. criminal law for prosecution of genocide, but Human Rights Watch brought a civil suit under the Alien Torts Act in the name of Rwandans resident in the U.S. who had suffered from the genocide. This suit, against Jean-Bosco Barayagwiza, resulted in a $105 million judgment against Barayagwiza, handed down in U.S. District Court on April 9. In the decision, Judge John S. Martin wrote that "the plaintiffs have overwhelm-ingly established that the defendant has engaged in conduct so inhuman that it is difficult to conceive of any civil remedy which can begin to compensate the plaintiffs for their loss or adequately express society's outrage at the defendant's actions."

SOUTH AFRICA

Human Rights Developments

South Africa's African National Congress (ANC)-led government continued its reforming drive during 1996, but also faced significant checks in its stated ambition to reduce some of the inequalities in South African society and introduce a culture of respect for human rights and the rule of law. While further legislation aimed at ending long-standing abuses was adopted and a draft constitution containing a strong bill of rights completed, the government faced and in some cases conceded to demands—in the context of rising public concern about violent crime—for repressive law-and-order measures. Following the completion in May of the draft constitution that was submitted to the constitutional court for certification, the National Party left the government of national unity (GNU) to become the largest opposition party. The Inkatha Freedom Party (IFP), which had not participated in the constitutional discussions, remained in the GNU. In 1996, South Africa ratified the African Charter on Human and Peoples' Rights.

A draft final constitution was adopted by the constitutional assembly in May to replace the interim constitution that came into force on April 27, 1994. Under the certification process provided by the interim constitution, the final constitution was subject to certification by the constitutional court to comply with a set of "constitutional principles." Although the court found that it "complies with the overwhelming majority of the requirements of the [constitutional principles]," it referred certain sections back to the constitutional assembly for amendment, including those relating to the powers of provincial and local government. The bill of rights, including protections for some economic and social rights, was certified, except for the right to collective bargaining for employers. The constitutional assembly reconvened in September to draft amendments to take into account the objections of the court. A revised draft was adopted on October 11, which was in turn to be submitted to the court for certification on November 18.

Local government elections went ahead in the Cape Town metropolitan area and in KwaZulu-Natal province in May and June, respectively, where they had been postponed from 1995 as a result of confusion over electoral arrangements and continuing political violence. In both cases, the vote took place without serious irregularities in the conduct of the poll and all parties accepted the results. The final results in KwaZulu-Natal showed that the ANC held urban areas, with the IFP continuing to prevail in the rural areas of the former KwaZulu "homeland."

Political violence nevertheless continued to simmer in KwaZulu-Natal. Reduced levels of violence in the province were at least in part due to more effective policing. Nevertheless, the nongovernmental monitoring organization, the Human Rights Committee of South Africa, recorded 374 deaths during political violence in KwaZulu-Natal as of the end of September. On the southern coast of KwaZulu-Natal, for example, a special investigation team arrested over one hundred people during 1996 and charged them in connection with offenses related to political violence. Among over thirty other suspects, three policemen from the Port Shepstone police station were charged with murder in connection with a Christmas Day 1995 massacre of nineteen people in Shobashobane. Initially suspended, they were allowed to return to duty in August, although the case against them remained pending. In Cape Town, gang violence led to the emergence of a vigilante response in the form of a group calling itself People Against Gangsterism and Drugs, which was responsible for the killing of a well-known gang leader in August.

A notorious massacre of the past was examined in the trial of former defense minister Magnus Malan and nineteen others. The defendants were accused of involvement in the 1987 massacre of fourteen family members of an ANC leader in KwaZulu-Natal, either directly, or through the design or management of a scheme in which individuals were trained by the South African Defence Force to carry out political assassinations or promote political violence. Three of the accused were discharged in May after the prosecution closed its case, including the former head of the South African Defence Force Department of Military Intelligence, Gen. Tienie Groenewald, on the grounds that the state had failed to submit sufficient evidence against them. In mid-October, the remainder of the defendants were acquitted, amid accusations that the prosecution had not been as well conducted as it might have been by the KwaZulu-Natal attorney-general.

In September, Eugene de Kock, commander under the previous government of the notorious, once secret Vlakplaas unit of the security police, was found guilty in August of six murders and eighty-three other crimes. In his plea in mitigation before sentencing, de Kock implicated senior members of the former government in "dirty tricks" activities against anti-apartheid activists and in the promotion of political violence by covert supply of weapons and other means. Among those named were previous presidents P.W. Botha, current National Party leader F.W. de Klerk, and a number of generals in the army and senior police officers. de Kock also said that South Africa had been behind the 1986 murder of Swedish premier Olaf Palme.

The National Commission on Truth and Reconciliation, sworn into office in December 1995, held hearings around the country during the year, at which past victims of rights abuses told their stories. The legislation establishing the truth commission empowered it to compile as full a record as possible of gross human rights violations during the period March 21, 1960 to December 6, 1993; to recommend the award of reparations to the victims, and to grant amnesty to perpetrators in return for full disclosure of the acts they had committed. Comparatively few perpetrators came forward during the year, and most of those who did apply for amnesty were already in prison, convicted of offenses which they claimed to be political. Political parties were also given an opportunity to present their views of the conflicts of the past. The National Party apologized for the suffering caused by apartheid, but once again failed to acknowledge that its policies of "separate development" in themselves were wrong. In a much fuller submission, the ANC accepted responsibility for the abuses carried out in its own camps in Zambia and Tanzania, while giving a detailed analysis of the context of its own armed struggle.

On August 9, national women's day, the truth commission held hearings dedicated solely to violations against women. Contemporary violations of women's rights also received attention during the year. A twenty-eight member parliamentary committee was established to monitor the commitments made by the government under the Convention for the Elimination of Discrimination Against Women, ratified in 1995, and at the 1995 U.N. conference on women in Beijing. A women's office was also established in the office of the president. Legislation establishing an independent "gender commission" was passed in June, although the body was not yet functional by November. The South African Law Commission announced that it was undertaking a review of the 1993 Prevention of Family Violence Act, under which over 20,000 interdicts (restraining orders) had been granted to victims of domestic violence by the end of 1995, addressing some of the weaknesses of the act criticized by lawyers and women's rights campaigners. In May, the government launched a national program of action for children, taking account of the 1995 ratification of the Convention on the Rights of the Child.

Police reform continued during the year. In August, an executive director was appointed for the Independent Complaints Directorate provided for in the 1995 police act to investigate complaints against the police, although the directorate was not yet functioning at the time of writing. Human rights organizations also expressed concerns that the directorate would have insufficient powers to be effective, and that anti-corruption units established in the police service at national level would not come under its control. Despite some efforts to take action against abusive officers, victim statements and court-authorized raids on police stations revealed that torture equipment, such as rubber hoods and electric shock materials, was still in use against criminal suspects or witnesses in many areas. Police corruption remained widespread, as did collusion with organized crime.

A national anti-crime strategy was announced in May, which included measures to improve investigation of crime, reduce corruption in the police, take action against gangs, promote victim support schemes, prohibit the carrying of firearms at certain gatherings, make bail conditions tougher and improve processing of cases in the courts. However, in the face of public demands for stronger action against violent crime, more repressive measures were also announced, including the construction of new "super-maximum security prisons." In September, the ANC announced that it would review its opposition to the death penalty. Legislation was passed allowing children accused of serious crimes to be held in prison or police detention cells, reversing earlier legislation, which limited detention of children to a maximum of twenty-four hours. However, a government report published in September confirmed allegations of abuse of children held in "places of safety," which hold children considered at risk in their home environment as well as youths that await trial.

Little progress was made toward prison reform during the year. The Correctional Services Transformation Forum, formed in

1995 to guide the process of reform in the prisons with participants from a variety of interested groups, was disbanded after failing to make significant progress. In April the prison service was officially demilitarized on the order of the minister of correctional services, but the measure was criticized both by prison officers and by human rights groups for being badly implemented. Prison disturbances took place at a number of prisons during the year: in two of the worst incidents, four prisoners were killed in a January riot in Barberton prison, and three in a September riot at Upington. In response to calls by human rights groups for the appointment of a prisons inspectorate, it was announced that an "inspecting judge" for the prison system would be appointed.

Although both the U.N. and the Organization of African Unity (OAU) conventions on refugees were ratified by South Africa in 1995, policy toward refugees and undocumented aliens remained problematic. More than 150,000 aliens were deported in 1995, and deportation continued at the same rate in 1996, usually without regard to a deportee's right to a hearing. Immigrants were often the target for police harassment, and routinely blamed by politicians and others, without good evidence, for the reported rise in crime. In June, a limited amnesty for nationals of countries within the Southern African Development Community (SADC) who were illegally resident in South Africa was announced in June, and in July SADC countries met with representatives of the U.N. High Commissioner for Refugees (UNHCR) and agreed to cooperate in formulating refugee policies.

South Africa's foreign policy exhibited a lack of strong leadership during 1996. Contradictory statements were issued on relations with Libya, Cuba, and Iran, in particular, as South Africa responded to U.S. and other criticism for its attitude to those countries. President Nelson Mandela led the international outcry at the execution of nine Ogoni rights activists in November 1995 that resulted in the suspension of Nigeria from the Commonwealth and other mea-sures (see Nigeria section). South Africa changed its stance during 1996, however, in the face of the reluctance of other African countries to take a strong position, and did not back the appointment of a special rapporteur on Nigeria proposed at the 1996 session of the U.N. Commission on Human Rights. South Africa followed the OAU in imposing sanctions on the government that took power in Burundi after a military coup in July. The second report of the Cameron Commission, investigating South Africa's arms trade, was published in March, and recommended wholesale reforms of the procedures for licensing arms sales: a decision to supply arms to the current government of Rwanda was taken in accordance with these new procedures. South Africa made contributions toward the peacekeeping efforts of the OAU and of the U.N. in Angola.

The Right to Monitor

There were no restrictions on the right to monitor human rights violations in South Africa during 1996. Nongovernmental human rights organizations, however, faced a budget crisis as foreign funding, directed to the nongovernmental sector before 1994, continued to be redirected to government projects. A number of independent statutory bodies mandated to monitor government activity began to function, including the Human Rights Commission, charged with promoting respect for human rights and investigating violations, and the Public Protector, charged to investigate misconduct in public administration. While there were criticisms of the first work of these bodies, they promised to perform a useful function in the future.

The Role of
the International Community

The contribution of other countries to human rights in South Africa during 1996 consisted largely of financial assistance to the ANC government's "reconstruction and development program" and to nongovernmental human rights organizations. A number of specifically human rights-related projects were announced during the year, including the creation of a European Union Foundation for Human Rights in South Africa, funded by the European Union (E.U.), South Africa's largest bilateral donor. The foundation was created to implement the E.U.'s human rights program in South Africa, with disbursements of US$19 million from 1996 to 1999. The E.U. also granted $2.4 million to the truth commission. USAID pledged $3.1 million to a consortium of nongovernmental bodies involved in public interest law and human rights under the umbrella of the National Institute for Public Interest Law and Research and pledged to spend a similar amount over the next financial year. In addition, USAID gave $9.5 million to the Ministry of Justice to train lawyers, judges, and magistrates; carry out law reform; conduct human rights education; and increase access to the judicial system. U.S. Peace Corps volunteers were scheduled to arrive in South Africa for the first time in January 1997. Canada promised to provide at least $4.4 million over four years to help upgrade South Africa's judicial system. Britain provided assistance toward redeveloping police training programs, and toward the restructuring of the defense force.

SUDAN

Human Rights Developments

The National Islamic Front (NIF) dominated Sudan's government, which had declared Sudan an Islamic republic. The civil war, underway since 1983 against the rebel Sudan People's Liberation Movement/Army (SPLM/A) and others and continued to be the context of massive human rights violations, including indiscriminate attacks on civilians and refusal of relief access to the needy, arbitrary detentions, mistreatment, and torture.

While giving lip-service to tolerance, during 1996 the NIF, an Islamist political party, continued its policy of using state power to coerce Islamization and force its interpretation of Islam upon Muslims, in violation of freedom of religion. Its politicization of religion and ethnicity made settlement of the war increasingly difficult. Although Islam was the state religion, only 60 percent of the population was Muslim. The Muslim population lived largely in the north, and most southerners remained Christians or practiced traditional African religions. The SPLM/A, initially a southern-based movement, continued to seek a united secular Sudan. Poor relations between Christian churches and the government, as well as the civil war, were deeply related to the north-south questions and the government's Islamization project. The government continued to characterize attacks on its poor human rights record as attacks on Islam.

In March, elections were held for president and legislative assembly but were boycotted by the opposition, as political parties remained banned and there were substantial restrictions on free speech, assembly and association. The governing NIF reinforced its political control through these elections, although as a political party it, too, was technically banned. The NIF's attempts to speak for all Sudanese Muslims were rebuffed by leaders of traditional Sudanese Sunni Muslim sects, two of which formed the backbone of the two largest political parties in Sudan, the Democratic Unionist Party and the Umma Party—both banned since the 1989 army/NIF coup.

Slightly greater press freedom permitted to local newspapers prior to the elections ended shortly after March. After repeated suspensions, the government finally closed *Al Rai Al Akhar*, the last independent paper then still open in July. At two state publishing houses, the government dismissed women journalists who demanded equal pay and laid off an additional 150 women and fifty men. Arrests of journalists continued in 1996.

Other forms of expression also remained tightly circumscribed. After former vice-president and well-known southern politician Abel Alier publicly called for resolution of the war in late 1995, he and others close to him were detained briefly and harassed in other ways. Several signatories of a June 1996 petition to the government calling for a multiparty system were arrested, others harassed.

As usual, the universities were sites of struggle between pro- and antigovernment students, in which government forces played a partisan role. At the private, independent Ahliya University in Omdurman, the triumph of antigovernment students in student elections in mid-1996 led to more violent clashes between student groups. Although pro-NIF student supporters and NIF militias attacked and destroyed university buildings during these clashes, none were detained and instead the government used this as a pretext to close Ahliya University permanently.

For the most part, however, efforts to secure the release of detained antigovernment activists did not meet with success. The government continued to hold security detainees for up to and sometimes beyond six months without charges or recourse to the courts. Unacknowledged places of detention, "ghost houses," continued to serve as informal security detention facilities where mistreatment and sometimes torture occurred. Victims of the most severe torture continued to be largely from Sudan's marginalized peoples, particularly those in or from the war-affected areas, such as the south, the central Nuba Mountains, and the Beja region in eastern Sudan.

According to the government, coup plotters abounded. Several alleged "plotters" were detained by security in January and released on bail in May, under close surveillance, possibly to be tried in a civilian court. Another thirty-one detainees (including ten civilians) were put on trial by a military tribunal in Khartoum in August for an alleged February coup attempt. The trial, in October still proceeding in the military intelligence area of army headquarters, was closed to the public. Human Rights Watch's request to observe it and for the public and the press to have access was ignored. In late September, one defendant, a civilian journalist, took off his shirt to show what he said were torture scars; other defendants claimed to have been

tortured. The defendants were charged with crimes that carry the death penalty. Another group captured in August in and around Port Sudan is expected to be tried before a military tribunal also.

Many of the almost two million displaced southerners and Nubas in the Khartoum area since the mid-1980s "illegally" built shanties and churches. These structures continued to be destroyed in disregard of international due process standards pursuant to an "urban renewal" plan. This plan would reverse population trends resulting from the ongoing civil war and the droughts of the 1980s, as Khartoum's population doubled to four million and the ethnic balance of the capital shifted away from its Arab base. Those displaced who arrived in Khartoum after 1990 had no right of tenure anywhere in Khartoum, not even in the dreary "official" displaced persons' camps. By late 1995 about 4.25 million war-affected inside Sudan—north and south—required some form of relief assistance. Another 556,000 were refugees in neighboring countries.

The war that had driven the displaced and refugees from their homes continued. The government's war abuses included targeted air attacks on civilian populations. On August 23, two helicopter gunships flew low and deliberately fired rockets and machineguns on civilians on market day in Kotobi, Western Equatoria, where 6,000 displaced persons were sheltering. Five civilians were killed and forty-five injured, and two churches were destroyed. Indiscriminate government attacks on concentrations of civilians included three bombing raids on the town center and market place in Maridi in Western Equatoria during July, in which three civilians were killed and twenty-three were reported wounded.

Civilians had no respite from human rights abuses in the central Nuba Mountains either. For example, on March 23 and 24, 1996, two villages in the Moro district were looted and destroyed by a joint army and Popular Defense Forces (PDF) militia raid, leaving 1,000 families destitute.

Slavery was an ongoing abuse. Government troops and government PDF militias had captured and enslaved women and children in army-sponsored raids on southern and Nuba villages for the past ten years. They were allowed, as a form of war booty, to take these civilians captive for use in domestic slavery or to sell. For example, on March 16, in southern Kordofan, a PDF attack on Mabior Deil, a village established by the government for the displaced in 1995, killed an estimated thirty-one and kidnapped at least thirteen women and children for slavery. The PDF reportedly enslaved twelve in another attack on Majok Kuom in Bahr El Ghazal on April 25, and seventy-one were reportedly enslaved by the PDF in attacks in the Abyei area of Kordofan in April.

Cmdr. Kerubino Kuanyin Bol, heading a government militia, brought the greatest destruction to southern Sudan in late 1995 and early 1996. Kerubino, a former SPLA founder whom the SPLA held prisoner in secret camps for over five years, escaped and in 1993 returned to his native northern Bahr El Ghazal. Since then, in alliance with the Sudan government, his troops routinely attacked, looted, and burned civilian villages, killing civilians, wiping out their cattle and grain, and sparking a need for emergency relief. The government frequently denied access to this region to nongovernmental organizations (NGOs) and to Operation Lifeline Sudan (Southern Sector), the U.N. umbrella agency charged with crossborder emergency relief to the internally displaced. It appeared that the government was trying to push civilians to migrate to government garrison towns, another example of the government's scorched earth or "draining the sea" counterinsurgency strategy, as in the Nuba Mountains.

In 1996, the most significant political development in the civil war since the 1991 SPLA split occurred when the leader of the 1991 split, Cmdr. Riek Machar, took his Nuer-based Southern Sudan Independence Movement/Army (SSIM/A) into an alliance with the government. Along with Kerubino, a Dinka, Machar signed a "Political Charter" with the government in April. Most of the

Sudan's known oil reserves lay within SSIM/A territory.

The Political Charter was the culmination of a government strategy, which did not break the war's stalemate but imposed a high cost on the south. With this charter, the Sudan government continued to actively prolong and deepen ethnic divisions between and among the two largest peoples in southern Sudan, the Dinka (mostly aligned with the SPLA) and the Nuer (mostly with the SSIA), with approximately 12 and 5 percent, respectively, of the entire population of Sudan. The government's strategy extended to arming and financing several other smaller, often ethnically-based splinters of the SPLA.

Unlike prior years, however, when the SSIA/SPLA conflict could be characterized as internal SPLA faction fighting, the government of Sudan was in 1996 directly responsible for the conduct of the Machar and Kerubino forces fighting against the SPLA. This stepped-up government orchestrated fighting among southerners led to more civilians killed, displaced and left destitute in 1996 than at any time since the height of SPLA faction fighting in 1993. The Dinka-Nuer fighting even spread to the Kakuma refugee camp in Kenya where six refugees were killed and over one hundred wounded in two days of clashes in mid-1996.

Compounding the ethnic divisions was the refusal of SPLA Commander-in-Chief John Garang to investigate and punish attacks on civilians by his troops, particularly attacks made across ethnic lines. In the largest recent attack, on July 30, 1995, Dinka SPLA forces attacked villages in the Nuer area of Ganyliel, killing more than 210 persons. Although eyewitnesses saw SPLA commanders and soldiers there, Garang said this action was not "ordered" by the SPLA, and told Human Rights Watch that investigating allegations of abuses by SPLA troops was "not a priority" for the SPLA.

An SPLA offensive starting in October 1995 recaptured several southern villages from the government, and was followed in early 1996 by stepped-up SPLA forced recruitment, including of young boys, from

Western Equatoria, and from refugee camps in Ethiopia and Kenya. On August 17, an SPLA commander detained six Catholic missionaries who had been critical of SPLA forced recruitment and other abusive practices in the Western Equatoria area of Mapourdit, but released them on August 28 after international protests.

New rebel actors in the war appeared in the east. The northern-based Sudan Alliance Forces (SAF) and the eastern-based Beja Congress, members of the opposition umbrella National Democratic Alliance (NDA) headquartered in Eritrea, began attacks on government forces inside eastern Sudan. Landmines were placed in the area, some left reportedly by opposition forces.

The Right to Monitor

No independent domestic human rights monitors were able to operate above ground in government-controlled Sudan. Following the 1989 coup, the government banned the independent Sudan Bar Association and the Sudan Human Rights Organization (SHRO). The original SHRO functioned out of Cairo, London and other cities as an organization in exile. Government supporters inside Sudan established an official organization also called SHRO, unconditionally supporting the government.

Dr. Ushari Mahmud, a linguist and human rights antislavery campaigner, was jailed by the incumbent government for twenty-two months (1989-91) in an attempt to force him to renounce his 1987 slavery study and, as of November, remained banned from travel.

The Role of
the International Community

Sudan continued to be isolated internationally, and its human rights record often criticized. Relations with most of the ten countries bordering Sudan were tense, and the governments of Egypt, Eritrea, Ethiopia, and Uganda alleged Sudan was contributing to destabilization there by backing rebel groups opposed to those governments.

In January, the U.N. General Assembly renewed its condemnation of Sudan's human rights record for the fourth consecutive year, and condemned its practices of institutionalized slavery. The U.N. Commission on Human Rights in April condemned human rights violations in Sudan in a resolution noting with "deep concern reports of grave human rights violations in the Sudan," as described in reports submitted by the special rapporteurs on the situation of human rights in Sudan; on extrajudicial, summary or arbitrary executions; on the question of religious intolerance; and by the chairs of the Working Groups on Arbitrary Detention and on Enforced or Involuntary Disappearances. The Sudan government, responding to pressure, lifted its two year ban on visits by U.N. Special Rapporteur on Human Rights in Sudan Gaspar Biro. His visit to Khartoum in August was marred by a government newspaper's incorrect quotation in which he is held to have denied slavery existed in Sudan. The special rapporteur replied that the Sudanese media had "grossly misrepresented" his views, and that he continued to receive reports of slavery.

The U.N. Commission on Human Rights in April resolved to establish three U.N. human rights monitors for Sudan, to be based in Uganda, Kenya and Eritrea; the government refused to accept U.N. monitors on its soil. As of November, however, the U.N. failed to establish the missions of the monitors. Also in mid-1996, the government invited the U.N. special rapporteurs on free expression and religious tolerance to visit.

European Union

The Africa-Caribbean-Pacific European Union Joint Assembly of the European Union condemned the human rights record of the government of Sudan for the fourth consecutive year in a resolution on March 22, and "also condemned the regime for its practices of institutionalized slavery." It called on the international community to outlaw the sale of armaments to the government. It further criticized the government and all factions of the SPLA for killings, massacres, torture, and other abuses of human rights. A similar resolution followed in late September.

United States

The U.S. government condemned the human rights records of both the Sudan government and the southern rebel factions in the State Department's *Country Reports on Human Rights Practices for 1995*. Although a 1993 U.S. State Department decision placing Sudan on the list of countries supporting "international terrorism" made Sudan ineligible for all U.S. assistance except humanitarian aid, the U.S. Congress in 1996 exempted SPLA-controlled areas of Sudan from the ban on U.S. development aid.

The U.S. took the lead at the U.N. Security Council early in 1996 on a resolution to impose sanctions on Sudan for its failure to extradite to Ethiopia three men accused of participation in the assassination attempt on Egyptian President Hosni Mubarak when he arrived in Addis Abba, Ethiopia, for the Organization of African Unity (OAU) summit meeting in September 1995.

In early 1996, the U.S. embassy in Khartoum withdrew its American personnel, citing security reasons. These diplomats, relocated to Nairobi, returned to Sudan for visits but their relocation hindered any active human rights role that the embassy might have played inside Sudan. The U.S. expelled from the Sudanese diplomatic mission at the U.N. a Sudanese diplomat with the portfolio of "human rights," accusing him of involvement in a conspiracy to bomb targets in the U.S.

Fatih Erwa, whose naming as ambassador of Sudan to Washington was rejected by the U.S. in 1995, was named Sudan's Ambassador to the U.N. in 1996. The 1995 rejection by the U.S. was presumed to have been motivated by Erwa's involvement in Juba in 1992 in hundreds of summary executions and "disappearances," including those of four employees of the U.S. Agency for International Development.

United Nations

Mild Security Council sanctions relating to the Addis Abba incident, including a downgrading of diplomatic relations and refusal of visas to government personnel by U.N. member states, were imposed on Sudan in May 1996. These were extended in August 1996 to a ban on Sudan Airways if the government continued to refuse to extradite the suspects, whom it claimed were not in Sudanese territory. But human rights was not on the Security Council agenda.

The United Nations Children's Fund (UNICEF), the lead agency in Operation Lifeline Sudan (OLS)(Southern Sector), won praise in an external review of OLS, specifically for its work in the south on advancing the implementation of the Convention on the Rights of the Child (CRC) and observance of humanitarian law. In the south, OLS (Southern Sector) engaged actively in human rights dissemination. It signed joint commitments on humanitarian principles, CRC, and international humanitarian law, called the "ground rules," with each of the SPLM/A, SSIM/A, and the SPLM/A-United, in early 1996. The OLS conducted field investigations of attacks affecting civilians, and asked the attackers to account for violations of the conventions. UNICEF family reunification of unaccompanied boys in SPLA custody in the south was started in mid-1996, a significant first for the SPLA.

A rare press release by the U.N. secretary-general in February sharply criticized the government for dropping several bombs near a marked International Committee of the Red Cross plane and U.N. personnel at two approved relief locations in southern Sudan.

The chronic and grave problem of government denial of relief access for reasons unrelated to need continued. The OLS faced stiff government resistance to access to fifteen southern relief locations with assessed need (of 140 locations requested). In addition, the government had since September 1995 refused to let the OLS operate its largest and most efficient plane, a C-130, sharply reducing OLS capacity to assist the needy even in areas where access was permitted. Because of a lack of infrastructure, fighting and landmines, most access to southern Sudan continued to be by air.

The C-130 issue was raised repeatedly with the government at high levels, without success, and was made public in July with a statement by the U.N. secretary-general followed by a World Food Programme press conference denouncing the impeded access, which threatened 700,000 southerners with hunger. Almost the next day, the government reversed its position and permitted OLS use of the C-130.

High-level U.N. pressure by Under-Secretary General for Humanitarian Affairs Yasushi Akashi convinced the government to permit OLS access to Pochalla, retaken by the SPLA in March 1996, where July floods seriously affected 15,000 to 25,000 persons. This permission only held for one month, however, not long enough to meet Pochalla's needs.

The most persistent gap in U.N. attention to human rights problems in Sudan remained the Nuba Mountains, where the Khartoum government for years blocked all human rights and emergency relief access except for agencies aligned with the government. In this blackout, it attacked civilian villages and forcibly displaced civilians to government-run "peace villages" where they were subjected to human rights abuses and pauperization. Despite repeated pleas, the U.N. has dodged this access issue.

This OLS failure came in for criticism in the external review of OLS, which stated that the U.N. approach of quiet diplomacy in the north "has achieved little beyond providing an impetus for the [government of Sudan] to expand its mechanisms of control and regulation. . . . the scope and coverage of OLS is determined on the basis of [government] approval, rather than actual need." This criticism was directed not only against the OLS inactivity in the Nuba Mountains but also with regard to internally displaced persons in the north, particularly in the Greater Khartoum area.

The United Nations High Commissioner for Refugees (UNHCR) reportedly did little to prevent the SPLA from recruiting some one hundred Sudanese boys from refugee camps in Kenya (June) and Ethiopia (March). The UNHCR also faced the challenge of resettling 260 former unaccompanied boys whom the SPLA sent to Cuba for schooling in the late 1980s.

Slavery complaints have been pending against Sudan for several years at the International Labour Organisation, the Working Group on Contemporary Forms of Slavery, and the U.N. Committee on the Rights of the Child. A government-promised slavery investigation due in August had not occurred as of November.

ZAIRE

Human Rights Developments

The human rights situation in Zaire continued to deteriorate in 1996 as anxiety over the country's future increased. Continued state-sponsored abuse—including harassment of opposition politicians and human rights activists, widespread arbitrary arrest, torture, rape, killings and looting by military and police, and government support for ethnic militias—raised doubts about the commitment of national political leaders to a promised 1997 transition to democracy. By organizing "controlled chaos," as some observers have labeled policies encouraging opposition groups to splinter and fostering regional and ethnic divisions—including the inter-ethnic battles and massacres that took place in North and South Kivu in 1996—President Mobutu Sese Seko sought to guarantee that he and his allies would remain in office indefinitely, even as Zaire inched toward national disintegration and the population found the struggle for daily survival increasingly difficult.

President Mobutu, now in his thirty-first year in office, regained a degree of international support in 1996 by exploiting the ongoing presence of Rwandan refugees in Eastern Zaire and promising to support upcoming multiparty elections. Within Zaire, President Mobutu remained the dominant political power, even as health problems limited his personal involvement in the day-to-day operations of government. Despite differences on some issues, Prime Minister Kengo wa Dondo generally supported and assisted President Mobutu.

Zaire's national legislative body, the High Council of the Republic-Transitional Parliament (HCR-PT), meanwhile suffered from deep divisions that limited its ability to check the president's power. After being forced out of his position as president of the HCR-PT in June 1995, Archbishop Laurent Mossengwo officially resigned in January. The legislative body was unable to agree on a successor, thus two vice-presidents, one a Mobutu loyalist and the other a critic of the president, shared leadership.

The political parties opposed to President Mobutu experienced divisions that raised doubts about their ability to present a unified opposition front in upcoming elections. Several opposition parties entered a newly reformulated cabinet in February, which prompted Etienne Tshisekedi, the leader of the major opposition alliance, the Sacred Union of Radical Opposition, to expel them from the group. In reaction to a second set of purges he initiated in April and May, Tshisekedi was himself ousted from both the Sacred Union and his political party, the Union for Democracy and Social Progress (UDPS) and replaced by his second in command, Frederic Kibassa-Maliba. The groups officially withdrew their claim that Tshisekedi was the rightful prime minister of Zaire, a position they had supported since his removal from office in 1993.

Meanwhile, despite promises from both President Mobutu and Prime Minister Kengo to hold presidential, parliamentary, and municipal elections in the coming year, the government undertook only limited preparations for a transition to democracy. A forty-four-member National Election Commission (CNE) was established in January to prepare for elections. In April the CNE announced that elections would be held in May 1997, but the president of the commission, Bayona ba Meya, immediately expressed doubts

about whether this timetable was realistic.

In September, less than a week after the first 116 of an expected 9,400 election delegates were installed, Georges Nzongola, one of two vice-presidents of the CNE and a prominent democracy activist, resigned from the commission in protest over the government's lack of serious commitment to holding elections. Nzongola complained, among other things, that less than 5 percent of the CNE's budget had been released by the government. Further hampering election preparations, the referendum on a new national constitution originally scheduled for December 1996 was postponed to February 1997, while the HCR-PT was unable to pass a law to govern the elections, despite going into extraordinary session in July for that purpose.

The conduct of President Mobutu and his supporters raised concerns about their commitment to free and fair elections. President Mobutu declared his candidacy even before the CNE announced a date for presidential elections, and army and police harassment of government critics during the course of the year seemed intended to prevent challengers from mounting an effective opposition. In March, soldiers broke up an opposition meeting and arrested several leaders, including Tshisekedi, who was briefly detained. Reverend Steve Hamaweja, president of the Christian Liberal Party, his eight year-old son, and another child of seven years, were detained and tortured in March, according to a letter Hamaweja smuggled out of detention. On September 7, Akerele Iyombi, president of the Congress Lokole Party, was arrested: she was briefly detained at a military camp in Kinshasa. Both Hamaweja and Iyombi had previously expressed an intention to run for president.

Anxiety over Zaire's political future was heightened in late 1996 by uncertainty about President Mobutu's health. Mobutu's September 7 announcement on Zairian national television that he was in Switzerland recuperating from prostate surgery fueled fears that the president's ill health could be used as an excuse to postpone the promised

1997 elections. Following speculation in Zairian newspapers about a potential army coup, the military high command in September publicly declared its loyalty to the institutions working for democratic transition, but this did little to dispel public apprehensions.

Zaire's persistent political crisis intensified the country's grave economic troubles. The government made no effort to address endemic high unemployment, massive inflation, and a deteriorating infrastructure. With little supervision and almost no financial support from the central government, administrative, judicial, and military officials at the local and regional levels participated widely in graft and corruption, exacerbating an already serious crime problem and increasing the level of insecurity among average Zairians.

The most serious and extensive human rights violations in 1996 occurred in Eastern Zaire, where the continuing presence of nearly 1.1 million Rwandan refugees sparked interethnic conflicts and provoked tensions between Zaire and its neighbors. Zairian authorities expressed concern that the presence of the refugees, who were concentrated in camps around Goma, Bukavu, and Uvira, would complicate the upcoming elections. They repeatedly proposed plans to encourage repatriation, but the refugees, many of whom were involved in the 1994 genocide and feared retribution if they return, resisted, and none of the repatriation plans were fully implemented.

For most of the year, the former Rwandan army and the Interahamwe militia groups responsible for the 1994 genocide in Rwanda continued to operate freely within the camps, using intimidation and violence to discourage refugees from returning to Rwanda. Insecurity in the camps forced international nongovernmental organizations and United Nations agencies to suspend operations various times during the year. In July, several expatriate workers were detained, interrogated, and beaten by the Zairian Camp Security Contingent (ZCSC), Zairian troops deployed by the UNHCR to keep order. In September, refugees boycotted a UNHCR census intended to determine the size of the refugee population.

The presence of the camps contributed to tensions in the Great Lakes region and a serious deterioration of relations between the governments of Rwanda and Zaire. Rwandan authorities claimed that guerrilla attacks on government officials and survivors of the 1994 genocide were being organized out of the camps in Zaire (see Rwanda section). Zairian government officials had, in fact, provided shelter to the former Rwandan army and Rwandan Hutu militias and helped them to re-arm. At the same time, Zaire had persistently refused to cooperate with the International Tribunal on Rwanda in seeking out, detaining or cooperating with the extraditing of persons indicted for genocide. In September, fighting between Rwandan and Zairian military around Bukavu left an undetermined number dead and drove hundreds from their homes.

Problems in the camps also helped to reignite ethnic conflicts that first erupted in the region in 1993. Worries that the Zairian government would forcibly close the camps in advance of the 1997 elections fueled calls among some exile leaders for the creation of an ethnic Hutu homeland in Eastern Zaire. Hutu refugees from Rwanda organized local Zairian Hutu populations in Masisi and Rutshuru zones into civilian militia groups modeled after the Rwandan Hutu militia groups known as the Interahamwe.

After several violent incidents in Masisi in late 1995 involving Hunde and Nyanga militia, known as Bangerima or Mai-mai, the Hutu militia launched a series of attacks, apparently seeking to drive other ethnic groups out of Masisi and Rutshuru. The Bangerima and Mai-mai counterattacked, and the conflict steadily expanded in the first months of 1996, killing hundreds and displacing more than 200,000. Zairian Tutsi, who were present throughout the region, were a primary target of both sides in the conflict. Through pillage, rape, and murder, the militia sought to drive Tutsi not simply out of their homes but out of the region.

Between February and July, more than 18,000 Zairian Tutsi fled into Rwanda and Uganda. Government officials were heavily implicated in the conflict. Regional and national officials, including the governor of North Kivu, helped to incite the violence with incendiary statements, while local officials both participated in attacks and profited from pillage. Soldiers and police supported both Hutu militia and the Bangerima/Mai-mai, depending on local circumstances and possibilities for profiting from the situation.

Political leaders in South Kivu also exploited anti-Rwandan and anti-Tutsi sentiments by inciting hostility and violence against the Banyamulenge, an ethnic group whose ancestors migrated from Rwanda and Burundi to Uvira, Mwenga, and Fizi zones in the early 1800s, substantially before colonial occupation. Formerly well integrated into Zaire, the Banyamulenge in recent years were increasingly lumped together with other Tutsi. In 1993, the National Conference, the gathering of representatives of political parties, nongovernmental organizations (NGOs), churches, and other groups that launched Zaire's transition to democracy, denied representation to the Banyamulenge, claiming that they, along with the Tutsi of North Kivu, were not Zairian but Rwandan, and they subsequently faced growing harassment and discrimination.

In late July 1996, two organizations serving the Banyamulenge were banned and several prominent individuals were arrested, including three Protestant pastors and two local chiefs. Subsequent attacks against the Banyamulenge community, estimated to number 400,000, by local ethnic militia drove thousands to flee, many crossing into Burundi and Rwanda. From September to as of this writing, violence intensified. In retaliation, armed Zairian Tutsis launched attacks against the Zairian security forces and the Rwandan refugee camps in October, forcing international aid agencies to pull out, leaving hundreds of thousands of refugees on their own. Zaire accused Burundi and Rwanda of supporting the incursions and of invading Zaire.

In late July 1996, two organizations serving the Banyamulenge were banned and several prominent individuals were arrested, including three Protestant pastors and two local chiefs. Beginning in September, local ethnically-based militia attacked the Banyamulenge, who number some 400,000, killing hundreds and causing thousands to flee into Burundi and Rwanda. In retaliation, the Banyamulenge, allied with other groups opposed to the Zairian government, attacked Zairian security forces and the camps housing Hutu refugees from Burundi and Rwanda. Zaire accused Rwanda and Burundi of invading Zaire. Although these governments denied having made such incursions, press reported seeing Rwandan soliders frequently on Zairian territory.

As the Banyamulenge drove north, other Tutsi forces, apparently assisted by soldiers of the Rwandan Patriotic Army, attacked refugee camps north of Lake Kivu, driving their populations into an enormous concentration at Mugunga. International aid agencies withdrew, leaving both refugees and displaced Zairians without assistance and raising fears of mass starvation or epidemic. The Tutsi rebels launched a decisive attack against Mugunga in mid-November, breaking the resistance of the soldiers of the former Rwandan army and militia who had been controlling the camp. As the defeated soldiers and militia fled westward, they sought to force the refugees to accompany them, but they were unable to control the huge numbers of people. Perhaps 100,000 refugees went with the retreating troops, either willingly or under duress, while an estimated half a million Rwandans returned home. Some welcomed the opportunity to retun once they had been freed of control by the former government; others apparently went back more reluctantly, because they saw no other choice possible.

Right to Monitor

Despite harassment from the police, military, and government officials, human rights organizations in Zaire remained impressively active and outspoken. The Zairian Association for the Defense of Human Rights

(AZADHO) regularly denounced corruption by government officials and abuse by the police and judiciary, releasing a major report in December 1995 on violence against women in Zaire and another in June condemning corruption in the judicial system. Other active groups included the Committee for Democracy and Human Rights (CDDH), the Voice of the Voiceless for Human Rights (VSV), the Heirs of Justice, and Grace.

Serious harassment of human rights activists occurred in North and South Kivu. In July, Didi Mwati Bulambo and three other workers for the Collective of Action for the Development of Human Rights (CADDHOM) in South Kivu were arrested following the publication of an article in CADDHOM's newsletter, *Mwangaza*, alleging corruption in the prosecutor's office of Kamitunga. The four were beaten and held in terrible conditions for two months before being provisionally released on September 16.

In August, the commissioner for Uvira zone in South Kivu banned MILIMA, a development and human rights NGO active among the Banyamulenge, and issued an arrest warrant for Muller Ruhimbika, president of the group. Ruhimbika earned government wrath for drawing international attention to the persecution of the Banyamulenge, providing information to the Carter Center and the U.N. Human Rights Commission's special rapporteur for Zaire.

Harassment of human rights activists and organizations was common in other parts of the country as well. For example, in March and April Ikutu Amba, chair of AZADHO in Idiofa zone in Bandundu, was interrogated several times and beaten by police, eventually forcing him to flee into hiding in Kinshasa. The interrogations followed Ikutu's denunciation of a local chief whom AZADHO accuses of ordering several thousand arbitrary arrests and illegal fines. During the final interrogation, the police confiscated keys to AZADHO's Idiofa office.

The Role of
the International Community

The international community focused almost exclusively on two issues in Zaire during 1996: the Rwandan refugees in eastern Zaire, and the transition process. The camps continued to present a serious dilemma for the international community, both before repatriation had taken place, and once the fighting began in eastern Zaire. The presence of the Rwandan refugee camps had resulted in increased arms flows into the region, growing insecurity, and environmental devastation. In addition, the Zairian authorities played a key role in re-arming the former Rwandan army, providing shelter and protection to them and other Hutu militias in eastern Zaire, and permitting these forces to carry out military training and raids into Rwanda. Although this close association between the Zairian security forces and the Hutu refugees in Zaire was well known, the international community did not respond adequately to end this collaboration. Once the violence began in eastern Zaire in October, Zairians were among the displaced.

Overall, efforts to gain President Mobutu's cooperation with international efforts regarding the refugee camps and the Great Lakes crisis took precedence over the human rights situation in Zaire. Mobutu benefited considerably from this situation, which he used to effectively end his international isolation. The clearest sign of his new stature internationally came in April, when France reinstated its assistance program to the Zairian government. All but humanitarian assistance had been cut off in October 1991.

United Nations

The main U.N. involvement in Zaire revolved around its role in overseeing the Rwandan refugee camps in eastern Zaire. In February 1995, the U.N. High Commissioner for Refugees funded Zairian troops that were deployed to keep order in the refugee camps, known as the Zairian Camp Security Contingent (ZCSC). Despite the well-established reputation of the Zairian military for abusing its own citizens, for the first several months the conduct of the force was regarded as acceptable. In 1996, however, the conduct of the ZCSC troops deteriorated, and they were responsible for abuses against refugees as well as against expatriate aid workers in the Goma area. UNHCR complained to Zairian authorities and some troop rotation reportedly followed, although there is no indication that any troops were investigated or prosecuted for their actions.

U.N. Special Rapporteur Roberto Garreton was a forceful advocate for human rights in Zaire. He published a strong report in January, and another one in October. After long delays and efforts to undermine the project, the government of Zaire agreed in September to permit the establishment of a small office by the U.N. High Commissioner for Human Rights in Kinshasa, tasked to provide information to the special rapporteur and to High Commissioner as well as to provide advice and support to local NGOs.

The secretary-general sent two assessment missions regarding the feasibility of elections and the U.N. role. Although the U.N. began providing technical assistance, it conditioned its participation upon measures including passage of the new constitution, disbursement of funds to the electoral commission by the government, and a clear demonstration from the government that it is serious about holding elections. At that point, the U.N. would be prepared to make a larger commitment.

Tensions between Zaire and the U.N. increased in September, when Zaire accused the UNHCR of assisting armed Rwandans to cross the border into Zaire to fight with Banyamulenge Tutsi against Zairian troops. Secretary General Boutros-Ghali sent a special emissary to Kinshasa to defuse those tensions.

Following the attacks on the refugee camps, the U.N. secretary-general proposed on November 7 that a multinational force be set up for humanitarian purposes to create safe corridors to enable Rwandan refugees to return home. The secretary-general also assigned a special envoy, Canadian Raymond Chretien, to travel to the Great Lakes region and to set the corridor plan in motion. On November 15, the U.N. Security Council approved the deployment of a Canadian-led multinational force until March 31, 1997, for the purposes of delivering short-term humanitarian assistance and providing shelter; assisting the UNHCR with the protection and voluntary repatriation of refugees and displaced persons; and establishing humanitarian corridors for the delivery of assistance and to help voluntary repatriation. As of this writing, the force had not yet been deployed.

European Union

Like other donors, European Union policy toward Zaire concentrated on the refugee camps and the elections, but the E.U. also contributed toward rehabilitation programs for Zaire in areas such as sanitation, infrastructure, and reforestation. Since the suspension of E.U. aid to the Zairian government in January 1992, the European Commission has allocated US$309.81 million for Zaire. In 1995, the E.U. allocated $176.46 million for Zaire; in 1996, the E.U. provided an additional $6 million for rehabilitation of infrastructure, and $2.5 million for the displaced from Kasai and Shaba.

The E.U. was also prepared to contribute to the estimated $250 million needed to conduct the Zairian elections, but did not place public conditions relating to human rights on E.U. assistance. In March, the troika of the E.U.—the then current presidency (Italy), the preceding presidency (Spain), and the next presidency (Ireland)—visited Zaire to discuss the transition to democracy and concerns about delays in its implementation. The delegation met with a range of Zairian officials, including President Mobutu.

The European Council of Foreign Ministers, meeting in Florence in June, mentioned the situation in Zaire in its final communique, though it only focused on the E.U. support for the transition process and the E.U.'s interest in assisting Zaire to prepare for the elections. At a meeting on October 1 and 2, the E.U. Council of Foreign Ministers agreed on "the urgency of continuing to prepare elections in Zaire irrespective of the political uncertainties there" and expressed its hope "that the UN Secretary-General would send his personal representative to Kinshasa as soon as possible."

United States

The crisis in the Great Lakes region drew the U.S. into closer involvement with Zairian leaders, especially President Mobutu. In an effort to gain his assistance on issues ranging from the Rwandan refugees in eastern Zaire to the regional arms flows to the crisis in Burundi, the Clinton administration muted its criticism of the government's human rights record, while promoting the transition to democracy.

In March, Prime Minister Kengo visited Washington and met with U.S. officials. State Department spokesperson Nicholas Burns said the U.S. noted the slow and "disappointing progress" toward a transition to democracy, and stressed that Zaire had to create an environment where "democratic values and practices can flourish."

In May, Assistant Secretary of State for African Affairs George Moose and other U.S. officials met with President Mobutu and Prime Minister Kengo to discuss the situation in Burundi. This was the highest level meeting between a U.S. official and President Mobutu during the Clinton administration. According to the State Department, the delegation also urged Zairian leaders to halt the arms flows through Zaire, to stop allowing their territory to be used as a base for insurgent forces in the region, to detain Rwandan war crimes suspects, and to separate intimidators from the refugee camps.

While a State Department statement was issued on May 21 condemning the ethnic violence in North Kivu, indicating that "Zairian military have in some cases either failed to intervene or actively assisted in the violence," the U.S. was reluctant to be too critical. In a July 1 response to a letter of concern about the violence by Senators Nancy Kassebaum and Russell Feingold, the chair and ranking member of the Senate Africa

Subcommittee, the State Department went so far as to praise the actions of the Zairian government.

ZAMBIA

Human Rights Developments

The run-up to the multiparty elections scheduled for November 18 saw a deterioration in respect for human rights. This was disappointing; Zambia had been heralded as a model for democracy after the peaceful transfer of power in November 1991, when the Movement for Multiparty Democracy (MMD) and its leader Frederick Chiluba gained a landslide victory over President Kenneth Kaunda and his United National Independence Party (UNIP).

The electoral registration process for the 1996 general elections was itself controversial. Fewer than 2.3 million people had been registered, less than for the last two elections in Zambia, in part because of voter apathy and lack of trust in the registration process. Registration was also marked with irregularities. There was evidence that duplicate National Registration Cards were issued to some voters and that duplicate names appeared on the rolls, while the names of others were arbitrarily omitted. There were also incidents where registration officers asked a fee for registration and turned away known UNIP supporters.

The ruling MMD deliberately blurred the distinction between party and state. In Lusaka's Soweto Market the MMD conducted a voter registration exercise, its militants pressuring people to put down their market store numbers and to confirm affiliation to the MMD in return for registration. Human Rights Watch/Africa also obtained documentation showing an MMD scheme to expand the police with its own supporters before the elections. The government also reportedly distributed relief maize and fertilizers as a campaign tool in the Chikankata by-election. Government officials had also threatened to deny state services to constituencies that did not vote for the ruling MMD. At the Makaika by-election in March, Deputy Minister for Education Newton Ng'uni said that while there were 660 desks to be delivered before the end of April, "if you vote for a UNIP candidate I will not deliver the desks."

The conduct of the MMD at the Moomba and Mkaika by-elections in April was also marked by other types of intimidation and violence. People were beaten up by party cadres. Camps of these party cadres were placed strategically close to polling stations. Houses belonging to UNIP supporters in Mkaika were burned down and physical violence was attributed to MMD supporters.

The main opposition party, UNIP, also engaged in electoral abuses. In the Moomba and Mkaika by-elections, UNIP cadres assaulted MMD supporters and villagers they suspected of supporting the MMD. UNIP leader Kenneth Kaunda neither condemned the violence nor appealed to his supporters to refrain from violence during the by-elections. Such inter-political clashes in the by-elections restricted freedom of movement among the villagers in these constituencies. Nor could politicians from both sides freely campaign, hold meetings or move around.

The government forced a radical amendment to the 1991 constitution through the MMD-dominated parliament in May, rejecting demands that major constitutional reforms first be agreed by a Constituent Assembly and subjected to a referendum, as proposed by the Mwanakatwe Constitutional Review Commission in 1995. Particularly controversial was a provision in the Constitutional Amendment act (1996) that imposed new requirements on persons seeking to hold the office of president. These included that the person be a Zambian citizen born to parents who are Zambian by birth or descent and that the person not be a tribal chief. These requirements appeared to be precisely tailored to disqualify specific opposition leaders from running for president, including former president Kenneth Kaunda. Some of the new restrictions appeared to violate the International Covenant on Civil and Political Rights, to which Zambia is a party. Articles 25 and 2 of the covenant guarantee to citizens the right "to be elected at genuine periodic elections" without "unreasonable" restrictions and without "distinctions" such as birth, national origin, or political opinion. The disqualification of all but second or third generation Zambians from office appeared unreasonable, especially in light of the transparent political motivation to exclude UNIP leaders from the race.

The constitutional amendment was vigorously challenged by opposition political parties, civic associations, human rights and women's groups, in part because it would damage the opposition's chances effectively to participate in the upcoming election. The article in effect banned UNIP leader Kaunda—who is partially of Malawian heritage—and UNIP's vice presidential candidate—a tribal chief—from running. On October 23 the UNIP announced that it would not field candidates in the elections scheduled for November 18 unless the contentious clauses of the constitution and amendment were removed or unless the elections were held under the provisions of the 1991 constitution before the 1996 amendment. Seven other opposition parties joined the boycott on October 24.

In June and July, a shadowy group called the "Black Mamba" was blamed by the government for a spate of bomb blasts and threats in Lusaka and on the Copperbelt, in Ndola and Kitwe. Most of the bombings caused minor damage but on June 6, in an attempt to defuse a bomb planted at Lusaka International Airport, one bomb disposal expert was killed and another seriously injured.

The arrest in early June of UNIP vice president Senior Chief Inyambo Yeta and seven other members of UNIP in connection with the spate of bombings increased uncertainty and fear. All were committed to the Lusaka High Court for trial and were charged with treason and murder in July. Two were released in early September. On September 27 the state closed its case after calling forty-three witnesses. The trial provided little evidence to suggest that these UNIP members were involved in any violent conspiracy against the state. It appeared that they were detained solely because of their political affiliation. On November 1, the remaining six were acquitted of treason and murder charges, there being no evidence to prove that they were linked to the "Black Mamba." According to the judge, more than one "terrorist group" existed. The responsibility for the acts attributed to "Black Mamba" remained unclear, though the defense lawyers in the "Treason Trial" attempted to prove that the "Black Mamba" bombings were the work of the government. But in judgment on November 1, Justice Peter Chitengi said there was no evidence to that effect either.

The independent press was also a target for government intimidation throughout the year. *The Post* newspaper was under particular attack. In February police arrested three of its editors and banned edition 401 before its distribution because it reported that the government was secretly planning to hold a referendum on the constitution without giving much advance warning to the public. That day's on-line edition was also banned, making it the first act of censorship on the Internet in Africa. The three journalists faced a minimum of twenty-five years in jail on charges under the Official Secrets Act, for receiving "classified information."

On February 22, the Zambian parliament made an unprecedented decision to try and sentence *The Post's* editor, Fred M'membe, Bright Mwape, the managing editor and columnist Lucy Sichone to imprisonment for an indefinite period. The sentence was recommended by the Standing Orders Committee following the publication of articles which claimed that certain parliamentarians lowered the dignity of the House. M'membe and Mwape, prisoners of conscience for the expression of their views, were, however, released in March after the Lusaka High Court ruled that they had been "wrongly sentenced" in absentia.

The judiciary came under attack from government supporters especially after the Supreme Court in January struck down pro-

visions in the Public Order Act, finding that the requiring of permits for meetings was a contravention of the Zambian peoples' constitutional rights. After a Parliamentary Code of Conduct tribunal found the then Legal Minister Remmy Mushota guilty in July of "subverting laid down procedures," for which he was dismissed from office, Mushota himself became the most outspoken critic of the judiciary. The campaign against it was never condemned by the office of the president, which, despite Mushota's disgrace, appointed him in August to the Citizenship Board of Zambia. This gesture of support appeared to have encouraged other government officials and the pro-government press to criticize the judiciary and "opposition" lawyers, such as those who defended UNIP's "Treason Trialists," and the Law Association of Zambia (LAZ).

One particular focus for these attacks was the championing of exclusivist ethnic politics, with the judiciary characterized as mainly deriving from Zambia's Eastern province or Malawi. George Kunda, the chair of LAZ was, for example, investigated by immigration officials for his nationality status.

The Munyama Human Rights Commission which had a mandate to investigate and establish reports of human rights abuses between 1972 and 1993, effectively the Kaunda government's human rights record, had its report published by the government in October, over a year after its submission. The government's White Paper on human rights, released at the same time, declared that a permanent human rights commission would be established which would submit annual reports to the president and parliament. It would also have the power to freely investigate complaints of violations, visit jails and detention centers, and to recommend to the president and parliament effective measures to promote human rights and provide compensation. But there was no clear directive in the report about accountability for past human rights abuses.

The Munyama Commission also investigated prison conditions. It found that conditions of prisons were appalling, with food insufficient or unfit for human consumption, widespread illness, denial of medical treatment, and prisoners being denied basic necessities such as soap and clothing. Five prisoners were reported to have died of starvation in Kamfinsa State prison, Kitwe in July. A High Court judge toured Lusaka Central Prison in September and was told that cells built for twenty inmates housed seventy. Prison Service public relations officer Augustine Phiri admitted in August that the average death rate of prisoners held by the service was 6.66 per month, attributing this to overcrowding.

The Right to Monitor

Zambia in 1996 experienced a growth in the number of organizations and individuals active in monitoring human rights. In early 1996 a coalition of many of these groups, the Committee for a Clean Campaign, was launched to monitor the run-up to the 1996 multiparty elections. The government's response was to increase its harassment of these local groups. Individuals from the Law Association of Zambia (LAZ), the Zambia Independent Monitoring Team (ZIMT), the Catholic Commission for Peace and Justice (CCPJ), and the Forum for Democratic Process (FODEP) were called "foreigners" by government ministers, trying in this way to undermine their public credibility.

Several Zambian groups engaged in human rights had reported that their phones are tapped. During a "Treason Trial" hearing Police Chief-Inspector Muleshi admitted in August that he had bugged *The Post's* telephone in violation of the Telecommunications Act of 1994. These human rights groups also reported threats from individuals whom they suspected were linked to government. The government also avoided meeting these groups at a senior level. By contrast, international human rights monitoring groups had experienced no government impediment, although government senior officials were reluctant to discuss human rights issues with them. The Commonwealth Human Rights Initiative sent a three person team to Zambia in late 1996 Its report, released on September

23, urged dialogue and compromise between all sides and called for donor unity in pressing the Zambian government to improve its record on good governance.

The Role of the International Community

The support of international aid of up to US$1 billion a year was vital to the progress of the economic reform program of President Chiluba. As Zambia's largest revenue earner, aid had accounted for some 70 percent of gross domestic product. In 1992, Zambia received about $1.2 billion in nonemergency aid, three times the average in Africa. But in 1996 the aid pledged was only $800 million, down a third from the 1992 figure. At the heart of the decline in donor commitments were issues of good governance, accountability, and democratic practice.

The World Bank's Consultative Group for Zambia (the "Paris Club") met in Bournemouth in December 1995. The donors indicated that the level of assistance in 1996 would be determined by the Zambian government maintaining the momentum of its economic reform program and "tangible" progress on governance issues. A strongly worded demarche was handed over to the government.

As 1996 progressed and the government showed itself little inclined to act upon its commitments to good governance, Western donors began to cut back bilateral aid, particularly balance of payment support. Norway led the way in May, suspending its balance of payments support. In the following months the European Union (E.U.) countries followed. Britain, Denmark, and Sweden all suspended balance of payments support for violations of good governance norms. Unusually, for the Japanese government, its Lusaka mission also issued a press release in August emphasizing the need for good governance.

European Union

The E.U. did not lead the initiative to push for improved human rights and good governance issues. The member states were at first divided over tactics. But by September there was a converging of views, with the exception of the Republic of Ireland whose diplomatic mission in Lusaka appeared less enthusiastic about publicly voicing human rights concerns there. In May 1996 the E.U. finally issued a demarche to the Zambian government over its Constitutional Amendment Act, drawing special attention to the exclusion from running in the forthcoming presidential elections of UNIP leader Kaunda. This was followed in September by demarches to both the government and opposition urging them to enter into "intensive dialogue." In November, the E.U. said it would closely monitor Zambia's preparation for elections and emphasized the need for the highest electoral standards. The E.U. expressed the hope that "even at this late stage, it will be possible to hold elections which are free and fair and acceptable to all parties."

United States

The United States played an important role throughout the year in pressuring the Zambian government to improve its human rights record. USAID announced in July that it was cutting aid to Zambia by more than 10 percent (worth $2.5 million) because of the recent constitutional amendments, especially the exclusion of Kaunda from standing for president. Planned U.S. government assistance for the 1996 fiscal year was $19,024,000 but USAID's assistance program in Zambia remained under continuous review and cuts in the 1997 financial year program were possible.

During her nomination hearing in June the U.S. ambassador-designate to Zambia, Arlene Render, strongly criticized the Zambian government's performance on good governance issues. Her concern was also shared by Senator Nancy Kassebaum, the chair of the Senate Africa Subcommittee, who, with Senator Edward Kennedy, wrote to President Chiluba in June raising "serious questions about Zambia's commitment to democracy."

HUMAN
RIGHTS
WATCH

AMERICAS

Human Rights Developments

In the Cold War environment of the 1970s and 1980s, governments in the region deflected human rights criticism by accusing those who documented human rights violations of being motivated by ideology, not principle. Though the accusations changed from those of prior years, in much of the region during 1996, human rights groups still faced unfounded criticism designed to discredit their work. Human rights monitors in many countries were accused of favoring criminals when they denounced police brutality or raised questions of due process violations, as if they were seeking to protect those who broke the law from effective law enforcement. In fact, governmental accusations against human rights monitors manipulated the genuine frustration of the region's populations with high levels of impunity, thus attempting to avoid accountability for their own conduct.

While serious laws of war violations continued to be committed by both sides in Colombia, and largely at the hands of the Shining Path in Peru, in other parts of the region, public security became the central issue. In Brazil, Colombia, Mexico, Haiti, and Guatemala, citizens reached a point of desperation because of criminal violence and began clamoring for a crackdown on criminals at any cost. Lack of faith in the justice system and frustration with impunity led to lynchings of suspected criminals in Mexico and Guatemala, while in Brazil, many sectors of society welcomed police brutality in crime control. Despite serious due process violations criticized by the international community, Guatemala executed two convicted murderers, the first use of the death penalty outside of the Caribbean and Guyana in a decade. Indeed, Latin America's trend toward abolition of the death penalty appeared on the verge of being reversed by governments eager to react to public insecurity.

Unfortunately, police forces almost everywhere in the region were part of the problem, rather than the solution, and in many countries were distrusted. A January 1996 survey by one of Brazil's leading pollsters showed that 88 percent of Rio de Janeiro residents believed the police were involved in organized crime. With very few exceptions, police forces were brutal, corrupt, and negligent in fulfilling their basic duties: investigating and apprehending criminals and protecting the population without committing abuses. Faced with allegations of human rights violations, police tended to close ranks rather than investigate and discipline violators. In many countries, police operated as if law enforcement and protection of human rights were incompatible.

Establishing effective judicial systems and forging professional police forces constituted an unanswered challenge to the region in 1996, although some positive steps were taken. In Honduras, the National Congress approved the constitutional reforms necessary to pass the main police force from military to civilian control. The earlier transfer of the police investigations unit from military to civilian hands greatly reduced abuses. In Guatemala, the government committed itself to reforming the constitution to remove the military from any involvement in law enforcement as part of ongoing peace talks with guerrillas. Problems with the military police were publicly acknowledged by the federal and some state governments in Brazil. Though São Paulo and other Brazilian state governments took steps to reduce police violence, Rio de Janeiro state authorities irresponsibly promoted "far west bonus and promotion programs," which rewarded police officers for "neutralizing" criminals, dead or alive.

In Mexico, federal and state authorities purged corrupt police officers but failed to prosecute those who committed human rights violations. Although the government of Venezuela sought to reorganize the judiciary, it made no significant advances in reforming its brutal and corrupt police force.

Haiti's newly created civilian police force lost credibility by carrying out acts of brutality and using excessive force. Although the Inspector General's Office showed initiative in investigating and administratively sanctioning wrongdoers on the force, criminal prosecutions lagged. And in the Dominican Republic, security forces committed more than thirty-five unjustified killings without prosecution.

Several governments in the region demonstrated a greater willingness to acknowledge serious human rights abuse. The government of Fernando Henrique Cardoso abandoned the defensive posture of past Brazilian governments and invited its critics to join him in formulating a National Human Rights Plan. If implemented, the plan would grant ordinary courts jurisdiction over human rights abuses committed by military police and codify the crime of torture, among other measures. The government of Guatemalan President Alvaro Arzú acknowledged the existence of gross human rights violations and impunity as the main obstacles to respect for human rights. Argentina's President Carlos Menem recognized the growing problem of corruption and police brutality in many provinces, including Buenos Aires. Even President Alberto Fujimori of Peru made uncharacteristic acknowledgments of injustices perpetrated by the "faceless courts" he set up in 1992 to try those accused of terrorism and treason.

Some governments also put into effect measures aimed at addressing persistent problems. The government of Guatemala announced the dissolution of the nationwide network of civil patrols, which had terrorized the countryside by committing serious abuses for fifteen years, and enacted legislation to give civilian courts jurisdiction over common crimes committed by the military. Peru's Congress finally agreed on the naming of the country's first human rights ombudsman, Jorge Santistevan, who quickly became active in promoting human rights. At Santistevan's initiative, the Congress approved a law creating a special commission to review the hundreds of cases of prisoners unjustly prosecuted by the faceless courts and make recommendations for presidential pardons. Unfortunately, Peru's Congress voted in October to extend the use of faceless courts for another year.

President Arzú took steps to increase civilian control over the military in Guatemala with the unprecedented removal of senior military officers accused of corruption. President Menem retired three of the country's top military officers, whom he deemed insufficiently supportive of his military reforms, leaving in his post army leader Gen. Martín Balza, who in 1995 had apologized publicly for the role of the army in the 1976-1983 "dirty war."

Bolivia's minister of justice, René Blattman, successfully pressed for measures to alleviate human rights violations related to counternarcotics policies, promoting legislative reform and setting up a government office to collect human rights complaints in the coca-growing Chapare region. In Mexico, President Ernesto Zedillo incorporated the language of human rights into his public discourse. This proved to be mainly symbolic, however; he took no meaningful action to address Mexico's enduring problems of abuses and impunity for human rights violations.

Other authorities rejected criticism outright. In what amounted to a reversal of his earlier support for human rights reform, President Ernesto Samper of Colombia, in an October 1 speech, recklessly dismissed criticism of Colombia's abysmal human rights record by asking, "What liberties and what human rights are valid amid anarchy and violence?"

The government of Rafael Caldera in Venezuela also displayed little tolerance for human rights criticism. In contrast with Venezuela's traditional openness, the government rejected credible reports from human rights monitors as well as the U.S. State Department.

The government of the state of Rio de Janeiro departed from the stance of Brazil's federal government, a significant fact for human rights in the state. On the day that Human Rights Watch/Americas released its January 1996 report on police violence, the governor responded, "We ought to stop these lies....They should worry about what is going on in Serbia." The Mexican government permitted an Inter-American Commission on Human Rights delegation to conduct an on-site investigation for the first time, but its Foreign Ministry continued to reject the findings of well-documented reports by nongovernmental human rights organizations.

Many of the region's most serious human rights problems endured. Police and military forces routinely tortured detainees and criminal suspects, especially in Brazil, Mexico, Peru, Colombia, and Venezuela. None of these countries—with the exception of Mexico—had modified their domestic legislation to specifically codify the crime of torture and establish effective judicial remedies for victims, as required by the U.N. Convention against Torture and Other Cruel, Inhuman or Degrading Treatment or Punishment, to which each of these countries are state parties. In Mexico, the courts failed to enforce legislation prohibiting torture, even in cases where evidence of torture existed.

Brazilian military police continued to commit unjustified killings in the course of official duty. In April, military police killed nineteen squatters blocking a highway in the Amazon state of Pará.

In Cuba, the government systematically violated the rights of freedom of expression, association, assembly, privacy, and due process of law. The Cuban penal code provided a solid legal foundation for the suppression of political dissidents.

In Colombia, political killings by the army, police, guerrillas, and paramilitary groups claimed an average of six lives a day in the first nine months of the year, and the government gave the army broad powers to respond to public disturbances, including nonviolent protests.

Armed opposition forces engaged in political assassinations in both Colombia and Peru at an alarming level. The Revolu-

tionary Armed Forces of Colombia (FARC) continued to use kidnapping as a means of financing its activities. The National Liberation Army (ELN) continued to use landmines indiscriminately throughout Colombia, leaving many civilian victims. The Shining Path in Peru was responsible for more than 200 political killings, including the March 6 assassination of community leader Pascuala Rosado Cornejo of Huaycán, after which they sought to blow up her body.

Throughout the region, impunity for human rights violations prevailed. Initiatives by the Arzú government in Guatemala failed to curb impunity, while fear of reprisals and incompetence on the part of judicial authorities combined with obstruction by the army led to setbacks in several notorious cases. The Chilean Supreme Court failed to seek justice for past human rights violations by systematically applying the amnesty law decreed by the military government in 1978. As in Chile, the amnesty law promoted by President Fujimori in Peru blocked the investigation and punishment of gross human rights violations.

In Honduras, the failure by police to enforce warrants undermined the efforts of civilian authorities to bring military officers who conducted "disappearances" and torture to account.

The Right to Monitor

Human rights monitors continued to face threats and physical violence without effective investigation, prosecution, or punishment of those responsible. On October 13, a gunman shot dead Josué Giraldo Cardona, a lawyer with the Civic Committee of Meta, Colombia, whose members have suffered systematic persecution by the army and paramilitary groups for years.

On October 20, human rights lawyer Francisco Gilson Nogueira de Carvalho was killed by machine-gun fire in the northeastern state of Rio Grande do Norte. Nogueira had been investigating connections between death squads and local authorities. In August, federal police opened a criminal investigation and a military judge filed a civil suit for alleged defamation by our Brazil office director, James Cavallaro, who wrote a newspaper article criticizing the acquittal of military officers accused of torture. Both cases were pending at the time of this writing.

In Mexico, human rights monitors faced serious threats, including those working for the Miguel Agustín Pro Juárez Human Rights Center. The center's director, Father David Fernández, and staff were threatened, apparently in response to the organization's documentation of military and police human rights violations. David Fernández was among those that Human Rights Watch honored in 1996 for their defense of human rights.

The Cuban government continued to prosecute human rights monitors and prevent access to the island by international rights experts, including the U.N. Special Rapporteur for Cuba, Amb. Carl-Johan Groth.

The Role of
the International Community

United Nations

The U.N. continued to play an effective role in Guatemala, through its human rights verification mission, MINUGUA, and through moderating important accords as part of the process toward a final peace agreement. Two years after MINUGUA opened its doors in November 1994, its countrywide presence greatly contributed to a significant reduction in politically motivated assassinations, "disappearances," and instances of torture.

The U.N. Human Rights Commission decided to open a permanent office in Colombia, under the auspices of the U.N. High Commissioner for Human Rights, to report on human rights violations. As of this writing, the office had yet to be opened.

In July, the U.N. Human Rights Committee issued a devastating report on Peru, recommending an end to the use of faceless courts, a repeal of the amnesty law, and dismissal from public service of human rights violators.

Prof. Nigel Rodley, the U.N. Special Rapporteur on Torture, released a critical report on Chile and conducted an on-site investigation in Venezuela.

Organization of American States

The crisis that paralyzed the Inter-American Commission on Human Rights (IACHR) in 1995 was in part addressed with the appointment of a new executive secretary, which allowed the commission in 1996 to renew its forceful efforts to improve human rights practices in the hemisphere. One example of the commission's revitalization was the granting of dozens of injunctions, sometimes with the participation of the Inter-American Court of Human Rights, to protect the lives of those facing imminent danger.

Unfortunately, the commission's annual report failed for the first time in over twenty years to include country-specific analyses, which resulted in a loss of what had been an important tool to promote human rights.

The court issued important rulings on cases of "disappearances" and extrajudicial executions. However, the court's decisions did not further develop jurisprudence to advance human rights protection, as they had in previous years.

As they have in past years, some countries, most notably Peru, Mexico, and Chile, proposed initiatives that would, if carried out, undermine the work of the IACHR. Under the pretext of strengthening the inter-American system for human rights protection, they campaigned in 1996 for reforms of the American Convention on Human Rights that would limit access to the commission by nongovernmental organizations and increase regional governments' political control over the system. These countries also promoted stricter confidentiality in the commission's findings, as opposed to the transparency that would foster greater respect for human rights.

United States

Free trade and antinarcotics efforts—not human rights protection—lay at the center of Washington's concerns for the region. The State Department's annual *Country Reports on Human Rights Practices for 1995* continued to reflect accurately the human rights problems in most countries, and the administration kept an open door to human rights monitors. Nonetheless, it pursued no comprehensive policy to encourage human rights protection. At the same time, administration efforts to address past abuses by the Central Intelligence Agency and Defense Department were notably inadequate.

Washington's apparent desire to cover up relations maintained by the CIA with human rights abusers obstructed Haitian efforts to prosecute human rights violators. The White House refused to return to Haitian authorities thousands of documents and items seized during the 1994 military intervention or to deport Emmanuel "Toto" Constant, the former paramilitary leader wanted for numerous egregious human rights abuses allegedly committed while on the CIA payroll.

The CIA's unwillingness to declassify documents related to human rights also limited prosecutors' work in Guatemala and Honduras. Although the State Department declassified many documents about Guatemala, the CIA and Defense Department failed to follow suit. Nor have those agencies responded to repeated requests by Honduran authorities for documents regarding Battalion 3-16, a secret military death squad that operated with CIA assistance in the early 1980s in Honduras.

The release in September by the Defense Department of excerpts from training manuals used by the School of the Americas in courses for Latin American military officers until 1991 confirmed critics' assertions that the school instructed its officer students to violate human rights. The manuals recommended assassinations and torture against guerrillas. In October, U.S. Defense Secretary William Perry apologized for the instructions and promised to review the school's curriculum. This fell far short of what was needed: a thorough and independent investigation with appropriate penalties.

In June, the executive branch's Intelligence Oversight Board concluded its investigation of the role of the CIA with regard to a number of human rights violations committed against U.S. citizens or their relatives in Guatemala. The report concluded that agency assets, or local employees, had committed serious human rights violations while on the U.S. payroll, but it failed to recommend adequate steps to prevent recurrence.

Each of these elements revealed a covert policy of support for methods, individuals, and institutions that violated human rights. Although the most serious abuses occurred during past administrations, the current U.S. leadership bore responsibility for investigating and punishing those who carried out the abuses, a task it largely failed to undertake.

Spurred by the Congress, the administration tightened its decades-old embargo on Cuba, a policy tool which has not only been ineffective in bringing about an improvement in human rights conditions, but has prevented the free exchange of information in violation of the International Covenant on Civil and Political Rights. To some extent, the embargo's ineffectiveness resulted from the fact that it was not part of a principled human rights policy but was instead a blunt tool for the overthrow of the Fidel Castro government.

The Work of Human Rights Watch/Americas

Our work in 1996 focused on seven countries—Brazil, Colombia, Cuba, Guatemala, Haiti, Mexico, and Peru—where the nature and extent of the violations, and the response of the state, raised urgent human rights concerns. We conducted missions, published reports, and advocated changes to improve the human rights situations in these countries, as well as highlighting thematic issues that arose elsewhere, such as human rights abuse associated with the drug war in Bolivia together with the Human Rights Watch special initiative on drugs and human rights; police brutality in Argentina and Paraguay, through meetings with Presidents Carlos Menem and Juan Carlos Wasmosy; and prison conditions in Venezuela.

In Brazil, our representative in Rio de Janeiro worked closely with local human rights groups, contributed to the elaboration of the government's National Human Rights Plan, and published articles in Brazil's major newspapers. Much of our work in 1996 focused on police brutality. In Colombia, we documented human rights violations by paramilitary groups allied with the military, the role of the U.S., as well as violations of the laws of war by government and guerrilla forces.

We encouraged European governments to adopt a more active role in pressing for meaningful change in Cuba. Although European governments have developed influence with the Castro government through dialogue and investment, they have not used this influence to secure meaningful human rights reforms. A representative of Human Rights Watch/Americas traveled to European capitals to discuss Cuban issues with European government officials.

In Guatemala, we strongly advocated that any amnesty law enacted not grant impunity for human rights violations or similar abuses by guerrillas, meeting with President Arzú, Defense Minister Gen. Julio Balconi, and U.N. representatives. One of our long-term objectives, the dissolution of the civil patrols, was announced in August, when its phased implementation began. As part of a friendly settlement negotiation with the government—based on a suit we filed with the Inter-American Commission on Human Rights—the first patrols to be dissolved were the abusive Colotenango patrols.

In Mexico, we monitored rural violence, torture by police, and the failings of the justice system. Together with the International Labor Rights Fund and Mexico's National Association of Democratic Lawyers, we filed a labor rights petition under provisions of the North American Free Trade Agreement, which was accepted for review by the U.S. Labor Department's National Administration Office. The Women's Rights Project of Human Rights Watch documented sexual discrimination in Mexico's *maquiladora* sector, including pregnancy testing of prospective female employees, (see Women's Rights Project section).

In Haiti, we pressed for accountability for abuses committed under past and current governments. In addition, we documented abuses by the new police force. Our Haiti researcher discussed these issues with President René Préval in June.

Within Peru, we continued to focus on violations committed by the faceless court system, urging an independent review of cases tried before these courts.

The failure of most countries in the region to establish accountability for human rights violations necessitated our continued use of the inter-American system to seek justice in individual cases. In partnership with the Center for Justice and International Law (CEJIL), which took the lead, and domestic human rights groups throughout the region, we were involved in nearly one hundred cases before the Inter-American Commission on Human Rights, and some cases pending before the Inter-American Court of Human Rights.

BOLIVIA

Human Rights Developments

Human rights violations continued to accompany the enforcement of drug laws in Bolivia during 1996, though they appeared to diminish in frequency and seriousness. Most abuses occurred in the Chapare, the tropical lowland region where poor peasants cultivated much of Bolivia's illegal coca, from which cocaine is produced. Impunity for abuses by the police remained a serious problem, even as Bolivian officials promised to establish mechanisms to investigate and sanction such abuses. This section focuses on human rights abuses associated with Bolivian counter-narcotics programs in the Chapare.

In 1995, under strong pressure from the United States, the Bolivian government began an aggressive coca-eradication effort that was strongly resisted by coca growers. Periods of negotiation alternated with outbursts of violence in the Chapare. As documented in *Bolivia Under Pressure*, published in May 1996 by Human Rights Watch/ Americas, the Bolivian government engaged in serious human rights abuses in its efforts to quell farmers' opposition to eradication and meet its goals. Abuses included excessive use of force, arbitrary detention, and the suppression of peaceful demonstrations, most frequently by the Mobile Rural Patrol Unit (Unidad Móvil de Patrullaje Rural, UMOPAR), the anti-narcotics police force. The improper use of firearms caused serious injury and several deaths during crowd-control operations, and police used tear gas indiscriminately in residential areas, without sufficient precautions to avoid harm to residents. Indeed, in May, Col. Luis Caballero, the commander of UMOPAR, acknowledged frankly and for the first time that UMOPAR agents had been responsible for abuses during confrontations with growers.

In 1996, the government's anti-narcotics efforts were largely free of the violent confrontations between coca growers and police that had occurred previously. Local human rights groups reported no new fatalities during coca-eradication missions, but arbitrary arrests and ill-treatment, including beatings of persons arrested or under questioning by UMOPAR agents, continued. Massive detentions intended to stamp out legal demonstrations or arbitrarily round up suspects without arrest warrants occurred in December 1995 and January 1996. In December, for instance, police arrested hundreds of women coca producers during a peaceful march from Cochabamba to La Paz. The following month, in an effort to close down coca markets, they detained 145 people in the Chapare without arrest warrants.

Further reports of abuses were documented by the Chimore Human Rights Office (Oficina de Derechos Humanos de Chimore, ODHC), established in the Chapare region by the Ministry of Justice in December 1995 to investigate and report human rights violations. In memoranda addressed in June to the Subsecretary for Human Rights at the Ministry of Justice, the director of ODHC, Godofredo Reinicke Borda, M.D.,

reported the receipt of thirty-six complaints of human rights violations during the previous six months, including the beating or ill-treatment of suspects at the moment of arrest. For example, UMOPAR police detained Irineo García Acuña on February 27 in the province of Carrasco. On March 4, when García was examined by Dr. Reinicke, he was found to have a fractured rib and severe bruising, which Reinicke attributed to the police beating. The UMOPAR commander in the Chapare failed to reply to an ODHC request for information on the case, however, and the special anti-narcotics prosecutor did not act against the officer in charge of the police unit.

UMOPAR agents also arbitrarily detained thirty-five peasants following an attempted robbery in May, according to ODHC, and failed to refer the investigation to the National Police, as the law required. Three of those detained, Nicolás García Balderrama, Gualberto Acosta Sánchez, and Feliciano Sánchez García, had minor injuries that showed that undue force had been used. On May 9, two UMOPAR agents detained and beat a fifteen-year-old girl, Valeriana Condori, during a coca-eradication mission in Uncía. Dr. Reinicke, who examined the victim on May 23, found signs of bruising still present. In several other cases, ODHC complained that the anti-narcotics prosecutor had failed to do anything to investigate allegations referred to him or to prosecute officers allegedly responsible for abuses.

The Inter-Institutional Human Rights Commission (Comisión Interinstitucional de Derechos Humanos, CIDH), a monitoring group composed of representatives of eight nongovernmental organizations, reported in September that UMOPAR agents raided and searched homes illegally during a coca-eradication mission named Operation Hurricane (Operación Huracán), and that UMOPAR agents failed to wear identification tabs on their uniforms. UMOPAR introduced the tabs in late 1995, as urged by local activists and in the Human Rights Watch/Americas report *Bolivia: Human Rights Violations and the War on Drugs*.

ODHC's efforts notwithstanding, impunity for abuses continued. Indeed, it appeared that ODHC's reports failed to prompt appropriate action by either the UMOPAR or narcotics prosecutors. Not only did the UMOPAR and the narcotics prosecutors fail to investigate charges, but in a meeting with Human Rights Watch/Americas in August, Minister of Government Carlos Sánchez Berzaín professed ignorance of cases of human rights violations committed in the context of anti-drug operations, although Human Rights Watch/Americas had been informed that the Ministry of Justice had already referred the cases to his ministry.

Bolivia's anti-narcotics efforts took place within the framework of Law 1008, which defined penalties for the illegal cultivation of coca and the processing and trafficking of cocaine, and which created special judicial procedures and institutions for drug cases. In our 1995 report, Human Rights Watch/Americas expressed concern that people charged under Law 1008 were not allowed, under any circumstances, to be granted bail and were forced to await trial in prison. In addition, those acquitted by the first-instance court had to remain in custody. On February 2, 1996, President Gonzalo Sánchez de Losada signed into law a measure designed to correct the more flagrant due process violations stemming from the law. The reform ensured that those acquitted could await review of their cases on bail, and that review by the higher court would be discretionary rather than mandatory. It also imposed a time limit of eighteen months for pre-trial detention, such that those held for longer without trial must be released. The reforms did not, however, affect Law 1008's blanket restriction on pre-trial release for all defendants accused of drug-related offenses. In meetings with Minister Sánchez Berzaín, Minister of Justice René Blattman, and Foreign Minister Antonio Araníbar Quiroga, Human Rights Watch/Americas recognized the advances but pushed for further needed reforms.

The Right to Monitor

We did not receive any reports that the government prevented or restricted human rights organizations from conducting their investigations and reporting their findings during 1996.

The Role of the United States

While primary responsibility for human rights violations rested with the government of Bolivia, the U.S. government shared responsibility because it financed, trained, advised, and equipped the UMOPAR, as well as the special narcotics prosecutors and other Bolivian anti-narcotics institutions. Historically, the U.S. failed to make effective protection of human rights a condition of U.S. counternarcotics support. It had not used its considerable influence to curtail abuses by the UMOPAR, nor had it pressed for the establishment of effective internal investigative and disciplinary procedures to ensure accountability for such human rights abuses.

In a welcome development in August, the United States and Bolivia signed an agreement on U.S. assistance to Bolivian counternarcotics programs that included significant human rights conditions. Indeed, in that agreement, the U.S. made its financial support conditional upon "regular and measurable progress" toward the human rights goals established in the agreement. (See Special Initiatives section, on drugs and human rights.)

BRAZIL

Human Rights Developments

The year in Brazil was marked by the striking contrast between the laudable goals extolled by the federal government in its National Human Rights Plan (hereinafter, the plan) and the grave human rights violations that continued to occur. On April 19, less than a month before the release of the plan—an historic initiative composed of a comprehensive series of short-, medium- and, long-term measures designed to prevent and re-

dress grave human rights abuse in Brazil—
Military Police near the town of Eldorado do
Carajás, in the Amazon state of Pará, opened
fire into a crowd of landless squatters, killing
nineteen and wounding dozens of others.
The Eldorado do Carajás massacre instantly
became a symbol of the abuses committed by
state agents and third parties in the increasingly tense conflicts between squatters, large
landowners, and police over land. Violations in other areas such as forced labor,
urban police violence, prison conditions,
abuses against minors, women, indigenous
peoples, and other minority groups such as
transvestites, continued.

The May 13 release of the National
Human Rights Plan capped eight months of
effort by the Ministry of Justice in conjunction with Brazilian and international nongovernmental organizations (NGOs) since
the president announced the plan on September 7, 1995, Brazilian Independence Day.
Human Rights Watch/Americas, among the
international organizations invited to assist
in the drafting process, participated in meetings with other NGOs and government officials—including Justice Minister Nelson
Jobim and Attorney General Geraldo
Brindeiro—to express our views on the plan.
The fact that the plan was a product of the
joint efforts of government agents and NGOs
marked an important shift in the federal
government's approach to the issue of human rights. Since the election of President
Fernando Henrique Cardoso, federal authorities have consistently recognized the existence of grave human rights violations, often
citing NGOs as the source of their information, and have sought to work together with
members of civil society to address these
violations. The plan constitutes a first critical step beyond mere recognition of abuses.
Still, almost two years after election, the
Cardoso administration has been unable to
pass legislation to achieve the goals elaborated in the plan. This failure, as explained
below, resulted primarily from a lack of
cooperation by other sectors of the federal
government.

For example, the Ministry of Foreign
Affairs continued to oppose ratification of
the Optional Protocol to the International
Covenant on Civil and Political Rights and
of the compulsory jurisdiction of the Inter-
American Court of Human Rights. Both
would force Brazil to submit itself to the
jurisdiction of international bodies authorized to examine claims of human rights
abuse. As a result, only the Inter-American
Commission on Human Rights could consider individual violations by Brazil.

The plan consists of a series of measures, which, with a few exceptions, must
pass both houses of Congress and be signed
by the president in order to become law. One
of the key measures contained in the plan,
known as the "Bicudo law" (named for long-
time human rights activist and Congressman
Hélio Bicudo), would transfer from military
to ordinary courts the jurisdiction over crimes
committed by uniformed police officers. On
May 9, just days before release of the plan, the
Senate defeated the original draft of the
Bicudo law, substituting a weakened version
that transferred jurisdiction only in cases of
murder, and then only once the case had
proceeded to trial. Rejection of the original
Bicudo law was widely received as a sign
that the Senate would not cooperate with the
president on the plan. Indeed at the time that
this report was written more than six months
after the plan's release, none of its measures
in the area of public security had passed the
Senate.

One key element of the plan concerns
the codification of the crime of torture. Ironically, on the very day that the Chamber of
Deputies voted to approve legislation
criminalizing torture, security agents of the
Chamber of Deputies beat until unconscious
magazine salesman Severino de Araújo
Maciel to force him to sign a false confession. This contrast demonstrated the vast
gulf between law and practice in this area. In
1996, torture continued to be practiced on a
routine basis in police precincts throughout
Brazil, by methods including the use of
electric shocks, near-drownings, burning with
cigarette butts, and the rape of criminal suspects with nightsticks, broomhandles, and

similar objects. In the overwhelming majority of cases, police officers who practiced torture were neither prosecuted nor dismissed. One exception was the August dismissal of two federal police officers involved in the October 1995 death of José Ivanildo Sampaio de Souza after his detention and torture in Fortaleza, capital of the northeastern state of Ceará. The decree determining the officers' dismissal was signed by President Cardoso, in accordance with Brazilian civil service law. Though clearly an important step, the dismissal of these two police officers underscored the need for reform of the civil service provisions that guarantee employment to police involved in grave human rights abuses, pending extended administrative proceedings. For instance, the 120 police officers involved in the 1992 massacre of 111 detainees at the Carandiru prison facility, in São Paulo, continued to serve actively. Many of those involved were promoted within the Military Police. Similarly, all of the military police involved in the April 1996 Eldorado do Carajás massacre continued to serve on active duty.

The constructive attitude of the Cardoso administration constituted a welcome relief from the hostile, anti-human rights policies of many Brazilian state government authorities. This tension between the generally pro-human rights position of the federal government and the entrenched, often violent policies of many states, constituted perhaps the greatest obstacle to the effective implementation of the National Human Rights plan. In Brazil's federal system, state governments maintain vast authority, over public security in particular. In many states, governmental authorities failed to curb abuses; in several instances, as detailed below, they promoted policies that violated fundamental human rights.

Police violence, particularly unjustified killings and summary executions, intensified in Brazil's major cities and in rural conflicts. In the city of Rio de Janeiro, press figures based on analysis of police reports noted a nearly six-fold increase in the number of civilians killed by military police from just over three (3.2) per month to more than twenty (20.55) per month since Gen. Nilton Cerqueira took over as head of the police in the State of Rio de Janeiro in May 1995. This surge in police killings was widely seen as linked to two policies given priority by the State Secretariat of Public Security. The first promoted—and the second authorized a pay raise for bravery—thus advertising that officers involved in fatal shootings which, at a minimum, raised doubts as to the veracity of the versions offered by the police involved, would be honored. General Cerqueira refused to consider our recommendation in an August interview that the pay raise and promotion for bravery only be available in cases with no civilian fatalities. Cerqueira told Human Rights Watch/Americas during that interview that "crooks are not civilians" and that "crooks are crooks, dead or alive."

In the northeastern state of Rio Grande do Norte, Deputy Secretary of Public Security Maurílio Pinto de Medeiros continued in that position despite vast evidence of his supervision of a death squad composed primarily of civil police officers. The State Prosecutor's Office determined that the death squad was responsible for at least thirty-one homicides and indicted several of its participants. Pinto de Medeiros faced charges in at least two incidents, and the Human Rights Commission of the Chamber of Deputies requested that he be dismissed. Despite this, in a July 1996 interview, Col. Sebastião Américo de Souza, Pinto de Medeiros's direct supervisor, told Human Rights Watch/Americas that the latter would remain in his post because "there was nothing on him."

Grave allegations of urban police violence also surfaced in the Amazon's major cities. In Manaus, press reports in late May exposed a death squad run by police officers responsible for killing twenty-two people. The victims were believed to be criminal suspects, detained and killed by the death squad. In Rio Branco, capital of the Amazonian state of Acre, a special operations battalion composed of military policemen went on a killing rampage to avenge the death of a police officer at the hands of a reputed drug dealer. According to a local prosecutor, the operations battalion cut off the arms, legs and genitals of one victim before gouging out his eyes and killing him.

In contrast to authorities in many other states, São Paulo government officials took several important measures to reduce police violence and professionalize the police force. In September 1995, the secretary of public security created a program to track officers involved in fatal shootings, providing them with psychological counseling and removing them from active duty, at least temporarily. The secretariat also created the position of ombudsman for human rights. In its first six months of operation, the ombudsman's office received and responded to 1,241 complaints, including 126 complaints of police violence. Largely as a result of these programs, the number of civilians killed by the São Paulo Military Police fell from roughly 500 in 1995 to 104 in the first six months of 1996. In August, Human Rights Watch/Americas representatives met with the governor of São Paulo and his cabinet to express support for their efforts to reduce police brutality.

Similarly, authorities in the northeastern state of Pernambuco made significant advances in the battle to prosecute violent police, death squad members (many of whom were police) and those involved in organized crime. In January 1996, the state government created a witness protection program in conjunction with the prestigious nongovernmental Office of Support for Popular Organizations (Gabinete de Assessoria as Organizacoes Populares, GAJOP). In its first six months of existence, the program assisted thirty-seven people in danger.

Witness protection—or its absence—was highlighted when Wagner dos Santos, the key witness in the July 1993 Candelaria massacre of eight sleeping street children in downtown Rio de Janeiro, returned to Brazil for the trial of the first of seven military police officers charged in the crime. Dos Santos, who survived being shot three times during the Candelaria incident and a December 1994 attack on his life, had been forced to leave Brazil. His protection, survival, and testimony were critical to the April 1996 conviction of former military police officer Marcus Vinicius Borges Emmanuel. Significantly, Officer Borges Emmanuel was tried and convicted to an extended prison term before a jury, rather than a five-judge military tribunal, because the killings were committed while the police involved were off-duty. Another Rio de Janeiro jury convicted Officer Borges Emmanuel in his second trial several months later. Two other police officers and a third person involved in the sale of a weapon used to kill the children were scheduled to be tried by the end of 1996.

Another important step forward in the battle to end impunity was the August conviction of Osvaldo Rocha Pereira for the 1987 murder of rural leader Paulo Fontelles. Rocha Pereira was hired to kill Fontelles by a security firm working for local landowners in the state of Pará. Underscoring the importance of prompt criminal investigation, Rocha Pereira had been at large for several years, and was brought to Pará to stand trial following his arrest on charges of involvement in death squads in the Baixada Fluminense section of Rio de Janeiro that had claimed the lives of dozens.

On September 20, the federal government and the state of São Paulo signed an accord to destroy the chronically overcrowded Carandiru prison facility and to build twenty smaller, better-run facilities. Human Rights Watch/Americas visited Carandiru in August and verified the abysmal conditions there. Carandiru, which in 1996 housed roughly 6,400 prisoners in units designed for 3,200 inmates, was the site of an October 1992 massacre in which State Military Police killed 111 detainees while suffering no fatalities themselves. As of this writing, no one had been brought to trial for the massacre.

Prison conditions throughout Brazil continued to violate international standards. Brazilian prison facilities remained overcrowded: Ministry of Justice figures released in October 1996 showed that more than 148,000 persons were held in facilities designed to accommodate roughly half that number of prisoners. Thousands of detainees and convicted prisoners were routinely held for weeks, months, and even years in holding cells within police precincts because of a lack of prison space. In larger facilities, revolts, like the March 29, 1996 incident in Goiânia in which prisoners seized a delegation composed of Goiás State authorities, holding them for almost a week, were not uncommon.

Detention conditions for minors also continued to be abysmal. In May, Human Rights Watch/Americas joined a group of Brazilian NGOs and the Center for Justice and International Law (CEJIL) in a petition denouncing horrendous conditions in three detention centers for minors in Rio de Janeiro. In those centers, youths were not separated according to age, size, or the gravity of the crime committed. Older, more violent youths abused others, both sexually and by beatings, apparently with the complicity of authorities of the detention centers. The Inter-American Commission on Human Rights ordered the Brazilian government to take immediate measures to separate the adolescents held in the three centers by age, size, and criminal infraction in correspondences sent in May and again in August, and the government initiated construction to comply with the commission's recommendations.

Increasingly violent conflict over land made headlines throughout 1996. On April 19 in Eldorado do Carajás, Pará, in order to evict a group of nearly 2,000 families occupying a state highway to force negotiations, the Pará state military blocked off opposite ends of the road, trapping the landless squatters. After a brief scuffle in which squatters tossed rocks and sticks, the police opened fire into the crowd of men, women, and children. The result was nineteen dead squatters and dozens of wounded. Coroners' reports demonstrated that several of the victims had been hacked to death with their own sickles and other farming instruments, killed from behind or at point-blank range. After the incident, the police registry of weapons could not be located. None of the surviving squatters were asked to identify individually the police officers involved. Three months after the killings, the State Prosecutor's office submitted a poorly supported indictment to the military courts.

In the aftermath of the massacre, more than 120 police were detained for four days in their barracks. Several officers were confined to their barracks for up to fifteen days, and the commander, Colonel Pantojas, was detained for thirty. At this writing, none of those involved was in detention, and, due to a recent amendment in military court jurisdiction, it remained unclear whether the case would continue in the military or ordinary courts.

Though particularly extreme, the Eldorado do Carajás massacre was not the only case of fatal violence over land in Brazil. According to the Pastoral Land Commission (Comissão Pastoral da Terra, CPT), through mid-September, at least forty-three people had been killed in land conflicts nationwide. In all of 1995, the CPT documented forty-one such deaths.

The CPT also continued to document grave cases of forced labor and degrading labor conditions approximating forced labor throughout Brazil. Figures for 1996 were not available at the time this report was released. Figures for 1995 showed that the number of individuals subjected to forced labor had risen to 26,047 from a 1994 figure of 25,193, according to the CPT.

In January, the government provoked concern among those who defend the rights of indigenous peoples when it issued Decree 1775/96 strengthening the procedural rights of large landowners and others claiming title to traditional indigenous people's lands and threatened the stability of tribal areas which were in the process of demarcation. As of this writing, the Ministry of Justice had rejected the vast majority of new land claims, although it had as yet not taken concrete action with respect to eight claims.

One important area of improvement was the passage on December 4, 1995 of Law 9,140/95, which authorized compensation for the family members of 136 persons "disappeared" during the military dictatorship (1964-1985), and established a seven-member commission to investigate additional claims for compensation in cases of state-authorized killings during the military dictatorship. Throughout 1996 the commission evaluated numerous requests for indemnification and had authorized payment to at least one hundred families by early October.

The Right to Monitor

The Brazilian government imposed no formal obstacles to human rights monitoring, and Brazil continued to maintain a well developed network of human rights NGOs. As in prior years, these groups nonetheless encountered threats, intimidation, and physical violence from police and large landowners.

On October 20, human rights lawyer Francisco Gilson Nogueira de Carvalho was killed by machine-gun fire in an apparent targeted execution while returning to his home in Macaíba in the northeastern state of Rio Grande do Norte. Nogueira had been actively investigating the participation of police in Rio Grande do Norte in a death squad reportedly coordinated by Deputy Secretary of State Maurílio Pinto de Medeiros.

In several instances in 1996, courts were used to intimidate and harass monitors with groundless suits based on their defense of fundamental rights. In August, Father Antônio Ribeiro of the CPT office in João Pessoa, capital of the northeastern state of Paraiba, was sentenced to a four-year and ten-month prison term for the crime of conspiracy, resisting arrest, trespassing, and failure to obey a judicial order. The conviction resulted from the priest's defense of poor, rural laborers involved in land disputes.

In another misuse of criminal investigation to harass human rights monitors, the Federal Police opened an inquiry in August to investigate charges that Human Rights Watch/Americas Brazil Office Director James Cavallaro had criminally slandered a federal judge in an April article published in the Rio de Janeiro daily, *O Globo*. The article published in *O Globo* criticized an oral sentence in which, according to press accounts, Judge Mário César Machado Monteiro had sought to justify the use of torture to interrogate criminal suspects. Despite the fact that his decision was criticized by numerous public figures, including the minister of justice, Monteiro filed separate civil suits against Cavallaro, the Rio de Janeiro daily *Jornal do Brasil* and two judges for defamation because of their criticism of his decision.

The Role of the United States

In 1996, the U.S. gave relatively little direct assistance to Brazil. For Fiscal Year 1997, the administration requested US$225,000 for training through the International Military Education and Training Program (IMET) and $1 million in anti-narcotics assistance. In October, the Brazilian government refused $600,000 authorized for anti-narcotics assistance, arguing that the amount was insignificant in comparison to the aid given to other South American nations.

In September, the U.S. embassy sponsored the visit of Gene Shur, director of the F.B.I.'s witness protection program. The visit highlighted the need for a federal witness protection program.

The State Department's analysis of Brazil in its *Country Reports on Human Rights Practices for 1995* accurately summarized the principal human rights abuses committed in Brazil. The report focused on the failings of the administration of justice, in particular the inefficiency and corruption of the judicial process, which rendered convictions of those who violated human rights extremely difficult.

CHILE

Human Rights Developments

Chile made slow progress in promoting human rights reforms, due to continuing opposition from the military and political right and the failure of the government of President Eduardo Frei to press for advances. Human rights violations from the past remained an openly debated and tense issue, as the Supreme Court and military appeals court continued to close unresolved "disappearance" cases, applying an amnesty law enacted by the military government that left power in 1990. Authorities downplayed abuses by the Carabineros police, including torture, while civilian and military officials used the courts to try to silence their critics.

The National Corporation of Reparation and Reconciliation (Corporación Nacional de Reparación y Reconciliación, CNRR), a government body set up in 1991 to continue investigating human rights violations that occurred during the military government, delivered its final report in August. Its investigations confirmed 899 more deaths and "disappearances" than had been documented by its predecessor, the Rettig Commission, bringing the total number of victims of such crimes during the seventeen-year period to 3,197.

Debate continued on the future of court investigations into such cases. Political negotiations on the so-called Figueroa-Otero proposals broke down in April. The bill, named for Minister of the Interior Carlos Figueroa and opposition leader Miguel Otero, was the latest in a series of unsuccessful government proposals aimed at ending court investigations into human rights violations committed during the military dictatorship. In exchange for curbing court actions, a concession to the military, the government had proposed several reforms to democratize Chile's 1980 Constitution, crafted by the military government. However, right-wing opposition leaders refused to accept the reforms, while left-wing members of the government coalition rejected legitimizing the amnesty law. Tensions surrounding the issue remained unresolved.

Regardless of the proposed Figueroa-Otero bill, the Supreme Court continued to apply Chile's amnesty law. During the first half of the year it closed six cases of "disappearances" and extrajudicial executions, involving twelve victims; the Martial Court, or

military appeals court, amnestied eleven cases, involving sixteen victims. Human Rights Watch/Americas met with the president of the Supreme Court to press for stronger human rights action on such cases.

The Supreme Court continued to close human rights cases in the second half of the year. For example, in August, the Second Chamber of the Supreme Court did so in a case involving the torture and murder in 1976 of Spanish United Nations official Carmelo Soria, and gave amnesty to two army officers implicated, Guillermo Salinas Torres and José Ríos San Martín. The case had been reopened on the orders of the Supreme Court in 1994 on the grounds that the amnesty was inapplicable due to Chile's obligations under an international convention on the prevention and punishment of crimes against diplomats. In June 1996, the investigating judge, Eliodoro Ortiz, declared the amnesty applicable, arguing that Soria did not have diplomatic status and that the treaty in question had been misinterpreted. The Supreme Court, despite its earlier verdict, ruled unanimously in support of this view. A group of parliamentarians tabled an unsuccessful impeachment motion against the judges who made the decision.

The Supreme Court also closed the case of Lumi Videla, who was detained by agents belonging to the secret police known as the National Intelligence Directorate (Dirección de Inteligencia Nacional, DINA) in September 1974 and held for several weeks in a secret detention center in Santiago. Her body was later thrown onto the grounds of the Italian Embassy.

While the Chilean courts tended to close human rights cases, Argentine police arrested Enrique Arancibia Clavel, a former DINA agent, in Buenos Aires, in January. The arrest followed the issuance of an arrest warrant by a federal judge, María Servini de Cubria, for the car-bomb attack that killed former Chilean Army Commander-in-Chief Carlos Prats González, then in exile in Buenos Aires, and his wife Sofía, in September 1974. In a positive move, the Chilean government appointed a lawyer to represent it in the

Argentine case.

An Uruguayan judge, Aída Vera Barreto, identified a body recovered from a shallow grave on an Uruguayan beach in April 1995 as that of Enrique Berríos, a former DINA chemical weapons expert and an associate of Michael Townley, the former DINA agent convicted in the United States for the murder of former Foreign Minister Orlando Letelier. Berríos had fled Chile in 1991 after being called as a witness in the Letelier case. His whereabouts were unknown until he turned up at a police station in Parque de Plata, Uruguay, in November 1992, and pleaded for assistance, claiming that he had been kidnapped. The police officer in charge offered to help but then returned him to his captors, members of Uruguayan military intelligence, at the insistence of senior Uruguayan military officers.

Abuses by the police, in particular by Carabineros, the uniformed branch, remained an issue of concern. In January, U.N. Special Rapporteur on Torture Nigel. S. Rodley concluded in his report on Chile that cases of torture were "sufficiently numerous and serious for the authorities to continue giving attention to the problem, and to translate official rejection of the practice into specific measures. The rapporteur had transmitted to the government 110 allegations since 1990, and concluded that ill-treatment of detainees bordering on torture was "very extensive." Government officials took issue with the report, including Secretary General of Government José Joaquín Brunner, who said that torture cases were "isolated."

Much-needed and far-reaching reforms to the Criminal Procedures Code, presented to Congress by the Ministry of Justice in 1995, were still under debate. The reforms would provide protections for detainees' rights.

Government, military, and police authorities continued to file defamation lawsuits against their critics, using the Law of State Security and the military penal code. In December 1995, Judge Rafael Huerta sentenced political analyst and former Pinochet minister Francisco Javier Cuadra to a suspended sentence of 540 days in prison and a fine of 100,000 pesos (approximately US$242) for a comment he made in a magazine interview alleging that some parliamentarians used cocaine. The Supreme Court upheld the decision after an appeals court ruled in favor of Cuadra. Human Rights Watch/Americas and the Center for Justice and International Law (CEJIL) brought this case to the Inter-American Commission on Human Rights in October, accusing Chile of violating free expression guarantees.

In May, the Inter-American Commission on Human Rights found Chile to be in breach of the freedom of expression provisions of the American Convention on Human Rights by banning circulation and distribution in Chile of *Impunidad Diplomática*, a book by Chilean journalist Francisco Martorell, released by Planeta editors in Argentina. Martorell was given a 541-day suspended sentence for libel in September 1995. The commission called on Chile to lift the ban, which amounted to prior censorship, and allow Martorell to return to Chile to promote his book, which he was not permitted to do. Human Rights Watch/Americas and CEJIL litigated on Martorell's behalf.

On October 29, police arrested Gladys Marín, who was accused of defaming Gen. Augusto Pinochet. The president of the Communist Party, Marín had called Pinochet a "blackmailer" during a speech marking the anniversary of the 1973 military coup. Others sued for defamation during the year included Socialist Youth leader Arturo Barrios, charged with insulting General Pinochet at a June 1995 ceremony in memory of "disappeared" Socialist leader Carlos Lorca; Nolberto Díaz, president of the Christian Democrat Youth, for comments on a radio show attacking conscription laws; Tomás Hirsch, president of the Humanist Party, for accusing a prison medical team of using unclean hypodermic needles during a prison HIV test; Manuel Cabieses, director of the left-wing newspaper *Punto Final*, accused of sedition for a front-page image of Pinochet; and Eduardo Maneses, lead singer of the rap group Black Panthers (Panteras Negras), for insulting the police in the lyrics of its song "War on the Streets."

The Right to Monitor

We did not receive any reports that the government prevented or restricted human rights organizations from conducting their investigations and reporting their findings during 1996.

The Role of the International Community

European Union

In July, the European Union (E.U.) signed a cooperation agreement with Chile pursuing enhanced economic, financial, and technical cooperation, and enabling Chile to become involved in trade talks between the E.U. and the Southern Cone Market (El Mercado del Cono Sur, Mercosur). "Respect for democratic principles and fundamental human rights" constitutes an essential element of the agreement. In June, prior to the signing of the agreement, the European Parliament passed a resolution deploring the Supreme Court decision in the Carmelo Soria case.

United States

Human rights remained a low priority in U.S relations with Chile, and the Clinton administration made no public interventions on human right issues during the year.

In July, U.S. Amb. Gabriel Guerra-Mondragon provoked a stern reaction from the Chilean government when he pointed out—correctly—in an embassy press briefing that the military was not fully subordinated to the civilian power. The ambassador's comments came in the midst of rumors, sparked by an article in the *New York Times*, that the Clinton administration was debating allowing sales of high-technology military equipment, such as F-16 fighter planes, to countries in the region. Chilean Minister of Defense Edmundo Pérez Yoma retorted that Guerra-Mondragon was "very wrong" in his comments about civil-military relations, and that the armed forces were constitutionally subject to the elected government. The U.S

embassy issued a clarification, stating that the ambassador's remarks had been taken out of context and saying that the State Department's annual human rights report noted that Chile's armed forces were subordinated to the president but enjoyed a "large degree of autonomy."

COLOMBIA

Human Rights Developments

Turmoil continued in Colombia as President Ernesto Samper confronted mounting evidence that he approved of drug cartel donations to his presidential campaign. A vocal opposition, intense U.S. pressure to resign, and his own resolve to remain in office apparently led the president to adopt authoritarian measures and cede broad powers to the army to govern. The result was a direct assault on the 1991 Constitution and its fundamental guarantees, with nefarious implications for human rights.

President Samper's measures had little effect on political violence or human rights violations, which remained numerous. In the first six months of the year, an average of three people a day fell victim to political killings, which totaled 522. As a percentage of such cases, paramilitary violence rose in comparison to 1995.

New evidence emerged in 1996 showing that the military continued to promote paramilitaries and used them to collect intelligence and assassinate Colombians suspected of guerrilla ties. For example, in Segovia, in the department of Antioquia, a government investigation led to the arrest of a captain who eyewitnesses said escorted six paramilitaries flown in from Medellín to a military base on April 22, then killed fourteen people and injured fifteen.

For their part, guerrillas committed violations of international humanitarian law, including political killings, kidnappings, the use of landmines, and attacks on civilian targets, including public buses. In a single incident, Revolutionary Armed Forces of

Colombia (Fuerzas Armadas Revolucionarias de Colombia, FARC) militants were believed to have murdered eleven men on the Osaka Farm on February 14. The National Liberation Army (Ejército de Liberación Nacional, ELN) also reportedly detained and disarmed three policemen and a soldier at a roadblock in the department of Norte de Santander on January 24, then killed them, burning one of the bodies.

According to police, a majority of the kidnappings registered over the first nine months of 1996 were the work of guerrillas. Some victims had no part in the conflict but were noncombatants seized for ransom. Although the FARC leadership purported to have stopped kidnapping, the practice continued, albeit described as "a peace tax." For its part, the ELN called its kidnappings a "war tax on the wealthy."

During the first half of 1996, President Samper governed Colombia under a "state of internal commotion," invoked after the killing of Conservative leader Alvaro Gómez on November 2, 1995, and extended through August. Although the measure never produced the capture of Gómez's killers, its stated goal, it did suspend key rights, like freedom from unwarranted search and seizure. The military was also authorized to circumvent local civil authority and petition the executive directly to declare "special public order zones" where more rights were suspended, like free movement. By the end of May, over one-third of Colombia was a "special public order zone." The governor of the department of Guaviare publicly criticized the executive for failing to notify him that his state would be placed under *de facto* military rule. After the Constitutional Court overturned President Samper's August 1995 declaration of a state of internal commotion, its members were barraged with anonymous death threats. Subsequently, the court did not challenge the November declaration of a state of internal commotion, limiting its actions to instead striking down a few measures imposed in its wake. In what was considered a public rebuke, in July 1996 President Samper introduced to congress a constitutional reform bill that would bar the court from reviewing states of internal commotion in the future and eliminate time constraints on such declarations, making them indefinite.

President Samper's dependence on extraordinary measures demonstrated that, far from following through on his inaugural promise to defend rights, he was convinced that soldiers must be allowed to operate outside the rule of law to be effective. Another constitutional reform bill he introduced would convert emergency measures into permanent legislation, including one that would authorize the military to investigate all crimes even in non-emergency situations.

A pro-military coalition of forty senators also presented six bills seeking to reform the constitution to curtail rights, including the legalization of preventive detention without a warrant for up to seven days and a prohibition of civilian investigations of military officers implicated in crimes. It took only six months for legislators to overturn a 1995 Constitutional Court decision barring active-duty military officers from serving on military tribunals, virtually ensuring that their record of impunity would remain intact.

In a marked shift from previous years, President Samper sharply questioned the dedicated Colombians who took seriously their roles as rights monitors, including Public Ombudsman Jaime Córdoba, who declined to stand for a second term after Samper chastised him for failing to defend the president against charges of corruption. Córdoba had also opposed President Samper's promise to reintroduce the death penalty for the crime of kidnapping, which would violate Colombia's obligations under the American Convention on Human Rights, terming it "the *coup de grace* to his deteriorating policy of the defense of human rights."

All was not negative in 1996, however. Efforts to improve the human rights record of the National Police bore fruit. President Samper signed into law a measure obligating Colombia to honor recommendations made by the Inter-American Commission on Human Rights, including the payment of reparations in human rights cases. The office of the Attorney General (Fiscal de la Nación) conducted credible investigations, though they produced few tangible results. Of special interest was the work of the Attorney General's Human Rights Unit, which handled selected human rights and international humanitarian law cases. One investigation led to an arrest warrant for Gen. (Ret.) Farouk Yanine Díaz, a central figure in the army's support for and promotion of paramilitary groups in the 1980s. Eyewitnesses testified to prosecutors that as Second Division commander, General Yanine had paid paramilitaries to kill nineteen men, then supplied the gunmen with information used to locate and kill them. Yanine, who finished his career in 1992 as the second-in-command of the Colombian military, taught at the Inter-American Defense Board College, which operated under the auspices of the Organization of American States in Washington, until his return to Colombia to face charges in October.

General Harold Bedoya, who became commander of the joint chiefs of staff in October 1996, accused the Human Rights Unit of being "infiltrated by the guerrillas." President Samper echoed these charges, in one War College address vowing to "prevent [soldiers] from having to constantly appear before court to respond to unfounded charges...by other enemies instead of carrying out their duties for the benefit of the country."

As investigators, the Procuraduría, in charge of investigations against government officials and administrative sanctions, fared worse. Two successive heads of the Procuraduría faced criminal charges for corruption, and the offices of the delegate for human rights and special investigations were largely dismantled. Far from seeking to fortify the Procuraduría, pro-military senators proposed a constitutional reform to eliminate its jurisdiction over the military, thereby ensuring impunity.

The available evidence showed that impunity remained the norm for soldiers who committed human rights violations. Even as the military denied complicity, the institution almost always filed a *colisión de competencia*, a jurisdictional challenge, with Colombia's Superior Judicial Council (Consejo Superior de la Judicatura) to shift cases from civilian to military jurisdiction. There was a consensus among human rights groups in Colombia that the council unfairly favored the military in such disputes. In one 1996 case, the council ruled that military officers who provided arms and uniforms to paramilitaries who helped carry out the 1991 massacre of seventeen people near Los Uvos, in the department of Cauca, should be prosecuted by military tribunals since such equipment was provided as part of the officers' normal duty. In October, General Bedoya suggested amending the constitution to allow military trials for civilians accused of terrorism.

The military argued that its tribunals were tougher and more efficient than civilian courts, citing a high conviction rate. However, their accounting made no distinction between trials for military infractions—like insubordination—and human rights violations. According to the Procuraduría, most convictions corresponded to infractions while most acquittals corresponded to human rights violations.

In the past, President Samper had promised to reform the military justice system, and in 1995 he convoked a commission to study such changes. As of this writing, however, the commission's effort had yet to be translated into legislation. An effort to establish criminal penalties for the crime of forcible "disappearance" continued to languish.

Other government actions also contributed to disturbing attacks on rights. Despite criticism from within the judiciary, the only step taken to reform the public order courts, or "faceless" courts, created to prosecute drug traffickers and guerrillas, was to limit the use of anonymous witnesses to a case-by-case review. Using anonymous judges and with severe restrictions on the right to a defense, these courts continued to violate the right to fair trial. The Defense Ministry continued to promote so-called rural security cooperatives of wealthy ranchers and businessmen who secretly provided troops with intelligence and formed groups to defend their property despite these groups' similarity to outlawed paramilitary groups.

The government also sought to muzzle unfavorable press. After reporters filmed soldiers firing on Caquetá coca farmers during an August protest of a U.S.-backed eradication campaign, the state-run National Television Commission (Comisión Nacional de Televisión) banned televised reports based on anything but official sources. It also barred news programs from showing any images related to the protests "that reflect situations of extreme human suffering," a move widely interpreted as an attempt to stifle protest.

Over 750,000 Colombians were internally displaced because of political violence, the single largest group in Latin America. A national study in 1995 found that paramilitary violence was responsible for 32 percent of all forced flight, compared to 26 percent caused by guerrillas and 16 percent by the armed forces. The problem worsened during 1996. Although the government developed a plan to assist the displaced, as of this writing it had failed to allocate funds to it. Guerrillas routinely used forced displacement as a tool of war, demonstrating that neither side was yet willing to honor Protocol II Additional to the Geneva Conventions, ratified by the government in 1995.

The Right to Monitor

Human rights monitors continued to carry out courageous work despite attacks and threats. Among those who most forcefully spoke out was Pedro Malagón, a congressman from the department of Meta and a member of the Patriotic Union (Unión Patriótica, UP). On June 20, 1996, armed men shot and killed Malagón and his seventeen-year-old daughter in Villavicencio, Meta's capital. Previously, Malagón had reported that army intelligence agents had offered a bodyguard US$10,000 to facilitate his murder. Josué Giraldo, also a UP member and a founder of the Meta Civic Committee for Human Rights, was himself murdered in Villavicencio on October 13, after receiving numerous death threats. On January 11, armed men shot and killed community activist Sylvio Salazar as he left his Medellín office. Salazar had worked to stem violence between gangs, police, and guerrilla-backed militias.

Threats remained common, particularly for lawyers who defended Colombians accused of rebellion, the charge that corresponded to support for armed opposition groups. On February 28, Reynaldo Villalba Vargas, a member of the "José Alvear Restrepo" Lawyers' Collective, received a condolence card for a client, Margarita Arregoces, from a paramilitary group calling itself "Colombia Without Guerrillas" (Colombia Sin Guerrilla, COLSINGUE).

Human rights groups and other nongovernmental organizations were also threatened for their work. Three groups working with families displaced by paramilitaries, including the National Association of Peasant Small-Holders/Unity and Reconstruction (Asociación Nacional de Usuarios Campesinos-Unidad y Reconstrucción, ANUC-UR), were described as "manipulated by the guerrillas" in an army report. In July, paramilitaries reportedly threatened ANUC-UR president Belén Torres.

Members of the Peace Brigades International based in Barrancabermeja also received threats from police and local paramilitaries. On June 13, a Peace Brigades member traveling by bus was apparently the target of paramilitaries who stopped public busses near Puerto Araujo. Armed men searching for "a foreigner" stopped the wrong bus, however, and the member was unhurt.

Human rights activists were often charged with slander by army officers. Although the courts rarely acted on these cases, including one filed by General Bedoya against Father Javier Giraldo, the director of the Intercongregational Commission for Justice and Peace (Comisión Intercongregacional de Justicia y Paz), the tactic was widely seen as an effort to silence critics.

Even international intervention—like

the invocation of precautionary measures by the Inter-American Commission on Human Rights—resulted in more, not less danger for monitors. According to one respected Colombian human rights group, "Within Colombia, this procedure has resulted in more pressure and intimidation as well as the complete control of the activities [of the threatened person] through the only measures taken: the assignment of bodyguards."

The Role of the International Community

In March, at the meeting of the U.N. Commission on Human Rights, Colombia successfully deflected efforts to increase international oversight of its human rights conditions through appointing a special rapporteur. However, sustained pressure by Colombian human rights groups and their international counterparts, including Human Rights Watch/Americas, obligated the government to agree to establish a permanent office in Colombia under the auspices of the U.N. High Commissioner for Human Rights. As of this writing, the office had yet to begin its work; however, human rights groups were hopeful that it would serve as both a collector of information and a source of pressure on the government to honor Colombia's commitments under international agreements.

Several commissions created under the auspices of the Inter-American Commission on Human Rights to study key cases, including the Trujillo massacre, failed to bear tangible fruit in 1996. In contrast, the Inter-American Court issued its first condemnation of Colombia ever on December 8, 1995, when it held the government responsible for the 1989 forced "disappearance" of Isidro Caballero and María del Carmen Santana. The only dissenting vote was Judge Rafael Nieto Navia, a Colombian, who argued that since the officer involved was suffering "mental difficulties"—an assertion unproved before any court—the state should be absolved of responsibility. The petitioners sought unsuccessfully to recuse Nieto from considering the case based on conflict of interest, since his son was the Colombian

Defense Ministry's legal adviser for international affairs and cases like this one.

For the first time since the U.S. Congress adopted a "certification" process for countries that received anti-narcotics assistance, Colombia was "decertified" in March. In July, the Clinton administration stepped up pressure by revoking Samper's U.S. visa, and exchanges between the two countries were bitter. Nevertheless, the United States remained a key supporter of the Colombian security forces, and Colombia remained the hemisphere's top recipient of U.S. military aid, most of which went to the National Police for drug interdiction and eradication. The Pentagon estimated U.S.-Colombian arms deals at $84 million in Fiscal Year 1996 and $123 million in Fiscal Year 1997—the highest level ever.

As U.S. campaign rhetoric turned to drugs, Congress approved the sale of lethal weaponry to Colombia's military, a troubling shift. In September hearings, Congress authorized up to twelve Black Hawk helicopters and twenty-two M-60 machine guns for shipment to the Colombian army even though, as administration officials noted, they sought no assurances that they not be used in the counterinsurgency operations where most human rights violations occurred. Indeed, the Colombian military had previously announced to the national press its intention to buy U.S. helicopters and launch a new offensive against guerrillas. Although past commercial arms deliveries amounted to less than $2 million per year, administration officials estimated that they could reach $35 million in Fiscal Year 1996 and $21 million in Fiscal Year 1997.

As of this writing, Human Rights Watch/Americas and the Human Rights Watch Arms Project were nearing completion of a report documenting the disturbing role played by the United States in Colombia's military-paramilitary partnership. Despite Colombia's disastrous human rights record, a U.S. Defense Department and Central Intelligence Agency (CIA) team worked closely with Colombian military officers on the 1991 intelligence reorganization, after which, in

1992 and 1993, dozens of people in and around the city of Barrancabermeja were killed because of their political activity. In addition, U.S. military authorities appeared to have turned a blind eye to abuses, even though they had acknowledged that training and weapons provided to Colombia for counter-narcotics purposes could be used in counterinsurgency operations where human rights violations might occur.

U.S. Ambassador to Colombia Myles Frechette offered support to the Attorney General's Human Rights Unit, a positive step. Likewise, the embassy met with international and Colombian human rights groups, an important message at a time when they faced threats and attacks. Within the embassy, a group vetted officers slated for U.S. training, disqualifying officers implicated in serious human rights abuses and thus sending an important message. The State Department's *Country Reports on Human Rights Practices for 1995* was widely considered an accurate portrayal of the situation, although Human Rights Watch/Americas criticized the report for imprecisely terming crimes committed by drug traffickers and guerrillas "human rights violations," rather than labeling them common crimes or, when appropriate, violations of the laws of war. We were aware of no public statements made by the ambassador or other U.S. embassy officials in support of human rights in Colombia in 1996.

CUBA

Human Rights Developments

The Cuban government continued to use intimidatory tactics and its unduly restrictive criminal laws to silence independent voices and emerging organizations in 1996. State security agents limited the activities of dissidents, nongovernmental organizations (NGOs), and Cuba's few independent journalists through intimidation, short-term detention, and in the most serious cases, prison terms or forced exile. Reinforcing the urgent

need for legal reform, authorities invoked penal code provisions such as "enemy propaganda," "contempt of authority," and "dangerousness" that criminalized internationally protected rights to free expression and association.

Vice-President and General of the Army Raúl Castro Ruz expressed the government's intolerance of minimal openings in Cuban civil society in a March 23 speech to the Central Committee of the Communist Party. General Castro dismissed what he called incipient *"glasnost,"* particularly the emerging independent press, as a threat requiring aggressive governmental control.

The Cuban government launched a crackdown against the Cuban Council (Concilio Cubano), a coalition of 135 NGOs, on February 15, shortly before the group's first national assembly to discuss nonviolent dissent. State security agents targeted Concilio members with harassment, short-term detention, and in several cases, criminal prosecution. The pressures against Concilio prevented the national meeting and continued with less intensity as of this writing. As part of the crackdown, Cuban authorities detained dozens of activists, including Dr. René Góme Manzano, who already had been disbarred, was then released after trial. On February 23, judicial authorities convicted Concilio's national leader, attorney Leonel Morejón Almagro, of "resisting authority" and "contempt of authority," charges frequently used to criminalize expression perceived to threaten the state, and sentenced him to fifteen months in prison. On February 22, a Cuban tribunal sentenced another Concilio leader, Lázaro González Valdés, to fourteen months on the same charges.

The Cuban government steadily harassed Cuba's emerging, independent journalists, several of whom were Concilio members. In the most severe cases, the authorities forced journalists to choose between exile or prosecution under criminal laws penalizing free expression or association. In May, after repeated detentions and threats of prosecution for "criminal association," the government forced Rafael Solano, the founder of

Habana Press, into exile in Spain. Roxana Valdivia Castilla, who founded the Patria press agency in Ciego de Avila, received similar threats. In June, she went into exile in the U.S. As of this writing, the government had not permitted exiled journalist Yndamiro Restano Díaz to return to Cuba, despite assuring him that he would be able to leave and return freely to the country after his 1995 release from prison. Cuban authorities sometimes harassed and detained exiled journalists' family members who remained in Cuba.

The Cuban government also exiled activists, such as Concilio member Eugenio Rodríguez Chaple, the president of the Democratic Block José Martí (Bloque Democrático José Martí). Cuban authorities detained him in February and threatened him with up to fifteen years in prison for "illegal association" and "enemy propaganda." He left Cuba for Spain on July 4. In June, a Cuban tribunal sentenced Radames García de la Vega and Néstor Rodríguez Lobeina, of the Cuban Movement of Youth for Democracy (Movimiento Cubano de Jóvenes por la Democracia), to internal exile, ordering them from Havana to their hometowns in eastern Cuba.

Conditions for political prisoners and the general prison population remained poor in Cuba. In violation of the U.N. Standard Minimum Rules for the Treatment of Prisoners, Cuban inmates languished in overcrowded cells with minimal provisions of food and medical assistance, frequently reporting significant weight loss and aggravated health problems. At several facilities, prison authorities reportedly beat prisoners, including minors, and subjected political prisoners and others who protested prison conditions to harsh measures, such as suspension of visits, transfers to remote areas far from family members, and prolonged confinement in isolation cells, in violation of the Convention Against Torture and Other Cruel, Inhuman, or Degrading Treatment or Punishment, which is binding on Cuba. Meanwhile, the government continued to bar access to prisons to domestic and international human rights monitors. Cuban au-

thorities last permitted the International Committee of the Red Cross (ICRC) access to prisons in 1989.

The Cuban penal code continued to criminalize "illegal exit," thereby violating Article 13 of the Universal Declaration of Human Rights, which protects the right to leave one's own country. In June, Cuban authorities charged Elier Orosa Remírez with this "crime," after the U.S. returned him from Guantánamo Bay. Orosa's treatment violated the May 1995 immigration agreement between the U.S. and Cuban governments, which provided that Cuba would not harass returnees.

The Cuban government refused legalization of independent organizations in 1996, including human rights groups, labor unions, and other NGOs, thereby leaving these groups' members at risk of prosecution for taking part in meetings. Years after Elizardo Sánchez Santacruz filed for the legalization of the Cuban Commission for Human Rights and National Reconciliation (Comisión Cubana de Derechos Humanos y Reconciliación Nacional, CCDHRN), the Cuban government continued to withhold legal recognition. Similarly, members of the Christian Liberation Movement (Movimiento Cristiano Liberación) were detained and intimidated after filing for government registration in March 1995, which they never received.

Cuba's Foreign Investment Law required all investors to hire employees through the government-controlled employment agency, which apparently selected workers based on political viewpoints. This discriminatory action and the government's refusal to allow independent trade unions violated Article 23 of the Universal Declaration of Human Rights, which guarantees nondiscriminatory access to jobs and the right to form and join trade unions.

The Right to Monitor

The Cuban government impeded the work of domestic and international human rights groups in 1996. The Concilio crackdown targeted all of Cuba's most prominent human rights organizations. The government did not allow human rights activists to participate in international conferences outside Cuba.

Once again, the Cuban authorities refused to allow the U.N. Special Rapporteur on Cuba, Amb. Carl-Johan Groth, who was appointed in March 1992, to enter the country and review human rights conditions. The government did not permit the ICRC to visit prisons, nor did it allow international human rights NGOs, including Human Rights Watch/Americas, to conduct on-site visits. At mid-year, an unnamed Cuban government source cited in the U.S. media attempted to discredit our work by falsely alleging that we funneled U.S. government money to Cuban NGOs.

On June 19, following four days of meetings with Cuban journalists, Suzanne Bilello of the U.S.-based Committee to Protect Journalists was detained by Cuban authorities, interrogated for several hours, and then expelled from the country the following morning. On July 12, Cuban immigration officials expelled Jacques Perrot, of the France-based Reporters without Borders (Reporters sans frontières), hours after his arrival in Havana. Harassment of local journalists intensified following these incidents.

In August, the Cuban government refused to renew the visa of Robin Diane Meyers, the United States Interests Section human rights officer, complaining among other things that she had distributed "anti-government literature," including writings about José Martí and George Orwell's *Animal Farm.*

The Role of the International Community

United Nations
While barred from entering Cuba, Special Rapporteur Groth actively tracked human rights developments. The fifty-second session of the Human Rights Commission again extended the special rapporteur's mandate and condemned Cuban human rights practices. The Cuban government unsuccess-

fully attempted to restrict the mandate of the U.N. Working Group on Arbitrary Detentions, which had censured Cuba in several cases.

European Union
The European Union (E.U.) publicly supported human rights in Cuba and successfully pressed for the release of several political prisoners, who were then exiled. The E.U. could claim few other positive results from its efforts, though. Europeans became complicit in human rights abuse by promoting investment in government-dominated projects that deny basic labor rights. Moreover, while urging further investment in Cuba, the E.U. did not exercise its leverage to insist on concrete improvements in human rights, such as penal code reforms or access for the U.N. special rapporteur.

To its credit, following the crackdown on Concilio Cuban, the E.U. froze discussions on a cooperation agreement with Cuba, which was due to include a human rights conditionality clause.

Organization of American States
In October, the Inter-American Commission on Human Rights condemned the Cuban government's July 1994 sinking of the *13 de marzo* tugboat, whose seventy-two occupants were fleeing Cuba. Forty-one people died in the attack, which the commission assailed as a violation of the rights to life and transit.

United States
On February 24, the Cuban Air Force shot down two civilian aircraft, killing four members of Brothers to the Rescue (Hermanos al Rescate), a Miami-based Cuban exile group. The incident sparked a prompt but indiscriminate U.S. government response. On March 12, President Clinton signed the Cuban Liberty and Democratic Solidarity Act (also known as the Helms-Burton law) into law, solidifying the thirty-year policy of isolation that had failed to bring human rights improvements to Cuba. The Helms-Burton law included provisions that restricted

the rights to free expression and association and the freedom to travel between the U.S. and Cuba, thus violating Article 19 of the International Covenant on Civil and Political Rights, a treaty ratified by the U.S. The Clinton administration's additional bars on communication, such as the suspension of direct flights between the U.S. and Cuba, also limited opportunities for the free flow of information.

The U.S. government continued to track closely human rights developments in Cuba in 1996. The State Department's Cuba section in its *Country Reports on Human Rights Practices for 1995* was thorough and reliable.

DOMINICAN REPUBLIC

Human Rights Developments

The government of the Dominican Republic was responsible for serious human rights violations in 1996, including extrajudicial executions and other police abuses and substandard prison conditions. Human rights activists highlighting these and other concerns found themselves the targets of government intimidation.

Dominican security forces, including the police, military, and the National Directorate for Drug Control (Dirección Nacional de Control de Drogas, DNCD), were responsible for the extrajudicial killings of more than thirty-five persons, including minors, from January to November. Government investigations of these cases were rare, and as of this writing, the Dominican courts had not convicted any state agent for the crimes. Among these cases, on April 22, members of a National Police (Policía Nacional, PN) unit killed José Luis Alvarez and Juan Villegas Castillo in the Villa Agrícolas section of Santo Domingo. On July 15, two police officers asked seventeen-year-old Valentín Vargas Martínez, a resident of the El Capotillo section of Santo Domingo, to give them

money; when he did not, both officers opened fire, killing him. Police shot to death another minor, nine-year-old Anthony Martínez, in Villa Altagracia on August 6. A DNCD unit in Santo Domingo chased Crispin Tiburcio to the shore of the river Isabela on May 26. When he fled into the water, the DNCD agents prohibited rescuers from assisting him, and he drowned.

Common inmates in Dominican jails and prisons suffered extreme overcrowding, food shortages, poor physical conditions, and beatings, knifings, and bullet wounds at the hands of guards and other prisoners. The government routinely failed to separate minors from adults in the prison population and, in a number of cases, reportedly denied minors sufficient protection from older prisoners, who forcibly prostituted them. At the country's largest prison, La Victoria, outside Santo Domingo, approximately 90 percent of the detainees had never been tried, according to the Dominican Human Rights Committee (Comité Dominicano de los Derechos Humanos, CDDH), some despite having spent up to six years in the facility. Prison authorities rarely separated pre-trial detainees from convicted prisoners.

The poor prison conditions led to frequent protests and prison violence. On May 11, for example, prisoners at the jail in Najayo rioted, leaving eleven inmates dead and fifty injured. In September, prisoners in several regions coordinated strikes, leading to one death at La Victoria and one each at prisons in El Seibo and San Francisco de Macorís.

Although prison conditions changed little in 1996, the government took positive steps by establishing a Children's Tribunal (Tribunal Titular de Menores) and a children's detention center in La Vega. Several hundred children remained in adult prisons as of this writing, however.

Two rounds of presidential elections in 1996, leading to the August 16 inauguration of Leonel Fernández Reyna, occurred without significant violence or irregularities. However, the government undertook several illegal, discriminatory measures in the pre-electoral period. In conjunction with public criticisms of an opposition candidate's alleged Haitian heritage, the government expelled over 3,000 Haitians, many of whom were legal residents and others who were Dominican citizens of Haitian descent. Dominican authorities seized and destroyed the national identity cards of numerous Dominicans of Haitian descent. The cards also served as proof of voter registration. The police and military conducting the expulsions routinely denied detainees their right to a hearing before expulsion. They also mistreated detainees and failed to allow them to notify family members or retrieve belongings. Shortly before the elections, then President Joaquín Balaguer made public statements challenging the right to citizenship of children born to Haitians residing in the country, in apparent contradiction of constitutional citizenship rights.

On May 27, the Dominican government refused Dr. Josefina Juan viuda Pichardo, the former attorney general for the national district, the right to return from Miami to the Dominican Republic. Dr. Juan, who had been receiving treatment for cancer in the U.S., was known for speaking out against alleged involvement of high-ranking Dominican government officials in drug trafficking. With the second round of presidential elections scheduled for June 30, a legal advisor to the government justified barring Dr. Juan's return on the grounds that her presence in the country would create "irritation, controversy, and conflict" at election time. In mid-June, the Inter-American Commission on Human Rights took action on her case, urging the Dominican government to permit her return. Shortly after the presidential election, the government announced that she could return, and she arrived in Santo Domingo on July 21.

Journalists also suffered pressures at election time. Television producer Nuria Piera and a photographer, Iris Lizardo, were attacked by ruling party members and accused of being "traitors" at June electoral rallies. Juan Bolívar Díaz, the author of *Electoral Trauma (Trauma Electoral)*, a book making accusations of fraud in the 1994 presidential elections, lost a defamation suit brought by Generoso Ledesma. The June 19 sentence appeared excessive: a six-month jail term and order to pay approximately US$214,000 indemnization.

Late in the year, the May 26, 1994 "disappearance" of university professor Dr. Narciso González Medina drew increasing national attention, largely due to the October 11 hearing on the case before the Inter-American Commission on Human Rights. Shortly before his disappearance González had published an article criticizing then-President Balaguer as "the most perverse" leader in the Americas and had called for civil disobedience in response to alleged fraud in the 1994 presidential elections. One year later, an investigating judge (juez de instrucción) had opened the case, but witnesses refused to comply with subpoenas, and police did little to enforce them. Late in 1996 however, the president reaffirmed his commitment to resolving the case and several witnesses provided declarations, including the Chief of the Armed Forces, Lt. Gen. Juan Bautista Rojas Tabar. Shortly after his appearance in court, Rojas made public statements leading the president to fire him on November 1. Two representatives of organizations working on González's case received telephone death threats near the time of Rojas' removal, in one case blaming their efforts for his firing. Other González supporters, family members, and witnesses also had faced death threats. Information emerged in 1996 that one witness, José Pérez, who reportedly saw Dominican soldiers detain González on May 26, 1994, was "disappeared" a few days later.

The Right to Monitor
Repeated threats from the Dominican government, as well as intimidatory incidents such as robberies of homes and vehicles without any items of value being taken, created a tense environment for Dominican human rights activists. In June, in full view of a crowd, two National Police officers fired repeatedly on Danilo de la Cruz, a member of the CDDH. De la Cruz had just spoken at a

press conference in El Capotillo denouncing the police role in the drowning death of Crispin Tiburcio (see above). The police reportedly opened an investigation of this incident but had made no progress as of this writing. Police publicly threatened to kill the president of the CDDH, Virgilio Almánzar, in October, shortly after he videotaped them roughing up several youths.

The Role of the International Community

The Inter-American Commission on Human Rights took swift action in the case of Dr. Josefina Juan viuda Pichardo (see above) in June 1996, urging the Dominican government to permit her return and guarantee her safety. In October, the commission heard Narciso González's case (see above) but had not reached any decision or settlement as of this writing.

The U.S. State Department's section on the Dominican Republic in its *Country Reports on Human Rights Practices for 1995* provided a detailed and reliable review of human rights concerns in the country.

GUATEMALA

Human Rights Developments

Political violence waned in 1996 as the government of President Alvaro Arzú Irigoyen made progress in peace talks with the Guatemalan National Revolutionary Union (Unión Revolucionaria Nacional Guatemalteca, URNG). The Arzú administration undertook several bold initiatives to address longstanding human rights problems and also demonstrated a greater degree of independence from the military than any previous civilian government.

The presence for a second year of a professional and effective United Nations human rights verification mission, the Mission of the U.N. in Guatemala (Misión de las Naciones Unidas en Guatemala, MINUGUA), undoubtedly contributed to the decline in politically motivated human rights abuse, by almost guaranteeing international scrutiny to those abuses that occurred.

Yet while human rights violations such as "disappearance" and extrajudicial execution motivated by ideology sharply declined during the Arzú government's first year, criminal violence—in many cases with the involvement of current or former security force elements—surged. Popular desperation at the unchecked violence prompted several lynchings in different parts of the country. At the same time, journalists, human rights monitors, political activists, trade union and peasant organizers continued to face terror tactics including abductions, torture, and death threats, in many cases from current or former security force members or their civilian allies who stalked their victims with impunity.

And while the government took several potentially significant steps toward ending impunity, none had produced concrete results as of this writing. In January and again in September, the government took the unprecedented steps of dismissing high-level army and police officers allegedly involved in organized crime. Among those cashiered were officers linked to notorious human rights violations. With U.S. encouragement, the government formed a special crime task force composed of police and prosecutors to solve new cases in which the security forces were implicated, or in which judicial or police authorities, human rights monitors or international observers became victims. The effectiveness of this unit was difficult to measure in its first months of operation.

In what may become an important precedent for the hemisphere, the Congress in June approved legislation channeling all trials of common crimes committed by the military into civilian, rather than military courts. Military courts would henceforth be limited to handling infractions of the military code of justice. A constitutional challenge to this legislation, filed by military officers, was not yet resolved by the Constitutional Court as of this writing. And in August, the Congress passed legislation creating a judicial protection unit to coordinate protection for judges, prosecutors, witnesses and others connected with criminal prosecutions who might come under threat, although this unit had yet to be funded.

Unfortunately, the accumulated weight of decades of terror rendered the judiciary unresponsive to such stimulants. Prosecutions of notorious human rights violations remained stalled in 1996, and in some cases suffered setbacks. While fear of the potential violent consequences of prosecuting human rights violators explained much of this inaction, negligence on the part of some prosecutors and judges also played a large part.

MINUGUA reported that members of the guerrilla URNG threatened civilians from whom it sought to collect "war taxes" early in the year, although these incidents dropped off after the guerrillas agreed in May to suspend the war tax. In October, the guerrillas turned over an elderly woman they had abducted in exchange for a guerrilla commander detained by the government.

Street children continued to suffer at the hands of police officers and private security guards. In April, two police officers raped sixteen-year-old Sandra Esmeralda Gómez Guevara while a third kept watch. Despite detailed testimony from the victim and an eyewitness, including physical descriptions and the names of two of the attackers, the police internal affairs unit did nothing to investigate the crime.

In June, two private security guards were sentenced to thirty years in prison for the murder of two street children and wounding of a third in 1994. This conviction, a rare achievement, was overturned by an appeals court on August 26, on the basis of a flimsy technicality. The owner of the security firm that employed the guards was a high-ranking and powerful former military officer.

During 1996, various street children and youths were the victims of shootings, many of which appeared to be linked to efforts at "social cleansing"; police and/or security guard involvement was suspected. Nine minors died as a result of these shootings, while three other youths were

knifed to death near Guatemala City in June. On September 20, sixteen-year-old street youth Ronald Rafael Ramos was shot in the head and killed by a uniformed Treasury Police officer in the town of Tecun Uman, on the western border with Mexico. The officer was not apprehended.

In September, on the other hand, Guatemala set a negative precedent for the hemisphere, becoming the first country in the region, outside of the Caribbean and Guyana, to use the death penalty in more than a decade. Two peasants convicted of raping and murdering a four-year-old girl in 1993 were executed by firing squad, despite international protests including a request from the Inter-American Commission on Human Rights of the Organization of American States to delay the executions until due process defects in the men's trial were resolved. The men had no attorney for several weeks after their arrest and were subsequently defended only by a law student.

On August 14, the Arzú government announced it would begin a gradual dissolution and disarming of the army-organized civil patrols which, since the early 1980s, have been responsible for innumerable human rights violations in rural areas. Human Rights Watch/Americas and others had pressed for the patrols' dissolution for many years but faced determined resistance from the military, which relied on the patrols for intelligence-gathering, political control of remote communities, and to carry out its dirty work of political repression. The welcome announcement that the patrols would be dissolved and disarmed encountered some resistance in subsequent months, including from patrollers and members of the army.

This announcement followed the 1995 dissolution of the network of military commissioners, civilians deputized by the army to carry out intelligence-gathering and local military recruitment. Yet many individuals who previously held that position continued to exercise power through intimidation in rural communities. This phenomenon was expected to reproduce itself with the civil patrollers unless the government aggressively investigated, prosecuted, and punished former patrollers and military commissioners who committed abuses.

Police feared former military commissioners and civil patrollers because they perceived these individuals as protected by the army. The Arzú government had little more success than its predecessors in detaining notorious patrollers or former commissioners wanted for human rights violations. Former military commissioner Victor Román Cutzal, wanted in connection with the murders of two human rights monitors in the department of Chimaltenango in 1994 and 1995, remained at large as of this writing, although a warrant for his arrest was issued in August 1995. Román had been briefly detained in 1994, but was released after the judge who ordered his detention was murdered in a still unresolved case. Three patrollers wanted for the murder of human rights monitor Tomás Lares Cipriano in April 1993 remained undisturbed in their communities near Joyabaj, Quiché, as did a group of patrollers wanted for the slaying of three villagers from Chel, in northern Quiché department, in December 1990.

Raúl Martínez, a former civil patrol chief in the Ixcán region who on two separate occasions took hostage representatives of international humanitarian organizations, continued to defy a May 1995 arrest warrant for several months in 1996. On April 30, 1996, in an apparently choreographed maneuver, Martínez appeared in court on a day in which the regular judge was sick and his substitute released Martínez on bond. Martínez's bond was later revoked, and on August 26, he was sent to prison in Cobán.

Other cases suffered disheartening setbacks in 1996, including the murder of human rights monitor Juan Chonay Pablo at the hands of civil patrollers as a human rights demonstration was winding down in August 1993. On April 25, a district court judge in Huehuetenango acquitted civil patrollers linked to the slaying after dismissing evidence from several eyewitnesses on the specious grounds that their participation in the demonstration disqualified their testimony.

An appeals court subsequently remanded for a new trial.

Prosecution of the alleged masterminds of the 1990 extrajudicial execution of anthropologist Myrna Mack Chang took one step forward and two steps back. The forward movement, including the indictment of Gen. (ret.) Edgar Godoy Gaitán, Lt. Col. Juan Guillermo Oliva Carrera, and Col. Juan Valencia Osorio by military judge Eriberto Guzmán, resulted from the persistence of the victim's sister, Helen Mack, and the special prosecutor handling the case, Mynor Melgar. But in June, new legislation transferring cases of common crimes to civilian courts brought a transfer of the case to a district court judge, who declined to take the case on the grounds that Guatemala's old criminal procedures code, rather than the code implemented in 1994, should govern the procedures. Helen Mack and prosecutor Melgar each appealed this ruling, without success at the appellate level, and were awaiting a decision by the Supreme Court as of this writing. Two years of investigatory work in the case would be discarded were the Supreme Court to ratify the district court judge's ruling. Fear of military reprisal pervaded the six-year proceedings in the Mack case; more than a dozen judges handled and passed it on; nearly all the witnesses fled the country; the police investigator was murdered, and one magistrate's bodyguard kidnapped, beaten, and threatened.

In proceedings for the October 1995 massacre of eleven repatriated refugees in the hamlet of Xamán, the judge hearing the case in Cobán released eight soldiers on bond a few hours after receiving the 5,000-page judicial file on the case. Although the judge was later fired by the Supreme Court and the soldiers' bond revoked, the case did not move forward in 1996. Nor was progress made in the case of Efraín Bámaca Velásquez, a guerrilla commander married to U.S. citizen Jennifer Harbury, "disappeared" and apparently extrajudicially executed after capture by the army in March 1992. Instead of pursuing strong evidence of Bámaca's murder at the hands of the army, Attorney General Acisclo Valladares expended considerable effort in a successful bid to convince the Constitutional Court to rule the Harbury-Bámaca marriage invalid, so that Harbury could no longer pursue the case in Guatemalan courts. Meanwhile, inaction by the prosecutor assigned to the case, Sylvia Jerez, enabled the army to further obstruct the judicial progress.

The military struggle that had provided the pretext for repression through the 1980s and early 1990s was coming to an end. On September 19, the government and the URNG signed one of the most significant and contentious of the substantive accords designed to form the basis for a comprehensive peace agreement. In the "Accord on Strengthening Civilian Power and the Army's Role in a Democratic Society," the government vowed to reform the constitution to remove from the military its role as the guarantor of internal security, and to grant it responsibility only for defending the nation from external threats. A single civilian police force was planned, the Mobile Military Police would be demobilized, and the army's troop strength reduced by one-third. The accord also allowed for a civilian defense minister for the first time. Additional provisions in the agreement were designed to disentangle the army from domestic spying, a practice that had enabled the army to identify and eliminate successive generations of civil society leaders.

Operational issues surrounding the formal end of armed conflict remained to be discussed between the government and guerrillas before a comprehensive peace accord could be signed; several aspects of this and previous accords, including the formation of a truth commission, would only come into effect at that moment.

The repatriation of refugees from Mexico slowed to a trickle in 1996 due to a combination of factors including continued concerns for physical safety following the Xamán massacre, limited access to land and material assistance, and the possibility of permanent resettlement in Mexico.

The Right to Monitor

Those promoting respect for human rights continued to suffer threats and harassment, and the government made no serious effort to investigate the threats. Journalists reporting on abuses by security forces also continued to be targets of harassment.

On February 28, four armed men driving a black vehicle with smoked-glass windows kidnapped radio reporter Vinicio Pacheco in downtown Guatemala City. The men drugged and tortured Pacheco and questioned him about his coverage of corruption and kidnapping rings before releasing him near Lake Amatitlán.

On April 1, residents of the village of Guineales, including civil patrollers, and a former military commissioner, attacked Julio Ixmatá Tziquín, of the human rights group Mayan Defense (Defensoría Maya). The group threatened to kill Ixmatá because of his human rights work and was about to set him on fire when relatives and neighbors intervened.

The bishop of San Marcos and attorneys working in his human rights office received death threats in February, and members of an indigenous human rights group in Chimaltenango were threatened by the so-called Avenging Jaguar (Jaguar Justiciero, JJ), which appears linked to current or former security force agents.

In April, May, and June, Father Daniel Vogt, a parish priest in El Estor, Izabal, who has faced repeated harassment and threats from local authorities because of his defense of peasants jailed on fabricated charges, received anonymous threatening telephone calls. In addition, Father Vogt and other residents of El Estor who had protested arbitrary acts by local authorities were threatened in obscene flyers distributed broadly in El Estor in June, September, and October. Although the government had committed itself, under instructions from the Inter-American Court of Human Rights, to protect Father Vogt, it failed to investigate the threats he received.

In June, Carlos Federico Reyes López, a member of the Guatemalan Forensic Anthropology Team, was twice threatened by unidentified armed men. A caller to the forensic team office made new death threats in August.

Widows of men massacred by the army and civil patrols in the early 1980s in the Rabinal area were threatened by former military commissioners, who stated in early September that there would be mass killings on September 15, the date the widows planned to commemorate the massacres.

Former human rights activists who in January became congressional deputies received death threats on several occasions. The "Group for the Recovery of the Guatemalan Army" (Por la Reivindicación del Ejército de Guatemala, PREGUA) issued public threats against deputies Rosalina Tuyuc, Amílcar Méndez, Nineth de Montenegro, as well as human rights monitors Carlos Aldana and Frank LaRue and several government officials. In September, the same deputies were again threatened, this time in a communiqué signed by JJ, which also listed labor and student activists, human rights monitors Ronalth Ochaeta, Carlos Aldana, Mario Polanco, and Helen Mack, and the human rights ombudsman, Jorge Mario García Laguardia, as potential targets.

The Role of
the International Community

United Nations

As noted above, the United Nations played an important and increasingly successful role in moderating peace talks between the government and guerrillas and in monitoring human rights violations through its respected verification mission, MINUGUA. Indications early in the year that the U.N. might allow a blanket amnesty to be included in peace agreements prompted Human Rights Watch/Americas to write to Secretary-General Boutros Boutros-Ghali and foreign ministers of nations assisting the peace process to insist that any amnesty negotiated between the government and guerrillas not include gross violations of human rights. On August 8, U.N. Under-Secretary-General for Political Affairs Marrack Goulding responded, assuring us that the U.N. could not condone any agreement that would violate the principles of human rights and international law upon which the United Nations was founded.

Guatemala also continued to benefit from scrutiny by U.N. Independent Expert Mónica Pinto, who through her December 1995 report maintained pressure on broad issues such as the end to the civil patrols, the removal of military influence from law enforcement, and demilitarization of the intelligence services.

United States

The Clinton administration's policy toward Guatemala remained entangled in the threads of a scandal—the 1995 revelation that a Guatemalan army colonel implicated in the cover-up of the murder of U.S. citizen Michael DeVine and the torture and possible execution of Efraín Bámaca had been on the Central Intelligence Agency (CIA) payroll even after his involvement in one of the cases had come to light.

In May 1996, the State Department declassified nearly 5,000 documents regarding human rights violations suffered by U.S. citizens or their relatives in Guatemala, as well as a handful of human rights violations against Guatemalan citizens since 1984. The declassification was a welcome move, which unfortunately was not followed by other agencies whose files were more likely to contain relevant information. U.S. intelligence and military agencies maintained intimate contacts with Guatemalan human rights violators for several decades and did not generally share information with the State Department. Intelligence agency files were thus more likely to contain information valuable to relatives of victims and prosecutors seeking to bring to justice those responsible. Not only have U.S. intelligence agencies and the Pentagon refused to open their files, they have also, according to press accounts, barred the State Department from releasing a handful of documents that attribute human rights violations and other criminal acts to the CIA-linked Guatemalan implicated in the DeVine and Bámaca cases.

A lengthy investigation into the Guatemala scandal conducted by the executive branch's Intelligence Oversight Board (IOB) was made public on June 28. The report confirmed that "several CIA assets [Guatemalans on the CIA payroll] were credibly alleged to have ordered, planned, or participated in serious human rights violations such as assassination, extrajudicial execution, torture, or kidnapping while they were assets— and that the CIA's Directorate of Operations (DO) headquarters was aware at the time of the allegations [of abuse]." The IOB also found that the agency "violated its statutory obligation to keep the Congressional oversight committees 'fully and currently informed'" of these instances and also neglected to inform officials within the U.S. embassy in Guatemala, the State Department, or the National Security Council.

While the IOB's report was hardhitting, its recommendations were insufficient to prevent recurrence of abuse. The report praised new guidelines issued by the CIA in February, which "generally bar" asset or liaison relationships with human rights abusers, but allow such relationships "in special cases when national security interests so warrant." The IOB added that the CIA operatives in Guatemala had previously ignored headquarter recommendations to avoid hiring assets involved in human rights abuse. Clearly the agency cannot be left to police itself on this matter, and the fact that the IOB report accepted CIA assurances at face value detracted from the report's credibility.

Overt U.S. military aid and training remained suspended for Guatemala, although the CIA reportedly maintained aid to military intelligence, purportedly on counternarcotics grounds. The administration resumed criminal investigations training programs for the police, which had been suspended in 1995. This move was warranted by the Arzú government's commitment to police reform.

HAITI

Human Rights Developments

President René Préval assumed office on February 7, 1996, marking a historic transfer of power from Haiti's first democratic government to its second. Despite a peaceful change of government, Haiti continued to suffer police abuses and political violence, in several cases at the hands of former soldiers, in 1996. However, the absence of widespread, systematic abuses ensured that Haiti's refugee outflow was negligible. The continued presence of both troops and civilian police of the United Nations Support Mission in Haiti contributed to the country's relative stability. In October, U.N. Secretary-General Boutros Boutros-Ghali recommended UNSMIH's extension beyond its November 30 expiration date.

The new civilian police force, the Haitian National Police (Police Nationale d'Haïti, PNH), which was created to replace the army and commenced operations in mid-1995, reached a full strength of over 5,200 agents in 1996. The PNH committed serious human rights violations, including extrajudicial executions, the unjustified or disproportionate use of lethal force, and beatings. Eradication of abusive practices by the police apparently will require thorough training and supervision. Yet, the new force lacked qualified leaders and was plagued by poor discipline and inexperience. These ongoing abuses went almost completely unpunished. While the investigative and disciplinary actions of an internal inspector general's office were encouraging, the judicial system lagged behind, making minimal progress on prosecutions of abusive police agents. In a troubling development, unknown assailants killed eight police agents between March and August.

The worst police violence occurred on March 6 in the Port-au-Prince shantytown Cité Soleil. Yet as of this writing, the Haitian judicial system had not prosecuted any wrongdoing as a result of that day. PNH agents extrajudicially executed at least six individuals in a disturbance that commenced when local residents gathered to protest the police killings of Jimmy Poteau and Eliphète Monval. A PNH agent had reportedly shot and killed Monval at a Port-au-Prince demonstration on March 4, 1996, after the demonstrator had slapped him. At the same demonstration, the PNH unit known as the Ministerial Security Corps (Corps de Securité Ministerielle, CSM) detained Poteau and eight others, later transferring only eight detainees to the Pétionville police station. Poteau, the apparent victim of an extrajudicial execution, was found on March 5 near Portaille Léogane with a bullet in his chest.

The crowd protesting Monval's and Poteau's deaths erected barricades on March 6 and allegedly attacked a passing police officer. An emergency call went out on police radios and most Port-au-Prince area police units responded. Several hours of pandemonium ensued as police roared through Cité Soleil in pickup trucks firing weapons and terrified residents fled for cover. Witnesses stated that many police agents were searching for members of a purported Red Army (Armée Rouge).

PNH agents conducting house to house searches on March 6 seized Frenel Louis from his home, took him outside, and shot him twice. Leaving him on the street, the police left the neighborhood, but returned shortly afterward and reportedly shot him again, killing him. Walson Marco was protesting with a youth group on March 6 when three PNH officers reportedly killed him, shooting him in the head, chest, and foot. Other March 6 shooting victims survived apparent police attempts at extrajudicial execution. A twenty-year-old man alleged that PNH agents took him from his home and beat him and two others while questioning them about the Red Army. When he said he did not know of such a group, the police told him to run and then shot him in the hip. Three police agents stopped a nineteen-year-old man and asked him if he was in the Red Army. He was too frightened to respond and began to run. Police officers reportedly shot him in the buttocks.

Police using excessive force wounded at least fifteen others that day. Maxim Destin was walking when he saw a police truck with at least eight armed, uniformed officers. Police fired at him as they passed, wounding him in the hip. Christol Bruno observed police in pickup trucks firing on demonstrators and then fled for his home. Police tried to force open his locked door and then fired through it, shooting him in the chin.

The Haitian police were responsible for additional summary killings in 1996, including the beating deaths of at least five detainees. In late June, PNH agents killed four detainees held at the Croix-des-Bouquets police station, near Port-au-Prince, including Fedner Descollines, whom they severely beat before throwing him in a latrine, where he was later found dead. On June 6, 1996, PNH agents beat one detainee to death and severely injured three others in the Carrefour police station.

On August 20, 1996, a leader of the Mobilization for National Development (Mobilisation pour le Développement National, MDN) party, Pastor Antoine Leroy, and member Jacques Florival were shot to death in Port-au-Prince. The U.S. embassy alleged that members of the Presidential Guard, a unit of the national police dedicated to presidential security, were responsible. Shortly thereafter, President Préval removed the unit's chief, deputy chief, and one other member. As of this writing, the Haitian government had commenced an investigation of the deaths but had not charged anyone for the killings.

Police leaders, who received eighty-six complaints of ill-treatment or torture in the first six months of 1996, acknowledged increasing police reliance on violent interrogation methods. Some police justified beatings when detainees were armed or accused of gang activity, and one officer excused beatings as a necessary police practice, since "these people are criminals." Detainees faced mistreatment during arrest and interrogation with punches, kicks, blows with pistol butts, batons, and pipes, and in one Port-au-Prince police station, with electric shocks.

Haitian police continued to use their

weapons in circumstances where lethal force was unjustified or excessive. On January 16, a group of employees went to the Haitian-American Sugar Company in Port-au-Prince to demand their paychecks. A large contingent of police arrived, attempted in vain to disperse the crowd, and then opened fire, killing Martha Jean-Charles and a six-month-old baby. Police also engaged in other misconduct, including the failure to respect appropriate arrest and search procedures, the carrying of impermissible weapons (such as Uzis or M16s), and the failure to wear uniforms and identification.

The Haitian government made only half-hearted efforts to establish accountability for past human rights violations and for ongoing police abuses during 1996. The U.S. government's refusal to return documents seized from the paramilitary organization, Front for the Advancement and Progress of Haiti (Front pour l'Avancement et Progrés d'Haïti), most widely known as FRAPH, and Haitian military headquarters in 1994 and its secret settlement with FRAPH's leader, Emmanuel Constant, directly impeded the prosecution of human rights crimes in Haiti. The U.S. also covered up information regarding Constant's alleged role in the October 1993 assassination of Justice Minister Guy Malary. A CIA memo detailing a meeting of Constant and other FRAPH leaders with Haitian military officers that month, reportedly to plan Malary's execution, was released late in 1996 as part of a civil suit against FRAPH.

U.S. forces seized approximately 160,000 pages of documents and other materials from FRAPH and military headquarters late in 1994, including "trophy" photographs of torture victims, videotapes, and passports. FRAPH reportedly was founded with CIA assistance and its director, Constant, received regular CIA payments. FRAPH members were responsible for human rights atrocities under the military government that ruled Haiti from 1991 to 1994. The U.S. withholding of evidence of human rights crimes from the Haitian government, including documents implicating U.S. agents, and its pro-

tection of Constant, obstructed the search for truth and justice.

In this context, the Haitian government-supported Commission for Truth and Justice completed its investigation and presented a final, 1,200-page report detailing human rights violations under the military government to then President Aristide in February. President Préval later did little to follow through on the truth commission's work, only releasing the report's recommendations at mid-year and announcing a limited distribution of the report in October. The justice minister declared in June that the ministry lacked sufficient funds to provide reparations for human rights victims. The committee for the enactment of the truth commission's recommendations and the Office of Citizen Protection (Office de la Protection du Citoyen, a human rights ombudsman) both lacked a staff and financial backing.

Haitian courts made limited progress in pursuing scores of criminal complaints presented by human rights victims. By late 1996, prosecutors obtained convictions in approximately thirty cases nationwide of abuses committed by soldiers, their accomplices, and members of FRAPH, but these cases reportedly were marked by light sentences relative to the gravity of the offenses. The Haitian government suffered a resounding defeat with the acquittal of two defendants accused of assassinating the justice minister, Guy Malary, on October 14, 1993. The prosecution of the Malary case was marred by the flight of the principal suspects, at least one under alleged U.S. protection, the government's inability to access army and paramilitary records held by the U.S., witnesses' fear of coming forward, and poor prosecutorial preparation.

Despite minimal progress, the successful prosecution of even a few human rights offenders demonstrated the possibility that when the government chose to do so, it could make genuine progress against impunity. Thus, the government's failure to provide justice for more human rights victims called into question its will to tackle this fundamental problem.

In 1996, Col. Michel François, the former Port-au-Prince police chief, who had been sentenced *in absentia* to life imprisonment for the 1993 murder of Aristide financial supporter Antoine Izméry left the Dominican Republic for political asylum in Honduras. Franck Romain, the former mayor of Port-au-Prince, whom the Haitian government indicted for his leading role in a 1988 massacre, accompanied him and also received political asylum. The Haitian government had not prepared extradition requests for either François or Romain as of this writing.

A Special Investigation Unit created in late 1995 and operating with international support continued investigating seventy-seven politically motivated crimes committed before, during, and after the period of military government, including the 1995 series of approximately twenty "execution-style killings." Yet, the most significant development regarding these twenty cases came from the U.S. government. In testimony to the International Relations Committee of the U.S. Congress on September 27, U.S. Amb. William Lacy Swing blamed the Presidential Guard for the May 22, 1995 killing of Michel J. Gonzalez and suggested that the unit may have participated in other killings. On October 22, the Republican majority of the committee charged in a public report that the Clinton administration had "information implicating" members of the Presidential Guard in at least six 1995 killings, as well as those of the two MDN leaders on August 20, 1996. In response to U.S. requests, the Haitian government removed several members of the unit. Despite U.S. allegations, neither the U.S. nor the Haitian government produced concrete evidence that the Haitian security unit had committed these killings.

The few successful human rights prosecutions and the stigma still attached to sexual violence against women discouraged Haitians who suffered rape under the military government from seeking the prosecution of their attackers. Meanwhile, women's organizations reported an increase in sexual violence. In April, the government took the positive step of ratifying the Inter-American Convention on the Prevention, Punishment and Eradication of Violence Against Women. The Ministry for Women's Condition and the Rights of Women prepared extensive recommendations for reform of Haiti's legal codes, including the redefinition of rape as a crime against the person rather than against morals, but the Justice Ministry had not acted on these changes as of this writing.

The Haitian public's frustration with the judiciary's ineffectiveness contributed to recurring vigilante violence. The June 1996 attack on three prisoners, who were dragged from a prison cell in the town of Roseaux prior to trial and hacked to death, highlighted a continued reliance on popular "justice." Disappointingly, the impunity that gave rise to these killings also was extended to those responsible for vigilante violence.

Under President Jean-Bertrand Aristide, the Haitian government had dismantled the army, but without a comprehensive policy against impunity these demobilized soldiers continued to threaten Haiti's security. In July, André Armand, the leader of the Organization of Soldiers Dismissed Without Cause (Rassemblement des Militaires Révoqués Sans Motifs, RAMIRESM), alleged that former soldiers were planning a *coup d'état*. Days later, he was shot and killed. On August 17, 1996, the government arrested fifteen former soldiers and several others at the MDN party headquarters and accused them of plotting against the government. Two days later approximately twenty armed men, reportedly in uniforms and thought to be former soldiers, fired on the Port-au-Prince police station, killing one bystander.

The improvements in prison conditions that commenced with the 1995 creation of a National Penitentiary Administration (Administration Penitentiaire Nationale, APENA) were sustained in 1996. Nonetheless, pre-trial detainees made up approximately 80 percent of the prison population, and prison authorities regularly held them with convicts. Overcrowding and substandard conditions persisted. There were fewer escapes, and the prison guards did not commit systematic human rights abuses. However, on November 28 and 29, 1995, prison guards reportedly beat child detainees at the Fort National prison. Subsequently, the government moved children to a separate facility and initiated procedures to separate children from adults in all detention centers. The Ministry of Social Affairs opened a Children's Tribunal (Tribunal pour Enfants) in December 1995.

The Haitian press functioned with minimal restrictions in 1996, and newspapers, radio, and television stations represented divergent viewpoints.

Minimum wage violations, retaliatory firings for union organizing, and sexual harassment, including dismissals for pregnancies, reportedly were commonplace in Haiti's workplace in 1996. Yet, the Ministry of Social Affairs lacked sufficient staff, vehicles, and resources to adequately monitor compliance with labor laws.

The Right to Monitor

The Haitian government created no obstacles to the monitoring work of domestic and international human rights organizations.

The Role of
the International Community

United Nations and
the Organization of American States

In June 1996, the U.N. reduced its troops in Haiti from 6,000 to 1,300, and the number of civilian police dropped from 800 to approximately 300. The mandate of the newly named UNSMIH extended until November 30. The U.N. troops contributed to greater security, while the civilian police provided training assistance to the Haitian police force. The U.N. Human Rights Commission extended the mandate of the independent expert on Haiti, Adama Dieng, for another year, requiring him to submit a report at the commission's fifty-third session.

The U.N./OAS International Civilian Mission in Haiti maintained a reduced presence, with approximately sixty human rights observers. The mission provided technical assistance to the justice ministry and police, and monitored human rights. The mission increased outreach and training for local organizations.

European Union

The European Union provided valuable support to improve prison conditions and contributed to judges' training. The French led UNSMIH's civilian police. However, the French government expelled Haitians from the French Caribbean departments of St. Martin and Guadalupe, without due process.

Canada

Sustaining a strong commitment to Haiti in 1996, Canada provided a significant portion of UNSMIH troops and civilian police, and technical assistance, particularly to the judiciary.

United States

The U.S. played a leading role in police and judicial reform and supporting elections as part of an overall aid package of US$120 million in 1996. Most U.S. troops departed Haiti early in the year. Despite this notable commitment, by delaying the return of the FRAPH and Haitian military materials to the Haitian government for over two years and by protecting FRAPH leader Emmanuel Constant, the Clinton administration impeded Haiti's progress on prosecuting human rights abuses. U.S. officials negotiating for the return of the seized items proposed limiting access to certain Haitian investigative and prosecutorial authorities with the apparent aim of avoiding retaliation against named individuals. The administration's further insistence on the excision of U.S. citizens' names apparently served the separate and illegitimate purpose of covering up possible U.S. complicity in political murder and other abuses, particularly the involvement of U.S. intelligence agents with the military government and FRAPH. In late September, U.S. officials announced plans to return these items to Haiti, but in fact, the administration had only arranged for delivery to the U.S. embassy there. As of this writing, the U.S. had not reached an agreement for the return of the documents and other materials to the Haitian government.

In June, the U.S. reached a secret settlement with FRAPH's leader, Emmanuel Constant, allowing Constant to remain in the United States. Several months after Constant was detained and found deportable by the U.S. immigration authorities, the Clinton administration decided to release him into the United States rather than return him to Haiti. The agreement allowed Constant to go free on June 14, 1996 and provided him with a work permit, but required that he not speak publicly. Constant also retained the option to choose deportation to a country other than Haiti or the Dominican Republic, subject to U.S. approval.

The U.S. Congress conducted several hearings on political violence in Haiti during 1996. The September testimony of Amb. William Swing, and the International Relations Committee Republican majority's public report revealed the administration's prior knowledge of alleged participation of the Haitian Presidential Guard in political killings in 1995 and 1996. As the year drew to a close, the need remained clear for the administration to conduct a thorough and impartial investigation into allegations that U.S. government agents or entities had been or were involved in serious human rights violations in Haiti in the past years.

HONDURAS

Human Rights Developments

In 1996, the attorney general's office, the national commissioner for human rights, and private human rights groups pressed forward with efforts to establish accountability for gross human rights violations which occurred in the 1980s. Their courageous initiatives were thwarted, however, by the refusal of the alleged perpetrators to appear in court, the failure of the police to carry out arrest warrants, and the inability of the judicial system to act independently when pressured by the armed forces. The government of President Carlos Roberto Reina took positive steps to institutionalize civilian control of the police and to reduce the excessive authority enjoyed by the military. The fact that on March 26, a grenade was thrown from a passing vehicle at the home of President Reina in Tegucigalpa, underscored the risks inherent in taking these positive steps.

Criminal charges were filed this year and arrest warrants issued for Maj. Manuel de Jesús Trejo Rosa and Col. Raimundo Alexander Hernández Santos for the murder of Nelson Mackay Chavarría and the attempted murder of Miguel Francisco Carias in 1982. Colonel Hernández was for many years operational commander of Battalion 3-16, a secret military intelligence unit responsible for scores of "disappearances" in the 1980s. Hernández, who had been continually promoted by his superiors despite his well-documented role in death squad activities, is now wanted for three separate cases of atrocities. He and Trejo remained at large as of this writing.

Eight retired and two active-duty members of the armed forces charged in 1995 for their role in the 1982 kidnapping, torture, and attempted murder of six student activists, also refused to appear in court. On February 19, the other fugitive in this case, Capt. Billy Fernando Joya Almendola, held a televised press conference. Still the police failed to detain him. In April, the civilian criminal investigations unit of the Honduran police detained former police agent Jorge Antonio Padilla Torres, who allegedly participated in the capture of the students, although he was later released for insufficient evidence.

On January 5, the First Appellate Court ruled that an amnesty law passed in 1991 applied in cases of members of the armed forces charged with "disappearances." President Reina and then-Armed Forces Chief Luis Alonso Discua Elvir publicly applauded the court's unfortunate decision.

On January 19, the Supreme Court of

Justice of Honduras unanimously overruled the lower court, finding that the amnesty laws passed in 1987 and 1991 did not preclude judicial investigation of human rights violations.

On June 24, Judge Celino Aguilera of the Choluteca district court issued arrest warrants for nineteen men charged in the case of the June 1982 forced "disappearance" and execution in June 1982 of Adán Aviles Fúnez and Amado Espinoza, among them police and military officers. On July 19, one of the men, Col. Aben Claros Méndez, appeared in court and was detained. However, when Claros provided an alibi, the judge granted him provisional liberty, even though Claros was under investigation for instigating, rather than directly participating in, the crime.

In April, the Reina government granted political asylum to two Haitians wanted for numerous gross violations of human rights in Haiti, in violation of international treaties which limit political asylum for individuals who have acted against the founding principles of the United Nations, which include human rights and international law. This unethical measure to protect Lt. Gen. Michel François and Col. Franck Romain helped those individuals escape justice in Haiti, where their alleged crimes included extrajudicial execution and torture. Human Rights Watch/Americas protested this decision to the Reina government, whose foreign minister, Délmer Urbizo Panting, responded, "The demands of Americas Watch [sic] have no importance for us...," according to press accounts.

We also protested the decision to appoint former Armed Forces Chief Luis Alonso Discua as the government's alternate delegate to the U.N. Discua had been linked to serious human rights violations and, according to U.S. documents declassified in 1996, had boasted of forming Battalion 3-16. Sending Discua to a gilded exile in the U.N.'s posh New York headquarters represented an affront to the United Nations' avowed purpose of promoting respect for human rights, not to mention providing an undeserved bonus for the general. Later in the year, Discua's status was downgraded to "advisor."

Local human rights groups continued to report homicides resulting from police abuse of authority, although at diminished levels compared with the 1980s and early 1990s. The exception to this positive trend was the performance of regional police commandos (COREs), which engaged in abuses including the extrajudicial executions of supposed criminals. The commander of CORE-7, Lt. Col. David Abraham Mendoza García, named in five different lawsuits, was charged with assassination, abuse of authority and violation of the duties of an official.

In a welcome move, the Honduran government ratified the United Nations Convention Against Torture and Other Cruel, Inhuman or Degrading Treatment in 1996. As of this writing, the National Congress was considering reforms to the criminal code which would codify torture as a crime and assign penalties of five to fifteen years to government officials who engage in torture, with lighter penalties for private citizens found guilty.

In another positive development, on September 8, 1995, the National Congress approved constitutional reforms necessary to pass the main police force from military to civilian control. A vote on the ratification of the constitutional reforms was expected before the end of 1996. Military control of the police was long identified as a source of human rights violations in Honduras, and abuses declined after the criminal investigations police was placed under civilian control in 1994.

In other areas, Honduras's record remained poor. Prison conditions continued to be substandard, and Honduras had one of the highest rates of incarceration of unconvicted prisoners in the world—more than 90 percent. The illegal detention of minors with adults was commonplace, in violation of the Honduran constitution and international human rights treaties to which Honduras is a state party. Several cases in which minors were physically and sexually abused by adult prisoners were reported in 1996 and one minor in prison, Carlos Enrique Jako, was murdered.

The Right to Monitor

A series of threats and attacks against human rights monitors, critics of the army, and those seeking justice in human rights cases demonstrated the continued dangers associated with the pursuit of truth and justice in Honduras. The authorities failed to prosecute anyone responsible for these attacks and threats.

On February 10, unknown men machine-gunned the vehicle of Carlos Turcios, a congressional deputy who had just spoken out against the naming of General Discua to the U.N. Security Council.

On June 17, two unidentified men shot dead public defender Marlen Zepeda in San Pedro Sula. Zepeda had received threats related to one of her cases and told friends she feared reprisals from the police.

The step-daughter of Dr. Ramón Custodio López, the head of the Committee for the Defense of Human Rights in Honduras, died under unclear circumstances on June 5. Mercedes Emilia Burgos Espinoza's death was reported as a suicide. Her car had crashed into an electrical post, and she suffered a gunshot to the head. On July 17, Dr. Custodio and the victim's mother publicly stated that she had been assassinated as a reprisal for Dr. Custodio's human rights work and that since her death, Custodio and his wife had received anonymous, threatening phone calls.

In July, the Public Ministry discovered about 4,000 background files on human rights advocates, government officials, judges, politicians, and journalists among the dossiers of suspected leftists—many of them victims of "disappearance"—in a military intelligence office. The files included such information as the floor plans of homes, the names of children, and the schools they attended. Although many files were obviously compiled in the 1980s, the content of others indicated that the military continued surveillance of civilians.

The Role of the United States

The United States owes a tremendous debt to Honduran victims of human rights abuses because of its substantial, prolonged support for human rights abusers in the military. Washington provided hundreds of millions of dollars in aid to the Honduran military in the 1980s, and engaged in a covert program of direct assistance to Battalion 3-16 which carried out scores of "disappearances" of suspected subversives. Moreover, those courageous Hondurans who reported on military abuses of human rights were rewarded with scorn and defamation from the U.S. embassy and State Department. These U.S. policies reflected Washington's desire to counter leftist forces in Central America, regardless of the cost to human rights.

As part of their efforts to investigate and prosecute military officers who commanded Battalion 3-16, the Honduran attorney general and the national commissioner for human rights have repeatedly requested the declassification of documents in U.S. agencies' files regarding Battalion 3-16. The most significant of these files may be held by the Central Intelligence Agency (CIA), which supported, trained, and worked closely with Battalion 3-16 during the 1980s, according to Honduran and U.S. government officials. While the State Department provided some materials in response to these requests in 1996, all other agencies failed to respond. The Clinton administration's failure to insist on CIA and Pentagon disclosure of information on Battalion 3-16 was a shameful betrayal of those seeking justice in Honduras and was most likely motivated by a desire to avoid embarrassing and incriminating disclosures about CIA involvement with human rights violators.

MEXICO

Human Rights Developments

Words versus deeds again posed the central human rights conundrum in Mexico during 1996. In a speech before United Nations

Secretary-General Boutros Boutros-Ghali in Mexico, President Ernesto Zedillo noted, "In Mexico, the government has a responsibility to exhaust all constitutional remedies to ensure that no serious violation of individual guarantees remains unpunished." Nonetheless, impunity remained a serious human rights problem throughout Mexico. Rural violence, police abuse, and torture also plagued the country, while attacks against human rights activists, journalists, and labor union members proved the difficulty of dissenting publicly in a country experiencing profound political and economic transformation.

To its credit, the Mexican government showed itself to be more open to some international human rights inspection than it had been in the past, hosting a delegation from the Inter-American Commission on Human Rights (IACHR), which is part of the Organization of American States. Mexico also reversed a long-standing refusal to allow the U.N. Special Rapporteur on Torture to visit the country, though the oral invitation issued before the U.N. Human Rights Commission in April had not, as of this writing, resulted in the setting of dates for such an investigation. Mexico had also not yet decided whether to accept the compulsory jurisdiction of the Inter-American Court of Human Rights, a possibility the government said it was considering.

Unfortunately, impunity for human rights violations—one key indicator of the political will to fight abuses—remained pervasive during 1996, and the government continued to deny that violations had occurred in even the most blatant cases. No soldier had been brought to justice for the violations committed by the military during the 1994 uprising of the Zapatista Army of National Liberation (Ejército Zapatista de Liberación Nacional, EZLN), including the Ocosingo Clinic massacre and Ejido Morelia extrajudicial executions.

The government also failed to take action against public servants responsible for torture and due process violations committed during a crackdown on alleged Zapatistas in 1995, documented in the February 1996 Human Rights Watch/Americas report, *Torture and Other Abuses during the 1995 Crackdown on Alleged Zapatistas*. On appeal, judges acquitted two of the supposed Zapatistas, Javier Elorriaga and María Gloria Benavides, a married couple, ruling in the Benavides case that police acted without a search warrant and that her confession had been forced through "physical and mental pressure." Sebastián Entzin, tried with Elorriaga on charges including rebellion, walked free after paying a fine for possession of a weapon and criminal association. More than a dozen other alleged Zapatistas detained in the 1995 crackdown, all of whom suffered serious abuses, remained in jail.

The conviction of seven alleged Zapatistas from Yanga, Veracruz state, highlighted the problem of torture in Mexico. Strong evidence existed to indicate that the detainees gave their testimony under torture, yet judges accepted their self-incriminating declarations. Mexico could rightly boast a series of federal and state laws that provide strong protections against torture and mandate punishment for those who practice it, but prosecutors rarely, if ever, applied the law. As of this writing, no police officer, soldier, or public official had ever served a sentence for torture in Mexico.

Several serious obstacles stood in the way of the eradication of torture in Mexico, including Mexican jurisprudence that established the principle of judicial immediacy. The principle permits judges to give greater weight to a detainee's first confession, which is more likely to be made under torture, even if the detainee later retracts it. A judge cited this principle in the Yanga case, for example. Moreover, prosecutors lacked the will to end the practice of torture. Often, if prosecutors charged torturers at all, they accused them of lesser crimes, like abuse of authority. Further, prosecutors acted as if to give the benefit of the doubt to those accused of torture, rather than initiate immediate and thorough inquiries into the accusations.

While human rights violations committed in the context of the Zapatista uprising have been well documented, rural Mexico suffered from violations that often occurred outside the national or international spotlight. Violence tore particularly at the northern zone of Chiapas state, which lies beyond the area where Zapatistas and the Mexican army faced off beginning in January 1994. There, operating with the tacit and sometimes explicit support of the government, groups of armed civilians, linked to the ruling Institutional Revolutionary Party (Partido Revolucionario Institucional, PRI), violently expelled their ideological opponents from communities. Opponents of the PRI were also killed, apparently for their political beliefs. In Tila municipality, Human Rights Watch/Americas interviewed refugees from Miguel Alemán, Nuevo Limar, Susuchumil, Tzaquil, and Usipá, all of whom were expelled from their homes because of their support for the Party of the Democratic Revolution (Partido de la Revolución Democrática, PRD). The victims identified their assailants as members of Peace and Justice (Paz y Justicia), a group founded in 1995 by members of the PRI. Peace and Justice members prohibited residents of Masojá Shucjá from traveling past the two communities on its border, Miguel Alemán and Crucero, for example, effectively holding them captive in Masojá Shucjá. On August 28, 1995, residents of Miguel Alemán expelled PRD members from the community, who took refuge in Masojá Shucjá, leaving behind their burning homes. They returned following an agreement reached on March 31, 1996, but the peace lasted only until May 18, when residents again burned the homes of PRD members and forced them to flee. In Tila, the Catholic church also came under attack, in large part because of its support for human rights work in the region.

In a long report on northern Chiapas released in October, the Fray Bartolomé de las Casas Human Rights Center (Centro de Derechos Humanos Fray Bartolomé de las Casas, CDHFBC) strongly criticized the government for acting in concert with progovernment groups committing acts of politically motivated violence and failing to punish those responsible for them.

In Bachajón, Chilón municipality, members of a PRI group know as the Chinchulines went on a rampage following the murder of their leader in May 1996. A long-standing community conflict came to a head following a vote for local authorities in which the PRI candidate lost. After the Chinchulines harassed members of the victorious group, people within the victorious group murdered the leader of the Chinchulines, Gerónimo Gómez Guzmán, which touched off violent attacks by his supporters. The Chinchulines burned houses and forced more than one hundred people to seek refuge outside the community. They also set fire to buildings belonging to the Catholic diocese, whose human rights organization, the Indigenous Rights Center (Centro de Derechos Indígenas, CEDIAC), had documented abuses committed by the Chinchulines for years. Witnesses interviewed by Human Rights Watch/Americas agreed that for several days after the attacks, state security police worked hand in hand with the Chinchulines to control the streets, including overseeing a roadblock at the entrance to the town. Only after strong national and international pressure did police arrest some two dozen members of the Chinchulines.

Chiapas state government officials denied the existence of any armed groups other than those committing common crimes.

Violent attacks were carried out by anti-PRI groups as well in Chiapas. In June, for example, gunmen killed four members of the PRI in Jonixtié, Tila. As noted above, those opposed to the PRI's domination in Chilón murdered the head of the Chinchulines; in Venustiano Carranza, members of the Casa del Pueblo, a community group, engaged in armed confrontations with the Alianza San Bartolomé, a group aligned with the PRI. The government, however, often favored the PRI participants in violence. Despite well-documented attacks by the Alianza San Bartolomé in Venustiano Carranza, for example, only members of the opposition Casa del Pueblo were arrested, according to the Coordinating Group of Nongovernmental

Organizations (Coordinación de Organismos No Gubernamentales, CONPAZ).

With the appearance of a new guerrilla group in Mexico, the Popular Revolutionary Army (Ejército Popular Revolucionario, EPR), the government tightened controls on social organizations in areas where the EPR moved publicly. On August 28, the EPR attacked targets including navy, police, and army posts in the states of México, Chiapas, Oaxaca, Puebla, and Guerrero, leading to a heavy deployment of troops in many parts of the country. In response in Guerrero, the army gave the strong impression that it suspected the entire civilian population and had decided to investigate civilians to find those they felt might be guilty of some crime. At roadblocks in some areas, soldiers required local residents to show identification and checked their names against a list. Troops reportedly carried out similar actions in other states where the EPR was thought to be present. In Oaxaca state, men believed to be state security officials kidnapped journalist Razhy González Rodríguez on September 17. González, who interviewed EPR members for the local weekly *Contrapunto*, spent two days in captivity, during which time his abductors questioned him about the armed group.

Authorities also moved to jail leaders of social organizations whose radical rhetoric made them suspect in the eyes of officials; some of the detainees reported being tortured in detention. Authorities arrested Omar Garibay, from the Marxist-Leninist Communist Party of Mexico (Partido Comunista de México/Marxista-Leninista, PCM-ML), on charges that included attempted murder. According to Garibay and his lawyer, the prosecutor initiated the investigation at 4:30 p.m. on June 14, even though the incident did not take place until almost 8:00 that night, indicating that authorities falsely accused him. Garibay was released in late October. In addition to his role in the Communist Party, Garibay was a leader of the Broad Front for the Creation of a National Liberation Movement (Frente Amplio para la Construcción del Movimiento de Liberación Nacional, FAC-MLN), a group of above-ground organizations suspected by authorities to be linked to the EPR. Other groups, such as the Southern Sierra Peasant Organization (Organización Campesina de la Sierra del Sur, OCSS) also suffered arrests. Hilario Mesino, an OCSS leader and Amnesty International prisoner of conscience, who was jailed in Acapulco, reported being beaten twice while in detention in attempts by authorities to force him to incriminate himself as a member of the EPR.

Tighter security measures coincided with what appeared to be mounting pressure against journalists and social activists. In February, the weekly *Proceso* magazine and daily *Reforma* published reports on surveillance of social activists on the part of government security agencies. Other pressures on activists also occurred during the year. On July 9, for instance, members of El Barzón, a national organization of debtors affected by high interest rates, found a bomb in their office in Nuevo León state. El Barzón had been active in protesting Mexico's economic policies. Prior to the discovery, several members of the organization had been threatened, including Liliana Flores Benavides, Nancy Rodríguez Villareal, and Marta Rodríguez Martínez. The perpetrators were not identified.

Physical attacks and threats also served to pressure journalists, many of whom covered topics related to corruption. In most cases, the assailants went unidentified, though it was widely presumed that the subjects of exposés were involved. In February, for example, Ninfa Deandar, who owns and runs the daily *El Mañana de Nuevo Laredo*, in Tamaulipas state, received anonymous telephone death threats. Later that month, unidentified assailants kidnapped reporter Raymundo Ramos as he left the newspaper's office, warning him to stop writing about the governor of Tamaulipas.

Labor activists continued during the year to face government restrictions designed to limit their effectiveness. As documented in a Human Rights Watch/Americas report released in September, *Labor Rights and*

NAFTA: A Case Study, pro-government labor unions and federations, along with laws and labor tribunals that favor the ruling PRI, combined with repressive government action to make independent union activity difficult. The case of the Single Union of Workers of the Fishing Ministry (SUTSP) exemplified the problem. After the Fishing Ministry was converted into the Ministry of the Environment, Natural Resources and Fishing in 1994, authorities prohibited SUTSP members from freely exercising their free association rights. After more than eighteen months of restrictions, the government called for elections so the ministry's workers could choose between SUTSP and a union supported by the PRI; SUTSP lost the vote, but only after being weakened by the government to the point where it was likely to lose. In June 1996, Human Rights Watch/Americas, the International Labor Rights Fund (ILRF), and Mexico's National Association of Democratic Lawyers (Asociación Nacional de Abogados Democráticos, ANAD) filed a petition on the case before the United States National Administrative Office (NAO), which is part of the Labor Department, under the labor rights side agreement enacted with the North American Free Trade Agreement (NAFTA). (See below.)

Violations of women's rights in the northern *maquiladora* sector were also common, as documented in *No Guarantees: Sex Discrimination in Mexico's Maquiladora Sector*, researched by the Human Rights Watch Women's Rights Project. To reduce the cost of pregnancy- and maternity-related benefits, major corporations from the U.S. and elsewhere systematically required women job applicants to take pregnancy tests so they could eliminate from the work pool women whose tests were positive. The government failed to investigate the violations fully or take steps to end them. (See section on Women's Rights Project.)

The Right to Monitor

The year started badly for human rights activists in Mexico, and it never improved. Rocío Culebro, director of the National Network of Civil Human Rights Organizations (La Red Nacional de Organismos Civiles de Derechos Humanos), received a series of threatening phone calls beginning on January 12, prior to a trip to the United States to discuss Mexican human rights conditions. That same month in Tijuana, Baja California state, Lourdes Felgúerez and Víctor Clark Alfaro of the Binational Human Rights Center (Centro Binacional de Derechos Humanos) received threats for their efforts to end torture by local police officers.

On March 27, unidentified assailants abducted Héctor Gutiérrez Ugalde, an assistant to National Human Rights Commission staff member Dr. Julián Andrade Jardí. After beating him severely, his abductors told Gutiérrez to deliver a threat upon his release: "Tell that woman we will get her, and her son, too." The reference was to Andrade and his mother, human rights activist Teresa Jardí, who at the time ran the human rights program of the Fund for Assistance, Promotion and Development (Fonda para la Asistencia, Promoción y Desarrollo, FAPRODE), a Mexico City-based human rights group. Then, on April 3 and 4, Teresa Jardí received anonymous death threats at her home in Mexico City.

The Miguel Agustín Pro Juárez Human Rights Center (Centro de Derechos Humanos Miguel Agustín Pro Juárez, PRODH) came under repeated attack. In a campaign designed to discredit PRODH's work, individuals claiming to be Jesuit priests falsely accused PRODH's director, Father David Fernández, himself a Jesuit, of being a guerrilla leader. On October 7, Fernández received a telephone death threat from a caller who said he would be killed following the murder of Pilar Noriega, who worked with PRODH on the defense of the alleged Zapatistas. That same morning, an anonymous note left at PRODH's office threatened the team of lawyers working with the group. The note contained details about the movements of Noriega that morning. PRODH lawyer Digna Ochoa and Noriega had received three prior death threats, each increasingly specific about the activities of the lawyers, indicating that they were under surveillance. One of the messages also threatened Enrique Flota, a lawyer who collaborated with the PRODH defense of the alleged Zapatistas. On October 24, Juan Salgado of the Mexican Academy of Human Rights (Academia Mexicana de Derechos Humanos, AMDH) received a telephone death threat after organizing a campaign in solidarity with PRODH staff and other threatened human rights activists.

In recognition of the important and necessary work done by PRODH, Human Rights Watch invited Fernández to participate in an annual event to mark the achievements of noted human rights monitors from around the world.

Other church-related human rights groups also came under attack. The Commission for Solidarity and Defense of Human Rights (Comisión de Solidaridad y Defensa de los Derechos Humanos, COSYDDHAC) received a series of threats addressed to Father Camilo Daniel Pérez, a founder of the group, which threatened him and members of the staff's family. In May, Bachajón's CEDIAC came under attack during the rampage by the Chinchulines (see above). On June 19, local media in Oaxaca state accused Msgr. Arturo Lona, the bishop of Tehuantepec, of arming local rebels. Following similar charges in 1995, assailants shot at Bishop Lona, but he survived unharmed. Throughout the year in Chiapas, CDHFBC labored under threat from organizations linked to the PRI, who impeded its field work and accused the staff of supporting attacks against the political party.

The Role of the United States

The United States continued to solidify government-to-government ties with Mexico, seeking an ever-closer relationship on fighting drugs, monitoring the common border, and military cooperation. As had been the case in past years, the State Department's *Country Report on Human Rights Practices for 1995* criticized Mexico, finding that torture "continues to be a serious human rights problem" and that "a number of murders were committed for ostensibly political reasons." Nonetheless, U.S. officials gave no indication that they factored their concerns into policy toward Mexico, except on cases related to U.S. citizens, though, to their credit, embassy officials met periodically with Mexican human rights activists.

The U.S. Department of Labor continued to work on labor rights issues in Mexico through the NAO. In July, the NAO accepted for review the three contentions contained in the petition submitted in June by Human Rights Watch/Americas, ILRF and ANAD: that Mexico violated its labor law by denying SUTSP free association rights; that provisions in Mexican law that limit to one the number of unions that federal employees can form in any entity, like a ministry, violate Mexico's obligations under international treaties to respect freedom of association; and that the Federal Conciliation and Arbitration Tribunal (Tribunal Federal de Conciliación y Arbitraje) is biased against unions independent of the ruling PRI. The NAO scheduled a hearing on the topic for December 3.

In June, the NAO released a hard-hitting report on a 1994 case, involving freedom of association violations in a Sony plant. "It is difficult for workers to register an independent union at the local level in Mexico," found the June 8 report, but given the lack of enforcement mechanisms within the side agreement, the report prescribed no compulsory remedy. In October, the NAO received a new petition, submitted by the Communications Workers of America, that accused the Maxi-Switch factory in Sonora state of violating freedom of association guarantees. As of this writing, the NAO was considering whether to accept the petition for review.

If the State Department ruled out the "stick" approach to promoting human rights, the "carrot" became more enticing during the year. For the first time ever, a U.S. secretary of defense visited Mexico in December 1995, during which time the Mexican and U.S. militaries agreed to explore closer cooperation in such areas as counternarcotics, force modernization, disaster relief, and education and training. As of this writing, the United States had approved the grant transfer of twenty UH-1H helicopters to Mexico's Defense Ministry, and President Bill Clinton announced that he planned to send fifty-three more during Fiscal Year 1997. In April, the U.S. began to train Mexican soldiers at Fort Bragg, Fort Campbell, and Fort Benning, the first such instruction for the Mexican military. Funded by the U.S. Department of Defense's anti-narcotics bureau, the soldiers returned to Mexico to train police in counter-narcotics tactics.

In addition to the anti-drug instruction, Mexico received US$1 million in International Military Education and Training (IMET) funds, more than double the amount provided in 1995. The State Department requested five times that amount for International Narcotics Law Enforcement (INL).

PERU

Human Rights Developments

During 1996, the government of President Alberto Fujimori adopted some positive steps toward protecting human rights, although violations of due process and torture remained as ingrained as ever and serious violations of international humanitarian law continued to be committed by the Shining Path (Sendero Luminoso) guerrillas. In a welcome, if overdue development, the Congress elected a People's Defender, (Defensor del Pueblo, or human rights ombudsman), whose task was to investigate and promote human rights. One of the ombudsman's first actions was to draft a bill, approved by Congress in August, setting up a special commission to advise President Fujimori on the granting of pardons to the hundreds of people unjustly imprisoned for terrorism since 1992, an initiative the government had been promising for years.

This positive development was overshadowed in October, however, when Congress voted to allow the so-called faceless courts responsible for these unfair convictions to function for a further year. Established as an emergency measure in 1992 to summarily convict terrorism suspects, these courts have been unreservedly condemned by the international community for violations of basic due process guarantees, which affect innocent and guilty alike.

Extrajudicial executions and "disappearances" committed by government forces in their continuing battle against armed opposition groups continued to decline, although local human rights groups reported several cases in the second half of the year. Violent state-sponsored abuse continued as police regularly engaged in torture as an interrogation tool; a practice facilitated by lengthy periods of police detention allowed under anti-terrorism procedures and by routine acceptance of coerced confessions as evidence in the faceless courts. In a July 1996 report, the U.N. Human Rights Committee stated it was "deeply concerned by persistent reports of torture or cruel, inhuman or degrading treatment..." Following the beating death of detainee Mario Palomino in a Lima police station in March, opposition deputies proposed legislation to codify specifically the crime of torture, assigning penalties appropriate for the gravity of the offense. However, the Congress failed to act on this proposal. By June some 928 police had been sacked for impropriety and criminal offenses, including those allegedly responsible in the Palomino case. In a rare example of a conviction for torture, in July a court in Huánuco sentenced two policemen to five and six years of imprisonment for beating to death a detainee, Jhoel Huaman García, in Cerro de Pasco in May 1995.

New doubts were raised about the effectiveness of measures to restore the independence of Peru's judiciary, which was shattered following President Fujimori's *coup d'etat* in April 1992. The future of the positive efforts being made by the National Magistrates Council (Consejo Nacional de la Magistratura) to restore the tenure of judges and prosecutors whose positions had become provisional after executive branch intervention in 1992, was called into question when Congress approved a law in June creating a Council of Judicial Coordination (Consejo de Coordinación Judicial) charged with overseeing the restructuring of the judiciary and with powers to fire judges and prosecutors. Control over this body was to be concentrated for a two-year renewable transition period in the hands of two officials, both considered to have close ties with the executive branch.

The Shining Path continued to resort to indiscriminate violence against civilians as well as the selective murder of their political opponents, violating basic standards of international humanitarian law. The Shining Path detonated two car bombs during the last week of July, when Peru celebrated its Independence Day. One exploded outside a Lima police station, killing a passerby and wounding several others. The other went off in the basement of an apartment block where Gen. Manuel Varela Gamarra, military chief of the Upper Huallaga region, lived, killing a taxi driver and injuring five people.

Some of the worst guerrilla abuses occurred in the departments of San Martín and Huánuco, in the Upper Huallaga valley. Among the victims was fifty-two-year-old Julio del Castillo Rodríguez, president of the Upper Huallaga Self-Defense Committtee, who was killed in Naranjillo on April 6 by six armed men wearing hoods. On June 1, six civilians, a soldier, and four guerrillas were killed when Shining Path members led by Oscar Ramírez Durand, a.k.a. "Feliciano," attacked a civilian bus traveling with a military and police escort near the town of Tocache, Nuevo Progreso. On the previous day, the same group had blocked traffic at the village of San Jacinto and searched travelers one by one, checking their names against a list of local leaders said to be targeted for assassination. On August 21, around one hundred guerrillas believed to belong to Shining Path blocked the road to Pucallpa and murdered Celso Estela Pérez, whom they had captured after he had gone to the defense of his brother Casimiro, a local government leader.

Red Path, a Shining Path faction led by Feliciano and opposed to the "peace accord" currently advocated by the imprisoned Shining Path founder, Abimael Guzmán, was the prime suspect in a wave of killings and threats against former Lima community leaders. On March 6 a Red Path unit assassinated Pascuala Rosado Cornejó, founder and leader of the self-help community of Huaycán, who had returned to the community after a period spent in Chile, where she had taken refuge due to repeated death threats from the Shining Path. Rosado's assassins shot her in the head, attempted to explode her body, and scattered leaflets. Several of Rosado's colleagues received death threats, and some left the country for security reasons. On July 30, four armed individuals shot and killed Epifanio Santamaría Rodríguez, a former leader of the community of San Martín de Porres, in Los Olivos, a Lima suburb. His assassins shot him at point-blank range in front of his daughter.

Red Path increasingly turned its weapons on former comrades in the Abimael Guzmán faction of the movement. On May 2, three men dressed in suits, who identified themselves as policemen, shot and killed a Shining Path leader, Víctor Rafael Hernández Ramírez, while he lay asleep in his home in Villa El Salvador, Lima. Before blowing up the body with a hand grenade, the assassins left a card saying "stamp out revisionists and capitulators, PCP Lima Base," a reference to the group that police believed were responsible for the Rosado killing. In July, four hooded individuals forcibly assembled the villagers of Huacrachuco, near Chimbote, harangued them, and then separated two brothers, Beltrán and Gonzalo Principe Herrera, and a third man from the rest. They then murdered all three, who were reported to be followers of the Guzmán line, placed placards on their bodies with the word "traitors," and fled in a van.

The number of killings and "disappearances" attributed to police and military forces continued a downward trend that has been maintained since 1992. However, the National Human Rights Coordinating Committee (Coordinadora Nacional de Derechos Humanos, hereinafter "Coordina-dora"), a respected nongovernmental network of human rights groups, reported several extrajudicial executions in the Upper Huallaga Valley at the hands of the army.

On August 23, soldiers detained seventy-two-year-old Nicolás Carrión Escobedo in the hamlet of Uruspampa, in the department of La Libertad, taking him to a military base. At 5:00 p.m., Carrión's body was removed to the morgue, and the autopsy revealed he had been stabbed in the chest; his body was lacerated and severely bruised in several places. Several witnesses saw soldiers detain María Cárdenas Espinoza, aged twenty-seven, on May 27 in the hamlet of Chinchavito, Huánuco department, where she worked as a cook. As of this writing, Cárdenas remains "disappeared."

Investigations to establish the fate of victims of "disappearances" in earlier years have been halted by the blanket amnesty law promulgated in June 1995. The amnesty law prevents the courts from investigating human rights violations committed in the course of the counterinsurgency war between 1980 and June 1995, ensuring complete impunity for those responsible. In July 1996, the U.N. Human Rights Committee condemned the law categorically and called on the government of Peru to repeal it, to compensate victims, and to ensure that perpetrators of human rights violations do not continue to hold public positions.

Local human rights groups continued to receive frequent, credible complaints of brutal forms of physical torture employed by the police and military against ordinary criminal suspects as well as persons suspected of terrorism. Neither the old nor young were immune. Cases documented in 1996 by the Coordinadora included eighteen-year-old Porfirio Carmen Pérez, whom police arrested on suspicion of theft in Aguaytía, Pucallpa, and allegedly shocked on the head with electricity, beat with a tire iron, and half-drowned to get him to confess to a robbery; police in Pucallpa also detained Pedro Manuel Ruiz Brock, and allegedly beat and sexually assaulted him in a police station; in August, soldiers from the Monzón military base, Huánuco, searching for a stolen assault rifle, were alleged to have brutally tortured and raped a suspect, Juana Ibarra Aguirre. The Coordinadora also documented the deaths, apparently as a result of torture, of two young army recruits, Rafael Delgado Chicchón and Willy Zalamir Obeso Olascagua, in army bases in Piura. The army denied responsibility.

On August 17 the government promulgated Law 26,655, which established an *ad hoc* commission empowered to review cases of persons unjustly convicted of terrorism or treason and make recommendations for presidential pardons. The commission was also empowered to recommend measures to strengthen human rights guarantees in terrorism and treason trials. The three-person commission was composed of the minister of justice; Father Hubert Lanssiers, a former prison chaplain and prisoners' rights activist; and the ombudsman, Jorge Santistevan.

The formation of the commission was a victory for the Peruvian human rights community, which had campaigned long and hard on the issue often in the face of grossly unfair criticism that it was in sympathy with armed opposition groups. One of the first prisoners released on the recommendations of the commission was journalist Alfonso Castiglione Mendoza, who was arrested in Huacho in April 1993 and sentenced in November 1995 to twenty years of imprisonment for terrorism. Mendoza had been tricked into renting a room to individuals who turned out to be guerrillas, and the evidence of his innocence in the trial was overwhelming. In May Human Rights Watch awarded Castiglione the Hellman/Hammett prize for politically persecuted or unjustly detained journalists. Forty-four more prisoners were released in October as a result of the first round of case evaluations by the *ad hoc* commission.

President Fujimori remained convinced that Peru's ordinary courts were incapable of prosecuting terrorism suspects. In his July state of the nation address, the president lamented that Peru lacked a "system of justice on which citizens and businesspeople, nationals and foreigners could rely. This is a reality we must overcome once and for all..." Yet mechanisms set up the previous month to coordinate a restructuring of the judiciary and the Public Ministry sacrificed judicial independence at the altar of efficiency. In the early hours of June 16, Congress approved a law ostensibly creating a Council of Judicial Coordination, a broadly representative body intended to improve coordination among the various agencies involved in the reorganization of justice. However, the law proposed that for a transitional period until December 31, 1998 (and extendable indefinitely thereafter) a four-member council, headed by a retired naval commander, José Dellepiane Massa, would take charge of the entire process of judicial reorganization. The law conferred new powers on the Executive Commission of the Judiciary (an administrative body created in December 1995 of which Dellepiane was also executive secretary) to "evaluate the suitability of" and, where necessary, suspend judges, supplanting the powers constitutionally exercised by the National Magistrates Council. It also interfered with the functions of the Magistrates' Academy, a training school for judges and magistrates established under the 1993 Constitution, by assigning Dellepiane control of training curricula. This concentration of powers to restructure the judiciary in a tiny circle of officials, one of whom (Dellepiane) was known to have close connections with the armed forces and the executive, marked a setback for judicial independence. The law sparked protests from members of the Supreme Court and the National Magistrates Association and led to the resignation of two prominent jurists from the Magistrates' Academy.

The Right to Monitor

On March 29 Congress appointed Jorge Santistevan de Noriega as Peru's first human rights ombudsman by an overwhelming vote. The post was established by the Constitution of 1993, and its duties defined by legislation passed in August 1995. The appointment, long delayed because of disputes over the official's powers and party squabbles over candidates, was widely welcomed, particularly by Peru's nongovernmental human rights community. It signaled, for the first time, official recognition of the importance of the defense of human rights by a government which in past years has treated human rights organizations with scorn.

Nongovernmental human rights monitors continued to suffer harassment and threats in 1996. As in earlier years, the targets were mainly lawyers working to secure convictions of perpetrators of human rights violations. On February 18 three masked individuals visited the home of Edith Luquillas González, a member of the Committee for the Defense of Human Rights in Pasco (CODEH-Pasco). Luquillas was out at the time, but one of her sisters heard the men threaten her safety in obscene language before leaving. Edith Luquillas and CODEH-Pasco have played a prominent role in campaigning for justice in the case of Jhoel Huaman García, tortured to death by police in May 1995. Shortly before the incident Judge Onesimo Vela Velásquez ordered that one of the police officers accused of Huaman's death, Rolando Alejandro Huere Orey, be released without charge.

Threats against human rights lawyer Gloria Cano Legua continued in 1996. Cano was working on the case of Tomás Livia Ortega, one of the survivors of the Barrios Altos massacre of November 1991. The court investigation was closed on July 13, 1995 following the promulgation of the amnesty law in June. Cano, a lawyer belonging to the Peasant Defense and Legal Advice Team, a member of the Coordinadora, received obscene and threatening messages on her telephone answering machine on March 25 and April 3, and on March 28 she discovered that an attempt had been made to force the lock of her office door.

On April 24, Angélica Matías Ronceros, legal advisor to the Association of Relatives of Victims of Terrorism, which is affiliated with the Coordinadora, received a telephone call from a man who greeted her with the words: "Hello, Angélica, I hope you enjoy your birthday, since its going to be your last!" This was one of a series of intimidating telephone calls and encounters with strangers experienced by Matías and members of her family, which began in February. Matías had suffered similar threats repeatedly during 1995. In some of the incidents, individuals claiming to be members of the National Intelligence Service (Servicio de Inteligencia Nacional, SIN) were involved.

The Role of
the International Community

United Nations
The U.N. Human Rights Committee, which monitors states' compliance with the International Covenant on Civil and Political Rights (to which Peru is state party) held hearings on Peru in New York and Geneva in 1996 and issued its "preliminary observations" on July 25. The committee's report categorically condemned Peru's amnesty law, saying it "prevents appropriate investigation and punishment of perpetrators of past human rights violations, undermines efforts to establish respect for human rights, contributes to an atmosphere of impunity among perpetrators of human rights violations, and constitutes a very serious impediment to efforts undertaken to consolidate democracy and promote respect for human rights and is thus in violation of article 2 of the Covenant..."

The committee also expressed "its deepest concern" about the laws which set up the faceless courts, which it said "seriously impair the protection of the rights contained in the Covenant for persons accused of terrorism..."

United States
Washington's human rights policy toward Peru evolved from "quiet diplomacy" to a warm embrace, a shift unwarranted by the limited improvements undertaken in Lima. U.S. officials increasingly spoke of close and improving relations with the Fujimori government, and almost never publicly raised human rights issues. In October, the Fujimori government used the visit of Gen. Barry McCaffrey, director of the White House Office of National Drug Control Policy, to launder the image of its scandal-ridden intelligence chief, Vladimiro Montesinos. U.S. officials took insufficient steps to publicly distance themselves from Montesinos during McCaffrey's visit, even while the press characterized his meetings with Montesinos as a gesture of support..

Montesinos, an advisor to SIN, which he is widely believed to control, reportedly worked for the Central Intelligence Agency. Montesinos had been repeatedly linked to an intelligence agency death squad responsible for serious human rights violations. In August, a drug kingpin on trial in Lima accused him of extorting large sums to enable the trafficker to transfer drugs without problems. Government officials promptly closed ranks around Montesinos and announced that there would be no investigation of the allegations. Human Rights Watch/Americas and the Washington Office on Latin America wrote to U.S. National Security Advisor Anthony Lake in September pressing for a public termination of any relationship the administration maintained with Montesinos. As of this writing, Lake had not responded.

In December 1995, the arrest and summary trial by a faceless military court of a U.S. citizen, Lori Helene Berenson, gave the U.S. a golden opportunity to make a forceful intervention regarding the abusiveness of faceless military courts. Berenson, who was linked by police to a plan by the Túpac Amaru Revolutionary Movement (MRTA) to kidnap parliamentarians, was convicted of treason and sentenced on January 11 to life imprisonment. The Department of State's acting spokesperson Glyn Davies stated on that day that "the United States deeply regrets that Ms. Berenson was not tried in an open civilian court with full rights of legal defense, in accordance with international juridical norms...[T]he United States remains concerned that Ms. Berenson receive due process. We have repeatedly expressed these concerns to the Government of Peru..." This statement stood out during a year otherwise marked by an absence of public criticism of the faceless courts by the U.S. government, and perhaps because it was unique, it had no discernible effect. Washington's plea for an open judicial hearing in a civilian court fell on deaf ears, and all Berenson's appeals were exhausted in secret hearings.

While the administration maintained an imperceptible profile on human rights issues, it increased security assistance to Peru aimed at combating narcotics. The administration spent approximately US$10 million in support of anti-narcotics efforts by Peru's police and air force in Fiscal Year 1996, and will spend a similar amount in Fiscal Year 1997. At the end of the 1996 fiscal year, President Clinton directed an additional $13.75 million worth of military equipment to the police and air force.

The Clinton administration deserved to be commended for using United States Agency for International Development (AID) funds to support human rights work in Peru, and especially legal aid for prisoners unjustly accused of terrorism. The U.S. contributed AID funds to four human rights groups that specialize in legal defense, including a legal team assembled by Father Hubert Lanssiers for the express purpose of defending innocent prisoners. This program, administered by Catholic Relief Services, has taken up 1,078 cases since the program began in 1995 and obtained the release of 274 prisoners, according to official AID statistics made available to Human Rights Watch/Americas in May. AID also contributed $50,000 to the office of the human rights ombudsman.

VENEZUELA

Human Rights Developments

Venezuela's police captured the attention of national and international human rights groups during 1996 for the brutality with which they carried out their work. System-

atic and widespread human rights violations, including torture and extrajudicial executions, were common, while impunity for the state agents responsible remained pervasive. As security forces acted abusively during the year, convicted criminals and detainees awaiting trial suffered prison conditions that violated international standards.

As of this writing, according to Venezuelan human rights organizations, state security forces committed at least 103 extrajudicial executions during the first ten months of 1996, and the number of torture cases increased over prior years. The La Poma Bakery (Panadería La Poma) case highlighted the brutality and impunity with which the Metropolitan Police of Caracas (Policía Metropolitana, PM) operated. After being called to the scene of a robbery on June 17, seven members of the PM, in the presence of witnesses and television cameras, arrested two suspected criminals. Hours later their corpses appeared at the Caracas morgue. The Criminal Court of First Instance issued an arrest warrant for the police officers involved in the operation. The Superior Court later revoked the order on the grounds that there was insufficient evidence. The higher court reasoned that, despite evidence that the police committed the killings, no one could be held responsible because the specific officers who had done so had not been identified. In another case involving Caracas police, this time in the city's Sucre municipality, officers working in the 24 de Julio neighborhood of Caracas detained José Luis Pimentel, whom they accused of being a criminal. According to the Network in Support of Justice and Peace (La Red de Apoyo por la Justicia y la Paz), municipal police officers detained him and took him to an alley, where they shot him to death. The Network in Support of Justice and Peace reported that he was arrested while playing chess and that his neighbors denied that the death followed an armed confrontation, as the police asserted.

Local human rights groups documented repeated violations in Apure state, along Venezuela's border with Colombia. The

Guasdualito-based Human Rights Defense Committee (Comité para la Defensa de los Derechos Humanos, CODEHUM) published a report in July documenting forty-seven cases, including such abuses as torture. On January 21, for example, officers of the Technical Judicial Police (Policía Técnica Judicial, PTJ) detained José Anicasio Rojas at his home outside the city of Guasdualito, transferring him to the PTJ station, where they blindfolded, handcuffed, and beat him. They tortured him by placing a plastic bag over his head. In Guasdualito, on February 19, Víctor A. Díaz Ojeda was detained and accused by the National Guard (Guardia Nacional, GN) and army of being a member of a Colombian guerrilla group. He was brought to the local military base, where he was tied to a tree, blindfolded, and tortured with electric current to his testicles. Similarly, GN officers detained Josué Coburuco and Gerardo Vargas on February 20 in the town of El Amparo. Accused of cattle rustling, and turned over to the army, they were tortured with electric current.

Indigenous peoples who lived along Venezuela's border with Colombia or Brazil also suffered human rights violations. The situation was especially serious in the states of Zulia, Amazonas, Bolívar, and Delta Amacuro. In the area of San Fernando de Atabapo, Amazonas state, members of the Baniba, Curripaco, Piaroa, and Puinabe ethnic communities frequently reported to local human rights groups that state security forces arbitrarily detained and mistreated them. For example, in January, Durifa Da Silva, an indigenous man from the community of Guarinuma, was arrested by police. The officers handcuffed and harshly beat him, then left him with serious bruises, on the banks of the Atabapo river.

Impunity for such abuses remained a serious problem. Four years after the bodyguards of then-President Carlos Andrés Pérez assassinated two Wayuú Indians in Zulia state, military and civilian courts continued to argue over jurisdiction, contributing to an unwarranted delay in the case. Similarly, more than three years after a massacre at Haximú, Amazonas state, in which sixteen Yanomami Indians were killed by Brazilian prospectors, the government had not undertaken an investigation, much less prosecuted those responsible. In September, the Inter-American Court of Human Rights ordered Venezuela to pay compensation for its responsibility in massacring fourteen fishermen in El Amparo in 1988, a case that the Venezuelan courts had failed to clarify. The Inter-American Commission on Human Rights, which forwarded the case to the court, found that the killings were carried out by a joint operation of the army, the PTJ, and the Office of Intelligence and Prevention Services (Dirección de Inteligencia y Servicios de Prevención, DISIP). The Venezuelan government did not contest the facts.

While the police and military acted brutally throughout the year, detainees faced abusive conditions in prison. Built to hold a population of just over 15,000 people, the prison system was jammed with 24,000 prisoners during 1996. Notoriously poor conditions led Human Rights Watch/Americas to send a delegation to the country in March 1996 to inspect eleven prisons. This trip was followed by a mission of the Inter-American Commission on Human Rights.

The extreme overcrowding, exacerbated by severe understaffing, inadequate material support, and violence, meant that the majority of Venezuela's prisoners were forced to endure appalling and degrading living conditions, in violation of the International Covenant on Civil and Political Rights and the American Convention on Human Rights, which established Venezuela's responsibility to treat inmates with dignity. Inmates routinely slept two or three to a bed, on the floor in passageways, or in filthy bathrooms. In Sabaneta prison, for instance, some inmates slept in hammocks strung in narrow pipe-access passageways between cell blocks.

Official violence against prisoners was also common. The GN maintained harsh control of a number of prisons, frequently engaging in collective punishment or arbitrary beatings of prisoners. The most violent incident involving the GN occurred on October 22. Early in the morning, National Guardsmen started a fire in La Planta prison in Caracas that killed at least twenty-five prisoners. Officers indiscriminately fired tear gas and incendiary devices into overcrowded cells of the prison's Ward 4. Prisoners who could not escape the cells, which were locked, burned to death. Venezuela's minister of justice reportedly described the attack as an "unjustifiable crime" and insisted that the responsible guardsmen be punished for their actions.

The large majority of inmates in Venezuela were pre-trial detainees, who were held with convicted prisoners. This resulted from Venezuela's extremely long criminal proceedings and systematic denial of provisional liberty to defendants awaiting trial, in violation of international standards that established Venezuela's responsibility to provide prompt trials.

Women prisoners, who constituted nearly 5 percent of the prison population, generally enjoyed somewhat better conditions than male inmates. With some notable exceptions, women's facilities tended to be newer, less overcrowded, and better maintained than men's installations, with proportionally larger staffs, less violence, and greater work and recreational opportunities. In the prison of Ciudad Bolívar, however, the women's annex was integrated into the larger men's facility, so that some fifty women prisoners were confined together with over 1,000 male prisoners.

Women prisoners also faced discrimination. While men were freely granted conjugal visits, women prisoners, except for a handful participating in a pilot program, were denied them.

The Right to Monitor

Human Rights Watch/Americas was not aware of cases of physical attacks on Venezuelan human rights monitors. Nonetheless, several incidents reflected official intolerance of human rights reporting and activism. This intolerance showed itself in the form of public criticism, part of a broader effort to discredit the work of nongovernmental organizations.

On several occasions government authorities labeled human rights monitors as criminals interested in spoiling Venezuela's international image. In this same vein, the government rejected the Venezuela section of the State Department's *Country Reports on Human Rights Practices for 1995*, stating that it was a "caricature" of the actual situation. The government also called into question the information provided to the State Department by Venezuelan human rights organizations.

Venezuela also rejected the findings of an Amnesty International report. Minister of the Presidency Asdrúbal Aguiar stated that the Amnesty International document was partial and based on biased methodology. Aguiar also sought to discredit the work of Venezuelan human rights organizations, whom he said provided Amnesty International with information "geared exclusively to placing blame on the Caldera administration."

The Role of the United States

U.S. Embassy officials in Venezuela maintained regular contact with Venezuelan human rights organizations, which was reflected in the Venezuela section of *Country Reports on Human Rights Practices for 1995*. The report presented an accurate description of human rights conditions in the country. Human Rights Watch/Americas was unaware, however, of any public statements from the embassy condemning human rights violations when they occurred during 1996.

The State Department's International Narcotics and Law Enforcement (INL) bureau disbursed US$500,000 to Venezuela during 1996, roughly the same as the preceding year. In an effort to assist Venezuela in the process of reforming its Code of Criminal Procedure, the United States Information Agency (USIA) sponsored training seminars for judges and prosecutors.

HUMAN
RIGHTS
WATCH

ASIA

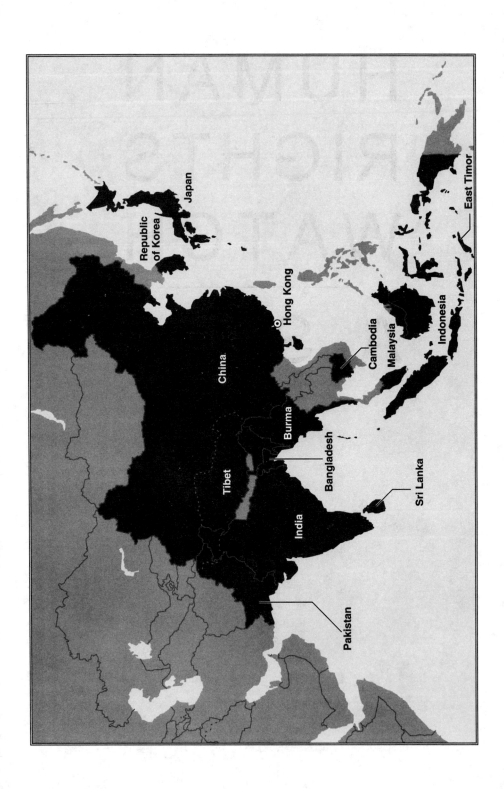

HUMAN RIGHTS WATCH/ASIA OVERVIEW

Human Rights Developments

In terms of human rights, Asia in 1996 was marked by major setbacks, minor progress and much unfinished business. On the one hand, there was an obvious deterioration of the human rights situation in Burma, Cambodia, China, and Indonesia. In addition to the arrest of over 1,000 supporters of the democracy movement in Burma during the year, forced labor and forced relocations in Burma's eastern provinces led to a massive exodus of refugees and migrants to Thailand. China's particularly harsh treatment of democracy advocates like Wei Jingsheng, serving a fourteen-year prison sentence, and Wang Dan, a former student leader who "disappeared" in 1995 only to surface in custody and be formally tried and sentenced to eleven years in prison on subversion charges in October 1996, were part of a more systematic effort to crush the political opposition. At the same time, China's arrests of busiess and banking executives during the year demonstrated that arbitrary detention was not restricted to political activists.

The utter disregard for the rule of law by Chinese authorities, even as some legal reforms were undertaken, did not bode well for Hong Kong and its transition to Chinese rule in 1997. Many activists in Hong Kong were already concerned by Chinese government statements and actions that signaled strict controls of the press and of political participation after the transition. In Indonesia, dozens of student activists under the age of thirty faced trial and certain conviction on political charges for taking part a nonviolent leftist political organization that the Soeharto government, with no evidence, charged with masterminding serious riots in Jakarta, the capital, in July.

If the level of state repression was high during the year, the demand from Asian citizens for basic civil liberties was greater than ever. If 1988 was the year of the pro-democracy movement for Burma, 1989 for China, 1990 for Nepal, 1992 for Thailand, 1993 for Cambodia, and 1995 for Hong Kong, 1996 was a banner year for Taiwan and Indonesia. The elections in Taiwan in March, in which 14,000,000 Taiwanese voters for the first time chose their president by direct and secret ballot after an open and lively campaign, was a stunning refutation of the "Asian values" argument that Asians care more about strong, efficient government than about popular participation. The elections also demonstrated that there was nothing inherently incompatible about Confucian cultural traditions and respect for civil liberties. The Indonesian democracy movement developed a new cohesion with the formation of an independent election monitoring group in March and the demand for accountable leadership that led to mass support for Megawati Soekarnoputri, daughter of Indonesia's first president, as an alternative to President Soeharto.

Major human rights problems remained unresolved in the region. In Kashmir, despite the holding of elections in May and September and a reduction in the frequency of confrontation between the military and various groups of armed insurgents, the level of summary executions of suspected militants by Indian security forces remained high. In Sri Lanka, initial optimism that the government of Chandrika Kumartunga, which was largely supportive of human rights, would be able to prevent violations of humanitarian law as its army waged war against the Liberation Tigers of Tamil Eelam (LTTE), was waning at the end of the year. The LTTE, whose violations of a cease-fire in April 1995 led to the resumption of the war, was responsible for serious violations of humanitarian law in the territory it controlled. In Bangladesh, all political parties were responsible for widespread violence and civil strife prior to elections in February and June.

Religion frequently intersected with

human rights in Asia, often with negative consequences. The Chinese government saw Tibetan Buddhism, Christianity, Islam, and millenarian sects, for different reasons, as serious threats to the legitimacy of the Communist Party and intensified efforts to regulate all. Clashes between Muslims and Christians, originating in unsolved political conflict and unprosecuted human rights abuses, erupted in East Timor in June as they had in 1995. A rash of church-burnings in Java in June, September and October, that the government failed to prevent, and the efforts, with clear communal overtones, of the Indonesian army in August to whip up anti-communist sentiment among Muslim groups following the arrest of members of a student leftist party, all suggested that the much-vaunted reputation of the Indonesian government for religious tolerance needed to be reconsidered. The taking of Kabul by the Muslim militia calling themselves Taliban or "students" signaled a period of grave discrimination against women; the group's seizure of former Prime Minister Najibullah from a U.N. compound and the subsequent torture and execution of Najibullah and his aides boded ill for human rights in Afghanistan. In Burma, the ruling State Law and Order Restoration Council persisted in a pattern of discrimination and abuse against the Muslim Rohingya minority in Arakan, in the north of the country.

At the same time, the fact that Bishop Carlos Ximenes Belo of East Timor received the Nobel Peace Prize was recognition of the critically important role religious figures can play as protectors of human rights. And there was some progress toward prosecuting communal violence in India, with the reinstatement of a commission looking into the role of the police in Hindu-Muslim riots in Bombay in 1993. In September, one Hindu man was prosecuted and convicted for killing two Sikhs in the course of a massacre of over 3,000 Sikhs in Delhi in 1984 in which police and ruling party officials took an active role; it was the first such conviction in relation to that massacre.

Several regional issues came to international attention during the year. The problems of migrant workers in Malaysia—Bangladeshis, Indonesians and Filipinas in particular—were highlighted with the trial beginning in June of Irene Fernandez, a Malaysian human rights activist charged with "false reporting" for her efforts to document abuses of migrants in Malaysian immigration detention centers. If her trial represented the efforts of one part of the Malaysian government to silence public criticism of the problem, other parts of the government took constructive steps during the year to curb abusive practices of labor recruiters.

Thailand's cabinet, in part because of pressure from a labor-starved business community, adopted a resolution in July giving temporary legal status, and therefore protection of some Thai labor laws, to almost 900,000 illegal migrant workers, mostly from Burma, Laos and Cambodia. But that welcome development was offset by the failure of the Thai government to crack down on illegal recruiters sending Thais, many of them women, to Japan and other countries. Of all the human rights issues in Southeast Asia, migration was one of the few on which systematic talks at an intergovernmental were taking place, both among national human rights commissions, within the Association of Southeast Asian Nations (ASEAN) and at a bilateral level between foreign and labor ministers of sending and receiving countries. In the Human Resources Development Working Group of the Asia Pacific Economic Cooperation forum (APEC), on the other hand, there was strong resistance to addressing the problem of migrant laborers, despite attempts by the Philippines government to get it on the agenda.

Bonded labor continued to be a major issue in South Asia. Both India and Pakistan failed to enforce laws prohibiting bonded labor, but in both countries, local nongovernmental organizations (NGOs) had produced a range of recommendations for governments and donor agencies for the identification and rehabilitation of bonded laborers, particularly children, and there was some prospect of greater international scrutiny of government enforcement procedures.

Another regional human rights issue, that of the Vietnamese boat people spread among camps in Malaysia, Hong Kong, the Philippines and Indonesia, came to a violent close at the end of the year with the formal end of the Comprehensive Plan of Action, the multilateral plan for repatriation and resettlement of Vietnamese asylum seekers, on June 30. As first-asylum countries rushed to close down their camps, their security forces often used disproportionate force against Vietnamese resisting forced return, although the resistance itself was often violent. Incidents of excessive force occurred throughout the first-asylum countries, including the January shooting death of one Vietnamese in Sungai Besi, Malaysia and the beatings of Vietnamese in Palawan, Philippines in February. Detention conditions for Vietnamese in Hong Kong continued to be a major concern, where some of the camps were expected to remain open in 1997 despite stepped-up efforts to repatriate those remaining. In a humanitarian move that could have been a model for other first-asylum countries, the Philippines in August permitted the remaining 1,000 Vietnamese to integrate locally.

Domestic and international advocacy efforts forced the issue of trafficking of Asian women and children for prostitution onto the agenda of governments in the region. In August, for example, Thailand announced a ten-year plan, the "National Policy and Plan of Action for the Prevention and Eradication of the Commercial Sexual Exploitation of Children," distributed at a world conference on the subject in Stockholm. While welcome, the plan focused only on those under eighteen, leaving the problems of older victims unaddressed, and it was not clear how implementation would proceed. The plan, however, gave too little attention to the prosecution of traffickers and promoters of commercial sex. Thailand has been a center of trafficking for prostitution, with Burmese and Chinese women trafficked into the country, and Thai women trafficked out.

One other development in the region was worth noting. Increased access by human rights organizations and pro-democracy activists to the Internet facilitated international advocacy campaigns on everything from Burma to bonded labor, but Asian governments for the most part treated the Internet with great suspicion. In January, the State Council in China issued a draft set of rules to regulate use of the Internet; subscribers were ordered to provide a written guarantee that they would not use the Internet for purposes "harmful to the state." In September, Chinese authorities deployed sophisticated technology to block subscriber access to as many as one hundred English and Chinese sites on the World Wide Web. In June, the South Korean government warned that the draconian National Security Law could be applied to attempts to circulate material about North Korea on personal computers; the warning came after a local newspaper carried an article on a Canadian Web page with a picture of Kim Jong Il, the North Korean leader. In July, Singapore announced a new licensing system designed to regulate the Internet and censor any material that might "undermine public morals, political stability and religious harmony." On September 4, the ASEAN countries announced an agreement to collectively regulate communication on the Internet. In the same month, Burma issued a new law which entailed a fifteen-year sentence for anyone importing, purchasing or using modems or fax machines without governmental permission. No known restrictions were placed on the use of the Internet in South Asia.

The Right to Monitor

Human rights organizations continued to be effectively banned in—and international human rights organizations banned from—North Korea, Burma, Vietnam, Brunei, Bhutan, and China/Tibet. In China, however, university-based legal aid organizations took on some functions of rights protection. Singapore had no human rights organizations operating freely in the country, but access to the country by international organizations was not a problem. Human rights monitoring continued to be a dangerous profession during the year, with two monitors killed in India: Kashmiri human rights lawyer Jalil Andrabi was abducted by Indian security forces and murdered in March, while Parag Kumar Das, an editor and activist from Assam, was killed in May. Fernando Reyes, a human rights lawyer, was killed in Zamboanga del Sur, the Philippines, and Kalpana Chakma, secretary of a women's organization in the Chittagong Hill Tracts, Bangladesh, was abducted by army gunmen in June and not seen thereafter. In Burma, twenty-one political prisoners who had attempted to send information about prison conditions to the U.N.'s special rapporteur on the country were beaten and given additional sentences of five and twelve years. In Indonesia, Cambodia, Malaysia, Pakistan and Nepal, human rights monitors faced various degrees of persecution and harassment.

National human rights commissions in the Philippines, India, and Indonesia continued to play an important role despite restrictions in their mandates, particularly in the case of the latter two. India's commission focused national attention on the problem of custodial violence; it was far less successful in raising concerns about abuses by security forces in Kashmir or the northeast. The Indonesian commission helped bring about prosecutions of soldiers in several key incidents during the year and issued a brief but stinging report on the government-backed storming of opposition party headquarters that led to the Jakarta riots in July

The year saw increasing joint action of NGOs across national boundaries, especially on Burma. From May 1 to 17, the Bangkok-based NGO coalition, Asian Forum for Human Rights and Development, sent a delegation of two Thais and two Filipinas to Burma to investigate human rights abuses. In a report issued from Manila in July, the group called on ASEAN countries to ban aid and investment and ban Burma from membership in ASEAN. At the trial of Irene Fernandez in Malaysia, international observers from Indonesia and Bangladesh as well as the United States were in attendance. In February and March, NGOs in Nepal hosted a series of meetings which brought together hundreds of Asian activists to coordinate advocacy on wide range of human rights concerns, from labor rights, the environment, health, and development, to protection of civil society and conflict resolution. November saw one of the largest gatherings of Asian human rights organizations for a regional meeting since the 1993 Asian preparatory conference for the Vienna World Conference on Human Rights, as hundreds of groups convened in Manila in conjunction with the APEC summit. Labor rights issues were high on the agenda.

The Role of the International Community

Security and commercial concerns dominated the international agenda in Asia throughout 1996, and most governments saw pressure on human rights concerns as jeopardizing those interests. The European Union held its first E.U.-Asia summit meeting in Bangkok in early March, at which the phrase "human rights" was barely mentioned. The U.S. maintained its low profile on human rights concerns in South Asia, with the exception of the child labor issue. Ensuring continued access to Asian markets and maintaining existing investments there were far more important to the industrialized countries than challenging Beijing, sanctioning Rangoon, conditioning Korea's entry into the Organization for Economic Cooperation and Development (OECD) on labor rights improvements, or protesting crackdowns on the political opposition in Indonesia.

As the World Trade Organization (WTO) prepared to hold its first ministerial meeting inDecember in Singapore, Asian NGOs debated the pros and cons of trying to include in the WTO Charter a "social clause"— a way of linking trade benefits to adherence to basic labor rights standards. Asian governments were virtually united in their opposition to an effort led by the U.S. and France to set up a working group on labor and environmental standards at the

Singapore meeting that would address many of the concerns raised by social clause proponents. The issue was also expected to be debated in the margins of the APEC summit in Manila in late November.

United Nations

The United Nations was much more visible as a human rights presence in Asia than in previous years. The Geneva-based U.N. Human Rights Centre continued to maintain an office in Cambodia, and its term was extended for another two years in an agreement between the center and the Cambodian government. Justice Michael Kirby stepped down as the special representative for human rights in Cambodia and was replaced by Thomas Hammarberg, former secretary-general of Amnesty International.

In July, Louis Joinet, head of the Working Group on Arbitrary Detention, visited China to begin discussions about the possibility of a more in-depth visit by the working group in 1997. Special Rapporteur on Torture Nigel Rodley visited Pakistan in February, but his effort to obtain permission from Indonesia to investigate torture in East Timor was unsuccessful. In Burma, a new special rapporteur was appointed by the Commission on Human Rights to replace Prof. Yozo Yokota, but as of November, State Law and Order Restoration Council (SLORC) had not permitted the new appointee, Rajsoomer Lallah from Mauritius, to visit.

No new ratifications of major U.N. conventions on human rights took place during the year, but a campaign was underway in Indonesia among NGOs and the government-appointed National Human Rights Commission for ratification of the Convention Against Torture and Other Cruel, Inhuman or Degrading Treatment or Punishment. The hearings in Geneva of the U.N. Committee on the Rights of the Child drew international attention to abuses against children in China and Burma, and in October, the hearing of the Human Rights Committee on the compliance of the United Kingdom with its obligations under the International Covenant on Civil and Political Rights, par-

ticularly with respect to Hong Kong, was a useful means of raising international concern about China's determination to avoid such reporting once Hong Kong returns to Chinese control in 1997. China also submitted a report to the U.N. Committee Against Torture on the steps it had taken to prevent torture. The report was used by NGOs to focus on the steps China had *not* taken and on the ongoing problem of torture in Chinese prisons.

The U.N. Human Rights Commission in Geneva suffered a severe blow to its credibility and effectiveness when, during its April 1996 session, the Chinese government used commercial threats and blandishments to block any discussion or vote on a resolution expressing concern about human rights abuses in China and Tibet.

Association of South East Asian Nations

The ASEAN ministerial conference in Jakarta in July, and the expanded ASEAN Regional Forum (ARF)—a forum for discussion of security issues, which included India, China, and Burma (as an observer)—resulted in a standoff on strategy toward Burma. ASEAN reaffirmed its commitment to "constructive engagement" despite pressure from mostly western countries to use its influence to bring more pressure to bear on SLORC to improve its human rights practices. Later in the year, however, as conditions in Burma further deteriorated, a growing split emerged within ASEAN over how to deal with Burma and how soon to grant it membership.

European Union

Human rights proved a particularly thorny issue in European-Asian relations. In March, as noted, Bangkok hosted the first E.U.-Asia summit, widely seen as an attempt by European leaders to use the APEC model to involve Europe more closely in the economic dynamism of East and Southeast Asia. The meeting involved twenty-five heads of state, and the only human rights issue that surfaced was East Timor, when the Portugese prime minister and Indonesian President Soeharto held bilateral talks. Some key E.U. countries, including France and Germany, apparently used the meeting to find a formula for avoiding sponsorship of a resolution criticizing China's human rights reccord at the U.N. human rights commission. When foreign ministers of many of the same European countries met their ASEAN counterparts in July in Jakarta, they were roundly criticized for focusing too much on human rights issues, particularly on Burma and East Timor.

Japan
Japan continued to play a cautious role on human rights in the region, using the leverage of granting, suspending or resuming Official Development Assistance (ODA) to advance human rights concerns only in the case of Burma, while security issues were the clear priority in its bilateral relations with China. This was also the case in South Asia, where Japanese authorities engaged India on nuclear discussions but refrained from directly addressing specific human rights problems such as Kashmir. Tokyo asserted its role as the world's leading aid donor by hosting, together with the World Bank, two international donor consortiums in 1996, on Cambodia and India.

Donors and Investors
The World Bank and the Asian Development Bank made little demonstrable progress in 1996 toward implementing their respective "good governance" policies, although the World Bank did show some interest in addressing the bonded child labor issue, especially in India.

Demands for increased corporate responsibility in Asia in terms of protecting human rights increased both domestically and internationally. The demands on footwear manufacturers, such as Nike, and mining companies, such as Freeport-McMoRan, both of which have operations in Indonesia, were particularly public. Light export-oriented industries, such as the manufacture of textiles, garments, and toys, and other industries such carpet-weaving, became more sensitized to the issues of child labor and worker rights abuses. In Burma, international investment became the target of selective purchasing legislation in several U.S. cities and states and of consumer boycott campaigns in other western countries, leading to the withdrawal of several companies from Burma. Apple Computers and Heineken were among those that pulled out. In some cases, companies responded with either cosmetic gestures or more serious efforts to monitor their own operations, but few were willing to work with local or international NGOs to assist in carrying out social audits or monitoring of internal guidelines, and the lack of transparency and accountability by the private sector remained a key obstacle to enhanced corporate responsibility.

An important emerging issue for the business community was the upcoming transfer of Hong Kong in July 1997, and how foreign investors would respond to human rights developments after the transfer. As the year ended, some U.S. business interests were already playing a positive role by sending clear signals to Beijing on the importance of maintaining the rule of law, protecting free expression, and stopping the spread of corruption from the mainland to Hong Kong.

The Work of Human Rights Watch/Asia
The year was marked by new initiatives on both research and advocacy, while Human Rights Watch/Asia continued to follow up on past work. On countries with strong NGOs, we worked with local groups to set priorities: bonded labor and migrant labor in South and Southeast Asia became research priorities in this way. But even in countries with no human rights organizations, such as China and Burma, the scope of our work widened beyond the traditional and ongoing concerns of arbitrary detention, torture and violations of freedom of expression and association. A major study of abuses in China's orphanages during the year sparked international outrage and provided new insights

into how the impact of a repressive state apparatus can reach beyond political and religious dissidents to touch the country's most vulnerable citizens—abandoned, orphaned and handicapped children—in a way that violated the most fundamental human rights. With regard to Burma, a report released in September on the human rights violations suffered by the Rohingya Muslim minority served as a follow-up to two earlier reports on that issue, but in focusing as much on repatriation and protection of returned refugees as on abuses inside Burma per se, it provided a new way of examining the problem. It also provided new opportunities to seek accountability from the Burmese government, including through international humanitarian and development agencies.

We continued to respond swiftly to particularly grave cases of abuse, issuing press statements and briefing materials, appealing to U.N. bodies, or meeting with officials of donor governments as the case warranted. The massive arrests in Burma in May and September, the crackdown on student and labor activists in Indonesia in August and September, and the formal indictment and trial of Chinese dissident Wang Dan in October were all occasions for emergency interventions. Likewise, whenever Asian human rights monitors abroad were attacked, we responded immediately, as in our protests over the killing of Kashmiri lawyer Jalil Andrabi in March and our decision to send a series of observers to the trial of Malaysian activist Irene Fernandez in Kuala Lumpur.

Hong Kong received particular attention during the year, as the transition to Chinese sovereignty approached in 1997. Our office in Hong Kong continued its emphasis on China, but staff also worked with local monitoring groups to generate more international attention to the steps taken by China that had or were expected to have deleterious effects on civil liberties.

While our research output was considerable in 1996—ten short reports, four book-length reports, two of them in collaboration with the Human Rights Watch Children's

Rights Project (CRP)—we devoted an equal amount of staff time and resources to advocacy efforts. An example was the campaign on bonded child labor in India, based on the report *The Small Hands of Slavery*, issued in September. The report itself involved three months of intensive research. When it was ready for publication, we undertook a process of detailed consultation with our Indian colleagues on the policy recommendations and on plans for follow-up. We then sent letters summarizing the recommendations to the key donor governments and agencies attending the annual meeting on development assistance chaired by the World Bank, which convened in Tokyo in September. We also discussed the issue with Japanese Foreign Ministry officials in advance of the meeting. Responses from several agencies including the World Bank suggested that some of the recommendations could be incorporated when projects to support industries known to employ bonded child labor, such as sericulture, came up for renewal. The report was used as evidence by local NGOs in Tamil Nadu in a case before the Supreme Court to abolish bonded labor in that state. A joint campaign of local, regional and international NGOs to eradicate the practice of bonded labor was expected to continue well into 1997.

Asia was a major focus of work at the U.N. during the year. We joined with other NGOs in lobbying for a resolution criticizing Burma's human rights record at the U.N. Commission on Human Rights, which ultimately succeeded. Despite the best efforts of our New York, Washington, Brussels and Hong Kong offices, however, and those of many activists worldwide, a resolution on China failed to come to a vote. In the course of intensive press work and discussions with European Union members on the China resolution, however, the Brussels office managed to secure a resolution from the European Parliament that helped force the E.U. countries at the commission to take a stronger position than they would have otherwise; that action provided a useful basis for further European lobbying on China. We raised several Asian issues in written submissions at the U.N. Human Rights Commission meeting in Geneva in April, including abuses in Chinese orphanages, concerns about trafficking of women from Burma to Thailand, and concerns about migrant workers in Asia. Staff submitted evidence on Burma at the hearing on the Committee on the Rights of the Child. In July, as in previous years, we submitted a petition on human rights abuses in East Timor to the U.N. Committee on Decolonization, noting that any discussion of East Timor's political status must be informed by an understanding of the pattern of human rights violations there.

The Washington, London and Brussels offices played key advocacy roles during the year. Human Rights Watch gave evidence on forced labor in Burma before the European Commission in Brussels and testified before the U.S. Congress four times on China and once each on Hong Kong, Indonesia/East Timor, and Pakistan. We also testified before the U.S. government's Presidential Commission on U.S.-Pacific Trade and Investment Policy. Through our Washington office, we maintained close and regular contact with embassies of Asian countries as well as with the World Bank, U.S. government agencies and the U.S. Congress. In July, a staff member traveled to Tokyo to meet with government officials, members of parliament, NGOs, journalists and others to continue a dialogue on human rights issues in the region and Japan's official human rights policy. We also published op-eds in Japanese newspapers during the year, as well as providing information about human rights concerns through other articles in the regional press.

In sum, the year in Asia was marked by increasing cooperation of local, regional and international NGOs, especially on issues such as labor rights and women's rights. Arbitrary detention and punishment of peaceful dissent continued to be major problems in countries where NGOs were not allowed to function, but condemnation of these practices from NGOs and governments in other Asian countries was increasingly common. The

political manipulation of religion by governments and opposition groups in many Asian countries raised the spectre of communal conflict in the years to come. Among donor countries and trading partners of Asian countries, business concerns continued to overshadow human rights, and the fear of losing contracts became a powerful incentive for many countries to avoid criticism of human rights abuses.

BANGLADESH

Human Rights Developments
Political violence among Bangladesh's major political parties dominated events in 1996 and led to widespread human rights abuses. A mid-year election ended the immediate crisis, but because authorities failed to disarm party cadres and prosecute leaders responsible for inciting the violence, it erupted again within a few weeks, although on a smaller scale. The conflict over land in the Chittagong Hill Tracts continued to take a toll on civilians as both the Bangladesh government forces and the guerrilla army, Shanti Bahini, carried out indiscriminate attacks. Army troops were also believed responsible for the "disappearance" of human rights activist Kalpana Chakma in June.

The political crisis stemmed from a long-standing dispute between the governing Bangladesh National Party (BNP) and the opposition, led by the Awami (People's) League, over charges of government corruption and vote-rigging. On November 25, 1995, after a yearlong boycott of parliament by the opposition, President Abdur Rahman Biswas dissolved parliament. Fresh legislative polls were announced for February 15, 1996, but all of the opposition parties pledged to boycott the polls unless Prime Minister Zia resigned beforehand; in the weeks leading up to the elections, they stepped up their campaign of strikes and street protests to force the government to accede to their demands. As the February vote approached, the political deadlock erupted in violence as supporters, youth wings and student fronts of all political parties battled with each other, and opposition groups fought with police, paramilitary Bangladesh Rifles (BDR)—both under the control of the Home Affairs Ministry—and the army, which had been called in by the election commission to retrieve illegal arms ahead of the election.

On February 4, still before the vote, at least 200 uniformed soldiers armed with guns and batons conducted indiscriminate raids in Charsayedpur village, taking three villagers into custody, rounding up and interrogating scores of others, and beating at least 200 residents, including women and children. The detainees were beaten and tortured with electric shocks. To Human Rights Watch's knowledge, the soldiers responsible were never prosecuted. In another incident, on January 31, 1996, some 150 students were injured and about ninety-five arrested as police, backed by BDR troops, raided Jagannath Hall, Dhaka University's dormitory for religious minority students and a stronghold of the Awami League student wing. Approximately thirty students were hospitalized as a result of the police attack. The police raid followed an exchange of fire between pro-government and anti-government factions on the university campus.

The polls themselves were marred by violence among rival political factions, intimidation of voters, and attacks on polling centers by opposition activists and credible allegations against the ruling party of vote-rigging in the uncontested election. At a protest rally in front of the national Press Club in Dhaka prior to the election, a speaker from the Awami League warned, "Anyone who goes to vote will come back dead." On and immediately before election day, several hundred polling stations across the country were gutted by opposition militants. Nationwide, an estimated sixteen people were killed and 500 injured in violent incidents over the two weeks leading up to the polls, forcing authorities to postpone voting in some areas.

In several incidents during the weeks before and after the February 15 election,

journalists were assaulted, harassed or arrested either because of their suspected ties to the opposition, or because they were reporting on or photographing police shootings and other abuses. On February 10, a photojournalist for the Dhaka-based daily newspaper, *Janakantha*, was severely beaten by BDR troops when he attempted to take a picture of the family of a ten-year-old boy who had been detained. A reporter for the daily *Banglarbani* was also badly beaten, and both men had their cameras confiscated. Another photojournalist with the Dhaka-based daily *Ajker Kagoj* (*Daily News*), was beaten by police after taking photographs of a clash between violent Awami League supporters and the police. He sustained a deep wound to his head. On February 29, 1996, *Ajker Kagoj*'s chief reporter was arrested under the Special Powers Act—a law which provides for detention without charge. The arrest was apparently meant to put pressure the newspaper's editor, Kazi Shahid Ahmed, an outspoken critic of the government, who was in hiding. The reporter was released on bail on March 31.

Gross mistreatment of criminal suspects by both police and judiciary were a problem outside the political sphere as well. In one case, Vladimir Lankin, a Russian citizen, remained on trial for the third straight year in 1996 on criminal charges. Neither the fact that he had been tortured into confessing by use of electric shock nor the illegal length of his trial moved the judge to speed sentencing; on the contrary, in mid-year, the judge himself caused an additional delay by taking a four-month "retraining" course. During the hiatus, Lankin's health deteriorated to the point that he had to be hospitalized.

The BNP won all but two of the 207 seats for which results were declared; new voting was ordered in the remaining ninety-three constituencies because of various irregularities and charges of vote-tampering. The opposition, led by Sheikh Hasina, declared the election "illegal" and organized strikes throughout the country to force a new election on its terms. On March 9 the opposition declared an indefinite non-cooperation movement that brought the economy to the brink of collapse. The country's emerging export-oriented garment-manufacturing industry suffered a heavy toll from lost production and from the closure of Chittagong port. In the first three months of 1996 alone, the fighting among supporters of rival parties, encounters between protestors and the police, BDR and army, and bomb and arson attacks by various political groups led to an estimated 120 deaths, thousands of casualties and widespread property damage.

Zia was sworn in as prime minister for a second term on March 19 while the opposition's non-cooperation movement gathered momentum. On March 28 thousands of civil servants staged a sit-in at the main government secretariat building in Dhaka, demanding the installation of a caretaker authority. On March 30, as the opposition prepared to orchestrate a siege of the presidential palace by thousands of supporters, President Biswas dissolved the newly-elected legislature and, as Zia stepped down, appointed ex-Chief Justice Habibur Rahman as chief adviser to head an interim government that presided over fresh national elections on June 12, 1996.

The polls were considered generally fair, although there were consistent reports of intimidation of the Hindu minority and in the Chittagong Hill Tracts, a largely tribal area. The vote brought the Awami League to power under Prime Minister Sheikh Hasina Wajed. Tensions between the new government and the army surfaced on August 13 when the government used the Special Powers Act to arrest three former army officers in connection with the 1975 assassination of Sheikh Hasina Wajed's father, former Prime Minister Sheikh Mujibur Rahman, and most of the members of his family.

Violence between rival student factions erupted again in August. On August 22 in Bogra, a clash left one student and one policeman dead. Police called in paramilitary units after students attacked a police station in Bogra on August 24. They opened fire on the students, some of whom were also allegedly firing guns; two students were killed. Prime Minister Hasina Wajed promised a judicial probe into the incidents. On August 25, after several days of student violence, hundreds of police raided residence halls at Dhaka University, arresting alleged outsiders and seizing numerous weapons. Opposition legislators staged a walkout of parliament denouncing "unprecedented police barbarity" against opposition students and supporters. September by-elections in several constituencies were also marked by violence, as the BNP raised uncorroborated allegations of vote-rigging.

In the Chittagong Hill Tracts, a low-intensity conflict continued between Bangladesh government forces and the Shanti Bahini, a guerrilla force that took up arms in 1973 after Bangladesh rejected their demand for autonomy and began settling Bengalis in the area. Officials say up to 8,000 soldiers, rebels and civilians have been killed in the protracted insurgency. Human rights groups have documented torture and extrajudicial executions of suspected Shanti Bahini supporters. These abuses and attacks by settlers drove thousands of tribal families to flee to northeast India. On August 14 the Tripura state government in India resumed the repatriation of 50,000 refugees. On September 11, Shanti Bahini militants killed thirty Bengali settlers, beheading most of them, in the Rangamati district of the Hill Tracts. Settlers' organizations vowed revenge.

In June, outspoken tribal rights activist Kalpana Chakma was abducted by unidentified gunmen and has not been heard from since. (See below.)

In August, protests broke out over a long-standing dispute between Bangladesh and Pakistan over the citizenship of Bengali-speaking residents of Pakistan who claim to be Bangladeshi, and Urdu-speaking "Biharis" in Bangladesh who claim to be Pakistani. Both countries deported "illegal" immigrants while failing to resolve the issue. On August 14, Pakistan's independence day, hundreds of "Biharis" scuffled with police in Dhaka, and a few tried to burn themselves alive to protest a delay in their repatriation to Pakistan.

The treatment of refugees from Burma remained a concern during the year. Bangladesh, though not a signatory to the U.N. Convention Relating to the Status of Refugees, became a member of the U.N. High Commissioner for Refugees (UNHCR) Executive Committee in 1995. This did not stop the government denying new arrivals the right to seek asylum. The strikes during February and March virtually halted all re-patriations of the remaining 50,000 Rohingya Muslims who had fled to Bangladesh in 1992. During this period, when interna-tional aid agencies and staff of the UNHCR were unable to travel to the refugee camps, there were reports of beatings and food dep-rivation in the two southernmost camps. By April several thousand new arrivals began entering Bangladesh, reporting an increase in forced labor and other abuses in Burma. (See section on Burma.) In an attempt to stem the flood, Bangladesh authorities jailed new arrivals or prevented them from reach-ing Bangladesh. In one incident in April, twenty-five asylum seekers, most of them women and children, drowned as their boat was being towed back to Burma by the Bangladesh Border Rifles. By the time the rains began in June, some 10,000 new arriv-als had entered Bangladesh. By the end of the year some 250 Rohingyas remained in appalling conditions in Cox's Bazaar jail (which had a capacity of one hundred) and the Bangladesh government continued to deny the UNHCR and nongovernmental or-ganizations access to all new arrivals, most of whom had taken shelter in the jungle.

The Right to Monitor
NGOs for the most part operated freely in Bangladesh. On the eve of the June 12 gen-eral elections, however, armed gunmen ab-ducted Kalpana Chakma, organizing secre-tary of the Hill Women's Federation, along with her two brothers, from their family home in New Lallyaghona village in Rangamati district. The gunmen attempted to shoot the two brothers, who managed to escape unhurt. One of Chakma's brothers identified Lieutenant Ferdous, an officer from

the Ugalchhari army camp, as one of the abductors. The army denied involvement in the kidnapping. As of November, there was no word on Chakma's whereabouts. In late August the government constituted a three-member committee to investigate the "disap-pearance" of Kalpana Chakma and identify the those responsible. The committee was also asked to propose suitable legal action and steps to prevent future incidents.

The Role of
the International Community
Bangladesh's donors expressed alarm at the country's slide into chaos in the early part of the year. The U.S. attempted without success to bring together the leaders of the BNP and Awami League to negotiate an end to the stalemate. Embassy personnel also privately expressed concern about the rising violence and electoral abuses during the February general elections. During the riots in Chittagong, the British ambassador visited several of the businesses destroyed or dam-aged by the mobs, and raised concerns with local authorities about the failure of the police to act promptly to protect citizens and property. A number of countries sent delega-tions to observe the June elections, including Japan, the European Union and the U.S.

Despite the violence committed by se-curity forces, arms transfers to Bangladesh from the U.S. and other governments contin-ued. In Fiscal Year 1996, the U.S. was esti-mated to provide US$4 million in foreign military sales, plus another $2.4 million in commercial sales, in addition to Interna-tional Military Education and Training (IMET) assistance budgeted at $250,000.

In July the Council of Europe approved a negotiating brief presented by the Euro-pean Commission to begin negotiations for trade and cooperation agreements with four Asian countries: Laos, Cambodia, Pakistan and Bangladesh. All agreements were to comprise a "human rights clause" whereby cooperation may be suspended in case of violations of human rights. On October 11, the European Commission announced that it was likely to start negotiations with

Bangladesh in early November. The agreement would seek to create a climate favorable to investment and exchanges between private sectors while strengthening the base for human rights. European negotiators announced that they expected some difficulties with the human rights clause.

BURMA

Human Rights Developments
Any hope that the July 1995 release of opposition leader and Nobel laureate Daw Aung San Suu Kyi might be a sign of human rights reforms by the ruling State Law and Order Restoration Council (SLORC) government were destroyed during 1996, as political arrests and repression dramatically increased, while forced labor, forced relocations, and arbitrary arrests continued to be the daily reality for millions of ordinary Burmese. The turn for the worse received little censure from Burma's neighbors, who instead took the first step toward granting the country full membership in the Association of South East Asian Nations (ASEAN) and welcomed SLORC as a member of the Asian Regional Forum, a security body.

Twice during the year there were mass arrests of opposition supporters. In June a new law was promulgated making even verbal criticism of the government an offense carrying a twenty-year sentence. Meanwhile in ethnic minority areas more than 85,000 people were forcibly evicted from their homes to military-run work camps or garrison towns. During the year U.N. Secretary-General Boutros Ghali's envoys were twice refused entry, and by October neither they nor the U.N. special rapporteur on Burma had received invitations to visit the country.

On November 28, 1995 the opposition National League for Democracy (NLD), led by Daw Aung San Suu Kyi, withdrew from the National Convention, condemning it as a "sham." (The convention had been set up by the government in 1993 to draft a new constitution.) The SLORC then banned the NLD

from returning, and the convention continued to meet despite having only seventeen elected representatives sitting with the 577 government-chosen delegates. It adjourned at the end of March and had not been recalled by the end of October. The NLD's boycott of the convention marked the beginning of a year-long confrontation between the SLORC and the NLD which led to the detention over 1,000 NLD supporters between November 1995 and October 1996. The majority of them were released after being detained for up to one month without charge, but more than eighty were still in custody by November, with half of those having received summary trials and sentences of seven to ten years. The true figure was almost certainly higher, as there was almost no information about those detained outside Rangoon.

On January 4, the NLD celebrated independence day in the home of Daw Suu. Twelve performers from a musical troupe who had come from Mandalay were arrested when they returned to their homes. Eight were released a month later, but four were charged under the 1950 Emergency Provisions Act for "spreading false news" and were sentenced to seven years each. On January 27, six NLD members were arrested for having written a poem to commemorate the 1991 death in detention of their colleague U Tin Maung Win. Three were released, but the others were sentenced to seven years. In April the NLD was refused permission to hold new year's celebrations in the compound of Daw Suu's house.

In May the NLD announced that it would hold a general party meeting to commemorate its election victory in 1990 and discuss future activities. This would have been the first time all NLD members of parliament had met since the 1990 election. In response, the government began arresting NLD MPs from their homes or off buses and trains as they tried to make their way to Rangoon. By May 27, when the meeting opened, 235 MPs and twenty-three party members had been detained. In response to international outrage at the detentions, the SLORC claimed that they were all being held in government guest houses and would shortly be released. In reality, most of those arrested were held in military compounds or military intelligence centers, and in Rangoon some were taken directly to Insein jail.

By the end of June all but twelve of those originally detained were released. Almost immediately notices appeared in the government-controlled media announcing the resignations, usually for "health reasons," of NLD members as elected representatives and as party members. By August thirty-five MPs had resigned. Daw Suu reported that they had done so under immense pressure from the SLORC, and at least one parliamentarian, U Chit Twe, was arrested for refusing to do so. In addition, the MP Dr. Aung Khin Sint (who had only been released after three years in jail in March 1996) announced his resignation in June but was seen in July standing with Daw Suu at the weekend meetings. He was subsequently rearrested on July 23, and was convicted and sentenced on September 13. No details were released about the outcome of his sentence. As of early November, a total of twenty-six elected NLD members of parliament remained in detention.

They were joined by yet more NLD members arrested between June and September. Key workers from the party's headquarters at Daw Suu's house and effective regional organizers were particularly targeted. On August 19, the SLORC announced the sentencing of twenty-eight people. These included U Win Htein, Daw Suu's assistant and spokesman, who was sentenced along with three others to seven years in prison for having had a video made showing barren fields to illustrate the failure of the government's agricultural policy; Win Htein was later given an additional seven years for unspecified offenses. Three other NLD members, including elected parliamentarian U Kyaw Min, were sentenced to ten years for allegedly inciting unrest among students; three others were sentenced to seven years; and nineteen people from the Chin state, including two MPs (U Do Thaung and Khun Myint Htun) and two monks were each sen-

tenced to seven years' imprisonment for allegedly having been in contact with exiled Burmese opposition groups. In the government press reports concerning the latter arrests, two U.S. citizens, including a representative of the International Republican Institute, were cited as their contacts abroad. On September 23, the same newspaper announced that a further nine students had been arrested for distributing leaflets outside Daw Suu's house.

Despite these setbacks, the NLD continued to push for its members' rights to meet and work as a political party. On September 27, the anniversary of the formation of the party, Daw Suu called a second party congress. The government's response was immediate and harsh. Armed troops blocked off all access to Daw Suu's house the night before the congress was due to begin and arrested 109 party members, including sixty-one MPs who had already arrived. Others were prevented from leaving their home towns. Over the next two days up to 800 supporters were arrested, as they gathered at the NLD's headquarters in downtown Rangoon or waited near the barricades to get a glimpse of Daw Suu. By October 2 the military had begun to release some of those arrested but some were thought to face long jail terms.

In addition to the arrests, two political prisoners died in detention during the year, and twenty-one prisoners were badly beaten for allegedly having attempted to send information about prison conditions to the U.N. Special Rapporteur on Burma. Among those beaten was U Win Tin, a founding member of the NLD who had been in jail since 1989 and was known to be in poor health. Win Tin was given an additional five-year sentence under prison rules, while the other twenty received between an extra twelve and five years each. James Leander (Leo) Nichols, an honorary consul representing Nordic countries and Switzerland in Burma, died in June after just two months in jail. He had a longtime heart condition which was exacerbated by his treatment in jail, where he was held in solitary confinement and pressured to sign false confessions. U HlaThan, an NLD parliamentarian, died in August from tuberculosis, reportedly linked to his being HIV-positive. Hla Than had been in jail since 1990, and concern was expressed that he may have contracted the AIDS virus while in jail, where doctors frequently reuse needles without proper sterilization.

Despite these arrests and news of the appalling treatment of political prisoners in jail, citizens continued to show their support for Daw Suu and the NLD. Thousands of people gathered outside the gates of Daw Suu's house every Saturday and Sunday to hear the NLD leaders speak. The intimidation of the crowds increased as the year progressed, with reports from June onwards that military intelligence personnel used videotapes of the meetings to identify civil servants or people who had relatives in the civil service, and threatened to dismiss them if they continued to attend the meetings. On September 27, barricades were erected across the main street leading to Daw Suu's house, and hundreds of supporters were arrested as they waited near the barricades to hear her. The barricades were taken up and then put back several times during October, and the weekend gatherings were effectively banned. As a counter-measure, the SLORC forced thousands of people to attend mass political rallies during June and July where the crowds pledged their loyalty to the government. All civil servants were threatened with dismissal if they did not attend the rallies, and school children, farmers and day laborers were ordered onto buses and taken to the rally sites.

The political impasse was not restricted to the SLORC's confrontations with the NLD. Just as important was the standoff between the SLORC and ethnic nationalities over the next chapter of the new constitution which must be agreed upon before the convention can reconvene. The chapter concerns the division of power between the central government and local government at the regional and state level; it was therefore the first attempt at political discussion between the armed ethnic groups who agreed to military cease-fires with the SLORC before the

end of 1995; as of late September the discussions were reported to be deadlocked.

Several of these groups, especially those from the Shan state, demanded increased political representation for the ethnic groups at the central level. Aware of the dangers of the democratic and ethnic opposition forming a common platform, the SLORC reportedly issued a stern warning to all ethnic representatives not to meet with Daw Suu or other NLD members.

In December 1995, five members of a Karen cultural organization in Rangoon were arrested and held for five days for having invited Daw Suu to join them for Karen New Year celebrations. Daw Suu herself was stopped as she was driving toward Insein township, where the celebrations were being held, and questioned for an hour in the nearby military headquarters.

For populations living in areas where armed groups have not yet signed cease-fires with the SLORC—southern Shan, eastern Karenni and Karen, northern Arakan and southern Chin states—1996 was another year of extensive repression and abuse by the Burmese army as it targeted civilians in an attempt to deny the rebel groups any local support.

The size of the military continued to grow, with an estimated 350,000 troops at year's end. This expansion lead to increased reports of forced conscription, particularly of boys under the age of eighteen, and many under fourteen.

In Shan state, former members of the Mong Tai Army of drug warlord Khun Sa formed new groups following his surrender in January. These groups, some of whom had already left Khun Sa in August 1995, were reported to have a total of 8,000 men under arms by July, but their presence led to intensified military operations by the Burmese army in Shan state. From early March onwards, the military began to force more than 450 villages in the area between Namsan, Kueng Heang and Mong Nai to move to sites along main roads or near army garrison towns. Over 60,000 people were affected by the orders. None of them received any food or financial help in the new areas, and those relocated near roads were forced to work with no pay to widen and improve the roads. Access to this area was strictly forbidden. As many as 10,000 people, mainly young men and women, were reported to have fled to Thailand, where they were refused permission to seek asylum and instead sought employment as illegal migrant workers.

In Karenni state, there was a renewed military offensive against the Karenni National Progressive Party (KNPP) in January, in which Swiss-made Pilatus aircraft were used to strafe KNPP positions and civilian villages. As the fighting died down, the SLORC began a new tactic in May when ninety-six villages from the Sha Daw area were forced to move to Sha Daw town. In June and July the relocation area was extended to southern Karenni state, near Ywathit town, just east of the state capital Loikaw. Altogether 25,000 people were reported to have been affected by the relocations by the end of the year. In the relocation sites, soldiers gave the villagers enough food for ten days but nothing else. Most of the relocations took place during the rainy season, compounding the difficulties for families forced to walk for days to the new sites and find shelter. Eight thousand people fled to Thailand, where refugee camps for the Karenni have been established since 1985, and the new arrivals reported that as many as 150 people, mainly children, had died in Sha Daw from malnutrition-related diseases.

In Karen state the SLORC also relocated thousands of villagers in the Kawkereik area, and thousands more were forced to build roads designed to improve the military's access to areas previously under the control of the Karen National Union (KNU), an armed opposition group. Villagers also suffered repression from the Democratic Karen Buddhist Army (DKBA), a group with close links to the SLORC, which forced people to move to their headquarters at Myaing Gyi Gnu. The DKBA also continued their attacks on Karen refugees in Thailand, frequently also robbing and killing Thai citizens.

In the western part of the country, over 10,000 people fled from Arakan state to Bangladesh during the year. There they joined the 50,000 refugees remaining from the 1991-92 exodus when 270,000 Muslims fled gross human rights abuses by the Burmese military. The UNHCR has been present in Arakan overseeing their reintegration since 1994, but it was unable to curb all but the most serious physical abuses. Forced labor, forced relocations, and the "disappearance" of men accused of working for the Rohingya rebel organizations continued. In addition the Burmese government implemented new restrictions on travel, requiring all Rohingyas (including returnees) to stay within their village boundaries. The SLORC continued to refuse to acknowledge the Rohingyas as full citizens, leaving them vulnerable to abuse and racial harassment. Despite the ongoing abuse suggested by the flight of so many new refugees to Bangladesh, over 5,000 refugees were repatriated during the year, and 15,000 were cleared to return by the Burmese government.

The Right to Monitor

While the government continued to prohibit the formation of indigenous human rights groups and no international human rights organizations were permitted official access to the country, the National League for Democracy worked to expose the arrest and illegal treatment of party members. In February, it was reported that the NLD had established a Legal Advisory Committee, headed by U Tin Oo, which would work to give legal assistance to those detained for their political opinions and activities. In March two letters from the Executive Committee of the NLD were sent to Gen. Than Shwe, chair of the SLORC, protesting the illegal detention of party supporters and requesting that those elected in 1990 be called to form a parliament. By the end of the year, however, increased intimidation and the arrest of key party members had largely stifled the NLD's voice.

U.N. bodies were refused access to the country during the year. In March the U.N.

secretary-general's representative, who had been mandated by the December 1995 resolution of the U.N. General Assembly to assist in the implementation of the resolution and the dialogue between all parties in Burma, was told that the government was too busy to receive him until August. By the end of September, the representative had still not received an invitation to go. Similarly, in April an International Labor Organization delegation which had received permission to visit the country and investigate the government's compliance with Article 87 of the ILO conventions (freedom of association) were told on their arrival in Bangkok, on a stopover to Burma, that their invitation had been rescinded. In June a new Special Rapporteur to Burma, Rajsoomer Lallah, was appointed by the U.N. Commission on Human Rights but by the end of October, he had not received any response to his repeated requests to conduct an investigative mission to the country as his mandate requires. No U.N. agencies working in Burma were permitted access or to give assistance to those forcibly displaced in the Karenni and Shan states.

The government's promotion of Burma as a tourist destination and relaxation of visa restrictions led to an increase during the year in the numbers of international activists who could visit the country. But Burmese whom they contacted were often detained for questioning or sometimes arrested and sentenced.

Increasing numbers of foreign journalists visited the country, often on tourist visas as the government introduced new restrictions on the press, both domestic and foreign. In May a number of foreign journalists had their visas revoked, preventing travel to Burma; in July the foreign minister admitted that the government maintained a blacklist of journalists who wrote "bad things" and later that month embassies issued a new warning with all visa applications that journalists posing as tourists in order to enter the country would be heavily fined and deported if discovered while in Burma. Throughout the year, the government used its control of all domestic media sources to issue increas-

ingly virulent attacks against foreign media. The government continued to jam broadcasts by the BBC and Voice of America and frequently disconnected the telephone line to Daw Suu's house at times when interviews had been prearranged. In April, the work of Human Rights Watch/Asia, Amnesty International, and Article 19 was attacked in an article in the magazine *Kyemon*, which accused these groups of "dancing to the CIA's [Central Intelligence Agency] tune."

The Role of
the International Community

During the year there was increased activity on Burma from the international community, but as western and Asian governments took very different approaches, it had little impact on the domestic situation. There was some good news, however. The release of Daw Suu, and her access to the international media, brought the situation in Burma to the notice of ordinary people everywhere, spurring grassroots campaigns in the west, and to a lesser extent in Asia, which pressed with gathering strength for governmental action. In the U.S., a campaign was launched to introduce legislation which would bring additional economic sanctions against the Burmese government should Daw Suu be arrested or in the event of "large-scale repression." By September the legislation, though somewhat weakened, came into effect.

Also in the U.S. students and ecumenical groups supporting an international boycott of Burma succeeded using state and city-level legislation to force several U.S. companies to withdraw from Burma. In Europe too, advocacy groups called for consumer boycotts to compel Heineken, Carlsberg and British Home Stores to leave Burma, while also pressing their governments and the European Union to introduce punitive sanctions. In Asia, a coalition of nongovernmental organizations repeatedly urged their governments not to admit Burma into ASEAN, while Malaysian groups also protested the state visit by Burma's premier Gen. Than Shwe in June 1996.

United Nations

Despite the adoption by consensus of a strong U.N. General Assembly resolution condemning Burma on human rights grounds in December 1995, there was little evidence of cooperation and coordination to press for human rights improvements as the year progressed. Governments seemed to consider the release of Daw Suu in July 1995 enough of an "improvement" to soften their stance toward the government, and some, particularly Burma's neighbors, continued to soften even after the arrest of scores of her supporters. Having requested the U.N. secretary general to assist in the implementation of the resolution, U.N. member states did little to assist his representative in gaining access to Burma.

The U.N. Special Rapporteur to Burma, Prof. Yozo Yokota, resigned from his position in April, citing a lack of political and financial backing from U.N. member states which had made it increasingly difficult to fulfill his mandate. His replacement, Rajsoomer Lallah, a former chief justice of Mauritius, was appointed in June. The SLORC had approached the U.N Human Rights Commission to put forward the name of a Filipino and refused to acknowledge Lallah's appointment.

European Union

As the internal situation deteriorated during the year, grassroots campaigns were able to push western governments into taking punitive measures to back up their rhetoric of condemnation. Following the death in custody of Leo Nichols, Denmark pushed for Europe-wide economic sanctions against Burma but failed to gain the support of Britain, France, and Germany. The Danish action did result, however, in the European Union reconsidering its position on Burma, and on October 29 the E.U. adopted a new legally-binding policy which maintained the existing embargo on arms and withdrawal of military personnel from embassies in Burma, and enacted a ban on visas for senior SLORC officials and suspension of high-level bilateral visits to Burma by E.U. government officials. The policy was due to be evaluated in six months, with a view toward extending it or taking further measures in response to developments in Burma. In addition, the British government placed a moratorium on all government-sponsored trade missions to Burma, although in September the chair of the Asia-Pacific Advisory Group, which works closely with the U.K. Department of Trade and Industry, led a private business delegation there and was assisted by the British embassy in Rangoon.

Also in Europe, the International Confederation of Free Trade Unions and the European Trade Union Committee brought a complaint against the SLORC and its use of forced labor, under the European Commission's legislation guiding the Generalized System of Preferences (GSP). The GSP program is designed to give developing countries preferential trade tariffs. The European Commission started an investigation in January, the first of its kind, and a decision was expected in January 1997. This could lead to full or partial withdrawal of GSP from Burma.

United States

In the U.S., the administration's Burma policy continued to respond to each crisis as it occurred, with no clear direction. Even when the SLORC accepted the "surrender" of drug warlord Khun Sa and allowed him to live in freedom in Rangoon, the U.S. found few ways of reacting. A reward of US$1 million was offered for his capture, but by the year's end there was no sign that he would ever face trial in the U.S. The U.S. led the international community in condemning the arrests in May and September, and on October 5 finally took action, implementing a visa ban on certain Burmese government officials and members of the military. The May arrests and the pending sanctions legislation in Congress prompted a mission of U.S. envoys to Asian states in June. The only concrete result was an agreement for increased coordination of policy toward Burma with Japan, but ASEAN countries took offense at what they saw as transparent posturing. China did not respond to the mission.

Asia

Japan, which was widely credited with having successfully pressed for the release of Daw Suu in July 1995, was forced by events in Burma to slow down its plan to resume aid. Japan's ambassador in Rangoon, Yoichi Yamaguchi, met with Aung San Suu Kyi several times and tried to foster a dialogue between the NLD and the SLORC.

When the Burmese government rounded up NLD members in May, Prime Minister Hashimoto quickly condemned the arrests. Japan's foreign minister, Yukihiko Ikeda, met with Burmese Foreign Minister Ohn Gyaw at the ASEAN ministerial meetings in Jakarta in June and protested a new law enacted by Rangoon banning public gatherings. At the same time, however, Japan actively supported Burma's bid to become a member of ASEAN.

China remained Burma's steadfast ally throughout the year, and there was also an increasing rapprochement with India and Bangladesh. In ASEAN, while economic investments from Singapore and Malaysia soared during the year, the question of Burma's entry into the regional grouping was an issue of contention. In keeping with their new economic relationship, Malaysian Prime Minister Mahathir and Singaporean Senior Adviser Lee Kuan Yew were the most supportive of SLORC, with Mahathir calling for Burma to be admitted as a full member of ASEAN during the July 1997 meeting in Kuala Lumpur, and Lee advising Daw Suu that she would be "impotent" if asked to lead the country. However, Thailand and the Philippines, both countries with an active and vocal community of nongovernmental organizations, voiced their concerns about the arrests in May and September, and called for a reconsideration of "constructive engagement." Their opposition did not extend to refusing Burma entry into ASEAN, but they were concerned not to rush the membership process. In November 1996 the ASEAN ministers met to reassess the timing of Burma's membership.

CAMBODIA

Human Rights Developments

The human rights situation continued to worsen in the third year following the withdrawal of the United Nations Transitional Authority in Cambodia (UNTAC). Political tensions rose between the two partners in the coalition government; political violence increased, as did restrictions on freedom of the press; and a pattern of impunity continued to favor those responsible for human rights abuses, including former Khmer Rouge officials.

In March, the ruling coalition partners, the royalist party Front Uni National pour un Cambodge Indépendent, Neutre, Pacifique, et Coopératif (Funcinpec) and the Cambodian People's Party (CPP), accused each other of failing to honor power-sharing agreements. Some CPP leaders also charged that the ambivalence of Funcinpec soldiers was responsible for the failure of the 1996 dry season offensive against the Khmer Rouge, which resulted in high casualties for the government soldiers, largely from landmine injuries. The war of words escalated further amid reports that both parties had moved troops into the capital, with CPP leader Hun Sen, at one point moving tanks near his residence to fend off what he claimed was a plot to assassinate him.

In one of the most dramatic developments of the year, former Khmer Rouge Deputy Foreign Minister Ieng Sary, along with two of his generals and between 1,000 and 3,000 soldiers, split with the main Khmer Rouge leadership headed by Pol Pot and entered into peace negotiations with the government. Ieng Sary had been tried *in absentia* in 1979 by an ad hoc tribunal called the People's Revolutionary Court of Phnom Penh for the political killings perpetrated under Khmer Rouge rule. He was found guilty and sentenced to death, along with Pol Pot. Nevertheless, King Sihanouk, under pressure from Co-Prime Ministers Hun Sen and Prince Ranarridh, granted Ieng Sary an amnesty on September 14 following negotiations between his faction of the Khmer Rouge and the Cambodian government. Ieng Sary made a public case for his pardon, claiming at a press conference on September 9 that he had no responsibility for the deaths of Cambodians under Khmer Rouge rule. The amnesty was one more illustration of the pattern of impunity that has characterized Cambodia's post-UNTAC history.

A law passed on October 26, 1994 that all but grants immunity from prosecution to government employees, including police, who commit abuses was used increasingly during the year. Under Article 51 of the Law on Civil Servants, a judge wishing to prosecute senior civil servants must file a request through the minister of justice to seek authorization from the Council of Ministers before the prosecution can proceed. Authorization from the head of the ministry involved is necessary for the prosecution of lower-ranking civil servants. An exception to the authorization process is made for civil servants who are arrested while in the act of committing a crime. The cumbersome authorization process all but ensured that government officials who abused human rights would go unpunished.

Article 51 drew criticism from the Ministry of Justice as well as from some provincial judges. However, it appeared from internal government documents that the government was not only committed to retaining this law, but that it was also proposing a similar provision for a draft law on military personnel.

The rising level of politically motivated violence was threatening to affect the local elections planned for 1997 and national elections in 1998. The opposition Khmer Nation Party (KNP), headed by former Finance Minister and National Assembly representative Sam Rainsy, opened its first offices outside of Phnom Penh in May despite government statements suggesting the party was illegal. In early May, a KNP official in Siem Reap province was fatally beaten and robbed of the registration forms of over 2,000 KNP party members, strongly suggesting a political motive for the killing. On May 17, three KNP officials were arrested by provincial police while traveling in Ang Snoul district in Kandal province to collect membership applications. The three were held for two days before they were released. Other KNP offices in Kompong Som and Prey Veng provinces and elsewhere in Kandal province were also subject to harassment, including intimidation by provincial officials and police.

On May 18, 1996, in another incident that may have been related to the attacks on the KNP, prominent journalist and KNP steering committee member Thun Bun Ly was murdered in Phnom Penh, in what appeared to be a politically motivated assassination. As of this writing there were no public results from the Ministry of Interior's investigation into the killing. Thun Bun Ly's death marks the first killing of a journalist in Cambodia since December 1994. He had been convicted in 1995 on charges of defamation and disinformation in two separate trials on the basis of articles published in his newspaper. He had lost his initial appeals but had appealed to the Supreme Court and was awaiting a decision. On the day that he was murdered, he had published an article in his newspaper *Oudamkati Khmer* (*Khmer Ideal*) about overhearing a threat on his life made by an officer in the anti-terrorist unit of the army.

Some officials of Funcinpec were also intimidated. Local newspapers reported in early June that in two Siem Reap districts, Funcinpec leaders were going into hiding each night for fear of attacks after being harassed by local police. First Prime Minister Prince Ranariddh, the senior Funcinpec leader, made specific references to incidents in which Funcinpec signboards had been torn down from provincial offices and to reports that the police in Kandal province (which surrounds Phnom Penh) had tried to prevent people from watching the Funcinpec television station. Ranariddh's public statements immediately drew a response from Second Prime Minister Hun Sen of the CPP, who, while not mentioning Ranariddh or Funcinpec by name, criticized in a speech those raising allegations of political violence.

Extrajudicial killings and torture of civilians, particularly those living in areas contested by the government and the Khmer Rouge, increased during the year. Abuses were particularly common in Battambang province, where the Khmer Rouge sought to cut Route 5, the major land route to Phnom Penh. Incidents included the arrest and torture in Battambang province of eight men in May on suspicion of carrying out activities for the Khmer Rouge. Each of these men was tortured during interrogation, resulting in the death of one of the eight. The Battambang police commissioner claimed that the man had killed himself in his cell after his interrogation by hanging himself with his own shirt and tying one end around a metal bar that was so low that he would have had to lift his legs off the ground in order to strangle himself. There were also at least five extrajudicial executions by police and soldiers in Battambang province. The victims were typically farmers who lived in villages in zones contested by the government and the Khmer Rouge.

The Cambodian government continued efforts to restrict the press. On June 28 Chan Rottana, the editor of *Samleng Yuvachon Khmer* (*Voice of Khmer Youth*) and a KNP member, was imprisoned upon losing his appeal to the Supreme Court of a February 1995 conviction for disinformation under the UNTAC press law for a satirical piece he published titled "Ranariddh is More Stupid than Hun Sen Three Times a Day." The Supreme Court also ordered that *Samleng Yuvachon Khmer* be shut down. Chan Rottana was released after serving one week in T-3 prison when he was pardoned by King Sihanouk. His arrest marked the first time since the U.N.-sponsored elections in 1993 that a journalist was imprisoned for the nonviolent expression of his opinions.

In another case involving a journalist, the editor of *Serei Pheap Thmei* (*New Liberty News*), Hen Vipheak, was imprisoned on August 23, when the Supreme Court upheld his conviction for disinformation.

He was convicted in May 1995 for an article he published headlined "Cambodia: Country of Thieves" and for a cartoon showing Hun Sen holding a gun to Ranariddh's head. The Supreme Court ruling upheld both the decision and the municipal court's penalty of a one-year jail term and a fine of five million riels ($US2,000), while reversing the Appeal Court's ruling that the newspaper be shut down as well. Hen Vipheak was jailed in T-3 after the Supreme Court ruling, but he too was released after a week in prison under a pardon issued by King Sihanouk, with the prior approval of the two prime ministers. Like Thun Bun Ly, Hen Vipheak was a KNP steering committee member.

The government's disregard for press freedoms, as well as for other fundamental rights, was also demonstrated by its treatment of several ethnic Vietnamese living in Phnom Penh who were affiliated with an anti-Hanoi Vietnamese-language newspaper published in Phnom Penh called *Tu Do* (*Freedom*). In March 1996, the government deported to Vietnam three ethnic Vietnamese men affiliated with *Tu Do*, resulting in the closure of that newspaper. The Cambodian Ministry of Interior alleged that these men were engaged in an attempt to destabilize and overthrow the government of Vietnam but provided no supporting evidence. It was not clear whether the men were Cambodian citizens illegally expelled to Vietnam or whether they were Vietnamese citizens whom the Cambodian government sent back to certain persecution in Vietnam. In early August, there were unconfirmed reports that one of the three had been released due to serious illness; the whereabouts of the other two men were unknown as of late 1996.

The Right to Monitor

Cambodian human rights groups continued to conduct investigations into abuses around the country. In addition, they conducted human rights training courses for government employees as well as for other nongovernmental organizations.

The United Nations Human Rights Centre, which maintains an office in Phnom

Penh, was able to carry out its activities without threats from the government, marking an improvement in relations between the government and the center over 1995. The term of the center was extended for two years by agreement with the Cambodian government. Justice Michael Kirby stepped down as the special representative of the U.N. secretary-general for human rights in Cambodia and was replaced by Thomas Hammarberg.

The Role of
the International Community

The U.N. Commission on Human Rights passed a resolution expressing concern over continuing abuses, including violence and intimidation directed at political parties and the press.

The U.S. and the United Nations International Drug Control Programme (UNDCP) criticized the increasing levels of drug trafficking in Cambodia and urged steps to control it, some of which raised human rights concerns. Among other things, the UNDCP drafted a stringent drug control law that includes provisions granting the police broad powers which, given current police practices, would increase the likelihood of arbitrary detention. Both the UNDCP and the U.S. government lobbied the Cambodian government heavily to pass the draft law, which as of late 1996 was before the National Assembly and was expected to pass easily.

Several governments, including Australia and the U.S., along with U.N. Special Representative Hammarberg, raised concerns about the increase in trafficking into prostitution of women and girls.

The European Union, meanwhile, began the process of negotiating a trade agreement with Cambodia. This first trade and cooperation agreement between the E.U. and Cambodia will include a reciprocal application of most-favored-nation treatment, development cooperation targeted on the poorest sections of the population, and protection of the environment. The agreement will be conditioned on respect for human rights and

democratic principles and will require approval by the European Parliament. In June, however, following a visit to China, Cambodian First Prime Minister Norodom Ranariddh told the press that Cambodia will not accept conditional aid from the E.U.

The Consultative Group (CG) on Cambodia, comprising Cambodia's major donors, met in Tokyo on July 11-12, convened by the World Bank and the Japanese government. Prior to the CG meeting and in a separate meeting the day before with the two Cambodian prime ministers, representatives of the U.S. and Australian governments raised concern over the absence of accountability for government abuses, including for human rights violations. The U.S. delegation specifically noted that "episodes of violence and intolerance of political expression in the past year have raised concerns about the direction Cambodia may be heading." The donors pressed for assurances that the 1997 and 1998 elections would go forward and be free and fair. The International Monetary Fund raised concerns that money from the sale of state forestry assets was not finding its way to the coffers of the Ministry of Finance. However, Cambodia's main donors once again granted unconditional aid to the Royal Government of Cambodia. These pledges amounted to US$501 million, some 44 percent of the total national budget for 1997.

Prior to the CG meeting, the European Parliament passed a resolution criticizing Cambodia's record on human rights, press freedom and the continuing destruction of forests.

The Clinton administration continued to address human rights issues largely in private. Publicly, the U.S. downplayed its concerns over the human rights situation in Cambodia, emphasizing instead that conditions represented an improvement over the period of Khmer Rouge rule. The U.S. Congress, on the other hand, was more vocal. In March, the House of Representatives adopted a resolution expressing concern about deteriorating human rights conditions in Cambodia; it urged that the issue be raised both at the donor meeting and during consideration of World Bank and Asian Development Bank projects in Cambodia. The Senate passed a similar resolution in September, focused on the projected elections and the need for continued U.N. human rights monitoring; it also sharply criticized King Sihanouk for giving Ieng Sary an amnesty that might allow him to form a political party and participate in the elections.

The U.S. Senate held up consideration of a bill granting Most Favored Nation (MFN) trade status to Cambodia for several months, mainly due to concerns about human rights. Unconditional MFN was finally signed into law by President Clinton on September 25.

CHINA AND TIBET

Human Rights Developments

The Chinese government stepped up its efforts to prevent socioeconomic change from disrupting the political system by tightening controls on freedom of expression and continuing to persecute political and religious dissidents. Business people also faced arbitrary detention and unfair trials. The government intensified repression in Tibet, Xinjiang and Inner Mongolia, made ominous moves in Hong Kong, and responded to criticism of its treatment of orphans by tightening controls on access to the state orphanage system. In a positive development, legal reforms passed by the National People's Congress in March seemed to herald some modest progress toward due process for criminal suspects. At the same time, international willingness to confront China on human rights issues reached a new low.

A fresh wave of arrests and sentences of the few remaining pro-democracy and human rights activists not already in prison or exile left the dissident movement effectively crushed. On October 30, 1996, Chinese authorities sentenced Wang Dan, the principal student leader of the 1989 Tiananmen Square protests, to eleven years in prison on charges of conspiring to subvert the Chinese government. He was accused of "colluding" with other dissidents, including Wei Jingsheng, to form discussion groups and appeal for the rule of law, criticizing the government in articles published abroad, accepting a scholarship at the University of California for self-study in Beijing, forming a mutual aid group with other dissidents, and accepting financial help from abroad. No foreign press or observers were permitted inside the courtroom.

Ten months earlier, in December 1995, the country's most prominent dissident, Wei Jingsheng, was finally brought to trial after more than eighteen months in incommunicado detention and sentenced to an additional fourteen years in prison on the political charge of "counterrevolution." In January 1996, he was sent to Jile Prison in Hebei, and in July, news surfaced that hardened criminals had been moved into his cell to provide round-the-clock surveillance. Denied fresh air and exercise, Wei was also refused proper medical treatment for a range of ailments contracted during his previous imprisonment.

A second Tiananmen Square leader, Guo Haifeng, reportedly was sentenced in September to seven years in prison for "hooliganism" for helping a third dissident escape to the United States. He served a previous four-year term. Liu Xiaobo, a literary critic who helped negotiate the withdrawal of students from Tiananmen Square on June 3-4, 1989, was seized on October 7, 1996 and administratively sentenced the next day to three years in a reeducation through labor camp. On September 30, he and dissident Wang Xizhe issued a statement calling for the impeachment of President Jiang Zemin and for meetings with the Dalai Lama over the issue of Tibet's autonomy. Wang, fearing imminent arrest, immediately fled China. The government not only accused him of illegally crossing the Chinese border, but threatened to punish all who assisted in the escape.

Veteran labor rights activist Liu Nianchun was "disappeared" in May 1995 for over a year only to resurface on July 4 when he received a three-year sentence of reeducation through labor over and above time in detention. Liu was sent to a remote prison camp in northeast China.

Other 1989 activists remained in limbo. Li Hai, a graduate philosophy student who spent a year in prison after June 1989, co-sponsored the 1993 "Peace Charter," then was arrested again in May 1995, was tried *in camera* on May 21, 1996 on charges of "leaking state secrets." As of November, he had not been sentenced. In September, Zhang Zongai, a former elected member of the Xi'an People's Congress who had spent five years in jail for denouncing the government crackdown on the 1989 pro-democracy movement, was tried on charges of "counterrevolutionary propaganda and incitement" for having written letters seeking guidance from the Taiwan news media on how to bring democracy to China; secondary charges against Zhang included communicating his political views by letter to a friend in the U.S. and conducting an interview with Wang Dan prior to the latter's renewed detention.

Xiao Biguang, a Beijing academic involved in the unofficial labor and church movements, was in detention for over two years before being given the maximum three-year administrative labor reeducation term in 1996. Among others who received administrative sentences during the year were Yao Zhenxiang, a long-time financier of Shanghai's dissident movement who fled to France in 1994 but was arrested soon after voluntarily returning to China in early 1996 having obtained official pledges for his safety; Tan Zihua, a Shanghai resident active during the Democracy Wall period (1979-81); and Chen Longde, a leading human rights activist from Hangzhou who had signed an open letter to the government in May calling for reevaluation of the 1989 pro-democracy movement.

Several political prisoners "freed" after serving their sentences in full were subjected to a variety of post-release restrictions and harassment. Chen Ziming, originally sentenced in 1991 to a thirteen-year term as a "black hand" of the 1989 pro-democracy movement, was released on medical parole for the second time on October 6, 1996. Parole conditions are stringent. Chen cannot step outside his door, use a telephone, meet with anyone except family members, or publish. Access to medical treatment for his testicular cancer, heart problems and high blood pressure must be negotiated through security officers. Chen's first parole came in May 1994, but was revoked on June 25, 1995, after he took part in a petition drive which asked that China tolerate peaceful political dissent.

Bao Tong, the most senior government official imprisoned after the Tiananmen Square crackdown, was released in May after serving his entire seven-year sentence, but instead of being allowed to return home, he was immediately transferred to the custody of a high-security government compound in the western suburbs of Beijing, where he continued to be held as of October, denied all access to the outside world apart from limited visits by members of his immediate family. His health continued to be a major concern, but access to medical care was restricted.

Torture of China's detainees and prisoners continued, as exemplified by Chen Longde's case. In 1996, one month after his conviction without trial, Chen leapt from a two-story prison walkway in an attempt to avoid repeated beatings and electric shocks from a senior prison official as punishment for his refusal to write a statement of guilt and self-criticism.

Police seized Wang Hui, wife of jailed labor activist Zhou Guoqiang, on May 15 and held her for more than a month. As a result of her treatment, including deliberate withholding of liquids, she tried to commit suicide by hanging. After the police cut her down, she was punished with a severe beating. No reason for Wang Hui's detention was ever given, but she had been active in pressing her husband's suit against the government. On September 22 she was detained again for unknown reasons.

Medical treatment continued to be denied to political and religious prisoners. Chen Ziming, for example, sentenced in 1991 to a thirteen-year term as a "black hand" of the 1989 pro-democracy movement, was believed to be extremely ill with testicular cancer. The Chinese government rejected quiet diplomatic interventions by foreign governments on his behalf.

Business executives and others involved in trade and finance were also at risk in 1996. Hong Yang, an official of the People's Bank of China who had been assigned to work at the Washington D.C. headquarters of the International Monetary Fund, was lured back to China as part of an IMF delegation in December 1995, tried in June for alleged corruption, and sentenced to eleven years, then retried after enormous pressure from the IMF and given a reduced sentence of five years—proving that sustained pressure in individual cases can be effective.

Xiu Yichun, a senior Chinese manager for Shell, and one of her counterparts at the China National Offshore Oil Corporation were detained in early February on charges of obtaining state secrets related to the financing and environmental aspects of Royal Dutch Shell's plans to build an oil refinery in Huizhou, east of Hong Kong. CNOOC was to be Shell's joint venture partner, and the arrests came shortly before Chinese Premier Li Peng was to visit the Netherlands to discuss the project. As of late March, neither family members nor colleagues had been allowed access to Xiu Yichun; as of August, Shell officials had not been able to obtain any additional information. Motivation for the arrests was unclear but may have reflected official concern that Chinese nationals working for foreign firms would use knowledge of local business practices to violate the law.

All labor rights activism outside the confines of the official All-China Federation of Trade Unions remained a major focus of government repression. A 1996 circular cautioned cadres against illegal unions and "anti-government" and "anti-socialist" tendencies lurking in state-owned enterprises. Police statistics showed that more than 12,000 strikes, rallies and other forms of industrial action took place nationwide during 1995. In January 1996 Zheng Shaoqing and Chen Rongyan each received two-year labor re-education sentences for organizing a half-day taxi strike in the southern city of Zhuhai early in the month; six others received one-and-a-half year terms; and the licenses of all those who took part were confiscated. The fate of most unofficial labor organizers in China generally remains unknown.

Government moves to restrict freedom of expression and access to information also took place, notably in the form of sweeping new regulations curtailing public access to the Internet; controls on foreign economic news services operating in China; and an insistence by Chinese leaders that the domestic press should report only "good news," avoid disclosing details of the widespread social unrest, and reflect the position of the government and the Communist Party.

The Internet controls, inaugurated by a draft set of rules issued by the State Council in January, required existing computer networks linked to the Internet to "liquidate" and "re-register" with the authorities and to use only those international linkage services provided by specified government departments. All subscribers were ordered to provide a written guarantee that they would not use the Internet for purposes "harmful to the state." This goal was further realized in September, when the government deployed sophisticated technology to block subscriber access to as many as one hundred English and Chinese sites on the World Wide Web, including the *Washington Post, Economist, Wall Street Journal*, CNN, and *Time* magazine; the Voice of America's Chinese service and, Hong Kong's Democratic Party; a home page of the Tibetan government-in-exile; and overseas dissident sites.

Chinese student efforts to use the Internet for mass mobilization resulted in a government ban in June and July on public protests against the erection by Japanese ultra-right groups of a lighthouse on the disputed Diaoyu Islands, sovereignty over which is claimed by both China and Japan.

In its response to common crime, the

government was indiscriminate. A massive, nationwide offensive on crime known as the "Strike Hard" campaign, the largest since the first such campaign in 1983, was launched in April. In the first six months of the campaign, hundreds of thousands of suspected criminals were arrested, tens of thousands sentenced, and at least 1,500 executed. In one reported case, in Shenzhen in September, the condemned person was executed in full view of several hundred onlookers, despite a long-standing law banning public executions. With its stress on "rapid arrests and rapid sentencing" (summary judicial procedures and government-set targets for the desired number of arrests by public security officials), the anti-crime campaign implied a high incidence of forced confessions, false convictions and wrongful executions. For the first time since 1983, the government extended the campaign to political, religious and ethnic "splittists and separatists." In September, despite officially published evidence that the draconian policy had failed to curb a steadily rising crime rate, the government announced that "Strike Hard" would henceforth be a permanent feature of China's law enforcement scene.

In the Tibetan Autonomous Region and Tibetan areas of Qinghai, Yunnan, Gansu, and Sichuan, the effects of a July 1994 policy conference on Tibet combined with the "Strike Hard" campaign produced more arrests of suspected independence supporters, a stepped-up campaign to discredit the Dalai Lama as a religious leader, crackdowns in rural areas as well as towns, a major push for ridding monasteries and nunneries of nationalist sympathizers, and the closure of those that were politically active. Monks who refused to sign pledges denouncing the Dalai Lama or to accept a five-point declaration of opposition to the pro-independence movement, faced expulsion from their monasteries.

In May, a ban on the possession and display of Dalai Lama photographs led to a bloody confrontation at Ganden and to searches of hotels, restaurants, shops, and some private homes. Over ninety monks were arrested; fifty-three remained in detention as of October despite Chinese official reports that none of the sixty-one arrested were still being held. At least one person and perhaps two others are known to have died in the melee.

Chinese authorities acknowledged that they are holding Gendun Choekyi Nyima, the child recognized by the Dalai Lama but rejected by Chinese authorities as the reincarnation of the Panchen Lama, "under the protection of the government at the request of his parents." Chadrel Rimpoche, the abbot in charge of the original search team, officially labeled a criminal and a "scum of Buddhism," has been missing along with his assistant, Champa Chungla, since November 4, 1995.

Security forces in Tibet used forms of torture which leave no marks against those suspected of major pro-independence activism. These activists were subject to recurrent "disappearance" during which they were subjected to extremes of temperature, deprivation of food and water, applications of electricity, and forcibly injected drugs. Those caught torturing often escaped with mild censure. A court in Shigatse in Tibet gave a county police chief a suspended jail sentence after convicting him of torturing a suspect. He reportedly told the woman, who spent sixty-five days in the hospital as a result of her injuries, "I am the government policy here. It's no use reporting this to anyone."

The Chinese government also tightened controls in two other autonomous regions, Inner Mongolia and Xinjiang. In December 1995, at least ten intellectuals who had formed a group called the Southern Mongolian Democratic Alliance were arrested, and police broke up peaceful protest demonstrations in support of the alliance. In June the region's Communist Party secretary called for an attack on "splittist" forces which, he said, were trying with Western backing to destroy China's unity. In Xinjiang, the nationwide anti-crime campaign was extended to include a wholesale police and army roundup of alleged Uighur separatists, some of whom were later executed. Underground religious groups were targeted for closure, and all publishing units were forbidden to publish products whose "contents violate party or government policies...." Access to Xinjiang was denied to foreign journalists.

Unofficial Christian and Catholic communities were targeted by the government during 1996. A renewed campaign aimed at forcing all churches to register or face dissolution, resulted in beating and harassment of congregants, closure of churches, and numerous arrests, fines, and sentences. In Shanghai, for example, more than 300 house churches or meeting points were closed down by the security authorities in April alone.

From January through May, teams of officials fanned out through northern Hebei, a Catholic stronghold, to register churches and clergy and to prevent attendance at a major Marian shrine. Public security officers arrested clergy and lay Catholics alike, forced others to remain in their villages, avoid foreigners, refrain from preaching, and report to the police anywhere from one to eight times daily. In some villages, officials confiscated all religious medals. In others, churches and prayer houses were torn down or converted to lay use.

Government statements and policies toward Hong Kong did not bode well for civil liberties after the transition to Chinese sovereignty on July 1, 1997. Its decision to prevent elected members of the Legislative Council from serving their full terms and instead to install an appointed "provisional legislature" to rule the territory for the initial year was one disturbing development. In June, China's top official on Hong Kong affairs said that demonstrations in Hong Kong advocating the overthrow of Chinese rule or independence from China would be banned after July 1997. He had earlier indicated that the Hong Kong press would be subject to vaguely defined but potentially sweeping restrictions including bans on any articles relating to Taiwan or Tibetan independence.

The Chinese government reacted to international publicity about conditions in state orphanages, exposed in a report by Human Rights Watch in January, by closing off access to many of the institutions to anyone not directly employed there, foreign or Chinese. It also responded to evidence of abuse of children in the Shanghai Children's Welfare Institute by detaining and harassing Chinese citizens involved in earlier attempts to investigate the problem.

The one area in which significant advances in human rights protection were made by the government during 1996 was that of legal reform, with the passage in March of a revised criminal procedure law and an administrative punishment law. The former law, among other things, provided for improved access by detained criminal suspects to legal counsel and made progress toward acknowledging the presumption of innocence. The latter, in theory, restricted police authority to sentence suspects without trial to long periods of administrative detention or to hold suspects in "investigative detention" without recourse to any judicial process. Other legislative revisions, however, increased by a month the maximum time-limit a detainee could be held without being formally arrested.

The Right to Monitor

While some legal aid clinics were operating at universities that allowed *de facto* monitoring of and action in support of human rights, no organizations that identified themselves as human rights organizations per se were permitted to function. Legal scholars could and did address problems in the criminal justice system, but anyone who spoke out on behalf of political prisoners or gave information on human right abuses to outsiders, including foreign journalists, risked arrest.

The Role of the International Community

The Chinese government's continued linkage between trade and human rights—threatening to restrict trade or foreign investment in retaliation for human rights criticism—paid major dividends in 1996. Human rights fell nearly to the bottom of the international agenda as Beijing defeated a half-hearted effort led by the European Union (EU) and the U.S. to pass a resolution at the U.N. Human Rights Commission. China's leaders traveled to various European capitals, and to Bangkok for the first E.U.-Asia summit, encountering little serious human rights criticism. And the Group of Seven (G-7) industrialized countries, at their annual summit in June,disregarded an opportunity to develop a long-term multilateral strategy to promote human rights in China.

The most damaging setback came at the U.N. Human Rights Commission session in Geneva in April, where a resolution criticizing human rights violations in China never even came to a vote. The resolution had been sponsored by the U.S. and the European Union, but the Clinton administration, concerned that it could not gather enough votes to win, was reluctant to lobby governments at the highest levels. Several countries of the EU were more concerned with increasing trade with China than with taking a strong stand in Geneva. The actions of the resolution's sponsors, even with a last-minute lobbying effort by the U.S., ended up being too little, too late, especially given the massive lobbying effort by China. By a vote in the commission on April 23 of twenty-seven to twenty, with six abstaining, China succeeded in pushing through a "no action" motion. A debate or vote on the resolution itself never took place.

No progress whatsover was made on access by humanitarian organizations to Chinese prisons and detention facilities, but the head of the U.N. Working Group on Arbitrary Detention did visit China in July and at the end of the year was trying to negotiate terms of reference for a more in-depth trip to China by the working group in 1997.

UNICEF, after initially saying it would begin a pilot project to help upgrade staff training in some orphanages, by June expressed disappointment at Beijing's "excruciatingly slow" reforms. Not only was UNICEF denied access to some of the institutions it sought to visit but the U.N. Com-

mittee on the Rights of Child, at its meeting in Geneva in June, complained about China's reluctance to provide infant mortality data.

China submitted reports during the year on its compliance with two international human rights treaties, the Convention on the Rights of the Child and the Convention Against Torture and Other Cruel, Inhuman or Degrading Treatment or Punishment.

European Union

The year began with massive international publicity on the mistreatment of Chinese orphans, sparking a swift response from western governments and international agencies. The European Parliament passed a strong resolution condemning abuses in Chinese orphanages, calling on Beijing to open all child welfare institutions to foreign observers, including UNICEF, and urging the EU to raise the issue during its E.U./ China Human Rights Dialogue in Beijing in later January, which it did. In addition, Chinese authorities responded to western criticism by taking first journalists, then diplomats on a guided tour of an orphanage in Shanghai. The U.S. State Department also publicly expressed concern about treatment of orphans and withstood a barrage of criticism from adoption agencies and some families of adopted children, concerned that criticism would lead to a decline in foreign adoption (as it turned out, adoptions increased substantially as a result of the publicity).

In January, the General Affairs Council of the EU adopted a long-term policy for relations between the EU and China, stressing economic engagement and a desire to bring China into the World Trade Organization, while addressing human rights and promotion of the rule of law through its political dialogue with Beijing. The European Parliament was due to draft its own response to the new China policy outlined by the European Commission at the end of 1995 and the European Council in 1996.

These developments set the stage for the E.U.-Asia summit on March 1 and 2 in Bangkok, where Chinese Premier Li Peng met with German Chancellor Helmut Kohl and French President Jacques Chirac, aiming to derail a resolution on China and Tibet at the U.N. Human Rights Commission in Geneva. With a US$2.1 billion Airbus sale in the works, and Li Peng set to visit Paris in April to finalize the deal, France was anxious to appease Beijing by backing off from an agreement with the U.S. to cosponsor the Geneva resolution. Germany, meanwhile, was China's largest trading partner in 1996, with bilateral trade of $18 billion and was also one of Europe's top investors in the country. Negotiations about possible Chinese concessions on human rights in exchange for dropping the resolution were ultimately futile, but the delay gave China a great advantage in lobbying governments worldwide at the highest levels, offering them trade and support in various U.N. bodies in exchange for their votes to keep the measure off the agenda.

Despite appeals on human rights in China and Tibet signed by over 200 French legislators and scattered protests, Li Peng's visit to Paris was hailed by Beijing as marking a "watershed" in its ties with France, and this was followed in July by a six-nation swing by President Jiang Zemin through Europe and Asia. When a vigorous debate on repression in Tibet erupted in the German parliament in June, and Beijing warned that German business interests in China could suffer, Bonn quickly scrambled to restore good relations. An invitation to German Foreign Minister Klaus Kinkel to visit China was temporarily withdrawn, but in September the invitation was renewed, and during his visit in October, Kinkel raised the cases of Wang Dan and Wei Jingsheng. Germany's president was expected to go to China in November. At about the same time relations with Bonn were patched up, Australia's prime minister, John Howard, was also threatened with trade retaliation for planning to meet with the Dalai Lama in Sydney; he proceeded with that meeting anyway.

United States

Human rights clearly took a back seat to commercial and strategic interests in U.S.-China policy throughout the year, as evidenced by the Clinton administration's announcement in July (presaged in a speech by Secretary of State Warren Christopher in May) that it would embark upon a series of high-level meetings with China aimed at improving Sino-U.S. relations, leading to reciprocal summit visits in Beijing and Washington in 1997 without specific human rights preconditions. The U.S. tacitly agreed to downplay human rights in pursuit of closer cooperation on security matters and other issues. The administration's 1994 "delinking" of trade and human rights was thus taken a step further, and President Clinton abandoned any possibility of using U.S. political or economic leverage with Beijing to exert pressure on human rights.

The shift in political will was particularly apparent in the U.S. agreement with China on copyrights, patents and other intellectual property rights issues reached in mid-June. The administration successfully rallied strong bipartisan Congressional support for use of possible trade sanctions to obtain the agreement, while arguing it would deal with other areas of disagreement such as human rights via "strategic dialogue." The debate on Most-Favored-Nation trading status in Congress focused, in part, on the value of "engagement" as the only tool to promote human rights progress but was heavily skewed by business lobbying to do away with the annual MFN renewal process entirely and by the administration's desire to promote "stable" relations with Beijing. By a lopsided vote (286 to 141), the U.S. House of Representatives voted on June 17 to support Clinton's renewal of MFN for another year, which the president proclaimed an endorsement of his overall "engagement" strategy. As political cover, the House adopted a nonbinding resolution citing China's poor human rights record, among other concerns, but mandating no policy changes.

The administration's engagement strategy produced few, if any, concrete results during the year. No prisoners were released due to U.S. bilateral or multilateral intervention, and any discussions about specific cases were relegated to closed-door meetings. In a meeting with Chinese Foreign Minister Qian Qichen in Jakarta in July, Secretary of State Warren Christopher raised human rights only in a general way, while touting the agreement for a series of high-level visits, including his own trip to Beijing in November (the first since his disastrous visit there in 1994), a prospective visit by Vice-President Al Gore, and a bilateral meeting between Clinton and Jiang at the APEC (Asia Pacific Economic Cooperation) forum in Manila in November. Two weeks earlier, presidential National Security Advisor Anthony Lake went to Beijing and reportedly discussed specific human rights cases, but announced no progress whatsoever, stressing instead the trend toward overall closer relations. Both meetings were also unsuccessful in restarting the formal bilateral human rights "dialogue" suspended by China in 1994.

Christopher met with Qian again at the U.N. in New York in September; human rights concerns, access to prisoners, Tibet and Hong Kong were discussed.

The State Department did issue public statements about specific political prisoners, for example, protesting the continued detention of Bao Tong following completion of his prison sentence, and urging the release of Fu Guoyong, a democracy activist sentenced in September. The U.S. embassy in Beijing, on the other hand, generally took a noticeably low profile on human rights as the new U.S. ambassador, Jim Sasser, who arrived in Beijing in February, concentrated on promoting U.S. business interests. The embassy did try to send an observer to Wang Dan's trial.

The administration supported putting China and Hong Kong on the agenda for discussion at the G-7 summit meeting in Lyon, France on June 27, and language for the final statement was apparently agreed upon; but the discussion was later reconfigured to respond to a major bombing in Saudi Arabia, and the China language was also deleted.

Members of the U.S. Congress contin-

ued to be outspoken on human rights throughout the year, sending letters to Secretary Christopher prior to his meetings with Chinese officials in Jakarta and New York; raising questions during Congressional hearings; lobbying the administration on policy decisions with human rights implications, such the Export-Import Bank's decision to provide export credits for the Three Gorges Dam project; called for a full-scale, independent investigation of abuses in Chinese orphanages and for multilateral efforts to ensure U.N. access to them.

On May 30, despite intense lobbying by some corporate interests, the U.S. Export-Import Bank announced it would not provide export credits to U.S. companies involved in the Three Gorges Dam Project. Though the decision was made primarily on environmental grounds, the human rights and social impacts of the project were clearly part of the decision-making process within both the bank and the White House, which had earlier recommended that the bank not fund Three Gorges. In July, the president of the Export-Import Bank, Martin Kamarck, visited China and there were indications that the bank might reconsider its decision if China took certain steps to meet its environmental criteria. Meanwhile, the Export-Import Bank of Japan was due to decide by mid-December 1996 whether it would provide loans to Japanese companies involved in Three Gorges.

Japan

In its policy toward China, Japan continued to emphasize nonproliferation and nuclear testing, for the most part downplaying human rights concerns. It did agree to co-sponsor the China resolution at the U.N. Human Rights Commission in April and encouraged China to uphold its international commitments in Hong Kong after the latter's return to Chinese sovereignty on July 1, 1997.

Through its Official Development Assistance (ODA) program, Japan provided China with more than $1.4 billion in aid in Fiscal Year 1996, making it China's largest bilateral donor. There were no known instances during the year of Japan's using its aid leverage for human rights improvements in China. Japan pledged its support for China's entry into the World Trade Organization.

World Bank Assistance
There were no efforts made, by any government, to restrain World Bank funding to China on human rights grounds; its annual lending to China totaled nearly $3 billion for the fiscal year ending June 30. However, a report by Harry Wu in October 1995 that a $125 million World Bank loan for an irrigation project supported forced labor camps in Xinjiang Province led to a World Bank investigation and congressional hearings in July 1996. The bank said it could find no evidence that its operations in Xinjiang benefited forced labor camps, though it acknowledged that the chief operator of its projects there, the Xinjiang Production and Construction Corps (XPCC), did administer such camps and was responsible for handling security and military in the province. This caused the U.S. Treasury Department to announce, in Senate hearings, that the U.S. would no longer support bank projects affiliated with XPCC until a clearer division was made between its military and civilian operations.

HONG KONG

As the year drew to a close, the chances that Hong Kong's autonomy would be maintained after the July 1, 1997 return to Chinese sovereignty seemed slim. The "one country, two systems" formula for the post-July Special Administrative Region (SAR) was already being systematically eroded, at least in the area of civil liberties, and the Chinese government seemed intent on repealing provisions in Hong Kong's Bill of Rights, dissolving the elected Legislative Council (Legco), undercutting the independence of the judicial system and the executive, and curbing freedom of expression and assembly.

Human Rights Developments
In September 1995, Hong Kong had held an election in which the pro-democratic forces won a majority of the twenty directly elected seats on Legco. On March 24, 1996, the Preparatory Committee, a body hand-picked by the Chinese government to handle transition matters, voted to disband Legco on July 1, 1997 even though its members would have served only two years of their four-year terms. The Preparatory Committee decided instead that in accordance with the Basic Law, the document worked out between Britain and China that will serve as Hong Kong's constitution after July 1, a 400-member Selection Committee would be empowered to select a provisional body to remain in place for one year. An elected body would thus be replaced by an appointed one, and it was not clear whether elections would in fact take place under Chinese rule after the one-year period.

Frederick Fung, chair of the Hong Kong-based political party called Association for Democracy and People's Livelihood who cast the one dissenting vote in this process, was immediately disqualified both from membership in the provisional legislature and from a place on the Selection Committee.

The provisional legislature would have the power to pass laws, approve a new budget for the SAR, and repeal or amend any law it deemed contrary to the Basic Law. The original Sino-British agreement to dissolve the legislature on June 30, 1997 and reconvene it the following day with no change in membership—the so-called through train agreement—was thus effectively scrapped. Pro-democracy activists and lawyers in Hong Kong voiced fears that the provisional legislature would revive draconian colonial security laws, pass new legislation on sedition, subversion and treason which could be used against the nonviolent political opposition, and institute the death penalty.

In addition to replacing the legislature,

China told a Hong Kong delegation in August that it was planning to set up provisional bodies to replace municipal councils and district boards but was "considering" allowing current members to stay on past 1997.

Freedom of expression also seemed endangered. In April, the deputy director of Xinhua news agency in Hong Kong, which acts as China's "embassy" in the territory, called on the Hong Kong government to "discipline" Radio Television Hong Kong (RTHK) for failing to give air time on demand to the Preparatory Committee. In June, Lu Ping, head of the Hong Kong and Macau Affairs Office under China's State Council, warned that after the transition the Chinese government would criminalize not only advocacy of certain viewpoints, such as support of Taiwan or Tibetan independence, but also merely publicizing those views. In July, China's information minister suggested that after 1997, local journalists in Hong Kong would be well advised to look to the press in China for "guidance" on what was proper to report. The Chinese government was known to be keeping a blacklist of Hong Kong journalists; the most common form of punishment for such reporters, according to the 1996 report of the Hong Kong Journalists Association, was simply to deny them entry to China. During 1996, journalists from the *Apple Daily*, *Next Magazine*, and *Open Magazine* were stopped at the Chinese border and forbidden to enter.

China continued to insist that it would not provide reports on the situation of human rights in Hong Kong to the U.N. Human Rights Committee set up under the International Covenant on Civil and Political Rights (ICCPR), in violation of its treaty obligation with the United Kingdom. Although the U.K. is a party to that covenant, and China is not, the two countries agreed in the 1984 Sino-British Joint Declaration that the covenant's protections would continue to extend to Hong Kong after 1997. At a meeting in February 1996, China and Britain agreed on a legal mechanism whereby approximately 200 multilateral international treaties would continue to apply to Hong Kong after July 1997; Beijing, however, excluded both the ICCPR and the International Covenant on Economic, Social and Cultural Rights from this list.

The fate of some eighty dissidents from the Chinese mainland currently in Hong Kong was a continuing concern, as human rights organizations and some foreign consulates stepped up efforts to ensure their resettlement to third countries before the 1997 transition.

The situation of Vietnamese asylum seekers in Hong Kong continued to be grim, as the Hong Kong government stepped up efforts to repatriate all remaining 14,000 residents of the Vietnamese camps before the transition. Conditions for camp inmates were worse than those for convicted criminals in prisons, particularly in terms of overcrowding and sanitary facilities. Violence was pervasive. On May 10, a major riot broke out inside the Whitehead Detention Center, sparked by asylum seekers who had been denied refugee status protesting forced repatriation. Camp inmates took guards hostage and burned twenty-six buildings and fifty-three vehicles. Hong Kong security forces used no lethal force in quelling the riot, but many observers believed that the inhumane and overcrowded conditions had contributed to the outbreak.

The Right to Monitor

Hong Kong human rights organizations operated freely, although they were increasingly concerned about their ability to do so after 1997. While the Basic Law guarantees freedom of association, it also, under Article 23, bans ties to foreign political organizations, and there is concern that after the transition, the provisional legislature to be appointed with Beijing's approval might pass legislation that construes ties to international religious, philanthropic, or human rights organizations as "political."

The Role of the International Community

It was clear that the international community was worried about the transition, particularly after China announced its intent to dissolve Legco. There was also widespread concern about the fate of the Vietnamese boat people.

On June 25, the Foreign Relations Committee of the U.S. Senate adopted a strongly worded resolution urging China not to proceed with plans to replace Legco. The full Senate passed the measure on June 28. The Clinton administration, while clearly unhappy with the move, refused to take a position on whether abolition of Legco would be a violation of the Basic Law, saying in July that it could not make a legal interpretation on a treaty to which it was not a party.

In the Fiscal Year 1997 U.S. foreign aid bill, signed by President Clinton on September 30, a requirement was inserted requiring Congress to provide additional reporting on the implementation of the Sino-British Joint Declaration, particularly with respect to the fairness of the election of the chief executive, the treatment of political parties, the independence of the judiciary, and the Bill of Rights. The legislation cited "deficiencies" in the report that the administration had submitted to Congress under the terms of the U.S.-Hong Kong Policy Act.

In July, at the annual ASEAN post-ministerial conference, and again in September at the United Nations, U.S. Secretary of State Warren Christopher raised concerns about Hong Kong with his Chinese counterpart, Foreign Minister Qian Qichen. National Security Adviser Anthony Lake had Hong Kong and the dissolution of Legco on the agenda when he visited China in July.

In the Asia-Pacific region, the Japanese government urged Beijing to uphold its international commitments on Hong Kong. On July 28, Australian Foreign Minister Alexander Downer warned China of international concern if pro-democracy members of Legco were not reappointed to the provisional legislature, and on September 16, Jeremy Hanley, a British Foreign Ministry official visiting Hong Kong, said that Britain would continue its efforts to persuade the Chinese government that dissolution of Legco was a "bad idea."

In July, the Canadian government offered to take mainland dissidents who would face persecution after the 1997 transition.

On July 18, the European Parliament adopted a resolution on the Vietnamese boat people, condemning the use of violence against asylum seekers, calling on U.N. member states to offer settlement to those with refugee status, and urging the UNHCR to extend its repatriation program to avoid deportations by force.

INDIA

Human Rights Developments

After taking office in June, India's new United Front government made several gestures that marked a change from previous governments' human rights policies, such as vowing to sign the United Nations Convention against Torture and other Cruel, Inhuman or Degrading Treatment or Punishment and allowing a visit by Amnesty International in July. However, it was not clear whether the government was prepared to address long-standing human rights concerns ranging from police abuse to bonded child labor. India also maintained its reputation as one of the most dangerous places in the world for human rights activists. The detention and subsequent murder of human rights activist Jalil Andrabi in Kashmir in March and the shooting death of Assamese activist Parag Das in May exposed the security forces' use of irregular militias to carry out abuses. By November, no one had been prosecuted in either murder. Human rights and environmental groups also came under increasing attack for their efforts to organize protests against large-scale development projects.

The tumultuous mid-year election that ousted the Congress government of Narasimha Rao resulted in a hung parliament and gave the Hindu-nationalist Indian People's Party (Bharatiya Janata Party, best known by its initials, BJP) its first opportunity to form a national government. After failing to win the support of any other party, the BJP lost a vote of confidence after only eleven days in office. On June 1 a coalition United Front government of left and regional parties assumed office and H.D. Deve Gowda became prime minister.

Parliamentary elections were also held in Jammu and Kashmir in May for the first time since 1989. Militant leaders called for a boycott, however, and there were widespread reports that security forces had forced voters to go to the polls. Shortly before the elections, the state government imposed a ban on any reporting that "directly or indirectly express[ed] lack of faith" in the state and federal constitutions or was deemed "prejudicial to the unity and integrity of the state and country"—apparent references to articles that might advocate a boycott of the elections or call for independence. State assembly elections in Jammu and Kashmir in September were also marred by reports of coercion and the arrests of leaders of the All-Parties Huriyat Conference—an umbrella group of parties opposed to the elections. Following the election, the National Conference party formed the first state government since 1990, and Farooq Abdullah, who together with Congress party leaders had been responsible for rigging state elections in 1987, again became chief minister.

Indian security forces in Kashmir continued their practice of arming and training local auxiliary forces made up of surrendered or captured militants to assist in counterinsurgency operations. These state-sponsored paramilitary groups, along with their counterparts in the regular security forces, committed serious human rights abuses, and human rights monitors and journalists were among the principal victims. On December 8, 1995, Zafar Mehraj, a veteran Kashmiri journalist, was shot and critically injured as he returned from an interview with Koko Parray, the head of the state-sponsored paramilitary group Ikhwan-ul Muslimoon. Although Mehraj had previously been threatened by both the security forces and some militant groups, in this case the evidence strongly implicated the state-sponsored militia force, Ikhwan-ul Muslimoon. Ikhwan-ul Muslimoon forces were also believed to be responsible for the murder of Farooq Ahmed Sheikh, a thirty-one-year-old pharmacist at the Soura hospital in Srinagar, on December 2, 1995.

Extrajudicial executions and torture by Indian security forces in Kashmir also continued. Ghulam Ahmed Bhat, an eighteen-year-old man who was deaf and mute, was summarily executed by troops of the Seventh Battalion of the Border Security Force (BSF) during a crackdown in Nawakadal, Srinagar, on December 21, 1995. During a visit to Kashmir in January, Human Rights Watch interviewed a number of torture victims who described severe beatings and the use of electric shocks. Civilians also continued to complain of assault, including sexual assault, by security forces during crackdowns. No prosecutions of security personnel for torture or murder were made public.

Militant organizations in Kashmir engaged in kidnapping and indiscriminate attacks on civilians. On January 4, fifteen Hindu villagers from the Barshala village in Doda were killed after unidentified gunmen reportedly ordered them to line up before separating Hindus from Muslims. Official sources claimed that Harakat-ul Ansar, a militant group, was responsible. A bomb exploded on December 3, 1995, at a crowded bus stop in Anantnag. At least eight civilians were killed and twenty injured. No group claimed responsibility. A bomb that exploded in the Sadar Bazaar business district of Srinagar in early January killed seven people and injured at least thirty-five others. The Jammu and Kashmir Islamic Front claimed responsibility. There was no word on the fate of four foreigners kidnapped by the Al-Faran militant group in July 1995.

Problems of impunity plagued the investigation into communal violence in Bombay. On January 23, Maharashtra Chief Minister Manohar Joshi terminated the Srikrishna Commission, which had been set up to investigate communal riots that had left over 1,000 dead in Bombay between December 1992 and January 1993. The riots, which followed the destruction of a sixteenth-century mosque in Ayodhya in the north Indian state of Uttar Pradesh, were orchestrated by police and other officials and political leaders, and targeted Bombay's Muslims. In response to petitions filed by human rights groups in the Bombay High Court seeking to revive the Srikrishna Commission, on May 28, 1996, the commission was reinstated. On October 18, eleven Muslims were sentenced to life in prison for the murder of six Hindus during the riots. However, as of November, not a single member of the police had been prosecuted for attacks on Muslims, nor had the commission's findings been made public.

In a long-overdue and welcome decision, on August 27, Judge Shiv Narain Dinghra sentenced eighty-nine men to five years rigorous imprisonment—the harshest category of imprisonment—for their roles in the anti-Sikh riots of 1984 in which more than 3,000 Sikhs were killed. In his judgment, Dinghra named senior Delhi police officials as the "real culprits" and accused them and their "political masters" of supporting the rioters and suppressing the truth about the killings. Several independent human rights groups had documented the involvement of police and Congress party officials in orchestrating the massacre. In September, Kishori Lal, a butcher from Delhi, was convicted of the murders of two Sikhs during the riots—the first such murder conviction in the twelve years since the riots. In June, H.K.L. Bhagat, a former Congress party minister, was indicted for his role in inciting and directing the rioters.

In a report to the Supreme Court on July 30, the Central Bureau of Investigation (CBI) named nine police officials responsible for the 1995 abduction of human rights lawyer Jaswant Singh Khalra in Punjab. The Supreme Court directed that the nine officers face trial for the abduction, that further investigations be carried out to ascertain the fate of Jaswant Singh Khalra and that key witnesses be offered protection during the investigations. On July 22 the CBI stated in a report to the court that it had found *prima facie* evidence that the Punjab police had secretly disposed of 984 bodies between 1990 and 1995, a period in which hundreds of Sikh men "disappeared" in police custody. In a separate case, former Director-General of Police K.P.S. Gill was sentenced to three months' rigorous imprisonment for slapping a female police officer. Gill has also been implicated in the torture and murder of hundreds of Sikhs in the police crackdown on the insurgency in Punjab. He has never been charged with these crimes.

Heightened attention to the problem of bonded child labor by organizations both within India and abroad helped spur some reforms by state governments. In a promising development, the newly elected government in the southern state of Tamil Nadu announced that implementation of the Bonded Labour (Abolition) Act (BLA) would be a priority and vowed to establish vigilance committees to oversee enforcement of the law throughout the state. The announcement prompted the formation of a coalition of nongovernmental organizations (NGOs) to work specifically on the issue of bonded child labor, focusing on rehabilitation and public education. At the national level, the Tamil Nadu NGOs, together with Delhi-based activists, began working with the new government on forming a national commission to oversee implementation of the BLA. In its 1994-95 report, the Ministry of Labor recommended raising the rehabilitation allowance for freed bonded laborers from 6,250 to 10,000 rupees (from approximately US$178 to $285). It was not clear, as of this writing, whether this recommendation had been implemented. As of November, there were no known prosecutions of employers who made use of bonded child labor.

Police arrests of street children, a frequent occurrence in railway stations throughout India, increased sharply in Bombay during July and August, the height of the monsoon. Street children using the Bombay Central Railway Station for shelter and employment were rounded up almost daily in a police campaign to "improve the quality of life" at the station by removing criminals and vagrants. The children were detained and beaten, often for the purposes of extortion, and then left without shelter. Lawyers filed a writ petition in the Bombay High Court asking for the court's intervention to stop the roundups and torture of street children.

Of the forty or so ethnic insurgent groups seeking autonomy in India's northeastern states, the most powerful operated in the states of Assam, Manipur, Nagaland and Tripura, carrying out attacks on security personnel, political assassinations, kidnapping, and murder of executives of key industries. The largest of these were the United Liberation Front of Assam (ULFA) and the National Socialist Council of Nagaland (NSCN). Civilians were frequent victims of Indian government counterinsurgency operations against these groups. In Manipur, deaths and "disappearances" of civilians at the hands of Indian authorities led to a series of strikes and demonstrations calling for independent inquiries, compensation and disciplinary action; journalists in Assam held a protest in May denouncing killings and harassment of their colleagues. The Armed Forces (Special Powers) Act, which grants the military broad powers to arrest and detain suspects, destroy property, and shoot to kill remained in place in the northeast. The law has been widely criticized for contributing to human rights abuses. Surrendered ULFA militants, called "SULFAs," aided Indian security forces in counterinsurgency and were also implicated in extrajudicial killings.

In Assam's Kokrajhar district, ethnic violence in May and June between members of the Bodo and Santhal tribes killed some eighty people and displaced at least 20,000 others when villages were destroyed by arson.

Between January and March 1996, more than 1,000 ethnic Nepali Bhutanese who had sought refuge in Nepal after their forcible eviction from Bhutan in 1990 began a peaceful march from the camps in Nepal through India to the Bhutan border. They were stopped from reaching the border by police in West Bengal, arrested and detained. Many of the marchers were beaten, and one died in custody. On July 5, 791 of them who had been detained since March were unconditionally released.

The Right to Monitor

Many human rights groups in India, particularly those based in major metropolitan areas, operated fairly freely in 1996. Those active in more remote rural areas who challenged the power of influential landlords or business owners, and those based in areas of conflict such as the northeast or Kashmir undertook considerable risks.

Jalil Andrabi, a prominent human rights lawyer and political activist associated with the pro-independence Jammu and Kashmir Liberation Front, was found murdered on March 27, 1996. According to eyewitnesses, Andrabi had been detained on March 8 by a Rashtriya Rifles unit of the army which had intercepted his car a few hundred yards from his home in Srinagar. The army repeatedly denied that Andrabi was in custody. Andrabi had previously received death threats from government-sponsored so-called "renegade" forces, and it was widely believed that Andrabi may have been handed over to such forces after his arrest. The bodies of some of the men believed to have been involved in the Andrabi's killing were later discovered in April; it was widely believed that they had been killed by the security forces. India's official National Human Rights Commission (NHRC) launched an investigation of Andrabi's killing, but as of November, no findings had been announced, and human rights lawyers complained of obstruction by the army and tampering with evidence from the post-mortem examination.

Parag Kumar Das, general secretary of the Assamese human rights organization Manab Adhikar Sangram Samiti (MASS), and editor in chief of the Assamese publication *Asomiya Pratidin*, was shot and killed by unidentified gunmen on May 17 as he was taking his son to school. The seven-year-old boy was wounded in the attack. A proponent for self-rule in Assam, shortly before his death Parag Das had published an interview in *Asomiya Pratidin* with the leader of the militant separatist group, ULFA. Das's colleagues in Assam suspected that his assassination may have been carried out by gunmen formerly associated with ULFA who had been working with the security forces.

On October 7, Warangal district police in the southern state of Andhra Pradesh threatened to "liquidate" Dr. Burra Ramulu and Amabati Srinivas, both members of the Andhra Pradesh Civil Liberties Committee, apparently because both men had called for judicial inquiries into police abuses against suspected members and supporters of the People's War Group, a Maoist guerrilla organization. Earlier that day, seven policemen had been killed by a land mine planted by the guerrilla group. On October 9, the Andhra Pradesh High Court ordered the state to provide protection to the two men.

In its annual report to Parliament on September 10, the NHRC accused the state government in Kashmir of concealing reports of human rights abuses by security personnel. At the same time, when provided with reports of abuse from independent human rights groups, the NHRC was seldom willing to push the authorities for impartial investigations. The NHRC vowed to make child labor and child prostitution a priority for its work in 1996; however, the commission recommended no specific reforms or programs to deal with bonded labor.

Activists who have organized protests against the environmental degradation caused by prawn aquaculture and the use of bonded labor on such farms have been harassed and arrested. On December 15, 1995, five activists of the Institute for Motivating Self-Employment (IMSE), an organization devoted to freeing farmers in Orissa from debt-bondage to landlords and money lenders and raising awareness about the harmful effects of aquaculture, were reportedly detained without charge after local police invited them to a meeting to discuss their work. On December 17, three IMSE activists who were protesting the arrest of their colleagues were also arrested. All eight IMSE workers were detained until January 19, 1996. When the director of IMSE and two human rights activists from Bangalore arrived to investigate the incident on December 20, their car tires were punctured by unidentified armed men who threatened them with "dire consequences" if they continued their investigation. The driver attempted to file a complaint, but the police refused to register the charges and instead detained the driver overnight. On returning to the car, the driver found that all documents had been removed.

Medha Patkar, leader of the Save the Narmada Movement (Narmada Bachao Andolan), was arrested by the Madhya Pradesh police on August 20. Patkar had organized a peaceful protest against the government's failure to provide rehabilitation to people ousted by the construction of a dam on the Narmada river. A number of activists were also beaten by police who broke up the demonstration. Patkar was held under a preventive detention law until August 30.

On June 27, police entered the villages of Mitihini and Khairi, in the Sonebhadra district of Uttar Pradesh, where villagers had protested forced resettlement to clear the area for an ash dike for the Rihand Super Thermal Power Project. A number of villagers were reportedly beaten, and thirteen protesters were detained.

The Role of the International Community

As had been the case in previous years, trade issues dominated international interest in India in 1996, and expressions of concern about human rights were limited to a few prominent cases. For example, the murder of Jalil Andrabi and the ongoing problem of child labor and bonded child labor led a number of countries to raise concerns with the government of India, both publicly and privately. However, the long-standing issue of impunity for the military in Kashmir and elsewhere in the country and the endemic problem of custodial violence received virtually no attention from the international community.

Following Andrabi's murder, on April

2, United Nations High Commissioner for Human Rights José Ayala Lasso called on the government of India to "undertake a thorough investigation ... with a view to establishing the facts and imposing sanctions on those found guilty of the crime."

The issue of bonded child labor received considerable attention at the World Bank convened donor meeting on India that took place in Tokyo in September, as a number of participant countries raised concerns about World Bank-funded projects that have made use of bonded child labor and about the need for donor involvement in rehabilitation efforts.

The European Council and the European Commission held talks in New Delhi with then Prime Minister Rao in early May, at which the EU agreed to support India's participation in the next E.U.-Asia summit. India was not invited to the meeting in Bangkok in March.

In late June, the European Commission issued its first official position paper on E.U.-India relations, outlining a long-term agenda for an "enhanced partnership." The paper focused on the impact of India's economic reforms in a democratic, multi-cultural society and was aimed at developing a framework for the E.U. to pursue its main interest in India: getting better access to India's "enormous market." There was a deliberate effort to downplay controversial issues, especially human rights. In the framework of an E.U.-India Partnership and Cooperation Agreement, signed in 1993 and conditioned on respect for human rights, an E.U.-India Joint Committee was set to meet in December 1996 in New Delhi. The joint committee was to outline specific priorities, including intensification of dialogue on "political issues" though the emphasis would clearly be on trade and investment; a business forum was scheduled for Brussels the month before. As the year ended, it was not clear what level of priority human rights would be given by the joint committee.

Most countries took a timid approach to the elections in Kashmir. Both the U.K. and the U.S. called on officials to ensure that the vote would be free and fair; however, neither publicly criticized widespread intimidation of voters by security forces. British Foreign Secretary Malcolm Rifkind also urged India to allow international observers at the polls. (The government did not permit international observers.) U.S. officials stated that they believed a fair vote could lead to "stability" and begin a political process. A visit to Srinagar by U.S. Ambassador Frank Wisner in August sparked criticism by most leaders of the opposition All-Parties Huriyat Conference, who refused to meet with Wisner because of what they claimed was his pro-India stand on the elections, and by opposition parliamentarians in New Delhi, who accused the U.S. ambassador of interference in an internal matter.

The U.S. embassy in New Delhi continued to relegate human rights concerns to a low priority. Although the State Department issued a strong statement condemning Andrabi's murder and calling for a "full and transparent investigation," embassy personnel expressed no further concern about reports of army obstruction of the investigation and the lack of progress in the case. Although the ambassador raised concern about child labor, the embassy played no notable role on any other human rights issue.

The U. S. Department's report on human rights was markedly less forthright about government abuses than had been the case in previous years. While attempting to characterize the situation in Kashmir as improving, the report completely failed to address abuses by state-sponsored militias. Elsewhere, the report appeared oblivious of documentation by Indian human rights organizations about deaths in custody and other abuses.

The U.S. continued to expand its program of military cooperation with India, holding special joint naval exercises and a visits to the U.S. by Chief of Army Staff Shankar Roy in September. Joint air force exercises and a visit to India by senior U.S. defense officials were scheduled for later in the year.

INDONESIA AND EAST TIMOR

The most serious riot in Jakarta in two decades in July underscored increasing tension in Indonesia as demands of various groups for more political participation, less abuse by the security forces, and a greater share of the economic pie continued to be met with repression. Jakarta was not the only site of unrest during the year; demonstrations followed by riots brokeout in Irian Jaya in March, July and September; in Ujung-pandang (South Sulawesi) and Ngabang (West Kalimantan) in April; and in East Timor in June.

Freedom of expression and association continued to suffer with opposition politicians, journalists, nongovernmental organization (NGO) activists, trade unionists, students, and an independent election monitoring group all facing various forms of harassment, in some cases involving arrest and torture. The government-engineered ouster of Megawati Soekarnoputri as head of the opposition party, Partai Demokrasi Indonesia (PDI), in June, and the arrests in July, August and September of dozens of student leaders and independent labor leader Mochtar Pakpahan were only the most severe manifestations of government intolerance of dissent. The government also attempted to fan fears of a resurgence of a communist threat in order to legitimize its actions against critics and to discredit opposition parties and their members.

At the same time, there were more prosecutions of military officers for human rights abuses—at least four cases involving over twenty men—than in any previous year. The prosecutions were welcome, but given other developments in Indonesia, it was difficult to conclude that they were evidence of a greater sense of the need for government accountability. In East Timor, a wide range of human rights violations continued to take place, compounded by increased training of civilian and paramilitary militias composed of East Timorese and by increasing incidents of religious and ethnic violence. The granting of the Nobel Peace Prize in October to two East Timorese was expected to increase international pressure for human rights improvements there.

The right to monitor the human rights situation in the country was compromised by the intimidation and harassment of NGOs that followed the emergence of KIPP, the election monitoring organization, and the crackdown on the student-led People's Democratic Party in July and August.

The July riots led to criticism of Indonesian government actions internationally, particularly from the European Parliament and the United States, and nervousness among foreign investors, but few concrete actions were forthcoming.

Human Rights Developments

The most significant political and human rights developments in the country surrounded the rise and removal of Megawati Sukarnoputri as a political opposition leader; the occupation of PDI headquarters in Jakarta by her supporters and their removal by army-backed paramilitary forces on July 27; the riots that followed; and the arrest and detention of members of a small leftist party that the government blamed for the violence.

In a clear violation of freedom of association, Megawati was ousted from the PDI in a special party congress held in Medan, Sumatra in June. The government ceased to recognize her as an official of the PDI, her supporters were removed from the PDI candidate list for the 1997 parliamentary elections, and her efforts in September to open a new office were thwarted by the government on the grounds that the office violated a zoning ordinance.

Following the Medan congress, Megawati supporters occupied PDI headquarters in Jakarta. On July 27, hundreds of youths linked to the newly installed PDI head, Soerjadi, backed by police and military personnel, forcibly entered and physically removed Megawati's supporters and set fire to the headquarters. The attack sparked a full-scale riot, affecting the area around the PDI offices and spreading into other parts of the city. Protestors stoned and set fire to more than twenty buildings; at least five people were killed and some 150 wounded. More than 200 people, including bystanders, were arrested; some of the latter were held up to five days and tortured to force confessions of involvement in the violence. Some 124 were later charged with crimes under the Indonesian criminal code and initially were denied access to lawyers. Virtually all of those formally charged were suspected Megawati supporters; meanwhile, none of the youths involved in the storming of the PDI headquarters were arrested.

The government, looking for a scapegoat for the riots, blamed a small leftist student-led organization called the People's Democratic Party (Partai Rakyat Demokratik, PRD) and its student, worker, peasant, and cultural affiliates. The PRD was accused not only of masterminding the riots but of being the new incarnation of the banned Indonesian Communist Party. By November 1, some thirty-nine students were in detention, at least five of whom had been tortured with electric shocks during military interrogation. Also in detention was labor leader Muchtar Pakpahan, general secretary of the Prosperous Worker's Union of Indonesia (Serikut Buruh Sejahtera Indonesia, SBSI), who was arrested at his home on July 30. Pakpahan was head of the NGO coalition supporting Megawati called the Indonesian People's Council (Majelis Rakyat Indonesia, MARI) which had the PRD as one of its members.

Both Muchtar and the head of the PRD, Budiman Sudjatmiko, who was arrested on August 11, were charged with subversion. While subversion is a capital offense, prosecutors were unlikely to seek the death penalty. The trials were expected to begin in late November or early December.

The government used the riots and the new "threat" posed by the PRD as a pretext for summoning and interrogating political critics. Prominent intellectuals such as Goenawan Mohammad, the former editor of *Tempo* magazine; former prisoner and internationally respected writer Pramoedya Ananta Toer; Bambang Widjojanto, head of the Indonesian Legal Aid Institute; and Megawati herself were among those summoned.

The Ministry of Information and the social and political affairs office of the armed forces, which had tried to suppress reporting about the dispute within PDI prior to the July riot, issued a strong warning afterwards to three tabloid newspapers about their coverage of events. Of the three, *Mutiara, Target,* and *Paron*, the latter had carried an interview with PRD leader Budiman Sudjatmiko that some said led to the discovery of his hiding place and subsequent arrest. Controls on the press continued through the end of the year; members of the Alliance of Independent Journalists, who defied bans on reporting and provided in-depth analysis of events in an underground magazine called *Suara Independen (Independent Voice)* faced dismissal and arrest. On October 28, police confiscated 5,000 copies of the magazine and arrested two printing press workers on charges of defaming the president and distributing an insulting publication.

The government's crackdown on the PRD was foreshadowed by its moves in April and May against the independent election monitoring group set up in March called the Komite Independen Pemantau Pemilu (KIPP), in which student and NGO activists were deeply involved. Thirty branches of KIPP sprang up across the country within three months of its founding; government harassment of NGOs linked to KIPP increased as a result, with KIPP meetings banned in Solo, Lampung and elsewhere. On April 22, the Medan office of theLegal Aid Institute was firebombed following a KIPP meeting, and the office of an NGO in Samarinda, East Kalimantan, whose members were active in the local KIPP branch, was raided the same month. Also in April, a local government office in Bogor, West Java, made public accusations that KIPP secretary general Mulyana Kusumah was affiliated with a communist group as a high school student, more than thirty years earlier. Newspapers and magazines were told they could no longer publish Mulyana's writings. The allegations seemed designed to discredit the election monitors.

In another example of violations of freedom of expression, prominent government critic and former parliamentarian for the United Development Party (UDP), Sri Bintang Pamungkas, was sentenced on May 8 to two years and ten months in prison on charges of "defaming the president." Bintang had been arrested and charged under Article 134 of the criminal code for remarks made during a lecture given in Berlin, Germany in April 1995 (*see* 1996 World Report). The sentence was upheld by an appellate court in October.

Political unrest erupted in several different areas of Indonesia during the year. In Irian Jaya, tensions resulting from the army killing of civilians in the Timika area in 1994 and 1995 remained high, with local groups convinced that the huge Freeport copper and gold mine that dominates the area bore some responsibility, directly or indirectly, for the problem. In February, a military court in Irian Jaya sentenced four soldiers to prison terms ranging from eighteen months to three years for killing three Timika villagers. A week after the trial, the then Irian Jaya military commander Major General Dunidja issued a booklet for soldiers on human rights and military professionalism, indicating a new sensitivity on the part of the army to human rights criticism.

Between March 10 and 12, thousands of Irianese took part in demonstrations of unprecedented scale in Timika following an incident in which a local man was injured and taken to the hospital by a Freeport employee. Rioters stormed and attacked security posts as well as property belonging to the mining company and its employees. The riot led to unfounded accusations that NGOs had organized it and complicated efforts to release twenty-six hostages seized by a guerrilla group, the Free Papua Movement (Organisasi Papua Merdeka, OPM), in January, in violation of international humanitar-

ian law. After negotiations to free the hostages failed, the Indonesian military mounted a rescue operation in May in which nine were freed and two were killed, apparently by Papuans but not by their immediate captors.

A second riot broke out on March 18 in Jayapura, capital of Irian Jaya, after the body of an independence leader, Thomas Wanggai, was returned for burial following his death in prison in Jakarta on March 12. Demonstrators were convinced Wanggai had been killed, although he seems to have died of natural causes.

Following the March riots and in light of the continued tensions between Freeport and the indigenous people within Freeport's contract of work area, the company indicated its intention to create a trust fund to be used for the benefit of the local community. On June 29, LEMASA (Lembaga Musyawarah Adat Suku Amungme), the representative body of the Amungme people, rejected the trust fund offer on the grounds that the funds would be channeled through the government rather than being given directly to the people. Disputes over that decision led to a demonstration on July 18 and subsequent allegations by the army that those who rejected the offer were subversives. Members of the Amungme group filed a class action suit against Freeport in U.S. district court under the U.S. Alien Tort Claim Act and the Torture Victim Protection Act of 1991. As of July 29 more than 1,000 individuals had joined in the suit against Freeport.

Another hostage-taking incident took place in mid-August 1996. Thirteen employees of the Djajanti Logging Company were taken hostage about sixty kilometers from the town of Timika. The Indonesian press reported that the hostage-takers were OPM members, but the circumstances surrounding the incident remained murky. Army spokespersons initially insinuated that WALHI, an environmental NGO that had been openly critical of Freeport's activities in Irian Jaya, and Tom Beanal, executive director of LEMASA, were somehow involved, but the allegations, yet another form of harassment against NGOs, were subsequently dropped.

On April 7, some 2,000 resident of the village of Ngabang, 186 kilometers east of the West Kalimantan capital of Pontianak, stormed an army camp to protest the severe torture of a local man named Jining. Jining was tortured because he drove by an army post too quickly. The army responded to the demonstrators with force, resulting in the death of a villager named Taku. On May 14, the National Human Rights Commission (KOMNAS) promised NGOs that it would investigate the incident, and the KOMNAS findings led to the prosecution of fourteen soldiers in July.

On April 22-24, riots broke out in Ujungpandang after student activists organized transport workers and others to protest a rise in transportation fares. Armored personnel carriers entered the campus of the Indonesian Muslim University (UMI), and in the ensuing turmoil, five students died. Three drowned after apparently jumping in a nearby river to escape army vehicles. Following an investigation by the government-appointed human rights commission, twelve soldiers were indicted on charges of procedural violations. On September 25, six of the twelve appeared in the Ujungpandang military court as their court martial began; in late October, the prosecutor recommended sentences of between five and six months for the accused.

A series of labor rallies took place during the year involving thousands of workers demonstrating for freedom of association and a higher minimum wage; Indonesia has only one legal trade union federation that is largely controlled by the government. One of the largest rallies took place in Surabaya, East Java, on July 8 involving 20,000 workers and led to the arrest of its student organizers on incitement charges. At year's end, it seemed likely that they would be charged with the political offense either of subversion or of "spreading hatred against the government."

Ethnic and religious violence increased in East Timor, some of it apparently deliberately provoked. In June, riots broke out in the town of Baucau after an Indonesian guard at a mosque in Baguia posted a picture of the Virgin Mary with a derogatory caption. The incident led to a protest march, security forces were called in to contain the demonstration, and upon their arrival, violence broke out. Over one hundred people were detained for their involvement in the demonstration.

Extrajudicial executions and torture continued in East Timor. In April 1996 a high school student, Paulo Dos Reis, was shot and killed by an Indonesian soldier after being suspected of resistance activities. Also in April Andre Sousa was shot and killed by an Indonesian soldier after he removed an Indonesian flag that had been flying at half-mast in honor of the death of President Soeharto's wife.

The Right to Monitor

Indonesian human rights organizations faced widespread harassment during the year throughout the country, although by year's end, fears of new regulations to curb their activities had not materialized. The alliance between human rights groups and pro-democracy activists in the formation of the independent election monitoring committee and the involvement of the largest human rights organization in the country, the Legal Aid Institute, in a coalition that supported Megawati and the PDI, led to tightened surveillance of NGO operations and intimidation of individual activists.

KOMNAS continued to function as a cautious but effective challenge to the military and helped bring about several prosecutions of soldiers accused of human rights abuses. KOMNAS at year's end was experiencing greater pressure from the government than ever before as a result of its preliminary findings of human rights violations in connection with the July riots, and there was widespread concern in Indonesia that the institution would emerge somewhat weakened as a result.

KOMNAS opened an office in Dili, East Timor, in July, but its effectiveness was compromised by the fact that it was located directly across the street from the district military command and was headed by a former prosecutor from the Indonesian island of Flores who did not speak the local language.

The Role of the International Community

The international community was sharply critical of Indonesia following the government's raid on the PDI headquarters in July and its subsequent actions against political activists. Other issues, such as East Timor and restrictions on freedom of expression, also received attention during the year at the U.N. and at the annual meeting of the World Bank-led donor consortium for development aid, the Consultative Group on Indonesia. Labor rights violations were the subject of debate in the U.S. as well as in the World Bank. But in general, governments studiously avoided linking trade privileges or arms transfers to human rights abuses. At the ASEAN Regional Forum, Jakarta largely succeeded in deflecting concerns about human rights as "interference in internal affairs," although it could not keep Burma off the agenda. The controversy over Freeport-McMoRan's role in Irian Jaya and abuses in the region had an impact on both U.S. and World Bank-provided political risk insurance programs provided to the company.

United Nations

A consensus chair's statement on East Timor was adopted by the U.N. Human Rights Commission in Geneva in April, reiterating concerns raised by the commission in previous years and calling for a clarification of the 1991 Dili killings, early release of detained East Timorese, and expanded access by international human rights monitors. But there was no attempt to promote a resolution despite Indonesia's continuing failure to respond positively to these recommendations. Meanwhile, the All-Inclusive Intra-East Timorese Dialogue continued, under the U.N.'s auspices, with a meeting in Austria from March 19-22. Nigel Rodley, the U.N. Special Rapporteur on Torture, tried but failed to obtain permission from the Indonesian government to visit the territory. The government said that, as U.N. High Commissioner for Human Rights José Ayala Lasso had just visited in December 1995, there was no need for Rodley to come.

Europe

In March, the first Asia-Europe (ASEM) summit in Bangkok became the occasion for unscheduled bilateral talks between Portuguese Prime Minister Manual de Oliveira Guterres and President Soeharto on East Timor, where Guterres offered partial diplomatic relations with Indonesia in exchange for the release of imprisoned East Timorese resistance leader Xanana Gusmao. Not only did Soeharto reject the offer, but efforts were underway in late 1996 to ensure that East Timor was kept entirely off the agenda of the 1997 summit.

The European Parliament, on June 20, adopted a resolution following the suppression of protests in Baucau, East Timor earlier in the month; the motion also called for a halt in all military assistance arms sales from the EU to Indonesia, for the release of all political prisoners, and for the dropping of charges against ousted parliamentarian Sri Bintang Pamungkas.

When European Commission Vice-President Manuel Marin met with Indonesian Foreign Minister Ali Alatas in Jakarta on July 26, he said that the EU and ASEAN were looking for ways to separate their trade and investment relationship from discussion of human rights issues, and suggested this might meet putting a freeze of any discussion of East Timor at an EU-ASEAN foreign ministers meeting scheduled for February 1997 in Singapore.

On September 19, the European Parliament met in plenary session and adopted a resolution on Indonesia condemning the violent seizure of PDI headquarters and calling for the release of peaceful activists. The resolution also urged that the U.N. Special Rapporteur on Extrajudicial, Summary or Arbitrary Executions undertake an investigation into the deaths that occurred during the storming of the PDI office.

German Chancellor Helmut Kohl visited Indonesia from October 26-29, and while he raised East Timor and other human rights issues in passing, the main subject of the trip was trade. He was accompanied by three ministers and seventy business leaders, and the trip produced agreements on the setting up of several large German-Indonesian joint ventures.

United States

In the U.S., concerns about East Timor caused some members of Congress to press for a broadening of the existing U.S. ban on small arms sales to Indonesia, but the Fiscal Year 1997 foreign operations appropriations bill adopted in September contained funding to continue an expanded International Military Education and Training (IMET) program, while continuing the existing restrictions on arms sales. In addition, prominent members of Congress in March protested the prosecution of Sri Bintang Pamungkas in a letter to Foreign Minister Alatas.

The ASEAN annual ministerial meetings took place in Jakarta from July 23-27. U.S. Secretary of State Christopher used the opportunity to meet with members of Komnas and said, in an unusually pointed barb at the Soeharto government, that the U.S. had a "deep interest" in encouraging "political pluralism" in Indonesia.

After the July riots, officials of the U.S. expressed concern both in Jakarta and in Washington. In August, thirty-six members of the House of Representatives wrote to Foreign Minister Ali Alatas urging Jakarta to respect the rights of those arrested, to ensure restraint by the security forces, and to cooperate fully with KOMNAS in its investigations.

Members of the House and Senate also urged the administration to suspend the sale of F-16 advanced fighter planes to Indonesia as a way of signaling U.S. concern about the decline in human rights; by the time a Senate hearing took place in September, the administration had put the sale on hold out of deference to congressional opposition, while

also stating its intention to proceed with the sale early in 1997. During a visit to Indonesia early in September, Assistant Secretary of State for East Asia and the Pacific Winston Lord failed to bring up the F-16 sale with Indonesian officials or suggest specific human rights improvements that would allow the sale to go forward. He did meet with NGOs and raised human rights concerns in his meetings with officials; he also briefly visited two detainees (Pakpahan and Budiman) in their detention cells, and in his public comments repeatedly gave the authorities credit for this gesture.

The U.S. Trade Representative (USTR) as of October had yet to issue a determination on whether to reinstate the formal review of Indonesia's Generalized System of Preferences (GSP) trade benefits on worker rights grounds. United States law conditions the program on progress in protecting labor rights in recipient countries. In September twenty-nine members of the House of Representatives wrote to USTR to urge reinstatement of the review, noting, in particular, the arrest of Mochtar Pakpahan and other labor activists. (The GSP program was newly funded by Congress in mid-1996, leaving the status of petitions filed in 1995 unaddressed; a petition on Indonesia calling for a review on worker rights grounds had been pending since August 1995).

Asia/Pacific

The Australian government did its best to avoid any criticism of Indonesia's human rights record. In August, Australian Foreign Minister Alexander Downer issued a weak statement following the July 27 riot, expressing the hope that conditions would return to normal quickly. But when Australian Prime Minister John Howard visited Indonesia in September, he avoided bringing up human rights altogether, despite pressure from Australian NGOs and members of parliament. The newly appointed Australian ambassador to Jakarta, John McCarthy, due to be posted in January 1997, told journalists he would avoid embarrassing the government publicly on human rights, while acknowledging that Australia was concerned about East Timor, freedom of expression, and other issues.

Japan also downplayed human rights concerns following the July crackdown, although the government did quietly urge Jakarta to release those detained solely for their peaceful political activity. Tokyo took no steps to review its large development aid program to Indonesia despite clear evidence of human rights violations.

Donors and Investors

At the World Bank-convened annual donors meeting in June, governments pledged $5.3 billion in development assistance for Indonesia, an increase of 7 percent over 1995 levels at constant exchange rates. In 1996, the bank loaned over $991 million to Jakarta and was the country's largest single donor. Some governments did express concern regarding Indonesia's human rights record in general terms, but no conditions were imposed and the bank congratulated the government on its overall economic performance.

In Irian Jaya, Freeport-McMoRan's $100-million political risk insurance contract with the U.S.-government-funded Overseas Private Investment Corporation, canceled in November 1995, was restored in April 1996 until the end of the year; the contract had been canceled on environmental grounds, though human rights concerns also were a factor. In September, the company itself abruptly canceled a separate $50-million political risk insurance contract with the World Bank's Multilateral Investment Guarantee Agency (MIGA), shortly before an investigation team from MIGA was due to leave for Irian Jaya to examine human rights and environmental problems surrounding the mine.

JAPAN

Human Rights Developments

Japan continued to confront allegations of poor prison conditions and discrimination in the legal system against foreigners, including women trafficked into the country for prostitution, migrant workers and Chinese dissidents who entered Japan as students. Its handling of the issue of "comfort women" who provided sexual services to the Japanese military during World War II continued to be controversial. Prime Minister Ryutaro Hashimoto's government was generally cautious in raising human rights concerns in other countries, particularly when dealing with its Asian neighbors where Tokyo has major economic and political interests at stake. The exception was Burma, subject of increasing concern and activism by the Japanese government in response to deteriorating conditions there. In its Official Development Assistance (ODA) program, Japan emphasized "positive linkage," offering assistance to governments in transition. Beyond its bilateral relations, Japan took some significant steps forward in 1996 by deciding to support the international campaign to ban land mines worldwide, and by announcing during a visit to Tokyo by President Clinton a joint program with the U.S. to build civil society and strengthen judicial systems in "new democracies." On the other hand, Japan continued to play a disappointing role in the U.N. discussions about an International Criminal Court, supporting the court in principle but slowing down the process of moving toward a diplomatic conference.

Within Japan, human rights abuses continued to occur during pre-trial detention and in prisons. Detention and prison facilities were characterized by draconian rules, arbitrary punishments, the use of prolonged solitary confinement, and severe restrictions on contact with the outside world. A number of lawsuits challenging the mistreatment of prisoners were filed over the course of the year. Indeed, there were over one hundred lawsuits pending in the Japanese courts that involved assaults by prison guards, the painful and degrading use of physical restraints as punishment, and other such abuses. The Center for Prisoners' Rights, a Japanese organization that litigates on behalf of prisoners, believed that as an increasing number of such suits were being filed, judges were becoming more inclined to rule in favor of prisoners.

Foreign workers in Japan continued to face major problems with the Japanese legal system, often not being provided with adequate interpretation or being informed of their rights, including their right to counsel, upon arrest for immigration or other offenses.

Asylum seekers faced major hurdles in Japan. In September, the Tokyo High Court rejected an appeal from a prominent Chinese dissident, Zhao Nan, for political asylum. His initial application was turned down by the Ministry of Justice in 1991, on the narrow technical grounds that he had not filed his original appeal for refugee status within sixty days of his arrival in Japan in 1989. The High Court upheld that ruling. Zhao Nan had been imprisoned inChina for two years from 1982 for his pro-democracy activities and continued his advocacy while in Japan. Since the 1989 massacre in China, no Chinese dissident has been recognized as a political refugee by the Japanese government, although at least forty-eight dissidents have obtained a special visa, renewable every six months, allowing them to remain in Japan. Zhao planned to appeal the ruling to the Supreme Court.

The treatment of some 200,000 so-called "comfort women" from China, Korea and the Philippines, forced by the Japanese army to serve as sex slaves during World War II, continued to receive international attention in 1996. U.N. Special Rapporteur on Violence against Women Radhika Coomaraswamy filed her report at the U.N. Human Rights Commission in April and urged the Japanese government to identify and punish those responsible for the use of sex slaves, to pay compensation to the victims, and to issue a public apology to the individual women in writing. Japanese officials questioned the accuracy of the report and lobbied unsuccessfully against its adoption by the commission. A voluntary fund established by the government began paying US$18,500 each to former sex slaves, which some NGOs and rights advocates welcomed and others criticized as insufficient either to fulfill the women's needs or to discharge the Japan's government's legal and moral responsibility.

The Foreign Ministry's annual report on ODA for 1995 (published in February 1996) noted that Japan was once again the largest bilateral aid donor worldwide, providing $14.5 billion in 1995. Among the top ten ODA recipients were major human rights abusers, including the governments of China (more than $1.4 billion) and Indonesia ($880 million), as well as India ($886 million) and Pakistan ($271 million). In describing implementation of the ODA Charter's provision calling for consideration of human rights conditions in giving aid, the Foreign Ministry emphasized Japan's efforts to assist newly emerging democracies or market economies in Mongolia, Cambodia, Vietnam, and countries in Africa and Central America. It also cited some examples of "negative linkage," where ODA was suspended due to human rights violations, including Nigeria and Gambia in 1994. In other cases, instead of cutting off aid, Japan "urged recipient countries to improve" human rights, such as Thailand and Peru; or it took steps to reduce balance-of-payments support assistance, as with Kenya and Malawi.

In Burma, Japan had suspended in principle most of its ODA in 1988 but following the release of Daw Aung San Suu Kyi in 1995 had moved to restore some limited grants assistance, such as $15.1 million for a nursing school, on "humanitarian grounds" and was preparing to restart major infrastructure projects.

Developments in 1996, however, pushed Tokyo to put any new ODA on hold and to take a tougher posture in response to the crackdown in Rangoon. Aung San Suu Kyi, in repeated interviews with the Japanese press, urged Japan to withhold aid and investment. Japan's ambassador in Rangoon, Yoichi Yamaguchi, met with her on several occasions and tried to play an intermediary role to help stimulate talks between her party, the National League for Democracy (NLD), and the government.

When the Burmese government rounded up NLD members in May, Prime Minister Hashimoto quickly condemned the arrests saying they "run counter to democratization" and publicly called on SLORC to hold a dialogue with the NLD. Japan's foreign minister, Yukihiko Ikeda, issued a strongly worded protest to his Burmese counterpart, who was visiting Tokyo at the time, calling the arrests illegal and "unacceptable to Japan." He also indicated privately that the increased repression would have a negative effect on Japanese investment in Burma. This message was followed up in July, at the ASEAN ministerial conference in Jakarta, where Ikeda again met with Burmese Foreign Minister Ohn Gyaw and protested a new law enacted by Rangoon banning public gatherings. At the same time, however, Japan actively supported Burma's bid to become a member of ASEAN.

Members of the Japanese Diet (parliament) urged Tokyo to go even further; a multiparty caucus called the "Diet Members' League for the Support of Myanmar's Democratization" issued a statement condemning the May arrests and urging Japan to "stop all cooperation" with Burma until those detained were released and the government began a dialogue with the opposition.

Reports in the Japanese press in June that Aung San Suu Kyi's arrest might be imminent provoked a warning from Tokyo that stronger action would be taken if she were detained, and the Foreign Ministry discussed possible contingencies for reacting to any further deterioration in conditions when two U.S. official envoys visited Tokyo to discuss Burma policy.

In contrast with its policy toward Burma, Japan reacted far less firmly to a major crackdown in Indonesia that began in July. While the government quietly urged Jakarta to release members of nongovernmental organizations and others detained solely for their peaceful political activity, it refused to condemn the violent arrests of those who occupied PDI (Democratic Party of Indone-

sia) headquarters, or the Indonesian government's use of the anti-subversion law. Tokyo took no steps to review its large ODA program to Indonesia. Foreign Minister Ikeda met with President Soeharto at the time of the ASEAN ministerial conference in July (prior to the crackdown); he raised the issue of human rights in East Timor during discussions with the Indonesian Foreign Minister Alatas.

Japan continued to downplay human rights in its relations with China, focusing instead on nuclear testing and regional security issues. Prime Minister Hashimoto met Premier Li Peng in Bangkok in March at the ASEAN summit meeting and urged China to support the Comprehensive Test Ban Treaty; he also pledged Japan's support for China's early entry into the World Trade Organization. The Chinese Foreign Minister visited Tokyo in March, but discussions were focused mainly on Taiwan. Early in 1996, the Japanese Foreign Ministry indicated it was considering putting a cap on ODA to Beijing in Fiscal Year 1996 due to China's nuclear testing program. But it continued to ignore the ODA Charter's human rights provisions in its relations with China. Amid tensions over Taiwan and the Diaoyu islands, the Japanese government was even more reluctant to raise human rights concerns with China except in the most general way. The Japanese government did, however, cosponsor the resolution on China at the U.N. Human Rights Commission in April, despite strong protests from Beijing, and it privately urged China to uphold its international commitments on Hong Kong during and following the transition to Chinese rule in 1997. Foreign Minister Ikeda noted this during a visit to Hong Kong in August following his meeting with Hong Kong Chief Secretary Anson Chan.

In Indochina, Japan stepped up its support of the governments of Vietnam and Cambodia. Foreign Minister Ikeda visited Vietnam in late July and signed aid agreements worth $3.6 million and offered economic and cultural aid worth $32.4 million over the next three years, primarily for bridge-building. In meetings with senior Vietnamese officials, he urged continued economic reforms and offered Japan's support in building up the legal system; otherwise, human rights were not explicitly on the agenda. On Cambodia, Japan cochaired with the World Bank an international donors' meeting in Tokyo on July 11-12 and arranged a separate meeting with the two Cambodian prime ministers and donor representatives to discuss the domestic political situation and plans for elections in 1997 and 1998. The Japanese ambassador to Phnom Penh underlined the need to prepare carefully for the elections in order to sustain donor support, but did not raise specific human rights concerns. Japan announced it would give $2.5 million for removal of landmines in Cambodia in 1996 and 1997.

In South Asia, human rights concerns were largely overshadowed by Japanese efforts to promote regional stability and denuclearization. Pakistan's prime minister, Benazir Bhutto, visited Tokyo in January and was urged to begin a dialogue with India on Kashmir. An ODA mission visited India in July, and though Japanese officials routinely discussed Kashmir as a source of tension and potential instability, they refrained from discussing human rights except by referring to the ODA Charter. In advance of an international India donors' meeting in Tokyo on September 16-18, cohosted with the World Bank, the Foreign Ministry ordered the Japanese embassy in New Delhi to investigate the use of bonded child labor.

In July, the Foreign Ministry cosponsored with U.N. University in Tokyo its second annual symposium on Human Rights in the Asia-Pacific Region. Though the seminar broke no new ground, it provided a useful forum to debate the pros and cons of establishing a regional human rights mechanism, and highlighted the positive role of NGOs throughout Asia.

The government announced in June, at the G-7 summit meeting in France, its plans to join the global campaign to ban land mines. Tokyo said it would hold an international conference in 1997 to support U.N.

landmine clearance, as well as assistance for landmine victims, and that it would cosponsor at the U.N. General Assembly a resolution promoting a total ban on landmines. On the other hand, Japan planned to continue to produce and use self-destructing and self-deactivating landmines until the enactment of an international treaty banning all antipersonnel landmines.

At the August session of the Preparatory Committee on an International Criminal Court in New York, Japan again argued for a lengthy negotiation process on the grounds that major legal issues had not yet been resolved. That position reflected Japan's lack of enthusiasm more generally about the whole concept of the ICC.

The Right to Monitor
Human rights groups in Japan faced no legal restrictions on their activities.

The Role of the International Community
The president of the European Commission, Jacques Santer, visited Tokyo in October 1996, but in his meetings with the prime minister, business leaders and others, he focused mainly on economic and trade relations, following up on the E.U.-ASEAN summit in Bangkok in March. He made only general references to the common interests of the E.U. and Japan in promoting "the rule of law, human rights, market principles (and) free trade," and called for greater coordination in development policies, especially in Africa.

The Clinton administration made some progress in 1996 to increase cooperation with Japan on human rights. The Administration sent two envoys to Asia in June to discuss policy toward Burma, and the discussions in Tokyo were considered productive by both sides. The U.S.-Japan Global Partnership Agenda, which had omitted human rights at Tokyo's urging, was updated during President Clinton's visit to Japan in April. A new component was added, aimed at encouraging the development of civil society in "democracies" by providing assistance with election preparation and monitoring and strengthening judicial systems. A working group meeting was projected for El Salvador to develop a pilot program with the Salvadoran government.

In preparation for the G-7 summit in France, Japan had agreed to the inclusion of human rights language on China, Hong Kong and Burma in the final communiqué, though this was later dropped. Informal contact and consultation took place during the year on other issues, including the resolution on human rights in China introduced at the United Nations Human Rights Commission in Geneva.

MALAYSIA

Human Rights Developments

Malaysia's harassment of nongovernmental organizations and its violations of freedom of expression were issues of concern during the year, and the arrest and trial of human rights activist Irene Fernandez, director of a women's and migrants' rights organization in Kuala Lumpur called Tenaganita, exemplified both.

On March 18, Fernandez, aged fifty, was arrested at her home and charged with "false reporting" under Section 8A(1) of the Printing Presses and Publications Act of 1984 in connection with a brief report Tenaganita had issued in July 1995 on the treatment of migrant workers in Malaysia's immigration detention centers. She was released on bail and was at liberty throughout the court proceedings.

The Tenaganita report, quoted widely in the national and international press, contained allegations of torture, mistreatment and deaths of migrant workers in the period 1994 to 1995 and focused in particular on a major detention camp outside Kuala Lumpur in the town of Semenyih. The report was denounced by the Home Ministry as defamatory, and when Fernandez's trial opened on June 10 in a Kuala Lumpur magistrate's court, the prosecution cited six-

teen statements it said were false. Unlike the Malaysian penal code, the Printing Presses and Publications Act places the burden of proof on the accused in defamation cases and assumes malice unless the accused can show that he or she took steps to verify the news. The charge carries a maximum penalty of three years in prison.

The trial, still going on at the end of the year and expected to continue through early 1997, became a *cause célèbre* among Asian NGOs and international advocacy groups working on behalf of migrants and women. NGOs were concerned that the charges diverted attention from the real problems of custodial abuse of immigrants and from state responsibility to investigate and prosecute those abuses. If there were errors in the report as the government alleged, the government could have provided a detailed refutation and given Tenaganita a chance to respond publicly or privately. Human rights activists were concerned that if NGOs were to be tried on criminal charges for errors in their publications and their daily activities disrupted as a result, freedom of expression and association both would be severely jeopardized.

The trial also led to questioning of Tenaganita's legal registration under the Companies Act, rather than the Societies Act. The latter has more onerous registration procedures and allows wider liability of personnel; as a result, many NGOs had elected to register under the former, but the government's investigation of Tenaganita suggested that more intense state scrutiny of NGO registration would be forthcoming.

The "false reporting" section of the Printing Presses and Publications Act, together with the Sedition Act, were used against opposition parliamentarian Lim Guan Eng from Malacca in a trial that opened in January and that many observers saw as an assault on free speech. In a lecture in January 1995, Lim had charged that a former Malacca chief minister, who also happened to be a powerful member of the ruling UMNO party, had raped a fifteen-year-old girl and that the girl had been detained for three years in a welfare home while the minister went free. The prosecution charged that his accusation constituted sedition because it instilled hatred and "aroused sentiments against the administration of justice in the country." The charge of "false reporting" was based on a pamphlet Lim had published with the title "Victim Jailed."

Lim's trial was adjourned shortly after it opened to await a federal court ruling on a landmark burden of proof case. The ruling, which came on July 26 was welcomed by civil liberties groups in the country, established that the prosecution must prove its charge beyond a reasonable doubt before the defense is presented. It was not clear when Lim's trial would resume.

In the government's efforts to avoid communal conflict, basic civil liberties sometimes suffered. By the end of the year, at least eighteen members of the banned Al-Arqam sect had been arrested under the Internal Security Act (ISA), and at least nine had been served with two-year detention orders. The ISA, which the government placed under review during the year, provides for indefinitely renewable two-year detention periods without trial for people considered a danger to state security. All eighteen detainees were accused of trying to revive the sect banned in 1994. The Malaysian government had accused it of "exclusivist" and "deviationist" teachings; press reports suggested that the ruling United Malay National Organization (UMNO) party was concerned about the extent of its business holdings.

The government closed the last transit camps for Vietnamese boat people at the end of June with the forced repatriation by ship of hundreds of asylum seekers from the Sungai Besi camp outside Kuala Lumpur. A riot broke out in which Vietnamese, reluctant to return, clashed with Malaysian security forces. Many of the Vietnamese employed violence, mostly throwing stones and molotov cocktails and in a few cases, fired homemade bows and arrows. On the other hand, the security forces responded with excessive force, firing on the Vietnamese, killing one man and injuring others.

The Right to Monitor
Malaysian human rights groups faced harassment and intimidation as noted above but were legally free to operate. The consequences for NGOs of the Irene Fernandez prosecution and trial were not clear at the end of year.

The Role of the International Community
The Fernandez trial attracted international attention particularly from countries, such as Bangladesh, Burma, Indonesia and the Philippines, whose nationals work as migrants in Malaysia. Observers from the first two countries attended sessions of the trial, as did a diplomatic representative from the U.S. embassy. In addition, when the government confiscated Irene Fernandez's passport in March to prevent her from traveling to Geneva for the U.N. Commission on Human Rights meeting, the U.S. made appeals on her behalf. Members of the U.S. Congress also protested her arrest and trial. In March, the Congressional Human Rights Caucus wrote a letter to Prime Minister Mahathir urging that all charges against her be dropped.

Malaysia appeared to take the lead within ASEAN on granting membership to Burma despite the latter's appalling human rights record.

PAKISTAN

Human Rights Developments
In the most significant human rights development in Pakistan during the year, the decade-old political and security crisis crippling Karachi entered a new phase as the government adopted a markedly more hardline stance toward the Immigrants National Movement (Mohajir Qaumi Movement, MQM), a political party representing Urdu speakers, about 60 percent of the population of Karachi. Both sides were responsible for severe human rights abuses: the government responded to the MQM's con-

sistent use of violence and intimidation by labeling the party "terrorist" and indiscriminately targeting its constituency.

Following mid-1995 when violence in Karachi reached record levels and security personnel were systematically attacked, the government initiated its latest and most brutal offensive against the MQM, which continued through 1996. Law enforcement agencies routinely used illegal and excessive force against suspected MQM militants with complete impunity. Although the offensive restored a measure of calm to Karachi city after years of spiraling violence—the death toll for the first half of the year was 300 people compared to more than 2,000 killings during 1995—the country's internal security apparatus was severely discredited in the process.

As part of a tightly coordinated effort with a streamlined chain of command headed by Home Minister Naseerullah Babar, the police, backed by paramilitary Rangers with sweeping powers of search and arrest, conducted systematic pre-dawn cordon-and-search operations in pro-MQM localities, indiscriminately rounding up all able-bodied males and parading them before informants for purposes of identification. Between July 1995 and March 1996 an estimated 75,000 Urdu speakers were reportedly rounded up in this way; toward the end of the year, hundreds remained in jail awaiting trial.

Several key MQM militants were the victims of extrajudicial executions, either during targeted police raids; or in custody, allegedly after being tortured or severely beaten; or in staged "encounters," often during transit between prisons. Police rationalized the illegal killings on the grounds that witnesses' reluctance to testify against militants in open court made it nearly impossible to secure convictions. Notorious MQM operative Naeem Sharri, accused of scores of murders, was among those summarily executed on March 11, in Karachi, without any court proceeding. His case sparked intense controversy, as strong evidence emerged to refute the police claim that Sharri had been killed in self-defense.

Between mid-1995 and mid-1996 at least 150 alleged militants were killed and 800 suspects arrested. The deputy inspector general of police (DIG) for Karachi, Shoaib Suddle, in March 1996 acknowledged the security forces' abusive conduct, although he rejected accusations that they routinely overstepped their authority. He told *The Guardian* of London, "[T]here have been a couple of cases where we also feel excessive fire power was used." To Human Rights Watch's knowledge no security personnel were prosecuted for illegal actions. Police authorities made no effort to ensure that proper post-mortems were conducted on the bodies of those killed in custody or in "encounters."

A surge in incidents of sectarian violence took place during the year, mostly tit-for-tat attacks by extremist Sunni and Shi'a groups in the Punjab and the North West Frontier Province (NWFP), that caused scores of casualties. Although some incidents were extremely serious, such as heavy fighting in mid-September in the NWFP town of Parachinar that left over a hundred civilians dead, the government failed to make a consistent or concerted effort to bring the perpetrators of religiously motivated violence to justice.

Government agents were involved in intimidation of the press during the year. Shaikh Aziz, a senior journalist working at the daily *Dawn* and Aftab Syed, the news editor of *The News*, were picked up and interrogated by intelligence agents in Karachi in June and September respectively. On July 5, district police warned journalists in Dadu, Sindh province, against reporting on alleged government harassment of a local opposition leader of national stature. Karachi police, on September 20, severely beat up several reporters and photographers and smashed their cameras. The journalists were covering the death of Murtaza Bhutto—brother of the prime minister and head of a breakaway faction of the ruling Pakistan People's Party—which had occurred during an "encounter" with the police earlier that night.

On October 20, in the town of Khuzdar in Balochistan province, the general secretary of the Khuzdar journalists' union, Hyder Baloch, was illegally confined for thirty-six hours by the local supervisor of the irrigation department for critical reporting. Gas, electricity and the water supply to Baloch's house were cut off, and his family members were harassed.

The press was given a boost, however, when the Lahore High Court dismissed a defamation action brought by Prime Minister Bhutto against a leading daily newspaper, *The News*, for reporting that Bhutto had requested the extradition of MQM chief Altaf Husain during a meeting with the U.K. Foreign Secretary Douglas Hurd. The court held that those holding public office must be open to criticism by a free press, which played an important role in exposing political corruption.

The status of women in Pakistan remained tenuous, with legal setbacks offsetting positive developments. On March 12, in a long- overdue step, President Leghari ratified the United Nations Convention on the Elimination of All Forms of Discrimination Against Women (CEDAW). However, like some other signatories to CEDAW, Pakistan's ratification included a debilitating reservation to the effect that treaty provisions in conflict with the national constitution would not be implemented. On June 10, the federal cabinet approved a draft bill to abolish the death penalty for women in all cases except for *hudood* (mandatory Islamic punishment) and *qisas* (retribution) crimes. While these steps were welcome, human rights would have been better served by abolishing the death penalty for everyone without exception and regardless of offense.

In a judgment that represented a stunning setback for women's rights in Pakistan, the Lahore High Court ruled on September 24 that an adult Muslim woman, even a widow or divorcée, cannot enter into marriage without the consent of her (male) guardian. Without consent she, as well as her chosen spouse, risks imprisonment on charges of fornication, which carries a maxi-mum punishment of death by stoning if the convict is *muhsan* (a sane, adult Muslim who has previously had lawful sexual intercourse) or one hundred lashes if the convict is not muhsan. The judgment had immediate implications for hundreds of women currently under arrest in connection with their marriages, usually on account of charges filed by their families for marrying without their consent. The court's decision denied women the constitutional guarantee of equal protection of the law and contradicted the principle of equality of the sexes enshrined in CEDAW.

At the end of the year, women's groups were hoping that a similar case—that of Saima Waheed—pending before a full bench of the same court would overturn the precedent, which had been decided by a single judge. Waheed, aged twenty-two, was fighting a case brought by her father to have her marriage judicially annulled because he did not consent to it. Meanwhile her husband and his family suffered reprisals: Waheed's husband was imprisoned in May 1996, for allegedly having had the marriage contract registered on a false basis, and was denied bail although charged with a bailable offense. After some of her husband's relatives were beaten up by thugs, the family went into hiding. Religious zealots attempted to pressure the presiding court by issuing threats of violence, attempting to bring arms into the courtroom, and launching a smear campaign against Waheed and her counsel. Because of such harassment, there was reason to believe that the lives of Waheed, her husband, her husband's family, and her counsel were in danger.

The institution of *karo kari* (black deed) or instant killings of suspected adulterers remained unchecked in rural parts of Balochistan, Punjab, and especially Sindh province. There were allegedly two such killings a day in the borderlands between Sindh and Balochistan, and in Sindh proper 246 karo kari murders were reported over a fifteen-month period ending in March 1996; in 148 of the cases, the victims were women. According to tribal custom, any man who suspects a female relative of sexual relations with a man to whom she is not married is obligated to kill both individuals immediately to preserve his family's honor. The police as a rule refrained from intervening or seeking to prosecute the perpetrators. In any event, convicted karo kari murderers rarely serve more than two years in prison.

Religious minorities in Pakistan continued to face discriminatory laws, such as those against blasphemy, which are used disproportionately against non-Muslim minorities and against the Ahmadi minority. The government, however, did address an issue which has served to marginalize minority constituencies in the political process. In February, the Bhutto government proposed, as part of an electoral reform package, the abolition of the separate electorate laws enacted by former President Zia ul-Haq in the 1980s, under which non-Muslims could vote only for candidates of their own communities standing for reserved parliamentary seats. The proposed law would give non-Muslims the right to cast votes for the general parliamentary seats as well as the reserved seats. Pakistan's main opposition party and the religious right objected to the proposed reforms, which have yet to be enacted into law.

In a far-reaching decision handed down on March 20, the Supreme Court of Pakistan put an end to the government's practice of appointing temporary or acting judges against permanent vacancies in the superior judiciary and delaying their confirmations for political purposes. The judgment also prohibited the government from transferring judges at will. The ruling was generally hailed as furthering judicial autonomy by giving judges security of tenure.

In view of mounting international criticism and threats of trade sanctions for its labor practices, Pakistan stepped up implementation of its child labor laws relative to previous years. Enforcement mechanisms were potentially strengthened through reforms that made the Ministry of Labor directly responsible for overseeing enforcement in conjunction with district-level vigilance committees. As one initial step, the Labor Ministry and the International Labor Organization launched a study to estimate the number of children in the workforce. In June the ministry reported that between January 1995 and March 1996 provincial labor departments conducted 7,003 raids on businesses suspected of employing child labor. Authorities prosecuted more than 2,500 employers, of which 395 were convicted and fined. Reflecting international demands, the labor minister asked the commerce ministry to institute a special marking scheme for carpets and footballs to certify that no child labor had been used in production. Human Rights Watch was particularly concerned about the use of bonded labor, including bonded child labor. It remained to be seen whether these efforts would have any significant effect on improving labor practices. There was no evidence of government resolve to tackle the problem of bonded labor in the agricultural sector.

November began on a dramatic note with a change in Pakistan's political leadership. On November 5 President Farooq Leghari dissolved the National Assembly and dismissed Prime Minister Benazir Bhutto's government, in a move he said was mandated by unchecked corruption, political violence and financial mismanagement. He appointed a "caretaker" government to serve for at least three months until constitutionally mandated elections could be held. The president cited systematic human rights violations, specifically the extrajudicial killings in Karachi (see above), as one of the reasons for dismissing the former government.

The Right to Monitor

Human rights lawyers in Pakistan faced threats of violence more from religious activists than from the government. Asma Jehangir, attorney for Saima Waheed in the case mentioned above, received death threats from those who backed her client's father's claim that a woman cannot marry without the consent of her guardian. A case involving a boy who reverted to Christianity after converting to Islam had to be adjourned because of the danger to the boy's attorney from religious extremists, who said the boy's reversion constituted apostasy.

In general, human rights organizations were free to criticize the government. On February 26 more than 2,000 lawyers staged a two-hour strike in Karachi to protest the conduct of law enforcement personnel in the anti-MQM offensive. A number of lawyers' professional associations deplored the blatant violations of law that characterized the government crackdown.

A bill allowing for greater government control of nongovernmental and "social welfare agencies" (NGOs) was pending before parliament at the end of the year. Under the bill all NGOs would be required to get their mandates or "constitutions" approved by a government Registration Authority. The authority would have the power to "dissolve" any NGO that it found to be "acting in contravention of its constitution." NGOs were concerned that the bill would enable the government to restrict their freedom of association and limit the scope of their operations.

The Role of
the International Community

Pakistan, along with Bangladesh, Bhutan, India, Maldives, Nepal, and Sri Lanka, signed a resolution to eliminate child labor adopted by a ministerial conference of the South Asian Association of Regional Cooperation (SAARC) held in Rawalpindi in August. The resolution called for an end to all forms of child labor by the year 2010 and of child labor in hazardous occupations by the turn of the century. It also espoused a commitment to move toward universal access to primary education by the year 2000. South Asian countries, including Pakistan, have come under international criticism and faced threats of trade sanctions over the use of child and bonded labor in industries and agriculture. In July, the U.S. House of Representatives unanimously passed an amendment to the appropriations bill to fund inspections of plants suspected of employing child labor in India and Pakistan.

Under the European Commission's legislation guiding the Generalized System of Preferences (GSP) trade program, the International Confederation of Free Trade Unions and the European Trade Union Committee brought a complaint against the government of Pakistan for the continued use of bonded labor in the country. The GSP program is designed to give developing countries preferential trade tariffs. By November the European Commission had still not decided whether to accept the complaint and launch an investigation.

U.N. Special Rapporteur on Torture Nigel Rodley visited Pakistan in February and March. His report, published in October, stated that "torture, including rape and similar cruel, inhuman or degrading treatment [were] rife in Pakistan."

In January, the U.N. Special Rapporteur on Religious Intolerance, Abdelfattah Amor, criticized legal restrictions on freedom of thought and worship in Pakistan. He decried the imposition of the death sentence for blasphemy as "disproportionate and even unacceptable." Amor also criticized Pakistan's *hudood* ordinances, which prescribe harsh punishments based on Islamic law for crimes such as adultery and alcohol consumption, and he requested that they not be applied against non-Muslims. He urged the removal of religious identifications from Pakistan passports.

The U.S. assistant secretary of state for South Asian affairs echoed Amor's comments at a U.S. Senate hearing on Pakistan's blasphemy laws in March. Also in March, the U.S. Trade Representative announced that Pakistan's preferential trade benefits under the Generalized System of Preferences (GSP) program would be suspended in three categories of goods (surgical instruments, sporting goods, and certain carpets) due to the insufficient steps taken by Pakistan to address the problem of child and bonded child labor.

In July, the Europe Council of Foreign Ministers authorized the European Commission to negotiate a new cooperation agreement with Pakistan, which would encompass significant provisions for the promotion of human development. Non-preferential and without a financial protocol, the proposed agreement would also include a clause on human rights, in principle allowing suspension of cooperation in cases of serious infringement.

REPUBLIC OF KOREA

Human Rights Developments

Three significant concerns in 1996 were symbolic of the ways in which the Republic of Korea undermined international human rights standards even as it played a largely positive role in defending those standards in international fora. Those concerns were the trials of two former presidents, the massive arrests and indictments of students participating in a banned unification rally, and the government's failure to change repressive labor laws.

The trials of former presidents Chun Doo-hwan and Roh Tae-woo on mutiny, treason and corruption charges provided the most spectacular example in Asia of the tension between the need for accountability for past human rights abuses and the importance of upholding international norms. Chun was sentenced to death in August in connection with his 1979 *coup d'etat* and the 1980 Kwangju massacre in which hundreds of people were killed; Roh was sentenced to twenty-two-and-a-half-years on similar charges.

While the verdicts were an extraordinary demonstration of how far Korea has come in its transition from the dictatorship of Chun to the democratizing government of Kim Young-sam, they also raised troubling questions about the use of the death penalty, the independence of the judiciary, and fair trial procedures. The court refused to accept the majority of defense witnesses. Some observers also charged that prosecutors appeared to be carrying out politically motivated orders from President Kim. Until October 1995 he had avoided advocating trials, maintaining that the cases of the ex-presidents should be evaluated by history. When he publicly announced he had changed his position, the prosecutors, who had already closed their investigations and declined to indict, immediately reopened the cases and proceeded quickly to indictments. An argument about the applicability of the statute of limitations which had been going on for several years was immediately resolved by passage of a new law in favor of the prosecution. Appeals of the two presidents were pending at the end of the year.

In late July as it has done every year, the Korean government banned the Pan-National Rally for Reunification, a student event organized under the auspices of Hanchongryon, the Korean Federation of University Student Councils, which campaigns for a confederation model of reunification with North Korea and the rapid withdrawal of U.S. forces. For nine days in August, some 26,000 police and other security forces mounted a violent offensive against the 7,000 students gathered at Yonsei University, many of whom used violence in return. Police detained 5,848 students and indicted 438 of them on September 17, thirty-eight under the National Security Law and the rest under the Act on Assembly and Demonstrations and the Law Against Violence. Another twenty-seven were kept in detention, and the rest were released.

Of those indicted, fifty-one had been sentenced by late October to prison terms ranging from eight months to three years. Korean human rights organizations reported that the police used beatings to demand false confessions from students in custody stating explicitly that they had instigated and engaged in violence.

While violence on the part of the students and excessive use of force on the part of security forces are to be condemned, President Kim Young-sam also bears responsibility for outlawing what could have been a peaceful demonstration, labeling it a "violent revolutionary pro-North Korean guerrilla operation" and insisting that student protests were no longer necessary now that he was president. Korean authorities, in an attempt to justify the violence, labeled Hanchongry as an anti-state organization and announced their intention to ban it, although a ban requires court action. As of November, that action was still pending.

On August 28, police carried out search and seizure procedures at student government offices at twenty-three universities. Immediately after the police search, Korea University officials closed the campus office of Hanchongry. On August 30, Seoul police closed Hanchongryon's internal communications network on the grounds that it had been used in support of North Korea. At the same time, the government made a decision to investigate the organization's home page on the World Wide Web. On September 2, Yonsei University authorities seized the facilities of the student newspaper, claiming it was prejudiced in favor of North Korea. A few days later, the government announced that all student newspapers would be investigated. Editors and writers at newspapers which praised North Korea would be prosecuted under the National Security Law (NSL). In addition, the Agency for National Security Planning and the police intensified their efforts to track down persons posting Internet messages "beneficial to North Korea."

The National Security Law itself remained a major human rights problem. In its response to Korea's 1992 report on fulfillment of its obligations under the International Covenant on Civil and Political Rights (ICCPR), the U.N. Human Rights Committee called the NSL "a major obstacle to the full realization" of the rights enshrined in the ICCPR. Article 7, section 1 of the law permits prison terms of up to seven years for anyone who "with the knowledge that he might endanger the existence or security of the State or the basic order of free democracy, praised, or encouraged, or propagandized for, or sided with the activities of an antistate organization." Other sections criminalize forming or joining such an organization and importing or disseminating materials in support of such organizations. Its repeal continues to be a major objective for Korean human rights and labor organizations.

In addition to those indicted under NSL provisions for participation in the student demonstrations, 264 people were arrested between January 1 and September 5 for NSL offenses. Almost fifty arrests were in connection with reopened investigations into organizations shut down in 1991-92.

On July 10, Yi Eun-soon, vice-president of the Women's Student Association at Kyoungsan University was arrested for producing T-shirts which included the name of a North Korean university. Police arrested Kim Jae-woo, chair of the Honam University Reunification Committee, on July 15 for allegedly showing a video to farmers about visits to North Korea. Although plans to show the video had been made, the event was canceled. Jang Dae-up was indicted in late June or early July for inserting a phrase from the Communist Manifesto into the student planner produced by the Sogang University Association. On August 28, Kwon Taek-hun chair of the Yongnam Student Council received a two-year sentence for distributing literature at a student meeting and leading a student demonstration in April. On February 3, Lee Eun-jin, a singer and Won Yong-ho, a publisher, were arrested for praising North Korea by disseminating a pro-North Korean songbook entitled *Song of Hope*. Dozens of other such arrests, in violation of the right to freedom of expression, took place during the year.

Labor rights also continued to be a major issue. Efforts to secure labor rights improvements as a condition for Korea's membership into the Organization for Economic Cooperation and Development (OECD), the exclusive twenty-seven-member club of developed nations, failed when Korea was invited to become a member in October, but in a precedent-setting development, a committee was created to systematically monitor Korea's labor practices.

Four major laws denying free expression and association and the right to collectively bargain through representative unions remained on the books in Korea: a ban on "multiple" unions which legitimizes company- and government-sponsored and "ghost" unions formed during the period of military rule; prohibition of third-party intervention in labor disputes by federations not recognized by the government; restrictions on the right to organize by teachers, many of whom work in the private sector; and mandated compulsory arbitration for "public interest workers," including those working in transport, utilities, public health, banking, broadcasting, communications and the post office.

In response to a complaint filed by the Korean Confederation of Trade Unions (KCTU) in January 1996, the Committee on Freedom of Association of the International Labour Organization (ILO) recommended that the government drop charges against the first president of KCTU, Kwon Young-kil, who had been arrested in late 1995 for giving a solidarity speech to the Seoul Subway Workers Union a year and a half earlier. The committee also called for repeal of the bans on third-party intervention (organizing activities by non-union personnel), union fundraising appeals, unimpeded union formation and the free election of union representatives.

The Right to Monitor

The government has placed no direct restrictions on the monitoring and dissemination of information about human rights violations but both the National Security Law and the ban on third-party intervention in labor disputes have been used to restrict human rights activities.

On October 2, the forty-eight-year-old monk Chin-kwan, co-chair of the Buddhist Committee for Human Rights, was detained on suspicion of violating the NSL for using telephone and fax to exchange information on dissident organizations' activities with Pak Tae-ho, chair of the Cho-sun Buddhist Alliance in North Korea. He also allegedly met three North Koreans at a hotel in Beijing in September 1995 and received from them $4,000 in travel expenses; and he allegedly traveled to Canada where he handed over materials about dissident organizations to a pro-North Korean overseas representative of the Pan-National Alliance for the Unification of the Fatherland. Chin-kwan is a prominent labor rights activist in KOHRNET, an alliance of Korean human rights organizations.

The Role of the International Community

The twenty-seven members of the OECD decided in October to admit Korea but required that Korea's labor rights practices be monitored on a regular basis. The decision had been delayed in part because of concerns over labor legislation and violations of worker rights.

Members of the European Union were particularly active in holding Korea to international standards. When a delegation of parliamentarians from Korea visited Brussels in October, Sir Leon Brittan, European Commission vice-president for external relations, said the E.U. favored Korea's membership in OECD but also noted that reforms in the labor laws would remain on the OECD's agenda even after Korea was admitted.

Given its "special relationship" with South Korea and its preoccupation with trade, security and North/South tensions, the U.S. was notably reluctant to press Korea publicly on human rights concerns, though the issue was raised privately by State Department officials. While supporting Korea's OECD membership, the U.S. also urged Korea to reform its labor laws, including during Secretary of Commerce Mickey Kantor's visit to Seoul in June.

SRI LANKA

Human Rights Developments

In December 1995, the Sri Lankan army captured the city of Jaffna, stronghold of the guerrilla group the Liberation Tigers of Tamil Eelam (LTTE, or Tamil Tigers). But by late 1996, it was clear that the war was far from over, and the human rights situation throughout the country remained grave. The LTTE continued to launch attacks on security personnel and civilian "collaborators" on the Jaffna peninsula, and after an initial period of restraint, soldiers retaliated in kind. In the northeast and in other parts of the country, both sides committed serious violations of human rights including extrajudicial killings, arbitrary arrests and detentions, torture and "disappearances," aided by emergency legislation applied nationwide as of April. Civilians were also killed by indiscriminate shelling and aerial bombardment. Nationwide, stringent government curbs on basic freedoms in the name of security narrowed significantly the space for civil society, and despite continued government efforts to account for past abuses by state forces, impunity remained a serious concern.

The year also saw a rise in political violence in southern Sri Lanka between supporters of the ruling People's Alliance (PA) party led by Prime Minister Chandrika Kumaratunge and its chief opposition, the United National Party (UNP). That violence had killed fifteen people by the end of September. Unprecedented labor unrest in crucial industries and services, including rubber, tea and coconut plantations, and the Ceylon Electrical Board, led to paralyzing strikes in the middle of the year. On May 31, the government resorted to emergency legislation to end the electrical strike, ordering arrests and threatening dismissals and confiscation of property. Human rights organizations protested the application of emergency regulations in non-security-related areas and noted that these laws were used by previous governments to dismantle trade unions.

Throughout 1996, the government maintained that a political settlement of the war was its goal but that LTTE violence made war necessary. A plan to devolve power to provinces defined partially along ethnic lines was central to peace proposals, but by November, no political consensus on this proposal had been reached in Colombo. The plan met with strongest resistance from extreme Sinhalese and Buddhist groups, but other parties also disagreed on key points.

Deliberate arbitrary killings of civilians escalated sharply in 1996. Bomb attacks attributed to the LTTE on Colombo's Central Bank building on January 31, and on a crowded commuter train in July, claimed a combined total of at least 160 civilian lives and injured some 1,550 people. The LTTE continued to conduct public executions of suspected informers and engaged in massacres and retaliatory killings of Sinhalese and Muslim villagers, torture and mistreatment of prisoners, forced conscription of children, and kidnapping, all in violation of the second protocol to the Geneva Conventions. Although Sri Lanka has not ratified Protocol II, many of its provisions are binding as a matter of customary international law.

Members of the security forces were also implicated in extrajudicial killings, as were Sinhalese and Muslim home guards armed by the Sri Lankan government and members of Tamil groups opposed to the LTTE who aided government forces in security and counterinsurgency operations. The largest deliberate attack on civilians by Sri Lankan soldiers during the year occurred in Trincomalee district on February 11, 1996, when army personnel from nearby camps went on a rampage in the village of Kumarapuram, killing twenty-four civilians, including thirteen women—one of whom was also raped—and seven children under the age of twelve. The massacre was apparently in retaliation for the deaths of two soldiers in an LTTE ambush. On February 26, a military court of inquiry found fourteen soldiers guilty of the killings, and the case was turned over to civil authorities. Eight army personnel were identified by witnesses as having taken part in the massacre. A magisterial inquiry was concluded, and the case was turned over to the Attorney General for a decision on indictment.

In Jaffna, army respect for civilians, initially high, deteriorated as LTTE violence increased. When troops occupied the city in December 1995, fewer than a few thousand civilians remained; some 350,000 people had been compelled by military operations and LTTE pressure to leave Jaffna and its suburbs for an area of the mainland called the Vanni, where the LTTE attempted to establish a headquarters in the town of Kilinochchi. By May 1996, Jaffna residents began to return home, and the government started to restore elements of civilian life, including schools and transportation. But after a suicide bomb blast killed more than twenty people in the city in July, residents complained of harassment at army checkpoints, and after the LTTE overran a military base in the northeastern Mullaitivu district in July, killing or capturing most of the garrison's 1,500 soldiers, army morale and respect for civilians in Jaffna deteriorated, evidenced by extrajudicial killings, "disappearances," and torture.

The LTTE lost Kilinochchi on September 29, after a two-month assault that displaced some 200,000 civilians. The majority fled to other parts of LTTE-held territory; more than 2,000 reached camps in southern India. On September 14, a UNHCR representative in Colombo warned the Sri Lankan government of a potential mass exodus from the Vanni to India, unless the government quickly restored food and other essential supplies.

Police and army personnel throughout the country, and particularly in Colombo and the northeast, continued to engage in sweeping "cordon and search operations," which resulted in the arbitrary arrests and detention of Tamil civilians and the mistreatment and torture of detainees. These sweeps intensified following major incidents in which the LTTE was implicated. After the bank bombing in late January, the government initiated joint army-police security operations in Colombo. The Human Rights Task Force (HRTF). a government body that monitors the rights of detainees, reported over 400 officially acknowledged detentions in Colombo the following month; others almost certainly went unreported. Tamils

detained in February reported beatings, torture and extortion by soldiers and police officers. In July, after the commuter train was bombed, 2,000 Tamils were detained for questioning in the northern town of Vavuniya, and some 500 others were arrested in sweeps in Colombo and Kandy.

Throughout the year, official and nongovernmental human rights workers complained of security force noncompliance with directives designed to protect the rights of detainees. Sri Lankan officials expressed private frustration over persistent physical mistreatment of detainees by police during interrogations, the army's use of illegal detention facilities, and severe torture in unofficial places of detention, but disciplinary or criminal action against perpetrators of abuse remained rare.

Tight control of war-related reporting made it difficult to gauge the level of police and army abuse. Censorship rules, in place from April 1996 until October 8, 1996, restricted references to actual or potential operations by the armed forces or the police; procurement of arms or supplies; deployment of troops, personnel or equipment; or official conduct or performance of state forces, including in international television broadcasts. Access to Jaffna and other war zones was strictly controlled.

In July, press reports indicated that 150 telephones belonging to some thirty-five journalists, including those from Agence France Presse, Reuters, and six Indian reporters, were being tapped by Sri Lanka's National Intelligence Bureau. In August, President Chandrika Kumaratunge said that she could not allow the media "to hinder the war effort of the Government with their malicious, false and damaging reports," and warned that two local newspapers, *The Island* and *Divaina,* must either be closed down or the government should "publish alternative newspapers to counter them."

The government continued to make administrative changes in 1996 designed to curb abuses and account for the tens of thousands who "disappeared" in the 1980s, but investigations into past abuses proceeded slowly and prosecutions were not forthcoming. Two of the three commissions appointed in 1995 to look into "disappearances" since 1988 were directed to terminate their work by the end of September, although they had not yet heard evidence in more than half of some 20,000 cases presented to them. On September 30 their mandate was extended for an additional three months.

In July, the Sri Lankan parliament approved the establishment of a permanent Human Rights Commission to handle public complaints on human rights abuse. In September, bowing to sustained pressure from Sri Lankan and international human rights groups, the cabinet approved ratification of the Optional Protocol to the International Covenant on Civil and Political Rights. The protocol allows individual complaints on violations to be taken to the U.N.'s Human Rights Committee. The Civil Rights Movement of Sri Lanka welcomed the decision, and urged the government to "take equivalent action under the Torture Convention by making the necessary declaration to enable individual petitions under that treaty as well."

In 1995 the government had created a committee to look into detentions under the Prevention of Terrorism Act and the emergency regulations. The purpose was to ascertain the number and identity of detainees under this legislation, to expedite cases, recommend releases, and improve conditions of detention. At the beginning of June 1996, officials confirmed that 658 persons were being held under detention orders, 150 of them in Colombo. Of these detainees, more than 600 were Tamils, many of whom had been held without trial for prolonged periods, ostensibly due to non-availability of Tamil translations of key documents.

The Right to Monitor

Despite a narrowing of the space for dissent that began in 1995, human rights organizations continued to operate openly and without legal restriction. Intervention by the Organisation of Parents and Families of the Disappeared (OPFMD) and the Civil Rights

Movement of Sri Lanka (CRM) in particular succeeded in extending the mandate of two commissions of inquiry into "disappearances" that were scheduled for termination.

Concerns remained over incidents of police harassment of persons associated with international organizations concerned with human rights, including the International NGO Forum on Sri Lanka, and Peace Brigades International, as well as possible threats to Sri Lankan human rights activists from other political forces, particularly the LTTE, which threatened harsh measures against clergy or nongovernmental organizations who cooperated with government rehabilitation efforts in Jaffna.

The Role of
the International Community

Western nations were virtually unanimous during the year in their condemnation of LTTE attacks on civilians and in their calls for a renewed dialogue between the LTTE and the government. Abuses by government forces received less attention by the international community, which perhaps feared that criticism could discourage ongoing human rights reforms. There were moves on the part of some countries with significant Tamil refugee populations to increase scrutiny of Tamil immigrants and consider laws restricting LTTE activity. Donors also vowed to provide aid for refugees relief and rehabilitation.

On January 12 the E.U. strongly condemned massacres of villagers in Sri Lanka by the LTTE and reiterated earlier appeals to both the Sri Lankan government and the LTTE to protect the civilian population. The fifteen-nation alliance stated that it believed that the Sri Lankan government's devolution proposals formed a basis for discussion on a settlement acceptable to all Sri Lankans. On February 6, the Italian presidency of the E.U. "strongly condemned" the bomb attack on Colombo's Central Bank.

The bombing of the Dehiwela railway station in Colombo on July 25, 1996 was condemned by the U.S. State Department, and called on the LTTE to renounce the use of terrorism. The E.U. also condemned the July bombing. It appealed to the LTTE to enter into political negotiations with the Sri Lankan authorities as soon as possible. Also in July, the Indian government extended its ban of the LTTE as an "unlawful association" under section 3 of the Unlawful Activities (Prevention) Act, 1967.

A U.S. delegation headed by Amb. Philip Wilcox, the U.S. State Department's coordinator for counterterrorism, visited Sri Lanka from August 18 to 23 to meet with senior officials of the Ministry of Foreign Affairs and security and intelligence au-thorities and voiced U.S. support for the Sri Lankan government's efforts to seek a peaceful negotiated settlement of the conflict.

In a September 16 meeting with Justice and Constitutional Affairs Minister Prof. G.L. Peiris, Canadian Foreign Minister Lloyd Axworthy announced that the Canadian government was considering legislation to restrict fundraising by the LTTE in Canada.

On October 1, U.N. Secretary-General Boutros Boutros-Ghali promised to support Sri Lanka's billion-dollar reconstruction program for the north once the war was over.

HUMAN RIGHTS WATCH

HELSINKI

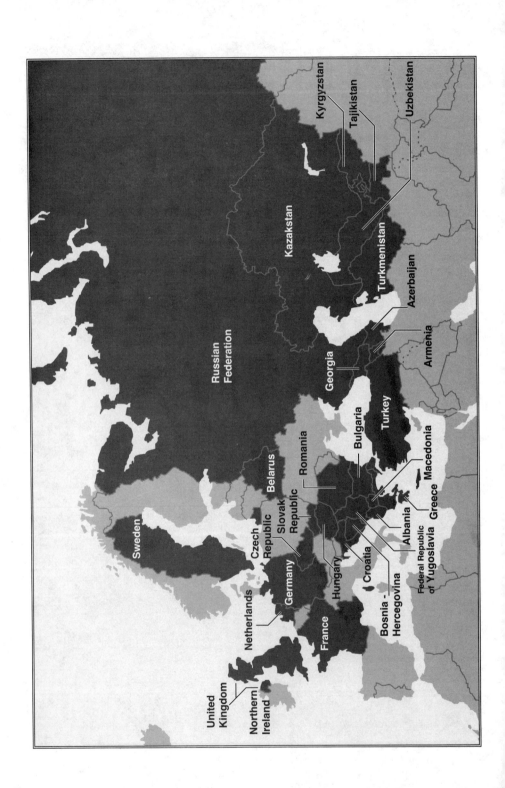

HUMAN RIGHTS WATCH/HELSINKI OVERVIEW

Human Rights Developments

While the international community continued to pay lip service to human rights principles in the Helsinki region, 1996 was notable for the wholesale subordination of these principles to political objectives in certain key countries, especially by the United States and the countries of the European Union. With regard to Bosnia-Hercegovina, the international community preached respect for human rights, democratic pluralism and accountability for past abuses, but did not insist on these principles if it meant delaying blatantly unfree and unfair elections. Shortly after Russian forces initiated a new offensive in Chechnya with massive violations of international humanitarian law, the Council of Europe, one of the regional institutions with a clear human rights mandate, admitted the Russian Federation (hereafter "Russia") as a member. By year's end, the governments and institutions considered most likely to speak out against human rights abuses had lost much credibility.

Especially in the case of the former Yugoslavia, where the atrocities of the war had been so severe as to warrant the establishment of the first war crimes tribunal since Nuremberg (the International Criminal Tribunal for the former Yugoslavia, ICTY), the rhetoric about accountability and justice proved largely hollow in 1996. By year's end, officials at the tribunal questioned how long they could continue without the arrest of indicted persons. These developments, along with the fact that those responsible for "ethnic cleansing" were still in firm de facto control of the region and that there was little prospect of accountability for gross abuses, had ominous implications for human rights, not only in the Balkans but throughout Europe.

Human Rights Developments

Among the gravest abuses during 1996 were those that occurred in the context of the armed conflicts in Bosnia-Hercegovina and in Chechnya. In both cases, civilians were the victims of executions and "disappearances," torture and other mistreatment in detention, and other gross violations of international humanitarian law.

In Bosnia-Hercegovina, Bosnian Serbs carried out a highly organized campaign of "ethnic cleansing," murder and rape in northwestern Bosnia even as diplomatic efforts toward a peace settlement intensified. The Dayton peace agreement, which went into force in December 1995, brought an end to the most severe of these abuses. Despite the successful implementation of the military provisions of the Dayton agreement, however, at the end of 1996, hundreds of thousands of civilians remained displaced, many with little hope of ever returning to their homes; ethnically and politically motivated killings, arbitrary arrests and detention, and the physical mistreatment and harassment of minorities by local authorities remained common; and those responsible for gross violations of human rights maintained power with little fear of being called to account for their crimes.

In Chechnya, civilians continued to suffer from indiscriminate and disproportionate fire until the August 1996 cease-fire. Russian forces routinely razed whole apartment blocks and heedlessly shelled residential areas throughout Chechnya, killing untold numbers of civilians.

Government forces were not the only ones to disregard international legal standards for the protection of civilians. Armed opposition groups in Chechnya, Georgia, Nagorno-Karabakh in Azerbaijan, Northern Ireland, Tajikistan, and Turkey also committed severe violations of international humanitarian law.

Torture and other forms of mistreatment remained routine during interrogations in Armenia, Azerbaijan, Bosnia-Hercegovina, Georgia, Kosovo (Federal

Republic of Yugoslavia), Russia, Turkey, Turkmenistan, and Uzbekistan, abusive officials were rarely held accountable, and confessions procured under torture were often admitted as evidence. Poor prison conditions and horrendous overcrowding also contributed to numerous deaths in detention in Azerbaijan, Bosnia-Hercegovina, Georgia, Russia, and Turkmenistan. Excessive use of force in dealing with prison disturbances led to at least fourteen inmate deaths in Turkey.

Respect for human rights and democratic principles deteriorated dramatically in Albania, Belarus, Kyrgyzstan, and Tajikistan, where government leaders, intent on maintaining political power, severely restricted the independent media, used the police and other state agents to restrict free assembly and association, and often resorted to fraud and electoral manipulation. The crackdown on political dissent was especially prominent in the period leading up to elections in Albania, Armenia, Bosnia-Hercegovina, Georgia, and Kyrgyzstan. Respect for human rights in Armenia, Azerbaijan, Greece, Kazakstan, Slovakia, Turkmenistan, and Uzbekistan remained poor.

Government officials recognized and feared the power of free expression and repeatedly tried to control or restrict critical speech. A journalist was beaten to death in detention in Turkey; journalists were arrested and prosecuted for their peaceful expression in Albania, Croatia, Russia, and Turkey. In Belarus, Bosnia-Hercegovina, the FRY, Turkmenistan, and Uzbekistan, government monopolies of the media limited citizens' access to diverse views and information. Throughout the region, vaguely worded laws that prohibit inciting public violence, defaming state institutions, and publishing state secrets, were used almost exclusively to punish peaceful, albeit critical, expression. The press also came under attack in Chechnya, where clearly marked press vehicles were shot at by Russian forces; in Chechnya, Russia, Tajikistan, and Uzbekistan, journalists were killed by unknown assailants or in crossfire.

Police brutality remained a serious concern in many countries in the region and was often justified by the growing crime rate. In Bulgaria, efforts to control organized crime were the pretext for the routine beating of citizens, destruction of property, and the complete disregard for due process by police forces. In Russia, a crackdown on crime resulted in the harassment, brutal mistreatment and arbitrary detention of persons from the Caucasus, especially Chechens.

Accountability for past abuses continued to be illusory in most of the region. In Bosnia-Hercegovina, Croatia, the FRY and Tajikistan, those who had committed serious abuses during times of armed conflict often showed total disregard for human rights and the rule of law in times of peace. Another devastating cost of the continued political influence exerted in the region by persons responsible for past abuses was the large number of refugees and internally displaced persons who remained displaced long after the military conflicts ended.

In refugee-receiving states such as the member states of the European Union, the rights of refugees were increasingly under attack and asylum seekers faced severe limitations on the right to appeal, detention for long periods, and, in some cases, refoulement.

Domestic violence, rape and other crimes of violence against women were seldom treated seriously by law enforcement officials in the region. Female victims of violence continued to be denied justice, including by the criminal justice system itself, in countries such as Albania, Bosnia-Hercegovina and Russia.

Ethnically motivated violence and discrimination against Roma continued to be pervasive in Bulgaria, the Czech Republic, Greece, Hungary, Romania, and the Slovak Republic. In one positive development, Roma appeared increasingly willing to seek legal recourse for human rights abuses.

The death penalty continued to be invoked in Albania and many of the countries of the former Soviet Union, including Georgia, Kazakstan, Russia, and Turkmenistan. In Bulgaria a move was underway to lift the

1990 moratorium on the death penalty. Routine denial of due process and the admission into evidence of confessions extracted under torture in many of these countries made the use of the death penalty all the more troubling.

The Right to Monitor

Although human rights groups made important contributions by documenting and opposing human rights abuses during 1996, a number of governments tried to interfere with their work. In countries such as Albania, Bosnia-Hercegovina, the FRY, Turkey, and Uzbekistan, human rights activists faced systematic harassment and surveillance by police and other government agents. Although the government of Uzbekistan tolerated some human rights monitoring to an unprecedented degree for that country, it continued to obstruct the registration efforts of independent human rights groups and to harass human rights activists. Turkmenistan remained one of the few countries in the world that, due to crushing government repression, could not boast a single in-country human rights monitor.

The Role of the
International Community

Europe

Many European institutions play an important role with regard to human rights: the Council of Europe and its attendant institutions—the Parliamentary Assembly, European Commission of Human Rights, European Court of Human Rights, and European Committee for the Prevention of Torture; the European Union, the European Commission and European Parliament; and the Organization for Security and Cooperation in Europe (OSCE) and its Permanent Council. However, these institutions had a mixed record on human rights in 1996. On the one hand, European institutions condemned abuses in Belarus, expressed concern over the state of democracy in Slovakia and, after some delay, criticized electoral violations in Albania. The Council of Europe's foreign minis-

ters, in a surprise move, postponed consideration of Croatia's application for membership in mid-May due, in part, to Croatia's poor human rights record. However, despite Croatia's continued non-compliance with the human rights provisions put forward by the council, Croatia was admitted as a full member in October. However, the European Union, the OSCE and the Council of Europe remained silent on the pervasive repression in Turkmenistan and the deterioration of respect for human rights in Kyrgyzstan.

In Bosnia-Hercegovina, where the OSCE was responsible both for organizing elections and monitoring respect for human rights, elections quickly became the primary focus of the mission, due in large part to the U.S. government's insistence that elections in Bosnia-Hercegovina be held before the U.S. presidential elections. European diplomats acknowledged that the time line created at Dayton had been unrealistic from the start because it had been determined largely by U.S. domestic considerations. However, the most powerful European governments were not willing or able to formulate a unified policy to counter that so forcefully pursued by the Clinton administration.

The European Union continued efforts to create a unified and increasingly restrictive asylum regime for its member states, leading in 1996 to increased detention, expulsions, and other measures that, in some cases, violate international standards and increase the risk of *refoulement*.

United Nations

United Nations monitoring missions in Croatia (Eastern Slavonija), Georgia (Abkhazia), Macedonia and Tajikistan were able to contribute significantly to regional stability. However, these missions often remained silent with regard to human rights abuses, opting instead to emphasize their security role. The UNHCR assisted in protecting vulnerable populations in Bosnia-Hercegovina, but failed to promote the safe return of refugees to Abkhazia and placed undue pressure on Tajik refugees in Afghanistan to return to their homes prematurely.

The U.N. Security Council condemned Croatia during the year for ongoing abuses against ethnic Serbs in the Krajina region of the country and for the government's failure to cooperate fully with the ICTY. However, it lifted sanctions against the Federal Republic of Yugoslavia and the Bosnian Serbs on October 1, following what it considered "successful" elections in Bosnia-Hercegovina without mentioning the parties' failure to cooperate with the tribunal, as required by the U.N.'s own resolution 1022, or the ongoing repression of ethnic minorities in Sandjak, Vojvodina and Kosovo.

In Bosnia-Hercegovina, the U.N. International Police Task Force (IPTF) often underplayed its mandate, especially with regard to the protection of vulnerable civilians. It did, however, cooperate with the International Implementation Force (IFOR) to remove checkpoints and, in some areas, individual IPTF units actively patrolled villages where ethnic minorities were being threatened. The IPTF also had the important task of vetting the local police forces, but at the end of 1996, this process was only beginning in the Bosniak-Croat Federation and had not yet begun in the Republika Srpska, while persons indicted for war crimes worked as Bosnian Serb police as late as October.

United States

The U.S. government's human rights policies in the Helsinki region were particularly disappointing in 1996. The Clinton administration continued to tout the importance of democratic principles in the countries of Eastern and Central Europe and the former Soviet Union, but it ignored electoral violations and fraud and remained silent about other human rights abuses to ensure that certain friendly governments remained in power.

The Clinton administration played the leading role in bringing about an end to hostilities in Bosnia-Hercegovina at the end of 1995 and thereby contributed to the single most significant human rights improvement in the region. However, the administration was willing to jeopardize the long-term success of the peace process because of short-term considerations. Although the administration paid lip service to the need for free and fair elections in Bosnia-Hercegovina, it insisted that the elections take place before they could be free and fair, largely because of Clinton's own reelection agenda.

The administration backtracked on its stated commitment to accountability. The U.S.-dominated IFOR refused to arrest persons indicted for war crimes, downplaying the extent of its authority and claiming that indictees would only be arrested if "encountered in the normal course of business." IFOR did everything it could not to encounter indicted persons, however, and did not arrest such persons even when, on several occasions, it came face to face with them.

In Russia, the Clinton administration refused to condemn massive humanitarian law violations in Chechnya during the Russian election campaign, clearly having decided that it would support President Yeltsin's reelection bid no matter what. Although the administration did criticize the abuses in Chechnya from time to time during the year, it failed to use the most important opportunities, such as the summit meeting between Clinton and Yeltsin in April, to press for improvements.

Similarly, the U.S. government disregarded numerous signs that the Albanian government of Sali Berisha was becoming increasingly intolerant of political opposition in the months leading up to the May elections in Albania and was noticeably slow to respond to widespread abuses during those elections. After some delay, however, the U.S. government took the lead in calling for a new vote. And the Clinton administration de-emphasized human rights concerns in Turkey, in part because of its concern about political stability, given the electoral success of the Islamist Welfare Party, and also because of regional security concerns related to the internecine Kurdish fighting in northern Iraq.

The Work of
Human Rights Watch/Helsinki

While maintaining broad coverage of and engagement in human rights developments throughout the Helsinki region, during 1996, a primary goal of the Helsinki division was to monitor and influence the human rights policies of the international community with respect to the former Yugoslavia. This emphasis was due to our recognition that the failure of the Dayton peace process—to achieve a peace built on respect for human rights and justice for the victims of gross abuses and to prevent the "success" of "ethnic cleansing" by insisting that refugees and internally displaced persons be able safely to return to their homes—would have devastating implications for human rights and the safety of ethnic minorities, not only in the countries of the former Yugoslavia but in every country in the Helsinki region.

Human Rights Watch/Helsinki continued systematically to document human rights abuses by all sides in the former Yugoslavia. However, the dramatically changed situation in Bosnia-Hercegovina—the presence of some 60,000 NATO troops, the influx of other international representatives into Bosnia-Hercegovina to monitor and enforce the peace agreement, and the potential for reconstruction aid—gave the international community new leverage over the parties. A priority, therefore, was to ensure that that leverage be used to obtain real human rights improvements. The Helsinki division kept the profile of human rights abuses high on the agenda of the international actors in Bosnia-Hercegovina and repeatedly reminded them of the human rights implications of policy options. We opened an office in Sarajevo and maintained a presence in the country throughout 1996.

Human Rights Watch/Helsinki repeatedly pressed for the arrest of persons indicted for war crimes by the ICTY, including through a June letter organized by Human Rights Watch/Helsinki to European and U.S. heads of state and government, which was signed by 204 organizations and prominent individuals in the U.S. and Europe. The Helsinki division also testified before the U.S. Congress and participated in a variety of international fora to urge international actors in Bosnia-Hercegovina to respond more assertively to ongoing human rights violations. In cooperation with the Human Rights Watch Women's Rights Project, we urged that human rights concerns of women be promoted and that any human rights training for Bosnian police include special training on responding to and investigating crimes of violence against women. We engaged in a concerted campaign prior to the September elections calling for the international community not to hold elections until conditions for free and fair balloting had been created. In June we released *Bosnia-Hercegovina— A Failure in the Making: Human Rights and the Dayton Agreement*, which concluded that the parties to the Dayton agreement had failed to comply with significant human rights provisions, that the international community had failed to insist on compliance with the legally binding obligations created by the Dayton accord and numerous Security Council resolutions, and called for the international community to use the means at its disposal to insist that the highest standards of human rights be upheld as prerequisites for economic aid and assistance. We also pressed the IPTF, responsible for overseeing the process of creating a new police force in Bosnia-Hercegovina, to assure that those responsible for gross human rights abuses are eliminated from the force.

Staff also exposed systematic abuses by the Croatian government against the ethnic Serb minority in the Krajina region after "Operation Storm." In April, we called for a delay, which was subsequently granted, in Croatia's admission into the Council of Europe and pressed for Croatia to be denied political and financial rewards until it cooperated with the ICTY. Human Rights Watch/ Helsinki also condemned restrictions on freedom of expression in Kosovo. conducted investigations in Kosovo, Sandzak and Vojvodina, and repeatedly urged the U.N. Security Council not to lift sanctions against the FRY until it also cooperated with the tribunal. A report released in June documented violations of civil and political rights in Macedonia.

In Chcchnya, we employed a three-pronged approach: documenting violations of international human rights and humanitarian law by both sides to the conflict, briefing international bodies on our most recent field research and formulating specific recommendations for their action, and pressing for accountability. We continued to document massive violations of the laws of war in Chechnya during missions to the region in January and October and released our findings in three reports during the year. Staff briefed the OSCE and the Council of Europe on atrocities committed by Russian forces and Chechen fighters and urged the Council of Europe, to no avail, to use the opportunity of Russia's application for membership to condemn such abuses. We also raised concerns regarding Chechnya at the fifty-second session of the U.N. Commission on Human Rights. Human Rights Watch/Helsinki opposed an amnesty for serious violations of the laws of war and pressed for accountability to be on the agenda of multilateral and bilateral meetings on Russia.

Human Rights Watch/Helsinki also conducted fact-finding missions to Stavropol and Krasnodar to expose the escalation of state-sponsored xenophobic violence, condemned the discriminatory implementation of anti-crime measures in Moscow, and worked to combat violations of the rights of refugees in the CIS. We played an active role in the UNHCR-IOM-OSCE conference on forced migration in the CIS held in Geneva in May, emphasizing the degree to which human rights abuses often cause migration and formulating recommendations to improve chances that refugees and internally displaced persons (IDPs) will be able to return to their homes in safety. Our Moscow office worked with the Women's Rights Project to oppose violence against women in Russia and to press for needed legislation on domestic violence (see section on the Women's Rights Project) and raised these concerns before the fifty-second session of the U.N. Commission on Human Rights.

In an effort to prevent a further deterioration in the human rights situation, during 1996 significant resources were devoted to exposing the alarming spread of serious abuses in several countries in the region. In June, the division sent its first mission to Belarus to document growing restrictions on the political opposition. In Armenia, Human Rights Watch/Helsinki protested against police violence in the wake of September 25 demonstrations following the elections and the ensuing crackdown on the political opposition and worked closely with Armenian human rights activists to bring international pressure on the government to address these concerns. Following the March release of our report "Human Rights in Post-Communist Albania," Human Rights Watch/Helsinki focused on the electoral fraud and post-electoral violence in Albania. Staff testified before the U.S. Congress on three occasions during 1996 regarding human rights in Albania and held numerous meetings to raise our concerns with the Clinton administration.

In 1996, Human Rights Watch/Helsinki intensified its efforts to engage the government of Uzbekistan in a dialogue on its human rights record and to exploit the government's desire for diplomatic and financial recognition by pressing the E.U., the U.S. government and other influential actors to insist on concrete improvements from the Karimov government. In May, Helsinki representatives met in Toshkent with senior government officials to discuss the findings of our November 1995 mission to Uzbekistan. A report entitled "Uzbekistan: Persistent Human Rights Abuses and Prospects for Improvement" was released in May. Throughout 1996, Human Rights Watch/Helsinki staff campaigned for the release of political prisoners in Uzbekistan, to obtain the registration of independent local human rights organizations in the country, to condemn widespread censorship, and to oppose impunity for state-sponsored abuses. To further its efforts in Central Asia, the Helsinki division opened a regional office in Toshkent in July and successfully pressed the government of Uzbekistan for its formal registration. Human Rights Watch/Helsinki also pressed the government of Turkmenistan for improvements in its human rights record during meetings in Ashgabat in June.

As part of our ongoing work on government destruction of villages in southeastern Turkey, Human Rights Watch/Helsinki released a report in June on the occasion of the U.N. conference on housing, Habitat II, documenting the failure of government programs to aid those forcibly displaced. We also protested the arrests of human rights activists during the conference, which was held in Istanbul. Human Rights Watch/Helsinki documented continuing torture of detainees, especially by Turkey's Anti-Terror units and also focused on the government's reprisals against victims of human rights abuse such as torture who seek recourse with the European Commission on Human Rights. "Turkey: Violations of the Right of Petition to the European Commission of Human Rights" was released in April. Helsinki staff also raised these concerns with the European Commission on Human Rights during meetings in Strasbourg. Numerous urgent appeals were sent to the Turkish government on cases of "disappearances," torture and restrictions on free expression, and we raised concerns regarding torture at the U.N. Commission on Human Rights. The Helsinki division, in cooperation with the Human Rights Watch Arms Project, also condemned the indictment of the publisher and translator of the Arms Project's November 1995 report "Weapons Transfers and Violations of the Laws of War in Turkey" for "defaming and belittling the state's security and military forces."

Human Rights Watch/Helsinki remained actively engaged in documenting and holding governments accountable for violence and discrimination against Roma, through fact-finding missions to and reports on the Czech Republic, Hungary, and the Slovak Republic. In cooperation with the Children's Rights Project, we also exposed the mistreatment of street children in Bul-

garia, a large majority of whom are Roma (see section on the Children's Rights Project). In Romania, we again urged the parliament to reject provisions of the criminal code that would continue to criminalize consensual sexual acts between individuals of the same sex.

Building on previous work on racism and xenophobia, Human Rights Watch/Helsinki launched an initiative to influence the asylum policies and practices of the states of the E.U., focusing in 1996 on Sweden, the Netherlands, the United Kingdom, Germany, and efforts by the E.U. to harmonize the asylum policies of its member states. In September 1996, we published "*Sweden: Swedish Asylum Policy in Global Human Rights Perspective*," which was released to coincide with the Swedish government's introduction of a proposed reform of the asylum law in parliament.

ALBANIA

Human Rights Developments

The Albanian government's respect for human rights continued to decline in 1996. Police violence, politicized courts, electoral manipulation and control of the media were systematically used by President Sali Berisha and his ruling Democratic Party to eliminate rivals and consolidate power.

The most public violations occurred at the time of Albania's third multiparty elections for parliament on May 26. Physical violence, ballot stuffing and voter list manipulation by state employees in favor of the ruling party occurred in numerous electoral zones. Opposition parties refused to recognize the results, which gave the Democratic Party 122 out of 140 seats in parliament.

The main opposition parties were denied permission to hold a protest rally in Tirana on May 28. Opposition leaders and demonstrators gathered nevertheless and were beaten by plain-clothed and riot police, including the deputy minister of the interior. Members of the international media, foreign election observers and human rights monitors watched the police attack and detain dozens of people, among them members of parliament and elderly protesters.

Electoral violations had, in fact, begun long before the vote. In late 1995, the so-called "Genocide Law" established a government-appointed commission to review the files of the communist-era secret police. Those who held high-ranking positions in the communist government or were found to have "collaborated" with the former secret police were banned from holding public office until the year 2002. The law did not provide adequate due process guarantees and punished individuals for their association with a now discredited group, rather than a specific criminal act. In the months leading up to the elections, the commission banned 139 individuals from participating in the elections, only three of whom were from the Democratic Party.

Before and after the elections, the government kept up its attack on the independent press. In January, the country's largest daily, *Koha Jone* (Tirana), and the newspaper of the opposition Socialist Party, *Zeri i Popullit* (Tirana), were accused of collaborating with the Serbian secret police, although no supporting evidence was made public. Shortly thereafter, the police confiscated six distribution vans owned by *Koha Jone*. On January 30, *Koha Jone* journalist Altin Hazizaj was arbitrarily charged with assaulting two police officers and held in detention for two days. On February 16, another journalist, Fatos Veliu, was detained and beaten by police in Saranda, allegedly because he had written an article about corruption in the local police.

On February 26, police detained and questioned the entire staff of *Koha Jone* about a bomb that had exploded that morning in Tirana. In connection with the bombing, a journalist from the newspaper *Populli Po* (Tirana), Ylli Polovina, was later fined U.S. $300 for "inciting public violence" because of an article he had written about the assassination attempt on Macedonian President Kiro Gligorov in November 1995. On March 12, the editor of *Populli Po*, Arban Hasani, was fined $2,160 for two articles that the court found to be capable of "inciting of national conflict" and "defamatory of the secret police" (SHIK).

A number of Albanian and foreign journalists were abused by the Albanian police during the May 28 demonstration in Tirana, including Gianfranco Stara and Spiro Ilo from Associated Press Television and Eduardo del Campo from *El Mundo* (Spain). Bardhok Lala from the Albanian newspaper *Dita Informacion* (Tirana) was abducted by the secret police after the demonstration, severely beaten and left for dead in a lake on the outskirts of Tirana.

Despite promises of reform, the Democratic Party maintained firm control of the state radio and television. Some private stations were tolerated, although there was still no legislation to allow for private electronic media. Most of the private stations avoided news or political reporting.

Throughout the year, the government continued to prosecute those it claimed were responsible for past crimes. At least thirty former communist officials were sentenced to long prison terms for various "crimes against humanity," such as ordering the shoot-to-kill policy on the border. At the same time, some former officials with close ties to the current government avoided prosecution. On March 15, four people were sentenced to between two and four years of imprisonment for trying to reestablish the former communist party (Party of Labor), which was banned in 1992. On September 16, another four people were convicted on the same charges.

On October 16, four days before municipal elections, the police arrested fourteen people it claimed were members of a communist terrorist organization that sought to overthrow the government. No evidence was made public, raising speculation that the arrests were timed as a campaign move before the elections.

Women's rights were another growing concern in 1996. Domestic violence was a serious and widespread problem that was virtually ignored by public officials.

The one area of improvement in 1996 was the status of the Greek minority in the south of the country. In August the Albanian government opened three Greek-language schools in areas where the Greeks had long requested minority-language education. Relations between Greece and Albania improved steadily throughout the year, although Albania's Greek minority still complained about job discrimination and the slow return of church property.

The Right to Monitor

The main human rights organization in the country, the Albanian Helsinki Committee, was denied permission to monitor voting in Tirana polling stations during the May parliamentary elections. Six weeks before the elections, its telephone line was cut. Foreign human rights groups, including Human Rights Watch/Helsinki, were free to investigate abuses in Albania during 1996, but were monitored by the secret police. Many foreign organizations observed the May 26 parliamentary elections without interference, although the government limited the number of monitors from the Organization for Security and Cooperation in Europe (OSCE) that could observe the October 20 municipal elections.

The Role of
the International Community

The international community's attitude toward the government of Sali Berisha changed radically after the May elections. Since coming to power in 1992, President Berisha had enjoyed the strong support of the international community, most notably the U.S. government, despite clear signs that human rights violations were repeatedly taking place. A number of top-ranking western officials visited Albania in the weeks preceding the elections, thereby lending credence to the Albanian government. In return, Berisha opened up Albania's ports and airstrips for NATO use and encouraged moderation among the ethnic Albanians in neighboring Kosovo and Macedonia.

After some delay, the U.S. government, the European Parliament and Council of Europe expressed their strong disappointment with the elections and encouraged the Albanian government to hold new elections as soon as possible. The U.S. State Department issued a number of statements that highlighted human rights problems and proposed possible solutions.

The OSCE sent two missions to monitor the parliamentary elections, one from the Parliamentary Assembly and one from the Office for Democratic Institutions and Human Rights (ODIHR). The report of the latter was substantially stronger than the report of the former and accurately documented most of the electoral violations. The Albanian government then accused some members of the ODIHR delegation of being communist sympathizers and limited the number of ODIHR monitors allowed to observe the October 20 local elections. Refusing to accept any limitations on mission size, ODIHR, as well as the Parliamentary Assembly, did not monitor the vote.

On April 20, the European Parliament criticized the May elections and urged the Albanian government to release political prisoners, a reference to Fatos Nano, leader of the Socialist Party, who has been in prison on political charges since July 1993. In June the European Parliament adopted a resolution urging European Union governments to make it clear to Tirana that closer cooperation with the E.U. is conditional on elections being held in full accordance with international standards. In September the European Commission released the second part of a $44 million E.U. financial aid package agreed upon in 1994. The Commission announced that the release was a result of Albanian authorities' introduction of a coherent set of political measures and economic reforms.

On October 2, the Albanian parliament ratified the European Convention on Fundamental Human Rights and Freedoms, as was required by Albania's accession to the Council of Europe in July 1995. However, the Albanian government failed to remedy other human rights concerns identified by the council, such as ongoing restrictions on freedom of expression and the lack of an independent judiciary.

ARMENIA

Human Rights Developments

The government's crackdown on the political opposition in September 1996 cast a pall on human rights. Given the 1995 ban on the Armenian Revolutionary Federation (ARF), Armenia's largest opposition party, and fraudulent 1995 parliamentary elections, the 1996 crackdown accentuated the government's intolerance of any real political opposition. The crackdown followed massive demonstrations on September 25 protesting election fraud in the September 22 presidential elections, in which incumbent Levon Ter-Petrossian defeated Vazgen Manukian by nine percentage points. Demonstrators marched to the parliament, where the Central Election Commission (CEC) was housed, and broke through gates to demand a recount. In the process they beat Speaker Babken Ararktsian and Deputy Speaker Ara Sahakian. In response, police brutally beat demonstrators and later arrested at least twenty-eight opposition leaders and supporters and CEC staffers. Among them, according to credible reports, Aghassi Arshakian, Kim Balayan, David Vartanian, Gagik Mgerdichian, and Aramad Zarkaryan, were brutally beaten; the latter required hospitalization for a fractured skull and broken nose and ribs. Attorneys for some of the detained, notably ARF leader Ruben Akopyan, were not permitted access to their clients.

In the wake of these events, police detained about 200 more individuals believed to have participated in the demonstration, President Ter-Petrossian banned public demonstrations and called in army troops to patrol Yerevan, and the Procurator General announced his intention to press charges of attempting violently to overthrow the government against Vazgen Manukyan and

seven other opposition leaders. Police closed the offices of the National Democratic Union (Vazgen Manukian's party), the National Self-Determination Association(a tiny opposition party), the Union of Constitutional Rights (a nationalist party), and Artsakh-Hayastan (an organization for the promotion of Karabakh issues). This crushing of opposition forces bore out Defense Minister Vazgen Sarkissian's September 25 warning that "After [the September 25] events, even if they win 100 percent of the votes, neither the Army nor the National Security and Interior Ministry would recognize such political leaders."

Credible reports indicate that electoral violations did not occur in those electoral precincts monitored by international observers; however, in the majority of districts without international observers, no local observers were allowed, dead people and minors miraculously appeared on lists of voters, soldiers were bused in with orders to vote for Ter-Petrossian, and ballot boxes were reportedly stuffed. The elections failed to win the approval of the OSCE ODIHR Election Observer Mission, which concluded that "very serious breaches" in the voting raised concern "for the overall integrity of the election process."

The ARF remained banned throughout 1996, while the Ministry of Justice reviewed its request for reinstatement. At the latest hearing (September 12), the Ministry of Justice rejected the ARF's registration papers, claiming that they lacked the requisite minutes of the ARF's founding congress. As of this writing the process had not been completed.

The trial of Vahan Hohvannisian, the ARF chair, and thirty other ARF members (also known as the "Dro" trial, after the name of an alleged secret armed section within the ARF that is charged with planning to overthrow the Armenian government) dragged on and, as of this writing, more than a year after its opening, had reached no conclusion. In a stunning display of bias, the Supreme Court judge presiding over the case accused two of the defense attorneys who had participated in a USAID trip to the U.S. of having been funded for the trip by the defendants' families.

The Armenian Ministry of Defense continued illegally to draft refugees from Azerbaijan and Nagorno Karabakh into the army and refused to give draft-age boys obligatory travel passes until they registered with their local draft board. Local draft boards on several occasions held hostage the parents of missing soldiers until the latter returned.

In April, the Ministry of Justice attempted to close Azg, the Ramkavar party daily, claiming that it needed to re-register under the auspices of the diaspora Ramkavar party, which is pro-Ter-Petrossian. The effort was unsuccessful.

The Right to Monitor
The Ministry of Justice refused to register the Committee for the Defense of Political Prisoners, basing its decision on its view that since there were no political prisoners in Armenia, such an organization was unnecessary.

The Role of
the International Community

Europe
In 1996 European institutions sought to include Armenia as part of an all-Caucasus strategy. In May the Council of Europe's committee of ministers voted in favor of having the Parliamentary Assembly consider Armenia's application for membership. In response to the September events, the council dispatched a mission to Armenia in early October. The European Union had been scheduled to sign an interim agreement underlying a broad trade and cooperation agreement with Armenia. It postponed a trip to Yerevan, where the signature ceremony was to take place, citing "security reasons."

United States
The second largest per-capita recipient of U.S. aid, Armenia received U.S.$95 million for FY 1996 under the Freedom Support Act,

a 100 percent increase in assistance since 1995. The Clinton administration's reaction to the September events marked an abdication of its responsibility toward human rights in a country in which it has a significant investment. The State Department's initial, weak statement in response to the crackdown, which merely called on both sides to exercise restraint, demonstrated a feigned ignorance of government practices, exercised throughout the past two years, aimed at cutting the opposition out of mainstream politics. A later statement expressed "concern for the future of those arrested."

The Clinton administration's response is even more inexcusable, given the scrupulous work of the U.S. embassy staff in Yerevan, which monitored the Dro trial, met with the relatives of opposition leaders arrested in the wake of the crackdown, and generally is extremely well informed on human rights violations.

Two high-level State Department visits were devoted to regional security and Nagorno Karabakh, and neither had a domestic politics or human rights component. The State Department did, however, acknowledge obvious cracks in Armenia's democracy in its *Country Reports on Human Rights Practices for 1995* and in a July 30 congressional hearing on the Caucasus. Additionally, on October 22, the Department of State called on the Armenian government to adhere to OSCE recommendations concerning the election law, but again failed to take the government to task for the brutal crackdown.

AZERBAIJAN

Human Rights Developments
The treason trials of President Heydar Aliyev's personal enemies, brutal treatment in detention, and continued repression of free speech stood in grim contrast to the Azerbaijan government's efforts to join international human rights institutions in 1996. Notably, on May 31, the parliament (Milli Mejlis) ratified the Convention Against Tor-

ture and Other Cruel Inhuman and Degrading Treatment or Punishment and several other human rights-related international conventions, and in June Azerbaijan received guest status with the Council of Europe.

But continued ill treatment in detention demonstrated how far Azerbaijan has to go in order to conform with Council of Europe standards and with the torture convention. At least two individuals died in pre-trial detention as a result of brutal beatings. Ilqar Samedov, arrested on narcotics possession charges on June 14, was sent to a hospital on June 15 and died on June 29 as a result, according to a coroner's report, "of blows to the head with a blunt object." After Samedov's transfer to a hospital, the case investigator refused to allow his father to see his dying son; moreover, police officials waited three days before making the death public. A member of the Islamist Revival Party died in April after seventeen days in the Ministry of National Security pre-trial facility.

Police routinely beat those detained at the Baku City Police Department. Victims included Col. Tofiq Qasimov, who was beaten for several days in January; Ramiz Jalilov, who received multiple injuries on September 30, 1995; Yashar Tezel (see below); and a young OPON (Special Police Detachment) member accused of participation in a 1995 coup attempt, whose parents reported to Human Rights Watch/Helsinki that police beat their son for two days and threatened to make him sit on a bottle in order to extract a confession from him.

Human Rights Watch/Helsinki also received credible reports from the attorneys and relatives of individuals charged in connection with various coup attempts that they were detained for as long as a month in the basement of the Presidential Special Department, deprived of meetings with attorneys, of running water, and of toilet facilities.

The fallout from three years of coup attempts and alleged assassination attempts on President Aliyev culminated in a series of trials and convictions marred by serious due process violations. In at least four cases, the

prosecution lodged accusations of participation in the March 1995 coup attempt long (up to a year) after the arrests of the accused on illegal weapons charges. These include Adyl Hajiev, sentenced in September to fourteen years of hard labor, Ramiz Jalilov (see above), a family friend of Rovshan Javadov (the 1995 coup leader); Rahab Qaziyev, brother of former Defense Minister Rahim Qaziyev (see below); and Gen. Vahid Musayev. The latter three were put on trial on treason charges. Investigators routinely denied defense attorneys access to these men.

Police arrested former State Secretary Panah Huseynov on April 16 on charges of misuse of state property, bringing to eleven the number of former state ministers in prison or awaiting trial. In connection with Huseynov's arrest, police also arrested Musavat party leader Arif Hajiyev (in violation of the immunity he enjoys as a member of parliament), allegedly for obstructing justice, and Turkish journalist Yashar Tezel, whom they released two weeks later. On April 18 police in Nakhchivan raided former president Abulfaz Elchibey's headquarters and arrested Qiyas Sadykhov, his former chief of staff, and his brother Niyas (whom they reportedly beat) for allegedly hiding Huseynov. Both were released in August.

The Supreme Court of Azerbaijan declined to retry former Defense Minister Rahim Qaziyev, who was sentenced to death in absentia in 1995 for major military defeats in Nagorno Karabakh and who was arrested in Moscow and extradited to Azerbaijan in April. Deputy Procurator General Isa Najafov told a Human Rights Watch/Helsinki representative in Baku that sentencing an individual to death in absentia did not violate due process, demonstrating a devastating lack of understanding of Azerbaijan's obligations under international law.

In May police in Nakhchivan detained the wife, son, brother and cousin of Sahib Huseynov, accused of plotting a 1993 failed assassination attempt on President Aliyev. The wife and son were detained for eight hours at the Nakhchivan airport; police brutally beat the brother in attempt to learn

Huseynov's whereabouts and later released him and his cousin. In early October, police in the Sharur district held "hostage" relatives of Popular Front Party member Kamal Talibov, and detained him on unclear charges.

Popular Front leader Arif Pashayev was released from prison under a May presidential amnesty, and former Minister of Defense Tofiq Qasimov was released from custody in February after intense public pressure and concern for his sharply declining health, but the reportedly trumped-up charges of treason remained.

The government continued to stifle political speech. Government censors routinely refused to allow publication of issues of opposition newspapers that contained articles criticizing President Aliyev, and the government closed the only independent television station in four counties. The Press and Information Ministry attempted to close *Avrasiya* (Baku), an independent daily newspaper, under the premise that its founders were not Azerbaijani citizens. In Lenkoran, *Lenkoran Hayati* (Lenkoran Life) journalist Israfil Agayev was sentenced to three years for libel in connection with an article critical of the local public prosecutor.

On October 22, university students Nasi Sharafkhanov and Bayram Ismailov received prison sentences of one and two years respectively, and their professor, Yashar Mammedli, was amnestied on charges of calling for the violent overthrow of the government, a step which violated free speech rights and was clearly aimed at intimidating the Popular Front Youth Organization, of which the students were leaders. The charges were related to anti-government leaflets they had distributed in January.

The Right to Monitor

Nakhchivan police routinely harassed Women's Rights Society activists at the Nakhchivan airport in an obvious attempt to block the flow of information to Baku on political prisoners in the area. The Ministry of Justice repeatedly refused to register the Committee for Human Rights and Democracy, citing, among other things, the

organization's failure to provide copies of the founder's passports, which is not among registration rules. The government continued to deny the International Committee of the Red Cross access to pre-trial detainees, but granted unhindered access to prisoners of war.

The Role of the International Community

Europe

The Council of Europe in June voted to grant Azerbaijan guest membership, and the European Union signed a partnership and cooperation agreement with Azerbaijan but, at the end of 1996, had not ratified an interim agreement. The European Parliament had not, as of this writing, given its assent to the agreement, which requires respect for human rights and democratic principles before it can be ratified by E.U. member states and Azerbaijan.

United States

The Clinton administration vigorously opposed a new bill that would tie U.S. aid to the Azerbaijani government to proportional aid to Nagorno Karabakh. U.S. aid was previously banned due to Azerbaijan's economic blockade of Armenia. The U.S. ambassador to Azerbaijan in private meetings with President Aliyev pressed for the release of Tofiq Qasimov and raised concern for the health of former Minister of Interior Iskandar Hamidov, now serving a fourteen-year prison sentence. Embassy officials also raised concern over the denial of registration to the Word of Life Church.

BELARUS

Human Rights Developments

Censorship and harassment of the independent media and trade unions, police brutality during public demonstrations, and presidential incursion on the power and independence of the parliament and judiciary punctuated the ever-worsening status of human rights in Belarus during 1996.

The anti-democratic tenor of the year was set by President Lukashenko's announcements that he would remain in office longer than the maximum two terms stipulated by the constitution, and "do away with" the "unnecessary" parliament. In December 1995 he issued a decree ordering government officials to ignore all decisions of the Constitutional Court that overturned presidential decrees; in June 1996 he proposed that the court's jurisdiction be vastly curtailed, and that the president appoint half the justices.

The government maintained a virtual monopoly over the media in 1996. Following the cancellation of their printing contracts in late 1995, three leading independent newspapers were forced to use printers in neighboring Lithuania. The only independent cable station was closed before the parliamentary elections on the pretext of needing transmitter repairs, but was allowed to reopen after agreeing never to broadcast political reports. In September, an independent rock music radio station that broadcast news was forced off the air due to "interference with government frequencies." Five independent weeklies had their bank accounts frozen. Individual journalists were also subjected to harassment in 1996, including physical attacks on Russian television reporters and the wife of a correspondent for Radio Liberty's Russian Service.

The government also directly interfered with dissident activities. During an April 26 march commemorating the tenth anniversary of the Chernobyl disaster, more than 200 of the close to 50,000 marchers were arrested and, after summary trials usually held inside their jail cells, given administrative sentences of three to fifteen days. Police beat many of the demonstrators, as well as innocent passersby, at the rally and again at police headquarters. The next day, Juri Khadyka and Vyacheslav Seivchuk, two leaders of the Belarusian Popular Front, a political opposition party that had sponsored the march, were arrested and eventually charged with organizing a mass disturbance. Similar

beatings and arrests occurred at a demonstration held outside the president's office on May 30, which had been organized to protest the continued detention of Khadyka, Seivchuk and seven other Ukrainians who had been imprisoned after the April 26 march.

Harassment of trade unions also continued in 1996. Following a subway workers' strike in August 1995, which special troops forcibly dispersed, all of the picketers were fired. Formal applications to hold pickets were subsequently rejected or severely restricted in size, and all unions were required to reregister with the government, in violation of International Labor Organization treaties. True to the presidential decree banning all trade union activities "in the interest of preserving public order," in May 1996 leaders of Poland's Solidarity trade union who were meeting in the Belarusian capital, Minsk, were detained and then deported by police.

The Right to Monitor

While local human rights organizations were not the direct subject of intimidation, government censorship of the independent press limited dissemination of information about human rights conditions in the country. In April, the Justice Ministry sent a letter to the Belarusian Popular Front, which had been openly critical of the government's human rights record, warning that it risked being banned. Police also illegally searched the party's office and arrested those present. The Belarusian Soros Foundation continued as in 1995 to be attacked in the government-owned media for its funding of independent newspapers and organizations working to promote democracy in the country. In addition, a presidential decree requiring the reregistration of all private organizations inhibited human rights monitoring. Human Rights Watch/Helsinki was not aware of restrictions placed on monitoring by international human rights groups.

The Role of
the International Community

In June, the International Labor Organization submitted a list of recommendations to the Belarus government concerning normalization of relations with trade unions and reported on violations of Belarusian trade unions' rights to the International Monetary Fund and the World Bank.

Europe
The Parliamentary Assembly of the Council of Europe conducted a number of investigations into the government's respect for human rights as part of its review of Belarus's application for membership in the council, which was pending in 1996. The European Parliament and the OSCE sent observers to the November and December 1995 parliamentary elections. In January the Parliamentary Assembly of the OSCE issued a report on its findings that criticized limitations placed on media coverage of the candidates. In May, a delegation of the European Parliament, in conjunction with a committee of the Parliamentary Assembly of the Council of Europe, appealed to Belarus authorities to refrain from harassing members of political parties and others who voiced dissenting opinions publicly.

In 1995 the European Union and Belarus signed a Partnership and Cooperation Agreement (PCA), of which respect for human rights and democratic principles is an essential element, and parts of the European Union worked actively to improve Belarus' compliance with its human rights obligations. In June the European Parliament's Foreign Affairs Committee asked the European Council of Ministers to postpone the entry into force of an underlying interim agreement "until there is evidence of an improvement in respect for the rule of law and democratic principle" in Belarus, but the European Parliament's Committee on External Relations recommended in July that the interim agreement be approved by the European Parliament. In May the European Parliament adopted a resolution expressing its concern about media censorship in Belarus and called on the European Union to support efforts to secure the immediate release of all prisoners of conscience there. In June the European Parliament adopted another resolution expressing regret about the worsening human rights situation in Belarus; as of this writing it had made no final decision on final ratification of the PCA.

United States
The U.S. record regarding human rights in Belarus was mixed. The State Department's *Country Reports on Human Rights Practices for 1995* was comprehensive and accurate and, in the wake of police brutality at public marches and government closure of an independent newspaper, the State Department actively urged the Belarusian government to observe its international obligations to comply with human rights standards. The State Department failed to issue any public protest when Belarusian Popular Front leaders Zenon Pazniak and Sergei Naumchyk were imprisoned in Belarus, but in August the U.S. Immigration and Naturalization Service granted the two men political asylum. Moreover, in November 1995, only seven weeks after the Belarus military shot down and killed two American balloonists— an act that the White House had labeled as deliberate—the U.S. Defense Department approved a $1,000,000 military aid package to assist Belarusian participation in NATO's Partnership for Peace exercises.

BOSNIA-HERCEGOVINA

Human Rights Developments
A U.S.-brokered peace agreement, negotiated in Dayton, Ohio, in November 1995 and signed in Paris on December 14, 1995, brought long-awaited peace to Bosnia-Hercegovina. The peace agreement ultimately succeeded in stopping the shelling and siege of cities and the mass slaughter of civilians. However, severe human rights abuses, including ethnically-motivated killings, expulsions and evictions, police brutality, and restrictions on freedom of movement, continued throughout 1996. Few of the refugees

displaced by the war were able to return to their homes in areas still controlled by other ethnic groups. National elections were held under conditions that fell far short of internationally accepted standards for free and fair balloting, with the predicted result of consolidating the political control of nationalist leaders who supported ethnic partition and continued to deny basic human rights to ethnic minorities.

Under the Dayton agreement, a NATO-led Implementation Force (IFOR) was authorized to separate the armed forces and to establish and maintain a "zone of separation" (ZOS) along the "inter-entity boundary line" (IEBL) which demarcated the division between the Republika Srpska and the Bosniak-Croat Federation (Federation). This mission was accomplished relatively quickly, considering the hostilities that had preceded the peace agreement. The Dayton accords also created mechanisms to oversee the implementation of the civilian aspects of the accords. These included the Office of the High Representative (OHR), an international police monitoring mission (the International Police Task Force, or IPTF) and a Commission for Human Rights. The Organization for Security and Cooperation in Europe (OSCE) was invited to establish a human rights and election monitoring mission and to supervise the holding of the first democratic elections in Bosnia-Hercegovina.

The human rights provisions of the agreement were largely ignored by the parties. All sides continued to hold prisoners of war well past the deadline set for their release. Only 217 prisoners had been released by the original January 19 deadline, leaving at least 645 in custody; figures could not be confirmed because the International Committee of the Red Cross (ICRC) was often denied access to places of detention. In February, the ICRC found eighty-eight unregistered Serb prisoners when it was finally allowed to enter a Bosnian government prison near Tuzla; other unregistered prisoners continued to turn up in the following weeks. A small number of Bosnian Serbs (at least eighteen) captured by Croatian army troops operating in western Bosnia in September 1995 were transferred to prisons in Croatia and had not been released by October 1996, in direct violation of the Dayton agreement.

By late February, the warring factions had withdrawn to the boundaries laid down in the Dayton agreement. Episodic violence continued to plague Bosnian-government-controlled Sarajevo until the city's complete reunification on March 19. The withdrawal of Bosnian Serbs from the areas of Sarajevo that had been under their control was marked by human rights abuses and massive civilian displacement. Warned by the Bosnian Serb leadership in Pale that it was dangerous to live in Bosniak-controlled territory and unconvinced by President Alija Izetbegovic's tardy assurances that they would be safe under Bosnian government rule, an estimated 60,000 to 70,000 Serb civilians fled their neighborhoods in Sarajevo for Serb-held areas before Bosnian government forces moved in. Armed bands of Bosnian Serb nationalists sought to terrorize those Bosnian Serb civilians who wished to remain in their homes. Moreover, after the Bosnian Serbs withdrew, Bosniak gangs followed suit by harassing the few remaining Bosnian Serbs. Most of the departing Bosnian Serbs were resettled in areas where there had previously been a Bosniak majority in order to prevent the return of Bosniaks and consolidate Bosnian Serb control over the area.

Ongoing tensions sporadically boiled over into conflict, especially between the nominal partners of the Bosniak-Croat Federation. Little progress was made on reuniting Mostar, creating a single army from the two sides, and otherwise strengthening the Federation established by the Washington Agreement in 1994, and the alliance continued to exist mainly on paper. Leaders on both sides, as well as NATO officials, periodically warned that the Bosniaks and the Bosnian Croats could easily slide back into war. The divided city of Mostar, scene of some of the worst Bosniak-Croat fighting, which was placed under European Union administration in 1994, continued to be the major flashpoint in the Federation, with numerous violent incidents against resident and transiting non-Croat civilians in west Mostar. Croat-Bosniak hostility occasionally flared up elsewhere: In central Bosnia, there were intermittent reports of beatings, expulsions, and house burnings by the rival groups. Local police were often complicit in such abuses, either by failing to provide protection to the targeted group or by actively participating in the violence.

Throughout the year, civilians were more often than not denied freedom of movement, and all sides continued to maintain illegal checkpoints on major roads in their respective territories. Refugees and displaced persons were generally unable to return to their homes, a guaranteed right under the peace agreement. Some displaced persons who tried to return to their homes, even for a short visit, were met by violent mobs, often organized by local authorities. In March, 800 Bosniaks had to be escorted by IFOR to visit grave sites in the Mostar area after Bosnian Croat soldiers refused to let them pass; Bosnian Croat police did likewise in the Kulen Vakuf area and other areas of Hercegovina under their control. In the same month, Bosnian Serb police prevented Bosniak refugees from visiting relatives or reclaiming homes in the Doboj area. Meanwhile, Bosniaks prevented Bosnian Croat refugees from returning to their homes in Bugojno and Vares. In late April, some 800 Bosniak and Bosnian Croat refugees scuffled with 1,500 local Serbs trying to prevent their return to their homes near Doboj. On April 29, a group of Bosniaks trying to circumvent an IFOR roadblock near Doboj ran through a mine field and were attacked by Bosnian Serbs at the other end; two Bosniaks were killed and five wounded. On the same day, Bosnian Serb mobs smashed the windows of buses taking Bosniaks to visit graves near their former homes in Trnovo.

In Prijedor, the local police chief, responsible for helping to organize concentration camps in 1992, handed out guns and incited the local population to prevent Bosniaks from crossing the IEBL to visit their homes. This went on for months, until finally, after a near shoot-out with IFOR, he was removed from office in September.

Throughout the year, minority populations continued to suffer ethnically motivated killings, arbitrary arrest and detention, physical mistreatment and harassment. There was little prospect for victims to obtain protection from local police and government authorities, who were often complicit in such abuses.

Government authorities on all sides continued the practice of politically-motivated resettlement in order to affect the ethnic composition of the resettled areas and to prevent the return of refugees and displaced persons. Meanwhile, several foreign host countries to refugees from Bosnia-Hercegovina including Germany, Austria, Switzerland and Slovenia, announced plans to begin early repatriation of refugees, despite ongoing persecution of those groups remaining in areas where they did not comprise the ethnic majority and a host of other serious security concerns.

By June, it was already clear that it would be difficult to conduct free and fair elections by September 14, the deadline established in the Dayton agreement. Limited movement throughout the territory, severe restrictions on the press along ethnic and political lines, and the increasing number of attacks and reports of intimidation of the political opposition made it impossible to create the "politically neutral environment" required by the peace agreement.

Despite the abysmal failure of the parties to the agreement to create free and fair conditions for elections, federal elections were held on September 14. Although the United States and it's ambassador to the OSCE, Robert Frowick, were strongly opposed to such a decision, municipal elections were postponed due to serious manipulation of the voter registration process, mostly by Bosnian Serb authorities, as well as concerns about security and freedom of movement for voters. The federal elections, which were held without violence, mostly due to low voter turnout and restriction of movement, were certified by the OSCE shortly thereafter, disregarding a call by the organization's own Election Appeals Sub-Commission for a recount based on allegations of vote fraud. On October 4, municipal elections were scheduled for late November by Ambassador Frowick, in direct contradiction to the recommendation of OSCE's head of the Independent Monitoring Mission and all twenty-five of his monitors, who believed that appropriate conditions for elections did not exist. Shortly thereafter, unable to ignore the OSCE's own logistical problems as well as deteriorating political conditions on the ground, Ambassador Frowick announced that municipal elections would be postponed until between April and June, 1997.

As of this writing, the newly elected Bosnian Serb representatives to the new parliament had not set foot in Sarajevo. Momcilo Krajisnik, president of the Republika Srpska, refused to participate in the inauguration ceremonies held in Sarajevo on October 5. Instead, according to *The Washington Post*, he met with indicted war criminal Radovan Karadzic three times on October 5, who ordered him not to go.

The end of large-scale fighting opened the way for journalists and investigators from the International Criminal Tribunal for Former Yugoslavia (ICTY) to begin serious investigations into alleged war crimes. ICTY investigators turned their attention to the mass graves around the Srebrenica area in Republika Srpska - an area from which up to 8,000 Bosniak males were still missing. However, the work of the ICTY was hampered by local authorities; grave sites were tampered with, and investigators were barred from some sites on many occasions during the year.

Under intense international pressure, some alleged war criminals were arrested, but the vast majority remained at large, and the parties, with the exception of the Bosnian government authorities, failed to meet their obligations under the Dayton agreement and U.N. Security Council resolutions to turn over persons indicted by the ICTY.

Indicted war criminals Gen. Ratko Mladic and Republika Srpska political leader Radovan Karadzic continued openly to defy the international community, repeatedly speaking to the press and, in the case of Karadzic, traveling right under the noses of American IFOR troops and IPTF monitors. Both men remained in office until U.S. pressure on Karadzic to disappear from the political scene resulted in his stepping down as "president" of Republika Srpska in mid-July. Most observers, however, believed that both Karadzic and Mladic continued to wield a great deal of influence.

The Right To Monitor

The Dayton agreement requires the parties to permit nongovernmental human rights organizations "full and effective access" for investigating and monitoring human rights conditions. Further, the United Nations Commission on Human Rights, the U.N. High Commissioner for Human Rights, the OSCE, and other intergovernmental or regional human rights missions were invited to monitor the human rights situation and to establish local offices.

Generally speaking, the parties in both entities permitted access by international human rights organizations, both nongovernmental and intergovernmental, although access for journalists and war crimes investigators was often impeded. Also, local human rights organizations did not travel outside their own immediate areas without international escorts for fear of possible threats and attacks from the other entity's authorities and/or civilians. The International Police Task Force (IPTF) was often prevented from investigating allegations of human rights abuses involving the police. In Banja Luka, for example, following the murder of two Bosniaks in police custody in late August/early September, the local chief of police refused to take action against the police officers responsible and failed to provide the IPTF with information about the investigation. Although eventually guaranteed access to all detention sites, the IPTF was also frequently obstructed in its efforts to investigate reports of illegal detentions or mistreatment in detention.

The Role of
the International Community

American and European support for the U.N. Security Council's decision on October 1 to lift sanctions against the FRY and the Bosnian Serbs was a low point in U.S. and European policy. The elections in Bosnia were not "free and fair," as required by the U.N. Security Council's Resolution 1022, nor were the parties cooperating with the war crimes tribunal, also stipulated in the resolution.

United States

The United States, after years of vacillation and taking a back seat to Europe, finally took the initiative in the peace negotiations in mid-1995. U.S. special envoy Richard Holbrooke, using extensive shuttle diplomacy, managed to bring the parties to the table in Dayton, Ohio, in November 1995, and the United States exerted significant diplomatic pressure throughout the year to keep the peace process on track. The United States also provided 20,000 American troops to IFOR, fully a third of the NATO forces sent to Bosnia-Hercegovina.

The Clinton administration also pushed hard to lay the groundwork for the fall elections, as stipulated in the peace agreement. However, it soon became obvious that the administration was determined to see elections held in Bosnia-Hercegovina whether conditions for free and fair elections existed or not. The Clinton administration feared that the failure to hold elections on time might be interpreted as a policy failure and could call into question the on-time departure of American troops from Bosnia in December 1996 - neither event would be welcome in an election year. Reports emerged that OSCE human rights staff were strongly encouraged by U.S. Ambassador to the OSCE Robert Frowick to report positive developments and to downplay the bleak human rights situation. As the elections neared, the U.S. administration replaced staff members and pressured Europeans associated with the mission to quiet criticisms of the process, even as reports about serious human rights abuses and manipulation of the voter regis-

tration process emerged, attacks on opposition members increased, and restrictions of access to the media continued.

One of the most disappointing aspects of the Clinton administration's policy was its refusal to involve U.S. troops within IFOR in apprehending indicted war criminals. The most glaring example of this policy occurred in mid-August, when American troops arrived at indicted war criminal General Mladic's headquarters as part of a weapons inspection team to confiscate more than 300 tons of illegal Bosnian Serb military hardware discovered by accident. Learning that Mladic was inside, the Americans quickly left the premises so as not to confront him (and thus the obligation to apprehend him) and returned at a later time after his departure. The Clinton administration also appeared to have signaled that it was satisfactory for indicted war criminal Radovan Karadzic to step down from political office, and that it would not press for his apprehension. Special envoy Richard Holbrooke was reported to have pressured Karadzic to "retire in Montenegro" and stated publicly that "... we have to get Karadzic either out of Pale or better yet move the capital of the Serb part of Bosnia from Pale to Banja Luka."

Europe

European leaders paid lip service to the need for arresting indicted persons, but remained indecisive when it came to action. Indeed France and United Kingdom, both countries with significant numbers of IFOR soldiers in Bosnia-Hercegovina, were not in favor of a clear "duty to arrest" clause when IFOR's mandate was being formulated. Throughout the year, they never provided the leadership so badly needed to secure IFOR arrests of those indicted for war crimes.

NATO and United Nations

IFOR troops were able quickly to enforce the military requirements of the Dayton agreement and, with the exception of sporadic confrontations especially with the Bosnian Serbs, IFOR's primary tasks of separating the armies of the parties to the conflict and creating a "zone of separation" was largely completed by February. Unfortunately, however, IFOR continued to define its mandate in the narrowest possible terms, thereby contributing much less than it could have to the peace process in Bosnia-Hercegovina.

IFOR and the IPTF did make significant efforts to remove fixed checkpoints throughout Bosnia-Hercegovina, but the parties continued to set up illegal checkpoints and to violate checkpoint rules by asking the ethnic identity of passengers. IFOR was also reluctant to play a leading role in preventing restrictions on freedom of movement and in protecting civilians. IFOR leaders emphasized that this was the responsibility of the parties, disregarding the fact that many of the abuses were being conducted by local authorities or tolerated by them.

Despite its clear authority to arrest persons indicted for war crimes, IFOR failed to apprehend a single person indicted by the ICTY. The U.N. Security Council Resolution 1031 called on all states to cooperate and comply with orders of the ICTY, and the Dayton agreement's Annex 1-A, Article 10 specifically refers to the obligation of all the parties to cooperate fully with ICTY. IFOR was therefore empowered to use force, which included the arrest of persons indicted by the tribunal, if any of the parties refused to hand over the indicted war criminals to the ICTY. After initially stating that it did not have the mandate to arrest indicted persons, NATO Secretary General Javier Solana later announced that IFOR indeed had the mandate and would arrest such persons if encountered in the course of normal business. However, IFOR failed to make arrests on several occasions when indicted persons, including both Karadzic and Mladic, were encountered, and it became increasingly clear that IFOR would go out of its way not to arrest indicted persons.

The IPTF, under the auspices of the United Nations, was slow to deploy and was not given adequate resources, such as communications equipment and vehicles, to enable effective action in the field. It's man-

date, formulated by the Security Council, excluded a possibility of arrest. The Bosnian Serb exodus from Sarajevo was the first real test of the IPTF, and it did not provide meaningful aid to victims of abuse. Many more Bosnian Serbs might have opted to stay in Sarajevo had they trusted the willingness or ability of the international community to protect them. However, IPTF and IFOR did little or nothing to provide protection for those who wished to stay. Statements to the press by IFOR and IPTF, such as "We can't guarantee anyone's security" did not help to reassure the population.

IPTF faced perhaps its greatest challenge in its efforts to restructure police forces throughout Bosnia-Hercegovina. The "vetting" process required police to reapply for their positions, during which those responsible for human rights abuses during the war or since the signing of peace agreement, as well as those who refused to cooperate with IPTF or were otherwise found in noncompliance with the Dayton accords, were supposed to be denied reemployment in the police force. Unfortunately, as of this writing, this process was still in its early stages in the Federation and had not even started in Republika Srpska, where local authorities failed to reach agreement with the IPTF on how to proceed. Meanwhile, in late October, a Boston Globe reporter discovered that four persons indicted for war crimes by ICTY were working as police officers in the Bosnian Serb towns of Prijedor and Omarska.

Pursuant to the Dayton agreement, High Representative Carl Bildt has authority for supervising all aspects of the civilian component. He has ultimate authority for conditioning reconstruction aid and can trigger reimposition of sanctions against the FRY and the Republika Srpska for failing significantly to comply with the peace agreement. Despite the substantial political and economic leverage at Bildt's disposal, he downplayed his authority throughout the year and generally refused to use his power to force substantive improvements in the parties' compliance with the peace agreement.

Instead, Bildt placed his trust in diplomatic negotiation and sent a clear signal to the non-complying parties that they would suffer no serious repercussions for failing to comply with the civilian provisions of the Dayton agreement. Bildt did make a very positive effort to deny aid to several towns in the Federation that had made little progress in the return of refugees and internally displaced persons.

Despite its own resolutions demanding compliance by the parties with the peace agreement and cooperation with the ICTY, the U. N. Security Council failed to take a strong stand regarding serious violations, most particularly the failure of the parties to cooperate with the tribunal and to permit refugees and displaced persons to return to their homes. It failed to use the leverage of Resolution 1022 when it suspended and later lifted the sanctions against the Bosnian Serbs. The Security Council failed to mandate IFOR to arrest those indicted by the tribunal, opting instead for the weaker language of "authority to arrest." The Security Council also undermined the IPTF by not giving it executive police powers.

BULGARIA

Human Rights Developments

Despite some progress in holding police officers accountable for violence directed at persons in custody, police misconduct remained a dominant human rights problem in Bulgaria throughout 1996. Police brutality was directed primarily at ethnic minorities, but attacks on ethnic Bulgarians and children were also commonplace.

Special police force units known as *Red Berets* routinely mistreat people on the pretext of addressing the burgeoning problem of organized crime in Bulgaria. On April 8, 1996, the Bulgarian daily *Standard* (Sofia) reported that forty masked policemen raided the offices of a private firm. The police beat some employees into unconsciousness, broke windows, and destroyed equipment. The

special forces executed a similar operation in late November 1995 in the Druzhba district in Sofia. *Standard* reported that eleven *Red Berets* stormed a cafe and beat several persons so severely that six victims required emergency surgery. No officer serving in the special forces has ever been charged with any offense related to such instances of police abuse.

Bulgaria made some progress in prosecuting police officers responsible for the deaths of suspects in custody. The Bulgarian daily *Twenty-Four Hours* (Sofia) reported on June 10, 1996, that a Sofia military court convicted six policemen of killing or helping to kill twenty-two-year-old Hristo Hristov in April 1995 after he had been arrested on suspicion of theft. The police beat Mr. Hristov to death in a police cell where his parents found him dead and handcuffed to a radiator. Four of the convicted officers received prison terms of between four and twenty years and two received suspended sentences.

Ethnically motivated violence continued to dominate the human rights landscape in Bulgaria in 1996. The Roma minority was specially targeted both by the police and by xenophobic "skinhead" groups. On March 25, 1996, an off-duty police officer in the city of Russe used his identification documents to gain entrance to a Roma home. The officer held Paun Marinov and Veska Marinova at gunpoint and, claiming that the couples' identification documents were not in order, demanded money. The couple refused to pay whereupon the policeman beat them and other members of their family. No charges were brought against the officer. In only one known instance have suspected police officers been prosecuted for mistreatment of Roma. On March 4, 1996, two officers were tried by the Pleven Military Court and sentenced to eight months in prison and suspended for three years for severely beating two Roma teenagers in Vidin in April 1995.

For the first time in the history of Bulgaria, a Roma man who was beaten by the police sued the Bulgarian Ministry of Internal Affairs for damages. On December 15,

1995, the Regional Court in the city of Pazardzhik ordered the Ministry to pay damages to twenty-two-year-old Kiril Yosifov. Mr. Yosifov was beaten and tortured by the police during an organized raid in his neighborhood on June 29, 1992. The court awarded Mr. Yosifov damages for the bodily injury and moral degradation he suffered.

Attacks against Roma by "skinhead" groups continued throughout 1996 and perpetrators were rarely prosecuted. Roma street children claim that they are attacked frequently and receive no assistance from the police. (See also *Children of Bulgaria: Police Violence and Arbitrary Confinement* in the Children's Rights Project section). On January 4, 1996, a group of twenty "skinheads" armed with knives and chains attacked several homeless Roma children who were sleeping at the railway station in Sofia. Eighteen-year-old Velichka Hristova Ognjanova was stabbed repeatedly. The "skinheads" were taken to the police precinct but later were released.

Freedom of expression suffered serious setbacks during 1996 as the Bulgarian government further infringed on the autonomy of the media. On September 5, 1996, the government passed the *Radio and TV Law*, over President Zhelyu Zhelev's veto, creating a National Radio and Television Council responsible for monitoring broadcasts and appointing directors to state radio and television. The law ensures that the ruling party has the power to elect the majority of council directors and gives directors power to cancel programs and suspend broadcast licenses by taking into consideration "universally accepted moral values" and the "protection of the national and spiritual values of the Bulgarian people."

Attacks on media freedom also resulted in the firing of seven senior journalists from Bulgarian National Radio(BNR) on December 18, 1995. In November 1995, the reporters signed a declaration accusing the management of BNR of censorship. According to the Bulgarian Helsinki Committee, the dismissals reflected "an atmosphere of lawlessness and administrative arbitrariness in the national electronic media."

In June 1996, Bulgaria's Minister of the Interior requested that the National Assembly lift the moratorium on the death penalty, first implemented in July 1990. As a condition of admission to the Council of Europe, Bulgaria was required to impose the moratorium on executions with the expectation that the death penalty would be abolished. As of this writing, the parliament has taken no action on the minister's request.

Attacks on gay people in Bulgaria appeared to grow in both frequency and scope. On July 9, police broke into the Sofia offices of the Flamingo Center, a publisher of gay- and lesbian-interest books, arrested staff, and confiscated office equipment and all publications. Two days later, a police raid resulted in mass arrests of both Bulgarians and foreigners at a "gay beach."

There was considerable harassment of several religious groups in 1996, including the imprisonment of Jehovah's Witness conscientious objectors to military service, police raids of religious meetings in private homes, and government interference in the election of religious officials within spiritual communities. In January, five Protestant sects issued a joint statement protesting systematic official and private discrimination against Protestants; as of this writing, there has been no official response.

The Right to Monitor
There were no reported violations of the right to monitor.

The Role of the International Community

European Union
In November 1995, the European Parliament adopted a resolution calling for Bulgaria and Romania to be removed from the list of countries whose nationals need a visa to enter the European Union. In March, Bulgarian government officials came to an understanding with the E.U. with regard to being removed from the E.U. visa "blacklist" in the near future.

United States

The U.S. granted Bulgaria permanent Most Favored Nation trade status (MFN) on July 18, 1996. There was no debate in the U.S. Congress over Bulgaria's human rights record, and the Clinton administration failed to raise concerns about human rights violations prior to the president's signing the MFN legislation.

The State Department's *Country Reports on Human Rights Practices for 1995* contained an accurate and thorough report on the human rights situation in Bulgaria.

CROATIA

Human Rights Developments

The human rights situation in Croatia remained poor in 1996. In particular, the few ethnic Serbs who remained in Croatia after the Croatian Army recaptured western Slavonia and the Krajina from rebel Serbs in the summer of 1995 faced discrimination and mistreatment by the government of President Franjo Tudjman. Few Serb refugees who fled these areas in the face of the army's offensive were allowed to return to their homes. In eastern Slavonia, which is still under Serb control but is slated to be gradually reintegrated into Croatia, the situation remained tense. Meanwhile, Croatia's increasingly autocratic ruling HDZ [Hrvatska Demokratska Zajednica] party, led by President Tudjman, frequently sought to suppress domestic political opponents and independent media.

Human rights violations against Croatia's remaining Serb community in the Krajina region included the summary execution of elderly and infirm Serbs and the wholesale burning and destruction of Serb villages and property. Most of the remaining Serbs were ultimately forced to flee the area, reducing the proportion of Serbs in Croatia's population from about 12 percent to between 2 and 3 percent. Local human rights monitors reported that an estimated eighty elderly Serb civilians were executed in the months

from November 1995 to April 1996, long after the Croatian government was in control of the region. The Croatian government was aware of the killing and did little to stop it.

By March, according to the UNHCR, 14,000 Krajina Serbs had applied for permission to return home, but only 2,500 applications had been approved, despite President Tudjman's assurances that Croatian Serbs who had not committed war crimes and were ready to accept Croatia as their homeland would be allowed to return. U.S. Ambassador Peter Galbraith and others expressed concern over the slow pace of repatriations. Moreover, Serbs living elsewhere in Croatia also suffered discrimination, especially in the workplace. In April, the government cut off funds to the Serb newspaper *Nas Glas* (Zagreb), citing the paper's "anti-Croatian stance."

The mistreatment of ethnic Serbs in the Krajina region did nothing to ease the fears of Serbs living in eastern Slavonia, scheduled by the U.S.-brokered Dayton peace agreement to be disarmed and brought back under Croatian rule by mid-1997. The area is patrolled by peacekeeping troops of the United Nations Transitional Authority in eastern Slavonia (UNTAES). According to many reports, local Serb leaders have encouraged Serb refugees from elsewhere to resettle in eastern Slavonia and, in a move inconsistent with the Dayton agreement, indicated that they would seek a referendum to determine whether the region should be returned to Croatian authority. However, in early May, the Croatian government adopted a program for the area's peaceful reintegration and passed a law granting amnesty to rebel Serbs who had not committed war crimes. Fifteen Serbs—including Goran Hadzic,"interim president" of the eastern Slavonia Serbs who had been sentenced in absentia to twenty years in prison for war crimes—were specifically excluded from the amnesty. In late September, Croatia drafted a new amnesty law covering all Croatian Serbs who took part in the 1991-95 rebellion, not only those living in eastern Slavonia. Article 3 of the bill listed twenty-one offenses not covered by the amnesty, including genocide, war crimes against civilians and prisoners of war, and the desecration of religious monuments. A U.N. spokesperson said on September 25 that the U.N. was "pleased with the new amnesty," and that "This should give a sense of confidence to the people in the region [eastern Slavonia]." According to UNTAES, demilitarization and demoblization was completed in eastern Slavonia without any problems by June 21.

President Tudjman's autocratic tendencies and impatience with democratic opposition surfaced conspicuously with several attempts to quash domestic critics. In October 1995, an opposition candidate won the mayorship of the capital, Zagreb. In December, Tudjman told the state news agency HINA (Hrvatska Informativna Novinarska Agenicija) that he would not "allow Zagreb, whose population count constitutes a quarter of the whole of Croatia's, to get a city or county authority that would oppose state policy." During the next five months, the opposition-dominated Zagreb City Assembly elected one mayor after another, only to have President Tudjman bar each one from taking office. Finally, in April, Tudjman dissolved the assembly and called for a referendum. In May, in a rare show of independence, the country's highest court annulled the dissolution. However, a legally elected mayor has not yet been appointed to Zagreb.

The regime also harassed Croatia's few independent media outlets. The HDZ dominated the electronic media and applications for broadcast frequencies by many independent TV and radio stations were rejected by the government. At the beginning of July, "Slikom Na Sliku," an independent television news program, was suddenly canceled without warning. In February, HRTV director Ivan Parac was replaced after accusing his predecessor, Antun Vrdoljak, a member of HDZ, of corruption. HDZ parliamentary deputies blocked discussion of Parac's charges, prompting an opposition walkout. Two weeks later, Deputy Prime Minister Borislav Skegro brandished a pistol in the face of a journalist from *Novi List*, one of Croatia's leading independent dailies which is based in Rijeka, an area where the HDZ has little support. In late March, the HDZ introduced press laws giving the government broad powers to launch legal proceedings against journalists for reporting vaguely-defined "state secrets" and for offending or slandering the president and other officials. The Croatian Journalists' Society and Croatian PEN Club denounced the law. Days later, tax authorities hit Novi List and an Italian minority periodical, *La Voce del Popolo* (Rijeka), with a dubious bill for U.S. $2.5 million for alleged customs violations. In May, citing environmental and property law violations, financial police temporarily closed down *Panorama* (Zagreb), an independent newspaper that had criticized Tudjman. On June 14, a reporter and editor-in-chief of *Feral Tribune*, an independent weekly in Split, were put on trial for satirizing President Tudjman under new legislation—an amended section of Article 71 of the Croatian criminal code—which mandates criminal punishment for journalists who defame top government officials. Although the slander trial ended with the acquittal of *The Feral Tribune* on September 26, the Croatian parliament immediately began reviewing a draft law on public information which would require all media sources to take out a compulsory insurance policy to fund any possible trials against them. Party leaders of the HDZ have already threatened to sue the editor of an independent weekly newspaper, *Globus* (Zagreb), for slander.

Croatia continued a policy of not cooperating fully with the International Criminal Tribunal for the Former Yugoslavia (ICTY). Persons indicted for war crimes continued to move about freely in Croatia. Ivica Rajic, a Bosnian Croat wanted by ICTY for having taken part in a central Bosnian massacre of Bosniak civilians in the village of Stupni Do, was spotted residing with his family in a motel owned by the Defense Ministry in Split. Dario Kordic, former leader of Tudjman's HDZ party in Bosnia-Hercegovina and indicted for killing Bosniak civilians during "ethnic cleansing" campaigns in central Bosnia, settled into an apartment in the capital and moved about Croatia unrestricted. Under American pressure, the highest ranking indicted Croat, Bosnian Croat Gen. Tihomir Blaskic, voluntarily gave himself up to the Hague on April 1. Meanwhile, in April, Zagreb's own war crimes tribunal made a show of trying eight Croatians for killing eighteen elderly Serbs after Croatian forces retook the Krajina. In mid-July, the court found no evidence to incriminate six of the eight and sentenced the other two for burglary.

The Right to Monitor

The Croatian government generally did not interfere with the activities of domestic and international groups monitoring human rights in their country; however, local groups were, at times, harassed and intimidated by local extremists. Human rights groups continued to work to prevent forcible evictions and other human rights abuses in their respective localities and brought their concerns to the attention of the local and national authorities. Many times, the results of their work were also published by the independent press. But, most distressingly, human rights monitoring efforts by local organizations in Croatia came under a steady barrage of criticism and threats from the leading political party and government headed by President Tudjman through the government-controlled media. Specifically targeted was the Croatian Helsinki Committee led by Ivan Zvonimir Cicak, and a number of Croatian intellectuals including Yale professor Ivo Banac who were labeled "anti-Croatian," "fascist," and even "enemies of the state."

The Role of
the International Community

United Nations

With NATO troops taking over peacekeeping duties in Bosnia-Hercegovina and most of the contested areas of Croatia retaken by Croat forces, the U.N.'s largely ineffectual peacekeeping force, UNPROFOR, was left mainly with the mission of patrolling eastern Slavonia. In January, the Security Council authorized a reconstituted 5,000-strong force led by retired American Gen. Jacques Klein and renamed the UNTAES. Klein was to oversee the region's demilitarization and the return of refugees, as well as its reintegration into Croatia by mid-1997.

In January, the U.N. Security Council passed a resolution condemning Croatia's human rights abuses in Krajina, including "Killings of several hundreds of civilians, systematic and widespread looting and arson, and other forms of destruction of property." The resolution called on Zagreb to stop blocking the return of refugees, to bring war criminals to justice, to restore Serbian property rights and to stop discriminating against the remaining Serb civilians. Under pressure, the Croatian parliament voted to reverse an earlier decision requiring Serbs who fled Croatia to reclaim their property within three months. But U.N. Secretary-General Boutros-Boutros Ghali, in an August report to the Security Council, criticized Croatia for continuing to violate the rights of the Serb minority and preventing the return of some 200,000 Serb refugees.

By late September, the U.N. had also clearly become frustrated by Croatia's failure to cooperate with the ICTY and extradite Bosnian Croat war criminals residing in Croatia. On September 20, "deploring the failure of the Croatian authorities to execute the arrest warrants issued by the ICTY," the Security Council called for the execution of those arrest warrants without delay. It remained unclear, however, what pressure—if any—the Security Council would be willing to exert on Croatia if it continued to ignore the warning.

In March, the tribunal issued a warrant for the arrest of Krajina Serb leader Milan Martic for a rocket attack on Zagreb in 1995. The tribunal also indicted several Serbian officers of the Yugoslav Army for their role in the massacre of some 261 people, including hospital patients, in the Croatian city of Vukovar during the 1991 war in eastern Slavonia.

European Union

On August 4, 1995, almost as soon as the Croatian Army launched its offensive in the Krajina area, the European Union announced that it was suspending negotiations on a trade and cooperation agreement with Croatia. The E.U. move appeared to be motivated by irritation with Croatia for having resorted to military means to regain control of its territory. As of mid- October 1996, negotiations between the E.U. and Croatia on the trade and cooperation agreement— which includes both a human rights conditionality and suspension clause—remained suspended.

Council of Europe

In April the Council of Europe's Parliamentary Assembly voted to admit Croatia as a member. Although the Council of Europe's Committee of Ministers was expected to confirm the decision of the Assembly soon after, it decided to postpone Croatia's membership into the Council indefinitely because of its disregard of commitments made in March. In early July the Committee of Ministers again specified various conditions that Croatia had to meet by September 30, before becoming a member of the Council of Europe. The conditions included allowing the safe return of Serb refugees from Krajina, recognizing the results of Zagreb's mayoral elections, ending the government's crackdown on the independent media, and cooperating fully with the ICTY, including the apprehension of suspected war criminals. On October 16, the Committee prematurely admitted Croatia as its 40th member stating that it had not been able to endorse such membership in May because Zagreb had at that time not fulfilled all conditions required for membership. However, despite Croatia's failure to apprehend indictees or allow most Serb refugees to return safely to Krajina, the Committee of Ministers now found it sufficient that Croatia had made promises to implement the Dayton agreement, cooperate with the ICTY, respect human rights and the rights of minorities, refugees and displaced persons, and allow freedom of the press and local elections.

United States

As architects of the Dayton Peace Agreement in Bosnia-Hercegovina, the overwhelming U.S. priority in the region was to ensure compliance by all three sides: the Bosniaks, the Bosnian Croats and the Bosnian Serbs. For the latter two, this often meant that U.S. diplomacy was conducted in the respective "mother" countries to make sure that Zagreb and Belgrade would exert pressure on their counterparts in Bosnia. Thus, the U.S. continued to pressure Croatia to support the fragile peace in Bosnia-Hercegovina, while at the same time overlooking, and often failing to condemn, the deteriorating domestic human rights situation in Croatia. Croatia, on the other hand, continued to support the HDZ's hard-line nationalists in Bosnia who resisted cooperating with the Bosniaks, their nominal partners in the American-brokered Federation. On August 17 and 18, at the seventh U.S.-sponsored meeting in as many months to strengthen the Bosniak-Croat Federation in Geneva, President Tudjman agreed to dismantle the Bosnian Croat, self-styled, para-state of "Herceg-Bosna" by August 31. However, once again Tudjman and Bosnian Croat leaders ignored the U.S.-brokered deadline without any repercussions from the Clinton administration.

CZECH REPUBLIC

Human Rights Developments

The Czech human rights record for 1996 was mixed. Despite the generally laudable reforms of Czech democracy, the government failed to ensure many basic human rights to the Roma minority. The continued effects of a discriminatory citizenship law and the state's unwillingness to combat growing racist violence revealed a pattern of discrimination along ethnic lines.

The biggest problem stemmed from the local police, who sometimes displayed an open sympathy for "skinheads," allowing them to hold unauthorized marches and threaten non-ethnic Czechs. Police were often slow to respond to Romani calls for help and hesitant to make arrests, even after a violent attack. In some cases, police themselves used excessive force against Roma.

Despite noticeable improvements in 1996, the judicial system did not always punish the perpetrators of racially motivated violence to the fullest extent of the law. When cases did go to court, the attack was often viewed as a "personal fight" rather than a premeditated act of violence against an individual on account of his race, ethnicity or color. Sentences were often light, which sent the message that such attacks are not considered serious.

Racist attacks—and the government's lack of response—were the most serious concern of Roma in the country. But Roma also continued to face state discrimination in other areas of daily life, such as education, housing and employment. They were often segregated in "special schools," denied residency permits and refused jobs, solely because of their race or ethnicity.

The issue that received the most international attention is the country's controversial citizenship law, which came into effect after the division of Czechoslovakia in January 1993. Although the law does not specifically refer to Roma, its requirements on residence, ancestry and criminality had a clearly disproportionate impact on Roma, and as such are discriminatory. In addition, many Roma who met all of the requirements of the law were arbitrarily denied citizenship by local officials.

As a result, many Roma living in the Czech Republic in 1996 did not have Czech citizenship even though they are long-time or lifelong residents of the republic. Those denied citizenship were unable to vote, run for office, participate in the privatization process or seek redress for wrongs committed against them during the communist regime. Some non-citizens had difficulty receiving permanent residence, which is necessary to receive social benefits from the state. An undetermined number of people

were deported to Slovakia, while others became stateless altogether. Although it is difficult to prove with certainty, evidence suggests that the law was drafted with the specific intent of hindering citizenship for Roma and facilitating their removal from the Czech lands.

Parliament passed an amendment to the law in April 1996 after substantial international criticism. According to the amendment, the Ministry of Interior may waive the five-year clean criminal record requirement, which is the clause that had prevented many Roma from obtaining citizenship. As of August, the ministry had waived the requirement for all sixty-two people who had applied. Even as amended, however, the law remains inconsistent with the Czech Republic's international commitments.

Parliamentary elections in June kept Prime Minister Vaclav Klaus in power. The far-right Republican Party won eighteen seats (an increase of four seats) with a blatantly anti-Roma program. Former high-ranking communist party officials and secret policemen were banned from running for office under a "lustration law" (screening law) that was extended until the year 2000 in September 1995. In February, the minister of the interior proposed that the Party of Czechoslovak Communists be prohibited from participating in the elections, since the party was banned in 1993, but the government took no action.

The Right to Monitor
Human Rights Watch/Helsinki was not aware of any attempts by the Czech government to impede human rights monitoring and reporting in 1996.

**The Role of
the International Community**

United States
Relations between the U.S. and the Czech Republic remained friendly throughout 1996. However, the U.S. Helsinki Commission did express frequent and pointed criticism of the citizenship law and its effect on the Roma

minority. The section on the Czech Republic in the State Department's *Country Reports for Human Rights Practices for 1995* was largely accurate.

Europe

The Czech Republic is, together with Hungary, Poland and Slovenia, considered a leading candidate for early membership in NATO and the European Union because these countries meet, or are close to meeting, essential conditions set out by NATO in 1995. These condition, among others, include internal democracy and civilian control of the armed forces.

FEDERAL REPUBLIC OF YUGOSLAVIA

Human Rights Developments

Human rights conditions remained a cause for concern in 1996 in the Federal Republic of Yugoslavia (FRY), despite Serbian President Slobodan Milosevic's efforts to shake off the country's pariah status after the Dayton agreement. Continued repression and police brutality in Kosovo, discriminatory practice with regard to minorities and the unlawful treatment of refugees perpetuated the pervasive atmosphere of xenophobia and ethnic nationalism. Government control of the media became more stringent, and independent media nearly ceased to exist. The government's continued antagonism toward the U.N. International Criminal Tribunal for the Former Yugoslavia (ICTY) underscored the FRY's defiance of the international community's efforts to seek accountability for war crimes perpetrated in the former Yugoslavia.

Minorities continued to face harassment, in part because of their ethnicity and in part because of the political threat they pose to the state since most non-Serbs identify with opposition parties. Opposition Serbs,

although never facing the level of intimidation and violence that Muslims and Croats faced during the war, nonetheless encountered serious harassment and limitations on their political participation that paralleled those imposed on minorities. Few attempts were made during 1996 to prosecute or hold accountable those who committed serious crimes against non-Serbs and Serb supporters of the opposition. Now, in the wake of the Dayton agreement on Bosnia-Hercegovina, the Serb political opposition and ethnic minorities continue to be marginalized by the Milosevic government - which, under international pressure, has changed its tactics, but not its aims.

The treatment of Bosnian Serb and Croatian Serb refugees was particularly troubling during 1996, as the government continued with its attempts to forcibly settle displaced persons in Kosovo, the Serbian-controlled sector of eastern Slavonia in Croatia, Sandzak and Vojvodina. The Serbian Helsinki Committee reported that Bosnian Serb and Croatian Serb refugees in Serbia were "the worst treated refugees in the war," noting that many had not been officially recognized as refugees by the Serbian government, and that in some instances this indeterminate status had been used to reduce the level of humanitarian aid, medical treatment and housing opportunities.

The government also interfered with the registration process of Bosnian Serb refugees for the September national elections in Bosnia-Hercegovina. Human rights groups in rump-Yugoslavia reported that local authorities obstructed efforts by refugees to vote by absentee ballot. In addition to failing to distribute ballots to many voters who had been promised that they would receive them by mail, Serbian officials were accused of coercing Bosnian Serbs to register to vote in the Bosnian Serb-held entity, Republika Srpska (RS), in areas of strategic importance to the RS authorities, and to vote exclusively for Bosnian Serb candidates. Methods used included misinformation, withholding of humanitarian assistance, fraudulent registration and mass public registration designed to intimidate those who might otherwise have registered in a non-Serb dominated municipality.

The status of resident minorities did not improve in Kosovo, where 1.8 million ethnic Albanians have faced systematic discrimination since 1989. In 1996, thousands of Albanians were harassed, detained or beaten by Serbian policemen who act with near total impunity. At least sixty ethnic Albanians are currently in Yugoslav prisons for political reasons after trials fraught with due process violations. The politically controlled courts consistently rejected overwhelming evidence that torture was used by the police and investigators to extract confessions.

Serb authorities continue to deny ethnic Albanians their right to free association and speech. All Albanian organizations face regular harassment by the police and security forces, including the maltreatment of activists and the arbitrary and illegal confiscation of office equipment. Albanian-language media is minimal, censored, and faces political and economic barriers imposed by the state.

In September, the Serbian government agreed to reopen Albanian-language schools in Kosovo, although it remains to be seen if the agreement will be respected. Before September, during 1996, many Albanian students and teachers were detained and beaten for wanting to study or teach in their native language. The police often confiscated money that had been collected for private Albanian-language schools.

Freedom of movement for ethnic Albanians in Kosovo remained limited. A large number of Albanians were denied passports by the rump Yugoslav authorities and could not travel; others were denied reentry into rump Yugoslavia after time spent abroad. A new citizenship law was passed by the parliament on July 16 which may result in statelessness for Kosovo Albanians. According to this law, a person from Kosovo may lose his or her citizenship if it is determined that he or she originally became a Yugoslav citizen by using documentation that the rump Yugoslav government claims to be false. There is a danger that this provision will be used arbitrarily to strip ethnic Albanians of their citizenship with no official inquiry or right to appeal specified. The creation of "stateless" Kosovo Albanians would be a violation of the FRY's commitments under international law to eliminate statelessness, in addition to leaving many with no voting or residence rights.

State control of media and efforts to prevent free expression continued in 1996. Freedom of the press within rump Yugoslavia was curtailed after the Serbian information minister declared in January that independent broadcasters would no longer be granted frequencies because their information was "anti-government, inaccurate and patently one-sided." Studio B, the last prominent independent television station in the FRY was nationalized in February; at the end of May, the popular Radio Smederevo left the ranks of independent radio stations in the country when it too was nationalized.

Facing growing criticism for having betrayed the Serb populations of western Slavonia and the Krajina region of Croatia, and western Bosnia, the Milosevic government took steps against its critics. Authorities detained opposition leaders on questionable charges and scheduled local, republican and federal elections simultaneously in November, thus making it difficult for opposition parties to distribute scant resources for any semblance of a free and fair campaigning process.

Although the FRY turned over two suspected "small fry" war criminals in early April and permitted the ICTY to open an office in Belgrade in August, the government refused to cooperate with the tribunal in other ways. Members of the Yugoslav Army, Milan Mrksic, Veselin Sljivancanin and Miroslav Radic, all indicted war criminals for their activities in the Croatian city of Vukovar in 1991, continued to reside in the FRY. The government did little to encourage the arrest and extradition of another fifty indicted persons believed to be in Republika Srpska. Several of the most infamous indictees were allowed to make very public appearances during 1996, with no repercussions. Sightings of indicted war criminal and Bosnian Serb Army General Ratko Mladic were embarrassingly frequent throughout Republika Srpska, and he was also allowed to move freely in the FRY, most notably attending a May funeral for an indicted war criminal General Djordje Djukic in Belgrade. Although not yet indicted by the ICTY, Zeljko "Arkan" Raznatovic—a notorious war criminal who partook in brutal ethnic cleansing campaigns in Bosnia-Hercegovina and Croatia—continued to hold a parliamentary position in the Serbian government.

The Right to Monitor
While the work of international and domestic human rights groups was carefully monitored by the state government, international human rights groups were more consistently allowed visas into the country in 1996 than they had been in the past. The work of organizations such as the Helsinki Committees for Human Rights in Serbia and Montenegro, the Humanitarian Law Center and the Serbian Civic League helped to maintain international awareness of human rights conditions in the country; the Democratic League of Croats in Vojvodina, the Council for the Defense of Human Rights and Freedoms in Kosovo, the Helsinki Committee of Sandzak, and the Kosovo Information Center also reported instances of abuse against their respective nationalities. Nonetheless, rights groups were far from universally respected: human rights activists in Kosovo, specifically from the Council for the Defense of Human Rights and Freedoms, were regularly harassed by Serbian police.

The Role of
the International Community

United Nations and Europe
Throughout 1996, Milosevic's continued support for the Dayton peace process was viewed by the international community as critical to its success. In an effort to keep the

Dayton peace process on track, the United States and the European Union opted to downplay human rights abuses within the FRY, as well as the government's continued ties to the war-criminal laden leadership in the Republika Srpska.

In late December 1995, in recognition of the role played by Milosevic in bringing about the Dayton peace agreement, the Security Council suspended the sanctions imposed mainly by Security Council Resolution 757(1992). These sanctions required member states to cease trading in any commodity, maintaining air traffic links, or participating in sporting or cultural events with the FRY; the lifting of these sanctions was to be contingent upon cooperation with ICTY, ceasing to aid the Bosnian Serbs, and cooperating with the U.N.'s embargo against Bosnia-Hercegovina.

The FRY's inner wall of sanctions was permanently lifted on October 1 after the OSCE ruled that the national-level elections were successful in Bosnia-Hercegovina. At the time of this writing, the so-called outer wall of sanctions remained in place, including denial of readmission into the United Nations, the OSCE, the International Monetary Fund, and other international organizations crucial to the FRY's full integration into the international community. According to an October 1995 decision by the European Union's General Affairs Council, long term economic assistance is conditioned on the implementation of the Dayton agreement, respect for human and minority rights, cooperation with the ICTY, and with respect to FRY "the granting of a large degree of autonomy within it for Kosovo."

United States
Throughout the year, the Clinton administration continued to meet with President Milosevic on issues related to the Dayton peace process, the ICTY, the state of affairs in Kosovo, and press freedoms in the FRY. In July, after two rounds of talks with U.S. special envoy Richard Holbrooke, President Milosevic was finally induced to demand that Bosnian Serb leader and indicted war

criminal Radovan Karadzic step down from any form of political activity in the Republika Srpska. This served the immediate aim of removing Karadzic from public view, while allowing Karadzic's Serbian Democratic Party, headed by nationalist elements far more extreme than he, to remain an OSCE-legitimized participant in the Bosnian elections. Although Milosevic's agreement with Holbrooke promised Karadzic's official withdrawal from political activities, even Holbrooke noted that Karadzic could still exercise power through hidden channels.

Although U.S. Secretary of State Warren Christopher told Milosevic in February that Yugoslavia will never achieve full acceptance into the international community until it reconciles the status of Kosovo, both U.S. and European governments gave up one of their most important bargaining chips for improvements in human rights in Kosovo by allowing the permanent lifting of economic sanctions in early October.

GEORGIA

Human Rights Developments

Human rights progress in Georgia stagnated in 1996. Abuses persisted, especially torture and other forms of mistreatment in detention, arbitrary detention, appalling prison conditions, use of the death sentence, corruption of law enforcement officials and the judiciary, and harassment of some political dissidents.

The cease-fires relating to the internal wars between the central government and the breakaway regions of South Ossetia (1992) and Abkhazia (1992-94) continued to hold, preventing a return to large-scale violations of the laws of war. Spontaneous returnees to Abkhazia suffered reprisals and death, and most of the estimated 250,000 people, overwhelmingly Georgian, who fled that region were afraid to return. The Georgian side made some progress in determining accountability for war crimes committed by Abkhazian fighters, but most war crimi-

nals from both sides went unprosecuted, fueling an atmosphere of lawlessness and impunity that adversely influenced general human rights protection.

The year got off to a mixed start. Monitors from the Organization for Security and Cooperation in Europe (OSCE) termed the November 5, 1995, parliamentary and presidential elections and the November 19, 1995, parliamentary run-offs "relatively open;" the assessments of the British Helsinki Group and others were generally less positive. There were overt attempts by the government to intimidate some opposition figures, and the OSCE reported that police interfered with some pre-election rallies. On the eve of the November 5 elections, authorities in the capital, Tbilisi, illegally closed the headquarters of the United Communist Party of Georgia and charged its presidential candidate, Pantileimon Giorgadze, with attempting to commit terrorist acts.

Neither Russian-sponsored peace talks on Abkhazia, recommended in July in Moscow, nor threat of sanctions against Abkhazia by the U.N. Security Council yielded positive results. Russian (formally Commonwealth of Independent States or CIS) peacekeepers began to implement their expanded mandate in Abkhazia in 1996, including responsibility for policing. CIS and U.N. monitors deterred an escalation of hostilities, but were unable to prevent sporadic violence and intimidation of returnees by local residents and Abkhazian police. On January 5, for example, six members of the ethnically Georgian Sanaia family in Shesheleti, Gali district, were reportedly tortured and murdered, and their two neighbors shot to death. The proximity of the village to several detachments of CIS peacekeeping forces and U.N. observers undermined faith in their ability to protect the hundreds of thousands of potential returnees to the region. Return was also deterred by the disappointingly slow progress in de-mining the Gali region; only 20 percent of the mines were removed by June, according to the U.N.

On June 18, the Georgian State

Prosecutor's office completed its investigation into acts of genocide and ethnic cleansing against Georgians in Abkhazia, naming some seventy people as organizers and several hundred as perpetrators of these acts. This step toward accountability for war crimes was encouraging, but only if these individuals are prosecuted and receive a fair trial. The investigation also reportedly neglected to review cases of abuse by Georgian combatants and is therefore only a half-measure at best.

Hopes were higher in 1996 for resolution of the conflict with the separatist region of South Ossetia. In May, the OSCE helped forge a peace memorandum in which the parties pledged to refrain from use of force or other forms of coercion and to "take all necessary measures to halt any illegal actions and any infringement upon the right of individuals on ethnic grounds." However, the failure to resolve the issue at the heart of the conflict—the region's status within Georgia—undermined hopes that signatories would honor this new pledge.

The government acknowledged police abuse to an unprecedented degree in 1996. According to the U.S. State Department's *Country Reports on Human Rights Practices for 1995*, Georgian prison officials themselves reported that forty individuals had died in pretrial detention alone from torture and abuse as well as poor conditions. According to the August 5, 1996, issue of the Georgian newspaper *Akhali Taoba* (Tbilisi), a review by the Procurator's office of police misconduct identified sixty-eight illegal searches, fifty-five attempts to hide a crime, seventeen illegal arrests, and an unspecified number of cases of severe mistreatment of detainees, including the use of electric shock. On August 14, the paper cited the Procurator's office and the Ministry of Internal Affairs as reporting that "dozens" of criminal proceedings had been initiated against police officers in 1996. However, it was unclear how many had been prosecuted and punished, if any. Moreover, no reduction in the routine police abuse or deprivation of basic due process rights was noted or, indeed, claimed in 1996.

Georgian law enforcement officials' frequent violation of the rights of detainees made the country's active use of death sentences in 1996 all the more abhorrent. The government did not provide pertinent figures requested by Human Rights Watch/ Helsinki, but some journalists and human rights groups reported that as of September there were forty-one individuals on death row, including several who were known to have been convicted on the basis of confessions extracted under extreme duress.

Press freedom was widely enjoyed, although self-censorship remained a problem, particularly in the government media. The September adoption of a law on state secrets that restricts some freedom of the media, and the de facto closure of independent TV channel Rustavi-2 on July 17, apparently for political reasons, raised some concern over the state of the independent media.

Pressure against some high-profile political opponents also continued in 1996. The trials and sentencing of several leading detractors of President Shevardnadze's administration, including former Defense Minister Tengiz Kitovani, paramilitary leader Vakhtang (Loti) Kobalia, and opposition members Nugzar Molodinashvili and Badri Zarandia, dealt a significant blow to the radical opposition.

The Right to Monitor

The government generally did not interfere with monitoring; indeed, theoretically it strengthened its own capacity for addressing complaints directly by adopting a law in May establishing the office of human rights defender (analogous to an ombudsman). As of this writing the office was not yet functioning. At the same time, the fact that a human rights activist, Giorgi Kervalishvili, requested political asylum in Germany in December 1995 claiming "constant moral and psychological pressure from the authorities" suggested that not all was well with indigenous monitoring.

The Role of
the International Community

United Nations
In the face of political stalemate, the UNHCR failed again in 1996 to promote the safe return of refugees and displaced persons to Abkhazia. Indeed, it closed its field offices in the conflict zone (an area experiencing spontaneous return and violence) due to budget cutbacks. In 1996, the U.N. focused instead on monitoring compliance with the cease-fire agreement, preparing human rights education materials, and developing human rights monitoring for the region. The U.N. extended the mandate for the U.N. Observer Mission in Georgia (UNOMiG) and its 136 military observers in Abkhazia, and thereby played a significant role in deterring human rights abuses there. Security Council resolution 1077 of October 22 established a human rights office in Abkhazia's main city, Sukhumi, as part of UNOMiG. The proposed program, to be jointly administered with the OSCE, would aim "to promote respect for human rights, protect the human rights of the population of Abkhazia,... contribute to a safe and dignified return of refugees and internationally displaced persons and report on human rights developments" there.

European Union
On April 22, the European Union signed a Partnership and Cooperation Agreement (PCA) with Georgia that enshrines respect for democratic principles and human rights. If approved by the European Parliament, the E.U.'s commitment to insisting on compliance will be monitored closely.

Council of Europe
On July 14 Georgia applied to upgrade its guest status at the Council of Europe to full membership. This opened a review process that will offer many occasions for the council to use its influence to secure improvements in Georgia's human rights record. According to an Interfax report of July 15, Secretary General Daniel Tarchys set an appropriately cautionary tone during his July visit to Georgia by stressing that full membership would not be granted until Georgia banned the death penalty and otherwise brought its legislation into conformity with European standards, and refrained from coercive methods to settle the Abkhazia conflict.

United States
The U.S. embassy made important interventions and paid much-needed attention to brokering peace in Abkhazia. The State Department demonstrated a sensitive and comprehensive understanding of human rights problems in its *Country Reports on Human Rights Practices for 1995*. By contrast, the U.S. was not known to have demonstrated similar concern about Georgian authorities' failure to investigate and prosecute its own troops for war crimes.

GREECE

Human Rights Developments
Despite its membership in the European Union and NATO, human rights violations persisted at an alarming level in Greece during 1996. Of particular concern were violations of minority rights, the maltreatment of immigrants, and restrictions on freedom of expression.

In September 1995, the governments of Greece and Macedonia signed an interim agreement that cleared the way for a normalization of relations. Although the accord guaranteed the free flow of movement between the two countries, tens of thousands of ethnic Macedonians who fled Greece after the civil war were still not allowed back into the country in 1996, even to visit relatives or attend funerals. In contrast, ethnic Greek political refugees were regularly allowed to return. The Macedonian minority in Greece continued to face discrimination, including restrictions on freedom of expression and association

Tensions increased in 1996 vis-a-vis

the Turkish minority in Western Thrace, in part brought on by the tension between Greece and Turkey over the Aegean islet of Imia (Kardak) and Cyprus. In August, after intercommunal violence left dead two Greek protestors in Cyprus, a gang of motorcyclists rampaged through Komotini, attacking Turks and Turkish-owned property. Police did little to stop the violence, though the prefect of the region condemned the violence and an investigation was launched against the police.

The Greek government continued to deny the existence of a "Turkish minority," as opposed to the religious identification of "Muslim" that is officially used. In 1995, for example, the European Commission of Human Rights declared the case of the late Dr. Sadik Ahmet, a former parliamentarian who had been imprisoned in 1990 for using the words Turkish and Turk, as admissible.

A major instrument used against ethnic Turks in 1996, as well as other minorities, was article 19 of the citizenship law, which allows the state to revoke the citizenship of non-ethnic Greeks who travel abroad without the intent to return. In 1995, the U.S. State Department reported that seventy-two individuals had been arbitrarily stripped of their citizenship; the Greek government claimed that forty-five of them had given it up voluntarily. In 1996, the article was used to revoke the citizenship of a number of non-ethnic Greek citizens who had traveled abroad. One such case concerned Mr. Hussein Ramadanoglu and his wife, who had gone to Germany to work in 1990. In April, on a regular visit to Greece, they were told that they had lost their citizenship.

Another area of concern is the selection of the mufti. A 1990 law gave the state the legal right to appoint muftis, whereas previously they could be elected by the community. In 1995, the elected mufti of Xanthi, Mehmet Emin Aga, served six months in jail; in 1996 both he and the elected Mufti of Komotini, Ibram Sherif, faced similar charges of holding an unauthorized office. On October 21, Ibram Sherif was found guilty and fined.

Ethnic Turks continued to face restrictions on freedom of expression, discrimination in hiring, especially for the civil service, expropriation of land, and poor access to education and other state services. On October 24, the Turkish-language Radio Icik went on trial for operating without a license in 1994 and 1995 even though all private radio stations operate without a license because of the state's failure to distribute them. One bright point in 1996 was the election of three ethnic Turk deputies in the September parliamentary elections and the entrance into Greek universities of forty-five ethnic Turks through the first affirmative action programs.

The Greek Orthodox Church continued to enjoy a privileged status under Greek law. Other religious communities experienced various forms of state discrimination, particularly Catholics, Protestants, Jehovah's Witnesses and Scientologists. In May, the Macedonian activist Father Nikodimos Tsarknias was tried for working as an Orthodox priest, since the Greek Orthodox Church had defrocked him in 1993. He was acquitted in three trials, but other charges are still pending. On October 7, a prosecutor in Athens asked for the Greek branch of the Scientologists, known as the Center of Applied Philosophy, to be disbanded.

Greece has a large number of foreign guest workers, most of them from neighboring Albania. In August, the Greek authorities undertook a massive campaign to detain and expel illegal immigrants, the third such campaign in the last three years. According to local human rights organizations, an estimated 7,000 Albanians were rounded up and deported; many of them complained of maltreatment by the Greek police and border guards. According to the Greek Helsinki Monitor, twenty-nine Albanians have been missing since March, when they were reportedly arrested by the Greek police.

Greece's Roma population, the country's most marginalized group, faced police abuse and discrimination in housing and education in 1996. In February, the police maltreated a group of Roma in the Aspropyrgos neighborhood of Athens. Two ethnic Albanian groups, Chams and Arvanites, also complained of state discrimination.

Early 1996 saw a series of riots in Greek prisons. Inmates complained about unsafe and unhygienic conditions.

The Right to Monitor

Human rights groups encountered difficulties from the state in 1996. In August and September, state security forces followed a Greek Helsinki Monitor and Danish Helsinki Committee delegation to minority villages in Thrace, as well as a Greek Helsinki Monitor meeting with a Macedonian activist in Florina. The family of a Greek Helsinki Monitor activist was harassed by the secret police, who wanted to know about her work. Minority leaders and human rights activists who defended their rights were often slandered in the media.

The Role of
the International Community

Europe

In September, the European Parliament released a critical human rights report on Greece that cited the imprisonment of conscientious objectors and restrictions on religious freedom, minority rights and freedom of expression. In 1996, the European Court of Human Rights condemned Greece for violations of religious freedom because the state had closed a place of worship of the Jehovah's Witnesses, which had been built without authorization.

United States

Relations between the United States and Greece remained friendly throughout 1996, although the State Department's *Country Reports on Human Rights Practices for 1995* did highlight a number of human rights concerns. Greek President Stephanopoulos was greeted warmly by President Clinton when he visited the United States in May. The U.S. also helped mediate a settlement in January between Greece and Turkey over the disputed Imia islet.

HUNGARY

Human Rights Developments

Hungary's record on human rights was mixed during 1996. The Hungarian government undertook efforts to address some of its most serious human rights problems, especially regarding the protection of minorities. The Hungarian parliament introduced an amendment to the criminal code to allow more effective prosecution of those who commit crimes against individuals because of their national, ethnic or religious affiliation. Hungary also reached agreement with Romania and Slovakia over the mutual protection of minorities, after several years of difficult and controversial negotiations. However, there continued to be significant human rights violations, especially against the Roma minority. Police brutality and mistreatment in detention also continued to be of concern.

There were numerous reports of physical mistreatment of persons in detention during 1996. The European Committee on the Prevention of Torture issued a report in February criticizing the mistreatment of prisoners especially in Budapest, accusing police of beatings, and stating that conditions in some jails were inhuman. In particular, the report drew attention to the Kerepestarcsa Center for detaining foreigners in the country, arguing that they suffered brutal treatment and conditions which were inhuman and degrading. Hungary has since closed the Kerepestarcsa Center and moved those inmates to other facilities. Another twenty detention centers were closed and others were upgraded during the year, according to Interior Ministry spokesperson Moricz Miklos.

The Hungarian minister in charge of the civilian secret services, Istvan Nikolits, came under criticism from the chair of the Hungarian parliament's human rights committee for authorizing a wide-ranging program of surveillance of all minorities in Baranja county in the south of the country. Nikolits argued that the program, entitled "The Protection of National and Ethnic Minorities" was launched in light of the Yugoslav crisis to protect the county's minorities such as Serbs and Croats from attack because of their nationality or family ties. However, the parliament's human rights committee expressed concern that such extensive surveillance had continued after the danger had subsided and without judicial oversight.

Roma continued to face a discernible pattern of open societal and governmental discrimination in education, the workplace, housing and access to public establishments. In addition, private acts of violence were often openly supported or passively tolerated by the police and criminal investigators. When investigations did lead to criminal charges, the charges were usually significantly less than the facts would seem to warrant. Frequently prosecutors denied that violent attacks against Roma were racially motivated, thereby making the maximum sentence for conviction much less than would be the case if racism were recognized as the motivating factor. Human rights and Romani organizations in Hungary reported that Roma are especially likely to receive discriminatory treatment in the judicial process, with longer periods of pre-trial detention and higher sentences when convicted.

Although police abuses and discrimination against Roma continued to be frequent, Roma victims appeared increasingly willing to seek remedies for such abuse through the judicial system. In a landmark discrimination case, a Roma man who had been refused service in a restaurant because of his ethnicity won a libel suit against the owner of the restaurant.

The Right to Monitor

There were no reports of any attempt by the government to impede the work of human rights monitors during 1996.

The Role of
the International Community

Europe

In general, Hungary was recognized by the international community as having made substantial progress in the area of human rights and democratic institution-building. Spanish Foreign Minister Javier Solana, the new secretary-general of NATO, identified Hungary as a serious candidate for NATO membership during 1996. In addition, Hungary was judged to have met the general requirements for admission to the Organization for Economic Cooperation and Development (OECD), including respect for human rights, democracy and an open market economy. Hungary also met the general requirements of European Union membership, including specific human rights requirements. However, the European Committee for the Prevention of Torture issued a report in 1996 on the mistreatment of persons in detention, which was highly critical of ongoing police abuse and conditions in detention facilities. On September 16, Hungary and Romania signed a treaty designed to permit the development of friendly relations between the two countries and full respect for minorities as foreseen in particular in the European Stability Pact signed on March 20, 1995, in Paris at the initiative of the European Union.

United States

The Hungary chapter of the U.S. State Department's *Country Reports on Human Rights Practices for 1995* was generally accurate in its analysis of human rights in Hungary, correctly emphasizing that Hungary had failed to prevent police brutality against Roma and crime suspects generally. The report also noted that due process rights, such as access to counsel and a speedy trial, are not consistently guaranteed in Hungary.

KAZAKSTAN

Human Rights Developments

The Kazakstan government generally observed the rule of law in 1996 and, indeed, took dramatic action in response to serious problems in its penitentiary system. However, its 1996 record continued to be marred by persistent abuse in detention, abysmal prison conditions, attacks on the media, and varying degrees of harassment of leaders of the ethnic Cossack and Uighur communities.

After almost a year's hiatus in which democratic electoral processes were suspended, in January President Nursultan Nazarbaev finally restored democratic rights by reinstating the parliament, which he had illegally suspended in March 1995 and replaced with unilateral rule by the president and his Cabinet of Ministers.

Also heartening was the Kazakstan government's response to the entrenched problem of appalling prison conditions and serious mistreatment of detainees. According to the local newspaper *Karavan-Blitz* (Almaty) of June 4, some 2,500 inmates died in Kazakstan jails last year. Kazakstan was also vilified in a July report by Amnesty International for holding fourth place in the world for the number of executions and for shocking mistreatment of inmates. The government pledged to initiate a "stage-by-stage transition" from death to life sentences, proposed a ten-year program to bring jail conditions up to international standards, and issued an amnesty in July that, according to local monitors, resulted in the release of several thousand inmates from among a total prison population of 78,000, and the reduction in sentence of unknown more. Sadly, the amnesty was justified publicly by citing the dropping crime rate rather than the necessity to reduce human rights abuse.

Parts of the media had to battle for their independence in court this year. Although Kazakstan enjoyed broad press freedom, the independent Kazakstan-American Bureau on Human Rights alleged that independent journalists were increasingly persecuted by the state, such as being charged with slander for expression of critical political opinions. The group also charged that a new censorship regime had been introduced by the State Radio and Television Committee. The independent Kazakstan newspaper *Dozhivem Do Ponedel'nika* was forcibly closed this year,

and in May, the procurator's office threatened closure of the widely read Russian newspaper *Komsomol'skaia Pravda* unless its publishers issued a statement of regret for having published the provocative views of Russian nationalist Aleksandr Solzhenitsyn. The newspaper complied, and threats of charges were dropped. At the same time, in September a Radio Liberty stringer won damages from local officials who detained him illegally on his way to cover the visit of a Chinese dignitary.

Two cases of imprisonment and abuse of Cossack leaders in late 1995 and 1996 set an ominous tone for ethnic relations. On October 28, 1995, Nikolai Gunkin, *ataman* (leader) of the Semirech'e Cossack Host, was arrested in Almaty on his way to register as a candidate in the elections to the lower house of parliament. On November 21 he was sentenced to three months of imprisonment under Article 183-1 of the Criminal Code ("organizing an unsanctioned meeting," which he claimed was a peaceful religious procession in January 1995). Two weeks before his sentencing, unidentified assailants broke into the home of Gunkin's defense attorney, Ivan Kravtsov, and assaulted his wife, Iraida, who had to be hospitalized. Kravtsov withdrew from the defense the following day. Gunkin alleged that, once in detention, he was attacked by prison guards and that they threw cold water on him to force him to end a hunger strike.

In an eerily similar case, on August 20, 1996, Nina Sidorova, head of the Russian Center and advocate for the rights of Cossacks, was arrested on charges of resisting police authority and contempt of court. She, too, was arrested months after her alleged crime, and only when she made a political claim (attempting to register her group as a social organization). In statements received by Human Rights Watch/Helsinki, Ms. Sidorova claimed she was repeatedly beaten by guards and, prior to meetings with visitors, was shut in a small dark space, an experience she found so traumatizing that she ultimately refused to see anyone from the outside. On September 11, her defense attorney, middle-aged Maria Larshina, was beaten with a heavy object by an unknown man loitering outside her home, requiring her to be hospitalized. On September 22, Ms. Sidorova was released on bail pending trial, a concession to international pressure.

The Right to Monitor

Monitoring generally took place unimpeded. The May 31 law on social organizations reaffirmed in principle government support for such groups as human rights organizations.

The Role of
the International Community

Europe

The OSCE monitored parliamentary elections in December 1995 and protested violations of the electoral process. The European Commission opened an official representative office in Almaty on April 12 and the European Union became the single largest donor to Kazakstan. Following President Nazarbaev's suspension of parliament in 1995, the European Parliament decided to withhold assent for the Partnership and Co-operation Agreement which was signed by the E.U. and Kazakstan in 1995. The agreement is conditioned on the parties' respect for human rights and democratic principles as set out in OSCE documents.

China

In April, Kazakstan government officials signed a pact with Chinese counterparts in Shanghai to strengthen their common borders. This was formalized by a July 5 joint declaration in which China and Kazakstan pledged, among other things, that "they are opposed to national separatism in any form and they will not permit any organizations and forces to engage in separatist activities in their respective territories against the other side." Because the Chinese government often paints its ethnic Uighur minority as separatist-minded saboteurs, this is undoubtedly an implicit reference to Kazakstan's Uighur population, which shares language and cul-

ture with Uighurs in neighboring regions of China. The commitment ensured that Kazakstan, among other signatory countries, would turn a blind eye to the "Strike Hard" crackdown against Uighurs the Chinese had embarked on several months before throughout China. The campaign reportedly led to hundreds of illegal arrests. The agreement prompted Kazakstan authorities to prevent Uighurs from staging a public rally during the Chinese president's visit in July, in violation of their right to freedom of assembly.

KYRGYZSTAN

Human Rights Developments

The continued government crackdown on independent or critical media, freedom of speech and association, and an alarming consolidation of power for President Askar Akayev marked a distressing trend for human rights in Kyrgyzstan in 1996. Additional causes for concern included the continued use of the death penalty, squalid prison and detention centers, and police brutality.

President Akayev won the December 24, 1995, presidential election with more than 70 percent of the vote. However, his victory came amidst allegations of constitutional illegality that elections had been called prematurely and that three out of six presidential candidates had been unfairly excluded from the electoral process on the grounds that they had not collected the required 50,000 signatures mandated by unreasonable 'oblast' (regional) proportions."

Freedom of speech and of association also came under fire on December 22, 1995, when Topchubek Turgunaliev, deputy chair of the political party *Erkin Kyrgyzstan,* and Dzhurmagazi Usupov, chair of the *Ashar* movement, were arrested for the distribution of leaflets critical of President Akayev prior to the presidential election. They were charged under article 128, section 2, article 129 and article 68 of the Criminal Code of Kyrgyzstan for slandering and insulting the president in printed and written forms and intentionally inciting national dissent. Having spent four months in pre-trial detention, each man was given a one-year suspended sentence.

Rysbek Omurzakov, a journalist for the *Res Publica* (Bishkek) newspaper was arrested on April 12, 1996, and sentenced to two years of imprisonment under article 128, part 3 (libel with accusations of treason or other state crime). Unofficial sources suggest that the arrest was also made in connection with distributing leaflets critical of President Akayev. Following an appeal on August 6, 1996, Omurzakov had his two-year prison sentence suspended ostensibly after the court took into account his character and the fact that he has a family to support but likely as a concession to public outcry over his arrest.

The February 10, 1996, referendum on a draft law on constitutional change was approved by more than 94 percent of the electorate. This violated the 1993 Kyrgyzstan constitution, which prohibits constitutional change by referenda. The referendum was also objectionable because it gave the president unilateral power to appoint all top ministers except the prime minister.

The Kyrgyzstan government in 1996 continued to implement the *propiska* (residence permit) system which, in conjunction with an internal passport, is required in order to obtain permission to leave the country. This system arbitrarily restricts freedom of movement, both internally and internationally, in direct contravention of article 12 of the International Covenant on Civil and Political Rights, to which Kyrgyzstan is signatory. In April, in a clear violation of freedom of expression and of association, the Kyrgyzstan government banned the ethnic Uighur society, Ittipak, for three months on the grounds that it was allegedly carrying out separatist activities that ran counter to the interests of the Chinese people. Kyrgyzstan law does not treat separatist activities as a criminal act; rather, the suspension was the result of an interstate agreement to quell separatist activities, reached in April between Kyrgyzstan, Kazakstan, Tajikistan,

and the Chinese government. The Ittipak society was barred from campaigning in the press and media or from organizing any meetings, demonstrations or other mass activities in Kyrgyzstan, in violation of its right to freedom of speech, association, and assembly.

The year 1996 was proclaimed "Women's Year" in Kyrgyzstan. President Akayev accordingly granted an amnesty to numerous female prisoners on March 8 (International Women's Day) and appointed a female vice-premier. However, in contrast to the fanfare, "Women's Year" was not marked either by the introduction of any specific legislation to give support or protection to women who face domestic violence and job discrimination, or the enforcement of existing anti-discrimination laws, most notably the 1979 Convention on the Elimination of All Forms of Discrimination Against Women, to which Kyrgyzstan is a signatory.

Kyrgyzstan in 1996 did not sign the Second Optional Protocol of the ICCPR on abolishing the death penalty; it retained the measure for fifteen peacetime and two wartime offenses and continued to pass the death sentence in 1996. According to one Kyrgyz human rights group, juveniles are among those being put to death.

The Right to Monitor
There were no reported violations of the right to monitor.

The Role of the International Community

European Union
The European Union was silent on specific human rights abuses in Kyrgyzstan. In addition to its substantial aid through the TACIS and ECHO programs, it was preparing to implement, pending ratification by all E.U. member states, the signed Partnership and Cooperation Agreement (PCA) between the E.U. and Kyrgyzstan. The PCA cites respect for human rights and democratic principles as an essential element of the agreement. The European Parliament approved the PCA in

November 1995.

United States

U.S. government aid was expected to be over US$50 million in 1996, reportedly in recognition of Kyrgyzstan's stability and democratic reforms. The U.S. government sent observers to the trial of Topchubek Turgunaliev and Dzhurmagazi Usupov and prepared a strong and comprehensive analysis of Kyrgyzstan's human rights record in its *Country Reports on Human Rights Practices for 1995.*

MACEDONIA

Human Rights Developments

Since declaring its independence in 1991, Macedonia has avoided the war in the former Yugoslavia and established a basic framework for the protection of civil and political rights. Nevertheless, the implementation of these rights has remained a problem. In 1996, the government continued to commit human rights violations against Macedonian citizens of all ethnicities.

The most sensitive issue is minority rights, since Macedonia is made up of numerous ethnic groups, including Albanians, Roma, Serbs and Turks. All of these groups reported state discrimination, especially in minority-language education and state employment. At times their complaints were politically motivated, but, in many cases, the state failed to abide by the non-discriminatory principles of international law.

By far the largest and most vocal of the ethnic communities is the Albanians who, according to official statistics, comprised almost one quarter of the population. Despite some minor improvements, Albanians were still grossly under represented in state jobs, especially the police force. Some voting districts in the western part of the country, where Albanians predominate, were three times larger than districts in the east inhabited primarily by ethnic Macedonians.

The most important issue for ethnic Albanians is education in their mother language. An attempt in 1995 to open a private Albanian-language university was deemed illegal by the state, and the university was ordered to shut down. Four of the university's organizers were imprisoned after a trial that violated international standards of due process; they were later released on bail while they awaited an appeal. In 1996, the appeals court confirmed the guilty verdicts but reduced each of the defendants' sentences by one year. One of the defendants, Milaim Fejziu, was subsequently released.

Albanians were not the only victims. All citizens of Macedonia, regardless of ethnicity, suffered from the country's weak democratic institutions.

A constant problem in 1996 was the excessive use of force by the police. A local human rights organization, the Macedonian Helsinki Committee, documented numerous cases of arbitrary arrest and abuse in detention. On August 9, a Romani woman, Rakiba Mehmed, died under unclear circumstances after being chased by the police in Skopje. The authorities claimed that she died from a heart attack, but eyewitnesses claimed that they saw her being beaten severely by the police. As of November, the government had not begun an official investigation.

The independence of Macedonia's courts also came into question after the election of some judges with close ties to the government. Despite the adoption of democratic legal standards, there were violations of due process in 1996. Defendants were sometimes held in detention longer than the twenty-four hours allowed by Macedonian law, did not have proper access to a lawyer or were denied the right to a fair trial.

The political opposition continued to complain about state efforts to restrict its work, such as phone tapping and police harassment. In March, the two largest opposition parties, the Democratic Party of Macedonian National Unity and the Democratic Party, submitted a petition with 150,000 signatures calling for new elections. Shortly thereafter, the government proposed, and parliament hurriedly passed, legislation that altered the guidelines for submitting citizens' petitions. In June, according to the new guidelines, parliament decided that new elections would not be held.

In January, the government decided to privatize the state-run media conglomerate *Nova Makedonija*, which had a monopoly on the printing and distribution of newspapers. As of October, the privatization process had still not begun. Many private television and radio stations exist in Macedonia, but their broadcasts were limited to their local areas.

The Role of
the International Community

United Nations and OSCE
The international community's priority was to maintain the territorial integrity and political stability of Macedonia. Toward this end, a 1,200 member United Nations Preventive Deployment Force (UNPREDEP) and an Organization for Security and Cooperation in Europe (OSCE) mission continued to monitor and report on the internal and external threats to the country. In the name of stability, however, both organizations voiced little public criticism of human rights violations committed by the Macedonian government. Macedonia established full diplomatic relations with the European Union on January 10. The E.U.'s PHARE aid program provided Macedonia with approximately US$30 million annually.

United States
The United States continued its support of the Macedonian government and the government's attempts to promote inter-ethnic dialogue. Approximately 600 U.S. soldiers participated in the UNPREDEP mission. High ranking Macedonian military delegations visited the U.S., and joint military exercises were held within the framework of the Partnership for Peace. The first American ambassador to Macedonia was appointed in March.

ROMANIA

Human Rights Developments
The Romanian government made an effort to improve relations with its ethnic Hungarian community in 1996, but made little progress toward guaranteeing protection of its Roma minority. Although mob violence against Roma decreased during 1996, it was replaced by systematic police raids on Roma villages. These raids were usually conducted without warrants and were characterized by the excessive use of force by police.

The Colentina neighborhood of Bucharest was raided four times in 1996 by officers from the 7th District police. On one such occasion, on June 6, 1996, fifty policemen invaded homes and forced residents into cars. When one victim asked to see a warrant, an officer replied that no warrants were required because the Roma were not legal residents of the neighborhood. The Roma were taken to the station where they were severely beaten and humiliated and fined for "illegal domicile" for squatting on land they did not officially own. The Roma allege that the Ceausescu regime promised the land to them when they moved to Colentina in the 1970s to work on construction sites. Residents claim they have tried to buy the land from city authorities, but their offers were refused. The Roma village of Bontida was also the target of similar raids; victims there claim the police beat people and fined Roma families regardless of whether their address registrations were produced or not.

Random police violence targeting Roma was also commonplace and routinely tolerated by the authorities, leaving Roma victims without legal recourse. On May 9, 1996, Mircea-Muresul Mosor, a twenty-six-year-old Rom from Comani, was shot and killed by the chief of police, Plut. Adj. Tudor Stoian, in Valcele. An official police communique issued after the incident alleged that Mosor lifted a stick and was about to strike the police chief when Pl. Adj. Stoian shot him. Mosor was taken to the hospital where he died. Testimony from Mosor's attending physician and the death certificate contradict the official police report. The death certificate states that Mosor was shot in the back, and Dr. Dan Jijau, the attending physician, confirmed that the bullet went through Mosor's back. The official communique is thus highly suggestive of police misconduct at several levels.

Freedom of religion and association suffered setbacks in 1996 as Romania continued to prohibit particular religious gatherings. On June 25, 1996, the Romanian government denied permission for an international convention of Jehovah's Witnesses in Bucharest in July. The government's General Secretariat declared that it considered "thoroughly inopportune the attempt to improvise such a meeting in Bucharest in July or at any time in the future." The government's denial came in response to concerns raised by the Romanian Orthodox Church in a communiqué dated June 21, 1996, accusing Jehovah's Witnesses of "irresponsibly contributing to growing violence and hatred in the world." On July 1, Hillary Clinton reportedly canceled a visit to a Romanian Christian church in protest over the government's decision to deny permission for the Jehovah's Witnesses' convention.

A move toward decriminalizing homosexuality in Romania was undermined by the adoption of an amendment to article 200 of the penal code that makes sexual acts between persons of the same sex punishable with imprisonment for six months to three years. The amendment was adopted by the Chamber of Deputies of the Romanian parliament on September 10, 1996, and produced a storm of international protest, including passage of a European Parliament resolution condemning the decision. Romania's parliamentary Mediation Commission overruled the Chamber of Deputies' decision on September 24, 1996. The commission opted for the text adopted earlier by the Romanian Senate which criminalized homosexual conduct only if such conduct resulted in "public scandal."

On July 11, 1996, Radu Mazare and Constantin Cumpana from the Romanian daily *Telegraf* were sentenced to seven months in prison and fined for libel in connection with a 1992 article about corruption in the Constanta city council. The journalists were charged under articles of the penal code providing criminal penalties for journalists who offend public officials and began serving the jail sentences on August 30, 1996. The use of criminal libel laws against journalists will continue to silence dissent against government officials.

The Right to Monitor
There were no reported violations of the right to monitor.

The Role of
the International Community

European Union
On September 16, 1996, Romania and Hungary signed a treaty designed to permit the development of friendly relations between the two countries and to foster respect for minorities as contemplated by the European Stability Pact signed on March 20, 1995, in Paris at the initiative of the European Union. The treaty includes a recommendation guaranteeing the rights of the Hungarian minority in Romania.

United States
In July 1996, the U.S. Congress approved a bill granting Romania permanent Most Favored Nation trade status (MFN). The House vote was delayed because some members expressed harsh criticism of President Ion Iliescu and the Romanian government. Former U.S. Ambassador to Romania David Funderburk, member of the U.S. House of Representatives from North Carolina, opposed Romania's MFN status upgrade charging the Romanian government with human rights abuses, including violations of freedom of expression and religion and discrimination against ethnic minorities. The U.S. State Department's *Country Reports on Human Rights Practices for 1995* catalogued

serious human rights abuses by the Romanian government, including the frequent beating of detainees by police, rampant discrimination and police violence against the Roma minority, and restrictions on freedom of expression and religion. President Clinton signed the permanent MFN bill on August 3, 1996.

RUSSIAN FEDERATION

Human Rights Developments

The Russian Federation's human rights practices did not improve in 1996 despite heightened expectations stemming from its admission into the Council of Europe and from President Boris Yeltsin's re-election campaign promises. The August 1996 Khasavyurt agreements ended twenty months of war in Chechnya and the hideous violations of humanitarian law that had so tragically characterized it. New laws sought to implement Council of Europe standards in the Russian criminal justice system, and two Constitutional Court decisions reinforced guarantees of freedom of movement and due process. But the systematic violations of the rules of armed conflict in Chechnya from January through mid-August, unabated police brutality, especially against non-ethnic Russians, and the continued failure to repeal the *propiska* (residence permit) system underscored the Russian government's indifference to its domestic and international human rights commitments.

In the second year of war in Chechnya, civilians were the victims of indiscriminate and disproportionate fire in most areas of Chechnya, causing anywhere from 18,500 to 80,000 civilian deaths since the start of the war in December 1994. For example, in the December 1995 battle for Gudermes, Chechnya's second-largest town, Russian forces pounded parts of the town with heavy artillery and surface- and helicopter-launched shells, killing at least 267 civilians.

In his re-election campaign, President Yeltsin promised to end the war in Chechnya, which resulted in the Nazran cease-fire agreement. Within days of Yeltsin's re-election on July 3, however, indiscriminate bombing in Gekhi and Makhety killed at least another twenty civilians, and soon thereafter indiscriminate and disproportionate bombing and shelling killed an untold number of civilians throughout villages of eastern and southern Chechnya. In the August battle for Grozny, Russian bombs and shells destroyed entire apartment blocks and at least one hospital, and hit residential suburbs with wild inaccuracy. Gen. Konstantin Pulikovskii's August 20 ultimatum to carpet bomb Grozny, giving the city's 300,000 civilians forty-eight hours to evacuate, fortunately dissolved as new peace negotiations began.

Dozens of civilians reported to Human Rights Watch/Helsinki and Memorial (a leading Russian human rights organization) that they were shot at as they attempted to flee hostilities in Gudermes, and that dozens were killed and wounded. In another glaring example of direct attacks on civilians, Russian helicopters opened fire on a column of buses and cars transporting civilians fleeing Grozny after the August 20 ultimatum; ten civilians were killed. In early March, Russian forces blockaded the village of Sernovodsk, home to 7,000 civilians (the majority of them displaced persons from Chechnya); they forbade civilians from leaving the village and international humanitarian relief organizations from entering until after shelling had already begun. According to Memorial, at least forty-five civilians were killed during hostilities. On March 15, Russian forces gave civilians a two-hour warning to leave Samashki, a village of 7,000, before shelling it. Such short notice proved fatally inadequate. Russian forces refused to allow Chechen men to flee past the Samashki checkpoint, forcing them to remain under the shelling.

In June, the Ministry of Internal Affairs closed PAP-1, Grozny's most notorious "filtration" camp. While this was clearly a positive development, Russian forces not only continued the practice of beating and torturing Chechen men—the vast majority of them civilians—captured at checkpoints and holding them in unofficial "filtration" points; they also used these civilians as hostages to be exchanged for Russian detainees. Memorial documented at least three incidents of Russian forces using civilians as human shields: in Samashki, in March, where villagers were forced to ride on an armored personnel carrier (APC) through the village; and in Grozny, where from August 9-11 a trapped group of Russian troops took up defensive positions in Hospital No. 9, refused to allow the staff to tend to their patients, and used hospital staff as shields against Chechen fire.

The exchange of prisoners and detainees unfolded haltingly during 1996, resulting in few releases, in violation of the "all-for-all" principle set out in the Khasavyurt agreement. Between 1,500 and 3,000 Chechens were missing as of this writing; many of them presumably languished in the Russian criminal justice system outside Chechnya, having been captured at checkpoints and "filtered" outside Chechnya. As of October 3, some 1,900 Russian soldiers were reported missing.

Journalists repeatedly came under fire in Chechnya. On August 6, at two separate checkpoints, helicopters fired on two groups of journalists, both of which were traveling in vehicles clearly marked "TV" or "Press." Fortunately no casualties resulted. Russian commanders repeatedly denied journalists access to towns and villages under fire, notably in Gudermes (December 1995) and Samashki and Sernovodsk (March 1996). Unknown assailants assassinated Russian journalists Nadezhda Chaikova in March and Nina Yefimova on May 8.

On January 9, Chechen rebels led by Salman Raduyev seized 2,000 hostages in Kizlyar, Dagestan, and herded them into the town's hospital. They subsequently took 160 of these hostages as far as Pervomaiskoe and distributed the hostages among the houses where they had taken up defensive positions against Russian forces. Russian forces then bombed Pervomaiskoe, killing approximately twelve hostages. Within Chechnya, rebels held twenty-eight construction workers hostage in Achkoi-Martan in December 1995 and about eighty-four energy sector workers in Grozny in March. Chechen fighters as a rule did not refrain from taking up positions in residential areas, and their attacks on Gudermes and Grozny endangered the lives of hundreds of thousands of civilians.

In a slight improvement over last year, the Russian military procuracy reportedly convicted twenty-seven servicemen (the vast majority of them draftees) for crimes against civilians, mostly non-combat-related murders and lootings. However, it failed adequately to investigate, let alone prosecute, the most glaring combat-related violations of humanitarian law.

Law enforcement officials in Moscow harassed and brutally attacked ethnic Chechens and other individuals from the Caucasus. On November 18, 1995, the Organized Crime Police (RUOP) beat and tortured Artem Arutunian, an ethnic Armenian, breaking two ribs. Police sent him to a hospital on November 20, apparently fearing he would die in their custody, and released him without charges four days later. Mr. Arutunian's attempt to sue for damages ended in threats on his life. On December 11, RUOP severely beat Islam Gashayev in a Moscow apartment, causing him to lose consciousness, as they arrested him for the alleged illegal possession of a single bullet. A court later sentenced Gashayev to three years of imprisonment. In February, RUOP police broke into the apartment of Olga Kurbanova, arrested her Chechen brother-in-law Sultan, beat him, held him for three days, and left him on the snowy streets of Moscow. Moscow riot police even raided a tuberculosis hospital where Chechen families—war refugees—were being treated and roughed up several patients on the pretext of a weapons search.

Rather than seeking to curb racially-motivated violence rampant in Moscow since 1993, the Moscow city government strengthened police discretion to verify passports and propiskas, which it uses overwhelmingly against dark-skinned people. In the two days following the July 10 and 12 bombing of Moscow trolley buses, police detained 5,770 individuals for violating city propiska and registration requirements. This extraordinarily high number suggests that many of the detentions were wholly arbitrary. Moreover, Mayor Yuri Luzhkov's televised remarks, expounding a theory of Chechen involvement only two hours after the crime in which he "warn[ed] the entire Chechen diaspora" and promised to rid the city of "bums and organizations . . . connected to systems of southern structures," set the tone for "Operation Cleanse"—raids on markets, dormitories and the like—and the implementation of presidential decree 1025 (see below), which followed. The beatings of dozens of Azerbaijanis during market raids caused at least two to be hospitalized during this period. In August, Mayor Luzhkov declared that "crime in Moscow bears no ethnic factor," but failed to note that crime-fighting indeed does.

Presidential decree 1025, which was issued on July 10 as a crime-fighting measure, singled out "vagrants and beggars," enabled the Moscow city and regional governments to prolong such individuals' involuntary detention in "social rehabilitation centers" for up to thirty days, and allowed the police forcibly to "remove" the homeless from Moscow. Under an August 27 mayoral decree implementing decree 1025, Moscow police renewed the practice, established in 1993, of detaining the homeless and shipping them out of Moscow on trains. The decree provoked confusion and criticism even from within the ranks of the police, but police nonetheless deported about 4,800 individuals within the first three weeks the decree was in force.

In a landmark April 4 decision, the Russian Constitutional Court found unconstitutional city ordinances in Moscow, Stavropol' Krai, St. Petersburg and other cities that require individuals to purchase propiskas. Despite the court's decision, by November the Moscow and Stavropol governments had not altered their propiska rules and in addition continued to enforce regulations on temporary residence that caused undue hardship for refugees and migrants.

Ethnic tensions that flared against Chechens in Stavropol in the wake of the 1995 Chechen rebel raid on Budyonnovsk generally ebbed this year, but the Stavropol Krai and local village administrations failed to return at least twenty-one families who were deported from their homes in June 1995. In isolated areas, local Cossacks and police harassed and detained without warrant ethnic Chechens on suspicion of harboring weapons.

Moscow authorities sharpened their hostility toward refugees from the former Soviet Union. Police in Moscow regularly raided hotels where Armenian refugees had been granted housing after fleeing Azerbaijan in 1989 and 1990, allegedly to check identification and search out illegal weapons. In one such raid in July, Moscow riot police severely beat one Armenian man and sexually abused three Armenian girls. The Federal Migration Service (FMS) staunchly maintained its policy of refusing to settle refugees permanently in Moscow, in violation of the law on refugees and the Russian housing code. It presided over the evictions of refugee families from Moscow hotels and sent the former to reportedly uninhabitable quarters far from Moscow. When a facility director (an FMS employee) hired a gang of thugs to intimidate resident refugees into leaving, the FMS did not react. More positively, amendments to the 1993 law on internally displaced persons provided for refugee advocacy organizations to play a greater role in refugee policy-making.

Russia not only refused to grant political asylum to dissidents and politicians from countries of the former Soviet Union, it extradited them without the benefit of a court hearing. At least five individuals wanted in their home countries (Azerbaijan and Georgia), mostly on treason charges, were extradited between November 1995 and November 1996. Perhaps the most glaring case was that of Rahim Qaziyev (see section on Azerbaijan), whom Russian authorities extradited to Azerbaijan within three days of his arrest in Moscow in April. On July 25, Moscow police detained Davlat Khudonazarov, an opposition candidate in Tajikistan's 1991 elections, in cooperation with an outdated Tajikistan Internal Ministry "wanted" list. He was released the same day under tremendous public pressure.

The case of environmental researcher Alexander Nikitin underscored the pervasive powers the Federal Security Service (FSB) continued to exercise over freedom of information and due process. On February 6, the FSB arrested Nikitin, a retired Russian navy captain, and charged him with treason for having released state secrets. The charges sprang from a chapter he wrote on nuclear submarine accidents entitled "The Russian Northern Fleet: Sources of Radioactive Contamination" for Bellona (a Norwegian environmental organization.) Due process violations marred the case from its very beginning and, although the FSB failed to provide evidence justifying his continued incarceration, the St. Petersburg district court refused to release him from pre-trial custody while he awaited trial.

In a positive development related to the Nikitin case, the Russian Constitutional Court in March struck down a provision of a 1995 law on state secrets that required defense lawyers in state secrets cases themselves to obtain security clearance.

Despite Russia's admission into the Council of Europe, the Duma (parliament) failed to adopt a moratorium on the death penalty, and fifty-three convicts were executed as of October, a pace on par with 1995. The newly-adopted criminal code, which comes into force on January 1, 1997, continued to list five capital offenses.

In compliance with Council of Europe requirements, the Council of Ministers issued a decree in June aimed at providing relief for the tens of thousands of individuals languishing in Russia's uninhabitable pre-trial detention facilities. While the decree called for changes in the code of criminal

procedure to facilitate the release of individuals whose case investigations had ended, it failed to address the need for wider change in the bail system, responsible for catastrophic overcrowding. These facilities have proven deadly: the nongovernmental Moscow Center for Prison Reform (MCPR) estimated that since 1994, 5,000 people have died while awaiting trial in Russia. In 1995, 242 people died in Moscow's Butyrka pre-trial prison alone, which houses about 6,500 inmates. The MCPR attributed the rise in pre-trial deaths to the lack of medical attention. Not a single facility was held responsible for criminal neglect in relation to the deaths.

The new criminal code and code of criminal procedure ignored women's need for justice in cases of sexual violence. It eliminated Article 118, which dealt with rape at the workplace, despite the widespread practice of sexual harassment in private enterprise. Moreover, the new code of criminal procedure retained articles permitting investigators and defense counsel to request character references for the victim and requiring her to confront her attacker in closed meetings at police headquarters. These practices—along with stonewalling and outright refusal on the part of police to process a victim's report—in part explained why only 2 to 3 percent of women who were raped reported the crime.

The Yeltsin administration began to accord needed attention to violence against women, doubtless the result of advocacy by a vibrant network of crisis centers. The government's white paper on improving the position of women, issued in January, noted a sharp rise in domestic violence (a 100 percent increase in reported cases between 1993 and 1994) and acknowledged that the majority of victims of domestic and sexual violence refrain from reporting such violence to the police. However, it only vaguely stated the need to develop criminal and civil sanctions for violence against women, proffered no guidelines for improving police response, and neglected to call for the adoption of a law on domestic violence, various drafts of which repeatedly failed to clear the

Duma Committee on Women, Family and Youth.

The central government's careful control of the broadcast media overwhelmingly favored President Yeltsin during the presidential election campaign, but with very few exceptions journalists enjoyed wide freedoms in Moscow and St. Petersburg. Careful research by the Glasnost Defense Foundation, though, revealed that in the provinces, local governors maintained a tight grip on the press, dealing with their critics—especially those who investigate government corruption—by threatening them or pressing libel or other fabricated charges.

The Right to Monitor

Russian human rights organizations operated mostly unfettered, and a June 13 presidential decree supported the human rights movement by, among other things, establishing within the Presidential Human Rights Commission a council of experts consisting of representatives of independent human rights organizations.

In Chechnya, however, Russian forces refused access to Sernovodsk and Samashki to human rights and humanitarian relief organizations and the press until up to ten days after it had completed mop-up operations. From January through the end of May, the Russian command denied the ICRC access to detainees, whereas in 1995 the ICRC had had access to nearly 700 detainees.

The Role of the International Community

United Nations

The office of the secretary-general called the events in Chechnya "tragic," but maintained a hands-off policy with regard to human rights abuses by the government. On August 20, when Grozny was in flames and hundreds of thousands of civilians were fleeing in response to General Pulikovskii's ultimatum to carpet-bomb the capital, Secretary General Boutros Boutros-Ghali's office stated that Chechnya was an "internal matter of the Russian Federation," failing to use his

authority to condemn the massive international humanitarian law violations that were clearly prohibited by United Nations treaties and, therefore, should never be considered solely an internal matter.

The Secretary General was mandated by the statement of the Chair of the fifty-first session of the Commission on Human Rights to report on Chechnya to the commission's following session. To request a report on a state with a permanent seat on the Security Council was exceptional in the commission's practice. Notably, in its section devoted to NGOs, the report cited NGOs' documentation of human rights and humanitarian law violations.

The fifty-second session of the Commission on Human Rights again declined to adopt a resolution on Chechnya, opting instead for a chair's statement. The statement requested another report from the Secretary General and called for individual accountability for human rights and humanitarian law violations.

The U.N. Committee on the Elimination of Racial Discrimination, in its conclusions and recommendations to Russia's periodic report, noted the rise in "racist attitudes" among local authorities, rightly connected racism with the propiska system, and expressed "grave concern for the use of excessive and disproportionate force" in Chechnya. However, it failed to emphasize the role played by the federal government in fostering racism.

European Union

The European Union, Russia's largest trading partner, focused its human rights concerns on Chechnya, albeit reactively, as distinct from its proactive 1995 approach. In November, just as the worsening hostilities in Chechnya pointed to the utter failure of a 1995 peace agreement, the European Parliament incomprehensibly approved ratification of the Partnership and Cooperation Agreement with the Russian Federation, which is conditioned on the respect for human rights and democratic principles. After squandering this important means of leverage, the European Parliament's strongly-worded statements on Chechnya had little impact. In January and July, the European Parliament issued welcome resolutions warning Russia that its conduct would threaten its relations with the E.U., but arch responses by the Russian Foreign Ministry underscored the ineffectiveness of such resolutions without enforcement mechanisms.

An E.U. presidency statement deplored the loss of life and hostage-taking and called for an immediate end to fighting. On March 25, the E.U. strongly condemned attacks on civilians during the wave of fighting in Samashki and Sernovodsk. In sharp contrast, E.U. Commissioner Hans van den Broek chose not to use a high-profile visit to Moscow a week earlier to urge the Russian side to curb abuse in Chechnya. To its credit, the E.U. troika advanced the U.N. Commission on Human Rights chair's statement, despite strong pressure from the Russian delegation.

On September 19, the European Parliament called on Russia to release Alexander Nikitin pending trial and to explain the charges against him.

OSCE

The OSCE Assistance Group (A.G.) in Grozny spoke out frequently and sharply against abusive conduct in the Chechnya war. Its March 25 report on human rights violations noted Chechen responsibility for taking civilian hostages and characterized Russian forces' attacks on towns and villages as "warfare against the civilian population. . . in clear excess of what could be described as military necessary [sic]." A.G. head Tim Guldimann, undaunted by repeated calls for his removal by Russian politicians and commanders, publicly raised concerns about such abuse on numerous occasions. In Vienna, however, the Permanent Council made no noticeable effort to pressure Russia on accountability for humanitarian law violations, squandering the unique influence the OSCE enjoys as the only intergovernmental organization with a mandate in Chechnya.

Council of Europe

The Council of Europe's vote to admit Russia four years after Russia's initial application clearly reflected the primacy of the organization's political concerns over its human rights mandate and unwittingly gave a stamp of approval to abusive laws and practices by the Russian government. The timing of the vote—just after Russian forces had razed Pervomaiskoe—demonstrated that the council was set on admitting Russia with no regard for human rights abuses, thereby damaging the council's credibility on human rights.

Upon Russia's admission to the council, the Parliamentary Assembly (PACE) immediately created an ad hoc committee on Chechnya with a mandate to monitor human rights in the region and to prepare a parliamentary hearing to facilitate negotiations. When the council attempted to stage the hearing in September, however, Russia pressured the council into cancelling it, emphasizing Chechnya as "an internal matter of Russia." In September the council activated Order No. 508 against Russia, which monitors compliance with human rights obligations among new member states. It adopted a statement of concern on the Nikitin case in February, assigned a special rapporteur in September, and dispatched a mission to St. Petersburg to express its concerns jointly with the European Parliament to procuracy officials.

United States

The Clinton administration periodically criticized Russian forces' conduct in the Chechnya war, yet maintained an obvious silence during President Yeltsin's re-election campaign. In January, Secretary of State Warren Christopher accurately characterized Chechnya as "one of the troubling signs of Russian reform under strain," and State Department Spokesperson Nicolas Burns called the war a "grave, grave mistake." Russian forces' operations in the months leading up to the June 16 and July 3 elections, however, not only failed to elicit a public response from the White House or

State Department but failed to become an issue in President Clinton's April 20 summit meeting with President Yeltsin and Warren Christopher's March visit to Moscow. After Yeltsin's re-election, the administration's public statements toughened considerably; in a private letter in August, President Clinton urged President Yeltsin to call off the threatened total bombardment of Grozny.

The Clinton administration maintained a puzzling public silence on the Nikitin case. President Clinton squandered an excellent opportunity to raise it at the G-7 nuclear safety summit in Moscow in April, and Vice-President Gore likewise failed to raise the case publicly during his July visit.

The Clinton administration slashed Freedom Support Act aid to Russia—which funded among other things useful democratization, rule of law, and human rights programs—by threefold in FY 1996, to U.S. $115 million. It played a central role in securing a colossal $10 billion IMF loan to Russia, the second-largest IMF undertaking in the institution's history.

SLOVAK REPUBLIC

Human Rights Developments

Freedom of expression, freedom of assembly and the rights of minorities were under continuous attack by the government of Vladimir Meciar in 1996. The secret service, police force and state media were all used by the government for political purposes.

The government continued to impede an impartial investigation into the 1995 kidnapping of Michal Kovac, Jr., son of President Kovac, who has been a strong critic of Prime Minister Meciar. In May, a policeman and key witness in the case was killed when his car exploded on the outskirts of Bratislava. The government claimed that it was an accident, but allegations of Slovakia's first political murder quickly arose. Editor of the independent newspaper *Sme* (Bratislava), Peter Toth, accused the Slovak Information Service and government circles of involve-

ment in the death. The government filed libel charges against him for "intolerance and gross and ungrounded attacks against the cabinet." On May 20, the police announced the case's adjournment for lack of evidence, despite credible charges of the government's involvement.

In April, parliament approved amendments to the penal code that were intended for the "defense of the republic." While the amendments were allegedly intended to protect the state, their vague terminology opened the door for the state to restrict freedom of speech, assembly and expression. The articles in question restrict the right of Slovak citizens and, in some cases, foreigners living in Slovakia to organize activities or express opinions that are deemed damaging to "state interests" or "subversive to the republic." As of October, no one had been charged under these articles.

On June 20, parliament passed a controversial Law on Foundations to regulate the work of nongovernmental organizations that the government claimed were "destroying Slovakia's image." The law required all foundations to have a minimum U.S.$3,200 endowment, an amount which may force some of the smaller, local foundations to close. More seriously, foundations must now register with the government, which may arbitrarily decide which foundations may operate in the country. According to the Third Sector, a local nongovernmental organization, one foundation was already refused registration.

In May, the Slovak parliament ratified a Slovak-Hungarian friendship treaty, which had been signed by the country's two prime ministers in March 1995. Despite this, the Hungarian minority still experienced discriminatory treatment by the government. The most controversial development was the January enactment of a new language law, which made it illegal to use any language other than Slovak in official state business.

The country's estimated 300,000 Roma also continued to suffer from state discrimination, especially in education, housing and employment. Violent crimes against Roma by "skinheads" continued to rise, and the police and local courts often did not take adequate steps to apprehend and punish those responsible.

The government maintained control of Slovak television and radio, using it to present its political views rather than objective information. On May 22, Ivan Lexa, head of the Slovak Intelligence Service, accused the independent media, including Radio Free Europe (RFE), *Sme* and Radio Twist, of creating an "anti-Slovak atmosphere." In February, the government threatened not to renew RFE's license, but a one-year license was granted on February 15. In March, the government's legislative council approved a restrictive media bill, although, as of October, it had not been passed by parliament.

The Right to Monitor

Human Rights Watch/Helsinki is not aware of any attempt by the Slovak government to hinder the monitoring or reporting of human rights during 1996.

The Role of the International Community

The international community expressed concern about human rights violations in Slovakia on a number of occasions. The foundations law, language law and penal code amendments all provoked statements of concern from the European Union, the Council of Europe and the U.S. government. In February, European Commissioner Hans van den Broek warned that a lack of democratic reform could threaten Slovakia's acceptance into the European Union. The European Union and American ambassadors to Slovakia reiterated this position in October. The U.S. State Department's *Country Reports on Human Rights Practices for 1995* accurately reflected the human rights situation in the country.

TAJIKISTAN

Human Rights Developments

After several years of slow improvement on the human rights front, renewed fighting between government and opposition forces, violent attacks on returnees and some minorities and political activists, and a series of apparently politically motivated assassinations made 1996 the worst year in Tajikistan since the end of its bloody civil war in 1992. The sporadic fighting that broke out in October 1995 generated a new wave of displaced persons, raising the number of internally displaced persons within Tajikistan to some 20,000 by late September, according to the International Committee of the Red Cross and the Tajikistan Central Refugee Department. The fighting also raised tensions throughout the country that hampered general human rights protection in other spheres of life.

The peace settlement process remained largely deadlocked, resulting in bleak prospects for the full and safe repatriation of the tens of thousands of individuals forced from their homes during the war. The renewed warfare centered around Tavil-Dara, about 150 kilometers east of Dushanbe, along a strategically important road that connects it with the buffer area between government- and opposition-held territories, and in Kurgan-Tiube, Komsomolobad and Gharm regions. Since there was little independently confirmed information emanating from the conflict zone, the true picture of the nature and scope of violations of the laws of war during the hostilities remained unclear. Reports, however, were disturbing. A February 8 ITAR-TASS report, for example, asserted that opposition forces had used government prisoners of war as human shields. Displaced persons feared return even after the hostilities subsided because the Tavil-Dara area had been heavily mined.

It was clear that the violations of the 1994 cease-fire created a serious humanitarian crisis for the civilian population. The U.N.-sponsored peace negotiation process extended the cease-fire agreements between the government and the United Tajik Opposition and elaborated on such issues as prisoner exchanges. However, the exchange set to take place before August 20 did not take place, and hostilities continued in blatant violation of the cease-fire.

Safe repatriation of the remaining approximately 19,000 Tajiks in northern Afghanistan (according to UNHCR figures from October) was impeded not only because of retribution against them upon return but because refugees in opposition camps in Konduz and Takhar were intimidated by camp leaders into staying on. Moreover, the UNHCR undertook measures to coerce the remaining 7,000 refugees in Sakhi camp near Mazar-I-Sharif in northern Afghanistan to leave prematurely by cutting their food and fuel rations to below generally accepted levels. Returnees, and regional minorities such as the Gharmis and Badakhshanis, faced harassment by neighbors and even law-enforcement officials, notably in Khotlon province, and the government was generally unwilling to safeguard their rights or prosecute the abuses.

High-profile assassinations in and around the capital kept the country in the grip of political terror in 1996, severely hampering free speech. The sluggish response or complete inaction of the police further eroded faith in law enforcement; as of this writing, for example, only one of the murders resulted in apprehension of a suspect. Among the most influential shooting victims were Muhiddin Olimpur, a BBC war correspondent (whose body was found on December 13, 1995); Fatkhullo Sharifzoda, the state mufti, and his wife, son, daughter-in-law, and one other (January 21, 1996); Russian Public TV (ORT) journalist Viktor Nikulin (March 28), the twenty-ninth journalist to be killed in Tajikistan since 1992; the elderly rector of Dushanbe Medical School Yusuf Iskhaki (May 6); Mohammed Osimi, former president of Tajikistan's Academy of Sciences (July 29); and Mahmud Idiev, head of administration of Tajikabad District (August 1). The abduction of the

opposition's representative to the U.N. talks, Zafar Rakhmonov, on February 24, symbolized the political lawlessness that reigned in 1996.

The government continued an ambiguous policy toward political dissidents in 1996. On January 12, President Imomali Rakhmonov granted pardons to three opposition figures his government had once imprisoned: Oinyhol Bobonazarova, Shodmon Yusuf, and Bozor Sobir. At the same time, the government attempted to extradite dissidents from Moscow on politically motivated charges. Mirzo Salimov, a journalist for the dissident Tajik newspaper *Charogi Ruz* (Dushanbe), was arrested on October 13 for insulting the president; and former presidential contender Davlat Khudonazarov was detained briefly in July. Both were released under public pressure, and the treason charges that had hung over Khudonazarov since 1992 reportedly were dropped.

Authorities in the northern province of Leninobod, in particular, repressed civil rights through police abuse. Police dispersed a disorderly crowd in Ura-Tiube on May 14, resulting in five deaths; they also severely beat Ikhromjon Ashurov, who had spoken at a rally in the regional capital, Khojent, breaking several of his ribs, and arrested him for "banditry."

The Right to Monitor

Monitoring by local residents was extremely limited in 1996. U.N. military observers were at times denied access to the conflict zone by government soldiers. Fear of retaliation against individuals who reported violations to UNMOT (U.N. Mission of Observers in Tajikistan) or the Organization for Security and Cooperation in Europe (OSCE) greatly limited the ability of Tajiks to enjoy the protection of even these foreign bodies. Throughout 1996, UNMOT observers were robbed, shot at, and prevented from gathering information on the fighting. UNHCR access to camps in Konduz and Tokhar in northern Afghanistan was limited. The International Committee of the Red Cross was denied access to the troubled Tavil-Dara region from April to September.

The Role of
the International Community

The presence of UNMOT, with its forty-four military observers, continued to help deter abuse. The 25,000 CIS (Russian) troops, which largely protect Tajikistan's borders and military objects, played a more ambiguous role: both target of attacks and non-neutral participant in operations in Kurgan-Tiube, Tursun Zade, and Tavil-Dara. (The Russian government denied allegations of the latter). The UNHCR and OSCE monitored violations on the ground and conducted some important interventions. However, no international body consistently protested or was able to secure prosecution of human rights violators, and all continued to play primarily a reactive rather than preventative role. The IMF and World Bank squandered their considerable influence by approving $22 million and $60 million, respectively, without conditioning the credits on improvements in human rights practices.

United Nations

The U.N.'s diplomatic and refugee protection work was generally disappointing in 1996. The U.N. extended the mandate of the ninety-four-member UNMOT through December 15, 1996, but was impeded by the government and the opposition from carrying out its full mandate. It also failed to secure meaningful progress at the negotiating table, looking on helplessly as fighting erupted again in violation of freshly signed extensions of the cease-fire agreement. Most alarming was the UNHCR/Afghanistan's actively abusive role in attempting to coerce the premature repatriation of refugees at its Sakhi camp in northern Afghanistan through reduction of survival rations, a violation of its own policy of voluntary repatriation. UNHCR/Dushanbe took inadequate measures to follow up on the welfare of returnees in Dushanbe.

Human Rights Watch/Helsinki is concerned that the UNHCR effectively handed over its protection function inside Tajikistan,

except in Dushanbe, to the OSCE before conditions of return reached a level of stability adequate to permit the less experienced organization to undertake successfully the protection of the returnees. The OSCE was unable to maintain all of the UNHCR's field offices, thereby reducing the international community's capacity to offer protection to returnees on the ground. The UNHCR also failed to respond to serious charges leveled in a May Human Rights Watch/Helsinki report.

OSCE

In addition to implementing its new protection mandate, the OSCE mission, operational in Tajikistan since early 1994, continued important monitoring of human rights abuse. However, it was slow in fielding a full staff, reducing its efficacy. At OSCE initiative, the German government financed the establishment of a governmental civil rights institute in 1996. In March, the OSCE also agreed in principle to sponsor a human rights mission in Tajikistan, although as of this writing it had not materialized. Disturbingly, the OSCE agreed that mission staff be appointed by the government, thus intrinsically jeopardizing the ability of the staff to be impartial in a highly divisive conflict.

TURKEY

Human Rights Developments

A caretaker government and two subsequent coalition governments beset by bitter internal conflict were unable to produce any substantive democratization improvements or human rights legislation in 1996, though individual government ministers did speak out on human rights issues, and some positive actions were taken. A vocal, mostly free press, a small, but active civil society, and hotly-contested elections coexist with persistent violations, such as disappearances in detention or under suspicious circumstances, extrajudicial killings, restrictions on peaceful free expression, torture, forced evacuations, and death in custody. In November, a right-wing militant wanted by Interpol and implicated in at least seven killings and the female director of the Istanbul police academy with links to the mafia were killed, and an ethnic Kurdish deputy who controls a village guard was injured, while all travelling in the same car. The accident raised serious concern about corruption and abuse of power in the security forces and led to the resignation of the Interior Minister, who had been with the group at the same hotel before the accident. As in 1995, the main issue affecting human rights was the armed conflict between government security forces and the PKK in southeastern Turkey. A state of emergency is in effect in ten provinces there.

After the fall of the DYP/CHP coalition government of Prime Minister Tansu Ciller in September 1995, new parliamentary elections were held on December 24, 1995. They, however, brought no conclusive results: the Islamist Welfare Party (RP) received a plurality of 21 percent. Efforts to form governments proved lengthy and difficult. The short-lived center-right ANAP/DYP minority coalition government of Prime Minister Mesut Yilmaz (ANAP) made promises about ending the state of emergency in southeastern Turkey and liberalizing policies concerning the linguistic and cultural rights of Turkey's ethnic Kurds. During a March 21 trip to eastern Turkey for the *Newruz* new year holiday shortly after the formation of his government, Yilmaz announced a new approach to the conflict in southeastern Turkey, promising, "a new, more human, more realistic and courageous approach to the Kurdish problem including, in particular, the lifting of the ban on the teaching of the Kurdish language." Ultimately, his government was able to accomplish little and collapsed in early June. Regrettably, it abolished the office of State Minister for Human Rights, which in the past two years was a strong proponent of human rights. It was not until the fall that a new government belatedly appointed someone to the post.

In July, Necmettin Erbakan (RP) become Turkey's first Islamist prime minister since the founding of the republic in 1923. His party, in an awkward coalition with former Prime Minister Ciller's True Path Party (DYP), made general reform promises but also was unable to accomplish much. While in opposition, Erbakan had spoken of an Islamic approach to ethnic and regional problems, in part an attempt to strengthen his party among ethnic Kurds. During his first news conference after the December 1995 elections, Erbakan promised that he would recognize a Kurdish identity: "A human being can come from any origin. It is God's decision. We cannot discriminate." He also suggested allowing some form of Kurdish-language television and education.

These promises were not incorporated into the government's coalition protocol, which stated that, "The spiritual and psychological aspects of the fight against terror will not be neglected nor will debates be allowed that weaken our security forces conducting this struggle," while vaguely promising to "remove the state of emergency having taken the necessary precautions." Shortly after taking office in July, however, Erbakan traveled to Bingol in southeastern Turkey, where he promised a return program for the inhabitants of more than 2,500 villages and hamlets depopulated in the conflict, mostly as the result of a government counterinsurgency campaign. A similar move by a previous government ended in failure. In a first step to end the state of emergency, which was last renewed for four months on July 31, a law was passed amending a number of laws, including one on provincial administration. This new law, however, was criticized by opposition deputies as "disguised martial law" as it strengthened certain police powers and made them valid for all of Turkey. In October, Erbakan stated that, "We don't have a Kurdish problem...We have a terrorism problem."

Some government actions to investigate and prosecute allegations of human rights abuses were welcome and, if carried out widely, would do much to improve the situation. The DYP/CHP caretaker government—especially State Minister for Human Rights Adnan Ekmen—quickly charged officers implicated in the killing of the journalist Metin Goktepe, though the trial lagged. In April, a trial was launched against village guards implicated in a February 5 killing in Diyarbakir. In June, a trial was launched against ten officers charged with torturing sixteen high school students in Manisa in January. In late September, Justice Minister Kazan ordered an investigation after a prison riot in Diyarbakir took ten lives and suspended three top prison officials. In October, Foreign Minister Ciller promised to reduce detention periods.

The armed conflict in southeastern Turkey continued, along with forced village evacuations, most by security forces. The majority of human rights violations—whether by state actors or others—took place in this region. Unrest expanded west toward the rural Alevi villages of southeastern and eastern Sivas province as the PKK and other armed opposition groups who sought to move into these areas clashed with security forces. Large-scale police detentions, blockades, and harassment further exacerbated the situation. A report issued in February on the Sivas events by three Democratic Left (DSP) parliamentarians stated that, "many of our fellow citizens have chosen to leave their villages because of this 'double-sided' pressure." In southeastern Turkey, so-called actor unknown death squad style murders of suspected PKK members and Kurdish political activists and intellectuals continued. Many such killings are believed to be directly or indirectly linked to security forces, a fact stated in a 1995 parliamentary report but not investigated. Such killings have also been perpetrated by two feuding wings of an illegal radical Islamist group "Hezbullah," both against each other and against targets mentioned above, though security forces have continued a crackdown on this group.

The Human Rights Watch Arms Project continued to monitor arms sales to the Turkish government and deliveries to the PKK and to highlight the abusive use of these weapons. In October, a trial began against the translator and the publisher of a Turkish-language edition of an Arms Project report on the abusive use of such weapons by both sides in the southeast.

Although banned by a wide variety of domestic laws and international treaty obligations, torture continued to be used widely as an interrogation method by police, especially by units of the Anti-Terror Section. Detainees are stripped naked and often subjected to electric shock, beatings, suspension by the limbs, squeezing of sexual organs, and high-pressure water hose. While various government officials acknowledged the use of torture—most recently former Justice Minister Firuz Cilingiroglu in January—and groups like the European Committee for the Prevention of Torture regularly conducted expert on-site investigations, the practice continued because prosecution of abusive police is sorely insufficient and prosecutors are able to hold certain suspects up to fifteen days without access to counsel or appearance before a magistrate, a period that can be doubled under a state of emergency.

In early January, sixteen mostly teen-aged high school students were detained in the city of Manisa on charges that they were members of or had links with Dev-Sol (DHKP-C), a radical, leftist, illegal armed opposition group. During their eleven-day detention, they were subjected to torture. A parliamentarian who represents the region, Sabri Ergul (CHP), went to the police station to get information about the youths and came upon some of the young people lying on the floor, naked and blindfolded. Medical reports confirmed the torture.

Torture and ill-treatment were a major cause of unlawful death in police custody. A case that shook all of Turkey was that of Metin Goktepe, a journalist for the leftist Istanbul daily *Evrensel* who was detained at noon on January 8 in Istanbul while covering a funeral of prisoners beaten to death during prison unrest. Other reporters witnessed his detention and other detainees reported speaking to him. Police detained roughly 1,000 individuals and held them in a sport center turned into a temporary holding facility. Goktepe's body was discovered eight hours later inside the facility. An autopsy indicated that Goktepe died of internal bleeding to the brain and body due to blows.

A weekly sit-down protest in Istanbul of families of those believed to have disappeared in police custody or under suspicious circumstances focused public attention on the problem as never before. Lengthy detention periods and police flouting of regulations requiring the immediate registration of detainees and the notification of their families exacerbated the problem. One such case was that of Talat Turkoglu, a left-wing trade unionist who had been imprisoned in the past and was convicted in late March of supporting an illegal organization. After reports that he was being followed by police, Turkoglu left Edirne on April 1 for Istanbul and was not seen again. Another case is that of Abdullah Canan, brother of former CHP parliamentarian, Esat Canan, who disappeared in Hakkari province in late January after reportedly being stopped at a gendarmerie check-point. His mutilated body was discovered a month later. An inquiry commission composed of three CHP parliamentarians—including former Culture Minister Ercan Karakas—issued a report calling for the investigation of a gendarmerie major who had conducted a raid on Abdullah Canan's village and then publicly threatened Mr. Canan after he opened a case against him.

Considerable free and open expression in both print and television coexisted with the punishment of free expression through restrictive laws, such as Penal Code Article 312 forbidding "racism," Article 8 of the Anti-Terror Law banning "separatist" propaganda, and the Law to Protect Ataturk (No. 5816). While the mainstream press also suffered restrictions, the main targets were leftist and pro-Kurdish publications or publishing houses or Islamists who question the secular basis of the state. In August, the Istanbul daily *Cumhuriyet* reported that in the first six months of 1996, 172 years of prison time had been given to free expression cases. The leftist daily *Evrensel* (Istanbul) was especially hard hit, with courts ordering its closure in April and May for periods of up to twenty days.

Prison unrest and the excessive use of force in dealing with it remained a serious problem. During a riot in Umraniye prison in Istanbul in January, four inmates were reportedly beaten to death in retaliation. During unrest in the Diyarbakir E-Type Prison in September, ten prisoners died in a similar incident. In July, a hunger strike among leftist prisoners led to eleven deaths due to starvation. While part of the strike was motivated by the prisoners' refusal to be moved from preferred barracks-style prisons to ones with individual cells, many of their demands—such as the desire to be close to their trial, not to be maltreated during transport, and access to proper medical care—fell clearly within Turkey's international obligations.

There was also pressure against political parties. Forty-one top administrators of HADEP, the pro-Kurdish party that took 4.5 percent of the national vote in December 1995 and came in first or second in many southeastern provinces, were arrested in July on charges of being linked to the PKK after a June party congress at which a Turkish flag was ripped down and replaced by a PKK one. Eleven were released in September; but the trial continued. Three HADEP members were murdered execution-style in June near Kayseri. In May, proceedings were started to close the "Labor" ("Emek") party because its charter contained "separatist" propaganda. Various judicial proceedings were also launched against the Freedom and Solidarity Party ("Ozgurluk ve Dayanisma Partisi").

Illegal armed opposition groups continued to commit serious abuses in 1996, such as extrajudicial executions. In spite of public statements to abide by Common Article 3 protecting civilians and other noncombatants, the PKK consistently and flagrantly violated it. Victims included families of village guard members, government employees such as teachers, and those perceived by the PKK as "supporting the state."

In March, an individual was assassinated in Adana for "cooperating with the state." In April, PKK leader Ocalan threatened that fifty Germans would "return home in coffins" if they vacationed in Turkey. In June, family members reported that the PKK executed a village headman in Tunceli province in front of them because the man's daughter lived with a Turkish army NCO. That same month a rocket attack on a television station in Diyarbakir killed nine, mostly woman and children. In August, after stopping a bus in Sivas, PKK members executed the tourism director of the Malatya police force and another individual. In July and twice in October, PKK suicide bombers posing as pregnant women or civilians detonated explosives strapped to their bodies, killing soldiers, police, and civilians. In January, the radical leftist group Dev-Sol (DHKP-C) assassinated Turkish industrialist Ozdemir Sabanci. In August, militants of the radical Islamists "Islamic Great Eastern Raiders Front" (IBDA-C) burned down the office of a journal.

The Right to Monitor

Turkey's active and vocal human rights monitoring groups, led by the Human Rights Foundation of Turkey(HRFT), the Human Rights Association(HRA), and the Islamist-based *Mazlum-Der*, faced trials, detentions, and the banning of their publications throughout 1996. Amnesty International's researcher for Turkey remained banned from entering the country, though a large A.I. delegation headed by President Pierre Sane traveled to Turkey in September.

In September 1996, the publisher of the Turkish translation of an Arms Project report on the conflict in Southeast Turkey, Ayse Zarakolu, and the translator, Ertugurul Kurkcu, were indicted under Article 159/1 of the Turkish penal code for "defaming and belittling the state's security and military forces." Their trial continues.

Both the HRFT headquartered in Ankara and the Rehabilitation and Treatment Centers for torture victims it operates in Adana, Ankara, Izmir, and Istanbul, faced

legal harassment. The pressure against the treatment centers, which have operated openly since 1990 and which receive U.N. and E.U. funding, was a first. In late 1995 a trial was launched against nine members of the HRFT board and the former head of the Balikesir Bar Association for an article in a foundation publication, *A Present to Emil Galip Sandalci*. The trial ended in acquittal in May. In March, charges were filed against the head of the Adana branch of the HRFT, Mustafa Cinkilic, and a doctor who consulted at the treatment center there, for "disobeying orders of an official" and "negligence in reporting a crime." The prosecutor charged that both men had a legal obligation to report to officials the torture cases of those who sought treatment. In September Dr. Sukran Akin of the Istanbul HRFT treatment center was charged with "operating an unlicensed health center"; in November, the trial ended in acquittal.

The pressure against the HRFT appeared to come from the fact that the data it gathered was widely used and quoted by news agencies and foreign embassies and governments: for example, the U.S. State Department *Country Report on Human Rights Practices* has often used HRFT data.

The HRA, which has 15,000 members and operates offices in most of Turkey's provinces, faced similar difficulties in 1996. In the areas of southeastern Turkey under emergency rule, the HRA operated formally only in Diyarbakir because of threats, detention and torture, and in the past, killings. In February, the Iskenderun HRA branch was raided and searched, and a case was opened under Article 8 of the Anti-Terror Law against seventeen HRA members and administrators for a bulletin issued on September 1, 1995, in connection with World Peace Day; the case ended in acquittal in October. In March, the Adana office was also raided and ordered closed for fifteen days, and a Hakkari branch board member was detained by police. In April, the Kirsehir branch was mysteriously set ablaze; seventeen individuals who protested this action were detained by police. In August, HRA Deputy Secretary

Erol Anar faced charges along with his publisher under Article 8 of the Anti-Terror Law for his book, *A History of Human Rights.*

The Role of the International Community

Europe

European organizations of which Turkey is a member or an associate all played a role in human rights developments in 1996: the European Union; the Organization on Security and Cooperation in Europe (OSCE); and the Council of Europe's European Commission of Human Rights and European Court of Human Rights.

On December 13, 1995, the European Parliament ratified a Customs Union Agreement between Turkey and the European Union. The customs union is intended to reduce trade barriers and tariffs. As part of the agreement, Turkey should receive U.S.$470 million in adjustment funds between 1996 and 2000. Shortly after ratification, the parliament passed a non-binding resolution on Turkey, calling on the E.U. Commission to "monitor permanently human rights and democratic developments in Turkey." The parliament, which has veto power over the allocation of adjustment funds, also called on the commission to prepare periodic reports on human rights and democratization in Turkey.

On September 19, the European Parliament passed a resolution criticizing Turkey for doing little regarding "improvements promised by the then Prime Minister, Tansu Ciller, in the areas of democratization and human rights..." Consequently, it decided to block the 1997 adjustment fund payment of $66 million. Previously, these funds had been blocked due to objections from Greece. On October 11, the E.U. Commission presented its annual report on relations with Turkey since the implementation of the customs union. The report, which parliament will debate, called on Turkey to strengthen individual freedoms and liberties.

Other European bodies were also active. In July, the OSCE parliamentary assembly passed a resolution calling on Turkey to improve its human rights shortcomings and promising further OSCE activity in this area. The European Commission of Human Rights, which acts as the screening mechanism for the European Court of Human Rights, continued to review cases brought by Turkish citizens. More than 800 applications from Turkey have been made to the commission since 1991. In September, the court found Turkey guilty of violating the European Convention of Human Rights concerning the destruction of an ethnic Kurdish village in southeast Turkey and ordered damages to be paid.

United States

While U.S. officials did not abandon human rights dialogue with the Turkish government in 1996, its overall emphasis and importance fell compared with 1994 and 1995, a period highlighted by high-profile visits by Assistant Secretary of State John Shattuck. The strategic value of the Turkish-American relationship was spotlighted, while human rights were downplayed. This shift can be explained by several factors: growing U.S. concern over stability in Turkey given the inability to form a government after the December 1995 elections; the January conflict with Greece over the disputed Kardak (Imia) islet in the Aegean; an unspoken official unease over the entrance of the Islamist Welfare Party into the government; and the internecine Kurdish fighting in Northern Iraq and the desire to extend Operation "Provide Comfort," which operates from bases in Turkey. The embassy in Ankara, however, was active in monitoring the human rights situation, including trials, and the State Department's *Country Report on Human Rights Practices for 1995* was accurate and forthright.

During a speech in March, U.S. Ambassador to Turkey Marc Grossman stated that "1996 has already been more challenging," but affirmed that" the United States supports a strong security partnership based on our shared interests." President Clinton did not mention human rights or democratization as one of the topics of his discussion with Turkish President Demirel in official statements released after a March meeting. In response to a Human Rights Watch/ Helsinki letter outlining human rights concerns in Turkey on the occasion of the meeting, President Clinton affirmed that "the promotion of democracy and human rights serves as the cornerstone of my Administration's foreign policy" and regretted not having reviewed the letter before the meeting. In early July, upon the formation of the RP/DYP government of Prime Minister Erbakan, Under Secretary of State Peter Tarnoff traveled to Ankara to reaffirm the Turkish-American security relationship. While in the opposition, Erbakan had stressed the need to reorient away from the West and toward the Islamic world. Commenting on Tarnoff's visit, a State Department spokesperson stated that, "The national interests of the United States in Turkey dictate that we will continue to be concerned by Turkey's full...participation in NATO, with the fulfillment of the vision that both Turkey and the United States have had, that Turkey should be associated with Western institutions like NATO...that democracy and human rights are important."

U.S. military loans (FMF) and economic support funds (ESF) were drastically reduced in 1996, part of a long-term trend. In March, the Clinton administration asked for $175 million in military loans and $60 million in economic support funds for Fiscal Year 1997. After various amendments were attached in the House of Representatives to ESF, Turkey rejected the funds. At the Conference Committee in September, these amendments were scrapped, and it was decided to allocate to Turkey $175 million in FMF and $22 million in ESF for FY 1997. As of this writing, the administration has still not authorized the sale of ten attack helicopters to Turkey despite reports that Prime Minister Erbakan specifically requested them. The sale is being held up because of human rights concerns raised within the administration and by a number of groups, including Human Rights Watch.

TURKMENISTAN

Human Rights Developments

The autocratic rule of President Saparmurad Niyazov insured that 1996 was another year of relentless oppression of almost all civil and political rights in Turkmenistan. The media were tightly controlled, slavishly praising the president and his policies; there were no public rallies; there was no political opposition within the country; and political dissidents were arrested or committed to psychiatric hospitals against their will, making Turkmenistan the only Soviet successor state known to continue this barbaric practice. The high degree of repression kept information about abuses minimal again in 1996, which limited international criticism of specific abusive acts and helped the government to operate in an atmosphere of impunity.

It is indicative that the only public shows of dissent in 1996 took place in prison. According to the Kazakstan newspaper *Karavan-blitz* (Almaty) of February 15, fourteen death-row inmates in an unidentified Turkmenistan prison reportedly took guards hostage to secure their right to judicial review of their sentence (granted automatically under international law). The result of the reviews was not known, but, according to the article, President Niyazov later declared that all death sentences should be reviewed. In August, prisoners in the city of Mary rioted to protest appalling prison conditions, particularly acute in the blistering August heat of this desert country; this was the second such riot in a year. According to government sources, one inmate committed suicide, two were killed, and seven were injured. In the wake of the uprising, President Niyazov fired senior prison officials but took no known steps to improve conditions.

Turkmenistan's population continued to reel from the crackdown against the public rally of July 12, 1995, which called for new parliamentary elections and was the first public act of dissent in the country since the early 1990s. Police dispersed the peaceful demonstrators and arrested scores of participants. On December 26, 1995, reportedly twenty-seven individuals arrested at the rally were sentenced in secret trials. Two journalists among them, Yovshan Annakurban and Mukhamad Muradly, were each sentenced to three years of imprisonment for "malicious breach of the peace." On January 11, 1996, presidential edict No. 1717 granted twenty of those men clemency and exonerated them. There is no confirmation of charges against or sentences for the remaining demonstrators; the arrest of Charymurad Amandurdiev, who had escaped arrest until February 1996, raised the number to eight in 1996.

One of the few political dissidents remaining in Turkmenistan, Durdy Murad Khodzha-Mukhammedov, co-chair of the banned Party of Democratic Development of Turkmenistan, reportedly was committed to a psychiatric hospital in Goek-Teppe on February 23 without medical necessity. He had been similarly confined once before, in 1994, but reasons for his release then, or for his confinement now, were unclear. Two other dissidents (Rufina Arabova and a fellow member of Khodzha-Mukhammedov's party Valentin Kopysev) were also believed to be held in psychiatric hospitals for political reasons.

The Right to Monitor

Intense and pervasive government repression precluded the functioning of any indigenous human rights monitors in Turkmenistan in 1996. A delegation from Human Rights Watch/Helsinki was granted high-level government meetings in June, during which it was given assurances of permission to conduct field investigations in the future. Fearing possible government reprisals against local residents, the delegation deliberately avoided meeting with victims or other independent sources of information during its stay.

Because of the complete repression of dissent, there was no reason to believe that the newly created parliamentary Institute of Human Rights and the Democratization of Society and the State (established on Decem-

ber 27, 1995) would be permitted to function as anything but a government show piece.

The Role of the International Community

The international community did not break from its inexplicable silence on human rights abuse in Turkmenistan in 1996, at best limiting expression of its concern to closed-door meetings. As a result, the government was not forced to make any improvements as concessions to outside pressure—the only pressure possible in this repressive state. Typical of the passive attitude was the statement made by a World Bank representative to Human Rights Watch/Helsinki during a March meeting that the bank took no action on Turkmenistan's well-known human rights abuses precisely because they were so bad.

United States

Except for its excellent *Country Report on Human Rights Practices for 1995*, the U.S. government is not known to have made any public condemnations of Turkmenistan's entrenched human rights practices. On September 14-16, Deputy Assistant Secretary of State Stephen Coffey traveled to Ashgabat to communicate concerns privately and to demand responses to specific cases of illegal arrest and detention. There was no known response as of this writing.

UNITED KINGDOM AND NORTHERN IRELAND

Human Rights Developments

Cease-fires declared by paramilitary organizations in 1994 led to calls for the repeal of Northern Ireland's draconian emergency legislation regime. In January 1996, with the cease-fires still in force, the United Kingdom (U.K.) renewed the Emergency Provisions Act (EPA) for another two years commencing in August 1996. In doing so, the

U.K. government ignored calls made in 1995 for the repeal of emergency legislation from the U.N. Human Rights Committee and the U.N. Committee Against Torture.

The emergency legislation regime severely curtails due process rights with decidedly compromised standards for arrest, detention, interrogation, and the right to counsel in comparison with universally accepted standards under international law. Since 1994, Human Rights Watch/Helsinki has called for the total repeal of the emergency legislation. In addition, European legal institutions have found the U.K. guilty on more than one occasion of human rights violations under emergency legislation provisions. The U.K. has failed to support its renewal of the emergency regime with credible proof required under European law that an emergency posing a "threat to the life of the nation" exists.

The Irish Republican Army (IRA) resumed its campaign of violence in February 1996 with a bomb at Canary Wharf in London. The bombing came only weeks after the International Body on Arms Decommissioning, chaired by former U.S. Senator George Mitchell, issued a report on January 24, 1996, recommending the de-commissioning of paramilitary weapons as a process parallel and integral to peace talks but not as a precondition to talks. After abandoning its cease-fire, the IRA claimed responsibility for seven bombs on the U.K. mainland. On October 7, 1996, the Provisional IRA resumed bombing in Northern Ireland with the explosion of two car bombs inside British army headquarters at Lisburn, southwest of Belfast, killing one soldier and injuring thirty people.

The Mitchell report also stressed the need for confidence building measures such as action on policing, prisoners, and an end to emergency legislation. Human rights groups have argued that issues of justice and accountability are at the core of the conflict and must be at the center of any attempt to broker a solution. They have been concerned that the lack of attention to human rights concerns by the U.K. has contributed to the failure of the peace process.

Despite the eighteen-month cease-fire, paramilitaries on both sides of the conflict continued to engage in punishment beatings and shootings in the course of community policing. Direct Action Against Drugs (DAAD), associated with the IRA, claimed responsibility for the deaths of seven alleged drug dealers in December 1995 and January 1996. *The Irish Times* (Belfast) reported in late January that the IRA had suspended its campaign of killing drug dealers because of its adverse impact on Sinn Fein's political credibility. DAAD resumed such killings on September 16, 1996, with the shooting death of Sean Devlin, a drug dealer who defied a previous IRA expulsion order by returning to Belfast.

The summer months in Northern Ireland saw continued controversy around the issue of marches by members of the Protestant community through predominantly Catholic neighborhoods. Concerns in particular centered around the breakdown in the rule of law when the police reversed an earlier decision to re-route a march at Drumcree away from a Catholic area under threats of violence from Protestant marchers. Human rights groups also were disturbed by the massive and indiscriminate use of plastic bullets by the security forces, which resulted in numerous injuries. Human Rights Watch/Helsinki has called for a total ban on the use of plastic bullets. Of further concern was the death of Dermot McShane who was killed when a British army vehicle ran him over during disturbances in Derry in July and attacks by police in riot gear on people seeking emergency treatment at a city hospital.

In late August, the U.K. government announced the establishment of an independent body, the North Commission, to review current arrangements for handling public processions and "associated public order issues in Northern Ireland." Given the public's lack of confidence in both the Royal Ulster Constabulary (RUC) and the autonomy of state appointed review commissions, there are reservations regarding the practical impact of the commission's recommendations.

The inquest system in Northern Ireland remained a source of concern. In the case of Patrick Shanaghan, killed by a loyalist paramilitary group in 1991, an inquest was only held after five years. The Shanaghan family withdrew from the inquest after being prevented from raising evidence that suggested official collusion in the death. Nine months before the slaying, Mr. Shanaghan had been warned by an RUC inspector that his life was in danger because his security files had fallen out of a military vehicle and were in the hands of loyalist paramilitaries. An independent inquiry stated that the killing was a very serious crime which "the authorities who claimed to investigate it did not take seriously."

Meanwhile, the official peace talks were beset by procedural wrangling, and little progress was made toward addressing substantive issues.

The Right to Monitor
There were no reported violations of the right to monitor.

The Role of
the International Community

Europe
On February 8, 1996, the European Court of Human Rights held in *Murray v. U.K.* that the restrictions on access to legal advice under the emergency legislation, coupled with the ability to draw adverse inferences from silence in the face of police interrogation, violated the European Convention on Human Rights guarantee of a fair trial. The U.K. government declined to amend the emergency legislation in response to the court's ruling but has indicated that it is studying the court's judgment.

United States
The Clinton administration remained actively involved in the peace process in Northern Ireland, although the administration generally failed to highlight the centrality of human rights issues to resolving the conflict.

The U.K. section of the U.S. State Department's *Country Reports on Human Rights Practices for 1995* cited the concerns expressed by the U.N. Human Rights Committee, the Committee on the Rights of the Child, and the Committee Against Torture about the U.K.'s failure to protect human rights in Northern Ireland. (For other problems in the U.K., see The Right to Asylum in the European Union section.)

UZBEKISTAN

Human Rights Developments
There were contrary tendencies of abuse and reform in Uzbekistan in 1996, although almost all human rights continued to be denied. The government maintained complete control of the media, and perpetrated or allowed the abuse of detainees and prisoners, interference with the independence of the judiciary, and a crackdown against members of the Islamic community. Nevertheless, the release of some prisoners of conscience, improvement in the right to monitor, and the federal authorities' greater willingness to address new abuses brought to their attention by international actors made 1996 a more promising year for human rights in Uzbekistan. Generally, the government's pledges of reform brought Uzbekistan greater international approval than its actual human rights record warranted. By year's end, increased attacks on dissidents suggested that the promises were empty words.

Perhaps the most pervasive violation of human rights in Uzbekistan remained denial of free speech, typified by total government control of the mass media and the widespread intimidation of journalists. A May 8 presidential decree and repeated presidential exhortations to journalists to be more critical of the government rang false. Media were still used fundamentally for state propaganda. The government attempted to boost its image in February by bringing a delegation of high-profile journalists from Russia to tour Uzbekistan, but it strictly controlled their movements during their stay. Several journalists who asked to remain anonymous reported that they had been threatened with loss of their jobs because their line of inquiry was displeasing to the government. In separate incidents, President Karimov and the head of the state television and radio, Shahnoza Ghanieva, deliberately misrepresented protests of abuse by Human Rights Watch/Helsinki representatives as statements that the organization had, on the contrary, found all reports of abuse to be unfounded.

The Russian-language media were particularly hard-hit in 1996. In February, Interfax correspondent Sergei Grebeniuk was found murdered. A police investigation did not result in any arrests, sending a chilling message to journalists, particularly Russians, in Uzbekistan. In January, Goskompechat' froze publication of the Russian Cultural Center's newspaper *Vestnik Kul'tury* (Toshkent) immediately after the first issue had appeared and, in August, Russian Radio Mayak was reportedly ordered closed beginning in January 1997. The information blockade was so severe that many Russian-speakers reportedly cited it as the reason for their emigration in 1996.

Abuse during arrest, detention, and incarceration remained serious problems in 1996. Residents were detained and interrogated without legal grounds and mistreated for the purposes of intimidation or extortion. The release of some political prisoners this year gave a crucial glimpse into abusive practices. According to testimony taken by a then-member of the Human Rights Society of Uzbekistan, Safar Bekjon was beaten 106 times during six months in Karshi prison, or almost once per day, and Gaipnazar Kushchanov was regularly beaten by guards, losing three teeth as a result, in Kyzyl Teppe pre-trial detention center.

Police entrapment of dissidents also continued in 1996. On August 12, police raided the home of Kochkar Ahmedov, a member of the banned Birlik movement. He was later accused of possessing several grams of marijuana and two pistol cartridges that allegedly were found during the raid. The charges fall into a well-known pattern of charges falsified by the police against dissidents. His trial had not begun as of this writing. The families of opposition figure Shukhrullo Mirsaidov, activist and Radio Liberty journalist Iadgor Obid, and independent cleric Obidkhon Qori Nazarov were badly harassed by the police in the capital, Toshkent, and threatened with eviction. Most dramatically, on November 9, Mr. Mirsaidov's son, Hasan, was kidnapped, beaten, threatened with death, and released— an uncanny revisiting of the same kidnapping and beating he and his father had suffered in 1995 in the darkest days of government repression. Freedom of association also remained severely limited in 1996. Genuinely alternative political parties remained banned for the fourth straight year.

The government continued to deny the existence of a state-sponsored crackdown on leaders of independent, as opposed to state-run, mosques and their followers in Toshkent and in the Farghona Valley. There, the government harassed, detained, fired from work, and illegally deported dozens of these individuals. On February 24, for example, some fifty security agents surrounded the Tokhtaboi mosque in Toshkent during prayer time, and a representative of the local administration announced that the mosque's prayer leader, Obidkhon Qori Nazarov, was dismissed from work. Then the forces reportedly beat some twenty people, put four under administrative arrest for alleged "hooliganism," fined others, and ordered his deputy, Tahir Ibrahimov, deported to Tajikistan, where his family lived. These events, coupled with the failure to find three high-profile clerics believed to have been "disappeared" by security forces—Abdulla Utaev (1992), Abduvali Qori Mirzo and Ramazanbek Matkarimov (1995)— silenced many Muslims.

At the same time, a June amnesty on the eve of President Islam Karimov's working visit to the United States liberated five prisoners of conscience: Rashid Bekjon, brother of exiled Democratic Party Erk leader Mohammed Solih; Abdulla Abdurazzakov;

Safar Bekjon; Gaipnazar Kushchanov; and Mukhammadnabi Mirkomilov. An August 7 amnesty released political dissidents Makhmadali Makhmudov, Tolibjon Artykov, Shavqat Mamatov and Khoshim Suvanov, and also reduced the sentences of other prisoners of conscience by a quarter to a half. But four new political arrests were also made: on February 13, three scholars affiliated with Samarqand State University—Kholiknazar Ghaniev, Bakhtiar Nabii-oghli, and Nosim Boboev—were arrested for possession of the banned *Erk* (Toshkent) newspaper. Under international pressure, the men were released on April 13 and the charges dropped.

The Right to Monitor

Despite some abuse of human rights activists, the right to monitor improved this year, as did the government's willingness to respond to reports of abuse. Fear of reprisals generally prevented local residents from investigating and reporting on violations of their own civil and political rights, however.

In March, secretary of the unregistered Human Rights Society of Uzbekistan Polina Braunerg and her son were arrested in Almalyk and interrogated about her "spying" activities. After international outcry, the case against her and her son was suspended but the charges were not dropped. At the end of 1995, when leading activist Mikhail Ardzinov was in the United States to receive a human rights award from Human Rights Watch, police reportedly broke into his Toshkent home, removed his telephone and camera, and sealed his apartment. During the September seminar of the OSCE's Office of Democratic Institutions and Human Rights, activist Ahmadjon Abdullaev was detained and interrogated for an hour after having met with a representative of Amnesty International, and others reported heavy surveillance. It is likely that the police's overnight detention and mistreatment on August 30 of John MacLeod, the director of Human Rights Watch/Helsinki's Toshkent-based Central Asia office, was meant as intimidation for his activities.

At the same time, some new doors opened to monitoring and reporting by local residents in 1996. An intense international support campaign secured eleventh-hour permission, illegally denied, for the long-banned Human Rights Society of Uzbekistan to hold its organizing congress on September 7. The congress was held without interference, epitomized by the presence of society chair Abdumannob Polat, who had returned to Uzbekistan for the first time since fleeing it for asylum in the United States in 1993. On June 14, the Ministry of Justice registered the nongovernmental Committee for the Defense of Human Rights, despite the group's failure to comply with all provisions of the law on social organizations, strongly suggesting that it enjoyed government backing: the ostensible reason for prior rejection of the registration application of the Human Rights Society of Uzbekistan had been its failure to meet all legal requirements.

International monitoring also expanded in 1996. The two-and-a-half-year visa ban on Human Rights Watch/Helsinki was lifted and a field investigation permitted in November 1995 as well as numerous high-level meetings. In July, a branch office was registered by the Ministry of Foreign Affairs (registration by the Ministry of Justice was pending) and began operating.

The parliament's human rights commission completed its first full year of activity as a channel for citizens to seek government intervention on cases of abuse. It was not active on cases of political harassment, but did give an unusually candid assessment of government impediments to monitoring (*Narodnoe Slovo*, Toshkent, July 16), such as that "the people responsible cannot be bothered to make the effort, or lack the basic competence [to do so], which means the state funds spent on checking endless complaints are wasted."

The Role of the International Community

With the exception of the U.S. government and OSCE and, to a lesser extent, the U.N. and the government of the United Kingdom, the international community left human rights off its visible Uzbekistan agenda in 1996. Attempts by Human Rights Watch/Helsinki to inform the international business community involved in Uzbekistan about state-sponsored abuse and urge that it use its influential voice to press for reform had no apparent impact in 1996.

United Nations

In February, the UNDP, in conjunction with ODIHR and the U.N. Centre for Human Rights, conducted a government needs assessment trip, which in part included human rights concerns, and submitted a proposed program for implementation. With the exception of representatives of the U.N. Centre for Human Rights and ODIHR, however, the delegation failed to act on information contained in a detailed briefing paper submitted by Human Rights Watch/Helsinki, and rejected opportunities to consult with local activists. A UNDP representative in Toshkent reported that the UNDP office had made some interventions during the year but declined to mention which.

European Union

On June 20, Uzbekistan and the E.U. signed an Agreement on Cooperation and Partnership which conditions implementation on respect for human rights as outlined in OSCE documents. However, that element was not stressed prior to the signing. On the contrary, during an April 8 visit to Uzbekistan, European Commissioner Hans van den Broek inexplicably praised Uzbekistan's "serious progress in ensuring that human rights were defended." The European Parliament can still use its power to reject final approval of the Partnership and Cooperation Agreement with Uzbekistan to show concern that Uzbekistan seriously breached its human rights clause even before the agreement was ratified.

OSCE

The OSCE worked actively in Uzbekistan in 1996. It helped promote a human rights dialogue with the Uzbekistan government by maintaining a regional liaison office in Toshkent, sending delegations, and conducting two seminars on human rights topics in the fall of 1996. Although these seminars fixed much-needed scrutiny on Uzbekistan's human rights record, neither ODIHR nor the OSCE as such insisted on making even minimum improvements a prerequisite for conducting the seminars and failed to insist at the planning stages on adequate participation by nongovernmental actors at all seminars. The addition of a full-time human rights officer promised to strengthen the otherwise lackluster human rights work of the OSCE's regional office.

United States

The U.S. remained in the forefront of international governmental efforts to address human rights concerns in Uzbekistan in 1996, but prematurely weakened its stance by dramatically enhancing its support for the government.

The embassy conducted important interventions on behalf of victims, paid welcome and rare attention to the crackdown against Muslims, and the State Department's Bureau of Democracy, Human Rights and Labor consistently stressed that the progress to date fell short of international commitments and submitted specific demands and case work to the government. The U.S. is likely to have won the release of five prisoners of conscience in June, encouraged an open exchange of information with the government, and also used its membership in the OSCE effectively to promote human rights.

But it also offered an unprecedented degree of support for Uzbekistan, based more on promises of reform than actual reform. The most dramatic evidence of the new policy came in June when President Karimov came to the U.S. for a "working" visit (functionally an official visit). The trip granted him a long-coveted meeting with the U.S. president (which took place on June 25), previously withheld as a sign of U.S. disapproval of serious ongoing abuse in his country. It also afforded him several weeks of photo opportunities and assistance in securing business contracts that reportedly almost tripled U.S. investment in Uzbekistan, but allotted only a single meeting in which to communicate human rights concerns (put to excellent use by Assistant Secretary of State John Shattuck and his staff). However, because of the new policy of conciliation, when U.S. human rights demands were almost entirely unmet by the end of the year, the U.S. seemed hesitant to use available leverage to ensure compliance in the future.

THE RIGHT TO ASYLUM IN THE EUROPEAN UNION

Human Rights Developments

The number of persons seeking asylum in Europe continued to decline in 1996. Following a record number of applications in 1992, European states imposed strict visa requirements on the nationals of most of the world's refugee-producing countries. Largely due to these restrictions on entry into Europe, the number of asylum applications filed in the first six months of 1996 fell to an eight-year low. The rate at which European states recognized asylum seekers as refugees under the Geneva convention relating to the status of refugees remained low, with many countries pursuing increasingly restrictive interpretations of their obligations under the convention. For example, in the first six months of 1996, excluding refugees accepted under the UNHCR's resettlement quota program, Norway recognized only five asylum applicants as convention refugees. Although many of the European Union (E.U.) member states also granted temporary protection regimes and residence permits on humanitarian grounds, these alternative categories of protection often accord asylum seekers fewer rights and benefits than those available under the convention.

Those asylum seekers who, notwith-standing entry restrictions, reached Europe and applied for asylum faced a variety of additional barriers. Asylum seekers who had what were deemed "manifestly unfounded" claims and those coming to Europe through "safe third countries" to which they could be returned were subjected to accelerated screening procedures. Many asylum seekers placed in these categories were detained, received inadequate information and assistance for navigating the asylum procedures, and were either denied a right of appeal or deported before a decision was reached on their appeal. In the U.K., the home secretary introduced legislation to extend application of accelerated procedures to all asylum seekers from countries on its "white list," proposed to include Bulgaria, Cyprus, Ghana, India, Pakistan, Poland and Romania.

Application of "safe third country" rules continued to place many asylum seekers in jeopardy of ultimate *refoulement* because most E.U. member states made little effort to ensure that the returned asylum seeker would be able to seek asylum in the third country. Moreover, as E.U. states returned asylum seekers to their eastern and southern neighbors through which they had transited, these "safe third countries" increasingly implemented "safe third country policies" of their own. Many asylum seekers expelled from E.U. territory allegedly bounced from "safe third country" to "safe third country" and, in some cases, were ultimately returned to their country of origin. In a major setback for asylum seekers, the German constitutional court held in May 1996 that restrictions on the right of asylum adopted in 1993, including a "safe third country" policy and limitations on the right to appeal, do not violate the German Basic Law.

Detention of asylum seekers in Europe was a persistent problem in 1996. Detention was most often employed in the cases of asylum seekers with uncertain identities or nationalities. The trend in many countries was to detain asylum seekers for increasingly long periods of time. In May 1996, the Belgian parliament adopted legislation providing for renewable two-month periods of detention for asylum seekers whose asylum application had been rejected. Both the United Kingdom and the Netherlands constructed new facilities in which to detain rejected asylum seekers and illegal immigrants. In many European countries, asylum seekers were detained in unsatisfactory, prison-like conditions for extended and sometimes indefinite periods of time. In Sweden, notwithstanding repeated complaints by the European Committee for the Prevention of Torture and government-appointed advisory committees, the authorities persisted in detaining asylum seekers in remand prisons, integrated with the criminal population and subject to the same strict prison visitation and recreation regime, in at least one case for as long as ten months. The Netherlands held rejected asylum seekers awaiting deportation at its Koning Willem II detention facility, widely criticized in 1996 for its allegedly arbitrary and excessive disciplinary regime.

The primary purpose of increased detention is to ensure that asylum seekers whose applications are denied can be expelled. In 1996, a number of European countries stepped up efforts to expel rejected asylum seekers and illegal immigrants. Threatened expulsions were the subject of hunger strikes, demonstrations, and suicide attempts throughout Europe. Activists claimed that many expulsions split families in violation of the right to respect for family life and imposed other forms of hardship on long-term residents of European states. Methods of expulsion employed by several European states also drew criticism in 1996. On several occasions, authorities were reported to have used excessive physical restraint and administered sedative drugs to resistant returnees. There was also widespread use of group expulsion to countries where human rights activists claimed the high-profile practice could draw attention to and endanger the returnees.

The fate of more than 700,000 asylum seekers from Bosnia-Hercegovina residing in western Europe continued to dominate political agendas in 1996. The Dayton peace plan signed in December 1995 identified the early return of refugees and displaced persons as an "important objective" of the peace process. By late January 1996, Germany, which shelters more than half of the Bosnian refugees in western Europe, had already announced plans to terminate temporary protection as of June 30, 1996, and to commence repatriation of refugees immediately thereafter, with a goal of repatriating 200,000 Bosnians by July 1997. Although conditions in Bosnia-Hercegovina forced Germany to abandon this initial plan, it subsequently set October 1, 1996, as the date after which the Länder (lands or states) could forcibly repatriate Bosnians. Switzerland also announced plans to begin the aggressive repatriation of Bosnian refugees in mid-1996, though repatriation had not occurred as of this writing. Other countries took a more generous stance toward Bosnian refugees, refusing to set a strict timetable for return and agreeing to pursue only voluntary repatriation in cooperation with the UNHCR. As a practical matter, implementation of large-scale repatriation proved impossible in 1996 due to the slow pace of reconstruction and on-going violations of human rights. (See section on Bosnia-Hercegovina) Nonetheless, because of these repeated threats of imminent repatriation, many Bosnians in western Europe lived under considerable stress and insecurity throughout 1996.

The Role of
the International Community

European Union
The European Union's efforts to harmonize asylum policies in 1996 continued to reinforce restrictive trends in member states' policies.

On March 4, 1996, the Council of Ministers formally adopted a "joint position" on "the harmonized application of the definition of the term 'refugee' in article 1 of the Geneva Convention of 28 July 1951 relating to the status of refugees." Reinforcing restrictive jurisprudence in France, Germany, Italy, the Netherlands, and Sweden, the joint position suggests that protection should be given only to those persecuted by state agents or with the encouragement or permission of state agents. This interpretation of the convention could be used to deny protection to, for example, Algerians whom the government cannot protect from persecution by insurgents or Somalians fleeing circumstances in which the government has collapsed altogether. The UNHCR strongly criticized this aspect of the joint position, describing the interpretation as contrary to the letter and spirit of the Geneva convention. The joint position constitutes a nonbinding political commitment by the member states, and in September the Swedish government proposed reform of its asylum law that would depart from both its past practice and the E.U. joint position by providing protection for victims of persecution by non-state agents, regardless of government complicity. It remains to be seen to what extent the joint position will be implemented by the other member states.

In support of member states' efforts to increase expulsion of rejected asylum seekers and illegal immigrants, in December 1995 the Council of Ministers adopted a "recommendation of concerted action and cooperation in carrying out expulsion measures." The recommendation listed principles to govern coordinated expulsions and identified measures to obtain cooperation from states to which third-country nationals are to be returned. In September 1996, the European Parliament adopted a resolution criticizing the council for its failure to consult the parliament on the December 1995 recommendation, deploring expulsion practices in certain member states (France, Spain, and Belgium, in particular), and calling for a "thoroughgoing study into the legislation and practices on expulsion and removal policies in the Member States of the European Union."

There was some progress in 1996 toward complete ratification of the 1990 Dublin convention, detailing rules by which one and only one member state of the European Union would be responsible for adjudication of an asylum application. The convention must be ratified by all member states before it can be implemented. Ireland and the Netherlands, the only two states that had not yet ratified the convention, were expected to do so by late 1996 or early 1997. In the meantime, in March 1996, a subset of the European Union member states celebrated the first anniversary of the entry into force of the Schengen convention, which also established rules for determining the state responsible for each asylum application. There were continued reports, throughout 1996, that the applications of asylum seekers sent to "safe third countries," both inside and outside Europe, were frequently not considered in the third country, sometimes resulting in refoulement. In numerous cases, adjudicators of the British Immigration Appeal Authority found insufficient evidence to conclude that other European countries, including France and Belgium, could serve as "safe third countries." Such decisions raise significant doubts about whether the "safe third country" rules embodied in member states' legislation and the Schengen and Dublin conventions comport with international commitments to safeguard against *refoulement*. The "safe third country" rules and other aspects of European asylum procedures were the subject of a critical resolution adopted by the European Parliament on November 14 in response to the Council of Ministers' 1995 resolution on minimum guarantees for asylum procedures.

HUMAN RIGHTS WATCH

MIDDLE EAST

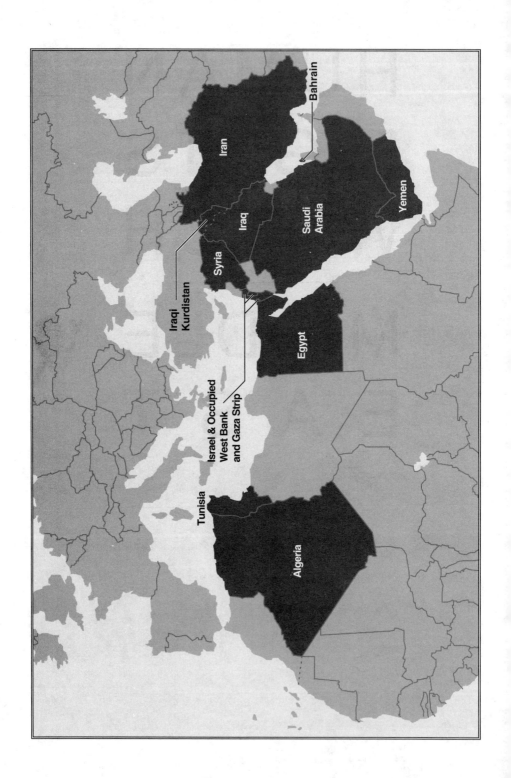

HUMAN RIGHTS WATCH/MIDDLE EAST OVERVIEW

Human Rights Developments

A preoccupation with political violence and the spread of militant Islamist movements tended to obscure the underlying reasons for the sorry state of human rights in the Middle East and North Africa. A combination of forces—a thriving civil society, a vociferous press, an independent judiciary, relatively free elections, regional human rights bodies, and effective third-party engagement—were potential remedies around the world to abuses such as mass arrests, torture, and the suppression of associations and media. But throughout much of the Middle East and North Africa, these accountability-enhancing factors were either nonexistent or weak, largely due to government pressure. Authorities therefore encountered relatively few constraints on their abusive conduct.

It was therefore unsurprising that human rights activists from the region, when discussing the priorities of their work, stressed the need to preserve the shrinking space that is permitted to institutions and forces that expose and protest abuses.

Of course, in some countries, authorities allowed no such space at all. Syria, Iraq, Saudi Arabia, Bahrain, and Libya allowed no independent media or human rights organizations. In these countries, open criticism of the government put a person at immediate risk of imprisonment or worse.

In those countries that allowed a measure of freedom of association and expression, governments chipped away at the exercise of these rights. In Algeria, Tunisia, Jordan, Egypt, and the Palestinian self-rule areas, former members of parliament, professors, writers, cartoonists and human rights activists were detained or imprisoned for peaceful political criticism.

In Egypt, a new press law limited conditions under which new newspapers could be established and criminalized expression deemed insulting to the president, although journalists and others successfully fended off more draconian legislation. A controversial move by the Lebanese government in September required the country's scores of privately owned but unlicensed radio and television stations, unrivaled in the region, to stop political programming immediately and cease all operations by November 30. Of the four television stations licensed in September, one was owned by the prime minister, another by the interior minister's brother, and the third—not yet in existence—by the speaker of the parliament.

Laws on defamation were misused to impose harsh penalties for criticism of government officials or institutions, chilling the press in Morocco, Algeria, and Tunisia. Palestinian journalists and human rights activists wound up in Palestinian jails for "insulting" President Arafat or appearing to question his policies. In Jordan, Leith Shubeilat, a prominent independent Islamist, received a three-year sentence because his criticism of government economic policies and the peace process with Israel was held to have violated the dignity of King Hussein. However, on November 8, he was released by royal decree.

Iranian journalists convicted of "publishing lies" or "defamatory" reporting on government policies were punished with lashes and prison sentences. Some of their outspoken compatriots risked even cruder punishments at the hands of well-organized zealots loyal to government factions, who shouted down, beat, or vandalized the property of dissidents. In Yemen, physical assaults on government critics by plainclothes thugs appeared to be one of the activities of the Political Security Organization, an agency that reported directly to the president.

Laws on associations and political parties were another means of hobbling independent institutions in countries that officially permitted them. In Lebanon, the Ministry of Interior refused to acknowledge receipt of the written notice required from newly formed organizations, turning what should be a *pro forma* procedure into a means of imposing an aura of illegality on the groups and scaring off their potential members. In Egypt, the newly formed Wasat Party was denied permission to function, as were most political parties that sought legal authorization under the Political Parties Law of 1977. In Tunisia, a law remained on the books that denied organizations considered to be "of a general character" the right to choose their own members; fortunately, an administrative court in 1996 exempted the Tunisian Human Rights League from this law.

Independent judges were an endangered species, where they existed at all. The Yemeni authorities threatened to reassign one of the country's foremost independent judges to a small village, and pressed for the Judges' Association to be opened to membership by prosecutors as well, a move judges held would impair its independence. Elsewhere, the executive authority sought to bypass independent judges and the fair trial guarantees of ordinary courts by prosecuting dissidents and critics in alternative court systems. President Mubarak ordered the transfer of the case of thirteen prominent Muslim Brothers from a civilian court to a military court, which handed out prison terms to seven of the defendants, a one-year suspended sentence to another, and allowed no appeals of the verdicts. In the Palestinian autonomous areas and in Bahrain, state security courts dispensed hasty and unfair justice. Nor were Syria's state security court disbanded during the thirty-fourth year of that country's state of emergency. And Israel tried West Bank Palestinians in military courts that failed to provide due process guarantees.

Torture was ingrained in many countries of the region in part because judges extracted no price for its practice—a pattern that persisted because it was either encouraged or tolerated by governments. Torturers were rarely punished, and judges routinely accepted into evidence confessions without probing defendant allegations that the confessions had been extracted through torture.

In Algeria and Tunisia, for example, defendants' rights to request a medical examination during their interrogation—their best chance for proving torture—was routinely violated, with no adverse consequences for the prosecution. In both countries, as in Saudi Arabia and Bahrain, uncorroborated confessions by defendants or by other suspects under interrogation were frequently the sole basis for convictions.

Despite the pervasiveness of violations, Human Rights Watch knew of only isolated cases over the last several years—in Israel, the Palestinian self-rule areas, and Morocco—where members of the security forces were punished in a transparent fashion for violently abusing the rights of civilians. Not surprisingly, all three were places where pressure was exerted on the authorities by some combination of local rights organizations, a relatively open environment for the press, and international pressure. Several other governments claimed to have punished abusers, but their vague assertions, which lacked verifiable details, failed to dispel suspicion that these claims were mere public relations gestures.

Human rights protection in the Middle East was weakened also by the absence of regional bodies other than nongovernmental organizations committed to promoting human rights. The main regional political institution, the Arab League, decried Israeli behavior toward Palestinians while pronouncing not at all on the human rights performances of its member states. The region had no counterpart to the Inter-American Court of Human Rights or the European Court of Human Rights (although all North African nations except Morocco, as signatories of the African Charter on Human and Peoples Rights, participated in the relatively weak African Commission on Human and Peoples Rights).

The Israeli-Palestine Liberation Organization peace process, despite the prospect for further Israeli military redeployment and greater Palestinian self-rule, yielded few human rights improvements during 1996. Invoking security concerns heightened by a series of suicide bombings, Israeli authorities at the highest level authorized harsh interrogation methods that, in practice, often amounted to torture, and imposed closures on the West Bank and Gaza Strip that restricted the movement of Palestinians more tightly than at any time since the Gulf War, devastating the Palestinian economy and creating a humanitarian crisis. Under pressure from Israel to "fight terrorism," the Palestinian Authority carried out mass arbitrary arrests, holding suspects without charge for lengthy periods or referring them to the State Security Court, where the chance for a fair trial was nil.

The several elections that took place in the region illustrated the weakness of institutional restraints on coercive state behavior. Egyptian authorities, not content merely to ensure a landslide for the ruling National Democratic Party in the late 1995 parliamentary elections, also cracked down on those who supported opposition candidates or protested voting fraud. Security forces arrested over 1,300 supporters of Islamist candidates between the two rounds, and barred meetings between some opposition candidates and the public.

Algerians, hungry for an opportunity to participate in normal political life after four years of strife, voted in large numbers in the November 1995 multiparty presidential elections. But the terms of the elections were dictated by the unelected government, which censored and harassed those favoring a boycott of the vote.

The elections in the Palestinian self-rule areas in January were relatively successful, thanks in part to the mobilization of Palestinian civil society and the engagement of the international community. The resulting legislative council emerged as the premier forum for airing human rights complaints against an increasingly repressive Palestinian executive.

The Iranian authorities manipulated the parliamentary vote in March and April primarily through the power of the Council of Guardians, composed of senior clerical figures and religious jurists, to disqualify candidates on the basis of politically motivated criteria and to nullify voting returns.

In Kuwait's parliamentary election in October, only 107,000 "first-class" Kuwaiti male citizens out of a total Kuwaiti population of about 700,000 were eligible to vote.

Syria continued to invoke the state of war with Israel to justify its emergency law. The governments of Tunisia and Algeria, meanwhile, focused on the challenge from Islamist militants as the grounds for curtailing rights and limiting dissent.

In countries that actually suffered repeated acts of political violence during the year, these acts became the pretext for circumscribing a broad array of rights and for attempting to discredit human rights concerns. The Egyptian government informed a U.N. committee that its investigation of torture in Egypt could be seen as "encouraging terrorism." The Algerian authorities blocked issues of an opposition weekly devoted to human rights on the grounds that they constituted an apologia for terrorism. In response to deadly bombings, the Israeli and Saudi authorities carried out mass and arbitrary arrests, often severely mistreating those brought in for interrogation.

To be sure, militant movements posed vexing security dilemmas and were major perpetrators of abuses. Some Islamist movements embraced indiscriminate violence and a discourse of extreme intolerance. Their deadly campaigns targeted civilians as well as security forces. Statements they issued threatened various groups and individuals on the basis of their beliefs or their ethnic or social identities. Islamist groups in Algeria continued to assassinate journalists, intellectuals and ordinary citizens in what was the region's bloodiest ongoing conflict during 1996.

Such targeting by militants of unarmed civilians, as also occurred in Israel and Egypt, violated basic norms of international humanitarian law. In Human Rights Watch's view, the prohibition of the intentional killing of civilians applies to all political violence, whether it is classified as internal strife or rises to the level of an armed internal conflict.

Although the region was spared full-fledged wars between states during 1996, Israel in April launched a major operation in Lebanon north of the zone it occupies in the south of the country, claiming as its justification Hizballah attacks on Israeli military and civilian targets. The intense seventeen-day conflict, which Israeli authorities named "Operation Grapes of Wrath," brought war to much of Lebanon, including Beirut, and to northern Israel. Israel, with its superior firepower and control of the skies, responded in a disproportionate fashion to Hizballah's mortar shells and Katyusha rockets, causing by far the most civilian casualties and damage to homes and civilian infrastructure. While it inflicted no Israeli civilian deaths during this conflict, Hizballah's indiscriminate fire toward towns in northern Israel violated humanitarian law, as did, on some occasions, its launching of artillery from or near civilian settlements.

In the deadliest single incident of this or any other conflict in the region during the year, Israeli artillery shells hit a United Nations Interim Force in Lebanon (UNIFIL) compound on April 18 in the town of Qana that was sheltering hundreds of civilians, of whom 102 died. Israeli authorities claimed that they were unaware Lebanese civilians had sought refuge at the base, and that they were aiming not at the base but at a nearby Hizballah mortar site. Investigations by the U.N. and Amnesty International into the pattern of Israeli artillery strikes cast doubt on whether the hits on the base were the result of an accident. Israeli officials rejected their conclusion.

Like the conflict in south Lebanon, the dispute in the Western Sahara dates to the 1970s. Although the cease-fire between Morocco and the Western Saharan liberation movement known as the Polisario Front remained in effect, there was no progress toward holding the U.N.-conducted referendum that both parties have accepted. In that referendum, Sahrawis would choose between independence or integration into Morocco. The free and fair nature of the referendum had already been compromised by evidence of U.N. partiality and a lack of control over the voter registration process, as well as by Morocco's intimidation and unfair conduct designed to influence the voter registration process. In May, the U.N. Security Council extended the U.N. operation's mandate but formally suspended the voter registration process, which had been stalled since September 1995 and was already five years behind schedule. This impasse put on hold the fate of some 100,000 to 165,000 Sahrawi refugees living in harsh camp conditions in southwestern Algeria, as well political prisoners and at least 1,900 prisoners of war being held by both sides.

The bleakness of the human rights picture in Iraq deserves special mention. The Iraqi people had to contend not only with a government that liquidated its critics, but also with post-Gulf War trade sanctions imposed by the U.N. Security Council. Because the Security Council and President Saddam Hussein could not agree on the terms of Iraqi oil sales that would pay for importing humanitarian goods, thousands of Iraqi civilians died from preventable illnesses and malnutrition-related causes. Meanwhile, in the Kurdish region in northern Iraq, whose de facto autonomy had been protected by a Western military alliance, fighting between rival political groups hobbled the local government set up in the aftermath of the Gulf War, attracted Iraqi and Iranian military incursions, and led to scores of arbitrary killings and other grave abuses. As always, Kurdish civilians were the big losers.

One positive note in 1996 was the increasing visibility of the women's movement in Morocco, Tunisia, Egypt, the West Bank and Gaza Strip, Jordan, Kuwait and elsewhere. Fighting abuses that ranged from the practice of female genital mutilation in Egypt to the denial of suffrage in Kuwait, women's rights activists struggled against prevalent interpretations of Islam that blatantly discriminated against women in many realms of life and contributed to a judicial laxness toward violence targeting women.

While its successes were modest, the movement's perseverance in the face of government pressures and social hostility insured that it would be one element of civil society that was certain to make itself heard in the coming year.

Working closely with women's organizations in the region, the Women's Rights Project of Human Rights Watch conducted fieldwork in Morocco and Egypt during 1996. In Morocco, we looked at discriminatory aspects, in the text and in practice, of the code of personal status, which relegates women to the status of minors throughout their lives. In Egypt, we began an investigation into problems of discrimination under the law and into violence within the family, including spousal abuse and female genital mutilation.

The Right to Monitor

About half the governments in the Middle East and North Africa tolerate some domestic monitoring of human rights. Groups in Israel, the West Bank and Gaza Strip, Jordan, Egypt, Algeria and Morocco all published reports that contained strong criticism of their respective authorities; independent groups also functioned in Tunisia, Lebanon, Kuwait, and Yemen.

However, during 1996, human rights activists in Syria, Tunisia, and the Israeli- and Palestinian-controlled areas of the West Bank and Gaza Strip were either detained or were serving prison terms handed down in past years. Activists in the Committees for the Defense of Democratic Freedoms and Human Rights in Syria (CDF) were serving the longest terms—up to ten years.

International human rights monitors could do field work in several areas with relative freedom, including Morocco, Egypt, Israel, the West Bank and Gaza Strip, Lebanon, Jordan, Kuwait and Yemen. Algeria allowed a mission by Amnesty International, despite its past criticism of the government's record. Iran allowed its first-ever mission by Human Rights Watch. Syria declined Human Rights Watch's requests for a visit, at least through the month of October, in con-

trast to its assent to a seven-week-long mission in 1995. Tunisia refused some groups while allowing others, only to subvert their work through heavy-handed and intimidating police surveillance. Human rights missions to Iraq were out of the question due to the risks they would pose for Iraqis who shared critical information, unless the scope of the mission was limited to assessing the effects of the U.N.-imposed sanctions. Saudi Arabia did not deviate from its policy of allowing no access for international organizations. Bahrain ignored a request for a formal mission by Human Rights Watch, which sent a researcher informally to the country.

The International Community

Western governments largely wrote off the promotion of human rights in the Middle East and North Africa, as if the political sensitivity and volatility of the region made human rights concerns an unaffordable luxury. The objectives of preserving the Israeli-PLO peace process, protecting friendly governments of oil-rich nations from internal and external threats, and checking the spread of militant Islamism led Western governments to downplay the promotion of human rights in the region.

The U.N. was engaged in human rights work in a number of countries. Special rapporteurs were assigned to cover human rights in Iran, Iraq and the Israeli-occupied territories. There was also some bold specialized work, such as the Committee against Torture's report on Egypt. But none of the major U.N. operations in the field featured as a chief part of their mandate the monitoring of rights conditions. (U.N. efforts to deploy human rights monitors inside Iraq were rejected by Baghdad.) UNIFIL in southern Lebanon carried out humanitarian work during Operation Grapes of Wrath, sheltering some 5,000 Lebanese civilians on its bases. It also organized convoys to evacuate residents who wished to flee the military conflict, and brought food, medicine, and other relief supplies to civilians unable or unwilling to leave their homes. UNIFIL vehicles and humanitarian aid convoys came under dangerously close Israeli fire during the conflict but its forces suffered no casualties.

On the other hand, the U.N. contributed to a humanitarian crisis and the continuing loss of life in Iraq through its six-year-old sanctions regime, as the Security Council and President Saddam Hussein again failed to settle on terms for Iraqi oil sales to generate the revenue that would enable the Iraqi government to purchase basic foodstuffs and medical goods desperately needed by the Iraqi people.

The European Union (E.U.) devoted its most significant effort in the region to projects in the Palestinian self-rule areas. It assisted in the well-run monitoring of the January elections, and pledged material assistance and training to the legislative council, which emerged as the leading forum for raising human rights concerns in the self-rule areas.

E.U. institutions occasionally raised human rights concerns elsewhere in the region during 1996, but did not do so in a systematic way. While a welcome resolution was passed by the European Parliament on the deterioration of rights in Tunisia, Syria earned E.U. praise for its economic policies and silence about its rights record.

Although the association agreements that the E.U. initiated with Tunisia, Morocco, and Israel contained a human rights clause, it remained to be seen whether this would have a practical effect on the trade and aid relationships that the E.U. was entering into with these countries.

United States

In an October 1995 speech, Assistant Secretary of State Robert H. Pelletreau declared, "The development of democracy and human rights—for the two go together—has been and remains central to U.S. foreign policy." And the assessments contained in the State Department's *Country Reports on Human Rights Practices for 1995* were comprehensive and appropriately critical. But the gap remained huge between the frank *Country Reports* and actual U.S. practice in attempting to develop democracy and human rights.

The U.S. had considerable potential leverage in the region. Aid to Egypt and Israel accounted for nearly half of the $12 billion that the U.S. spent on foreign assistance worldwide. The U.S. was the world's leading exporter of conventional arms to the Middle East and North Africa, which was the largest purchasing region in the developing world. For the most part, the U.S. declined to condition these aid and arms-trading relationships on improvements in human rights practices.

In 1996, President Clinton and his cabinet secretaries largely avoided the subject of human rights in the Middle East, except in their frequent denunciations of terrorism. Assistant Secretary of State for Democracy, Human Rights and Labor John Shattuck had not been to the region since early 1994, although a trip was under discussion for late 1996. Chief responsibility for articulating policy concerning human rights developments was left to Assistant Secretary Pelletreau.

In his October 1995 speech, Secretary Pelletreau cautioned that U.S. support for democratic principles, and by implication human rights, "needs to be viewed in the context of other priorities," which he listed as securing peace between Israel and Arab states, maintaining Israeli security and well-being, assuring stability in and commercial access to Persian Gulf countries, supporting U.S. business interests, and combating terrorism and the proliferation of weapons of mass destruction.

Overall, it was not a good year for the U.S. administration in the Middle East. The Arab-Israeli peace negotiations stalled and at times appeared close to collapse; the Israeli-Lebanese border again erupted in war; militant opposition groups in Saudi Arabia launched deadly attacks against U.S. military targets; and both the Iraqi and Iranian military launched incursions into the foundering, Western-backed Kurdish autonomous enclave in the north of Iraq.

Under these circumstances, the U.S. spent much of its time putting out policy fires and little time promoting human rights.

Apart from the *Country Reports* there was no public expression of concern for the human rights behavior of Syria or Egypt, both key players in the Arab-Israeli peace process. Senior U.S. officials voiced understanding for Israel's harsh response to Palestinian suicide bombings in February and March, although that response quickly amounted to harsh collective punishment for all Palestinians. In April, when heavy fighting erupted between Israeli and Hizballah forces in south Lebanon, U.S. officials repeatedly condemned Hizballah targeting of Israeli civilians but spoke not a word of public criticism of Israeli indiscriminate bombardment and disproportionate attacks that killed or injured hundreds of Lebanese civilians.

Keeping Israeli-Arab negotiations afloat also meant that the Clinton administration attention to serious human rights abuses by the Palestinian Authority (PA) was confined to high-profile cases such as that of Dr. Eyad al-Sarraj, and was offset by high-level U.S. emphasis on the need for the PA make "combating terrorism" its highest priority, whatever the cost in human rights.

With regard to its allies in the Persian Gulf, the U.S. came close to covering up for human rights abuses during the year. Here, the *Country Reports* were revealing. The chapter on Saudi Arabia indulgently presented the government's brand of religiously cloaked repression as "rigorously conservative" while discrediting the opposition groups as "rigidly fundamentalist." In testimony to the House Committee on International Relations in September, Assistant Secretary Pelletreau acknowledged that "internal tensions exist in many GCC [Gulf Cooperation Council] states—notably Bahrain" but went on to say, "All the GCC states are able to work with internal opposition effectively," implicitly condoning by omission the repressive practices of many of the GCC governments, Saudi Arabia and Bahrain in particular.

In North Africa, a region of less strategic interest to the U.S. than to France, U.S. policy was more engaged. Human rights formed a regular component of statements by U.S. officials concerning Algeria, albeit with an emphasis on "democratic rights" such as press freedom and political participation, at the expense of torture and summary executions—abuses whose victims were primarily Islamists and their sympathizers. The U.S., through an active embassy staff, also showed concern for Tunisia's relentless persecution of opposition and human rights activists. But Secretary Pelletreau's unseemly praise, while visiting Tunisia, for President Ben Ali's attachment to human rights signaled to governments that the U.S. was ready to tone down human rights criticism in exchange for the pursuit of U.S.-backed policies in other realms, such as support of the Israeli-Arab peace talks.

The Work of
Human Rights Watch/Middle East

The division devoted much of its resources to addressing humanitarian crises and working to preserve the fragile space in which civil society can function. We also increased the number of collaborative efforts with other nongovernmental organizations, our advocacy at the U.N., the number of our publications that were translated into Arabic, and our Farsi-language broadcast work.

In the realm of armed conflict situations, we sent delegations to Lebanon and northern Israel beginning in May to document violations of the laws of war during Israeli-Hizballah fighting. Together with the Arms Project of Human Rights Watch, we issued our first report on the subject, *Civilian Pawns: Laws of War & Use of Weapons on the Israel-Lebanon Border*.

Humanitarian issues of another kind were covered in a study of Israel's closure of the West Bank and Gaza Strip. That report argued that as an occupying power, Israel was ultimately responsible for ensuring the welfare of the Palestinian population under its occupation and, by its indiscriminate and debilitating closure of the territories, was in breach of that solemn duty.

Human Rights Watch staff met with Israeli officials to discuss the recommendations of both reports, and urged donor countries to give priority to addressing the closure of the territories in their démarches with Israel. Staff also met with Hizballah officials to stress that the targeting of civilians, whatever the supposed justification, was a violation of humanitarian law. Human Rights Watch wrote to Secretary of State Warren Christopher and Syrian President Hafez al-Asad, urging them to press both Israel and Hizballah to cease their violations of the laws of war. Articles on the conflict by Human Rights Watch staff appeared in the *Boston Globe*, the *Washington Post*, the Arabic daily *Al-Hayat* (London) and other media. We also raised our concern, in letters to Secretary Christopher and in a meeting with the State Department's Special Middle East Coordinator Dennis Ross, that the U.S. was ignoring human rights in its support for the peace process.

A mission in July examined abuses and intimidation tactics for which the Palestinian Authority was responsible in the West Bank and Gaza Strip. Human Rights Watch testified before a U.S. House of Representatives committee on that subject on July 23. We also urged donor countries to address the subject at an international donor meeting in Washington in September. In October, a mission probed allegations of the use of excessive force toward civilians during the fierce clashes that broke out between Israeli forces and Palestinians in late September.

Highlights of the year included our first-ever authorized mission to look at human rights in Iran. A report, issued before the first round of parliamentary elections, documented how authorities disqualified independent candidates or undermined their ability to compete. Throughout the year, in written interventions and press interviews, particularly Farsi-language radio broadcasts heard in Iran and elsewhere, we criticized repressive laws and the persecution of independent journalists and thinkers. In Human Rights Watch's annual awards ceremony for human rights monitors in November, we honored a courageous Iranian lawyer and rights activist, Shirin Ebadi.

Although Syrian authorities did not approve our request for a mission during the first ten months of 1996, we issued two reports based on our seven-week visit in 1995 and on follow-up research, and wrote four times to President Asad. A report *Syria's Tadmor Prison: Dissent Still Hostage to a Legacy of Terror*, published in April, called on authorities to discontinue the practice of transferring civilians to this infamous military facility. We recommended that authorities provide detailed information to families about relatives who died or were executed at Tadmor over the last sixteen years. *Syria: The Silenced Kurds*, issued in October, detailed violations of the rights of the Kurdish minority, including denial of citizenship and arbitrary state actions against suspected Kurdish political activists. The report included a detailed response from the Syrian authorities.

The report on the Kurds publicized the existence of the *maktoumeen*, a subcategory of some 75,000 stateless Syrian-born Kurds. In October, a Human Rights Watch representative briefed the U.N. Committee on the Rights of the Child about stateless Syrian Kurdish children.

Work on the government of Lebanon's record included a mission in July and August and three letters to the Lebanese government. We condemned the curfew that was imposed on Beirut and all other large cities on February 29 that prevented citizens from participating in peaceful demonstrations. In August, we protested tactics of the Interior Ministry that in recent years had prevented nongovernmental organizations from obtaining legal status pursuant to Lebanese law; the letter was reprinted in the Beirut daily *An-Nahar*. We wrote again in October about continuing "disappearances" of Lebanese civilians and Palestinian refugees in Lebanon who were detained by Syrian security forces and transferred to Syria. All of these letters went unanswered. On October 17, Human Rights Watch staff questioned Prime Minister Hariri at a public appearance in Washington about Lebanese complicity in the disappearances.

Our work on Egypt focused on the

expanding role of the military justice system in civilian political life, restrictions on freedom of association, and the erosion of free expression and tolerance. We visited Egypt in November 1995, and wrote an open letter to President Mubarak about the repressive climate in which the upcoming parliamentary elections would be held. We also investigated the military court trial of eighty-one Muslim Brothers and attended the session at which the verdicts were announced. On November 25, 1995, we issued a press release in Cairo jointly with the Egyptian Organization of Human Rights (EOHR) that announced the availability of reports issued separately by both organizations concerning the trial. We returned to Egypt in July and issued a detailed press release in advance of the August military court ruling in the trial of another thirteen Muslim Brothers.

A mission to Tunisia in March studied the elaborate campaign of the authorities to monopolize all discussion about human rights conditions in the country, including the persecution of human rights monitors and interference with the work of domestic and international human rights organizations. Our subsequent interventions, which included open letters to President Ben Ali and interviews with the press, focused on the repressive measures taken against Tunisians who raised their voice about human rights.

In keeping with our policy of according top priority to defending human rights activists who face persecution, we intervened not only on behalf of Tunisians, but also on behalf of Algerian human rights lawyer Rachid Mesli when he was abducted by security forces, Palestinian human rights workers who were arrested by the Palestinian or by the Israeli authorities, and Syria's Nizar Nayouf, an imprisoned human rights activist held in solitary confinement in a military prison. We also defended political figures when they faced persecution because of the nonviolent expression of their views. A letter to Jordanian authorities in February criticized the prosecution of Leith Shubeilat (see above).

Human Rights Watch protested to Brit-ish authorities on their efforts to deport outspoken Saudi dissident and asylum applicant Muhammad Mas'ari in response to pressure from Saudi authorities. We also wrote to the chairmen of three British defense firms that had lobbied their government to satisfy Saudi demands with regard to Mas'ari, drawing their attention to Saudi Arabia's dismal rights record and the unseemliness of their urging Britain's democratic government to take measures against a critic of the Saudi record.

Human Rights Watch conducted a research mission to Bahrain and interviewed Bahraini exiles elsewhere in the region. A long article about Bahrain by Human Rights Watch staff appeared in the July issue of *Le Monde Diplomatique*. An abridged English-language version appeared in *Middle East Report* and prompted a reply from Bahrain's ambassador to the U.S. We also briefed U.S., French, and British officials about the situation in Bahrain, and presented our concerns to the embassy of Bahrain in Washington.

Our collaborative efforts with other organizations in 1996 went beyond our frequent joint communiques with other U.S.-based human rights organizations. These included: an August 1 letter co-signed by the Moroccan Organization for Human Rights and the Paris-based Reporters without Borders urging Syrian President Asad to release eight imprisoned journalists; a September 23 letter to President Ben Ali on the deteriorating human rights conditions in Tunisia, co-signed by Amnesty International and three other organizations; an October 1 letter co-signed by nine other groups urging the U.S. administration to address the human rights dimensions of the crisis in northern Iraq; and a joint declaration condemning the Egyptian court decision that declared Professor Nasr Abu Zeid an apostate for his writings on Islam and ordering his wife's divorce from him.

We enlisted twenty-one human rights, women's rights, Arab-American and Muslim organizations to sign the declaration, which was translated into Arabic and widely circulated.

ALGERIA

Human Rights Developments

The year began with much hope for progress in ending Algeria's civil strife. The high turnout for the November 1995 presidential election, despite threats from Islamist armed groups against those who voted, appeared to give incumbent Liamine Zeroual a mandate to break the political deadlock.

But the year since the election disappointed those who looked to the president to initiate a meaningful opening toward opposition parties. Zeroual announced a referendum on constitutional reform to be held in November 1996, and plans to hold legislative and municipal elections sometime in 1997. Despite formal consultations with Algeria's political parties, the government seemed to dictate the terms of these initiatives with minimal input from the parties.

The lull in political violence around the presidential elections proved short-lived. Murderous attacks by Islamist groups, government-organized "self-defense" militias, and the regular security forces brought the estimated death toll since 1992 to more than 50,000. Precise data was notoriously elusive on how many persons were killed, by whom and why they were targeted, owing to strict government censorship and the hazards of investigating the violence. In addition, responsibility for most killing went unclaimed, and the sources of warnings and claims could not always be authenticated.

The endemic violence dated to 1992, when the military-backed government canceled the all-but-certain victory of the Islamic Salvation Front (Front Islamique du Salut, FIS) in parliamentary elections, outlawed that party and declared a state of emergency that remained in effect in 1996.

The decentralized armed resistance was composed of FIS loyalists and radical breakaway factions. Some Islamist groups targeted civilians in blatant violation of the most elemental humanitarian norms, assassinating relatives of security-force members as well as journalists, intellectuals, popular singers, and other figures whose personal politics or profession they deemed hostile to their Islamist enterprise. Car bombs and other explosive attacks took the lives of hundreds of civilians and caused tremendous damage to public and private property.

The regular security forces and militias also committed gross abuses, including extrajudicial executions, "disappearances" and torture. Persons arrested by the security forces were sometimes later found dead, their deaths attributed to armed clashes or attempted prison escapes.

The practice of administrative detention, permitted under 1992 emergency laws, was employed little if at all in 1996, and the camps housing administrative detainees since 1992 have been closed. Despite this welcome development, large numbers of Algerians continued to be arrested and held without charge. Persons seized by armed plainclothesmen, acting without arrest warrants, have "disappeared" for two years or longer in secret, unacknowledged detentions. That the security forces were responsible for abductions was evident from eyewitness accounts of the arrests, the testimony of some who were seized and later released, and reported sightings of some of the "disappeared" by other prisoners at detention centers. But families and lawyers found it impossible to obtain any information from authorities about the status and location of those who had been seized in this manner.

Suspected Islamists were frequently subjected to torture during interrogation. Human Rights Watch received testimony from a twenty-seven-year-old engineer arrested in December 1995 who underwent many of the methods commonly employed: "An interrogation session began with blows to my private parts, and was followed by questions. Then blows at my head. The blood flowed from my nose. A torturer they called 'Ten' began with the 'washrag' method: a washrag soaked in cleaning fluids stuffed down the detainee's mouth....The interrogation lasted three days, that is thirty-six hours of ... blows, [beatings with] electric cables, the 'washrag,' deprivation of food and water..." There were also credible reports of electric shock being used on detainees.

Arrests and detention often violated procedures set forth in Algerian law. Suspected Islamists were held incommunicado beyond the legal limit of twelve days while their families were not informed of their whereabouts. Their right to a medical examination to document physical mistreatment was routinely ignored by investigating judges. Then, when defendants repudiated statements made under interrogation on the grounds of coercion, judges systematically refused to rule them inadmissible or to investigate the allegations, noting the absence of medical certificates that would corroborate torture allegations. Suspects were routinely convicted on the basis of confession evidence, and legal safeguards against torture did not function.

The arrest of human rights lawyer Rachid Mesli showed how the security forces flouted laws even when handling a well-known figure. On July 31, Mesli was arrested on a street in an Algiers suburb by four armed individuals who did not present a warrant or identify themselves. His family did not know if he had been arrested by police or abducted by one of the groups responsible for countless assassinations. It was not until one week later that his whereabouts were confirmed, when he was brought to court. He was charged with associating with armed groups and remanded to prison.

In another case, Abdelqader Hachani, a senior FIS leader held in pretrial detention since January 1992 on charges of inciting the army to rebel, demanded unsuccessfully to be brought to trial. Other FIS activists, such as lawyer Ali Zouita, also spent years in detention without being tried.

Authorities claimed that the security forces were held accountable for their behavior but provided no information about cases where agents responsible for rights violations have been disciplined. One human rights lawyer observed that prosecutors refrained from investigating abusive security-force members because the prosecutors, who have as a group been targeted by armed groups, depend on those forces for their personal protection.

Paramilitary "self-defense" groups, active in rural areas and trained and armed by the security forces, were also implicated in willful killings of unarmed civilians, extortion, and other lawless behavior.

Public liberties remained severely limited by state-of-emergency restrictions. Political meetings required prior authorization. Parties favoring a boycott of the 1995 presidential election were sometimes refused permission to hold gatherings. State-controlled television ignored their positions and activities, and pro-boycott newspapers were sometimes confiscated.

The private press in Algeria engaged in lively debate on social and economic policy, but remained completely shackled in its coverage of security-related events and alleged security force abuses. Newspapers whose coverage departed from the official communiqués on security developments risked confiscation of their print run, legal harassment and imprisonment of editors and journalists. While coverage of atrocities attributed to the Islamists was permitted, newspapers were able to allude to security force abuses only indirectly, such as by publishing interviews with human rights activists.

On September 3, an appeals court upheld the three-year suspended sentence of Chawki Amari, cartoonist for the daily *La Tribune*, for a satirical cartoon that "profaned" the Algerian flag. He had spent one month in pre-trial detention. *La Tribune* was suspended for six months, and its publisher and editor were given one-year suspended sentences.

Government harassment came on top of an assassination campaign against journalists that had much of the press corps living and working in mortal fear. In the twelve months beginning in October 1995, sixteen Algerian journalists and press workers were murdered. In most instances, no one claimed responsibility for the attacks, although Islamist groups were suspected in a large portion of them. *Al-Ansar*, a newsletter published in Stockholm that presented itself as a mouthpiece of the Armed Islamic Group (Groupe Islamiste Armé, GIA), reported that group had claimed responsibility for a February 11 car bomb near the Maison de la Presse that killed three journalists from the daily *Soir de l'Algérie*.

The FIS remained banned, its two principal leaders serving sentences in an unknown location and unable to communicate with the outside world. Lawyers for one of them, Ali Belhaj, had no access to their client even though new charges were pending against him.

FIS figures in exile continued to make statements during 1996 repudiating violence directed against civilians, claiming that armed groups it said were outside FIS control, such as the GIA, who were responsible for such attacks. In an interview published in the *Al-Hayat* (London) on August 8, Abdallah Anas, a FIS figure in exile, declared, "The FIS follows red lines and denounces anyone who crosses these lines. These lines include the blind violence that is expressed through the assassinations of women, children and foreigners and the bombing of public places." It was not possible to ascertain if and to what extent the FIS, with its legal status revoked and its leaders in prison, attempted to use its remaining influence on the ground to curtail the deliberate and methodical attacks on civilians that have given Algeria's Islamist groups such notoriety.

The Right to Monitor

Human rights monitoring is hampered by the high level of political violence and the climate of fear. Exposure and discussion of human rights abuses were impeded also by press censorship regarding "security" matters. Authorities confiscated three issues of *La Nation* in March when that opposition weekly tried to publish a series of articles on human rights in Algeria. The Ministry of Interior accused the paper of "publishing false and biased reports, bordering on justification for terrorism and criminal violence."

Local organizations and lawyers whose clients include human rights victims encountered a wall of silence when inquiring with the authorities about specific cases of "disappearances," torture and other abuses.

The semi-official Human Rights Monitoring Body (Observatoire National des Droits de l'Homme, ONDH) devoted most of its public efforts to condemning violations attributed to "terrorists." The ONDH's token coverage of abuses attributed to the authorities seemed designed to create an impression of even-handedness but did not reflect the gravity of the government's abusive record.

To Algeria's credit, the government permitted Amnesty International, the main international group attempting to carry out on-site investigations in Algeria, to conduct a mission in 1996, despite its record of strong criticism of the government's conduct. Prior approval was required, however, both for international human rights organizations and journalists to enter Algeria. That approval was often delayed and in some cases not granted.

The Role of the International Community

United Nations

U.N. Secretary-General Boutros Boutros-Ghali responded to a request from Algerian President Zeroual to dispatch observers for the November 1995 presidential election, as did the Arab League and the Organization of African Unity (OAU). The seven-person U.N. team was "intended to show support for the election process," the secretary-general's spokesperson told Human Rights Watch on November 10. This goal was laudable. But the price of the observers' presence should have been appropriate statements of concern regarding government control over the election process, including harassment and censorship of those who favored a boycott of the vote. In fact, the monitoring team was too small to be anything but symbolic and it never made its findings public. Its mere presence, however uncritical and ineffective, helped the Algerian government to exaggerate its claims about the credibility of the election.

France

French policy remained largely supportive of the Algerian government during 1996, despite sporadic flare-ups in relations between Algiers and its former colonizer. President Jacques Chirac and the government of Prime Minister Alain Juppé were appropriately firm in condemning atrocities attributed to Islamists, including several that took the lives of French citizens, but remained circumspect on government repression.

France, Algeria's largest trading partner and the Western country most concerned with developments in that country, has provided the equivalent of nearly US$1.2 billion per year in assistance, mostly in the form of government-backed credits. France has also played a key role behind the scenes in lobbying international financial institutions to re-schedule Algeria's $32 billion external debt on terms sought by Algiers. France is concerned with the impact at home of Algerian instability, given its large population of North African origin; the influx since 1993 of Algerians fleeing that country's repression, violence and economic decay; and a rash of bombing attacks in France in 1995 that were traced to the Algerian conflict.

Overall, French preoccupation with Algeria declined in 1996, due partly to the cessation of bombings in France and the receding prospect of an Islamist victory.

In October 1995, President Chirac had hinted at impatience with the sluggish pace toward political normalization in Algeria. For the first time he ventured that it would be "legitimate" for France to link its assistance levels to the pace of democratization in Algeria. But a month later, he praised the Algerian presidential election as having taken place "under the best democratic conditions." Paris appeared to disengage somewhat in the ensuing months, as Zeroual failed to use the good will he had won through the elections to broaden political participation. In early August, Foreign Minister Hervé de Charette conducted the first French ministerial visit to Algeria in three years, a visit intended to give a boost to relations between the two countries.

Earlier in the year, France had announced plans to reduce the low-interest credits it provided Algeria. The stated reason was budget tightening; at no time did French officials suggest that the cuts indicated disapproval of the government's record on human rights or its reluctance to widen the field for political participation. There were in fact no visible signs that France was raising these issues with Algiers.

United States

U.S. policy remained one of qualified support for the government, while insisting that American influence was limited. The U.S. backed rescheduling of Algeria's external debt but provided no bilateral economic or military assistance. Washington held no illusions about the Algerian government's human rights record, as the State Department's *Country Reports on Human Rights Practices for 1995* made clear.

Principal Deputy Assistant Secretary of State David Welch cautioned in October 1995 congressional testimony that "purely military means" could not end Algeria's conflict. Apparently encouraged by the high turnout in the 1995 presidential elections, President Clinton in December indicated in a letter to President Zeroual that the U.S. was prepared to support him as he took steps to broaden and accelerate the process of reconciliation. Assistant Secretary of State Robert H. Pelletreau later termed the policy "positive conditionality."

Visiting Algiers on March 20, Pelletreau told the press that the process of reconciliation should include "all Algerians who reject violence and terrorism and accept the rule of law, be they secular or Islamist." The government should engage in "a vigorous pursuit of a policy of political inclusion," and this should include "pragmatic elements of the FIS," Pelletreau told the Council on Foreign Relations in New York on May 8.

U.S. officials subsequently raised human rights concerns in public on several occasions, focusing on restrictions on press freedom and freedom for political parties to function. These interventions, although welcome, were notable for the human rights concerns they did not mention, namely those whose principal victims were suspected Islamists and their family members—summary executions, torture, and "disappearances"—and continued impunity for abuses by the security forces.

The chief U.S. concern was the establishment of a credible political process. Pelletreau told the Senate Foreign Relations Committee on April 12 that in order to judge whether the forthcoming legislative elections are "credible, open and democratic," the U.S. could "suggest the kinds of questions [Algeria] will need answers for: Will political parties be free to hold meetings and campaign? Will the Algerian press be free to print articles without intimidation by terrorists? Will the government continue to censure and seize newspapers?"

To these worthy criteria for "positive conditionality" the U.S. could have added demands for curtailing the sometimes deadly abuses that security forces commit with impunity against suspected Islamists and their relatives.

BAHRAIN

Human Rights Developments

The end of 1995 and beginning of 1996 saw a resumption of widespread street demonstrations and clashes with security forces, mainly over issues of political reform. Serious, extensive and recurrent human rights abuses continued in the form of arbitrary detention, abusive treatment of prisoners, and denial of due process rights. Virtually all of those detained in connection with the political unrest belonged to Bahrain's majority Shi'a community. However, the Sunni ruling Al Khalifa family's broad denial of basic civil and political rights, such as freedom of speech and assembly, affected all Bahraini citizens.

Bahrain's current political crisis goes back to the second half of 1994, when demonstrations protesting high unemployment

rates in Shi'a villages and neighborhoods intersected with a island-wide campaign for political reform, initially manifested in a series of petitions calling for restoration of the parliament that was disbanded by decree in 1975. As well as, freedom for political prisoners, and permission to return for hundreds of Bahrainis forcibly exiled or prevented from returning because of their political activities. Widespread street demonstrations erupted following the December 1994 arrest of Shaikh Ali Salman, a young preacher active in the unemployment and political reform campaigns. The government, without disclosing evidence or specifying any legal offense, summarily and forcibly exiled Salman and three other activist clerics in January 1995, in violation of international law and Bahrain's constitution.

On April 1, the government detained five prominent Shi'a community leaders, including Shaikh Abd al-Amir al-Jamri, the informal head of the main opposition grouping, the Bahrain Islamic Freedom Movement, and an elected member of the disbanded parliament. The five were held for between five and six months without charge and without access to legal counsel.

Jailhouse negotiations between the government and Shaikh al-Jamri and his colleagues produced an "understanding" that led to the release of hundreds of detainees beginning in mid-August 1995, signaling a period of relative calm. On September 26, a day after his own release, Shaikh al-Jamri reiterated that "[t]he parliament comes at the top of our [list of] demands," but that "dialogue between the opposition and the government" was continuing around demands for the release of all detainees and permission to return for those exiled. The government, however, publicly denied the existence of any agreement.

By late October 1995, new petitions were announced and the atmosphere again grew tense. Clashes erupted again in December 1995 and January 1996, following the late November Supreme Court affirmation of a death sentence in the case of a security force member murdered in March

1995. Shaikh al-Jamri and seven other community leaders were arrested on January 22. A Ministry of Interior official, referring to demonstrations and attacks on property as well as the deaths of about two dozen citizens and three security personnel, told Reuters that "[t]here is proof, evidence and documents supported by pictures which prove the group's involvement in the incidents and would be submitted to the legal authorities." As of October 1996, the prisoners were still being held without access to counsel, none had been formally charged with any offense, and no evidence had been disclosed. Al-Jamri was allowed a brief family visit for the first time in September 1996; over the course of 1996 several of his close relatives were also picked up for lengthy periods of interrogation and detention without charge.

On February 7, 1996, Ahmad al-Shamlan, a defense lawyer and longtime leftist critic of the government, became one of the very few Sunni opposition activists to be detained. His arrest followed the distribution to Agence France-Presse of a statement of the Popular Petition Committee demanding the reinstatement of the elected parliament. The same week the government banned a seminar organized by the Uruba Club, an elite cultural association, entitled "Democracy and Shura," in which al-Shamlan was to participate. Through the state-dominated media the government accused al-Shamlan of being a conduit for foreign funds in support of the protests. But when he was finally brought before a State Security Court panel in mid-April, his charge sheet dealt with an article he had written one year earlier, faxes found in his office from the Bahrain Freedom Movement in London, a record of a London phone call from Mansur al-Jamri inquiring about his jailed father and sister, and the statement of the Popular Petition Committee in his possession. The court, in an unusual move possibly related to al-Shamlan's high profile in the region and internationally, released him on bail and in May acquitted him of all charges.

An undetermined number of Bahrainis were detained in 1996 for authoring or possessing documents relating to the political demands of the opposition, and several journalists working for international agencies were called in for interrogation. Another figure associated with the Popular Petition Committee, Sa'id Abdallah Asbool, was detained without charge for one week in April 1996, during which time he was interrogated about contacts with a visiting BBC reporter. In May, a Bahraini taxi driver and an Omani resident married to a Bahraini, were detained and reportedly tortured under interrogation for accompanying a BBC television reporter. The Omani, Abd al-Jalil al-Usfur, was released after three months and deported; the Bahraini, Sayyid Hussain, is believed to be still in detention.

Numerous arrests and preemptive closings of mosques and other meeting places early in 1996 confined demonstrations and street protests to Shi'a towns and villages, which were heavily patrolled and frequently subject to nighttime raids by security forces. Large-scale street demonstrations for a time gave way to attacks, including some with small explosive and incendiary devices, against public installations, banks, luxury hotels, and shopping centers. There were also unclaimed arson attacks against restaurants and shops frequented by expatriate workers. In the most serious of these, in March, seven Bangladeshi workers were killed.

In early June, the government announced the discovery of a previously unknown organization it identified as Hizballah Bahrain-Military Wing, charging that the unrest of the previous eighteen months was part of an Iranian-inspired and financed plot to overthrow the government. The government's claim was received with skepticism, since no evidence was presented other than "confessions" obtained from detainees who had been held for weeks or months without access to lawyers.

The State Security Law, decreed in 1974 over the nearly unanimous objection of the elected National Assembly, allowed the Ministry of Interior to detain persons for up to three years without trial. At least 3,000 persons were arrested between December 1994 and October 1995, of whom about 800 were formally charged. According to Bahraini defense lawyers, the majority of these were tried before the State Security Court; some were charged under the penal code and tried in ordinary courts. Many of those not charged had been released by the end of 1995, but an unknown number continued to be held in detention. Large-scale and indiscriminate arrests resumed in January 1996.

Human Rights Watch, on the basis of interviews with persons who had been detained and with defense lawyers, identified a pattern in which warrantless arrests were carried out in night raids on homes of suspects involving some ten to fifteen armed members of the security forces. Community leaders and middle-aged professionals suspected of involvement in the petition campaigns, as well as young men suspected of organizing or participating in demonstrations or attacks on property, were seized from their homes in this manner, typically between midnight and 4 a.m. Young men, and often members of their families, were often beaten and their homes ransacked.

Bahraini defense lawyers told Human Rights Watch that persons charged with offenses were typically brought before the State Security Court months and often as much as a year after their arrest. In these cases, the accused got to see a lawyer only on the day they first appeared in court, and uncorroborated confessions were often the sole basis for conviction. Defense lawyers and former detainees told Human Rights Watch that beatings and other forms of physical abuse were commonly used to secure confessions and information. Defense lawyers also said that over the past year the confessions on which defendants were convicted became increasingly formulaic, using the same wording and phrasing.

There were no known instances of officials being held accountable for human rights abuses.

In March 1996, the government decreed that offenses specified in fourteen ad-ditional articles of the penal code, such as arson, use of explosives or firearms, and physical or verbal attacks on public officials, would henceforth be considered offenses punishable under the State Security Law. Between March and October, 156 persons were sentenced to prison by the State Security Court. The number of those held without charge at any one time in 1996 was estimated at between 1,000 and 2,000.

Article 134 of the penal code, one of the articles currently under the jurisdiction of the State Security Court, targeted acts of speech by making it a punishable offense to "reveal news or statements or false hearsay on the internal situation of the state, thus weakening the financial confidence of the state or undermining its posture." It further restricted freedom of assembly by making it a punishable offense to "attend without official permission a conference, meeting or public debate held outside, or participate in any form in its work, with the purpose of discussing the political, social and economic affairs of the State of Bahrain, such that it weakened the financial confidence of the state...."

The Right to Monitor

Bahrain had no locally-based human rights organizations. Two Bahraini groups based outside the country and made up of exiled and expatriate critics of the government—the Bahrain Human Rights Organization (BHRO) and the Committee for the Defense of Human Rights in Bahrain (CDHRB)—compiled information on detainees and other issues. The BHRO said its request to the Bahraini government for permission to operate inside the country was not answered.

The government of Bahrain denied repeated requests by Human Rights Watch and other international human rights organizations to conduct formal missions and to meet government officials in the country. A Human Rights Watch researcher did visit Bahrain informally in 1996, and found persons there eager to discuss human rights issues but at the same time extremely apprehensive about the consequences should their contact with Human Rights Watch become known. Responding to an article published by the researcher after the visit, Bahrain's ambassador to Washington wrote on October 30 that the article was "full of misinformation and false accusations," but did not identify these inaccuracies. He added that "terrorist actions are a direct threat to and violation of the basic human rights of the Bahraini people," and that "the government of Bahrain...will use all means available to it within the law to protect its citizens."

The Role of
the International Community

The Arab World
The government of Bahrain enjoyed the unreserved public support of Arab governments of the Persian Gulf, particularly in the forum of the Gulf Cooperation Council. Saudi Arabia in particular indicated support for the government with regard to the internal unrest. Prince Nayif, the Saudi minister of interior, said in November 1995 that, "Saudi Arabia will not hesitate at any time in responding to any request from Bahrain...and the security of Saudi Arabia and Bahrain together will be for the service of the Bahraini people." Prince Sultan, the Saudi minister of defense, told the BBC in March that, "We are prepared to stand forcefully by Bahrain if the need arises."

In February, a delegation of eight Kuwaiti parliamentarians attempted to visit Bahrain to petition Amir Isa to negotiate with the opposition, but they were turned back at the airport.

Among Arab governments outside the Gulf, notably Jordan and Egypt, Bahrain also found considerable support. Jordan was widely reported to have seconded security personnel to the Bahraini government.

United States
Bahrain was the operational headquarters for the U.S. Navy's Fifth Fleet, and some 3,000 U.S. military personnel and dependents were stationed there. The U.S. maintained complete public solidarity with the government of Bahrain on the latter's dismal record, with the sole exception of the Bahrain entry in the State Department's *Country Reports on Human Rights Practices for 1995.* That entry was reasonably comprehensive and candid, although it understated the extent to which people have been detained for exercising the right of free speech as distinguished from participation in demonstrations and clashes with the authorities. It asserted misleadingly that Shaikh al-Jamri had been accused of "a wide variety of security-related crimes"; in fact such accusations consisted of unattributed statements in the government-controlled press and reflected a highly expansive definition of "security-related."

The State Department report also gratuitously denigrated the human rights monitoring of the BHRO and the CDHRB by grouping them with the Bahrain Freedom Movement and the Islamic Front for the Liberation of Bahrain, which made no claim to being human rights organizations, and by dismissing them all as "viewed by many local observers as espousing a political, rather than a purely human rights, agenda." The entry further mischaracterized them as "small numbers of emigres living in self-imposed exile," thus downplaying the government's use of forcible exile to punish political dissidence. Rather than assessing directly their allegations of abuse, the report attacked the BHRO and the CDHRB by innuendo as having "reportedly received funding from sources hostile to the Al Khalifa regime."

The U.S. consistently skipped opportunities to criticize Bahrain's abusive record. Defense Secretary William Perry made several visits to Bahrain during 1996 but, as of October, had made no public comment on the human rights situation. On January 25, Assistant Secretary of State Robert Pelletreau said that unrest in Bahrain "is brought about by a fairly high level of unemployment and some unrest in Bahrain's Shi'a community. It is urged on and promoted by Iran, across the Persian Gulf.... [Bahrain's leaders] are dealing with it, in my view, in a responsible way that deserves our support." On May 7,

Pelletreau, at the United States Information Agency Foreign Press Center, reiterated that Bahrain's difficulties "are sometimes fanned by flames from Iran.... We believe that the government is taking steps to address this situation and that the government deserves the support of its neighbors and other friends as it tries to deal with an ongoing difficult problem." In early March, during a visit of Crown Prince Shaikh Hamad bin Isa to Washington, State Department spokesperson Nicholas Burns stated that human rights did not arise in Secretary of State Christopher's meeting with the Crown Prince, but that "[t]he issue has come up numerous times in our relationship with Bahrain through Ambassador David Ransom and others."

The U.S. accounted for US$700 million in arms deliveries to Bahrain in the 1988-1995 period, out of total deliveries of $800 million. The State Department congressional presentation for Fiscal Year 1997 estimated U.S. military sales to Bahrain at $160 million in Fiscal Year 1996 and $330 million in 1997. These military supplies were mainly for the use of the Bahrain Defense Forces, which was not acknowledged to have been involved in internal security operations. Expatriate residents of Bahrain told Human Rights Watch, however, that tear gas and other projectiles were fired from foreign-supplied helicopters into villages during clashes.

In late May 1996, Gen. John Shalikashvili, chair of the Joint Chiefs of Staff, visited Bahrain, where he said, "We support Bahrain's efforts to ensure its stability, and we continue to accuse Iran as a threat to the stability of the region." Two weeks later, following the purported confessions of alleged Iranian-backed coup plotters (see above), Bahrain released portions of a letter from President Clinton to the Amir which stated, "the U.S. fully supports Your government and sovereignty and safety of Bahrain's territories," and praised his expansion of an appointed Consultative Council as reaffirming "your government's commitment to economic and social development and political reconciliation." In September, Secretary

Perry returned to Bahrain to arrange for the basing of twenty-three additional U.S. Air Force F-16s for use in patrolling the southern Iraq "no-fly" zone. Former President George Bush also visited Bahrain in March, and publicly commended the authorities for their handling of the protests: "I salute the government of Bahrain for preserving order and for guaranteeing for every Bahraini citizen a secure environment."

EGYPT

Human Rights Developments

Human rights conditions continued to deteriorate in Egypt, the most populous country in the Arab world and recipient of the second largest annual U.S. aid package, after Israel. Restrictions on freedom of expression and association, and the use of military courts to prosecute nonviolent civilians, remained major issues in 1996. Security forces operated with impunity, and armed Islamist militants deliberately killed civilians, targeting in particular Egyptian Christians in southern villages and foreigners in Cairo. The emergency law, continuously in force since 1981, was scheduled to remain in effect until May 1997.

On November 23, 1995, the Supreme Military Court sentenced fifty-four prominent Muslim Brothers to prison terms ranging from three to five years with hard labor. They included former members of parliament, university professors, and others who had intended to run as independents in the November 29 parliamentary election. They had been charged with membership in a proscribed organization (the Muslim Brotherhood has been banned since 1954), but had not been shown either to have used or advocated violence. The proceedings did not meet international fair trial standards, including the right to appeal to a higher tribunal. The prosecution of these nonviolent Islamists was a blatant move by the state to disenfranchise members of the country's largest political opposition movement and thwart its participation in electoral politics.

The two-round election on November 29 and December 6, 1995, for 444 parliamentary seats, produced an overwhelming victory for President Hosni Mubarak's ruling National Democratic Party. But the results were clouded by violence, arbitrary arrests of supporters of opposition party and independent candidates, and massive irregularities at the polls, all of which were documented by Egyptian nongovernmental organizations (NGOs), which mounted an unprecedented election-monitoring effort. Twenty-six people lost their lives in the violence surrounding the first round of the voting, the Center for Human Rights Legal Aid (CHRLA) reported, including five in Kafr al-Sheikh when security forces used force to disperse citizens who protested vote rigging and other fraudulent practices.

In a letter published by the *Washington Post* on December 26, 1995, the Egyptian ambassador to the U.S., Ahmed Maher El Sayed, stated that "the elections were conducted freely" and that "no step backward has been taken." But Court of Cassation judges saw it differently; as of October 2, they had nullified the election results for seats in 200 constituencies in response to legal challenges from losing candidates, the Egyptian Organization for Human Rights (EOHR) reported.

The unfair election process spurred the formation of the Wasat (Center) party, whose founding members were, in large part, younger members of the Muslim Brotherhood. One of the party's founders, Abu al-'Ala Madi, said in January that the party endorsed "action through the peaceful, democratic approach" and were "convinced of the need for involvement, pluralism, and dialogue." In January, Madi submitted the party's application for legal status to the Party Affairs Committee, the government-appointed body that licenses political parties. It was widely believed that Madi's prominence as a leading force behind the new party was the reason for his arrest in April and his imprisonment until August, when he was acquitted by a military court (see below). In

May, the party's application for legal status was denied. The founders immediately filed an appeal, but told Human Rights Watch they did not expect the case to be heard before December 1996. Members of political groups were barred from engaging in political activity prior to obtaining a license; violators faced up to five years in prison if convicted, pursuant to December 1992 amendments to the 1977 Political Parties Law. The Party Affairs Committee had systematically denied licenses to new political groups since the law came into effect in 1977. "Since the law was issued in 1977, no single political party has been formed through the approval of the committee. Instead, a court decision has always been required to legitimize any political party," EOHR noted in a July 1993 report.

At the same time that peaceful Islamist activists were imprisoned or otherwise blocked from participation in politics, armed militants carried out deliberate and arbitrary killings of civilians. Egyptian Christians in southern Egypt, including children, bore the brunt of this violence. These killings were apparently carried out by members of the military wing of the Islamic Group but, as in similar killings in past years, there were no claims of responsibility following any of the incidents. On April 18, eighteen Greek tourists were killed outside a Cairo hotel by four gunmen. Two days later, the Islamic Group claimed responsibility, stating that Israeli tourists had been the intended targets "because they often stay in this hotel."

The state continued to execute suspected Islamist militants who were sentenced to death by military courts for "terrorism" offenses that included but were not limited to murder. Six men were executed on June 2, bringing the number of executions to fifty-four since the trials of civilians in military courts began in late 1992. In an apparent paradox, the government continued to prosecute Muslim Brothers in military courts for peaceful political association, while it tried some militant Islamists accused of violent offenses in the state security court, where civilian judges presided. The explanation that Egyptian lawyers have offered for this dual justice system is that authorities have resorted to military courts in cases where the evidence was too weak to withstand the scrutiny of civilian judges.

In April, thirteen more Muslim Brothers were arrested, including university professors, former members of parliament, elected officers of professional associations and university faculty clubs, and candidates for parliament in 1995. Some of them also were founders or supporters of the Wasat Party, such as Abu al-'Ala Madi. The proceedings began in the civilian judiciary, but on May 11 the case was transferred to the military court by presidential decree. The defendants were charged with "running, in violation of the law, an organization called the Muslim Brotherhood, the aim of which is to advocate undermining the constitution and the laws," and "recruiting new elements with the aim of inciting the masses against the present government." No evidence was presented during the trial that the defendants had engaged in violence or the planning of violence. On August 15, the court sentenced seven of the defendants to three years in prison, including Mahmoud 'Ali Abu Riyyah and former member of parliament Hassan Judah (both in their seventies and in poor health), issued a one-year suspended sentence to 'Abd al-Azim 'Abd al-Majid al-Maghribi (a bedridden merchant also in his seventies), and acquitted five, including Abu al-'Ala Madi and his Wasat party colleagues.

Prison conditions remained abysmal, particularly in newly opened high-security facilities where suspected Islamist militants were held in almost complete isolation from the outside world. EOHR documented the gross neglect, physical abuse and inadequate medical care suffered by 4,000 inmates at Fayyoum (opened in 1995), and by another 300 prisoners at Aqrab (opened in 1993), where a ban by the interior minister on visits by lawyers and family members had remained in effect since December 20, 1993, despite successive court rulings against such bans. Both prisons were controlled by State Security Investigation (SSI), the elite internal security arm of the Interior Ministry. On June 17, the commander of Aqrab, accompanied by thirty soldiers, carried out a search of the inmates' cells. When it was discovered that medical student Gamal Osman had a watch and pocket radio, he and the nineteen other inmates in his section "were ordered out of their cells, stripped...of all their clothes, and were flogged [on] their backs, feet and buttocks," EOHR reported in September. When a pen was found on Ali Naser in the search of another section of the prison the same day, he and his seventy-nine cellmates were similarly punished.

There continued to be no transparency in official investigations of suspicious deaths in SSI custody and, as a result, SSI torturers enjoyed impunity. The case of Islamist defense lawyer Abdel Harith Madani, who died in SSI custody in April 1994 presumably under torture, was all but forgotten. The head of the human rights unit in the Egyptian Foreign Ministry told Amnesty International (AI) delegates in November 1995 that the investigation of Madani's death was continuing, although AI noted that it was unable to obtain from the ministry "details as to the methods and procedures" used to investigate deaths in custody.

The government's extreme sensitivity about deaths in custody extended to cases involving the police. This was evidenced by the banning of a story in the July 14-20 issue of the weekly *Middle East Times* (Cairo) about a Cairo woman who learned on June 18 that her husband had been hospitalized after being tortured at a police station in Manshiyet Nasr. She reportedly visited him at 'Ain Shams hospital the next day, before he died from what doctors said was a brain hemorrhage. The article cited details of four other cases in the same week in which suspects had been brutalized at the same police station and suffered injuries. All four victims had filed complaints, but reportedly the police obstructed prosecutors' investigations. A few weeks after this story was banned, Ahmed Higazi, a suspected Islamist militant, died in custody at SSI headquarters in Cairo.

In a decision that generated international condemnation, the Court of Cassation on August 5 upheld the June 1995 ruling of the Cairo Court of Appeals that declared Cairo University professor Dr. Nasr Abu Zeid an apostate and, on this basis, ordered that he be separated from his Muslim wife, university professor Dr. Ibtihal Yunis. EOHR noted that the ruling was "the first of its kind in the modern history of Egypt's judiciary, where a man and his wife are separated against their will because of the religious views and interpretations expressed by one of them." One of the reasons that the decision generated apprehension in Egypt was because of the dangerous precedent that it set: Egypt's highest appeals court had affirmed the legal power of a civil court judge to declare a Muslim intellectual an apostate solely on the basis of his scholarly writings. Sheikh Yousef al-Badri, who took a lead in initiating the legal action against Abu Zeid in 1993, expressed satisfaction with the August 5 decision: "No one will even dare to think about harming Islam again...we have stopped an enemy of Islam from poking fun at our religion."

In yet another legal twist in this complex case, the Court of Urgent Cases in Giza ruled on September 25 in favor of a motion submitted by Dr. Abu Zeid's lawyers to suspend implementation of the appeal court's June 1995 order that the couple separate. Islamist lawyers responded with pledges to appeal the stay. The Giza court's decision left untouched the ruling that Dr. Abu Zeid was an apostate. Lawyers for the couple were preparing further legal challenges as this report went to press.

Another freedom of expression battle raged in 1996 as pro-government and opposition journalists united in efforts for the repeal of Law No. 93 of 1995, which mandated preventive detention and imprisonment for vaguely worded offenses such as "publishing false or biased rumors, news and statements or disconcerting propaganda" if such material "offends social peace, arouses panic amongst people, harms public interest, or shows contempt for state institutions or officials." Scores of journalists had been investigated and prosecuted under this law, particularly for defamation and slander. The much awaited replacement law, drafted in 1996, aroused additional criticism; it mandated prison terms of up to five years for "inciting hatred of the regime" and one year for publication of material that "insulted the president of the republic." On June 15, President Mubarak bowed to the mounting pressure and by decree removed the penalties specified in Law No. 93 from the penal code. The new press law, approved by parliament on June 18, accommodated many of the journalists' concerns but limited conditions under which new newspapers could be established and criminalized expression deemed insulting to the president.

The Right to Monitor
The Egyptian human rights movement was one of the most dynamic and sophisticated in the Arab world. Despite the increasing international recognition of Egyptian human rights organizations, the government continued to treat them with hostility and has denied official legal status to EOHR, the oldest independent rights groups in Egypt. In an interview with the *Middle East Times* on May 27, President Mubarak stated that rights groups "interfere in the internal affairs of the country....They are just defending terrorists and criminals. Do they defend the interests of the innocent man on the street who has been injured by violence?" Interior Minister Hassan el-Alfi, in an interview in *Akhbar al-Yom* (Cairo) on June 15, claimed that the groups "are used by many agencies to influence societies and peoples. They all work for political purposes which are no secret to anyone."

Indeed, SSI officers from Mr. el-Alfi's ministry harassed Egyptian human rights activists throughout the year and directly interfered with their organizations' work. In July, six SSI officers arrived after midnight at the home of one human rights worker and questioned him about a complaint that his group had sent to the minister of interior. Another activist was summoned to SSI's

Cairo headquarters earlier in the year and questioned for two hours by a senior officer about his organization's publications.

At least one long-established organization was forced to negotiate with SSI for permission to hold human rights training courses, and throughout 1996 it was prohibited from holding seminars and workshops in major Egyptian cities. Some of the local NGOs invited to training sessions were summoned by SSI and instructed not to attend. At one of these events, participants from fifty local NGOs were expected. The night before, according to the organization's director, "the place was surrounded by SSI guards, and an SSI officer told me at midnight, 'No way. We'll even prevent you by force.' He told the hotel manager to remove our posters."

SSI officers also singled out prominent Egyptians and pressured them to remain publicly silent about issues such as the Wasat Party and the clampdown on the Muslim Brotherhood. One was threatened by an officer who criticized an article that he had written in an Egyptian newspaper. In another incident, the person involved told us that he received a "friendly visit" from a high-ranking officer, who wanted to know what he had said in meetings with international human rights organizations and journalists. Fear prevented these people from publicly disclosing and protesting this intimidation, and inhibited others from coming forward with accounts of direct and indirect pressure.

The Role of
the International Community

United Nations
The annual report of the U.N. Committee against Torture, issued in July, included a summary of the results of the committee's confidential procedure on Egypt, a three-year inquiry that concluded in November 1994 and involved extensive contact between the committee and Egyptian officials. The committee's conclusion, which was adopted by consensus in May, was that "torture is systematically practiced by the security forces in Egypt, in particular by [SSI], since in spite of the denials of the Government, the allegations of torture submitted by reliable non-governmental organizations consistently indicate that reported cases of torture are seen to be habitual, widespread and deliberate in at least a considerable part of the country." The committee also found that "judicial remedies are often a slow process leading to the impunity of the perpetrators of torture," and noted "with concern that no investigation has ever been made and no legal action been brought against members of [SSI] since the entry into force of the Convention [against Torture and Other Cruel, Inhuman or Degrading Treatment or Punishment] for Egypt in June 1987." The committee noted that the Egyptian government "did not avail itself of the opportunity it had been offered to clarify the situation" by accepting a visit to Egypt by the committee members participating in the inquiry.

The committee reported the attempt by Egyptian authorities to prevent the public release of its findings, and quoted from an extraordinary letter it had received from the government, which stated that disclosure of the findings "might be interpreted as signifying support for terrorist groups and would encourage the latter to proceed with their terrorist schemes and to defend their criminal members who engage in acts of terrorism by resorting to false accusations of torture. In other words, it might ultimately be interpreted as signifying that the committee is indirectly encouraging terrorist groups not only in Egypt but worldwide."

United States
Egypt remained a key U.S. regional military ally and a reliable partner in the U.S.-led Arab-Israeli peace process. U.S. aid to Egypt included $1.3 billion from the Foreign Military Financing Program and $815 million in Economic Support Funds. As in past years, there was no evidence that the Clinton administration used the significant leverage that this aid provided to insist that the gov-

ernment take specific steps to improve its human rights performance. Instead, U.S. senior officials signaled in public remarks that Egypt's position as an ally was secure, reinforcing the long-standing impression that public criticism of Egypt's human rights record remained off-limits, with the sole exception of the accurate and damning assessments in the yearly State Department's *Country Reports on Human Rights Practices.*

The U.S.-Egyptian Partnership for Economic Growth and Development, an initiative launched in 1994 by Vice President Al Gore to support privatization of Egypt's economy, has as one of its goals the building of "mutually beneficial economic and commercial ties between the two countries." In a statement on June 12 to the International Relations Committee of the U.S. House of Representatives, Secretary Pelletreau lauded President Mubarak's "personal commitment to accelerate economic reform and liberalization," but was silent on political reform.

At a joint press conference with President Mubarak in Washington on July 30, President Clinton reaffirmed "the close partnership between the United States and Egypt." Secretary Pelletreau told the House Committee on International Relations on September 25 that during Mr. Mubarak's visit there was discussion of "the need for Egypt to maintain momentum in its creation of a business environment favorable to investment, including the implementation of policies to spur privatization, liberalize trade, develop a unified commercial code, create a dispute settlement process, and protect intellectual property rights." Regrettably, Secretary Pelletreau did not list human rights as a factor that also enhance the investment environment, nor was he able to report that torture and other abuses in Egypt had been on the agenda of the July discussions.

IRAN

Human Rights Developments

As international debate focused on how to influence Iran's foreign policy, with the U.S. adopting stronger sanctions and Europe pursuing a policy of "critical dialogue," human rights developments were influenced mainly by domestic concerns. Personal freedoms suffered, public executions increased, and advocates of reform within the framework of the Islamic revolution found a less tolerant climate in which to express their views.

The government announced the discovery of "spy rings" on several occasions. In January three "U.S. spies" and two "Iraqi spies" were charged with espionage in Kermanshah. Later in January six "U.S. and Israeli spies" were charged in Tehran. In February the government announced the arrest of six members of a "Qatari spy ring." In April, Information Minister Ali Fallahian announced the arrest of twenty-nine "Turkish spies" in western Azerbaijan province. In June, thirty-three members of an "enormous espionage organization," centered in Tehran and Orumieh and composed mainly of public employees, were arrested. The proceedings against these suspects, all of whom could face the death penalty, took place mostly in secret and failed to comply with international standards for a fair trial. The outcome of the proceedings was unknown as this report went to press.

The authorities took harsher measures against convicted criminals in 1996. After an absence of several years, public executions resumed with the hanging of two convicted murderers in the Tehran suburb of Narmak in January. They had each been given seventy-four lashes prior to being taken to the gallows. Reports of the execution of large numbers of convicted drug traffickers also resumed in the Iranian press after several years' absence.

On May 15 five young men whom the government claimed had been convicted of rape and murder were executed in Tabriz and their bodies driven through the streets hanging from construction cranes. These public executions brought to an end street protests that had occurred in Tabriz on an almost-daily basis following the removal of a popular candidate from the ballot for parliamentary elections (see below).

The first round of the election for the 270-member parliament, or *Majles,* took place on March 8. Arbitrary bans on candidates and political parties, and restrictions on freedom of expression and assembly for opposition candidates, greatly restricted the rights of citizens to participate in selecting their representatives. The government-appointed Council of Guardians vetoed some 44 percent of the 5,121 declared candidates. The twelve-person council, composed of senior clerical figures and religious jurists, tightly controlled access to the electoral process by assessing such matters as candidates' "practical adherence to Islam" and support for the principle of "rule by the pre-eminent religious jurist (*velayat-e faqih*)."

The constitution provides for the Majles to be elected directly by the people and for the Council of Guardians to play a supervisory role in the process. Many argued that by excluding candidates in a summary and arbitrary manner the council overstepped its constitutional powers. Its decisions to exclude candidates and to annul voting results in some cities were the most troubling aspects of the parliamentary elections and violated the right to political participation, which is upheld in international human rights treaties to which Iran is a State Party.

Fifteen supporters of the Freedom Movement, a banned but tolerated political party, presented themselves as candidates. Only four made it through preliminary vetting, three of whom were excluded before polling day. By that time the party had announced its intention to withdraw from the election, complaining that government restrictions made it impossible to communicate with the public. Other tolerated opposition parties, like the Iran Nation Party and the National Front, boycotted the elections.

The government's tolerance or support for violent religious zealots known as Parti-sans of the Party of God (Ansar-e Hezbollah) undermined the meaningful participation of parties from outside the closed circle of the clerical leadership in the elections. Hezbollahi-led mobs disrupted their attempts to hold press conferences, political rallies, and other public gatherings.

After the voting, the Council of Guardians summarily annulled the results in eight cities, including Iran's third largest, Isfahan. On April 6 the council accused some candidates of using antirevolutionary slogans, making illusory promises and vote-buying. It neither identified those candidates nor substantiated its claims. In other cities where first-round results were annulled, no reason was provided, suggesting that the Council of Guardians was unhappy with the election results, not the process.

On April 19 the election committee in Tabriz, a body reporting to the Council of Guardians, removed Muhammad Ali Chehregani's name from the ballot. His campaign had highlighted issues of cultural discrimination against the Azari minority. This summary measure prompted as many as 40,000 people to demonstrate in Tabriz. Security forces broke up the protest and detained more than 600 people, according to local press reports.

The government also stepped up attacks on the press. Newspapers that published critical commentary risked suspension and prosecution. In November 1995 the government lifted the ban on *Tous,* a Mashad daily supportive of radical clerics critical of President Rafsanjani. But editor Mohammed Sadegh Javadi-Hesseri was subsequently arrested and sentenced to six months imprisonment and twenty lashes for "defamatory" reporting on government policies. In January the press court sentenced Abolghassem Golbaf. publisher of the monthly *Gouzarish.* to three months in prison in a case brought by Agriculture Minister Issa Kalantari, in violation of the procedures for prosecutions before the press court. Neither of these sentences had been carried out as of November 1996.

On January 27 a Tehran press court

convicted *Gardoun* editor Abbas Maroufi of "publishing lies." For this offense he received a sentence of six months in prison and thirty lashes. There were many violations of fair trial procedures in the prosecution, including the introduction of new charges during the proceedings without new evidence and without giving defense lawyers time to prepare. Maroufi left the country without serving his sentence but has repeatedly stated his willingness to return if he will be permitted to continue to publish his magazine.

Minister of Culture and Islamic Guidance Mostafa Mir Salam wrote in the Tehran daily *Keyhan* on February 8, "the press does not understand its limits" and acts "without wisdom and common sense." More than 190 journalists wrote an open letter to President Rafsanjani to protest the minister's remarks and to criticize arbitrary attacks on press freedom. On March 14, *Bahman*, the Tehran newspaper that published this open letter, received a suspension order from the Press Advisory Board for its critical reporting. That ban was overturned by an appeals court in September.

In February the Ministry of Culture and Islamic Guidance announced that it would impose pre-publication censorship on all books, a unprecedented measure in Iran's modern history. Previous policy had left publishers with the obligation to abide by guidelines and subject to penalties if they violated them. The new policies prompted deputy minister Ahmad Masjed Jamei to resign, saying he would "not accept responsibility for them."

In July agents from the Intelligence Ministry raided the home of a German cultural attaché as he hosted a group of Iranian writers. The six writers in attendance, together with their spouses, were detained overnight. In September security agents raided the home of prominent writer Farhad Koushan, where a group of thirteen writers were holding an informal weekly gathering. The writers were released in the early morning hours after being warned to halt such meetings.

Hezbollahi-led mobs loyal to factions or individuals within the leadership (see above) harassed government critics of all kinds, burning property, beating individuals and disrupting gatherings with impunity. On May 12, a Hezbollahi mob prevented philosopher Abdol Karim Soroush from delivering a lecture at Amir Kabir Technical University. In an open letter to President Rafsanjani sparked by this incident Soroush noted that he had turned down all previous invitations to speak, and canceled his university classes "in the interests of the country," but had not gained anything from this approach. He added, "I have gradually lost my professional and personal security as the brazen have become more impudent." Hezbollahi militants attacked two Tehran cinemas showing the film *Indian Gift*, which they thought to be corrupt even though it had been approved by government censors. They assaulted audiences and vandalized the cinemas.

Hezbollahi mobs demonstrated in the streets of Tehran against women bicyclists in April, criticizing also President Rafsanjani's daughter Faezeh Hashemi, a leading vote-winner in the parliamentary elections, who had supported women's right to ride in public. The authorities ceded to Hezbollahi demands, limiting women to riding on segregated paths out of sight of men.

Restrictions on personal liberty had a harsh impact on women. In November 1995, the Basiji, the anti-vice branch of the security forces, announced that it had detained 86,000 suspects in the previous twelve-month period. Most of them were thought to have been women detained for violating the dress code, which required covering the hair and wearing a flowing somber-colored body garment. The new penal code, which went into effect on July 9, substituted fines and prison terms for the penalty of lashes for violators of the dress code. One positive development for women was the reform of the divorce law in November 1995, enabling women to obtain a divorce even if their husbands did not consent.

A contraction of basic liberties was

apparent in the treatment of religious minorities. For the first time since 1992, death sentences were imposed on followers of the persecuted Bahai faith. On January 2, a revolutionary court in Yazd sentenced Zabihullah Mahrami to death for apostasy. Mahrami had announced his conversion to Islam during the early days of the revolution in the hope of avoiding trouble for his family, but after arranging for his daughter to marry a Bahai in late 1995, the authorities conducted hearings to examine Mahrami's religious beliefs. Finding him an unrepentant Bahai believer, the court sentenced him to death. Kayvan Khalajabadi and Bahman Mithaqi, imprisoned since 1989 for taking part in Bahai activities, had their death sentences confirmed by the Supreme Court. All three remained in prison as this report went to press.

Members of Protestant Christian churches also continued to suffer persecution for their beliefs. Only two Protestant churches that conducted services in Farsi, the Assembly of God churches in Tehran and Rasht, remained open. The murder of three leading Protestant clergy in 1994 had a devastating impact on the Protestant community. In November 1995, church sources reported the detention of Reverend Harmik Torosian, an Assembly of God pastor in Shiraz.

Religious persecution was not confined to non-Muslims. Followers of Shi'a Muslim clerics who had expressed opposition to the interpretation of Islam promoted by the government remained in detention in Qom, the center of Shi'a learning. For example, at least eighteen followers of Grand Ayatollah Mohammad Shirazi had remained in detention without charge since November 1995.

"Anti-vice" raids by the security forces on private homes continued. One such operation in June, in a wealthy Tehran neighborhood, resulted in the fatal fall of a young man from an eighteenth-story window. Accounts differed as to whether he was pushed by the police or slipped while trying to escape.

The new penal code, reflecting a harsher approach to law enforcement, gave prominence to corporal punishments like lashing and amputations of fingers, hands, and toes. Although the previous code provided for such punishments, they were rarely imposed. The new code simplified procedures for imposing corporal punishments, prescribed them for a wider variety of crimes, and reduced judges' discretion to impose alternative sentences. Six repeat offenders convicted of theft had the fingers of their right hands amputated soon after the implementation in July of the new code, in prison and in the presence of other convicted thieves.

Many Iranian asylum seekers in Turkey were summarily returned to Iran by Turkish authorities without their claim for political asylum being assessed by Turkish authorities or the United Nations High Commissioner for Refugees (UNHCR). This long-established practice took place without any mechanisms in place for monitoring the fate of the asylum-seekers who had been forced to return to Iran. There were also cases of individual refugees whose claims had been recognized by the UNHCR, and who in a few cases had even been accepted for resettlement in third countries, being subjected by Turkey to refoulement to Iran. No information was available of the treatment of those returned by Iranian authorities.

The Right to Monitor

For the first time since 1991, the government agreed to permit the U.N. special representative on the human rights situation in Iran, Maurice Copithorne, to visit the country. His visit in February was preceded by visits by two rapporteurs of the U.N. Commission on Human Rights. The special rapporteur on religious intolerance visited in December 1995, and the special rapporteur on freedom of expression in January 1996. Also in January, the government for the first time permitted a fact-finding mission by Human Rights Watch, albeit under near constant undisguised surveillance. Authorities did not authorize visits by other international human rights groups.

This partial openness to international

monitoring was a welcome change from the obstructive attitude of recent years. However, the extension of invitations to international monitors was not matched by any relaxation of the prohibition of independent domestic monitoring. Iranians who made critical comments about the human rights situation risked harassment by the authorities or attack by Hezbollahi mobs. Under the new penal code, the crime of espionage was defined so broadly as to criminalize the passing of almost any type of information about country conditions to foreigners, potentially criminalizing the transmission of human rights information to international bodies, and in violation of international law guaranteeing the right to receive and impart information. U.N. Special Representative Copithorne remarked in his report to the commission that "even the concept of human rights is not well understood" by the Iranian government.

Human Rights Watch honored Tehran lawyer Shirin Ebadi as a human rights monitor in 1996, in recognition of her work for human rights and legal reform in Iran.

The Role of
the International Community

United Nations
In April the U.N. Commission on Human Rights passed a resolution strongly condemning Iran for wide-ranging violations and renewing the mandate of the special representative on the human rights situation in Iran. Finding no satisfactory Iranian response, some European countries dropped their effort to offer a more conciliatory resolution in return for an explicit pledge by Iran not to take any action to carry out the death sentence decreed against British author Salman Rushdie in 1989. In August the Subcommission on the Prevention of Discrimination and Protection of Minorities also passed a resolution condemning the government's involvement in the killing of dissidents in exile.

European Union
European governments and the European Parliament voiced frustration with the failure of their "critical dialogue" policy toward Iran to modify Iranian policy. Although human rights violations inside Iran were explicitly included in the European policy, they were rarely highlighted among the issues on the agenda.

In February the European Parliament adopted a resolution urging Tehran to give assurances it would not carry out the *fatwa* sentencing Salman Rushdie to death, and urged the E.U. to increase pressure on the Iranian authorities to issue such a declaration. In July, the European Parliament again raised the Rushdie case and urged the European Council of Ministers to review its "critical dialogue" policy if the Iranian government refused to make sufficient concessions in this regard.

At a meeting of European foreign ministers in March, Germany's Klaus Kinkel, a leading defender of the policy, told the press that "we are close to the red line." He said that the E.U. would continue to seek to moderate Iran's behavior through dialogue, "but not at any price." Dutch Foreign Minister Hans Van Mierlo was even more outspoken, while at the same time rejecting U.S. efforts to stiffen sanctions against Tehran. In August, Danish foreign minister Niels Helveg Petersen announced his government's withdrawal from the "critical dialogue," explaining, "I cannot point to one single improvement as a result of critical dialogue."

United States
The U.S. has no diplomatic relations with Iran and asserts that it is a pariah state. Iranian leaders, meanwhile, habitually refer to the United States as "the Great Satan", or as the leader of "global arrogance." In 1996, human rights conditions inside Iran played only a minor role in the competition between the Democratic administration and the Republican-controlled Congress to show who was toughest on that country's government. Alleged support for international terrorism led the list of reasons behind moves to pun-

ish Tehran, including adoption of a law imposing sanctions on non-U.S. companies that invest in that country.

U.S. pressure on governments, the private sector and multilateral bodies certainly hindered Tehran in its efforts to attract foreign capital and investment. However, the impact of the sanctions policy on human rights was difficult to gauge.

Assistant Secretary of State Robert H. Pelletreau, speaking on May 14 in Tampa, Florida, said, "We have deep objections to several of Iran's policies, including its support for terrorism, pursuit of weapons of mass destruction, support for Hamas and other violent groups seeking to derail the [Arab-Israeli] peace process, subversion of other governments, and a human rights record which is deservedly condemned by the international community."

U.S. officials, in public statements on Iran, occasionally mentioned human rights conditions but rarely highlighted them. The Iran chapter in the State Department's *Country Reports on Human Rights Practices for 1995*, while generally accurate, spoke in broad generalities and presented few revelations, reflecting the lack of engagement on human rights conditions in U.S. policy.

IRAQ AND IRAQI-KURDISTAN

Human Rights Developments

The Iraqi government continued to engage in a broad range of gross abuses that systematically deprived its citizens of their most basic human rights. As the U.N. sanctions regime entered its seventh year, Iraqi civilians continued to suffer and die from malnutrition and illness in what had become a public health crisis. In northern Iraq, which remained for most of 1996 outside Baghdad's direct control, the major Kurdish political parties and Iraqi forces engaged in violations of human rights law.

Human Rights Developments in Government-Controlled Iraq

The government sustained a climate of fear and repression through a broad array of human rights violations. Throughout 1996, persons involved in or suspected of opposition to the government, especially those who held positions of responsibility within the government and military, were targets of arbitrary arrest, "disappearance," torture, and extrajudicial execution. Several waves of arrests and executions involving dozens of military officers were reported in May, June, and July following what the government claimed were foiled or failed coup attempts. By the beginning of 1996, the U.N. Working Group on Enforced or Involuntary Disappearances had over 16,100 unresolved cases of Iraqi "disappearances," more than for any other U.N. member state. There were continued reports of executions of detainees, though such incidents were hard to verify. For example, the Tehran-based Supreme Council for the Islamic Revolution in Iraq (SCIRI), an Iraqi Shi`a opposition organization, reported that in mid-March the government executed 500 detainees held in Abu Ghraib prison located west of Baghdad for their alleged involvement in the March 1991 uprising against the Iraqi government. The government reportedly prevented relatives of those executed from holding public mourning ceremonies for their dead.

Fierce repression in the southern marshes continued as the government employed artillery and armored divisions in several attacks against villages there throughout the year. The government targeted this area in part because it was a base for small armed resistance groups and a refuge for army deserters. According to SCIRI, the government shelled villages indiscriminately and arbitrarily arrested hundreds of persons there.

Iraqi courts imposed penalties of amputation, branding, and death against persons convicted of theft, corruption, currency speculation, and military desertion. The Permanent Mission of Iraq to the U.N. stated in an August 23 letter sent to Human Rights

Watch that the government had repealed decrees imposing amputation and branding as penalties for the offense of military desertion. Human Rights Watch was unable to verify this claim or to determine whether such forms of punishment had in fact ceased, but noted that the penalties still applied to other categories of offenders.

The continued imposition of harsh U.N. sanctions contributed to a massive public health crisis marked by malnutrition and increasing levels of infant mortality. In response to Iraq's invasion of Kuwait in 1990, the Security Council, cognizant of the dependence of Iraq's economy on oil exports, passed resolutions blocking all Iraqi exports and freezing Iraqi assets abroad. It thereby severely constrained Iraq's ability to pay for imports of food, medical supplies, and other basic goods. These resolutions also prohibited all imports except essential humanitarian items.

Resolution 687 (1991) conditioned the lifting of this embargo on a determination by the Security Council that the Iraqi government had complied with demands made in that resolution, including the destruction of its chemical, biological, and nuclear weapons programs and the payment of reparations to Kuwait. The Security Council to date had not made such a determination.

In response to Iraq's worsening public health crisis, the Security Council passed resolutions authorizing a one-time sale of US$1.6 billion worth of oil provided that Iraq agreed to U.N. supervision of the distribution of supplies and the deduction of some 40 percent of the proceeds for U.N. expenses and war reparations. President Saddam Hussein rejected these conditions as infringements on Iraq's sovereignty, thereby putting this principle ahead of ensuring the most basic material needs of his people.

Resolution 986 (1995) offered basically the same conditions for permitting the annual sale of up to $4 billion worth of oil sales to enable Iraq to purchase humanitarian supplies. On May 20, 1996, the two sides signed a Memorandum of Understanding (MOU) on the terms of this resolution. However, at the time of this writing, implementation remained stalled.

The combined impact on the basic welfare of the civilian population of the sanctions and of the air attacks of the 1991 Gulf War was catastrophic. Chronic food shortages and skyrocketing food prices kept the population on a "semi-starvation diet," according to the World Health Organization, leading to increased incidence of diseases such as marasmus and kwashiorkor.

A 1995 report by the U.N. Food and Agriculture Organization (FAO) indicated that child mortality—defined as the rate of death among children under sixty months of age—had quintupled since 1990. Based on these results, two of the FAO report's authors estimated over 500,000 sanctions-related child fatalities between 1990 and 1995. According to a joint FAO-World Food Programme assessment mission conducted in 1995, four million Iraqis, most of them children and pregnant or nursing women, were at serious risk of malnutrition. Drinking-water and water-treatment systems, significantly damaged during the Gulf War, continued to operate at limited capacity due to the inability to import spare parts. Shortages of basic and specialized medical supplies led to sharp increases in infectious, parasitic, and water-borne diseases, according to a 1996 report by the independent, New York-based Center for Economic and Social Rights. Since September 1990, the Iraqi government maintained a food rationing system in areas under its control, which according to the 1995 FAO report met only an estimated one-third of caloric needs in 1996.

The U.S. mission to the U.N. contested the link between sanctions and the health and nutrition crisis, accusing Baghdad of allocating scarce resources to such projects as the construction of palaces. Human Rights Watch could not ascertain the resources at the government's disposal and the portion of those resources allocated to alleviating the humanitarian crisis.

Human Rights Watch believed that the United Nations was bound by customary norms of international humanitarian law.

Thus, its economic sanctions—the coercive means employed in pursuit of the objectives of resolution 687—must conform to these legal requirements.

Article 54 of Protocol I to the 1949 Geneva Conventions prohibits the use of starvation of civilians as a method of warfare. International law permits belligerents some latitude in prescribing conditions to ensure that shipments of food and medicine are not diverted from civilian to military uses by their adversaries. However, humanitarian deliveries cannot be blocked for motives other than preventing diversion, such as to punish a civilian population in retaliation for its government's actions.

While resolution 687 did not prohibit the import of basic necessities, it blocked Iraq's ability to generate the foreign exchange it needed to purchase adequate amounts of them and thereby contributed to the malnutrition and health-care crisis described above. Furthermore, while various U.N. agencies maintained relief operations in Iraq, these did not resolve the civilian population's food deficit.

Further Article 54 concerns arose when implementation of the oil-for-food deal was delayed in late August and early September despite significant progress by the Security Council and Iraq toward reaching an agreement on how supplies would be distributed and on mechanisms for preventing Iraqi diversion. Edward Gnehm of the U.S. mission to the U.N. stated on September 3 that the conditions for the implementation of the MOU no longer existed, voicing concern for the safety of U.N. personnel responsible for distribution of the relief supplies. But the ability of U.N. agencies such as the World Food Programme to distribute goods to civilians largely without interruption during the fighting in the north raised suspicion that the U.S. motive for delaying the MOU was to punish the Iraqis for the military incursion there.

Since then, U.S. concerns for observer safety apparently receded. Subsequently, however, Iraq reportedly withdrew from a prior committment to allow freedom of movement of observers, while the U.S. refused to discuss the oil pricing formula until this and other issues were resolved. At the time of this writing, with resolution 986 enacted, a MOU signed, and a detailed distribution plan accepted, the enormity of the suffering in Iraq underscored the responsibility of the Security Council and Iraq to resolve these issues and commence as rapidly as possible the oil sales that would permit humanitarian relief to reach the Iraqi people.

Human Rights Developments in Iraqi Kurdistan

Iraqi Kurdistan remained for most of the year under the control of the two main political parties, the Kurdistan Democratic Party (KDP), headed by Masoud Barzani, and the Patriotic Union of Kurdistan (PUK), led by Jalal Talabani, in their respective zones of influence. The Kurdish administration, established in 1991 after the Iraqi military's withdrawal from parts of Iraqi Kurdistan (see below), was increasingly hobbled by KDP-PUK rivalry. Both parties operated separate military forces, secret police forces, and detention centers. The PUK and the KDP committed a wide array of abuses, including the detention of suspected political opponents; torture and ill-treatment of detainees; and the failure to investigate—or even to acknowledge—such abuses adequately. In addition, the PUK and KDP were responsible for the extrajudicial execution of dissident political activists.

On January 11, PUK troops reportedly ambushed a motorcade of leaders of the Labor Party for the Independence of Kurdistan, a small pro-independence Kurdish party, near Arbil. Twenty persons died in this attack, including Muhammad Amin al-Hallaq, a well-known activist. On June 16, thirty inhabitants of the village of Kelkin died in a KDP attack on villages inhabited by members of the Sourchi tribe, according to the Iraqi Kurdish Tribes Society, a London-based organization affiliated with the Sourchis. The society stated that the KDP killed tribal chief Hussein Agha after capturing him alive. The KDP disputed these casualty figures as too high and stated that the fighting had erupted after a member of the Sourchi tribe suspected of spying for the PUK had resisted KDP efforts to arrest him.

In late August, Iraqi ground forces and artillery units intervened on behalf of the KDP after KDP-PUK fighting broke out earlier that month, and in the process helped the KDP recapture Arbil, the regional capital. Although the Iraqi army left Arbil by September 2, Iraqi secret police continued to operate there. This renewed presence was of particular concern to members of many Iraqi opposition groups who had flocked to Iraqi Kurdistan in order to carry out their political activities outside of Baghdad's zone of influence. According to the Iraqi National Congress (INC), an umbrella organization for a number of Iraqi opposition parties, advancing Iraqi forces summarily executed ninety-six captured INC military personnel in Qushtapa, south of Arbil, on September 1 and later executed nineteen INC officers at its military headquarters in Arbil. After the capture of Arbil, there were reports of arrests, detentions, and executions of opponents of the Iraqi government and of the KDP. The Iraqi National Turkoman Party released the names of thirty-six of its members it said had been detained by the Iraqi secret police; it also reported that several of these detainees had been executed on September 3. The Islamic Action Organization said that Iraqi forces detained and later executed forty of its members. Various opposition groups reported that members detained by the Iraqi army and secret police were transported to Mosul and Kirkuk, cities that remained under Baghdad's control.

The PUK-KDP fighting and the intervention of the Iraqi army caused a significant displacement of civilians. According to the United Nations High Commissioner for Refugees, 50,000 refugees were camped on the Iranian side of the Iran-Iraq border by mid-September; Iranian officials estimated another 100,000 to 150,000 persons were internally displaced on the Iraqi side. Fighting near the Seiran-Band refugee camp between the KDP-Iraqi forces and PUK-Iranian forces on September 18 led to the deaths of up to fourteen refugees and the wounding of forty-seven others. These events aggravated Iraqi Kurdistan's chronic humanitarian crisis. According to the U.N. Inter-Agency Humanitarian Programme, approximately 650,000 persons, or around one-sixth of the population, were dependent on some form of humanitarian assistance. The local population faced not only the U.N. sanctions regime, but also an embargo from government-controlled Iraq during most of the year.

The Right to Monitor

Given the tight controls on free expression and the pervasive presence of Iraqi secret police, no independent human rights organizations functioned in government-controlled Iraq. The government repeatedly refused to grant a visa to Max van der Stoel, the U.N. special rapporteur on Iraq. Monitoring human rights conditions through contact with persons inside Iraq posed significant dangers to correspondents there. Iraq continued to reject the recommendation of the U.N. Commission on Human Rights to allow for the stationing of human rights monitors on its territory.

The state-controlled Iraqi press did not report on human rights violations. While the government often granted visas to foreign journalists wishing to cover the effects of the sanctions, the climate of fear and the presence of government-appointed minders prevented reporters from gathering much information on other human rights issues.

Prior to the KDP takeover in August, human rights groups in Iraqi Kurdistan operated openly, though not without risk of detention or other harassment by the KDP, PUK, or Iraq. After the Iraqi intervention and the increased presence of Iraqi secret police in the area, those human rights monitors who did not flee adopted a lower profile, although, in contrast to the situation in government-controlled Iraq, they were able to function to some extent.

The Role of
the International Community

United Nations
The Security Council continued to implement a series of resolutions aimed, among other things, at disabling Iraq's capacity for the manufacture, deployment, and use of certain weapons of mass destruction. (On the humanitarian effect of the U.N. sanctions, see above.) The U.N. Special Commission (UNSCOM) charged with the on-site inspection and destruction of Iraq's biological, chemical, and missile capacities oversaw in May and June the destruction of the al-Hakam plant near Baghdad, which U.N. officials stated could produce biological weapons. The Commission on Human Rights had since 1991 provided for a special rapporteur on Iraq. Chief among the commission's recommendations was the stationing of human rights monitors in Iraq, a call that went unheeded.

The U.N. Inter-Agency Humanitarian Programme, in coordination with the Iraqi government, maintained a relief effort to mitigate the impact of the sanctions on the Iraqi people. The operation was coordinated by the U.N. Department of Humanitarian Affairs and is implemented by U.N. agencies and some sixty international nongovernmental organizations (NGOs). This program provided over $1.2 billion in humanitarian relief in the five years ending in April 1996.

United States
In 1991, in the aftermath of Baghdad's harsh suppression of rebellions in southern and northern Iraq, the U.S., in conjunction with the U.K. and France, established a "safe haven" in northern Iraqi Kurdistan and "no-fly" zones in the north and south of Iraq, claiming authority from Security Council Resolution 688. These resulted in the withdrawal of the Iraqi army from much of Iraqi Kurdistan, which led to an improvement in the human rights situation there. The "no-fly" zones shielded the de facto Kurdish self-rule region and inhabitants of the south from Iraqi air strikes, though they did not prevent ground attacks in the north by neighboring Iran and Turkey or Turkish air attacks against suspected Turkish Kurdish rebel bases in northern Iraq.

Statements by U.S. officials emphasized that human rights were not among U.S. strategic interests in the region. In a television interview on September 17, Secretary of Defense William Perry explained that while the U.S. maintained a "humanitarian interest" in the Kurds of northern Iraq, its "vital interests" lay in the Arabian Gulf's oil fields. Similarly, Assistant Secretary of State Robert H. Pelletreau told the House Committee on International Relations on September 25 that U.S. efforts were focused on minimizing Iraq's threat to the U.S.'s regional allies through a strategy of containment, and that a "strong U.N. sanctions regime" was a part of this strategy.

The U.S. response to tensions in northern Iraq in mid-1996 reflected this priority. After the Iraqi army's actions in Iraqi Kurdistan in August and September, the U.S. response on the ground was to launch missiles against military installations in southern Iraq and to expand the southern "no-fly" zone. This move, while perhaps reassuring to U.S. allies in the Gulf, was of little direct benefit to the population at immediate risk from the military operation in the north of the country. To its credit, the U.S. agreed in September to evacuate and provide asylum to Iraqis employed by the Office of Foreign Disaster Assistance and other U.S. government agencies in northern Iraq, and later did the same for members of CIA-supported opposition groups active there. But, by early November, Washington had not agreed to evacuate or protect persons working for U.S. or other NGOs.

The U.S. continued to criticize publicly Iraq's human rights record. However, it did not give a high priority in its efforts at the U.N. to the stationing of human rights monitors there.

ISRAELI-OCCUPIED WEST BANK AND GAZA STRIP

Human Rights Developments

This section covers only developments in the West Bank and Gaza Strip. The conflict in southern Lebanon and northern Israel is discussed in the Middle East overview section.

As suicide bombings, a change of government in Israel and political disagreements stalled implementation of the Oslo peace accords, human rights were again subordinated to political objectives in the West Bank and Gaza Strip.

Between February 25 and March 4, a series of four suicide bombings in Israel caused fifty-eight deaths, most of them of civilians. Responsibility for the attacks was claimed by the militant Islamic Resistance Movement (Hamas) and Islamic Jihad. The government responded by imposing the strictest "closure"—the sealing of the West Bank and Gaza Strip—in the history of the occupation. Since late March 1993, the West Bank and Gaza had been under a general closure that prevented Palestinians without Israeli-issued permits from traveling into Israel or Israeli-occupied East Jerusalem, including for transit between the occupied territories. The army regularly tightened this closure by restricting the movement even of those Palestinians with valid permits. In an unprecedented step following the four suicide bombings, the Israeli army also blocked internal movement in the West Bank for ten days, effectively placing Palestinian residents under town arrest.

A humanitarian crisis ensued as Israel virtually halted the entry of food, medical, and relief supplies into the West Bank and Gaza. Personnel, patients, and ambulances were prevented from reaching health-care facilities, leading to at least nine probably avoidable deaths during the first ten days of the closure. The army also placed entire villages and camps under twenty-four hour curfew, arrested relatives of bombing suspects, including minors, and sealed and demolished the homes of nine bombing suspects, leaving innocent family members homeless. These measures appeared to be aimed at punishing the Palestinian population more than at preventing specific acts of violence. In their scale and indiscriminate nature, these measures amounted to collective punishment, which is proscribed under international law.

This intensified closure was gradually eased in April and May, but the general closure of the West Bank and Gaza, in place since late March 1993, continued. In addition to its adverse impact on health care, the general closure prevented regular access to schools and universities for hundreds of Palestinian students who were denied permits, often arbitrarily. By mid-September, no Gaza students had received permits to transit Israel in order to attend West Bank universities.

Onerous restrictions on the movement of goods, which Israel said were necessary for security reasons, further impoverished Palestinians. Israel also further reduced the number of Palestinians permitted to work inside Israel, although Israel had suppressed the local economy throughout the occupation, rendering Palestinians heavily dependent upon jobs inside Israel. These restrictions made it difficult or impossible for Palestinians to meet their basic needs, and violated Israel's obligation under the laws of occupation to ensure the basic welfare of the population.

Binyamin Netanyahu, the leader of the Likud party, was elected prime minister on May 29. During the ensuing months, the peace process came to a virtual halt and tension between the Palestinian Authority (PA) and Israel mounted. Partial redeployment from Hebron, the last major Palestinian city under direct Israeli military control, was delayed further as the Israeli government insisted on modifications to the original agreement. Israel continued to confiscate land in the occupied territories to expand settlements and build bypass roads for settlers. In addition, it demolished dozens of Palestinian homes, as well as a center that provided services to the handicapped in East Jerusalem, on the grounds that they had been built without difficult-to-obtain permits. In August, the cabinet formally lifted a moratorium on the construction and expansion of Israeli settlements in the occupied territories.

Against this background, Prime Minister Netanyahu decided, on September 25, to open a new entrance to a controversial ancient tunnel for use by tourists near Muslim and Jewish holy shrines in Jerusalem. This decision triggered protests throughout the West Bank and Gaza and violent clashes soon erupted, involving, in some cases, Palestinian police and armed civilians exchanging fire with Israeli soldiers. In other cases, such as an incident that took place in Jerusalem's Al-Aqsa Mosque compound on September 27, Israeli soldiers fired rubber bullets and live ammunition at Palestinians armed with stones and bottles. In three days, over 1,300 Palestinians were injured, and at least sixty-two Palestinians and fifteen Israeli soldiers died. Once again, the Israeli army placed residents of the West Bank under town arrest and imposed a total closure, impeding access to medical supplies, medical treatment, and food.

During the first eight months of the year, prior to the September 1996 clashes, six Palestinian civilians had been killed by Israeli security forces.

Following the 1995 "Oslo II" Agreement, Israel released about 1,000 Palestinian prisoners but, in areas that remained under its control, continued cracking down on suspected Islamists and opponents of the peace accords, arresting an estimated 1,400 more Palestinians on security-related grounds. These roundups, which included many arbitrary arrests, began in late December 1995, just prior to Israeli redeployment from major West Bank cities and population centers, and intensified following the suicide bombings in February and March.

On September 18, according to official Israeli figures, 2,335 Palestinians were serving sentences in Israel for security-related offenses, and an additional 677 were undergoing interrogation or awaiting trial. Another 294 Palestinians were being held in administrative detention, without charge or trial. Ahmed Qatamesh, the longest-held administrative detainee at the time, had completed his fourth year in detention without charge. In addition, 148 residents of other Arab countries, nearly two dozen of whom had already completed their sentences, remained in Israeli detention.

Throughout the year, the Israeli General Security Service (GSS) continued to subject Palestinian detainees to torture and ill-treatment during interrogation. The government renewed, at regular intervals, the authorization to use harsher methods of interrogation in "exceptional" cases. These methods were not made public but, according to extensive documentation by human rights groups, they included violent shaking, which had caused at least one death in 1995, abusive body positioning, beating, hooding, and sleep deprivation. In January, the Labor government introduced legislation which, while purportedly outlawing the use of torture, authorized the use of "pressure" against suspects. This draft law was expected to codify the government-appointed Landau Commission's approval, in 1987, of the use of "moderate physical pressure" which, in practice, amounted to sanctioning torture and ill-treatment. It had not been brought to a vote in the Knesset by the time this report went to press.

Prior to redeployment from parts of the occupied territories in 1994 and 1995, Israel transferred thousands of prisoners and detainees to facilities inside Israel. This violated Article 76 of the Fourth Geneva Convention, which requires that protected persons be held in the territories under occupation. The detention of Palestinians inside Israel impeded regular access to them by West Bank and Gaza lawyers, especially during closures. This policy also prevented regular family visits during closures, in violation of Article 116 of the Fourth Geneva Convention.

In July, the daily *Yediot Ahronot* (Tel Aviv) published an interview with Ehud Yatom, a former senior official in the GSS, in which he admitted to murdering two Palestinian bus hijackers in 1984 by crushing their heads with a large stone. GSS foul play had always been suspected in the case, since a newspaper had run photos of the Palestinians being taken alive from the bus, but details of an official inquiry were never made public. Despite Yatom's reported confession to these extrajudicial executions, the government initiated no action against Yatom or other senior officials who had been at the scene. Yatom later denied having committed the murders, reportedly after being reprimanded by the GSS for holding an unauthorized interview with the press.

The Palestinian Authority (PA)

The human rights situation in the areas of the West Bank and Gaza Strip that were under Palestinian self-rule deteriorated steadily during the year. Intolerant of internal opposition to its policies and under intense pressure from Israel and the United States to "combat terrorism," the PA conducted mass and often arbitrary arrests of suspected militants and opponents of the peace process. In the aftermath of the February-March suicide bombings, an estimated 1,000 to 1,500 people were rounded up, often arbitrarily, and several hundred remained in detention by October. Most of those detained were never charged with a criminal offense or put on trial.

Torture and ill-treatment by security forces occurred regularly during interrogation and led to at least one death: twenty-six-year-old Mahmoud Jumayal, who died in Nablus on July 30 as a result of severe beating and burning. Detainees who did not undergo interrogation, however, were not generally ill-treated.

The number of security agencies grew to at least eleven, but their respective duties seemed ill-defined or overlapping. Competition among the agencies, which appeared accountable to no one but Palestinian Authority President Yasir Arafat, encouraged abusive conduct. The police and security forces also lacked training and were implicated in dozens of beatings and unlawful shootings, including at least six "accidental killings." Many of the security agencies operated their own detention facilities, some of them in secret locations; thus, family members, lawyers, and human rights activists could not obtain prompt and reliable information about the whereabouts of detainees.

Security forces routinely beat and dispersed demonstrators demanding the release from Palestinian custody of uncharged detainees. On March 29, Palestinian security forces raided the campus of an-Najah University in Nablus, where students were protesting the large-scale arrests by both the PA and Israel. Security forces fired their weapons in the air, beat students with clubs, and used tear gas, injuring twelve students. During a massive demonstration in Tulkarm on August 2, following the death in detention of Mahmoud Jumayal, the police opened fire on demonstrators, killing one and injuring several others.

On January 20, an estimated 75 percent of eligible voters turned out to elect a president and an eighty-eight member legislative council. Local and international monitors characterized the rather rushed elections as generally free and fair, but identified violations. During the electoral campaign, both Israeli and Palestinian authorities sought to silence opponents of the elections and the peace accords through arrests, intimidation, and detention of some candidates and their supporters. The PA also denied candidates equal access to the media it controlled. In East Jerusalem, Israeli forces prevented candidates from campaigning in the city, and later created an intimidating atmosphere by filming voters and impeding some residents and Palestinian election observers from reaching polling sites.

The Palestinian legislative council, whose inaugural session was held on March

7, emerged as the primary forum for independent debate within Palestinian society, on issues such as human rights and accountability. The council passed several resolutions calling for the release of detainees held without charge, raised concerns about the use of torture, and challenged President Arafat's attempts to impose his will on the council. These exchanges were rarely reported in the Palestinian press, however, and the PA only occasionally responded to the council's demands or questions.

Although there was no formal censorship, Palestinian newspapers practiced self-censorship and rarely printed anything that could be construed as critical of the PA—particularly of President Arafat or his security policies. The PA had sent a clear warning against criticism when its forces detained *Al-Quds* (Jerusalem) editor Maher Alami, who had refused PA orders to publish an article on the front page of the Christmas day 1995 issue about President Arafat's meeting with the Greek Orthodox Patriarch. Numerous journalists were detained, usually briefly, and at times beaten. For example, in April Associated Press photographer Khaled Zghari was beaten until he lost consciousness after photographing a demonstration demanding the release of Hamas prisoners in the West Bank.

The Palestinian State Security Courts, established in February 1995, continued to exercise jurisdiction over both security and criminal matters. By October 1996, the courts had sentenced over fifty people in trials that violated basic due process guarantees. Trials were held at night and often lasted only minutes, and defendants did not have the right to legal counsel of their choice or the right of appeal.

The Right to Monitor

Although Palestinian groups monitoring human rights in the West Bank and Gaza came under pressure from the PA, none was closed or prevented from carrying out its activities. While authorities usually refused official visits by human rights organizations to detention facilities and detainees, they often permitted visits by lawyers and human rights activists in their individual capacity. On September 1, the International Committee of the Red Cross (ICRC) and the PA signed an agreement granting the ICRC regular access to all detention facilities and detainees in the self-rule areas. A similar agreement signed in 1994 had not been implemented.

The PA continued its past practice of targeting specific activists for harassment and short-term arrests, creating a climate of intimidation and fear. Dr. Eyad Sarraj, commissioner-general of the quasi-official Palestinian Independent Commission for Citizens Rights, was detained twice in 1996, after having been arrested and released in December 1995. He was arrested for eight days in May, after criticizing the PA's human rights practices in a *New York Times* interview. He was rearrested on June 10 and detained for seventeen days on trumped-up charges of drug possession. During his detention, Sarraj was denied access to his lawyer and subjected to physical ill-treatment on one occasion.

Mohammed Dahman, director of the Addameer Prisoner Support Association, was arrested on August 12 and detained for fifteen days. He was brought before the State Security Court and charged with publishing false information after issuing a press release raising questions about the death of a Palestinian detainee.

In Israel, the ongoing closure prevented West Bank and Gaza lawyers and rights groups from reaching prisons inside Israel. The closure also prevented Palestinian journalists, even those accredited by Israel, from entering Israel and East Jerusalem. For several weeks following the closure imposed in February, Israeli authorities barred not only Palestinians but also most non-Israeli and Israeli civilians from entering and leaving the Gaza Strip, preventing local and international relief and human rights groups from assessing the crisis and providing assistance. Immediately following the closure imposed after the violent clashes of September, most non-Israeli and Israeli civilians, including journalists but not settlers, were again barred from entering the West Bank and Gaza.

On February 4, 1996, Israel imposed a six-month administrative detention order on Sha'wan Jabarin, fieldwork coordinator at the Ramallah-based human rights organization Al-Haq. Jabarin had been administratively detained on five previous occasions, and had already spent almost thirty months in detention without charge or trial. His administrative detention order was renewed for another six months on July 27. Riyadh Za'aquiq, who worked for Defence for Children International in Hebron, was placed under administrative detention for six months on June 17. On August 19, Israeli authorities detained Bashar Tarabieh, a consultant for Human Rights Watch, while he was on vacation in his native Golan Heights. Tarabieh spent a week under interrogation in an Israeli jail, where he was subjected to hooding, painful shackling in a chair and sleep deprivation. He was released without charge. Al-Haq researcher Riziq Shuqair was shot and injured by Israeli soldiers while conducting field work during the September clashes in Ramallah.

The Role of
the International Community

The United Nations continued to monitor human rights through its Special Rapporteur on the Occupied Arab Territories Including Palestine.

European Union

European governments provided economic assistance both to Israel and the PA, through the European Union (E.U.), the World Bank-administered multilateral aid program, and bilateral agreements. The E.U. was the largest single donor to the PA, with US$404 million in assistance between 1993 and 1996 and a commitment to provide an additional $63 million annually until 1998. On October 1, the European Council of Ministers authorized the European Commission to negotiate an interim agreement on trade and cooperation with the PA. Both the E.U., through a

US$11.25 million program in 1996 for the promotion of human rights, democracy and civil society, and individual European governments actively funded and provided training to the Palestinian police and were involved in institution-building projects. The E.U. sent 300 election observers to the West Bank and Gaza for the January election and coordinated the international election observation operation.

Despite this leverage, however, European countries appeared fearful of disrupting the peace process and did not act determinedly to stem abuses, particularly when committed by the Palestinian security forces who they helped fund and train. European governments and the E.U. did privately condemn human rights violations by the PA throughout the year, but generally shied away from public pronouncements. Norway, among others, publicly condemned abuses in high-profile cases such as the arrest of Sarraj and the death of Jumayal (see above).

With regard to Israeli violations, European governments signaled the harm inflicted on the Palestinian population by the Israeli closure and raised this issue at the Washington follow-up meeting to the Sharm al-Sheikh conference.

Following the September clashes, the E.U. General Affairs Council issued a strong declaration urging both sides to "avoid resorting to disproportionate force," and reaffirmed the applicability of the Fourth Geneva Convention to East Jerusalem and other occupied territories. When asked by the European Parliament if the council was considering the possibility of suspending an E.U.-Israel Association Agreement, which is explicitly conditioned on respect for human rights, the council responded that its declaration was "quite explicit about what we [the E.U.] expect from Israel." As an immediate step, the European Parliament suspended $6.8 million in direct financial assistance to Israel, charging that its actions were jeopardizing the peace process.

United States

The United States, despite its stated goal of

promoting human rights and respect for the rule of law in the Middle East, and the detailed documentation of both Israeli and PA abuses in the State Department's *Country Reports on Human Rights Practices for 1995*, largely ignored human rights protection in its public dealings with Israel and the PA.

Israel remained the largest recipient of U.S. bilateral assistance, with over $3 billion in economic and military assistance, $50 million in counterterrorism assistance and nearly $2 billion in available loan guarantees in 1996. Yet, except for the section on Israel in the *Country Reports on Human Rights*, the U.S. maintained a public silence in the face of violations. On March 5, in response to a question about whether the United States had given Israel a blank check in responding to the four deadly suicide bombings, Secretary of State Warren Christopher said, "They're going to be taking firm action. Those will be the decisions of Israel." This statement, like many others by U.S. officials, ignored clear evidence that Israel had repeatedly carried out arbitrary arrests and tortured suspects.

The Clinton administration appeared concerned that any public criticism of then-Prime Minister Shimon Peres might jeopardize his chances of winning the upcoming Israeli elections. The U.S. did not publicly criticize the strict closure imposed in February, in spite of its tragic humanitarian consequences. However, the U.S. did, according to State Department officials, privately encourage Israel to implement specific measures aimed at mitigating the impact of the closure—particularly by facilitating the entry of food, medicines, and building materials into Gaza.

Both Israel and the U.S. repeatedly urged President Arafat and the PA to do more to prevent "terrorism." It was only after the PA engaged in repeated waves of often arbitrary arrests and torture of detainees that both governments praised President Arafat for showing determination in the fight against "terrorism." The implicit message sent by the U.S. in 1996—to both Israel and the PA—was that abuses carried out in the

name of security were justifiable and would not be publicly criticized. In spite of continuing evidence of extensive due process violations in the State Security Courts, no U.S. official retracted Vice-President Al Gore's praise of these courts in 1995. But following the repeated arrests of human rights activist Dr. Eyad Sarraj, for example, the U.S. consul general in Jerusalem met twice with President Arafat to convey U.S. concerns and urge Sarraj's release, and an officer from the U.S. embassy in Tel Aviv met with Sarraj in prison.

During the violent clashes over the Jerusalem tunnel in September, the U.S. abruptly withdrew support, for a mildly-worded U.N. Security Council resolution calling for "the immediate cessation and reversal of all acts which have resulted in the aggravation of the situation" and "for the safety and protection of Palestinian civilians." The resolution was passed by fourteen votes to zero, with the U.S. abstaining.

The U.S., a major participant in the international donor effort in the West Bank and Gaza, had obligated $225 million in assistance managed by the U.S. Agency for International Development between September 1993 and September 1996, more than half of which had been disbursed by the end of Fiscal Year 1996. Many of these programs were aimed at democratization, institution-building, and ensuring free elections. The U.S. also provided the PA about $13 million in police and medical assistance.

At the international level, the March 12 "anti-terrorism" summit convened in Sharm al-Sheikh, Egypt represented a lost opportunity: the statement issued at the end of the conference focused on preventing "terrorism" without reference to the human rights standards that have been so frequently trampled in pursuing that goal.

SAUDI ARABIA

Human Rights Developments

The Saudi government, an absolute monarchy, continued to violate a broad array of internationally recognized civil and political rights. It allowed no criticism, political parties, or other potential challenges to its rule. The government employed arbitrary arrest and incommunicado detention, torture, corporal and capital punishment to suppress and intimidate opposition.

Women faced institutionalized discrimination affecting their freedom of movement and association and their right to equality in employment and education. Labor laws banned the right to organize or bargain collectively. Many foreign workers, especially domestic workers, worked under oppressive conditions as the government and the courts provided little protection from exploitative employers.

Throughout 1996, the conduct of criminal trials fell far short of international norms. Saudi law did not guarantee detainees the right to counsel, made no provision for notifying families of arrests, and imposed no maximum time limit on the duration of pretrial detention. Article 4 of the Basic Law of 1992 waived the few protections offered detainees for being held in connection with "crimes involving national security," a category so broadly defined as potentially to extend to nonviolent opposition to the government. Article 20 of Imprisonment and Detention Law No. 31 of 1978 established flogging, indefinite solitary confinement, and deprivation of family visits and of correspondence as means of disciplining pre-trial detainees. There were reports that judges often accepted uncorroborated forced confessions as the sole basis for conviction.

The trial and execution of four persons held responsible for the November 13, 1995 bombing of the Saudi Arabian National Guard training center in Riyadh highlighted some of the deficiencies of the criminal justice system. That blast killed six persons, including five U.S. military personnel, and wounded sixty. On April 22, Saudi television broadcasted the "confessions" of four Saudis— Abd al-Aziz Naser al-Mi'tham, Riyad Suleiman Ishaq al-Hajri, Muslih Ali A'idah al-Shamrani, and Khalid Ahmad Ibrahim al-

Sa'id—arrested in connection with the bombing. According to Amnesty International, the four had reportedly been arrested two months before the announcement and subjected to torture. Their confessions were almost identical, and all implicated Dr. Muhammad al-Mas'ari of the Committee for the Defense of Legitimate Rights (CDLR), a London-based opposition group whose sharp denunciations of the Saudi government are regularly faxed to recipients in many countries including Saudi Arabia. The government executed the four, supposedly after a trial, on May 31.

Those doubting the authenticity of the confessions tended to view the implication of al-Mas'ari in the Riyadh attack as one of a series of Saudi government efforts to discredit and suppress him and the CDLR. These efforts included an attempt to pressure the U.K. to deport him (see below). According to the CDLR, on August 25 and 28 Saudi authorities arrested five of al-Mas'ari's close relatives living in Saudi Arabia, and had not released them by early October.

Shaikh Safar bin Abd al-Rahman al-Hawali and Shaikh Salman bin Fahd al-Audah, two prominent Sunni clerics arrested in 1994, remained in detention without charge or trial. The American Islamic Group, a California-based nongovernmental organization, stated that repeated efforts by various groups to obtain official information about the basis for the clerics' detention were fruitless. According to the CDLR, Shaikh al-Audah led a hunger strike in April to protest his continued detention and the deterioration of conditions in al-Hayer prison, where he was being held.

The June 25 bombing at the King Abdul Aziz base at al-Khobar, which killed nineteen U.S. military personnel and injured 386, was followed by a campaign of arrest and detention of suspected opposition activists. Hundreds of warrantless arrests were carried out in al-Qatif, Sayhat, Turaif, al-Jarudy, Um al-Hamam, and al-Awamiya by the Directorate of General Investigations (*al-Mabahith al-Amma*, or simply *al-Mabahith*), the secret police of the Ministry of Interior.

By early October, the campaign had not ended, with up to 2,000 persons remaining in detention, according to Saudis who monitor human rights developments in Saudi Arabia.

The government has long discriminated against the Shi'a community, which comprised about ten percent of Saudi Arabia's population and resided primarily in the Eastern Province. Shi'a faced unequal access to social services and government jobs, especially in the national security sector. The government rarely permitted the private construction of Shi'a mosques or community centers, and even sought to prohibit Shi'a religious instruction in private homes.

In March 1996 Saudi authorities initiated a campaign of arrests and detentions in the Shi'a community. By early September, twenty-three Shi'a clerics and religious scholars were in custody, according to the Alliance of Clergymen of Hijaz (*Tajammu' Ulema' al-Hijaz*), a clandestine opposition group. The government also seized many persons' passports at airports and border crossing points without legal justification, arbitrarily limiting their freedom to travel.

In early October, an estimated 200 Shi'a political prisoners remained in detention, according to independent Saudi sources monitoring human rights developments in Saudi Arabia. One case that gave particular cause for concern was that of eighteen-year-old Muhammad al-Zein al-Wa'il of the Awali district of Madina. According to the London-based Al-Haramain Islamic Information Center, al-Wa'il was arrested by Saudi forces in July and subsequently held incommunicado. During a prior arrest in 1995, the Mabahith had accused him of insulting the Prophet and his companions, an accusation sometimes leveled against Shi'a and which carries the death penalty. During his prior detention, he suffered physical and psychological abuse to such an extent that he required hospitalization after his release, according to the Center.

Non-Saudi detainees were also mistreated and denied due process. Human Rights Watch/Middle East interviewed an American engineer detained in July in the course of a business trip to Saudi Arabia. Saudi authorities arrested him at the airport upon his arrival and detained him in prisons in three different Saudi cities for a total of thirty-eight days. According to the engineer, who requested anonymity, his interrogators said that they had no charges against him but merely wanted information he allegedly had obtained about Saudi opposition groups when he was living in Saudi Arabia. He stated that during most of his detention he was held in solitary confinement and received insufficient food and medication. At one point his interrogators threatened to beat him. For thirty days they refused him any contact with his family, a lawyer, or the U.S. embassy. Saudi authorities only confirmed his detention to the U.S. consulate in Dammam seven days after his arrest.

The government owned all domestic radio and television stations and allowed the domestic privately-owned print media no margin to criticize. The government controlled senior staffing decisions at publications as well as their editorial content. Topics such as corruption, arms deals, and the country's financial difficulties were off-limits. Private satellite dishes were outlawed, but were unofficially tolerated.

The Right to Monitor

Saudi controls on freedom of expression and harsh suppression of dissent meant that no human rights organizations could operate in Saudi territory. Mail or telephone contact with persons in Saudi Arabia that touched on criticism of the government posed significant dangers to Saudi correspondents. No international human rights organization has in recent years been authorized to conduct a mission to Saudi Arabia. In October 1995, Saudi Ambassador to the U.S. Prince Bandar ibn Sultan extended an informal invitation to Human Rights Watch to visit Saudi Arabia. Follow-up phone calls subsequently made by Human Rights Watch to determine the modalities of the visit went unanswered.

The Saudi government's pressure on opposition organizations, as well as groups involved in human rights reporting, extended beyond its borders. Fearing Saudi efforts to have them deported and reprisals against relatives in Saudi Arabia, some individuals involved in London-based human rights and opposition groups chose to operate anonymously.

Foreign journalists required visas to enter Saudi Arabia and were often refused access.

The Role of
the International Community

United Kingdom

In January, the Home Office announced that the U.K. had decided to refuse without substantive consideration the application of Dr. Muhammad al-Mas'ari (see above) for political asylum. It sought instead to deport him to Dominica, which had agreed to take him.

This move came as a result of pressure from British defense contractors who were alarmed by Saudi threats, made both in public and private, that Saudi Arabia would cut lucrative defense contracts with British firms if al-Mas'ari were allowed to continue his opposition activities in the U.K. The *Times* (London) quoted Ann Widdecombe of the Home Office as saying, "British interests as a whole do require his removal. We have got enormous export considerations." Britain sold over US $2.2 billion worth of goods to Saudi Arabia in 1995.

The deportation effort was blocked by the Immigration Appellate Board, which on March 5 ordered the Home Office to reconsider al-Mas'ari's asylum claim on the merits, ruling that the government had tried to "circumvent for diplomatic and trade reasons" its obligations under the U.N. Convention Relating to the Status of Refugees. The government subsequently abandoned this effort and granted al-Mas'ari the right to remain in the U.K. for four additional years. Subsequently, Defense Secretary Michael Portillo said in an interview with the Arab press that London was searching for another country that would take al-Mas'ari.

United States

Saudi Arabia is the base for approximately 5,000 U.S. soldiers and is also a leading customer for U.S. arms and other exports. As in the past, the U.S. subordinated human rights concerns to maintaining the political and trade status quo. Besides the State Department's *Country Reports on Human Rights Practices for 1995*, the U.S. rarely if ever raised publicly Saudi Arabia's human rights record. Instead, U.S. policy emphasized the defense of the Saudi government against regional and internal opponents.

The *Country Reports* chapter reflected this emphasis. While it contained a detailed and relatively comprehensive overview of human rights violations in Saudi Arabia, it was marred by attempts to discredit the opposition while bolstering the government's legitimacy. For example, it stated, without substantiation, that the government "enforces adherence to the precepts of a rigorously conservative form of Islam—a position that enjoys near-consensus support among Saudi citizens." And while the official brand of intolerant Islam was "rigorously conservative" opposition groups facing government repression were characterized as "rigidly fundamentalist."

On April 22, after the announcement of the confessions of persons detained in connection with the Riyadh bombing case (see above), U.S. Ambassador Raymond Mabus stated that he was "extremely gratified that the government of Saudi Arabia has arrested four people responsible for the bombing," *The New York Times* reported. The ambassador thus implied that the detainees were guilty before this had been proven at trial.

The U.S. government participated in the investigations into the al-Khobar bombing by sending sixty agents of the Federal Bureau of Investigation (FBI) to assist the Saudis. While FBI Director Louis Freeh on many occasions publicly criticized the Saudis for not allowing the FBI access to the suspects, he did not publicly voice any concern over Saudi Arabia's mistreatment of detainees and its failure to adhere to due-process standards in criminal investigations.

SYRIA

Human Rights Developments

Syrian citizens remained under the tight control of a powerful state system in which opposition political parties and independent nongovernmental organizations were not permitted, the elected parliament functioned as a rubber stamp, and daily newspapers and other media served as government mouthpieces. Peaceful dissent was criminalized; political detainees and prisoners suffered harsh treatment, including extraordinarily long imprisonment for nonviolent offenses. In Syria, the rule of law was supplanted by the continuing state of emergency, in force since 1963, which granted broad, unchecked powers to the vast, multi-layered security apparatus.

President Hafez al-Asad, who in November 1996 celebrated twenty-six years in power, ruled unchallenged. By keeping a watchful eye on suspected domestic critics, punishing severely those who dared to speak out, and limiting the access of journalists and international human rights organizations to the country, the government made information-gathering and timely reporting about the human rights situation extremely difficult.

In a welcome development, a large number of political prisoners—reportedly up to 1,200—were released beginning in late November 1995 in a presidential amnesty, most of them held since the 1980s because of suspected links to the Muslim Brotherhood. This left some 2,700 political prisoners in Syria, the Paris-based Committees for the Defense of Democratic Freedoms and Human Rights in Syria (CDF) calculated. Among the remaining prisoners were those suspected of affiliation with the nonviolent, secular political opposition, many of them held since the 1980s and early 1990s and serving ten-and fifteen-year prison terms handed down by the state security court on charges based on the exercise of their rights of freedom of association and expression. Their trials, flouting fair trial standards, took place between 1992 and 1994.

Some of these prisoners were denied proper medical care, and others were transferred to military prisons. Forty-three-year-old poet and journalist Faraj Bayraqar, who has been imprisoned since 1987 and was sentenced to fifteen years by the state security court in 1993, suffered from injuries sustained during torture and reportedly could not walk unassisted. Thirty-four-year-old writer and human rights activist Nizar Nayouf remained in Mezze military prison in Damascus, where he was, since 1993, reportedly held in solitary confinement. Another twenty-one prisoners—all alleged to be members of two unauthorized leftist political groups—were transferred to the infamous Tadmor military prison because they refused to sign statements of support for the government and repudiating their past political activities as conditions for release. Some of these men had also been in custody since the early 1980s; all of them were tried by the state security court in 1994 for vaguely formulated offenses, such as "opposing the goals of the revolution," and sentenced to terms ranging from eight to fifteen years.

There were reports of continued arbitrary arrests in 1996. Forty Kurds were arrested in Aleppo and 'Ain Arab during *Nayrouz* ("new day," in Kurdish), the traditional Kurdish celebration of spring. In May, following a series of unclaimed and as-yet-unexplained explosions in Damascus and other cities, security forces reportedly rounded up scores of citizens, including some 400 from the Turkoman minority and smaller numbers of Kurds in Damascus, Aleppo, and areas in the north.

Suspected members of unauthorized political groups continued to be detained without charge, interrogated and mistreated by security forces. One Syrian activist who was detained in 1996 in the Palestine Branch of Military Intelligence in Damascus told us that he was first given a pen and paper and asked to write his life story before he was questioned by a high-ranking officer. Then he was blindfolded and handcuffed, and beaten every ten minutes on an hourly basis until the following day as interrogators sought to elicit a confession that he was a member of an illegal political party. "If you die, we have ten doctors to say that you died of natural causes," his interrogator allegedly told him.

The government also maintained its policy of keeping political opponents behind bars for many years without trial or beyond the expiration of their sentences, despite advanced age or the onset of life-threatening illnesses. Journalist Rida Haddad died in a Damascus hospital on June 17, eight months after his release from prison. He had been arrested in October 1980, held without charge for fourteen years, and then sentenced by the state security court in 1994 to fifteen years, including time already served. Haddad suffered from leukemia but was not released until October 1995, after serving his full prison term.

The persistence of this pattern of treatment raised grave concern about the fate of other long-term prisoners who had became seriously ill. One of them was Mustafa Tawfiq Fallah, a fifty-nine-year-old Syrian army officer who was sentenced to fifteen years in prison in 1971 but continued to be held illegally in Mezze prison long beyond the expiry of this term. It was reported in 1996 that Fallah was suffering from heart and kidney disease, among other ailments. As of this writing, we were aware of no response from Syrian authorities to calls for Fallah's release. In June, CDF named thirteen prisoners whose medical condition it described as critical, including lawyer and opposition political activist Riad al-Turk (detained without charge since 1980); lawyer and human rights activist Aktham Nouaisseh (sentenced to nine years by the state security court in 1992); and Faraj Bayraqdar, the poet mentioned above. The others were: Abbas Abbas, Nu'man Abdo, Safwan Akkash, Wahij Ghanem, Mustafa Hussein, Muhammed Kheir Khalaf, Issa Mahmoud, Ahmad Hassan Mansour, Nizar Mradni, and Munif Mulhem.

Human Rights Watch in 1995 documented the demand that political prisoners sign loyalty oaths to the government, abandon political activity, and collaborate with

security forces, as conditions for release. This practice not only continued in 1996, but a group of twenty-nine long-term prisoners were reportedly punished by transfer in January 1996 from Adra civilian prison to Tadmor military prison for refusing these demands. As of this writing, the prisoners reportedly had no contact with the outside world because family visits were not permitted. They were all arrested between 1981 and 1990 and were not tried by the security court until 1994; they were serving prison terms of up to fifteen years for alleged membership in three unauthorized political groups (the Party for Communist Action, the Communist Party-Political Bureau, and the pro-Iraqi Ba'th Party). Two of the prisoners, Safwan 'Akkash (arrested in 1983, serving a fifteen-year sentence) and 'Ammar Rizk (arrested in 1990, serving a twelve-year sentence), reportedly have serious health problems.

In 1996, Syrian security forces in Lebanon detained Lebanese citizens and Palestinian refugees, who then "disappeared." Some of these abductions began with short-term detention, interrogation and torture at Syrian intelligence headquarters at the Beau Rivage Hotel in Beirut, followed by transfer to Syria and imprisonment there without charge or due process. In one 1996 case, after a high-ranking Syrian officer called at the home of a Lebanese citizen and took him away, family members made inquiries at the local office of Syrian security. "First they said that they didn't have him, then they said that he was being questioned for a few days and would be released. After some days, they said that he was moved to Anjar [a Syrian detention facility inside Lebanon, near the Lebanese-Syrian border] and probably was in Damascus," a relative said. The family later was able to confirm this.

Using influence, bribery, or a combination of both, families sometimes learned where their relatives were detained in Syria and visits were permitted. One Lebanese, who was taken in 1994 and as of this writing continued to be held in a Military Intelligence facility in Damascus, saw his wife every two weeks. In other cases, families searched for "disappeared" relatives at Lebanese prisons and detention facilities, only to be informed that the person was not in custody and "probably" was in Syria. Inaction by Lebanese authorities in such cases only exacerbated the fear felt by victims' families, who insisted that names and other identifying details remain confidential. Lebanese lawyers identified Col. Rustom Ghazali as the officer in charge of Syrian intelligence in Beirut, and Gen. Ghazi Kan'an as the head of Syrian intelligence in Lebanon.

The Kurdish minority of some eight to ten million people continued to suffer from state-sponsored discrimination, and those Syrian-born Kurds classified by the interior ministry as "foreigners" (*ajanib*, in Arabic) or "unregistered" (*maktoumeen*) were officially rendered stateless. Authorities maintained various bans on the use of the Kurdish language, establishment of Kurdish private schools, and the publication and circulation of books and other materials written in Kurdish. Suspected Kurdish political activists were dismissed from their jobs at state-owned companies and from educational institutions were they were studying, and were prevented from traveling abroad by blocks upon the renewal of their passports.

In the continuing legacy of a controversial 1962 census in Hasakeh governorate in the northeast that stripped many Syrian-born Kurds of their citizenship, over 142,000 men, women and children—by the government's own count—remained arbitrarily denied of a nationality, in violation of international law. They were not permitted to vote or own property, hold public-sector jobs, or be issued passports.

The Right to Monitor

Syrians were not permitted to criticize any aspect of President Asad's rule or to monitor openly the human rights situation, much less publish and distribute information about abuses. Fear of arrest severely hampered the collection of information and its dissemination to the outside world. The state's clampdown in 1991-1992 on activists associated with CDF, the nascent human rights movement inside Syria, continued to have its intended chilling effect. Suspected CDF leaders and activists were prosecuted in the state security court in 1992 in an unfair trial and sentenced to prison terms of up to ten years. Their imprisonment continued to be a grim reminder of the consequences for Syrians who dared to criticize the state.

In a troubling change of the policy that prevailed in 1994 and 1995, Syrian authorities did not consent to visits to Syria in 1996 by international human rights organizations that sought to carry out field research. The government continued to delay its response to a Human Rights Watch request, pending since July 1995, for another investigative mission.

The Role of
the International Community

United Nations

In July, Human Rights Watch provided detailed information to the U.N. Human Rights Committee about the stateless Kurds in Syria. On the basis of this submission, the chair of the committee met with Syrian representatives in Geneva, and asked that their overdue report on the country's compliance with the treaty be submitted as soon as possible and that it put special emphasis on the situation of the Kurdish population in Syria.

European Union

European Union countries account for over 55 percent of Syria's annual exports, giving the E.U. substantial influence as a key trading partner; additional clout is provided by a five-year aid package worth US$178 million. Despite these potential levers to press for human rights improvements, the E.U. has long shown little political will to press for substantive improvements in Syria's dismal human rights situation. It continued its policy of public silence in 1996, sparing President Asad the constructive criticism that the government merited.

The joint press release issued on June 11 after the second meeting of the European Union-Syria Cooperation Council at the ministerial level omitted mention of human rights. Instead, the joint statement lavished praise on Syria, cited the improvement and expansion of its "political ties" with the European Union, and noted the common interest in "security, stability and prosperity throughout the Mediterranean." It added that "both sides were pleased to note that since 1994 the resumption of financial assistance had enabled cooperation to enter a very active phase." Emphasizing reforms geared toward economic modernization, the statement continued, "The E.U. is prepared to support Syria in this course of action and to help it to create a favorable climate for the modernization and development of its economy."

United States

For the seventeenth consecutive year, Syria was precluded from receiving U.S. aid because it was included on the State Department list of countries that sponsor terrorism, along with Cuba, Iran, Iraq, Libya, North Korea, and Sudan. State Department spokesman Nicholas Burns tempered the news of Syria's continuing stigmatization by inclusion on this list, which was disclosed in February, with these conciliatory words: "We have a much more regular set of contacts with the Syrian government [compared to the other states on the list]. We may not like everything the Syrian government does...but we do have a dialogue with the Syrian government which is a mature dialogue." And, as in past years, frequent high-level diplomatic contacts between the two countries continued, including face-to-face meetings in Damascus between Secretary of State Warren Christopher and President Asad in April, as the secretary attempted to broker a cease-fire in the fierce fighting between Israel and Hizballah.

Assistant Secretary of State Robert H. Pelletreau made clear in an address on August 21 that U.S. interests in the Middle East include "first and foremost, achieving a just, comprehensive, secure and durable Arab-Israeli peace." He added that Syria was central to this process: "We have long felt that

peace between Israel and Syria is essential for closing the circle of peace and producing a comprehensive settlement. We are committed to working toward this goal." The administration indeed continued its efforts to facilitate Syrian-Israeli negotiations. But, as in previous years, the administration's exclusive focus on the peace process left its spokespersons publicly silent about Syria's rights record.

To the best of our knowledge, the only public criticism by the Clinton administration during the year of Syria's human rights performance appeared in the State Department's *Country Reports on Human Rights Practices for 1995*. The assessment of Syria noted accurately that President Asad rules with "virtually absolute authority," security forces operate "outside the legal system," torture in detention is "widespread" and state security court trials "fundamentally unfair," freedom of peaceful assembly and association "does not exist," and freedom of speech and press is restricted "significantly." Secretary Pelletreau repeatedly stressed in 1996 that one of the U.S. policy goals in the region is promotion of "more open political and economic systems and respect for human rights and the rule of law." Despite the damning assessment of Syria in *Country Reports*, we could find no evidence of how the administration pursued its professed policy of promoting human rights in its bilateral relationship with Syria.

TUNISIA

Human Rights Developments

Tunisia remained a tightly controlled state where police surveillance, repressive legislation and trumped-up charges against opposition politicians and rights activists contributed to a climate of fear that stifled nearly all public criticism of President Zine Abidine Ben Ali. The government devoted enormous efforts to presenting its human rights record in a favorable manner that bore no relation to reality.

The harshest repression was reserved for suspected Islamists and their families. Authorities, exploiting domestic and international concern over a spillover of the conflict from Algeria, had since 1990 prosecuted and jailed thousands of suspected members and sympathizers of the banned Renaissance (Nahdha) party on charges relating to nonviolent expression and association. The arrests continued in 1996 despite an absence of political violence in Tunisia since the early 1990s. Intolerance of dissent extended to nonviolent leftist groups as well, whose members continued to be arrested during 1996.

Interrogation under torture was reported by some detainees. For example, three students who were arrested on suspicion of belonging to unauthorized leftist groups in November 1995 and who were held beyond the ten-day legal limit for incommunicado detention said they were beaten and suspended in contorted positions, dunked in tubs of water and subjected to food and sleep deprivation. Eight leftist suspects were subjected to much the same methods during their interrogation in August, according to lawyers who saw marks of abuse on them when they were brought to court.

Human rights lawyer Nejib Hosni, who has been imprisoned since June 1994, was transferred to a cell inside the Ministry of Interior in November 1995 to be questioned about new charges. Hosni told his lawyers that there he was subjected to repeated beatings, electric shocks to his feet, food deprivation, and confinement in a tiny cell with no bed. Demands for an inquiry into the allegations from his lawyers, human rights organizations, and the Tunisian Bar Association produced no response.

Hosni was given an eight-year sentence in January 1996 on a charge that he forged a signature on a contract in 1989. The government insisted that the case involved nothing more than a common criminal offense that the court had judged fairly and independently. The New York-based Lawyers Committee for Human Rights, which closely examined the dossier, argued persuasively in a 1996 report that Hosni's prosecution and stiff sentence were motivated by his outspoken denunciation, both in Tunisian courtrooms and to international observers, of human rights abuses. Hosni was due to stand trial in late 1996 on new charges of weapons possession, charges that observers also characterized as dubious.

Hundreds of Islamists and smaller numbers of leftists were serving jail terms for such offenses as distributing or possessing illegal tracts, belonging to unauthorized political parties, attending unauthorized meetings, or insulting state institutions or officials. Many more were in prison for providing or soliciting financial assistance for the families of Islamist prisoners.

In 1996, even prominent members of the legal opposition were imprisoned for their criticism of the government. Mohamed Mouada, president of the Movement of Social Democrats (Mouvement de Démocrates Socialistes, MDS), was convicted in February on trumped-up charges of treason, as a "Libyan agent," and sentenced to eleven years in prison. He had been arrested October 9, 1995, the very day that he went public with a critical letter addressed to President Ben Ali complaining about the lack of genuine pluralism, citing as an example the May 1995 municipal elections that gave the ruling Democratic Constitutional Rally 4,084 of 4,090 seats.

Mouada's MDS colleague Khemais Chammari was jailed for his efforts to defend Mouada. Chammari, a parliamentarian and well-known human rights activist, received a five-year sentence in July for faxing abroad documents from the evidentiary file in the case against Mouada, a charge that Chammari steadfastly denied.

Tunisia's governmental and private press were almost indistinguishable in their delivery of the official line. No direct criticism of the government appeared in any legal publication or on radio or television. Newspapers, both official and private, launched smear campaigns on cue against critics of Tunisia's human rights record, while blacking out the critics' words that prompted the backlash. Foreign publications were permitted to circulate only when they contained no negative coverage.

The court system was widely viewed by human rights observers as subject to political pressure. Defendants who alleged mistreatment while under interrogation were only rarely granted their right to a medical examination, and trial judges routinely gave no weight to claims that confessions had been tainted by torture or ill-treatment. But to the government's credit, some international observers were allowed at controversial trials.

Authorities insisted that human rights abuses were rare and that offenders were punished. According to an official booklet issued in July, since 1988 there have been five convictions of law-enforcement officers for use of violence against prisoners to obtain a confession, and 127 convictions for the use of violence against citizens without due cause by law enforcement officers. Such claims could only be met with some skepticism, since the government, citing confidentiality rights, never divulged verifiable details about such cases.

Punishment of political prisoners did not end with completion of a prison term. Many were dismissed from their jobs, had passports confiscated, and were compelled to report to the police one or more times daily. The police also commonly harassed the families of Islamist prisoners. Human Rights Watch received reports in 1996 of policemen suggesting to wives of Islamists that harassment would end if they divorced their imprisoned husbands, and questioning them about their sources of money when their children wore new clothing.

Law No. 75-40 of May 14, 1975 permitted passports to be confiscated "for reasons of public order and security, or if Tunisia's reputation might be harmed." In 1996, many human rights activists, persons with links to opposition movements, and ex-prisoners were denied the right to travel; official justification was provided only rarely.

Article 305 of the code of criminal procedure permits prosecution of Tunisians for violations of Tunisian law for acts committed abroad that fall within the broad definition of "terrorism" found in article 52b of the criminal code. Political activities that were perfectly legal in the countries in which they took place put Tunisians at risk of arrest and prosecution the moment they set foot again in Tunisia. For example, student Hafez Ben Gharbia served more than one year in prison for participating in an "unauthorized" meeting and demonstration in Germany in 1988, before authorities released him in 1996, following sustained international pressure.

The Right to Monitor

The government of Tunisia devoted remarkable energy to cultivating an image of respect for human rights while doing its utmost to bar independent monitoring of its record. It boasted of the presence of independent human rights organizations inside Tunisia while routinely posting plainclothes police outside their offices in order to intimidate members and potential clients.

The independent Tunisian Human Rights League (Ligue Tunisienne des Droits de l'Homme, LTDH) was able to do a modest amount of monitoring, although its critical communiqués were ignored by the Tunisian media and virtually all of the LTDH's efforts to communicate and meet with officials were ignored.

Tunisians suspected of criticizing the government's human rights record while abroad risked confiscation of their passports or worse. On October 7, Salah Zeghidi, a vice president of the LTDH, was arrested upon his return to the country, after participating in a public forum in Paris on human rights in Tunisia. He was interrogated about his contacts and activities abroad and released one day later. Moncef Marzouki, a former president of the LTDH who had faced continuous harassment for his outspokenness on human rights, was detained upon his return to the country in April and interrogated for several hours about who he met in Paris. His passport was also confiscated, less than two months after it had been returned to him following a previous period during which he was prevented from traveling.

Representatives of international human rights organizations were either barred from Tunisia or were allowed in and then followed by plainclothes police in a usually successful effort to deter Tunisians from speaking to them. The president of the Paris-based International Federation of Human Rights (Fédération Internationale des Droits de l'Homme, FIDH) was turned back at the airport in May on his arrival to conduct a mission. The Tunisia researcher for Amnesty International remained barred from the country, although that organization was permitted to send trial observers in 1996.

Human rights activists risked severe harassment. In addition to the Hosni and Chammari cases (see above), Frej Fenniche, the executive director of the Tunis-based Arab Institute of Human Rights, was arrested at Tunis airport on May 10 and interrogated for four days about human rights documents found in his luggage. During a hearing on the charges against Fenniche of "defaming state institutions" and "disseminating false information," authorities subpoenaed the president of the LTDH, Taoufik Bouderbala, for questioning about telephone conversations, which the police had wiretapped, between him and the president of the FIDH.

Rights activists were victims of suspicious crimes. Automobiles belonging to three members of the LTDH were vandalized or stolen in December 1995, an odd coincidence in a country where such crimes are uncommon. The following month, a visiting human rights researcher on assignment for the Ford Foundation had his computer and notes stolen from his hotel room at the end of his visit, while US$1,500 in cash lay untouched nearby.

The government of Tunisia tried to make more credible its attempt to monopolize the human rights discourse by cultivating a host of government-organized "non-governmental" organizations ("GONGOs"). These entities, with plausible-sounding names like Young Lawyers without Borders, appeared to have had few if any substantive programs on the ground in Tunisia, but could be relied upon to issue indignant joint communiqués in response to criticism of Tunisia from human rights organizations abroad.

The Role of the International Community

European Union

In July 1995 Tunisia became the first southern Mediterranean country to sign an association agreement with the European Union (E.U.), whose member nations accounted for three-quarters of Tunisia's foreign trade. The accord stipulated that relations should be founded on "reciprocity, partnership, and co-development in respect for democratic principles and human rights." Acting in that spirit, a delegation from the European Parliament visiting Tunisia in October 1995 sought a meeting with jailed MDS president Mohamed Mouada. Authorities refused their request. In May 1996, the European Parliament for the first time adopted a resolution critical of the "deterioration" of the human rights situation in Tunisia. The long-overdue resolution, which provoked a sharp response from Tunisia's parliament, called on the European Council and Commission to urge the Tunisian authorities to "alter their policy toward the democratic opposition and honour their international human rights commitments." In June the Tunisian parliament ratified the E.U. association agreement.

France

France, Tunisia's chief trading partner, enjoyed good relations with its former protectorate, which it saw as an island of stability in the region. President Jacques Chirac nonetheless appeared to step back somewhat during 1996 from the warm embrace he gave President Ben Ali during a state visit to Tunis the previous October. At that time he saluted Ben Ali as "the man who personified the new Tunisia...leading his country ever further down the road of modernization, social peace and democratic progress." The French president held no meetings with opposition or human rights figures during his visit, as his predecessor, François Mitterand, had done. He further delighted his hosts by voicing no human rights concerns publicly during this visit, and by announcing that bilateral aid to Tunisia would jump to 1.1 billion francs ($220 million) in 1996 from 594 million francs in 1995.

But Chirac was reportedly embarrassed when, three days after his departure, the police arrested MDS president Mouada (see above). He commented that France would follow the case "with attention" and hoped that justice would be "transparent." But senior French officials abstained from publicly criticizing human rights abuses throughout the year, except to say, upon the conviction of Mouada in February, that they had "taken note" of the judgment, a bland comment that nonetheless elicited an indignant response from Tunis.

A planned state visit to Paris by Ben Ali in September was canceled at the last minute, reportedly by the Tunisians. This spurred press speculation that the Tunisian president feared human rights criticism in France, and that the French government was frustrated with the lack of measures taken by Tunis before the planned visit to resolve some of the high-profile rights cases. But French authorities again abstained from commenting publicly on human rights and, in a publicized phone conversation with Ben Ali, Chirac proposed that the visit take place in 1997.

United States

The U.S. no longer provided Tunisia bilateral economic or military aid, but there was close military cooperation and Tunisia received $816,000 to train officers in the U.S. In 1996 Tunisia became eligible to receive grants of excess U.S. defense articles.

The State Department's *Country Reports on Human Rights Practices for 1995* showed familiarity with rights conditions. However, it noted misleadingly that the number of human rights complaints declined during 1995, as if the number of complaints filed truly reflected the number of abuses

committed in a country where authorities intimidated those who complain.

According to Tunisian human rights activists, the U.S. embassy in Tunis stood out among Western embassies for its monitoring of rights developments; staff met regularly with human rights monitors, observed political trials, and raised cases with Tunisian officials. According to the State Department, human rights concerns were also raised during 1996 at the ministerial level.

Although engaged on the subject, the U.S. did not wish human rights concerns to interfere with good relations, since Washington and other Western states appreciated Tunisia's support for the Arab-Israeli peace accords, its liberalizing and relatively healthy economy, and its apparent political stability and success in stemming Islamist radicalism, especially considering its proximity to Algeria and Libya.

In the past, U.S. officials urged, in their infrequent public comments on Tunisia, greater respect for human rights and pluralism. Regrettably, the most significant public statement on the issue during the past year signaled that U.S. praise on human rights could be a payoff for following the "correct" policies in other spheres. In his comments after meeting with President Ben Ali in Tunis on December 14, 1995, Assistant Secretary of State Robert H. Pelletreau said, "We appreciate Tunisia's strong support for the Peace Process, its support for the agreement in Bosnia, and its policies of economic liberalization, political enlargement and respect for human rights and the rule of law at home."

YEMEN

Human Rights Developments

The government of President Ali Abdallah Salih, which prevailed in Yemen's 1994 civil war, further constricted civil and political rights in that country. In 1996 Yemen's human rights profile compared unfavorably with the relative tolerance that had characterized the four years following the May 1990 unification of the Yemen Arab Republic (North Yemen) and the People's Democratic Republic of Yemen (South Yemen) and that ended with the civil war. In addition, the tribal-Islamist alliance embodied in the Reform (Islah) Party headed by Shaikh Abdallah al-Ahmar, the speaker of the Parliament, represented a coercive force somewhat autonomous from that of the state and the ruling General People's Congress party, further contributing to constraints on the exercise of basic civil liberties and human rights.

At the same time, government control over Yemeni society remained less encompassing than in many other states in the region. Perhaps most significantly, human rights activists and political critics of the government were able to look to the courts as a frail but nonetheless useful defender of their constitutional rights to publish and to speak out.

The Political Security Organization (PSO), an agency that reported directly to President Salih and operated without any written authorization, was responsible for the harassment, beating, and detention without charge or trial of a number of government critics, and contributed to an atmosphere of intimidation. The PSO's plainclothes agents also infiltrated and harassed the independent press, syndicates, and civic associations, in some cases forcing those organizations to cease their activities. Persons seeking to work for any government institution, such as Sana'a University, required clearance from the PSO.

The most serious instance of punishment outside any framework of law was the abduction in December 1995 of Abu Bakr al-Saqqaf, a sixty-one-year-old professor of philosophy at Sana'a University and columnist in *Al-Ayyam*, an independent newspaper published in Aden. Al-Saqqaf, who had been named minister of education by the secessionist government in 1994, had been abducted and beaten previously, in January 1995, but continued to write articles criticizing the government's policies toward the southern part of the country. According to al-Saqqaf, unidentified men seized him near his home and threw him into a car without license plates. He said they demanded that he stop writing articles critical of the government as they beat him with sticks and an electric baton, fracturing his skull, breaking several teeth, and inflicting bruises on his torso. Al-Saqqaf and others charged that his assailants belonged to the PSO. The Ministry of Interior denied this and claimed to be investigating the second abduction, but no findings or arrests had been announced as this report went to press. Al-Saqqaf also faced harassment in the form of dismissal from his university post, but was reinstated by a court order.

Human Rights Watch received reports of similar attacks in the course of 1996. On July 11, Arafat Jamali Madabish, a reporter covering parliamentary affairs for the Socialist Party-affiliated newspaper *Al-Thawri* (Aden), was assaulted inside the parliament by guards and subsequently detained for several days without charge before being released. On August 19, Abd al-Ilah al-Marwani, a lawyer active in civil liberties cases, was attacked outside a court in Ibb, reportedly by persons known to be connected to the PSO. According to a letter from the Lawyers' Union to President Salih, al-Marwani had been "attacked [physically] several times" in connection with his representation in court of opposition newspapers.

Other forms of harassment of government critics were frequent. In December 1995, security officials at Sana'a airport interrogated and confiscated the papers of Dr. Muhammad Abd al-Malik al-Mutawakkil, a political science professor at Sana'a University and vice-president of the independent Yemeni Organization for the Defense of Liberties and Human Rights (YODLHR), and Hisham Basharahil, editor of the independent daily *Al-Ayyam* (Aden), on their return from academic conferences abroad. In February 1996, the government arbitrarily withheld the salary of Dr. Abdu al-Sharif, professor of political science at the

Sana'a University, following a lecture he delivered at Georgetown University, in Washington, DC, on human rights and democracy in Yemen. Yemeni officials threatened Dr. Sharif and Dr. Muhammad Zabara with arrest and physical harm upon their return to Yemen because the *Yemen Human Rights Report* newsletter, which they co-edit, had directly referred to President Salih's responsibility for human rights violations.

Opposition parties and independent organizations and publications critical of government policies were generally given legal status but faced routine harassment. Trade unions, professional associations, and other independent organizations were often the target of government efforts to manipulate their governing boards by packing meetings and replacing government critics with supporters. The government closed down the opposition weekly *Al-Shura* from mid-1995 through mid-1996, ostensibly because leadership of the party to which it is affiliated—the Union of Yemeni Popular Forces—was being contested by a government-backed former member.

Sana'a was the site of a January 1996 UNESCO-sponsored seminar on press freedom, which adopted a "Declaration on Promoting Independent and Pluralistic Arab Media." Unfortunately, the principles of the declaration were repeatedly breached in 1996 by legal and extralegal attacks on independent media and publications affiliated with legal opposition parties in Yemen. Fuad Bamatraf, the director of radio broadcasting in the southern port city of Mukalla, was arrested while covering clashes between demonstrators and security forces in mid-June (see below). Authorities also blocked distribution of the opposition newspaper *Al-Tagammu* (Aden) in connection with the same events, and the government-owned 14th October Printing Press subsequently refused for more than a month, for no stated reason, to honor its contract to print *Al-Tagammu*, forcing the paper to suspend publication. In August Salem al-Hilali, a cartoonist for *Al-Tagammu*, was banned from publishing his cartoons and PSO officers prevented an exhibition of his cartoons in Aden.

Al-Ayyam, an independent Aden-based weekly critical of the government, was also the target of harassment and intimidation. On September 28, plainclothes security officers entered its offices to seize journalist Abd al-Rahman Khubara, who also reports for Radio Kuwait. Khubara's colleagues intervened, saying he could not be taken without a warrant. The officers left without Khubara but lay in wait outside, forcing him to remain in the office with colleagues overnight for fear of arrest. *Al-Ayyam* published a front-page account of the incident the next day, following which the PSO desisted. Khubara had been detained and interrogated by PSO officers for four days in 1995. On September 30, Muhammad al-Saqqaf, a physician and writer, appeared voluntarily for interrogation at the office of the attorney general in Sana'a and was charged with "publishing false information with malicious intent"—a violation of Yemen's press law—because of articles he had published critical of government preparations for parliamentary elections scheduled for April 1997. A trial date had not been set at the time of writing.

The *Yemen Times* (Sana'a), an English-language paper often critical of the government, charged in its July 1 issue that the PSO was effectively in control of the central post office, opening incoming mail and dumping copies of the *Times* that were addressed to international subscribers. On July 7, President Salih accused the *Yemen Times* and *Al-Ayyam* of "dubious practices." "I am directing an early warning to them because I know that the minister of information is hesitant to take legal measures against the papers," the president stated, according to *Al-Sharq Al-Awsat*, a London-based Arabic daily, "but I shall take the appropriate measures at the appropriate time."

Clashes between crowds and security forces erupted in Mukalla in June 1996 in an episode that reflected widespread perception of discrimination by the northern-based government against southerners. The disturbances were set off by a state prosecutor's remark, during a court hearing on a lawsuit filed by two southern women against the police for wrongful arrest and sexual molestation, to the effect that all southern women were "whores." Over the course of several days of rioting, police fired on unarmed demonstrators, injuring seventeen. Although the court later ruled in favor of the two women and against the arresting officers, the incident illustrated the problems arising from the replacement of virtually all local security forces and government officials by northerners after the 1994 civil war.

The Mukalla case also highlighted the fact that the courts, alone among institutions of government, on occasion challenged abuses and attempts to restrict civil and political rights. Much of the credit rested with one judge in particular, Abd al-Malik al-Gindari, in the west Sanaʻa court, who ruled, for example, that Professor Abu Bakr al-Saqqaf should be reinstated, that the weekly *Al-Shura* could be closed only by a court order, thus allowing the weekly to reappear, and that the government could not shut down the independent Hadarim Welfare Association merely because it had received material support not routed through the ruling General People's Congress party. The government threatened to reassign Judge al-Gindari to a small village, and also pressed for the Judges' Association to open its membership to prosecutors as well, a move judges argued would seriously impair its independence.

Prison conditions varied widely, and generally did not meet international standards. There continued to be an undetermined number of prisons not established or regulated by law that were associated with the PSO and with different ministries and high officials, including, reportedly, Speaker of Parliament Sheikh al-Ahmar. Many, possibly thousands of prisoners remained in detention for common crimes after many years without documentation regarding their trials or sentences. This reflected both a lack of resources devoted to the court and prison systems and a lack of political will to remedy the situation.

There were few reported cases of severe physical abuse of political detainees. There was, however, at least one case in 1996 of a suspicious death in detention. Ahmad Saʻid Bakhubira, thirty-five, was arrested in mid-June for allegedly being in contact with the National Opposition Front. PSO officials refused to cooperate with efforts of his father to locate him, and seventeen days later his body was discovered in a Mukalla hospital morgue. According to the YODLHR, Bakhubira's father has filed a complaint against the PSO and refused to accept a payment offer of 50,000 riyals (about US$400). The case received wide press coverage in Yemen.

One of Yemen's most egregious and long-standing cases of wrongful incarceration remained unresolved in 1996. Mansur Rajah, an activist with the leftist National Democratic Front, had been arrested in July 1983 and charged with the murder of a man in his village in Taʻiz province. He was interrogated, reportedly under torture, for nine months, in order to compel him to release the names of other NDF activists. He was convicted of murder and sentenced to death in March 1984, a sentence that had been upheld on appeal but had not yet been ratified by the Presidential Council. Yemeni human rights activists considered him to have been framed; in any event his trial in March 1984 was patently unfair, and Amnesty International has long regarded him as a prisoner of conscience.

The Right to Monitor

There were two main organizations based in Yemen working on human rights issues. The Yemeni Organization for Human Rights (YOHR) describes itself as a 30,000-member nongovernmental monitoring organization. It was headed by Hamud al-Hitar, a judge who was a strong proponent of the rule of law and judicial autonomy. In the period since the civil war, the YOHR protested illegal detentions, press closures and physical attacks on intellectuals. However, apparently in response to government pressure, the YOHR lowered its profile considerably in 1996.

The Yemeni Organization for the Defense of Liberties and Human Rights was set up in February 1992. In its first annual report, in 1994, the YODLHR recorded civilian deaths and injuries in the civil war as well as detailed information on security officers accused of rights violations, cases of illegal detentions, and the names of civil servants illegally dismissed. Although President Salih had ordered it to cease functioning, and the Ministry of Social Affairs denied license, the YODLHR operated legally in 1996 on the basis of a fifteen-year license from the Ministry of Cultural Affairs. The organization had to close its Sana'a office for lack of funds, but maintained an office in Aden and, after dispatching lawyers in response to clashes in Mukalla (see above), established a branch there as well.

There was a parliamentary human rights committee. Although headed by Yahya Mansur Abu Usba, a member of the opposition Yemeni Socialist Party, the group was rendered ineffective by its large GPC/Islah majority.

Amnesty International conducted an official mission to Yemen in 1996. There was an ICRC representative resident in Yemen, and the ICRC had access to prisons.

HUMAN
RIGHTS
WATCH

UNITED STATES

Human Rights Developments

Human Rights Watch continued to focus on immigration practices, police abuse, detainees' and prisoners' rights, the death penalty, and issues of discrimination in the United States. During 1996, through new legislation and the persistence of established abusive practices, U.S. authorities at federal and state levels undermined the rights of vulnerable groups, making the year a disturbing one for human rights. The fact that the U.S. hosted the XXVI Olympics in July, and presented itself aggressively as a leader in human rights and democracy through the vehicle of the Games, underscored yet again the importance of pressing the U.S. government to accept the full authority of international human rights standards; Human Rights Watch issued a report focusing on the Olympic venues of Atlanta and the state of Georgia with this goal in mind.

Legislation

Throughout the year, politically popular proposals made by Congress and the White House contributed to the accelerated erosion of basic due process and human rights protections in the United States. Despite his public proclamations in support of civil and human rights, President Bill Clinton displayed a startling lack of will to preserve rights under attack, and in some cases took the lead in eliminating human rights protections. Among the seriously flawed bills passed and signed into law were provisions to limit habeas corpus appeals, undermine prisoners' rights to bring lawsuits to address inhumane custodial conditions or treatment, and inhibit the ability of individuals fleeing persecution to seek asylum in the U.S. or challenge decisions about their immigration status. The new laws, all of which were opposed by Human Rights Watch, quickly led to court challenges that were pending as of this writing.

In April, President Clinton signed into law the Anti-Terrorism and Effective Death Penalty Act of 1996, which, among other objectionable provisions, allowed the use of secret evidence to deport legally admitted immigrants and imposed unprecedented restrictions on habeas corpus appeals for all defendants. The new law limits federal court review of state court convictions except in cases where the previous state court decision was "unreasonable." The new restrictions were imposed despite the fact that 40 percent of state cases carrying the death penalty, when reviewed in federal courts, have been found to contain harmful constitutional errors and have been overturned. The constitutionality of the new law was immediately challenged in court.

The effect of the new restrictions was particularly dramatic in death penalty cases because the new law's rigid time limits would deter lawyers from taking on complex capital cases. Coupled with the elimination of federal support for legal programs that provided representation for persons facing the death penalty, the new law left many death row prisoners without essential legal advice. Civil liberties organizations and Human Rights Watch had reported on innumerable examples of poor representation in capital cases that had led to death sentences; new restrictions on habeas corpus appeals, coupled with funding cuts for legal assistance, further endangered these defendants' lives.

The Prison Litigation Reform Act, which became law in April 1996, made it more difficult to initiate a lawsuit to improve treatment of inmates, or to monitor court orders to improve conditions stemming from such lawsuits. This, despite the fact that lawsuits have historically been the only reliably effective way to improve deplorable custodial conditions and abusive treatment. The bill's backers in Congress explained that they were merely attempting to curtail frivolous lawsuits, ignoring prisoners' rights advocates and other experts who cautioned that the new law was overly broad and would certainly result in serious abuses going undetected and uncorrected. In July, Human Rights Watch joined prisoners' rights groups in challenging the constitutionality of some provisions of the PLRA in the case of *Plyler v. Moore* in the U.S. Court of Appeals for the Fourth Circuit; the case was pending as of this writing.

In September, Congress passed and President Clinton signed the Illegal Immigration Reform and Immigrant Responsibility Act of 1996. In correspondence, Human Rights Watch warned legislators and President Clinton that these provisions prevent asylum seekers from exercising their internationally protected right to seek and enjoy asylum and undermine the prohibition on the expulsion or return (refoulement) of refugees as set out in international human rights treaties and U.S. law regarding treatment of asylum seekers.

Among other objectionable sections, the legislation contained new summary exclusion procedures that allow immigration officers to decide, on the spot, whether a person arriving at a port of entry without proper documentation has a credible asylum claim. If the asylum claim is not found credible by the officer, an administrative appeal is available—presuming the individual knows to appeal without benefit of legal counsel. The new law is based on the flawed presumption that those entering the U.S. without documentation, or with fraudulent papers, do not have legitimate asylum claims. In fact, individuals fleeing persecution often have no opportunity, or ability, to obtain proper documentation.

Human Rights Watch also opposed the legislation's unreasonable and arbitrary deadlines on asylum applications. Once the bill became law, individuals seeking asylum in the U.S. were required to file an application within one year of arrival. Human Rights Watch has long contended that the many obstacles to filing an asylum claim often prevent asylum seekers with legitimate claims from filing in a timely manner, and that their failure to meet arbitrary deadlines should not affect their cases.

In one of the most far-reaching provisions of the new law, the historic role of the federal courts in reviewing Immigration and Naturalization Service (INS) decisions was severely restricted. One section of the new law effectively bars class-action lawsuits against the INS, thus eliminating a crucial check on a notoriously mismanaged agency. Just after the bill was signed into law, Attorney General Janet Reno reportedly filed motions to dismiss four of five class-action suits brought by hundreds of thousands of illegal immigrants who claim they were wrongfully disqualified from the government's 1980s amnesty program.

Immigration Policy and Practice

In addition to the new legislation, other developments made treatment of immigrants within the U.S. a continuing concern for Human Rights Watch. The April 1, 1996 televised beating of two border-crossers by Riverside County sheriff's deputies, which also featured an audiotape of a California Highway Patrol officer using a racial epithet, exacerbated tensions between Latino communities and proponents of strict anti-immigration policies. The incident also led to renewed calls for new policies to address frequent post-chase beatings by law enforcement agents. A letter from Human Rights Watch to U.S. Attorney General Reno, urging examination of this problem, went unanswered.

We continued to investigate human rights violations committed by personnel of the INS, particularly the U.S. Border Patrol, along the southwestern U.S. border. In June, a Human Rights Watch fact-finding mission to the border region found continuing and serious incidents of the apparent use of excessive force against border-crossers, legal residents, and U.S. citizens. In addition to complaints of rough treatment and beatings, we investigated: a Douglas, Arizona Border Patrol agent who reportedly shot, from within his vehicle, at a man on the Mexican side of the border, hitting him in the back; an El Paso, Texas agent under investigation for allegedly sexually assaulting two Guatemalan women, and repeating the offense after summoning a nearby trainee to watch; and Border Patrol agent Charles Vinson, who allegedly raped a Salvadoran woman crossing alone in a remote area near the San Ysidro, California port of entry in December 1995, and who went on to face criminal charges. Vinson had previously avoided dismissal despite shooting dead a seventeen-year-old border-crosser in 1990 and provoking numerous complaints from fellow agents, who regarded him as a "loose cannon."

The low priority given to these kinds of human rights violations by the Clinton administration and Congress was troubling in light of the dramatic growth of the INS's southwest border program in recent years. In 1993, there were approximately 3,400 Border Patrol agents along the southwest border. By the end of Fiscal Year 1996, there were 5,014 agents, and the immigration bill enacted in September 1996 authorized 1,000 new agents for the next five fiscal years, meaning that by Fiscal Year 2001 there should be approximately 10,000 Border Patrol agents—a tripling of the force in an eight-year period. Hiring surges in the past have resulted in the rushed recruitment of individuals unsuitable for any law enforcement work, and in long delays in checking recruits' qualifications and background; under such circumstances, ill-qualified or violent recruits remain undiscovered until beyond the probationary period and become almost impossible to dismiss later.

Furthermore, as thousands of new agents were quickly put in place during 1996, agents being promoted to supervisor positions were not receiving adequate training. INS officials acknowledged that supervisor training programs were overwhelmed, raising the alarming prospect of new, possibly unfit agents managed by untrained supervisors. In addition, Justice Department oversight agencies tasked with monitoring and investigating allegations of abusive treatment were not growing in proportion with the huge increase in INS personnel.

In response to criticisms of the complaints, investigatory and disciplinary procedures used by the INS and the Justice Department's Office of the Inspector General, the INS convened a Citizens' Advisory Panel (CAP) to review the shortcomings of the current system and to make recommendations to the Office of the Attorney General for improvements. As of this writing, eighteen months after its first meeting, the panel was preparing its recommendations. Considering the CAP a worthwhile endeavor to improve flawed procedures, Human Rights Watch participated in many of the panel's meetings. We remain convinced, however, that external, independent citizen review of complaints against INS personnel is the only way to gauge the extent of abusive conduct and to ensure accountability when violations do occur.

Many detainees in INS custody endured mistreatment, poor conditions, and inadequate legal representation in facilities around the country. The increasing reliance on privately run contract facilities or local jails and state prisons to house individuals in INS custody raised serious questions about the INS's lax oversight of those institutions. Following the June 1995 detainee uprising at the INS contract facility in Elizabeth, New Jersey—due in large part to poor conditions and mistreatment by the facility's staff—the INS published a self-critical report, acknowledging the oversight failures at the facility. Yet, in subsequent correspondence with Human Rights Watch, the agency revealed that essential reforms had not yet been authorized or implemented.

The Human Rights Watch Children's Rights Project conducted an investigation into the treatment of minors in INS custody in California and Arizona. The research focused on issues such as access to information, legal representation, and family members; ability to communicate in the detainee's native language; assignment to county juvenile detention or remote facilities; duration of detention; and INS cooperation with local advocates and attorneys attempting to assist the children. A report on the findings was in preparation as of this writing.

Police Abuse
Abusive conduct by law enforcement personnel was not limited to mistreatment of immigrants and asylum seekers. Police bru-

tality remained one of the most controversial and pervasive human rights problems in the United States in 1996. Police officers in a number of cities were accused of serious human rights violations, including unjustified shootings and severe beatings, with many victims asserting that these abuses were racially motivated. And even while Congress approved funding to hire thousands of new police officers in cities around the country, there was no concomitant effort to improve flawed civilian review boards, police internal investigation procedures, or the low rate of prosecution for criminal civil rights violations. According to the most recent Justice Department national data available, of 8,575 complaints reviewed under the federal civil rights statutes in 1994, only seventy-six cases were filed for prosecution—less than 1 percent.

One aid in quantifying the problem of police abuse would be the collection of data about incidents of excessive force nationwide, as required by the 1994 crime bill. The Bureau of Justice Statistics, an office of the Justice Department, initiated test programs to collect these data, but progress was slow, and it appeared that obvious sources of information, such as civilian review boards that exist in the majority of large cities, were not being used.

The Justice Department did pursue its new power to bring civil injunctions against any police department that exhibited a "pattern or practice" of abusive treatment. In the city of New Orleans, the Justice Department initiated a wide-ranging investigation into misconduct in the notoriously brutal police force. And in October, the Justice Department stated that it was expanding its investigation of the Los Angeles Police Department, focusing on the use of excessive force and racially motivated misconduct. In either city, the Justice Department has the authority to seek a court order to force the department to remedy the problems it may identify.

Prisons

During 1996, protecting prisoners' rights in the United States became more difficult. At a time when the country's prisons and jails held over 1.6 million people—giving the United States one of the largest incarcerated populations of any country in the world, as well as one of the highest per capita rates of incarceration—legal protections for prisoners kept shrinking. In addition to the Prison Litigation Reform Act described above, the Supreme Court continued eroding past prisoners' rights precedents and exempting prisons from meaningful judicial scrutiny. In *Lewis v. Casey*, the Supreme Court restricted prisoners' legal remedies by imposing strict procedural requirements on suits challenging a prisoner's lack of access to the courts. Prisoners must now show that the constitutionally inadequate law libraries or lack of legal assistance in their prisons actually hindered them in litigating a meritorious underlying claim. This put many prisoner litigants in a double bind: it is precisely when the access scheme provided by the prison is most deficient that a prisoner is most likely to be unable to put forth his or her arguments well enough to make that showing.

Conditions in U.S. prisons, meanwhile, remained frequently unacceptable and inhumane. In a January report, U.N. Special Rapporteur on Torture Nigel Rodley wrote, "Conditions at certain maximum security facilities were said to result in the inhuman and degrading treatment of the inmates in those facilities." The special rapporteur specifically noted reports of poor treatment at the H-Unit of the Oklahoma State Penitentiary and the Secure Housing Unit (SHU) at Pelican Bay prison in California.

In July, as part of the continuing trend toward harsher treatment of criminals and prisoners, Congress began serious consideration of legislation that would allow juveniles to be held with adults in confinement. Human Rights Watch joined with a dozen human rights and children's rights groups to oppose the legislation; the problematic proposals were eventually dropped. The Human Rights Watch Women's Rights Project concluded a major investigation into custodial sexual misconduct in U.S. prisons. Research was conducted in California, Georgia, Illinois, Michigan, New York, and the District of Columbia. Researchers investigated prisoners' complaints alleging rape and other sexual abuse committed by prison guards, as well as allegations of poor accountability for guards who engaged in this misconduct. The Georgia findings were included in the July 1996 Human Rights Watch report on human rights abuses in that state (see below).

The Death Penalty
Thirty-two executions were carried out in the U.S. during the first nine months of 1996, a pace short of the record-setting 1995 total of fifty-six. Challenges to the death penalty statute in Texas (a state that accounts for a large percentage of executions each year) and to the habeas corpus provisions in the counter-terrorism bill explained the relative decrease. Human Rights Watch wrote to governors and clemency boards as each execution date approached, citing our opposition to capital punishment in all cases and noting particular areas of concern in each case. We also wrote about the application of the death penalty as part of a comprehensive report on human rights abuses in Georgia (see below).

Compliance with International Standards
Since 1994, the U.S. has been party to the Convention Against Torture or Other Cruel, Inhuman or Degrading Treatment or Punishment and the International Convention on the Elimination of All Forms of Racial Discrimination (CERD). Both treaties require reports to the United Nations, describing the nation's treaty compliance. The U.S. compliance reports on both treaties were due in November 1995, yet, as of mid-November 1996, neither report had been submitted to the relevant United Nations committee. Human Rights Watch wrote to Secretary of State Warren Christopher in October 1996, urging immediate submission of the CERD report and suggesting that the U.S. report cite specific practices or incidents relevant to the treaty's provisions, rather than recitation

of U.S. law that should, but does not always, protect U.S. inhabitants from treatment prohibited by the treaty. Human Rights Watch also reported on racial discrimination in the U.S. criminal justice system to the U.N. Commission on Human Rights in April.

Other important human rights treaties, including the International Covenant on Economic, Social and Cultural Rights, the Convention on the Elimination of All Forms of Discrimination Against Women, and the Convention on the Rights of the Child, remained unratified. Also during the year, the administration took no action toward signing or ratifying core International Labour Organisation conventions intended to protect basic labor rights. This, despite the United States' support for linkage between trade and labor rights at the World Trade Organization and in international trade agreements.

Human Rights and the Olympics
In July, Atlanta, the capital of the southern state of Georgia, hosted the XXVI Olympic Games after boasting in its International Olympic Committee application that it was "for many the modern capital of human rights." In light of this claim, Human Rights Watch and other international and local human rights groups took the opportunity to review the human rights record of Atlanta and the state of Georgia. In our report, *Modern Capital of Human Rights?: Abuses in the State of Georgia*, we found that state officials and public policies contravened fundamental human rights principles in a wide range of settings in Georgia.

For example, Atlanta police officers have used excessive force, including unjustified shootings and severe beatings, and have otherwise abused their power without coming before external civilian review and without punishment through internal department procedures. Georgia's death penalty law has led to capital punishment primarily for the poor and for African-Americans—particularly when the victim of the crime is white. This discriminatory impact, which has been documented in exhaustive studies excluding for all other variables, has compounded the abuse inherent in the death penalty itself. Drug laws have been enforced disproportionately against black drug offenders, who are arrested for cocaine-related offenses at seventeen times the rate of whites (even though studies show more whites are cocaine offenders) and who receive 98 percent of the life sentences handed down in drug cases.

We also found custodial conditions in the state to be alarming. Many local jails have been so overcrowded and physically deteriorated, and jail officials have neglected prisoners' welfare so shamefully in so many areas, that the U.S. federal government threatened to sue eleven Georgia counties over jail conditions. Women in prison suffered sexual harassment and intimidation, and sometimes rape, at the hands of their guards. And minors in state custody faced extremely poor custodial conditions, have been subjected to cruel restraints and punishment forbidden by international standards, and were held in overcrowded facilities with little educational or other programs to occupy them.

We also found that lesbians and gay men in Georgia faced hostility ranging from harassment under the state's anti-"sodomy" law, to openly discriminatory firing of gay employees by state officials and others, to verbal threats and physical attacks; victims of discriminatory treatment in most parts of the state have had no effective recourse, because discrimination on the basis of sexual orientation is not prohibited. The report described a positive development, with repercussions in Georgia and elsewhere, in the U.S. Supreme Court's decision in *Romer v. Evans:* the May decision struck down a discriminatory provision of the Colorado state constitution, thus endorsing civil rights protections for lesbians, gay men, and bisexuals in that state and preventing new laws or policies that would permit discrimination against gay people.

Finally, the report described attempts to limit freedom of expression in Georgia, noting that socially conservative groups, parents, and elected officials have sought to restrict artistic expression and sex education. The free flow of information via electronic communication has also been curtailed: citing concerns ranging from terrorism to trademark theft, Georgia lawmakers passed laws that restrict rights to free expression and privacy on-line.

Neither the governor of Georgia, Zell Miller, nor Atlanta Mayor Bill Campbell responded to our report, despite the inclusion of scores of detailed recommendations and letters accompanying the report to their offices, expressing interest in working together to ameliorate the problems we identified. In a positive development, the U.S. Department of Justice began a "pre-investigation" to determine whether there was sufficient information in our Georgia report to warrant opening a formal investigation into the children's institutions. This investigation would be similar to one initiated by the Justice Department earlier in 1996 into deplorable conditions in Louisiana's juvenile detention facilities; that investigation was spurred by a Human Rights Watch Children's Rights Project report released in 1995.

THE ARMS PROJECT

The Human Rights Watch Arms Project monitored and sought to prevent the transfer of weapons and the provision of military assistance and training to governments or armed groups that committed gross violations of internationally recognized human rights or the laws of war. A corollary of this was to promote freedom of expression and freedom of information about arms and arms transfers worldwide. In addition, the Arms Project sought to eliminate weapons which as a class were, or should have been, prohibited by the laws of war, without consideration of the human rights record of the country or group possessing them. These were weapons that are by their very nature indiscriminate or cause superfluous injury.

The Arms Project was established in 1992 amidst the myriad changes that were triggered by the end of the Cold War. As, throughout the world, the logic of conflict lost its East-West overlay, the arms trade that fueled conflicts similarly shed its overarching ideological motivations, replacing them, with the exception of a few conflicts in which the perceived national interests of the supplies still played a significant role, with the profit motive. Decisions about arms sales were increasingly based less on the geostrategic importance of the buyer than on the perceived need to shore up flagging weapons industries at home. The result was an unbridled proliferation of weapons in areas of ethnic and territorial conflict.

While the overall trade in conventional weapons declined, the trade in small arms and light weapons appeared to be growing, and a fresh generation of weapons was being developed under secret budgets. Moreover, new control mechanisms, like the U.N. Arms Register and international arms embargoes against specific countries, were few, and there was little effective enforcement. And contrary to early expectations raised by the end of the Cold War, weapons of mass destruction were abolished, and the threat of proliferation, catastrophic accident or precipitate use continued.

The new order that emerged following the collapse of the Berlin Wall required a new theory for containing conflict and building peace. The construction of solutions based on ideological interests gave way to a problem-solving approach to local and international conflict. Institutions like the United Nations and the Organization for Security and Cooperation in Europe (OSCE) projected themselves, not always successfully, as neutral forces that police conflicts, promote reconciliation through negotiation, disarm soldiers and insurgents alike, and monitor elections around the world. This new role required a detailed knowledge of local conditions and strong investigative capabilities, qualifications that the supranational bodies rarely possessed. Nongovernmental organizations (NGOs) were primed to fill the

vacuum, monitoring post-conflict arrangements, putting pressure on authorities to comply with both long-standing and newly accepted international standards and conventions, and serving as early-warning beacons when things go wrong. Within this context, the Arms Project pursued five separate but related approaches that formed the underpinnings of our perception of what the new theory of change required from us as a human rights organization.

To act as a whistle-blower: One of the Arms Project's tasks was to reveal the reprehensible activities that governments and other armed forces tenaciously sought to conceal. Such activities included, among others, the illegal use of weapons in conflict, arms transfers to abusive forces, and the production of banned weapons. Through investigation of such practices, the Arms Project was able to embarrass and stigmatize offending authorities, and to galvanize members of the international community to exert pressure to halt abuses and the arms supplies that fuel these.

To build human rights concerns into efforts at conflict prevention: In the view of Human Rights Watch, human rights abuse fueled conflict, as did the supply of arms to abusive forces. Our approach to this problem was to seek to minimize the human cost of conflict and also contribute to its containment by raising the cost of abuse and of supplying arms to abusers. Information unearthed by the Arms Project provided new ammunition to international coalitions seeking to discourage warring sides from recourse to violent breaches of international norms.

To be a standard-setter: The Arms project was in the forefront of efforts to establish new homes and standards for the production, trade and use of arms, and of interpreting existing standards. In a fast evolving world, new technology yielded new weapons and new practices at a steady pace, and both had the potential for abuse. New norms were required to regulate the development and use of new armaments. The fact that there had been so little documented use of chemical and biological weapons this century was largely due to the fact that a universally accepted norm against the use of these weapons had existed since 1925. The Arms Project, by conducting research and highlighting the connection between the arms trade (or particular weapons systems) and abuse, could build on popular outrage to establish norms regarding weapons transfers and production.

To promote accountability and transparency: Few domestic or international mechanisms existed to enforce freedom of information about arms transfers. The Arms Project made creative use of the Freedom of Information Act (FOIA) in the U.S., using documents obtained under FOIA to put pressure on the U.S. government to release additional documents. The Arms Project also supported the creation of the U.N. Register of Conventional Arms, and was pushing for the creation of a parallel register for light weapons and small arms. On the issue of accountability, the Arms Project was increasingly targeting individual weapons producers and weapons exporters. As Human Rights Watch was seeking to hold corporations accountable for human rights violations that occur as a result of their activities or as part of their production process, the Arms Project was conducting parallel research on landmine producers. By tracing the flow of weapons back to its origins, the Arms Project sought to press governments to rein in their own citizens involved in the sale of arms to abusive forces.

To engage and mobilize new human rights constituencies: Last but not least, the Arms Project was contributing to efforts aimed at strengthening the international human rights movement. In 1996, the Arms Project started to bring nongovernmental organizations (NGOs) into its circle of allies in two target countries, Turkey and Lebanon. These NGOs included natural allies, like human rights organizations, but also trade unions, teachers' associations, women's groups, peace groups, lawyers' unions, charitable organizations, and others. Basing ourselves on the presupposition that human rights enforcement and conflict prevention were best served by local remedies generated from within a strong and thriving civil society, we hoped that these organizations would bring extra pressure to bear on policymakers in the U.S. and the E.U. to comply with arms export regulations and remind Turkey, Israel, and Syria of their human rights obligations under existing treaties. This effort placed concrete tools in the hands of victims of abuse, contributing to their empowerment and, in the long run, the strengthening of their societies.

Within the framework outlined above, in 1996 the Arms Project was involved in the following programs.

Banning Landmines

During 1996, the movement toward a global ban on antipersonnel landmines gained tremendous momentum. It appeared to have become a question not of whether there will be a ban, but rather when. During the past year the International Campaign to Ban Landmines (ICBL) grew from 350 NGOs to nearly 700 in about forty nations. Not coincidentally, the number of governments expressing public support for an immediate ban grew from fourteen to about fifty.

After negotiations on revisions to the Landmines Protocol of the 1980 Convention on Conventional Weapons (CCW) deadlocked in Vienna in October 1995, governments resumed talks in Geneva for one week in January 1996 and two final weeks in April/May 1996. The results were criticized by the ICBL and the International Committee of the Red Cross as grossly inadequate and unlikely to make a significant difference in the human suffering and socio-economic dislocation caused by mines.

Yet, even as the revised protocol was formally agreed to on May 3, 1996, it was clear that the movement to ban antipersonnel mines had overtaken the CCW process as the only humanitarian solution to the global mines crisis. Government after government announced its support for a total and immediate ban, including many NATO nations, and numerous nations unilaterally prohibited production, export and use. Nations that had bans already in place, such as Austria, Belgium, Canada, Germany, the Netherlands, New Zealand, Norway, the Philippines, Sweden, and Switzerland were at the forefront of the move to ban antipersonnel mines. The Organization of American States passed a resolution in June 1996 calling for a hemispheric mine-free zone and the six Central American presidents announced in September 1996 that they were banning all production, stockpiling, trade, and use of antipersonnel mines, creating in effect the world's first mine-free zone.

The U.S., on the other hand, issued a highly anticipated new policy statement on antipersonnel mines on May 16, 1996 that was criticized by the ICBL and the U.S. Campaign to Ban Landmines (USCBL) as long on rhetoric but short on action. Indeed, it could be argued that the U.S., which under the new policy continued to cling to the use of so-called smart mines in all circumstances, and long-lasting "dumb" mines at least in Korea, had become part of the problem, not a promoter of the solution. The highlight for the U.S. was the signing into law in February 1996 of the Leahy amendment requiring a one-year moratorium on the use of antipersonnel mines beginning in 1999.

At the urging of the ICBL, the government of Canada convened a historic meeting of fifty pro-ban governments in Ottawa in October 1996. The governments agreed to a final declaration committing them to a ban, and to an agenda for action that set out specific steps at the national, regional and international levels necessary to achieve a ban.

In the most important development of the year, and perhaps the history of the campaign, Canada made the dramatic announcement that it would host a conference in December 1997 at which states would be invited to sign a treaty totally banning antipersonnel mines. Belgium indicated its intention to hold a preparatory negotiating conference in June 1997.

As one of the most active members of the Steering Committee of the ICBL, the Arms Project played an important role in these developments. The Arms Project was also instrumental in the growth of the USCBL, which evolved from a loose coalition to a highly organized campaign during 1996. The Arms Project served as the chair of the Steering Committee of the USCBL. The Arms Project collected information identifying U.S. producers of landmine components, which was used by the USCBL to launch a stigmatization campaign calling on all manufacturers to get out of the business.

Banning Chemical and Biological Weapons

In 1996, the Arms Project continued to develop its network of experts, who agreed to serve as a resource to the organization, and to contact other organizations, both governmental and nongovernmental, concerned about the proliferation of chemical and biological weapons (CBW). This year the Arms Project responded to reports of the use of chemical weapons in Chechnya, Libya, Papua New Guinea, Sri Lanka, Sudan, and Uganda. Although we were able to establish through our network of contacts that there was little credible evidence to support these allegations, we remained interested in further information about these cases. The Arms Project was involved in a major investigation of the alleged use of chemical weapons by Bosnian Serb forces during the war in the former Yugoslavia. This investigation was still in progress in November 1996.

The Arms Project continued to monitor the state of CBW proliferation and maintained files on all countries that potentially possess or were developing chemical or biological weapons. This effort was supplemented with FOIA requests to different branches of the U.S. government. In addition to obtaining relevant information about U.S. knowledge of CBW proliferation, we saw the FOIA option as a way of fostering greater transparency and accountability when U.S. government officials reported a growing number of CBW possessor states but failed to name the countries of concern.

In 1996 the Arms Project also looked at the impact of the breakup of the former

Soviet Union and declining defense expenditures in Russia, the former East Bloc, and the industrialized states on CBW proliferation. Weapons, or materials for weapons, might have been sold to states seeking chemical or biological weapons, and scientists with the technical expertise to develop CBW could have sold their services to these countries. The Arms Project closely monitored all reports of transfers of CBW munitions, materials, or expertise.

Human Rights Watch also continued to push for ratification of the Chemical Weapons Convention. Recently the Arms Project joined a coalition of organizations urging U.S. senators to ratify the convention. Human Rights Watch also supported negotiations toward a verification protocol for the Biological Weapons Convention.

Engaging and Mobilizing New Human Rights Constituencies

In 1996, the Arms Project began to explore ways of involving other NGOs in efforts to curb the transfer of arms to abusive forces. In this context, we met with scores of NGOs in Turkey, Lebanon, and Israel in an attempt to identify both potential partners and appropriate mechanisms to activate in the pursuit of greater protection of civilians in conflicts in southeastern Turkey and southern Lebanon/northern Israel. Our aim was to persuade human rights NGOs to add arms transfers to their agenda to the extent that such transfers could be linked to abuses of human rights. Likewise, we encouraged other NGOs to add both human rights concerns and arms trade-related issues to their agendas to the extent that arms transfers and human rights abuses had an impact on their work and their effectiveness within their own societies.

In the case of Turkey, we provided NGOs with the names and fax numbers of key officials in the U.S. government and E.U. institutions to facilitate communications, and we suggested particular courses of actions that could be taken. These included protesting the (now frozen) sale of Super Cobra helicopters by the U.S., as well as the pending sale of Eurocopters by France. We

were also seeking to engage the U.S. and the E.U. concerning both their role in the arms trade to Turkey (through their domestic obligations to link arms transfers to human rights conditions in recipient countries) and the human rights obligations to which they and the Turkish government had committed themselves.

In the case of Lebanon, we began a collaborative project with the Center for International Human Rights Enforcement in the West Bank to persuade the parliaments of E.U. member states to condition ratification of the recently signed Trade Association agreement between the E.U. and Israel on the establishment of mechanisms of human rights enforcement. The agreement had useful human rights language but lacked implementing measures. Israeli and Lebanese NGOs had a role to play in providing human rights information to the various European parliaments involved and in placing added pressure on parliamentarians to raise the profile of human rights in E.U. trade agreements.

By mobilizing indigenous NGOs around specific agendas, we sought to expand our circle of human rights allies in various parts of the world that were wracked by conflict, assisting them in their work and at the same time improving our own research and advocacy activities.

Investigating the New Generation of Antipersonnel Weapons

Based on the success in banning blinding laser weapons in 1995, in 1996 the Arms Project started research in the area of other next-generation antipersonnel weapons—often deceptively characterized as "nonlethal" weapons—focusing on the humanitarian implications of acoustic weapons, directed-energy weapons, non-laser blinding weapons, and weapons that use illegal chemical and biological components. Our aim was to prevent the development of weapons that either clearly indiscriminate (i.e., incapable of discriminating between combatants and civilians) or cause unnecessary suffering in the terms of international humanitarian law.

"Nonlethal" weapons were being touted as a humanitarian panacea to the brutalities of war. They fell into an emerging category of weapons that were purportedly designed not to kill but to disable, and that included weapons ranging from anti-movement foams, glues and lubricants to super-caustic acids, high-power microwaves, blinding lights, infrasound and genetically engineered targeted weapons. Although many of the weapons in this category did not yet exist, they did exist as ideas, while some were already in development. The Pentagon had hidden a number of these programs in "black" (i.e., secret) budgets. One way or another, there was no doubt that weapons employing new technologies would emerge over the coming years—with humanitarian implications that merit careful scrutiny. The first Department of Defense directive establishing a policy on "nonlethal" weapons was signed on July 9, 1996.

We were concerned that some of the nonlethal weapons that were being "thought up" and developed (or even deployed) could violate international humanitarian law, just as we found was the case with tactical laser weapons that blind. In our view, the term "nonlethal" was a misnomer at best: some of the so-called nonlethal weapons did kill (often depending on the distance the target finds itself from the weapon); others made it easier for the target, once disabled, to be killed with lethal weapons. Moreover, international humanitarian law prohibits weapons that are indiscriminate (like landmines) or cause "superfluous injury or unnecessary suffering." Protocol I to the Geneva Conventions of 1949 adds that parties to the protocol are under an obligation "[i]n the study, development, acquisition or adoption of a new weapon, means, or method of warfare...to determine whether its employment would, in some or all circumstances, be prohibited" by the protocol or "any other rule of international law." The review of the humanitarian effect of new weapons at the development stage was a particular concern of the Arms Project. In the case of blinding lasers, we argued that these weapons were inhumane

(causing unnecessary suffering) and repugnant to the conscience of humankind, as they do severely disabling, irreversible and uncorrectable damage to one of the vital senses. (These problems are compounded in countries with poor medical and health facilities).

Each new "nonlethal" weapon will have to stand the test of humanitarian law. Our task will be to distinguish the "bad" ones from the "good" ones, and then to stigmatize and prevent the development and use of those that are found to violate international law. In addition, we were concerned that the Pentagon was not carrying out the required review of the humanitarian law implications of the use of "nonlethal" weapons that are currently in development. In 1996, the Arms Project began an investigation of U.S. and foreign programs on acoustic and other directed-energy weapons, paying special attention to military efforts to assess the medical and health effects of these weapons.

Curbing Arms Transfers to Human Rights Abusers

In 1996, we continued our work in documenting the role of the arms trade in violations of human rights and international humanitarian law, and in seeking to curb the transfer of arms in those cases in which weapons have contributed significantly to abuses. Our activities focused on Turkey, the Great Lakes district in Central Africa, Angola, and Colombia. The Arms Project also completed a project on Israel/Lebanon, and started an investigation into the role of arms in the war in Sudan.

Turkey

Following the release of the report, *Weapons Transfers and Violations of the Laws of War in Turkey*, in November 1995, we focused our energies on drawing attention to the report and its recommendations, and putting pressure on the various parties involved to carry out some of the reforms proposed by us. Our activities included:

Issuing a statement at the end of 1995 to denounce a controversial proposed sale by the U.S. of 120 Army Tactical Missile Systems (ATACMS) to Turkey: This was the first foreign sale of the U.S.'s most advanced ground-to-ground missile. We protested the sale on the basis of Turkey's record of systematic human rights abuses and violations of the laws of war in the southeast, including the indiscriminate use of a variety of weapons and, on a number of occasions, the direct targeting of civilians. The sale had been under consideration by the U.S. for a number of months, but was not previously approved, primarily because of human rights concerns. Although it was unlikely that Turkey would use this particular weapon in its conflict with the Workers' Party of Kurdistan (PKK), Human Rights Watch held that approving this sale at a time of heightened concern about Turkey's human rights record would send the wrong message to the government of Turkey. Despite our attempt to block it, the sale was approved in early 1996.

Participation in an ad hoc campaign to block the sale of ten Super Cobra attack helicopters to Turkey: The campaign was coordinated by the Arms Transfer Working Group (ATWG) in Washington, of which the Arms Project is a long-standing member, and was joined by other U.S. NGOs, including Amnesty International, the Helsinki Commission, and the American Association for the Advancement of Science. In meetings with U.S. policymakers we communicated our concern about the proposed sale of a category of helicopters that our research in 1995 had shown to have been used in international humanitarian law violations in Turkey. In March, we signed on to a letter protesting the proposed sale that was sent by the ATWG coalition to Secretary of State Warren Christopher. As a result of the pressure that came out of these joint efforts, the proposed sale of the Super Cobras was frozen.

Drafting an action plan for Turkish NGOs: After we had discussed our report with a number of NGOs in Istanbul and Ankara in November 1995, we proceeded to draft an action plan enabling Turkish NGOs to directly protest any proposed U.S. or E.U.

arms sales to Turkey. This action plan was completed in April 1996, and distributed in Turkish shortly thereafter.

Providing information: Based on our investigations into and advocacy regarding misuse of weapons in Turkey, we contributed to a decision of the U.S. Senate Appropriations Subcommittee for Foreign Operations to request a report from the State and Defense Departments on efforts by the administration to monitor use of U.S. military aircraft, including helicopters, in Turkey. The report was due by June 1, 1997.

Protesting repression: In September 1996, the publisher of the Turkish translation of our report, Ayse Zarakolu, and the translator, Ertugurul Kurkcu, were indicted under Article 159/1 of the Turkish penal code for "defaming and belittling the state's security and military forces." Human Rights Watch vigorously protested this outrageous attempt by the Turkish government at stifling free expression, which was aimed not as much at Human Rights Watch, the author of the report, as at those who had made the information collected by Human Rights Watch available to the Turkish public. Human Rights Watch sent an observer to the first hearing in the trial, in Istanbul on October 18. A second hearing was scheduled for November 23.

Great Lakes
District of Central Africa

The Arms Project initiated work on Burundi after 1995 research on the Rwandan genocide showed the importance of exposing the role of outside actors in empowering governments or rebel forces to carry out highly abusive military campaigns. In the case of Rwanda, we published a report on arms shipments to both the government and the rebels of the Rwandan Patriotic Front (RPF) in early 1994, only two months before the start of the genocide. The report was largely ignored at the time. We then published a follow-up report in May 1995, based on research in 1994-95, in which we pointed a finger at France, Zaire, China, and some other countries for having provided direct military aid to the Rwandan government during the genocide, or for having facilitated the transshipment of arms to the defeated government's forces after these had been driven from Rwanda to eastern Zaire in the summer of 1994. This report received wide coverage, and led to strong language in a U.N. Security Council resolution in June 1995, calling for the deployment of international military observers at airfields in Zaire. Following Zaire's refusal to cooperate with the Security Council, the council then created an International Commission of Inquiry into arms shipments to Rwandan rebel forces. In its investigation, this commission based itself largely on the accusations made by the Arms Project, and in its second report in March 1996 it presented conclusions that were in accord with our findings.

The establishment of a formal mechanism by which to enforce the U.N. arms embargo concerning Rwanda and to investigate alleged violations of the embargo had set an important precedent, and may have been a deterrent to those states that had sought to advance their geostrategic interests in Central Africa by supplying weapons to their local allies. The situation in Burundi in 1996 was near-explosive, and had some of the characteristics that marked the run-up to the genocide in Rwanda in 1994. Human Rights Watch therefore called on the United Nations to institute an arms embargo on Burundi as well, and made efforts to expand the International Commission of Inquiry's mandate to include Burundi. To add power to our recommendations, we undertook an investigation of the role of the arms trade in fueling the conflict in Burundi, which was in progress as of this writing. We also met with government officials in South Africa in October to express our concern about the involvement of South African nationals in illegal arms trafficking and other military activities in areas of Africa wracked by highly abusive conflicts, including the Great Lakes district.

Angola

Our research on Angola had focused on the role of continuing arms shipments to both the government and the UNITA rebels in the wake of the 1994 peace accords—the Lusaka Protocol—in clear violation of the international arms embargo. In February 1996, the Arms Project and Human Rights Watch/Africa jointly published *Angola—Between War and Peace: Arms Trade and Human Rights Abuses since the Lusaka Protocol.* The report concluded that despite the signing of the Lusaka Protocol, extensive human rights abuses continued to be committed by both sides.

Moreover, both sides continued to acquire additional weapons. The Lusaka Protocol prohibits both sides from resupplying their military forces with "any military equipment, lethal or otherwise." Furthermore, U.N. Security Council Resolution 864 (September 1993) clearly prohibits the sale and supply of any military or petroleum products to UNITA, and U.N. Security Council Resolution 976 (February 1995) calls on both the government and UNITA "to cease any acquisition of arms and war materiel." Although arms shipments declined in 1995, new weaponry, especially from Russia and the Ukraine, reached the government. These were not merely pre-1995 orders; as the year progressed it was evident that the government was still purchasing new arms and military equipment. UNITA brought in new weapons both over land and on secret flights from Zaire and Congo to airstrips in the diamond-rich Lunda provinces. Sporadic but fierce fighting continued in the diamond areas throughout 1995.

Human Rights Watch called on the U.N. to institute an unambiguous and comprehensive arms embargo on Angola, applicable to both the government and UNITA, and to encourage member states to submit information on past weapons exports to Angola to the U.N. Register on Conventional Arms. Human Rights Watch called on the governments of South Africa, Zaire, and Congo, in particular, to assist the U.N. in its attempts to monitor UNITA sanction-busting; to stop mercenaries from their countries or who transit their countries from operating in Angola; and, in the case of Zaire, to take all measures to stop the use of Zaire as a conduit for the illegal arms trade (a recommendation that echoes recommendations we have made to Zaire with respect to Rwanda in 1995).

In response to the report, the Angolan government issued a statement denouncing our "false allegations," but indicated that it had committed itself to halting the import of arms and terminating its contract with a major South African security outfit. After intensive lobbying by Human Rights Watch, the U.N. Security Council adopted language in a resolution on Angola in May 1996 that reflected our human rights concerns, including a call on both parties to destroy their stockpiles of landmines and a call on member states to reinforce the weapons ban. Later in 1996, we launched a renewed investigation of further shipments of arms to both the Angolan government and UNITA.

Colombia

In 1996 the Arms Project with Human Rights Watch/Americas completed its investigation of the lethal nexus between the Colombian military forces and irregular paramilitary death squads, and the role of the U.S. government in reorganizing the military intelligence network in Colombia, which relies heavily on paramilitaries in the army's campaign against insurgents. A joint report by the Arms Project and Human Rights Watch/ Americas released in November concluded that a team of the U.S. Department of Defense and the Central Intelligence Agency worked closely with Colombian military officers on the 1991 reorganization of the military intelligence apparatus, which made paramilitary groups a key component. Working under the direct orders of military high command, paramilitary forces incorporated into military intelligence networks conducted surveillance of legal opposition political figures and groups, operated with military units, then carried out attacks against targets chosen by their military commanders. In some regions in Colombia, the military armed and equipped paramilitaries, patrolled with them

and used them as guides, and issued weapons licenses to known paramilitary leaders. In some cases, the military gave orders on whom to kill and when.

Research by Human Rights Watch also shed light on the "strategy of impunity" pursued by the Colombian military. The deeds of officers who work with para-militaries, brought to light again and again by the government's civilian investigators, have been systematically covered up by the military justice system, allowing these same officers to return to the field and continue their work of organizing, directing and deploying paramilitary groups.

The U.S. military authorities, in addition to making recommendations about the restructuring of Colombian intelligence in 1991, turned a blind eye to abuses, even though they have acknowledged that training and weapons provided to Colombia for counter-drug purposes may have been used in counterinsurgency operations during which human rights violations have occurred. Human Rights Watch has also obtained evidence showing that U.S. military personnel continue to advise and train the Colombian military, including the navy, and work in areas where the military maintains a partnership with paramilitaries.

Human Rights Watch made a number of recommendations to the Colombian government, the U.S. government, and the international community. In Colombia, we called for an end to the "strategy of impunity," urging, among other measures, investigation and prosecution of officers suspected of involvement in abuses. Human Rights Watch called on the U.S. to immediately suspend all military aid, sales and other forms of military and security assistance to Colombia until there is an end to the abuses committed by military-supported paramilitaries.

Lebanon/Israel

In April 1996, Israeli forces carried out a large-scale military operation in Lebanon, dubbed "Operation Grapes of Wrath." The Arms Project, in collaboration with Human Rights Watch/Middle East, had just completed a study on the ongoing conflict in southern Lebanon and violations of international humanitarian law by both Israeli forces and Hizballah guerrillas. Our report was released in May, updated to reflect preliminary findings about the most recent round of fighting. This report, *Civilian Pawns: Laws of War Violations and the Use of Weapons on the Israel-Lebanon Border*, described attacks on civilians on both sides of the border, and devoted special attention to the weapons used in the conflict. Most of Israel's arsenal derived from U.S. military assistance and sales. We were particularly concerned about Israel's illegal use of phosphorus and flechette shells in civilian areas. Hizballah, which had allegedly received most of its weaponry from Iran via Syria, was criticized for indiscriminately firing Katyusha rockets into northern Israel.

The Arms Project visited Israel, Lebanon, and Syria in May to release the report and discuss our findings with policymakers from all the parties concerned. We also met with a large number of NGOs in Israel and Lebanon to explore ways of effectively pressing both parties to protect civilians during the conflict. The Arms Project, in cooperation with Human Rights Watch/Middle East, also investigated Israeli attacks on civilian power transformers in Lebanon during the April operation.

The United Nations International Standards and Multilateral Measures

According to figures released in 1996, aggregate world military spending continued to decline in 1995, although the downward trend is tapering off. This trend also did not represent the entire world, for although there were heavy reductions in the western industrialized states and Russia, military spending continued to increase in certain countries and regions, notably the Middle East and Southeast Asia. The United States was the predominant arms supplier to the developing world in 1992-1995, according to the U.S. Congressional Research Service. The U.S. earned US$40.6 billion (constant 1995 dollars) from arms transfer agreements, 45.3 percent of all developing world agreements. During this period, France, the second leading supplier, accounted for nearly 21 percent of all arms transfers to the developing world, valued at $18.8 billion.

The major 1995 supplier to the developed world—in terms of contracts signed— was Russia with $6 billion in arms transfer agreements (39 percent). The United States was second with $3.8 billion (24.6 percent) and France was third with $2.4 billion (15.6 percent). In actual deliveries of arms during 1995—based on contracts signed previously—the United States led with $9.5 billion, 44 percent of the total, and the United Kingdom was second with $4.5 billion, or 20.8 percent of such deliveries.

In 1996, more states submitted information to the (voluntary) U.N. Register of Conventional Arms. As of October 7, ninety-one states had replied to U.N. requests for information. Although this information continued to contain inaccuracies and notable omissions, the register was an important source of information on the global arms trade and fostered transparency and accountability. The register continued to cover only seven categories of major weapons systems; it did not include the international trade in light arms.

In July, representatives of thirty-three states met in Vienna, Austria, and established the Wassenaar Arrangement on Export Controls for Conventional Arms and Dual-Use Goods and Technologies. Participating states agreed to control all items set forth in the list of dual-use goods and technologies as well as the munitions list with the aim of preventing unauthorized transfers or re-transfers of these items to a region or a state of serious concern to the participating states. To facilitate the future work of the Wassenaar Arrangement and possibly expand and enhance it, the participants also created a secretariat in Vienna. The next Plenary of the Wassenaar Arrangement was scheduled for December 1996 in Vienna.

The Convention on the Prohibition of the Development, Production, Stockpiling and Use of Chemical Weapons and on Their Destruction (the Chemical Weapons Convention, CWC), continued to garner signatures in 1996. By the end of October, the required sixty-five states had ratified the convention, which was therefore scheduled to come into force after 180 days, i.e., in April 1997. Except for the U.S. and Russia, nearly all the world's large chemical producers had already ratified. Soon after the deposition of the sixty-fifth instrument of ratification in October, the Organization for the Prohibition of Chemical Weapons in The Hague was expected to expand its staff and convene the first session of the Conference of State Parties, which will be responsible for the treaty's implementation.

There were few developments with respect to the Biological and Toxin Weapons Convention (BWC) in 1996. The BWC has review conferences every five years to assess progress on adherence to the Convention. At the end of the conference, the final document, agreed on by consensus, reports on the state of progress on each article. The Third Review Conference in 1991 called for an examination of possible verification regimes to the BWC. The next review conference was scheduled to take place in Geneva at the end of 1996. In 1994, an ad hoc group was established by a special conference to draft a legally-binding protocol for strengthening the BWC. This group met twice in 1996 and was expected to continue to meet in 1997.

Unfortunately, confidence in the BWC had declined since the last conference because of the admission by the Russian Federation in 1992 that despite being a codepository of the BWC in 1975 it had an offensive program until March 1992; disclosures in 1995 that Iraq had developed and deployed biological weapons; and reports that the private religious cult Aum Shinrikyo in Japan had been close to developing a biological weapons capability.

International Arms Embargoes

The U.N. Security Council imposed arms embargoes eleven times since 1966, nine of these since 1990. At the end of 1996, U.N. arms embargoes were still in place against Iraq, Liberia, Libya, Somalia, and UNITA in Angola. The Security Council's decision in August 1995 to lift the arms embargo provisionally against the government of Rwanda became final in September 1996, but the embargo remained in place against former Rwandan government forces in states neighboring Rwanda. (The forces of the government ousted in 1994 were based primarily in eastern Zaire.) The 1991 arms embargo against Yugoslavia came to an end in June 1996 within months after it was revealed that the Clinton administration had decided not to object to Iranian arms shipments to Bosnia in 1994. In August 1996, the Security Council threatened to consider an arms embargo against Burundi if that country's leaders and rebels did not begin unconditional talks by October 31.

The embargoes that remained in place in 1996 were enforced to lesser or greater effect depending on the interest and political will of the international community in every particular case. The sanctions committees routinely established as part of the arms embargo mechanism were under a mandate to collect information regarding implementation of those embargoes and recommend ways to increase their effectiveness. However, in the case of Rwanda, the U.N. Security Council created the additional framework of an International Commission of Inquiry regarding the sale or supply of arms and related materiel to former Rwandan government forces in the Great Lakes region, following revelations made by the Arms Project in May 1995 about arms shipments to these forces. The commission was primarily a fact-finding body composed of serving military and police officers. While it did not have the legal powers or the resources of a police force or investigative agency, it actively investigated reports on the sale or supply of arms and related materiel and the provision of military training to former Rwandan government forces.

In its second report in March 1996, the commission concluded that "it is highly probable" that the U.N. arms embargo had been violated in at least two instances that were brought to light in the May 1995 Arms Project report, *Rearming with Impunity: International Support for the Perpetrators of the Rwandan Genocide*. In its report, the commission criticized the U.N. sanctions process, pointing to the lack of U.N.-based information and the slow response time to events. For example, the commission was created some sixteen months after the adoption of the arms embargo on Rwanda in May 1994 and a month after the Security Council decided to lift the embargo provisionally on supplies to the (new) government in Kigali. The commission also stated that if Security Council resolutions are to be properly implemented and the commission's recommendations for this are adopted, "sufficient additional resources must be made available" to implement them.

Among its recommendations, which the Arms Project supported, the commission proposed that U.N. observers be stationed in Zaire to monitor implementation of the arms embargo and that particular governments should investigate allegations against their nationals or companies located within their borders in connection with possible sanctions busting. In addition, the commission recommended creation of sanctions committees that would have expanded functions and suggested parallel systems within individual countries that would aid in implementing and enforcing arms embargoes. The commission also recommended that countries bordering a country under an arms embargo should help maintain a data bank on the movement and acquisition of small arms, ammunition, and materiel.

At the end of October, the commission had completed its third report, but by the middle of November the Security Council had yet to release it to the public. Having obtained a leaked copy, the Arms Project issued a press release on November 11, calling on the Security Council to publish the report forthwith and act upon the Commission's conclusions and recommendations. In its report, the Commission showed

how arms continued to flow to the former Rwandan government forces, and how these forces raised funds and conducted military training in refugee camps in Zaire and Tanzania. In response to these findings, Human Rights Watch called on the United Nations and the international donor community to implement effective controls to enforce the international arms embargo against the former Rwandan government forces; to extend the mandate of the International Commission for the period of at least another year; to encourage member states of the United Nations to take legal actions against their nationals involved in arms trafficking in violation of U.N. arms embargoes, even if said individuals are operating in third countries; and to encourage states in the Great Lakes area to establish a regional arms register as a way of encouraging transparency about the arms trade and as a first step toward curbing the supply of weapons to armed forces engaged in human rights abuses.

The process to end the arms embargo imposed in September 1991 on all deliveries of weapons and military equipment to Yugoslavia began in November 1995. In Resolution 1021, the Security Council set out provisions for a termination of the arms embargo in stages. All provisions of the embargo were terminated in March 1996, with the exception of those related to heavy weapons, mines, military aircraft, and helicopters. The Security Council terminated the remaining provisions in June 1996.

In April it was revealed that the Clinton administration had decided two years earlier not to object to Iranian arms shipments to Bosnia at the height of the war in the former Yugoslavia. In testimony before the House International Relations Committee in April 1996, Undersecretary of State for Political Affairs Peter Tarnoff said the Clinton administration had feared for the survival of the Sarajevo government. U.S. officials were quoted as insisting that the administration was not obliged to impede the Iranian shipments under the terms of the U.N. Security Council embargo. Undersecretary Tarnoff said U.S. representatives were told to respond to inquiries by the Croatian government regarding the arms shipments by stating that they had " no instructions" on the matter. He also testified that the U.S. had no contact with the Iranian government regarding the weapons.

United States

The key U.S. initiative to control the proliferation of conventional arms around the globe in 1996 was its support for the formation of the Wassenaar Arrangement (see above). Aside from this new initiative, aimed at stopping the flow of weapons to only a handful of "rogue states," U.S. arms trade policy continued to be one more of promotion—for economic reasons—than of control.

The Arms Project had for several years promoted the establishment of both a U.S. and European "code of conduct" for arms transfers that would, among other things, prohibit arms exports to governments that did not respect human rights. In July 1996, a bill based on this concept, sponsored by Senator Hatfield and Senator Dorgan, was defeated in the Senate by a vote of 65-35. Though a loss, the debate and recorded vote put advocates of the code in a good position to advance the proposal in the next Congress.

President Clinton announced a new landmines policy in May 1996 that had by November resulted in little new concrete action (see above).

The vote for U.S. ratification of the Chemical Weapons Convention (CWC), scheduled for September 12, was postponed at the last minute when former Senator Bob Dole, the Republican candidate for president, sent a letter to the Senate majority leader opposing ratification. Opponents proposed two deliberately impossible amendments to the ratification measure. One declared that the treaty would not come into effect until the CIA certifies it is able to verify CWC compliance with "high confidence," and the other that it would not take effect unless North Korea, Libya and Iraq ratified it. As Dole's letter placed Republi-

can supporters of the CWC in a difficult position, the Clinton administration decided to postpone the vote, thereby ensuring that the U.S. would not be one of the original sixty-five state parties to the CWC.

Because the 104th Congress ended in September 1996, it became clear that the treaty would again have to be reported out of the Senate Foreign Relations Committee before it could be voted on by the entire Senate. The Convention was expected to come up for a vote again early in 1997, possibly still before its entry into force in April.

THE CHILDREN'S RIGHTS PROJECT

Human Rights Watch established the Children's Rights Project in 1994 to work with the organization's regional divisions and other thematic projects to investigate abuses that uniquely affect children and for which unique campaigning initiatives are needed. It was to deal with abuses carried out or tolerated by governments and also those perpetrated by armed opposition groups, such as the use of children as soldiers; and to fill the significant gap between child-oriented development and relief aid and traditional human rights work that focuses on the civil and political rights of adults, by devising effective research and advocacy strategies to work toward an end to the abuses that expressly affect the rights of children. Moreover, the project served as a link between international and national children's groups and the human rights community.

Children continue to be particularly vulnerable to exploitation. In many countries, children as young as nine were forced to become soldiers, to kill or be killed, to be victims of atrocities or, sometimes, to take part in them. In other countries, children as young as five or six slaved as bonded laborers, their childhood mortgaged as they tried to pay off loans made to their families. In many countries, children were forced into prostitution, snatched by strangers, or sold by their families and even trafficked from one country to another while governments ignored their plight.

The Children's Rights Project worked to hold governments accountable for failing to respect and protect children's basic human rights, especially the rights to life and freedom from torture and ill-treatment.

The Work of
the Children's Rights Project

During 1996 the Children's Rights Project, working with Human Rights Watch's regional divisions, researched and campaigned to bring to light the plight of bonded child laborers in India; police violence against street children in Bulgaria, India, Guatemala, and Kenya; ill-treatment of children in correctional institutions in Bulgaria and in Georgia and Colorado in the United States; abuses of unaccompanied minors by the U.S. Immigration and Naturalization Service; the effects of genocide on the children of Rwanda; and the torture of children by police in Turkey. The project also released a short report, *Children in Combat*, on child soldiers that pulled together the research of Human Rights Watch in eight countries over the past several years.

Child Slaves (Bonded Child Labor)

Bonded child labor took place when a family received an advance payment, sometimes as little as US$17, to turn over a child (sometimes as young as five or six years old) to an employer. Typically, the workplace was structured so that the child could never repay the advance. In some cases, bonded child labor was generational: many years earlier a family member was pledged to an employer and each successive generation was forced to provide a replacement worker.

In September the project released a report with Human Rights Watch/Asia, *The*

Small Hands of Slavery: Bonded Child Labor in India. Based on a two-month fact-finding mission, the report described in detail the use of children who worked as bonded laborers in six industries in India: silk, beedis (hand-rolled cigarettes), leather, silver, gemstones, and carpets. Our researchers interviewed more than one hundred bonded children (some as young as five) as well as lawyers, social workers, human rights activists, employers, and government officials. We concluded that, bonded child labor existed throughout India, and that conditions for these children are harsh, unhealthy and sometimes dangerous.

We worked closely with Indian non-governmental organizations (NGOs) on strategies for change. At the donors' meeting of governments and intergovernmental organizations that provide aid for India, nine of the eighteen delegations stressed the need to abolish bonded child labor. The World Bank agreed to look into its funding of the silk industry, in which we revealed the existence of bonded child labor. World Bank President, James D. Wolfensonn, told press in India that funding for projects using child labor would be ended. The report received remarkable press coverage in India and abroad. Moreover, the Indian government and the World Bank agreed to establish pilot programs on child labor.

Killing and Abuse of
Street Children by Police

Street children throughout the world continued to be reported killed or subjected to physical abuse by police. Moreover, they were frequently arbitrarily and illegally detained by police, sometimes for long periods of time.

Although much had been written about street children, almost all research and writing dealt with social and economic issues—health, poverty, AIDS, prostitution, glue-sniffing, and other drug abuse—in isolation from the political conditions in which they arise. With the exception of the massive killings of children in Brazil and Colombia, often by police, on which we reported in

1994, little attention was paid to the plight of these children, and almost none to the constant physical and psychological abuse carried out against them by police. Our 1995 report, *Children of Sudan: Slaves, Street Children, and Child Soldiers*, described police abuse of street children. We continued this focus in 1996 with work on police violence against children in Bulgaria, India, Guatemala, Kenya, and Turkey.

In September the project released *Children of Bulgaria: Police Violence and Arbitrary Confinement*, which documented abuses committed against Roma (Gypsy) street children by police, on the street, upon arrest, and in detention. We found that police routinely harassed children and used physical force to make them leave areas of safety and shelter. Police also conducted warrantless round-ups of street children upon suspicion of theft or for the alleged purpose of finding runaways. Street children were detained for many nights in police lockups in degrading and inhumane conditions, with no judicial review of the legality of their detention. They were often beaten by police upon arrest and while in detention, especially during interrogation sessions. Moreover, police did little to protect Roma children from attacks by "skinheads" and other street gangs. Children refrained from complaining to police about such attacks, fearing ill-treatment.

In November we released *Police Abuse and Killings of Street Children in India*, based on a month-long investigation in four of India's five largest cities: Bangalore, Bombay, Madras, and New Delhi. The report documented a consistent pattern of arbitrary and illegal detentions, torture, extortion, and even killing of street children for reasons as trivial as "making faces" at police, or for no reason at all. Police were rarely, if ever, prosecuted, or even disciplined, for these acts. Comprehensive recommendations made in 1979 by India's National Police Commission to eliminate police abuses were never implemented.

We called on the Indian government to implement the Police Commission's reforms.

to ratify the 1984 U.N. Convention Against Torture and Other Cruel, Inhuman or Degrading Treatment or Punishment, and to take specific steps to eliminate police abuse of street children. We worked with Indian NGOs to develop strategies to further these aims.

In September we sent fact-finding missions to Kenya and Guatemala to investigate the treatment of street children by police in those countries.

In October we sent a mission to Turkey to investigate police torture of children during interrogation, a subject addressed in a 1990 Human Rights Watch report.

Conditions in Children's Institutions

International standards provided both broad and specific protections for children in the justice system. These included the Convention on the Rights of the Child (Article 40), the International Covenant on Civil and Political Rights (Articles 10, 14), the Standard Minimum Rules for the Administration of Juvenile Justice, the U.N. Rules for the Protection of Juveniles Deprived of their Liberty, the U.N. Guidelines for the Prevention of Juvenile Delinquency, the Standard Minimum Rules for the Treatment of Prisoners, and the African Charter on the Rights and Welfare of the Child (Articles 16, 17).

Children in countries throughout the world were confined in dreadful conditions in detention or correctional facilities (training or reform schools), and sometimes in adult prisons. The public was generally not concerned about these conditions, perceiving these children as violent criminals (although studies in the U.S., for example, indicate that only between 10 and 15 percent of incarcerated juveniles had committed violent acts). These children were powerless to change their treatment and, generally, had no one to speak for them.

In 1995 the Children's Rights Project released *United States: Children in Confinement in Louisiana*. The report described conditions in all four secure correctional institutions for children in the state, based on interviews with more than sixty children, as well as state officials, judges, lawyers, social workers, and others concerned with juvenile justice. We found pervasive brutality by guards, overuse of isolation and the misuse of restraints—handcuffs and, on occasion, shackles—in violations of international standards. In a quite remarkable success for the project, the U.S. Department of Justice opened a formal investigation into the institutions in June 1996, based on our report.

We followed the Louisiana report with a report on correctional institutions in the state of Georgia. Unfortunately, Georgia officials refused permission for us to visit the facilities or talk with the children. However, in March we interviewed lawyers, social workers, judges, children, and others with experience in the correctional institutions there. We found that children were confined in shamefully overcrowded, squalid and unsanitary institutions with inadequate educational and exercise programs. As a result of overcrowding, these institutions were dangerous places for weaker children who were preyed upon by older, tougher juvenile offenders. In some facilities, four boys shared housing space intended for one. Moreover, we found disciplinary measures that were inappropriate and excessive. These included an overuse of confinement in isolation cells (sixty-three days in one case) and locking children in their cells for long periods of time. Moreover, four-point restraints, with children bound to a bed by wrists and ankles for long periods of time, were used as disciplinary measures, as well as to restrain children who were believed to be suicidal. Our findings were part of the Human Rights Watch publication, *Modern Capital of Human Rights?: Abuses in the State of Georgia*, which was released in July.

The U.S. Department of Justice began a "pre-investigation" to determine whether there was sufficient information in our Georgia report to warrant opening a formal investigation into the children's institutions. Also, we were working with the American Bar Association's Juvenile Justice Center to try to effect changes in the institutions.

During 1996 we also carried out a fact-finding mission to Colorado to look into conditions in children's institutions there.

In 1996 we investigated the treatment of unaccompanied children by the U.S. Immigration and Naturalization Service in Arizona, California, and Illinois. The investigation included children's access to lawyers and interpreters, their treatment by guards, and their placement in juvenile correctional facilities.

In our report on the children of Bulgaria we examined the procedures by which children as young as eight were confined for up to three years, without due process, to correctional institutions known as Labor Education Schools, for minor offenses and for status offenses, that is, offenses that would not be crimes if committed by adults, e.g. truancy, running away from home and "incorrigibility." Conditions in these schools were harsh and impeded, rather than improved, a child's well-being. Children told us of hunger, cold, and extreme and summary disciplinary measures, including severe beatings by staff members, reductions in diet, and confinement in an "isolator."

We presented our findings to Bulgarian authorities and, to the U.N. Committee on the Rights of the Child, in October, with detailed recommendations for reform of the Bulgarian juvenile justice system and the conditions of confinement for children whom courts have found to be delinquent.

The 1996 Kenya and Guatemala missions also looked into the procedures by which children were sentenced to institutions and the conditions there.

Child Soldiers
Children under eighteen—often as young as nine or ten—were used as soldiers around the world in international, and, more often, internal armed conflicts. These children were often equipped with fully-automatic assault rifles. They killed others (often children) and were themselves killed or grievously wounded. They witnessed and sometimes took part in atrocities. They were deprived of education and a normal childhood. Rehabilitating them and reintegrating them into a

peaceful society once hostilities ended was an immense and difficult problem.

The Children's Rights Project had issued three detailed reports on the use of children as soldiers: *Easy Prey. Child Soldiers in Liberia* (1994), *The Lost Boys: Child Soldiers and Unaccompanied Boys in Southern Sudan* (1994), and *Children of Sudan: Slaves, Street Children, and Child Soldiers* (1995). In 1996 we continued our advocacy with a short report, *Children in Combat*, that summarized our information on the use of child soldiers in eight countries around the world.

We continued our advocacy efforts on several fronts. First, we took part in a Belfast conference on children in low-level conflicts, which was part of a U.N. Study on the Impact of Armed Conflict on Children. We also provided information for the study, and later took part in editing and providing suggestions that were incorporated in the final report, which was presented to the U.N. General Assembly in November 1996. We worked with a coalition of children's and other organizations to maximize the impact of the report.

We provided information and carried out advocacy efforts in connection with the U.N. Working Group on raising the minimum age for participation in armed conflict. That group, setup by the Commission on Human Rights, met twice to draft an optional protocol to the Convention on the Rights of the Child that would raise the minimum age from fifteen to eighteen. The U.S. government, which had not ratified the convention, played a strongly negative role during the drafting of the optional protocol, resisting raising the age to eighteen and insisting that the protocol not take effect until ratified by twenty-five countries (in other human rights documents the number needed has been ten). We worked unsuccessfully to persuade U.S. officials otherwise.

In an effort to examine the impact on children of the Rwanda genocide, we sent a mission there in 1996. The mission focused on the roles played by children during the slaughter, the treatment of children by the former government's forces which carried out the genocide and by the forces of the current government, the conditions in which children were held afterwards, and discrimination suffered by imprisoned children because of their ethnicity.

Orphans in China

In January Human Rights Watch/Asia released *Death by Default: A Policy of Fatal Neglect in China's State Orphanages*, which described the starvation, disease, and unnatural deaths of thousands of abandoned orphans in state custodial institutions. The Children's Rights Project played an active advocacy role in bringing these findings to NGOs and intergovernmental organizations like UNICEF and the World Health Organization (WHO). In an effort to influence UNICEF programs in Chinese orphanages, we arranged a meeting for Dr. Zhang Shuyun, who had smuggled out of China vital information on the Shanghai orphanage, and Ai Ming, an orphan who spent the first twenty years of his life in that orphanage, with UNICEF officials. We also met with the WHO in Geneva concerning our findings and recommendations and to persuade the WHO to take action on the plight of the orphans. With Physicians for Human Rights, we arranged for Dr. Zhang a meeting with physicians to enlist their help in influencing Chinese officials to reform orphanage practices. We also prepared a report for the U.N. Committee on the Rights of the Child, discussed below.

This year the Children's Rights Project honored as a human rights monitor Krassimir Kanev, the chair of the Bulgarian Helsinki Committee (BHC), a Bulgarian nongovernmental organization founded in 1992. The BHC issued a detailed study of Labor Education Schools (juvenile correctional facilities) in 1996, and was active in protecting children's rights in other areas.

Work with the United Nations

During 1996 the Children's Rights Project conducted advocacy efforts with the U.N. Committee on the Rights of the Child,

UNICEF, and the World Health Organization.

The U.N. Committee on the Rights of the Child, the treaty body charged with monitoring compliance with the Convention on the Rights of the Child, was a forceful and effective group that welcomed input from NGOs. The committee received reports from states signatories to the convention, questioned officials closely on the state's compliance, and made cogent recommendations for change. In addition, the committee persuaded the U.N. General Assembly to create a special study on the impact of armed conflict on children. It also persuaded the U.N. Commission on Human Rights to establish the working group on the minimum age for armed conflict.

In the last two years, the Children's Rights Project submitted to the committee reports on the treatment of children in the justice systems in Jamaica, Northern Ireland, and the state of Louisiana (the committee agreed to receive that report although the U.S. was not yet a party to the convention). In many cases the committee urged the offending government to take the steps we had recommended.

In February 1996 the project presented both written and oral reports to the committee concerning the plight of orphans in China, mentioned earlier. The committee strongly criticized the Chinese government for the deaths we disclosed, and used many of the suggestions and recommendations that we had made to the committee.

In June the Asia division of Human Rights Watch presented written and oral reports to the committee on the status of children in Burma.

In October the project presented written and oral reports to the committee on police violence and arbitrary confinement of street children in Bulgaria, and an oral report on the plight of Kurdish children in Iraq, based on a report released by our Middle East division.

A written statement was also submitted to the Commission on Human Rights on the use of children as soldiers in armed conflicts, calling for the convening of a third session of the Working Group on raising the minimum age for participation in armed conflict. The project sent a letter to the U.N. High Commissioner for Refugees (UNHCR) urging it to take measures to prevent the conscription of underage boys from UNHCR refugee camps by the Sudan People's Liberation Army. The project learned that such conscription continued as recently as March and April of 1996.

The project called on the U.N. special rapporteur on torture and the U.N. Working Group on Arbitrary Detention to investigate police violence against street children and arbitrary detention in Bulgaria and India. We asked the U.N. Working Group on Contemporary Forms of Slavery, UNICEF, the International Labour Organization (ILO), and the WHO to press the Indian government to observe national and international laws forbidding bonded child labor.

The Role of the United States

One hundred and eighty-seven countries had ratified or acceded to the Convention on the Rights of the Child. Only five countries had not done so: Cook Islands, Somalia, United Arab Emirates, Switzerland, and the United States. The Clinton administration signed the convention in February 1995, but did not forward the convention to the Senate for ratification. Jesse Helms, the chair of the Foreign Relations Committee, had described the convention as a "pernicious document" and had vowed not to hold hearings on its ratification. Human Rights Watch supported U.S. ratification of the convention.

In February 1996 the U.S. continued to be a major stumbling block in the meetings of the Working Group to Draft an Optional Protocol to the United Nations Convention on the Rights of the Child on Participation of Children in Armed Conflict, that·sought to raise the permissible age for taking part in armed conflict from fifteen to eighteen. The U.S. permitted seventeen-year-olds to enlist in the armed forces with parental permission, and was opposed to raising the minimum age to eighteen. The working group was to meet again in 1997.

On a more positive note, in June the U.S. Department of Labor again held hearings on child labor, having issued two reports on the use of child labor and bonded child labor in the manufacture of products exported to the United States. In June Labor Secretary Robert Reich recommended four steps for ILO members to take on child labor: increase global public awareness of the problem; insist that international financial institutions such as the World Bank fully integrate the child labor issue into their decisions; adopt additional international laws against exploitative child labor; and provide resources for education and law enforcement.

THE WOMEN'S RIGHTS PROJECT

Women's Human Rights Developments

Women's rights activists left the 1995 Fourth World Conference on Women in Beijing armed with a Platform for Action adopted by 189 governments who had committed themselves to improving respect for women's human rights. In 1996, women around the world pressed their governments to live up to these promises by, among other things, ensuring in law and in practice the equality of women and men, repealing laws that discriminate on the basis of sex, removing gender bias in the administration of justice, and combating violence against women, whatever its causes. Following the Beijing conference, some governments stepped up efforts to promote women's rights: the South African parliament ratified the Convention on the Elimination of All Forms of Discrimination Against Women (CEDAW); the legislature in Nepal introduced legislation to allow women to inherit property; and the governments of Colombia and Ecuador

passed laws to protect women in cases of domestic violence. But these important steps will have little impact if they are not backed up with changes in government practice.

Aware that governments often must be compelled to follow up policy pronouncements with on-the-ground implementation, the Women's Rights Project worked in 1996 to monitor women's human rights developments in Egypt, Kenya, Mexico, Morocco, Russia, Rwanda, and the United States and to expose the gap between government rhetoric on women's human rights and the reality of the continuing abuse of those rights. In addition to these countries, during 1996 we conducted missions to investigate violations of women's human rights in Pakistan, South Africa, and the United States.

Egypt

In September 1996, the Women's Rights Project began to investigate problems of legal discrimination against women in Egypt and violence against women in the family, including spousal abuse and female genital mutilation (FGM). Although Article 40 of the Egyptian Constitution guarantees women equality under the law, numerous laws deny women rights that are accorded to men. Egypt's nationality law provides a striking example of women's unequal status under the law by denying women who marry non-Egyptians the ability to pass on their Egyptian nationality to their children. In February 1996, the Egyptian People's Assembly adopted an omnibus law on children but rejected draft language reforming the nationality law. An estimated 250,000 Egyptian women thus continued to suffer the consequences of unequal citizenship; they must obtain visas to allow their "foreign" children to live in Egypt and must pay for state education and health services to which Egyptian citizens are entitled. No similar restrictions are placed on male Egyptians who marry non-Egyptian women. The Mubarak government resisted efforts to reform this law and thus accord women the full benefits of citizenship. The government defended its position by arguing that a law conveying citizenship on children of non-Egyptian fathers presents a threat to security: as citizens, these children would, among other things, be required to serve in the army.

Other forms of legal discrimination underscored the secondary status of women. The criminal code, for example, allows a husband to receive a reduced penalty—three years maximum—for killing his wife if he can prove that he killed her to defend his honor. Women who kill their husbands for whatever reason are subject to the standard punishment for murder: prison and hard labor for a term between three years and life. Throughout 1996, reports of such "honor" killings and the light sentences given in response to them appeared frequently in the Egyptian press.

Human rights and women's advocates provided evidence that domestic violence was a widespread and seldom acknowledged phenomenon in Egypt. Initial research conducted in 1996 by the New Woman Research Center and El Nadim Center for Victims of Violence indicated high levels of spousal abuse and widespread acceptance of men's right to beat their wives. Despite growing awareness of the scope of the problem, the government made no statements acknowledging or condemning domestic violence. Moreover, advocates stated that law enforcement authorities, ranging from police to judges, tended to dismiss domestic violence as a private matter between husband and wife. Women were successful in filing domestic violence complaints with police only when they were prepared to insist on their right to do so. Although domestic violence by definition is committed by private individuals, states nonetheless are obliged under international law to protect women's lives and physical security. Further, where states routinely fail to prosecute domestic violence because of the sex and status of the victim, they deny women equal protection of the law.

Female genital mutilation (FGM), also known as female circumcision, continued to be widespread in Egypt despite government condemnation of the practice. A demographic and health survey funded by the U.S. Agency for International Development (USAID) and released in late 1996 estimated that 97 percent of girls in Egypt underwent FGM. In July 1996, Minister of Health Ismail Sallem announced his intent to enforce a ban on FGM; the announcement followed the highly publicized death of an eleven-year-old girl on July 12 consequent to FGM performed by a barber. The government's ban, however, was not consistently enforced, and the decree actively banning the practice had not been issued in writing or distributed to state medical facilities as of early November. In August 1996, a fourteen-year-old girl died after being subjected to FGM, in this instance performed by a doctor. And, in October, press reports indicated that two young girls, ages three and four, bled to death after a government doctor tried to circumcise them in their homes.

Following the health minister's July announcement, a doctor and professor at Ein Shams University, Munir Mohamed Fawzy, filed a lawsuit against Minister Sallem challenging the ban on FGM as unconstitutional; Fawzy argued that FGM is both required by Islamic law and medically desirable. In a September 29 court hearing, the judge postponed consideration of Fawzy's case until November 1996, and the hearing had not taken place as of this writing.

The Egyptian People's Assembly rejected an attempt to ban FGM explicitly as part of the law on children adopted in February 1996. In doing so, members of parliament argued that the criminal law—which prohibits severing a part of the body without medical necessity—provides adequate legal recourse.

Kenya

Since 1993, the Women's Rights Project has monitored the treatment of Somali women refugees in camps in northeastern Kenya in order to follow continuing problems of rape of women in the camps and to make broader policy recommendations to the U.N. High Commissioner for Refugees (UNHCR) about the protection of refugee women. Our 1993 report, *Seeking Refuge, Finding Terror: The Widespread Rape of Somali Women Refugees in North Eastern Kenya*, documented the Kenyan government's indifference to cases of sexual abuse, notably rape, against Somali refugee women in the northeastern Kenyan camps. Follow-up missions in 1994 and in 1996 found important changes in the UNHCR and Kenyan government's response to the widespread incidence of sexual violence and significant achievements in protection of women refugees. Among other measures, the UNHCR organized a program for Somali refugees to plant "live" fences (several rows of thick bushes) around the refugee camps to discourage incursions by bandits. The UNHCR also conferred greater responsibility on the refugees, including refugee women, for establishing security in their camps and addressing the issue of sexual violence.

The UNHCR has continued to offer human rights training to Kenyan police officers and has taken other steps to offer material support to the police, including the construction of a police post near the refugee camps, and advocated for the protection of refugees with the Kenyan government. Counseling, medical and legal services have been instituted for rape survivors, and procedures have been put into place to ensure that medical and police reports are filed as a matter of routine practice.

The result has been a significant decline in the incidence of rape, a number of successful prosecution of rapists, and improved protection provided by Kenyan police officers. Reported rapes of refugee women and children have declined by more than half, from over 200 cases in 1993 to seventy-six in 1994 and seventy in 1995. While these figures cannot be deemed to reflect the actual incidence of rape because of the ever-present factor of under-reporting, they do indicate a clear trend. However, problems continued to exist. First, rapes occurred when women and girls left the relative security of the camps in order to tend livestock and find firewood. It is most frequently young girls who engage in these tasks, and since late

1994, they have constituted a higher percentage of rape victims. Second, justice continued to elude most rape survivors. Long distances to the nearest court, coupled with an overburdened court calendar, have caused long delays in the few cases which have been prosecuted. Lastly, through 1996 there were still no women police officers posted in the area, despite assurances from the Kenyan government that it would assign policewomen to the area once housing was constructed.

Mexico

During investigations conducted in 1995 and 1996, the Women's Rights Project found that the Mexican government had failed to protect women workers from pregnancy testing and other discriminatory treatment in export-processing factories (maquiladoras) along the U.S.-Mexico border. In *No Guarantees: Sex Discrimination in Mexico's Maquiladora Sector*, released in August 1996, the Women's Rights Project concluded that major U.S.-based and other corporations that own or subcontract maquiladora factories routinely subject prospective female employees to mandatory urine testing and invasive questions about their contraceptive use, menses schedule, or sexual habits in order to screen out pregnant women and deny them jobs. Some maquiladoras have mistreated or forced to resign women who have become pregnant shortly after being hired. While the Mexican government has been aware of this discrimination, it has done little to protect women from pregnancy-based sex discrimination and instead has allowed U.S. and other corporations to flout Mexican federal labor law protecting women workers from discrimination.

Women victims of pregnancy-based sex discrimination were extremely reluctant to challenge the discriminatory hiring practices of Mexico's maquiladoras because they depended almost exclusively on work in that sector to support themselves and their families. For the most part, women who worked in the maquiladoras were heads of households, had little work experience outside the manufacturing sector, were undereducated for work in other sectors, and were ill-informed about their labor rights.

Women's reluctance to challenge workplace discrimination has been compounded by an official labor-adjudication system that was ill-equipped to investigate and remedy pregnancy-based sex discrimination. The Mexican government's labor-resolution mechanisms could not be accessed by most victims of pregnancy-based sex discrimination because these mechanisms only examined cases in which people already had an established labor relationship with an employer. Pre-hire sex discrimination prevented pregnant applicants from establishing such a relationship. Moreover, even were female employees to challenge workplace discrimination, they would face government officials who largely have failed to investigate, or who have refused to address the problem because maquiladoras were a major source of employment and foreign-income earnings. Our research showed that some labor officials feared reprimand from higher officials in Mexico City if they were to seek to enforce Mexico's labor laws in the maquiladoras.

In responding to the Women's Rights Project report, the Mexican government took the position that it was not illegal for employers to try to determine a female job applicant's pregnancy status in order to avoid placing the woman in a position that would endanger her life, physical and mental health, or that of her fetus. However, this view is inconsistent with both Mexican and international law. Mexico's federal labor code prohibits an employer from refusing to hire someone for reasons of either sex or age. The International Covenant on Civil and Political Rights (ICCPR) and the Convention on the Elimination of All Forms of Discrimination against Women (CEDAW) both prohibit discrimination. Moreover, the Mexican government failed to address the fact that corporations such as Zenith and General Motors had stated publicly that their only reason for screening prospective employees for pregnancy was not to protect them but to deny them work and avoid paying legally mandated maternity benefits.

Morocco

In late 1995, the Women's Rights Project spent two months investigating the effects of Morocco's discriminatory family code, or Moudawana, on women's status. The Moudawana regulates, among other things, legal capacity, marriage, divorce, and inheritance. In each of these areas, the Moudawana grants different rights to women and men and consistently renders women's autonomy subject to male guardianship and authority. The condition of never being a full and independent agent has serious consequences for women; they have been married without their consent, forced to undergo virginity exams, denied access to divorce and to child custody, and left with little recourse in situations of domestic violence. Moreover, although women's political rights and their access to education and employment are in theory protected by Moroccan law, discrimination in the family code limits women's autonomy and thus creates obstacles to women's full enjoyment of these rights.

Women's inequality in marriage begins before the union is finalized. A girl's or woman's consent to marriage is required, but it is rarely exercised contrary to the wishes of a father or other male relative. A woman of any age is prohibited from contracting marriage without the permission of a male guardian. Men over the age of eighteen are not required to seek anyone's permission to marry. Moreover, the Moudawana also requires women—and not men—to provide information about their marital and sexual history before receiving a marriage certificate. For example, the law requires that a woman disclose whether she is a "spinster-celibate" or has been previously married.

Women's status as legal minors also denies them equal participation in marriage and divorce, which can leave them particularly vulnerable to domestic violence. The Moudawana requires that a woman obey her husband and submit to his authority; custom condones even the husband's use of force in dealing with her refusal to submit. Women who attempt to leave abusive marriages have been thwarted by their unequal access to divorce: men may divorce their wives without cause or a court proceeding, while women must have specific grounds and court approval. The law compounds the unequal status of women in the marital relationship by allowing men up to four wives simultaneously. The law does require that wives be notified of their husbands' intent to marry again and that judges authorize polygamous marriages, but wives have no power to consent to or reject their husbands' decisions. Nor do women have the right to contract polygamous marriages themselves.

The Moroccan government has refused to eliminate sex discrimination from its laws. The only reform of the Moudawana, undertaken in 1993 after intense pressure from women's organizations, reaffirmed specific discriminatory laws. Morocco defended this discrimination as intrinsic to its laws based on Islamic jurisprudence. Judges and magistrates charged with interpreting Morocco's family code have reinforced the discrimination embedded in the law by undermining and resisting women's efforts to exercise their rights. Magistrates in the Moudawana courts have been hostile to divorce proceedings initiated by women. And, even where the courts do rule in favor of respecting those women's rights that are protected by law—for example, providing financial support for women divorced by their husbands or recognizing women's right to control their own property—the lack of enforcement mechanisms or meaningful penalties have made it easy to evade compliance with such judgments.

Russia

Political and economic change in Russia have in no way been matched by improved respect for women's rights. In fact, abusive practices such as sex discrimination and violence against women have flourished virtually unchecked in recent years. The Women's Rights Project visited Russia in April-May 1996 to investigate the barriers to justice faced by survivors of sexual and domestic violence. This mission followed our 1995 report, *Neither Jobs Nor Justice: State Discrimination Against Women in Russia*, revealing both widespread employment discrimination on the basis of sex that was practiced, condoned, or tolerated by the government and the role of Russian law enforcement agencies in denying women their right to equal protection of the law by failing to investigate and prosecute violence against women.

Our 1996 mission documented how police, prosecutors, state forensic doctors, and the criminal code itself created substantial obstacles that prevented women's complaints of violence from being successfully investigated and prosecuted. The police often rejected reports of violence against women, particularly those alleging spousal abuse. In cases of sexual violence, police officers and prosecutors often suggested that the women provoked the rape or that her report was fabricated. Women reporting crimes of sexual violence also faced difficulties in obtaining a referral by an official evidence center for a required medical examination. Such referrals, which must be authorized by police or prosecutors, are not provided unless the complaint is accepted. In some cases investigators refused to give women referrals to the evidence center. In other cases, investigators often did not inform women of the importance of being medically examined as soon as possible or spoke to the woman for several hours, thus delaying her medical exam and risking the loss of valuable evidence, or told women to go to the evidence center days after filing their reports. Consequently, women often did not have the medical evidence necessary to support a rape conviction.

In response to public outcry about violence against women, the Russian parliament drafted a family violence law in 1995, which is designed to prevent domestic violence. This draft family violence law languished in the parliament in 1996 and was not expected to pass. Many activists asserted that the law did not contain sufficient criminal penalties for domestic violence and would be a setback in protecting women from violence. For example, crisis centers would have to obtain a state license to operate. This licensing provision was already included in a social welfare law passed in 1996. Many nongovernmental organizations (NGOs) criticized licensing as a tool to allow the government to close any crisis center that it does not want functioning.

The state's failure to address violence against women was compounded by its unwillingness to combat sex discrimination more generally. In 1996, Russian women continued to confront unchecked employment discrimination in law and in practice. New labor legislation effective July 1, 1996 increased the number of occupations forbidden to women, despite an appeal by fifty-three women's organizations asking parliament to ensure that the draft legislation provided equal opportunities for women. In addition, the request of women's groups that the new labor law prohibit employers from denying women jobs because of their sex was rejected.

Throughout 1996, women's rights NGOs experienced significant difficulty in getting access to government officials. In July 1996, only one women's rights activist was invited to the hearings on the draft family violence law. This activist was only given a few days notice and did not receive a copy of the draft bill prior to the hearings.

Rwanda

During the 1994 genocide, Rwandan women were subjected to sexual violence on a massive scale, perpetrated by members of the infamous Hutu militia groups known as the Interahamwe, by other civilians, and by soldiers of the Rwandan Armed Forces (Forces Armées Rwandaises), including the Presidential Guard, and directed or permitted by administrative, military and political leaders in an effort to further their political goals. In April 1996, investigators from the Women's Rights Project and Africa division traveled to Rwanda to document this widespread

sexual violence and current problems facing Rwandan women in the aftermath of the genocide. A report released in September 1996 by Human Rights Watch and the Féderation Internationale des Ligues des Droits de l'Homme titled *Shattered Lives: Sexual Violence during the Rwandan Genocide and its Aftermath* found that, during the genocide, women were individually raped, gang-raped, raped with objects such as sharpened sticks or gun barrels, held in sexual slavery (either collectively or through forced "marriage"), or sexually mutilated. These crimes were frequently part of a pattern in which women were raped after they had witnessed the torture and killing of their relatives and the destruction and looting of their homes.

Women from both the Tutsi and Hutu ethnic groups were raped, although the preponderance of victims were Tutsi. The extremist propaganda which exhorted Hutus to commit the genocide specifically attacked the sexuality of Tutsi women, which it said had been used to dominate the Hutus. During the genocide, attackers frequently expressed their intent to use rape as a means to degrade and destroy the Tutsi community.

One result of the genocide is that Rwanda has become a country of women. An estimated 70 percent of the population is female, and some 50 percent of all households are headed by women. Regardless of their status—Tutsi, Hutu, displaced, returnees—all women are facing overwhelming problems because of the upheaval caused by the genocide, including social stigmatization, poor physical and psychological health, unwanted pregnancy—the National Population Office in Rwanda estimates that some 2,000 to 5,000 children have been born of rape—and increasing poverty. Yet, the Rwandan government, international donors, and the U.N. Human Rights Field Operation based in Rwanda have not addressed the past and present problems facing women, and there continued to be a lack of services designed to assist women victims of human rights abuses.

In addition to the social and personal

trauma resulting from the injuries suffered from sexual violence, women also faced dire economic difficulties in large part due to their second class status under Rwandan law. General practice has established that under Rwandan customary law, women cannot inherit property unless they are explicitly designated as beneficiaries. Accordingly, thousands of widows and orphaned daughters had no legal claim to their late husbands' or fathers' property or finances because they are women. Thus many women were destitute, living in abandoned houses or with relatives or friends, struggling to make ends meet, to reclaim their property, and to raise children. Hutu women whose husbands were killed or were in exile or in prison accused of genocide, dealt with similar issues of poverty as well as with the recrimination directed at them on the basis of their ethnicity or the alleged actions of their relatives. The Rwandan government had initiated a legal commission to address these issues and to introduce legislation to allow women to inherit equally with men, but the reforms were expected to take a long time.

The prospects for justice for Rwanda's victims of rape and other forms of sexual violence were grim during 1996, at both the national and international levels. The Rwandan judiciary faced systemic and profound problems that have made the likelihood of justice for both the genocide perpetrators and their victims a remote possibility. Over 80,000 prisoners were being held without trial in prison, and the judicial system was still not functioning. However, even should the system begin to function, rape victims will face specific obstacles, including that police inspectors documenting genocide crimes for prosecution are predominantly male and have not been collecting information on rape. At the international level, the International Criminal Tribunal for Rwanda (ICTR), which is tasked with bringing the organizers of the genocide to justice, opened trials in September 1996. In its first two months, there were no indictments for rape, although rape constitutes a war crime and a crime against humanity.

The Rwanda tribunal has faced serious resource constraints and continues to confront problems of staffing and methodology. (See below.)

United States
Throughout the year, we continued our investigation into sexual abuse of women in U.S. state prisons. The investigation covered eleven state prisons in the north, south, east, and west of the country and included interviews with the U.S. federal government, state departments of corrections and district attorneys, correctional officers, civil and women's rights lawyers, prisoner aid organizations, and over sixty prisoners formerly or currently incarcerated in women's prisons in California, Georgia, Illinois, Michigan, New York, and the District of Columbia, the nation's capital.

Our research indicated that the United States has the dubious distinction of incarcerating the largest known number of prisoners in the world, of which a steadily increasing number are women. Since 1980, the number of women entering U.S. prisons has risen by almost 400 percent, roughly double the incarceration rate increase of males. Fifty-two percent of these prisoners are African-American women, who constitute 14 percent of the total U.S. population. According to current estimates, more than half of all female prisoners have experienced some form of sexual abuse prior to incarceration. Many women are incarcerated in the 170 state prison facilities for women across the United States, and more often than not, they are guarded by men.

The custodial sexual misconduct occurring in the prisons we investigated takes many forms. We found that male correctional employees have vaginally, anally, and orally raped female prisoners and sexually assaulted and abused them. We found that short of using actual or threatened force, male officers have exploited their ability to provide or deny goods and privileges to female prisoners to secure sexual relations from them. In some instances male officers have engaged in sexual contact with female prisoners without using force or offering material reward in violation of their professional duty. In addition to engaging in sexual relations with prisoners, male officers have used mandatory pat-frisks or room searches to grope women's breasts, buttocks, and vaginal areas and to view them inappropriately while in a state of undress in the housing or bathroom areas. Male correctional officers and staff have also engaged in regular verbal degradation and harassment of female prisoners, thus contributing to a custodial environment in the state prisons for women which is often highly sexualized and excessively hostile.

Our report, *All Too Familiar: Sexual Abuse of Women in U.S. State Prisons*, was released in December.

The Role of
the International Community

United Nations

The work for advancing women's rights within the U.N. system rests in significant part with the U.N. Commission on the Status of Women (CSW). At its fortieth session in March 1996, the CSW met to review its mandate in light of the Fourth World Conference on Women, held in Beijing in 1995, and to establish a five-year work plan to make itself a more effective lobby for women's rights within the U.N. system. The session was intended to lay the groundwork for implementing the Beijing Platform for Action into the twenty-first century. The CSW adopted resolutions on, among other things, the mainstreaming of women's human rights within the U.N., trafficking of women and girls, and violence against women migrant workers; agreed on a method of work for dealing with the implementation of the Platform for Action adopted at the Beijing conference; and set a provisional agenda for its next session.

The U.N. General Assembly similarly took its cue from the Beijing Conference, and, in December 1995, adopted a series of resolutions encouraging U.N. agencies to raise the profile of women's rights in their work and governments to increase efforts to fight violence against women.

Consequent to efforts to integrate women's human rights into all U.N. human rights work, the U.N. Commission on Human Rights also played an increasingly important role in promoting respect for women's rights. At its 1996 session, the commission adopted resolutions condemning violence against women and advocating the full integration of women's human rights into the human rights work of the U.N. The commission acknowledged that fulfilling these commitments is critical to improving the quality and consistency of U.N. monitoring of women's human rights. Yet the commission refrained from committing itself to specific steps advocated by nongovernmental organizations (NGOs) and instead reiterated general promises that had been made at previous sessions and inconsistently implemented. Secretary-General Boutros Boutros-Ghali, in his report to the Human Rights Commission on the extent to which violations of women's human rights have been addressed in U.N. human rights work, noted that some progress had been made in integrating women's human rights into the U.N. human rights program but recognized that changes in policy had not consistently resulted in changes in practice.

Special Rapporteur on Violence Against Women Radhika Coomaraswamy reported to the Human Rights Commission on violence against women in the family as a human rights abuse in 1996, in the second report of her three-year term. She also submitted her first report on a specific human rights problem—sexual slavery imposed by the Japanese military during World War II. The rapporteur denounced the Japanese military's forcing of women and girls from across Asia into sexual slavery and called for the government to apologize to and compensate each individual survivor. The Japanese government strongly opposed this report and urged other delegations not to support the rapporteur's findings. Ultimately, however, the commission adopted the special rapporteur's report in its entirety.

The war crimes tribunals for the former Yugoslavia and Rwanda are important areas in which to assess the international community's commitment to the examination of abuses against women as methods of warfare, such as rape and sexual slavery, and the need to ensure that such abuses are investigated and prosecuted. Human Rights Watch has supported the work of the international tribunals for both the former Yugoslavia and Rwanda since their creation and publicly called on all governments to support the tribunals and to cooperate with their work. An international procedure, which condemns genocide and holds the perpetrators accountable, will send a message that the international community does not tolerate impunity for such crimes.

In 1996, the Women's Rights Project focused particularly on the International Criminal Tribunal for Rwanda (ICTR). From the beginning, the Rwanda tribunal faced serious resource constraints and problems of staffing and methodology, and with regard to gender-based crimes, these problems were magnified throughout 1996. In contrast to the former Yugoslavia tribunal, where rape was prominently condemned as a war crime and indictments brought against alleged rapists, the ICTR appeared to be allowing rape, yet again, to be overlooked as a crime. As of November 1996, there were no indictments for rape, despite the widespread sexual violence which occurred during the Rwandan genocide (see above).

The lack of rape indictments in Rwanda was largely due to a lack of political will among those responsible for the investigations. There was a widespread perception among tribunal investigators that rape was somehow a "lesser" or "incidental" crime not worth investigating. Some at the Rwanda tribunal also held the mistaken view that Rwandan women would not come forward to talk about rape. The initial interviewing techniques used by investigators were poorly designed to gain the confidence of the women and elicit rape testimonies. Furthermore, inadequate measures were put into place to protect those who gave evidence from retali-

ation.

The ICTR did take some steps to address the problem of sexual violence. In July 1996, the tribunal created a sexual assault committee to coordinate the investigation of gender-based violence. The committee began to operate in October, with the aim of addressing strategic, legal, and methodological questions confronting the investigations. However, the Witness Protection Unit based in Arusha, Tanzania, did not put into place mechanisms to ensure that women who testified would be protected from reprisal as well as to provide necessary support services. In the absence of immediate steps to address these problems and collect testimonies from rape victims, time was running out for including evidence of rape in cases to be brought before the judges. In October 1996, Canadian judge Louise Arbour replaced Richard Goldstone as chief prosecutor of both tribunals and, in an October 7 letter to the Women's Rights Project, pledged that allegations of sexual assault would be vigorously investigated and prosecuted and announced that she would seek to establish a sexual violence investigation team to operate from Kigali, Rwanda.

The impact of the Beijing conference—and its emphasis on protecting women's human rights as key to improving their status—was reflected in parts of the U.N. that previously overlooked women's concerns. Governments that gathered in Istanbul in June 1996 at the U.N. Conference on Human Settlements (Habitat II) vowed to protect and promote women's human rights. Governments specifically pledged to secure gender equality in all housing and community development planning and urban and rural policy. The Habitat consensus agreement recognized that discrimination against women and family violence were causes of women's restricted access to shelter and homelessness. Governments attending the conference agreed to eradicate, and provide legal protection against housing discrimination against women; ensuring women equal access to land and their ability to retain control and use of their homes, land, and property; and undertaking legal and administrative reform to ensure that women have equal access to economic resources, including inheritance rights, land, property, credit, natural resources, and technology. Moreover, governments committed their efforts to promoting shelter and basic services to survivors of family violence and recognized the need to pay special attention to the needs of poor women and victims of sexual exploitation. Finally, governments recognized that there are various forms of the family, affirmed that marriage must be entered into voluntarily, that husband and wife must be equal partners, and that the rights of family members must be respected. The Habitat commitments, however, were not backed up with resources for implementing them.

United States

In 1996 the Clinton administration continued to make strong general statements in support of women's human rights. These statements, however, did not always translate into specific policies. Moreover, on the domestic front, although the Clinton administration stated its support for ratification of CEDAW, the Senate failed to ratify this human rights treaty, leaving U.S. women cut off from access to important international human rights protections.

At the U.N. Commission on Human Rights, Amb. Geraldine Ferraro, head of the U.S. delegation to the commission, spoke out strongly in defense of women's rights as human rights. She condemned violence against women and the denial of women and girls of access to food, education, health care or property because of their sex. Ambassador Ferraro expressed the U.S. government's desire to see every nation fulfill the commitments made in the Beijing Platform for Action and underscored the U.S. intent to make good on its own promises. She offered two examples of U.S. efforts to implement the Beijing platform: the national campaign in the U.S. to fight violence against women, and new programs of the U.S. Agency for International Development (USAID) to encourage women's participation in micro-enterprises.

Although the U.S. clearly is making an effort to address women's rights concerns, it can still be very slow to take concrete initiatives in this regard. It was not until over two years after the genocide in Rwanda and more than one year after the creation of the tribunal that the U.S. dedicated any specific resources to the prosecution of rape by the Tribunal, or even gave any high-level public recognition to the existence of this problem. In October 1996, during his visit to Tanzania, Secretary of State Warren Christopher took the welcome step of designating US$650,000—of a total of $5,650,000 for the Rwanda tribunal—for the prosecution of rape and other genocide-based crimes. The U.S. has yet to turn its attention to ensuring that funding to the Rwandan judiciary and the U.N. Field Operation in Rwanda also be used to assist in bringing to justice the perpetrators of rape and other abuses against women.

The U.S. did take an initiative early on in post-genocide Rwanda by establishing a fund for Women in Transition in Rwanda, which in 1995 provided $1,000,000 to assist women, particularly widows, in their efforts to grapple with the economic and social upheaval of life after the genocide. Such programs are part of an increasing and welcome effort by the U.S. government to provide women with assistance as an integrated element of its development and democracy programs. Thus, with regard to Bosnia, President Clinton announced on June 29 that the U.S. would contribute $5 million to establish the Bosnian Women's Initiative. The funding was aimed at providing women with business development loans and skills training and ensuring them access to resources like day care, legal services, and education. In a similar effort in Asia in 1996, USAID started projects in Asia—to train women workers in their legal rights and strategies to protect them—and in the newly independent states of the former Soviet Union (NIS)—to promote new legislation to guard women's rights in the process of economic transition.

The State Department's *Country Reports on Human Rights Practices for 1995* included its most comprehensive reporting to date on violations of women's human rights around the world. Increased reporting, however, did not necessarily translate into greater integration of women's human rights into U.S. policy toward specific abusive governments. For example, although the U.S. acknowledged in its *Country Reports* that discrimination and violence against women occurs in Russia, it made limited efforts to incorporate remedies for such problems into its assistance programs for Russia. Despite awareness, for example, that Russian police consistently failed to respond to and investigate violent crimes against women, none of the $2.5 million for the law enforcement assistance program in Fiscal Year 1996 went to training Russian police on investigating such crimes. Only after representatives of Human Rights Watch briefed staff of the U.S. Congress on violence against women in Russia and a Senate subcommittee then earmarked $1 million for support of law enforcement training programs to address violence against women, did the State Department commit to training programs targeting this problem.

In another example, the *Country Reports on Human Rights Practices for 1995* noted that while there existed statutory equality between men and women in Mexico's labor codes, employers frequently require women to certify that they were not pregnant at the time of hiring. Nevertheless, in a meeting with a Human Rights Watch representative in Mexico City, an official at the U.S. embassy then in charge of labor issues argued that such discrimination did not constitute a human rights violation, suggesting that maquiladoras actually discriminated against men because they preferred to hire people they could pay less: women.

In order for the administration to translate its general commitment to women's rights into consistent policy, it must coordinate the sources of that policy with those responsible for carrying it out. The State Department senior coordinator for international women's issues could have played a critical role in augmenting U.S. integration of women's rights into its foreign policy. Unfortunately, the potential of this position went largely untapped in 1996 because, after the first appointee resigned in April, the post was vacant until September. Moreover, the exact mandate of the position remains unclear, and the Department has failed to ensure that the special coordinator has both the resources and access to play an effective role in ensuring that women's rights issues are fully reflected in the human rights policies of the U.S. with respect to abusive governments.

In Beijing, the U.S. had committed itself to establish a White House Inter-Agency Council on Women (IACW) to implement the platform for action adopted in Beijing, to improve the protection of women's rights in the U.S. and to increase the visibility of women's rights in U.S. foreign policy. The IACW began by pledging to cooperate with NGOs to develop a national action agenda to be revealed at a conference on women and girls on September 28, 1996—one year after the Beijing conference. But no national action agenda was drafted. Instead, at the September meeting, members of the IACW presented several initiatives undertaken in areas relating to the Beijing Platform for Action and discussed priorities for implementation. The measures touted at the national conference addressed important concerns—a nationwide, twenty-four-hour domestic violence hotline; providing loans to women who have little access to credit; promoting gender equity in education; and increasing research in breast cancer—but they failed to raise women's human rights as a priority.

This omission came despite the efforts of the Women's Rights Project and others to press the U.S. to make women's human rights a priority post-Beijing. In December 1995, the Women's Rights Project wrote to Secretary of State Christopher, urging the U.S. government to match its stated commitment to uphold women's rights around the world by co-sponsoring a U.N. General Assembly resolution aimed at increasing U.N.

support for efforts to combat violence against women. The resolution called, among other things, on the administrator of the United Nations Development Fund for Women (UNIFEM), in consultation with the secretary-general and other competent U.N. organs and bodies, to establish a trust fund within its existing structure that would consolidate UNIFEM's existing efforts to combat violence against women around the world and to ensure that its programs have adequate funding. The U.S. government was among the last to support this resolution.

The U.S. Congress, meanwhile, maintained a mixed record on international women's human rights in 1996. As noted above, the Senate failed to ratify CEDAW. At the same time, the Congressional Working Group on International Women's Human Rights, composed of fifty-six members of both houses of Congress and both parties, denounced violations of women's human rights in Bangladesh—the abduction of the leader of a women's federation; in Peru— repeated threats of rape and harassment against a human rights lawyer; and in Rwanda—the sexual violence during the 1994 genocide. Formed in April 1994, the working group sends urgent letters in support of women who are at imminent risk of abuse or who require international support in their search for justice for past abuse.

The Work of the Women's Rights Project

The work of the Women's Rights Project focused on gathering detailed documentation of violations of women's human rights in a variety of countries and on conducting extensive advocacy campaigns to combat and eliminate the abuses that we identified and publicized. Our efforts highlighted three areas of critical concern to women around the world: compelling governments to acknowledge and to end their own complicity in violence against women, even when carried out by private individuals; ensuring that women's rights are not trampled in the process of economic transition or development; and securing accountability in international

and national fora for violence against women in situations of conflict.

Bosnia-Hercegovina

Human Rights Watch has consistently monitored the human rights situation in Bosnia-Hercegovina since the outbreak of war and campaigned in defense of those victimized by "ethnic cleansing," war crimes—including rape—and other violations of human rights.

The Women's Rights Project also has worked to ensure that the process of reconstruction includes promoting respect for women's rights and ensures women's involvement in their country's political and economic future. In December 1995 the Women's Rights Project and other human rights and women's rights organizations wrote to Amb. Madeleine Albright, U.S. permanent representative to the United Nations, urging that implementation of the Dayton Peace Accords on Bosnia-Hercegovina respond specifically to the human rights concerns of women and support women's critical role in rebuilding their country. We joined forces again in February 1996 to raise women's human rights concerns in a letter to Jock Covey, chief-of-staff of the office of the high representative of the peace implementation process.

We and other members of this coalition then met in May 1996 with Assistant Secretary of State for International Narcotics and Crime Robert Gelbard to urge that the International Police Task Force (IPTF) deployed consequent to the Dayton Accords in Bosnia-Hercegovina, Eastern Slovonia, and Republika Srpska be responsive to women's human rights concerns. We urged that training for IPTF officers address women's human rights and that these forces have expertise in or be trained in responding to and investigating violent crimes against women, including domestic violence and sexual assault. We also stressed that permanent police officers to be trained by IPTF must be screened for a history of human rights abuse, including abuses against women.

The Women's Rights Project also

worked with U.S. Senate staff to call on USAID to integrate attention to women's rights into its economic development and humanitarian assistance to Bosnia-Hercegovina.

Kenya

The Women's Rights Project continued to raise the problems of women refugees with UNHCR and with the Kenyan government. We called on UNHCR to integrate protection measures for refugee women, such as those instituted in the Kenyan camps, into its overall refugee protection strategy, and to replicate such measures as a matter of course in all refugee situations. This issue was raised by Human Rights Watch with UNHCR officials at the time of an UNHCR Executive Committee meeting in Geneva in October 1996, and included in a Human Rights Watch discussion paper on refugee protection directed at that meeting.

Mexico

In August 1996, with the release of *No Guarantees: Sex Discrimination in Mexico's Maquiladora Sector,* the Women's Rights Project initiated a campaign to persuade the Mexican government to denounce pregnancy discrimination as sex discrimination; to investigate and stop such discrimination in the labor force; and to compel corporations active in the maquiladora sector to stop discriminating against women workers. The Women's Rights Project cooperated with Mexican and U.S. nongovernmental organizations to include gender-specific discrimination in the maquiladoras among the issues in workers' rights education campaigns. In October 1996, we wrote to Mexico's secretary of labor, Javier Bonilla García, expressing concern that the Mexican government seemed unwilling to honor its international obligation to protect its female citizens from discrimination and in fact appeared to countenance and rationalize this sex discrimination as a "protective" measure. In November we also wrote to the thirty-three corporations named in *No Guarantees* to ascertain the concrete measures they intended to take

to eradicate pregnancy-based sex discrimination in their Mexican factories. These companies included General Motors, Zenith, and Johnson Controls, among others. The campaign included working with U.S. and Mexican groups to focus on specific corporations for reform, urging them to stop exporting sex discrimination and to end discrimination in the hiring process in their Mexican maquiladoras.

Russia

As a follow-up to our April 1996 investigation into the Russian government's response to sexual and domestic violence, the Women's Rights Project met with staff of the U.S. Congress to brief them on our findings, as well as with representatives of the World Bank. The meeting in Congress led to the designation of US$1 million to train law enforcement and judicial authorities to recognize, investigate and prosecute crimes of violence against women. We urged the World Bank to ensure that the programs it supports, particularly employment agencies and retraining programs, do not foster the gender discrimination that has prevented Russian women from participating fully in Russia's economic life.

Rwanda

In the process of establishing the International Criminal Tribunal for the Former Yugoslavia, women's rights activists made significant gains in pushing the international community to recognize rape and other forms of sexual violence as war crimes and in securing the promise of accountability for such crimes. Human Rights Watch worked consistently throughout 1996 to ensure that these gains were not lost for women in Rwanda. Human Rights Watch held several meetings with members of the staff of the International Criminal Tribunal for Rwanda (ICTR), including the chief of investigations and the deputy prosecutor in Kigali as well as the legal advisor of the sexual assault committee based in The Hague, to call on the Rwanda tribunal to investigate and prosecute sexual violence and to step up efforts to improve the ability of its investigators to investigate such abuse. In June, Human Rights Watch protested to the Rwanda tribunal after a number of indictments were brought against Jean-Paul Akayesu, a local official of Taba commune. Rape was not among the charges, despite the widespread sexual violence in the Taba area during the 1994 genocide. Human Rights Watch called on the tribunal to investigate the reports of sexual violence in the Taba area in order to determine whether Mr. Akayesu bore command responsibility for the sexual violence in his area. In August, Human Rights Watch participated in forming a coalition of eighty-five women's rights and human rights organizations which wrote to the Rwanda tribunal to ensure that the progress made by the International Tribunal for the former Yugoslavia to prosecute rape not be undercut by a failure to pay appropriate attention to the crime of rape in Rwanda. Human Rights Watch also pressed U.S. State Department officials to ensure that its programs to and support of the Rwandan government and the Rwanda tribunal addressed the needs of Rwandan women.

United Nations

Only in 1993, at the World Conference on Human Rights, did the United Nations embrace the notion that women's rights are human rights. In the three years following, the Women's Rights Project pressed the U.N. to defend women's human rights more consistently and forcefully. For example, although government compliance with CEDAW is monitored by a committee, it has no power to consider individual complaints of human rights violations. We have joined other nongovernmental organizations in calling for an optional complaints procedure that would provide redress for women whose domestic legal systems have failed them and a way of applying and interpreting CEDAW's standards. At the end of 1995, Human Rights Watch wrote to the assistant director of the U.N. Division for the Advancement of Women to express our strong support for an optional protocol introducing the right to petition to the CEDAW committee.

Key to raising the visibility of women's human rights at the U.N. is enhancing the status of the bodies that have traditionally handled these issues. The U.N. Commission on the Status of Women (CSW), for example, has second-class status within the U.N. system as well as in the eyes of many governments. In 1996, at the CSW meeting itself, as well as in meetings with U.S. government officials and with our colleague organizations, we sought to strengthen the work of the CSW, to enhance the quality of U.S. government representation to that body, and to foster greater participation by NGOs in its session. Our efforts with respect to U.S. government participation were severely hampered by the Clinton administration's failure to appoint a U.S. representative until just ten days before the start of the CSW session, giving the delegate little time to prepare, giving the NGO community little time to communicate its concerns to the U.S. delegation, and casting doubt upon the seriousness of the U.S. approach to the CSW. Nonetheless, we met with the head of the delegation after her appointment and pressed for a series of reforms to expand CSW's influence in the U.N. At the CSW session itself, the Women's Rights Project pressed to have stronger human rights and gender-specific language included in two Philippines-sponsored resolutions, one on trafficking of women and girls and the other on violence against women migrants. The Women's Rights Project met with delegates of the Philippines, Canada, and the U.S. to urge them to ground the language of the two resolutions in international human rights instruments, including taking note of the gender-specific violence women migrants face.

Unlike the CSW, the U.N. Human Rights Commission had, until the early 1990s, paid little attention to women's human rights. Women's rights activists have consistently pressed the commission to integrate women's human rights into its reporting and monitoring, but, as noted above, have met with limited success. One exception to this pattern came in 1994 when the commission appointed the first Special Rapporteur on Violence Against Women, Its Causes and Consequences for a three-year term. In 1996, the Women's Rights Project worked to ensure that resolutions in specific countries expressed concern over women rights and that the commission step up its integration efforts. Prior to the fifty-second session of the U.N. Human Rights Commission, Human Rights Watch urged Amb. Geraldine Ferraro, head of the U.S. delegation, U.S. Assistant Secretary of State for Democracy, Human Rights and Labor John Shattuck, Amb. Paolo Torella of the European Union, and the representatives of the permanent missions to the U.N. to make women's rights one of their priorities at the first commission meeting after the Beijing conference. Human Rights Watch advocated that the commission's resolution on Rwanda emphasize investigating and prosecuting sexual violence and that a resolution on the former Yugoslavia stress protection of women's physical security and training of international police to respond to crimes of violence against women. We also urged support for a resolution on violence against women and called for a resolution setting forth concrete measures by which the commission would integrate women's human rights more fully into its work. The commission adopted both resolutions, although it declined to commit itself to the specific actions we recommended for integrating women's human rights into its work.

In statements submitted to the Human Rights Commission, Human Rights Watch drew attention to the worldwide problem of domestic violence and the failure of governments to prevent, condemn, and punish such crimes. We urged the commission to call on governments to denounce and criminalize domestic violence, to protect women from such assaults, and to uphold women's rights to equal protection of the law. Human Rights Watch also reported to the commission on the trafficking of women and girls into forced prostitution, on abuses against women migrant workers, and on sexual abuse and degrading treatment of women in prisons in

the United States. Women's Rights Project reports documenting forms of violence against women—from unpunished wife murder to forced virginity exams—were cited in the special rapporteur's report to the full session detailing violence against women in the family and states' failure to protect women's human rights.

The Women's Rights Project worked on increasing international understanding of the critical link between the respect of women's human rights and the improvement of women's social and economic status with our advocacy in preparation for Habitat II, the United Nations Conference on Human Settlements, in Istanbul in June. We proposed specific amendments to the Draft Agenda for the Global Plan of Action that would specify the range of housing problems women face as a result of violence and statutory discrimination and other abuses of their human rights. We urged that women's heightened vulnerability to becoming homeless consequent to acts of violence be recognized and addressed, stressed the need for legal reform in order to provide equal and nondiscriminatory access to property and land, and recommended that strategies to cope with the shelter requirements of returnees and internally displaced persons must account for the specific needs and vulnerabilities of women, including the protection of their personal safety. The final Habitat action agenda did specifically commit to protect and promote women's human rights, including with respect to women's equal access to property and resources and to promoting housing for victims of violence in the home.

The Women's Rights Project also participated in and coordinated campaigns protesting specific violations of women's human rights. In March 1996, we wrote to the prime minister of Malaysia to express deep concern about the arrest of Irene Fernandez, director of Tenaganita, a women's rights organization in Kuala Lumpur. Fernandez stood trial for false reporting in connection with a July 1995 Tenaganita press release on abuses against migrant workers in Malaysia's immigration detention centers.

In 1996, the U.S. Board of Immigration Appeals (BIA) for the first time recognized that female genital mutilation may constitute persecution and grounds for political asylum. Fauziya Kassindja had sought asylum on the grounds that she would have faced the threat of violence—in the form of FGM— had she been compelled to return to her native Togo. In an April 1996 letter to Immigration and Naturalization Service (INS) Commissioner Doris Meissner, Human Rights Watch supported her asylum application. We also expressed our dismay about the abusive treatment Kassindja had endured during her confinement in the Esmor detention facility in Elizabeth, New Jersey. On June 13, the BIA granted Kassindja asylum. Responding to our letter, the INS stated its support for the position that forced female genital mutilation can be a basis for asylum.

In a September 1996 letter to Prime Minister Benazir Bhutto of Pakistan, we protested the denial of the right of twenty-one-year-old Saima Waheed to marry the person of her choice. We also worked that month with Human Rights Watch/Middle East on a statement signed by a coalition of human rights, Arab-American, women's rights, and academic organizations condemning an Egyptian court decision declaring Cairo University professor Nasr Hamed Abu Zeid an apostate and ordering his separation from his wife, Prof. Ibtihal Yunis, on the grounds that she, a Muslim woman, could not remain married to an apostate. The organizations protested the court decision as violating the rights to marry and to freedom of expression. We also denounced the discriminatory effects of the ruling on Dr. Yunis, given the limited rights granted divorced women under Egypt's family law. On September 25, another court suspended implementation of the June 1995 ruling ordering the couple's separation.

United States

As part of our ongoing work on the sexual abuse of women in U.S. prisons, the Women's Rights Project continued to participate in efforts to oppose the passage of the Prison Litigation Reform Act (formerly known as the "Stop Turning Out Prisoners" legislation). After the legislation was passed and signed by President Bill Clinton in April 1996, we continued to monitor its impact on the ability of women prisoners to receive redress for rape and sexual assault committed by prison guards. On October 1, Women's Rights Project staff met with representatives of the Justice Department to urge them to monitor more vigorously the problem of sexual misconduct by guards in U.S. state prisons and, in particular, to improve its internal system for documenting complaints of such abuse as they are lodged with the department.

During 1996, we actively promoted the U.S. government's implementation of the Beijing Platform for Action and pressed the Clinton administration to fulfill its commitments to protect the human rights of women in the U.S. and throughout the world. We continued to urge the U.S. government to ratify CEDAW. We also participated in local and national efforts to build a grassroots campaign to educate women about CEDAW and mobilize for its ratification. As part of our ongoing effort to persuade the U.S. government to fully integrate women's human rights into the foreign policy process, we urged the U.S. to condition aid and trade benefits to other countries on enacting laws and committing resources to the investigation and prosecution of crimes of violence against women and on enacting reforms to discriminatory laws.

SPECIAL INITIATIVES

The complexity that human rights work has acquired, and the diversity of opportunities for advocacy and action, have increasingly demanded that Human Rights Watch undertake cross-regional or thematic initiatives involving a specialized focus or expertise.

At times, those initiatives consist of a single opportunity to make our voice heard on a crucial issue, but often they take the form of campaigns that have become a sustained part of our program. Some of these activities undertaken or maintained in 1996 included the following:

Prisons

Human Rights Watch has conducted specialized prison research and campaigns for prisoners' rights since 1987, to focus international attention on prison conditions worldwide. Drawing on the expertise of the regional divisions of Human Rights Watch, our prison project has investigated conditions for sentenced prisoners, pretrial detainees, immigration detainees, and those held in police lockups. The work is distinctive in the international human rights field in that it examines conditions for all prisoners, not only those held for political reasons. In addition to pressing for improvement in prison conditions in particular countries, the prison project seeks to place the problem of prison conditions on the international human rights agenda. We believe that a government's claim to respect human rights should be assessed not only by the political freedoms it allows but also by how it treats its prisoners, including those not held for political reasons. Our experience has repeatedly shown that a number of democratic countries that are rarely, if ever, a focus of human rights scrutiny are in fact guilty of serious human rights violations within their prisons.

The prison project has a self-imposed set of rules for prison visits: investigators undertake visits only when they, not the authorities, can choose the institutions to be visited; when the investigators can be confident that they will be allowed to talk privately with inmates of their choice; and when the investigators can gain access to the entire facility to be examined. These rules were adopted to avoid being shown model prisons or the most presentable parts of institutions. When access on such terms is not possible, reporting is based on interviews with former prisoners, prisoners on furlough,

relatives of inmates, lawyers, prison experts and prison staff, and on documentary evidence. The prison project relies upon the U.N. Standard Minimum Rules for the Treatment of Prisoners as the chief guideline by which to assess prison conditions in each country. Prison investigations are usually conducted by teams composed of a member of the project's staff or advisory committee and a member of a Human Rights Watch regional division's staff with expertise on the country in question. Occasionally, the prison project invites an outside expert to participate in an investigation.

The project publishes its findings in reports that are released to the public and the press, both in the United States and in the country in question, and sent to the government of that country.

In previous years, the project conducted studies and published reports on prison conditions in Brazil, Czechoslovakia, Egypt, India, Indonesia, Israel and the Occupied Territories, Jamaica, Japan, Mexico, Poland, Romania, South Africa, the former Soviet Union, Spain, Turkey, the United Kingdom, the United States (including a separate short report published on Puerto Rico), Venezuela, and Zaire.

The Enforcement of Standards

The U.N. Standard Minimum Rules for the Treatment of Prisoners is the most widely known and accepted document regulating prison conditions. Unfortunately, these standards, although known to prison administrators virtually all over the world, are seldom fully enforced. Based on extensive research over the years, we concluded in our 1993 *Human Rights Watch Global Report on Prisons* that the great majority of the millions of persons who are imprisoned worldwide at any given moment, and of the tens of millions who spend at least part of the year behind bars, are confined in conditions of filth and corruption, without adequate food or medical care, with little or nothing to do, and in circumstances in which violence— from other inmates, their keepers, or both— is a constant threat. Despite international declarations, treaties and standards forbidding such conditions, this state of affairs is tolerated even in countries that are more or less respectful of human rights, because prisons are, by their nature, out of sight, and because prisoners are, by definition, outcasts.

With the goal of translating good standards into sound practice, Human Rights Watch continued in 1996 to advocate the creation of a U.N. human rights mechanism to inspect prisons. Our prisons expert closely monitored the progress of the Working Group on the Optional Protocol to the Convention against Torture, convened by the U.N. Commission on Human Rights to devise a universal system of visits to places of detention. There were several issues of particular concern to Human Rights Watch, including, most notably, the confidentiality of the proposed system. In order to ensure the system's effectiveness, Human Rights Watch strongly believes that government non-cooperation should be grounds to justify a departure from the rule of confidentiality.

The United States
In 1996, as the country's prison and jail population swelled to 1.6 million—giving the United States one of the largest populations of prisoners in the world, as well as one of the highest rates of incarceration—legal protections for prisoners continued to shrink. Most notably, the deceptively named Prison Litigation Reform Act (PLRA) effectively hobbled the federal courts in their efforts to remedy even the most egregious prison abuses.

Alarmed at the accelerating trend toward impunity for prison abuses, Human Rights Watch stepped up its monitoring of prisons and jails in the United States. In July, we released a report titled *Modern Capital of Human Rights? Abuses in the State of Georgia*, which focused in part on the dangerous, filthy and deteriorating conditions of many Georgia county jails and reported on the Georgia prison system's use of excessive force. At our International Film Festival, in June, we worked to draw public attention to

the revival of chain gangs in the United States by screening and speaking about the current relevance of the film classic, "I Am a Fugitive from a Georgia Chain Gang." In mid-1996, we were active in efforts to oppose proposed legislation that would allow states to hold juveniles in adult prisons. Finally, along with other prisoners' rights advocates we filed an *amicus curiae* brief in *Plyler v. Moore*, a federal court case challenging the constitutionality of the PLRA.

A primary focus of our research, reporting and advocacy effort in 1996 was the sexual abuse of prisoners. One investigation, concluded by the Women's Rights Project along with our prison specialist, documented the custodial sexual abuse of women prisoners in state prisons in five states and the District of Columbia (see Women's Rights Project section). A second investigation, begun in mid-1996 and ongoing as of this writing, examined the abuse of male prisoners. In both contexts we found that inmates suffered rape, sexual assault and sexual harassment. Although in men's prisons the perpetrators of these abuses were usually other prisoners—very often with the deliberate acquiescence or even encouragement of prison staff—while in women's prisons the staff personally participated in abuses, the circumstances were in many ways strikingly similar. Despite the devastating psychological impact of this most personally invasive of human rights violations, there were few preventative measures taken in most jurisdictions. Another disturbing reality common to both men's and women's prisons was that perpetrators of abuse were rarely disciplined in any meaningful way. Even in brutal instances of rape, criminal prosecutions were exceedingly rare—indeed, almost nonexistent when the victim was male—and administrative sanctions were usually light: a short stay in segregation for an abusive prisoner, a transfer for an abusive guard.

Human Rights Watch also continued to collect information on conditions at supermaximum security prisons (known as "maxi-maxis"). We first called attention to the proliferation of such facilities, which have the harshest conditions of all U.S. prisons, in our 1991 report on prison conditions in the United States.

In April we inspected the Secured Housing Units (SHU) of the Wabash Valley Correctional Institution, a super-maximum security facility in Indiana, as a follow-up to a prior visit to the state's other such facility. Our mission focused on the problems of prolonged social isolation, sensory deprivation, excessive use of force by guards, use of physical restraints as punishment, racial discrimination, lack of educational, recreational and work opportunities, inadequate medical care, lack of due process in assignment decisions, and restrictions on contact with family members. Held in solitary confinement in small, sterile, continuously lit cells, and deprived of almost all human contact over a period of years, SHU prisoners were treated in a manner that was injurious to their human dignity and that boded poorly for their eventual reintegration into society.

Venezuela and Japan

In March, Human Rights Watch conducted a mission to Venezuela during which our investigators visited eleven prisons and met with a wide variety of government officials, including the minister of justice, in charge of the prison system, and the minister of defense, in charge of the National Guard, which controlled several militarized Venezuelan prisons. Although conditions varied somewhat from facility to facility, we found that the Venezuelan prison system was generally characterized by severe overcrowding; rampant inmate-on-inmate violence, including rape; custodial abuse, particularly by members of the National Guard; impunity; corruption; lack of provision for basic needs, including medical needs; extremely long criminal proceedings and systematic denial of provisional liberty to pre-trial detainees, so that the large majority of inmates remain unsentenced for three years or more; a poorly maintained physical infrastructure; and few work, educational, and recreational opportunities.

The wide national press coverage of the mission, both in newspapers and television, put pressure on the government to take steps to respond to the stagnating prison situation. Within a few days of meeting with the Human Rights Watch delegation, the Venezuelan minister of justice made a personal visit to a notorious Caracas prison that the delegation had discussed with him. Interviewed upon leaving the prison, the minister acknowledged that conditions were "terrible" and promised reforms, beginning by ordering the release of pre-trial detainees held beyond their maximum possible sentence.

Working closely with a Japanese prisoners' rights group that filed a number of prominent legal challenges to the treatment of prisoners in Japan, Human Rights Watch was active in the press and before the United Nations to prod the Japanese government to institute reforms of its prison system. Our 1995 report on Japanese prisons condemned the widespread use of solitary confinement, the restrictions on contacts between prisoners and the outside world, the obsessiveness about rules, and the draconian punishments that characterized the Japanese system.

Corporations and Human Rights

A shift in the terms of the debate over corporate social responsibility for human rights occurred in 1996. In the previous two years, corporations and governments had touted the positive impact of business and trade in enhancing respect for human rights in countries with widespread violations. They had promised that corporations would bring greater respect for essential human and labor rights, such as freedoms of association and expression, as well as an end to cruelty and discrimination and inequality on the basis of ethnicity or gender. However, during 1996 multinational corporations in several product sectors—Royal Dutch/Shell, British Petroleum, Total, Unocal, Freeport-McMoRan, Nike, Disney, Heineken, and Carlsberg— were placed on the defensive by damaging exposures of corporate complicity in human rights violations. Throughout the year CEOs and corporate directors were stung again and again by charges that their companies had abused workers and propped up repressive governments. Accounts of child labor and sweatshop working conditions stirred public opinion to become human rights issues of broad popular concern. Corporate management defended its presence abroad by citing the advantage of company wage scales over local ones.

These issues were initially publicized by a growing number of activist groups. Frequently, these organizations brought workers on tours of the U.S. to publicize their situations. Extensively covered in the news media, the charges were taken up by consumers and grassroots organizations in Europe, Asia and North America. In a few instances, this had an important positive effect. After protests in Denmark and the Netherlands, both Carlsberg and Heineken decided to sell their shares of a proposed brewery in Burma. Liz Claiborne also decided to end its sourcing from Burma. At the height of the exposures of corporate complicity with human rights abuse, in July, *The Economist* magazine, reflecting the shift, observed that multinational corporations were increasingly worried about protests against their activities in developing countries. The same issue editorialized that when governments failed to uphold international human rights, the moral burden of responsibility shifted to corporate management.

However, with billions of dollars' worth of investment and profit at stake, most of the business community resisted pressure. Generally corporations in oil, mining and heavy manufacturing made no pretense of concern. A small number in the apparel and footwear industries reacted to negative publicity by expressing a commitment to human rights and took limited steps to address the problems.

The Role of Governments

Government reaction to reports of abusive practices associated with corporate presence varied. The authorities in countries where these practices occurred frequently have erratic or poor human rights records Simultaneously, they promote ambitious economic development plans that invite foreign investment and they court corporations by offering conditions that will be attractive to them. Governments in China, Indonesia, and Mexico, for example, are all too willing to ignore irresponsible corporate practices.

In the countries where the companies are headquartered, governments are caught between their promotion of global corporate investment and the expectations they profess about investment advancing human rights. In 1996, political considerations and growing pressure forced many governments to take these issues seriously, yet did not lead to effective or credible policies. There were some exceptions, however. In Germany, the debate on child labor associated with the carpet industry in South Asia intensified due to mounting public concern. Based on consumer outrage over the use of child labor, the German government, beginning in 1993, gave serious consideration to the issue. Initially, Bonn funded the Rugmark campaign, a consumer-based effort to promote rugs produced without child labor. By 1996, the government shifted tactics to mix support of Rugmark and the Indian government-sponsored label with a preference for educational programs for children in South Asia. Nevertheless, the German government granted loan guarantees to Siemens and ABB for work on China's controversial Three Gorges Dam, which had been criticized internationally for environmental risks and the forcible relocation of more than one million residents of the areas affected by construction.

In October, the European Parliament debated charges against British Petroleum of complicity in human rights abuses in Colombia through the financing of units of the armed forces of Colombia to protect a jointly owned pipeline. The parliament passed a resolution condemning BP for funding death squads in Colombia. The following day, the company denied all allegations and appeared prepared to take an uncompromising position.

In the United Kingdom, Lord Frank Rudd and York Member of Parliament Hugh

Bayley joined the York Oxfam Campaign Group in calling on five top clothing retailers—Marks and Spencer, C & A, Next, Sears and the Burton Group—to guarantee humane conditions for the workers who made the apparel sold in their stores. Such activism was not echoed more centrally in Prime Minister Major's government, however.

The Canadian government's interest in these issues was equally lukewarm. In 1996, Canada's Department of External Affairs and International Trade raised the possibility of promulgating a voluntary code of conduct for Canadian businesses operating internationally. Prime Minister Jean Chretien, a strong proponent of Canadian corporate activity abroad, was confronted by a thirteen-year-old Canadian child labor activist, Craig Keilburger, during a January trip to India. Only after receiving scathing press coverage for initially refusing to meet Keilburger did the prime minister raise the issue of child labor publicly and mention possible sanctions for goods made by child labor imported into Canada.

The U.S. government, which has led the debate on corporate social responsibility for human rights, exemplified the contradictions in governmental efforts to address the issue. It engaged in several initiatives that generated needed attention to the issues and conveyed a sense of movement while failing to formulate effective programs. For example, in March 1995, the U.S. government had announced "Model Business Principles" for U.S. companies operating abroad; it then did nothing with them in 1996.

Due to the exposure of sweatshop conditions in developing countries, the revelation of widespread sweatshops in the U.S. and the discovery of Thai slave labor in an El Monte, California garment factory, the use of sweatshop labor became a major issue in the U.S. For example, Guess, Inc. and sixteen sewing contractors were charged with violating minimum wage and overtime regulations in a lawsuit. In June, in response to these concerns, Rep. George Miller, a member of Congress, called on retailers and manufacturers to voluntarily use labels on their goods stating that they had not used sweatshop labor and that they do permit independent monitoring of subcontractor plants. Following this initiative, on July 15-16, 1996, the U.S. Department of Labor hosted a "Fashion Industry Forum," which was billed as an educational forum (largely for the industry) on the so-called "No Sweat" initiative. No Sweat was launched as an effort to label garments No Sweat to show they were not made in sweatshops. It was modeled after the "Dolphin Safe" tuna label and the Rugmark label. However, as of mid-November, three months later, there had been no follow-through.

On August 2, president Clinton launched another initiative: the Fair Labor Coalition. In a photo-perfect Rose Garden ceremony, the President brought together at the White House the television personality and clothing entrepreneur Kathie Lee Gifford, Nike Chair Philip Knight, and representatives of apparel corporations L.L. Bean, Liz Claiborne, Phillips Van-Heusen, Tweeds, Patagonia, Nicole Miller, Karen Kane, Warnaco, as well as the most important U.S. garment trade union, Unite, the National Consumer League, and the Interfaith Center on Corporate Responsibility, an important and activist shareholder group.

Knight presented a vision of his objectives:

> For the past twenty-five years, Nike has provided good jobs, improved labor practices and raised standards of living wherever we operate, including here in the U.S. What we've come to realize is that we need to do a better job of publicly describing the actions we've taken to promote fair labor practices in newly emerging market societies, including the development of a code of conduct, internal monitoring and external audits.

The results of the coalition's work were scheduled to be known after six months, when its members would provide nonbinding recommendations to the president.

As timely as these high-profile initiatives were, it was not at all clear that they would affect specific corporate practices and lead to meaningful human rights improvements in and beyond factories internationally. As with the 1995 "Model Business Principles," there was a real danger they would be little more than window-dressing.

In October, the U.S. Department of Labor published a comprehensive and accurate assessment of corporate compliance with voluntary codes of conduct addressing the use of child labor. The report showed that while there was decreased use of child labor in the Americas, little progress had been made in Asia, where the practice is much more prevalent.

The importance of these issues was not only felt at the federal level. In a significant development, cities debated adopting selective purchasing ordinances to prohibit public entities from buying goods or services from corporations doing business in Burma. In 1995, the city government of Berkeley, California, had adopted such a measure. In 1996, the state of Massachusetts passed a law banning contracts with firms doing business in Burma.

Nongovernmental Organization Initiatives

Shareholder groups, concerned pension funds and progressive money managers began to see corporate human rights practices as one criterion for investment decisions. Increasingly involved in shareholder resolution actions at companies in which they held stocks, these groups sought to identify standards by which to hold corporations accountable. At the same time, nongovernmental organizations concerned with corporate responsibility, including human rights groups and others, relied on both exposure of fact and consumer education.

In the Netherlands, Dutch activists mounted a campaign against Heineken Beer's $30 million part-ownership in a brewery in Burma. When Heineken withdrew, company CEO Karel Vuursteen acknowledged the role that concern about corporate reputa-

tion had played in the decision.

In the U.K., Germany, and South Africa protestors engaged in a series of actions against Royal Dutch/Shell after the hanging of Ken Saro-Wiwa and eight other Ogoni activists in Nigeria in November 1995. Concerted efforts were made to introduce critical statements at the company's annual general meeting in London on May 15.

In Canada, Development and Peace collected nearly 90,000 signatures on petitions urging Nike to agree to independent monitoring of its subcontractors.

In the U.S., the National Labor Committee, Press for Change and the Guatemala Labor Education Project were very active in exposing conditions abroad.

In 1996, while continuing a dialogue with corporations, Human Rights Watch increasingly emphasized its research and advocacy by issuing reports linking corporate operations with violations of human rights, labor rights and women's human rights. The Human Rights Watch Women's Rights Project's report *No Guarantees: Sex Discrimination in Mexico's Maquiladora Sector* documented the Mexican government's failure to protect women from pregnancy testing and other discriminatory treatment in major U.S.-owned export-processing factories along the U.S.-Mexico border. Naming names, the report cited General Motors, Sunbeam Oster, and Zenith, among others, for engaging in sex discrimination and mistreatment of pregnant workers. (*See* Women's Rights Project.) Human Rights Watch/Asia and the Human Rights Watch Children's Rights Project released *The Small Hands of Slavery: Bonded Child Labor in India*, documenting the enslavement of millions of child workers through debt bondage. The report formulated extensive recommendations to end bonded child labor. (See India.)

In the last few years, a small "leadership" segment of the corporate community has emerged, representing largely the apparel and footwear industries. It meets regularly—sometimes with NGOs, including Human Rights Watch—to discuss codes of conduct and implementation. Unfortunately, nearly all these companies are opposed to transparency in the monitoring process.

In 1996, Human Rights Watch met with corporate representatives from a range of companies to discuss issues of mutual interest. This included meetings with business groups and companies concerned with China to discuss our assessment of the deteriorating human rights situation there and the effect of arbitrary state action on both business and individual human rights. We also met with companies implicated as complicit in governmental human rights abuse to review their policies and press for institutional change.

Human Rights Watch/Middle East took a strong stand criticizing the role of British corporations in pressuring the British government to deport exiled Saudi dissident Dr. Muhammed al-Mas'ari, a spokesman for the Committee for the Defense of Legitimate Rights (CDLR). Human Rights Watch/Middle East wrote the chairs of the arms corporations Vickers and GKN, both British corporations, citing their reported part in the decision to expel Dr. al-Mas'ari in violation of British law. Vickers is a leading manufacturer of arms and weaponry and a large supplier to the Saudi military. Human Rights Watch/Middle East protested the company's reducing al-Mas'ari's right to an asylum hearing to the status of an obstacle to British business and the company's business. (*See* Saudi Arabia.)

We also strengthened our cooperation with groups regularly working on these issues: shareholder activists, investment research groups, and progressive pension funds. Recognizing differences in orientation, Human Rights Watch shared its research findings with pension fund managers. We also brought Indonesian activists together with portfolio managers.

The Corporate Response

Some corporations displayed a flatly intransigent attitude to human rights criticism of their practices. Before and after the hanging of Ken Saro-Wiwa, Royal Dutch/Shell provided both increased financial investment and a diplomatic public relations shield for the Nigerian government. In newspaper advertisements Shell ran in Europe, the company blamed Saro-Wiwa's execution on those protesting his unfair trial. Likewise, in response to criticisms of its practice of sex discrimination against women workers in its Mexican maquiladoras, the Zenith Corporation, now owned by the South Korean conglomerate Goldstar, acknowledged the use of the practice without apology. In a letter to our Women's Rights Project, the company justified the discrimination—which is illegal under Mexican law—by citing the prevalence of pregnancy testing in "the local labor market." In October, despite specific concerns over human rights and environmental issues surrounding the construction of the Three Gorges Dam, in China, the Swiss-Swedish company ABB, a major turbine manufacturer, requested risk guarantees from the Swiss government for the export of its equipment for the dam. The U.S.-based Caterpillar corporation mounted a fierce campaign against a White House-initiated recommendation to deny loan guarantees for U.S. companies involved with the dam. The burgeoning international movement on Burmese human rights drew varied corporate reactions: as noted above, some apparel manufacturers pulled out, as did Pepsi-Cola, while the oil giant, Unocal, remained indifferent to protests.

In October, two large British supermarket chains, Sainsbury and the Co-op, launched a six-month project to develop codes of conduct to improve conditions for workers making their own label products. The companies acknowledged that their interest was prompted by consumer concerns. The supermarkets promised to develop their codes based on a "Third World suppliers charter" initiated by the Fairtrade Foundation, an organization which is backed by Oxfam and Christian Aid.

In the U.S., the exposures generated spiraling media coverage, as activist groups targeted individual celebrities. Television personality Kathie Lee Gifford faced charges that the clothing line bearing her name and sold by the WalMart chain of stores was made by child labor working under appalling conditions at Global Fashions in Honduras. This was followed by complaints from immigrant garment workers at an illegal sweatshop in lower Manhattan, in New York City, that they had not been paid after producing garments for Gifford. Days later, in June, following the National Basketball Association finals, star Michael Jordan's public image was tainted by reports that Air Jordan sneakers marketed by Nike had been produced by sweatshops in Indonesia.

Following the wave of negative publicity against Kathie Lee Gifford and Nike, more businesses discussed corporate social responsibility for human rights. But for the growing sector of the corporate world expressing interest in human rights (still mainly in the consumer-sensitive apparel and footwear industries), it became clear in 1996 that more than the mere pronouncement of a corporate code of conduct was necessary. Local organizations and international groups, increasingly sophisticated in pressing for concrete results, began insisting on both practices specifically tailored to ending abuses and transparent and independent monitoring of their implementation. But even the "leadership" companies remained cool to independent monitoring of their human rights plans or practices.

Drugs and Human Rights

Human Rights Watch continued to document and challenge human rights violations caused or exacerbated by efforts to curtail drug trafficking. We insist that anti-drug policies be pursued within the framework of internationally recognized human rights; that respect for such rights cannot be sacrificed to anti-drug objectives. In this second year of a multi-year initiative to subject drug programs to close human rights scrutiny, we addressed abuses in the United States and Bolivia.

In July, the Human Rights Watch report, *Modern Capital of Human Rights?: Abuses in the State of Georgia*, focused in part on race and drug law enforcement in the U.S. state of Georgia. The report was the first international human rights assessment of any anti-drug policies in the United States. Drawing on computerized statewide databases, the study statistically documented stark racial disproportions in the arrest and incarceration of Georgia's drug offenders. Our data analysis for the years 1990 to 1995 revealed that while both black (principally African-American) and white Georgia residents used and distributed drugs, black residents were far more likely to be arrested and incarcerated for drug offenses. Black residents were arrested for cocaine-related offenses at seventeen times the rate of whites. Blacks were arrested for drug possession at rates greatly exceeding their estimated share of the total drug-using population; the arrest rate for whites was, conversely, much lower than their share of the drug-using population. Blacks arrested for drug offenses were imprisoned at twice the rate of whites. A black eligible for a life sentence for drug offenses was five times more likely to receive it than an eligible white; as a consequence blacks received 98 percent of the life sentences imposed for drug offenses.

International human rights law affirms racial equality and condemns conduct that has an unjustifiable racially disparate impact. Assessing whether the harsh impact of drug law enforcement on blacks in Georgia contravenes human rights guarantees requires scrutiny of its goals and methods. In our analysis of racially disparate arrest rates, for example, Human Rights Watch concluded that the rates reflected the comparative advantages for the police in making drug arrests in low-income neighborhoods in which drug transactions were easier to detect and for which there is strong community and political pressure. Such reasons are scant justification, however, for discriminatory arrest patterns. We urged Georgia to assess its drug goals and policies and to consider alternatives to current patterns of criminal law enforcement that would reduce adverse racial disparities while continuing to respond to social concerns about public drug dealing and drug abuse.

In the southern hemisphere, we continued to monitor closely the human rights implications of anti-narcotics programs in Bolivia that were supported and funded by the United States. Several positive developments tracked recommendations made in our 1995 report, *Bolivia: Human Rights Violations and the War on Drugs*. Bolivia enacted legislation in early 1996 to reform provisions in the country's drug law which we had criticized for containing glaring violations of human rights principles; name tags were provided to anti-drug police to end the anonymity which had hindered identification of those who committed abuses; and the Ministry of Justice established a human rights office in the coca-growing region of the Chapare, as we had urged, so that victims of abuses had a more reliable mechanism for reporting abuses.

In May 1996, following new research conducted in the Chapare, we published a second report on abuses connected with Bolivian policies of drug law enforcement. *Bolivia Under Pressure: Human Rights Violations and Coca Eradication*, is a detailed study of the violence and human rights abuses that accompanied Bolivia's effort to meet the coca eradication goals imposed by the United States. The report includes a series of specific recommendations for steps the Bolivian and U.S. governments could take to improve the performance of the Bolivian narcotics police. A few months after the report was released, the U.S. and Bolivian governments signed letters of agreement covering U.S. anti-drug assistance to Bolivia. The agreements included human rights provisos that followed closely most of the recommendations made by Human Rights Watch. The agreements called, for example, for the development of regulations for proper police search and arrest procedures; for police training emphasizing human rights and providing courses in crowd and riot control to minimize the potential for violence and personal injury; and for the development of a police internal affairs office to investigate, discipline or recommend for prosecution police who violate basic human rights stan-

dards. Continued United States government support for Bolivia's anti-narcotics programs was made conditional on "regular and measurable progress" toward these goals. Salary supplements paid to Bolivian anti-drug personnel by the United States may be withdrawn if "there is reason to believe" the recipients have engaged in human rights violations.

In the latter part of 1996, we prepared a set of generic recommendations for conditions that should be incorporated into all decisions concerning anti-narcotics assistance to Latin American governments and began work to secure their adoption by the Clinton administration.

Freedom of Expression

The defense of the right to free expression remained a major focus of the work of Human Rights Watch in 1996. We documented and/or protested a variety of challenges to this basic right, most commonly involving abuses against journalists or against members of the political opposition, often in the context of national or regional elections. "Insulting the honor or dignity of the president or the state" is a charge used frequently to suppress free expression.

Among the countries in which we conducted free expression work in 1996 were: Albania, Algeria, Bangladesh, Belarus, Cambodia, China, Egypt (including the case of a Cairo University professor who was declared an apostate on the basis of his academic writings and ordered to be separated from his Muslim wife), Hong Kong, Indonesia, Jordan, Russia (including the case of Aleksandr Nikitin, who was arrested on treason charges for passing on information about the environment), the Slovak Republic, Syria, the Sudan, Tunisia, Turkey (including the trial of the translator and the publisher of a Human Rights Watch report), Turkmenistan, and Uzbekistan. Human Rights Watch/Asia sent observers to the trial of Irene Fernandez, accused in Malaysia of "false reporting" for publishing a report on abuses against migrant workers. Human Rights Watch/Americas, together with the Center for Justice and

International Law (CEJIL), was involved in 1996 in three complaints brought before the Inter-American Commission on Human Rights for violations of the right to free expression protected under the American Convention on Human Rights.

We also raised free expression questions involving the United States, most notably in our report on the state of Georgia, where freedom of expression is undermined by local school boards and by state assembly resolutions that have condemned the state's public broadcasting system and have opened up broad new possibilities to prosecute Internet users. We participated in a challenge to the state of Arizona's new law requiring public employees to use only English in the course of performing their official duties, arguing that this violates international legal protections of language rights.

Freedom of Expression and the Internet

In 1996 Human Rights Watch expanded its work on freedom of expression in cyberspace. In February Human Rights Watch became a plaintiff, together with nineteen other organizations and individuals, in a suit brought in the U.S. by the American Civil Liberties Union challenging the Communications Decency Act (CDA), an amendment to a sweeping telecommunications bill signed by President Clinton in February 1996. Human Rights Watch objected to the CDA because it criminalizes on-line communication that is legal in other media, specifically communication that might be deemed "indecent" or "patently offensive" to minors. These vague terms go much further than the prohibition of pornography on the Internet, a prohibition legally in force before the act. Ironically, the act would criminalize speech that is protected by the United States Constitution's first amendment when uttered aloud or printed in a newspaper. Human Rights Watch was also concerned that the effort to censor indecent communication could impede the work of our own and similar organizations, which transmit graphic accounts of human rights abuses that we believe are necessary to con-

vey fully the suffering that these abuses cause. The CDA was ruled unconstitutional by a panel of judges in June; the government then appealed the case directly to the Supreme Court.

The year witnessed increasing attempts by governments around the world to censor electronic communication. In January, for example, the State Council in China issued a draft set of rules to regulate use of the Internet; subscribers were ordered to provide a written guarantee that they would not use the Internet for purposes "harmful to the state." In May, responding to such attempts to restrict the use of the Internet, Human Rights Watch published *Silencing the Net: The Threat to Freedom of Expression On-line*. The report documents the wide range of methods currently being used to restrict the Internet, recommends principles for governments and international and regional bodies to follow when formulating public policy and laws affecting the Internet, and sets forth the international legal principles governing on-line expression.

Human Rights Watch also participated with several coalitions of on-line rights groups to protest Internet censorship agreements by the G-7 countries and the ASEAN nations, and a specific instance of on-line censorship in Germany. We wrote a letter to the Singapore government protesting its restrictive Internet policies and another to the Indonesian government to protest an arrest related to on-line communication.

Hellman/Hammett Grants

Human Rights Watch administers the Hellman/Hammett grant program for writers who have been victims of political persecution and are in financial need. The program gives between US$150,000 and $200,000 to writers all over the world. Established in 1989, the grant program is funded by the estates of Lillian Hellman and Dashiell Hammett, American writers who were victimized for their political beliefs and associations during the U.S. anti-communist "witch hunts" of the early 1950s. With this experience in mind, Ms. Hellman left the legacy to provide support for writers who have been persecuted for expressing political views.

In addition to providing much-needed financial assistance, the Hellman/Hammett grants focus attention on repression of free speech and censorship by publicizing the persecution that the grant recipients have endured. In some cases the publicity is a protection against further abuse. In other cases, the writers have requested anonymity because of the dangerous circumstances in which they and their families are living. In 1996, forty-four writers from twenty-three countries received Hellman/Hammett grants, including nine from China, seven from Nigeria, four from Vietnam, and three from Iran. Among the recipients in 1996 were the following:

Ayaz Akhmedov, founder of an underground satirical journal in Azerbaijan, was convicted of publishing articles that were "insulting to the honor and dignity of the president."

Mina Assadi, poet and journalist, fled from Iran to Sweden where she has continued to speak in opposition to Iranian censorship and despotism, both in the Shah's regime and by the Islamic Republic.

Bei Ling Huang, poet and literary critic, was repeatedly harassed by the Chinese government for his role in the Democracy Wall movement of 1979 and the underground literary movement of the 1980s.

Ernest Brima, journalist, fled from Sierra Leone in 1991 and from the Gambia in 1995 because of persecution following articles he wrote about military politics in Africa.

Arief Budiman, author of articles criticizing the political system in Indonesia including a sharp critique of newspaper closings in 1994, was dismissed from his position as professor of development studies at Satya Wacana University.

Alfonso Castiglione Mendoza, journalist, was convicted, despite a complete lack of incriminating evidence, of collaborating with terrorism by Peru's infamous "faceless" courts and sentenced to twenty years in prison.

Chen Dongdong, Chinese poet, was banned from all official poetry activities and from publishing because he had defended free expression and refused to cooperate with police.

Choi Chin-Sop, South Korean journalist, was arrested in a roundup of alleged members of a pro-North Korea "spy ring," was tortured to confess and sentenced to three years in prison.

Joseph Couture, Canadian journalist, was harassed by police after he discovered that the police were using an investigation of child pornography as cover for a crackdown on gay men.

Ali-Asqhar Haj Sayed Djavadi, Iranian novelist and journalist, fled to France under threat of execution for having warned about religious fundamentalist efforts to gain monopoly control of the state.

Do Trung Hieu, Vietnam, was tried and sentenced to a fifteen-month jail term for distributing "malicious documents" detrimental to the government, charges apparently stemming from his personal memoirs which include comments on Communist Party efforts to suppress the Unified Buddhist Church.

Ge Hu, arrested for protesting the June 4, 1989, Beijing massacre and sentenced as a "counterrevolutionary," was denied health care in prison.

Haluk Gerger, respected Turkish writer on nuclear weapons, was convicted of "spreading separatist propaganda" and is facing three more law suits for articles he wrote for the now-banned, pro-Kurdish newspaper, *Ozgur Gundem.*

Julio Godoy, journalist, was driven into exile after writing about coup plans against the Guatemalan government.

Hoang Minh Chinh, Vietnamese political theorist, has spent most of the last thirty years in prison and under house arrest for promoting reformist views.

Zubeida Jaffer, South African journalist, was harassed, tortured, and incarcerated for nine years for covering the anti-apartheid and trade union movements.

Kalala Mbenga Kalao, Zairian journalist, was arrested five times in four years, tortured, and had his home destroyed for reporting information critical of the government.

Karasaev Khusein, who writes of the epic storytellers and folk people of Kazakstan, was imprisoned as a member of the Social Turan Party although the party did not exist.

Martha Kumsa, journalist, an Oromo Presbyterian in Ethiopia, apparently targeted because of her religion and ethnic origin, spent nine years in prison without charge and finally fled to Canada.

Liu Nianchun, Chinese essayist, novelist, and poet, was first arrested for his role in the Democracy Wall movement of 1979 and has been repeatedly harassed and imprisoned since.

Meng Junliang, widely recognized as one of China's outstanding modern poets, has been in continuous conflict with the police due to his insistence that freedom of expression is a necessary prerequisite for writing real literature.

George Owuor, Kenyan journalist, was interrogated, beaten, and detained for reporting on human rights issues and official corruption, including articles exposing embezzlement by President Moi's ruling party and election fraud.

Miro Salimov, Tajik journalist, was charged with calling for the violent overthrow of the government, insulting the honor and dignity of the president, and inciting ethnic conflict over an article about why the Russian army in Tajikistan could not be considered a peacekeeping force.

Adnan Abbas Salman al-Sayegh, Iraqi poet and playwright, fled to Jordan and then Lebanon in the wake of government efforts to censor and ban his work for containing passages that the government claims are hostile lies.

Pari Sekandari, Iranian journalist, novelist, and poet, fled to Paris where she received death threats from Islamic militants and was advised to move to a secure address outside of the city.

Wang Donghai, Chinese essayist and poet, editor of an important dissident jour-

nal, was sentenced to two years in prison for his role in pro-democracy demonstrations.

Wang Xizhe, famous for his pro-democracy writings during the 1970s, was sentenced to fourteen years in prison for disseminating "counterrevolutionary propaganda" and "inciting the masses" to defy the state.

Kunle Ajibade, Christine Anyanwu, George Mbah, Ben Charles Obi, and Dapo Oloronyomi, five Nigerian journalists, were all targeted by the military government shortly after an alleged coup attempt.

The Hellman/Hammett grants were awarded after nominations were reviewed by a five-person selection committee composed of writers and editors. In the course of the year, the selection committee approved four additional grants to writers who needed emergency funds to help them leave countries where they were in immediate danger.

Academic Freedom

The Academic Freedom Project (formerly known as the Committee for International Academic Freedom) was formed in 1991 by Human Rights Watch and a group of U.S. university presidents and scholars in recognition of the critical role that education plays in the development of civil society and the frequent targeting of educators and students by the world's more repressive regimes. When professors, teachers and students are harassed or imprisoned for exercising their rights of free expression and inquiry, when their work is censored, or when universities are closed for political reasons, the project sends protest letters and cables to appropriate government officials and publicizes the abuses in the academic community.

In the past year, the Academic Freedom Project wrote about situations in China, Egypt, Guatemala, Israel's Occupied Territories, Nigeria, South Korea, and the Slovak Republic.

The project members urged the Chinese government to overturn the conviction of Wang Dan, a leader of the student protests in Tiananmen Square.

In Egypt, the project members inquired

about the arrests of four university professors who were accused of founding an illegal political party even though Egyptian law recognizes the right of every citizen to establish and join a political party.

A letter to the president of Guatemala expressed concern for the safety of student leaders at the University of San Carlos Law School who were harassed and received death threats as a result of their efforts to have the police who were responsible held accountable for the violence resulting from attacks on students who were demonstrating against bus fare increases.

The project members expressed concern about arbitrary restrictions on travel that deny Palestinian students and faculty access to universities in the West Bank and the Gaza Strip and urged Israeli President Benjamin Netanyahu to revise procedures so that students can resume their studies.

Project members wrote Gen. Sani Abacha asking that the Ministry of Education rescind the ban on national activities by unions at Nigerian universities.

A letter to South Korean President Kim Young-Sam urged him to revoke the fines and prison terms imposed on teachers who signed the "Declaration for Genuine Educational Reform."

Two letters protested the dismissal of Alena Brunovska, the director of Academia Istropolitana in Bratislava.

The project members include twenty-eight university presidents and scholars. Its co-chairs are Jonathan Fanton of the New School for Social Research, Hanna Holborn Gray of the University of Chicago, Vartan Gregorian of Brown University, and Charles Young of the University of California at Los Angeles.

Lesbian and Gay Rights

In 1995, Human Rights Watch adopted a policy opposing state-tolerated violence, detention, prosecution and discrimination on the basis of sexual orientation. In 1996, the organization put this policy into practice in a major report and a lawsuit.

Anti-gay legislation, violence, harass-

ment and discrimination were among the human rights problems detailed in the report, *Modern Capital of Human Rights? Abuses in the State of Georgia*, released in July to coincide with the Olympic Games in Atlanta. These problems, although acute in Georgia, are often found elsewhere in the United States as well. The report exposed the failure of law enforcement officials to prosecute cross-burning, arson, and vandalism against gays and lesbians as well as the sluggish police response to investigating and solving cases involving murder or direct physical attacks. This distaste for protecting the rights of gays and lesbians results in the vast majority of such crimes never being reported to the police. Georgia also has a shameful record of state-sanctioned employment discrimination and lacks laws to prohibit such discrimination in the private sector—so that even a mother who publicly decried the murder of her gay son by a group of teenagers with baseball bats had no recourse when, as a consequence, she lost her job. Intolerance of lesbians and gays became a highly visible issue before the Olympics as one Georgia county adopted a resolution condemning "lifestyles advocated by the gay community" and another county swiftly did the same. The Atlanta Committee for the Olympic Games withdrew plans to have the Olympic torch carried through the first county; faced with that prospect, the second rescinded its own resolution, despite death threats to one of the county commissioners. Human Rights Watch urged the repeal of anti-gay laws and ordinances, the prohibition at the federal, state and local levels of discrimination based on sexual orientation, and the reauthorization of the Federal Hate Crimes Statistics Act, which has a provision requiring the collection of statistics regarding anti-gay bias crimes.

The prison specialist of Human Rights Watch also began research on sexual abuse and rape of prisoners, examining, among other issues, the vulnerability of gay prisoners to rape. Our initial research highlighted as an area for further investigation the striking reluctance of prison officials to intervene when a victim is perceived as homosexual.

Human Rights Watch and other human rights organizations also attacked discrimination against gays and lesbians in the context of a landmark U.S. asylum case. In March, we submitted a "friend of the court" brief in the case of *Pitcherskaia v. INS*, an appeal of a denial of asylum to a Russian lesbian activist. Alla Pitcherskaia had been arrested and beaten by the police numerous times because of her association with lesbians, expelled from medical school, dismissed from jobs, forced to undergo state medical "treatment" as a lesbian, and threatened with long-term institutionalization, medication and electroshock therapy. Nevertheless, her application for U.S. asylum was denied. In its decision, the Board of Immigration Affairs had called into question the applicability of Attorney General Janet Reno's earlier determination that sexual orientation could be a basis for claiming persecution on account of membership in a social group. Our brief argued that as a matter of both U.S. and international law, persecution on account of sexual orientation is a basis for asylum. Following the submission of our brief, the Immigration and Naturalization Service admitted to misstatements in its brief and moved to correct the administrative record to reflect the view that gays and lesbians do constitute a particular social group; this was done, however, with the intent of avoiding a federal court decision that might settle the issue once and for all in U.S. law.

During 1996, the Human Rights Watch Children's Rights Project requested the American Psychiatric Association to look into cases of alleged psychiatric "treatment" of young people to change their sexual orientation. Although homosexuality was dropped from the official compilation of mental disorders in 1973, there had been reports that the diagnostic category of "Gender Identity Disorder" had been used instead to institutionalize children who manifest what are perceived as gay or lesbian traits.

Legal Advocacy and Standard Setting

An increasingly important strategy of Human Rights Watch is bringing evidence, arguments, and cases before courts and international bodies empowered to hear individual complaints and provide redress. Human Rights Watch strongly believes that it is vital to present human rights abuses to these fora, not merely to publicize them and win redress for victims but also to advance principles of protection of rights so that they become part of international and national law.

Human Rights Watch also strongly supports the creation of an effective international criminal court under U.N. auspices to pursue war crimes and crimes against humanity. In 1996 we worked with other human rights groups and with several national governments toward that end, as described below. In addition, we continued our vigorous advocacy of high-level indictments and prosecutions by the U.N.'s war crimes tribunals on the former Yugoslavia and Rwanda (*see* Helsinki and Africa overviews, sections on the relevant countries, and Women's Rights Project).

In 1996, as well, Human Rights Watch continued to press for the development of new human rights standards in international law through advocacy to international bodies and in international conferences. Among our efforts were promoting the adoption of minimum humanitarian standards in the rules of war, examining the effect of "lustration" and "repentance laws" in curtailing impunity, urging the recognition of the right to adequate housing, and defending the protection role of the United Nations High Commissioner for Refugees (UNHCR). We also participated in work related to the reform of NGO access to the U.N.

Legal Advocacy

United States federal courts

United States law allows federal courts to hear cases in tort brought against foreign nationals for "crimes against the law of nations" committed in foreign lands. This unique feature of the country's legal system has become an important tool in stigmatizing perpetrators of crimes against humanity by making sure that the United States does not become a safe haven for them when they leave office in their countries. Since 1980, several cases have been brought against torturers and abusers of other fundamental rights, and successive court victories have turned this litigation strategy into an important advocacy tool. In the late 1980s, Human Rights Watch joined other organizations and law firms in bringing three such complaints against the former "lord of life and death" of Buenos Aires, Gen. Carlos Guillermo Suárez Mason, who had fled Argentina shortly after the return to democracy and was living in golden exile in San Francisco. We won default judgments for our clients, and eventually Suárez Mason was extradited to Argentina.

In 1996, we had another resounding victory, in the case of *Mushikiwabo v. Barayagwiza*. The federal court for the Southern District of New York entered a $105 million judgment under the Alien Tort Claims Act against the leader of one of the Rwandan extremist groups who launched that country's genocide. With the assistance of the law firms Debevoise & Plimpton and Carter, Ledyard & Milburn, we represented several Rwandan nationals whose relatives were tortured and killed in the genocide of April and May 1994. The defendant, Jean Bosco Barayagwiza, was served in May 1994 when he visited the United Nations, and since then had lived in France and Zaire. The judgment stated that "the plaintiffs have overwhelmingly established that the defendant has engaged in conduct so inhuman that it is difficult to conceive of any civil remedy which can begin to compensate the plaintiffs for their loss or adequately express society's outrage at the defendant's actions." In awarding the victims $1.5 million in damages for every relative they lost during the genocide, Judge Martin declared: "This Judge has seen no other case in which monetary damages were so inadequate to compensate the plain-

tiffs for the injuries caused by a defendant. One cannot place a dollar value on the lives lost as the result of the defendant's actions and the suffering inflicted on the innocent victims of his cruel campaign."

Human Rights Watch has also assumed the role of plaintiff in litigation on behalf of human rights. This year, we joined nineteen other organizations and individuals in *American Civil Liberties Union v. Reno*, a suit challenging the Communications Decency Act which President Clinton signed into law in February. The act subjects to criminal sanction those who are the source of "indecent" or "patently offensive" communications on the Internet if those communications are accessible to persons under eighteen years of age. These vague terms, based on community standards and taken from the area of broadcast licensing, go much further than the prohibition of pornography on the Internet, a prohibition legally in force prior to the Communications Decency Act. Ironically, the act would criminalize speech that is protected by the United States Constitution's first amendment when uttered aloud or printed in a newspaper. We submitted evidence that under the vague standards of the act, even our on-line reports of human rights abuses such as trafficking in women, sexual torture, or rape, could subject us to criminal penalty. Although our reporting is sometimes graphic and explicit, we believe this is necessary to fully convey the suffering these abuses cause. A special three-judge panel struck down the Communications Decency Act's provisions as unconstitutional, and the U.S. government appealed the case directly to the Supreme Court under special procedures contained in the act. The Supreme Court was expected to consider this case and another, closely related case in 1997.

Under the Freedom of Information Act, it is possible to compel disclosure of information and documentation that exists in United States government archives. Human Rights Watch pursues administrative requests for release of material that we consider vital to human rights documentation. In 1996, we joined other organizations as plaintiffs in a case to compel disclosure of the satellite and aerial photographs that reportedly showed Bosnian civilians from the Srebrenica safe haven being rounded up in a soccer field before being killed. We initiated this request in August 1995, shortly after U.S. Ambassador to the U.N. Madeleine Albright showed these records to a closed session of the Security Council.

Briefs amicus curiae and advisory letters

Human Rights Watch, in conjunction with other human rights advocates, also submitted *amicus curiae* or "friend of the court" briefs in major U.S. cases during 1996. Two such cases challenged restrictive legislation. The Prison Litigation Reform Act, which became law in April, revised the ground rules of challenging abusive prison conditions through the courts, making it extremely difficult to bring a successful case. One effect of the act was to make it much less attractive for states to enter consensual agreements with plaintiffs to remedy prison conditions, by subjecting consent decrees to onerous requirements. In *Plyler v. Moore*, we filed a brief challenging the Prison Litigation Reform Act's provisions that allow states to unilaterally and immediately end existing consent decrees covering prison conditions, arguing that this termination of a judicial injunction violated the Constitution of the United States. Oral argument was set before the Fourth Circuit for December.

We also participated in a challenge to an amendment in the state of Arizona's constitution that requires public employees to use only English in the course of performing their official duties. With the assistance of the law firm Paul, Weiss, Rifkind, Wharton & Garrison, we filed an amicus brief in *Arizonans for Official English v. State of Arizona*, urging the Supreme Court to affirm the Ninth Circuit's decision striking down the law. Our argument was that the law's restrictions would violate international legal protections of language rights. Contrary to the appellant's claim that the law furthered

social unity, we cited worldwide examples where official language restrictions actually fostered communal tensions and in many cases, violence.

In the area of political asylum, Human Rights Watch has also made submissions where there was a danger that individuals might be forced back to a country where they faced a danger of persecution. In *Pitcherskaia v. INS*, we urged the Ninth Circuit Court of Appeals to affirm that persecution on account of sexual orientation can be a basis for refugee status in the case of a Russian lesbian activist who had been forced to undergo "medical treatment" by state authorities. Our brief was prepared by the law firms of Mayer, Brown and Platt and Hughes, Hubbard and Reed.

In June, Human Rights Watch and Amnesty International wrote to the Canada's minister of immigration, urging against the deportation of a former Honduran military officer, Florencio Caballero. Caballero, who had been pressed into serving as an interrogator with an elite intelligence unit, fled Honduras in 1986 and promptly contacted Human Rights Watch to relate his intimate knowledge of Honduran death squad activities. With no assurances of protection or compensation, Caballero provided critical testimony to both the Inter-American Commission on Human Rights and the Inter-American Court of Human Rights. The latter, relying in part on Caballero's testimony, found Honduras accountable for systematic state-sponsored violence and "disappearances" in the landmark 1988 case *Velásquez-Rodríguez*. Several other witnesses in that case have been killed. In August, a Canadian federal court granted leave for judicial review of the denial of asylum to Caballero.

Human Rights Watch also wrote in April to the head of the U.S. Immigration and Naturalization Service to urge that Fauziya Kasinga's claim for asylum be recognized, based on the fact that she would face the threat of female genital mutilation should she be compelled to return to Togo. Astonishingly, the immigration judge in her case failed to recognize female genital mutilation as persecution, and assumed she would be able to avail herself of police protection against such a threat. We called on the INS to ensure that all authorities in the asylum review process be trained on the nature of gender-related persecution and the lack of state response to such violations. Human Rights Watch also condemned Ms. Kasinga's mistreatment while in immigration detention and called on the INS to ensure that asylum seekers are not detained unnecessarily or subjected to inhuman or degrading treatment.

The Inter-American Commission and Court

Human Rights Watch/Americas, working in conjunction with the Center for Justice and International Law (CEJIL), is participating in close to one hundred cases before the Inter-American Commission on Human Rights (IACHR) and the Inter-American Court of Human Rights on behalf of the victims of human rights violations.

Our docket before the IACHR was very active in 1996. The commission declared admissible the case of *Narciso González*, a well-known university professor who allegedly was "disappeared" by state agents of the Dominican Republic. In *Maria Arena, et al.* we challenged Argentina's Federal Penitentiary Service practice of subjecting women and female children visiting inmates to vaginal inspections. As a result, the Argentine government set out to reform relevant legislation. In 1996, the IACHR found Chile in violation of Article 13 (freedom of expression) of the American Convention on Human Rights for barring the circulation of a book by Francisco Martorell, titled *Diplomatic Impunity*, according to the commission, a clear case of prior censorship. In the case of *Father David Fernández* and other Centro Prodh human rights activists who had been threatened in Mexico, the commission granted an injunction against the Mexican government and opened an investigation. The commission also referred to the Inter-American Court of

Human Rights three of our cases against Peru for arbitrary detention, forced disappearance and cruel and inhuman treatment of persons accused of terrorism.

During 1996 evidence was presented to the court in the case against Nicaragua of *Jean Paul Genie Lacayo*, who was allegedly murdered by the military under the command of Humberto Ortega.

The court issued judgments on the merits of two of our cases. In January, after Argentina acknowledged its responsibility in the case of *Baigorria and Garrido*, two persons "disappeared" by the police in April 1990, the court issued a judgment ordering the government to pay damages. The parties proceeded to negotiate a friendly settlement. In a case of the "disappearance" of a school teacher and union activist, *Isidro Caballero and Maria del Carmen Santana*, the court found Colombia responsible in December 1995, and proceedings began in 1996 on the issue of reparations. In six more of our cases, the court ordered either compensation to the victims of human rights abuse or injunctions to protect persons in imminent danger. In the case of *Carpio* against Guatemala, the court upheld protective measures for the widow of a former presidential candidate, his daughter-in-law, and the prosecutor investigating Carpio's 1993 assassination.

International Criminal Court

Events in 1996 highlighted the urgent need for the early establishment of an effective international criminal court (ICC). The start of the trial of Dusko Tadic, the Bosnian Serb charged with murder and torture at the infamous Omarska detention camp, the fiftieth anniversary of the Nuremberg prosecutions, the failure to apprehend senior Serb and Croat officials indicted by the International Criminal Tribunal for the Former Yugoslavia as well as ongoing crimes against humanity in Burundi and war crimes in Chechnya, underscored the need to establish accountability for the most serious human rights crimes.

Progress toward an ICC continued during 1996 as negotiations proceeded slowly.

The U.N. General Assembly voted in December 1995 to move the drafting process to a higher stage by convening a Preparatory Committee on the Establishment of an International Criminal Court to discuss and "draft texts, with a view to preparing a widely acceptable consolidated text of a convention" as a step toward a diplomatic conference to finalize the treaty creating the court. The decision to initiate a preparatory committee was agreed to after weeks of intense closed negotiations in which China obstructed a resolution.

The preparatory committee met for two three-week sessions during 1996. In the March-April session the delegates focused on the major political questions arising from the International Law Commission's (ILC) Draft Statute. The U.N. had mandated the ILC, a group of internationally recognized legal scholars, to create a draft statute, which the ILC completed in July 1994. At the preparatory committee meeting there were major differences over the court's subject matter jurisdiction, independence for the prosecutor, and the relationship between the proposed court and national jurisdictions. On the relationship between the Security Council and the court there was a clear polarization between the five permanent members of the Security Council and virtually all other delegations. By the end of the session it was widely felt that most of these questions would only be resolved by senior officials at a diplomatic conference of plenipotentiaries.

The August session focused on the more technical legal questions: general principles of criminal law, fair trial and the rights of the defendant, judicial cooperation, and court organization. Five working groups produced a compiled text including many proposals but only limited consolidated text. The delegates fell short of producing a consolidated text due to obstructionism by France, which introduced an entire alternative draft statute, and the sheer volume of various government proposals.

After intense informal negotiations at the end of the August session, the preparatory committee adopted a recommendation that called for an additional nine weeks of preparatory work to be completed by April 1998. The recommendation cited a 1998 diplomatic conference as a realistic goal.

The October-November debate at the General Assembly's Sixth Committee focused on the pace of the future negotiations. Those states supporting the early establishment of the court sought a resolution calling for a 1998 date for a diplomatic conference. They pressed for the ICC negotiations to be given priority and allocated six weeks during 1997. Other states opposing the establishment of an effective court were resistant to specific time commitments.

The permanent members of the Security Council played a primarily negative role toward the court. France, supportive of the court in 1995, reversed its position and by April called for wording that would require Security Council approval for every case on the court's docket. At the August session its massive alternative draft statute slowed progress. On the most important substantive issues the United States's interventions were aimed at limiting the court's effectiveness and independence. U.S. delegates opposed an independent prosecutor, supported Security Council control in situations involving international peace and security, while providing valuable leadership in the discussion on the technical legal issues. Citing a strategy of "deliberative momentum," the U.S. opposed an early conference date. China made clear that it opposed the early establishment of the court and in August called for a minimum of twelve additional weeks of preparatory work.

One of the most significant developments of the 1996 negotiations was the emergence of a bloc of states united around the need for an effective court. This group, representing diverse geographical regions, grew in size, negotiating skill and commitment during 1996. Composed of African, Latin American, Caribbean, European, Arabic, and Micronesian states, this group, "the likeminded states" or "friends of the Court," became a major force on behalf of the ICC.

By the August preparatory committee meeting, these "like-minded states," claiming thirty members, were regularly meeting to plan strategy and coordinate tactics.

Human Rights Watch attached great importance to the establishment of the ICC as a key mechanism to strengthen defense of human rights. During 1996 we continued to work in our own name and in collaboration with human rights, legal, religious, and international policy organizations. We prepared and circulated written commentaries outlining our position on the essential issues before the preparatory committee. Staff members vigorously encouraged the "like-minded states" to work as a bloc. To help expand their ranks we successfully lobbied states with a demonstrated commitment to accountability for human rights abuses committed under a previous regime. Through numerous interviews and articles Human Rights Watch raised the issue broadly in the press.

Human Rights Standards

U.N. and OSCE

In February, Human Rights Watch participated in the session of the ECOSOC (Economic and Social Council) Working Group reviewing consultative arrangements between the U.N. and NGOs. We joined with several other human rights organizations supporting the process, that was to open the U.N. to national organizations, but we opposed the suggested language stipulating that human rights organizations would have to fulfill additional requirements in order to be granted consultative status. In the course of the next several months, we repeatedly stressed our concerns, in lobbying and in joint statements with a number of fellow human rights organizations. Eventually, in July, ECOSOC approved a toned-down but still objectionable version of the resolution, in which human rights organizations were singled out for additional requirements to obtain consultative status with the council.

Also in February, we sent an open letter to the Organization for Security and Cooperation in Europe Human Dimension conference, which was considering the adoption of minimum humanitarian standards for the rules of war. Such standards would be especially useful in setting an indisputable baseline of humanitarian conduct for all parties to hostilities, particularly in situations where the application of the Geneva Conventions is unclear. Rather than supplanting existing humanitarian law, the standards are intended to reinforce basic principles such as the protection of civilians, even where it was debatable whether hostilities had risen to the level of sustained armed conflict, and they would bind all parties, regardless of whether a conflict was internal or international. In September, the U.N. secretary-general organized a workshop on the standards in Capetown, at which it was decided to begin a formal analytical study that may ultimately result in a General Assembly resolution on the standards.

In April, during the session of the U.N. Commission on Human Rights, we issued a statement in Geneva in which we raised serious concerns about a draft resolution presented by Cuba which had a potential to drastically limit the mandate of the U.N. Working Group on Arbitrary Detention. Eventually, Cuba withdrew its draft, and a different resolution was adopted.

Impunity

In May, we submitted a memorandum to the U.N. Special Rapporteur on Impunity, dealing with three developing areas of law. The first was the emerging right to know the truth concerning gross human rights violations. This right derives from the obligation in international law that states "ensure" rights and provide effective remedies, and pertains not only to victims and their families but also to the public at large. The second area was the practice of lustration—the purging of officials associated with an old regime— that is especially prevalent in the newly democratic states of Eastern Europe. In this case, we raised concerns that lustration penalizes individuals for their association with a group or organization rather than for their own actions, and pointed out the numerous procedural rights that can easily be violated by such practices.

Finally, we discussed the potential abuses inherent in repentance laws, a form of plea-bargaining practiced in Peru and Colombia among other states. In these countries, basic fair-trial standards often do not apply to persons implicated in criminal activity by *arrepentidos* (the "penitent" seeking to plea-bargain) who use the laws to gain lenient treatment for themselves. We recommended that courts must play an extremely vigilant role to ensure that confessions under such a system are not coerced, that they are corroborated wherever possible by independent evidence, and to ensure that the most culpable do not use the laws to their freedom by implicating others who have less information to trade.

Right to Monitor

The third major U.N. conference on international human rights of this decade took place during 1996—Habitat II, on the subject of housing and shelter. On the eve of the final preparatory conference in February 1996, Human Rights Watch strongly critiqued the draft conference agenda for failing anywhere to recognize that adequate housing is a universal human right, embodied in numerous treaties, including the International Covenant on Economic, Social and Cultural Rights. Citing our research, we demonstrated where violations of civil and political rights led directly to violation of the right to housing, and urged that this integral relationship between rights be recognized in the conference's final document. In May, we wrote to U.S. Secretary of Housing and Urban Development Henry Cisneros, criticizing the U.S. move to weaken the rights language in the document, and in June we updated our overall concerns regarding the draft final document and released the updated report in Istanbul to conference participants. The Habitat II final document differed significantly from its earlier drafts and incorporated several of the points made in statements by Human Rights Watch and our colleagues in the human rights community.

Refugee Protection

In September, Human Rights Watch presented the UNHCR Executive Committee with a discussion paper titled "Protection in the Decade of Voluntary Repatriation." The context for this paper was concern that UNHCR's protection function had been compromised because of the agency's and governments' heavy emphasis on repatriation as the solution of choice to refugee crises. Our paper documented instances where UNHCR was pressured into participating in supposedly voluntary repatriation exercises where conditions in the country of origin were arguably unsafe, or where the governments of origin or asylum were uncooperative and impeded UNHCR's protection function. We welcomed the publication of UNHCR's new handbook on voluntary repatriation, which emphasizes that return is voluntary where there is an "absence" of coercive measures to push refugees from a haven, such as a reduction in food rations. We also welcomed new protection guidelines on responses to sexual violence against female refugees. But in both cases, we emphasized that practice falls short of UNHCR's standards. More guidance is needed on UNHCR's role where the optimal conditions for voluntary repatriation do not exist, as in the case of Rohingyas returning to Burma from Bangladesh, or Sri Lankan Tamils who were pressured to return "voluntarily" from India. Likewise, we recommended that UNHCR put into place internal procedures to handle sexual violence against women refugees as soon as reports come in from the field, and to ensure that refugee women are integrally involved in formulating protective measures, as in Kenya where the number of reported rapes of Somali refugees decreased by half once such steps were taken.

As of this writing, Human Rights Watch is preparing to issue the paper publicly, expressing concern that the protection division of the UNHCR staff appeared to have been marginalized in recent internal reorganization.

Congressional Casework

Human Rights Watch continued to work closely with three casework groups composed of members of U.S. Congress: the Congressional Friends of Human Rights Monitors, the Congressional Committee to Support Writers and Journalists, and the Congressional Working Group on International Women's Human Rights. All three groups are bipartisan and bicameral.

Human Rights Watch initiated the formation of these groups to enable concerned members of Congress to write letters to governments that commit or condone violations against human rights monitors, writers and journalists, or gender-based abuses of women's human rights. Human Rights Watch supplies the groups with information about appropriate cases of concern; the groups, in turn, determine which cases they would like to pursue.

The goals of the congressional casework groups are three-fold. Most important, their letters help to pressure governments to end their persecution of human rights monitors, writers and journalists, and women; abuses which are either committed or routinely tolerated by governments. Second, members of the congressional groups are informed about these important incidents of violence and intimidation. Finally, copies of letters are sent to U.S. ambassadors in the relevant countries to inform them about cases of concern and to local press from the countries in question so that they in turn can bring additional attention to human rights violations.

The Congressional Friends of Human Rights Monitors

The Congressional Friends of Human Rights Monitors, formed in 1983, was composed of twenty-eight Senators and 106 Members of the House of Representatives during the 2nd Session of the 104th Congress. Steering committee members were Sen. Daniel Patrick Moynihan, Sen. James Jeffords, Rep. Tony Hall, and Rep. Constance A. Morella. In 1996, the group focused its attention on writing urgent action letters about time-sensitive cases of death threats, attacks, and unwarranted arrests of human rights monitors, to the heads of state in Algeria, Colombia, Croatia, Guatemala, Israel, Mexico, Palestinian Authority, Peru, Tunisia, and Uzbekistan.

The Congressional Committee to Support Writers and Journalists

The Congressional Committee to Support Writers and Journalists was formed in 1988 and was composed of seventeen Senators and seventy-four Members of the House of Representatives during the 2nd Session of the 104th Congress. Members of the steering committee were Sen. Bob Graham, Rep. Jim Leach, and Rep. John Lewis. In 1996, the committee condemned murders, attacks, and arbitrary arrests, as well as acts of censorship against reporters and publications, through letters to the heads of state in Cambodia, Cuba, Indonesia, Ireland, Mexico, Peru, Poland, Russia, and Turkey.

The Congressional Working Group on International Women's Human Rights

The Congressional Working Group on International Women's Human Rights, which was formed in April 1994 to promote accountability for violations of women's rights worldwide, is a bipartisan group composed of twenty-four senators and thirty-six members of the House of Representatives. The four members of the working group's steering committee are Sen. Patty Murray, Sen. Olympia J. Snowe, Rep. Jan Meyers, and Rep. Joe Moakley. In 1996, the group wrote letters of protest on abduction, threats, and rape to the heads of state in Bangladesh, Peru, and Rwanda.

HUMAN RIGHTS WATCH INTERNATIONAL FILM FESTIVAL

The Human Rights Watch International Film Festival was created to advance public education on human rights issues and concerns using the unique medium of film. Each year, the Human Rights Watch International Film Festival exhibits the finest human rights films and videos in commercial and archival theaters and on public and cable television throughout the United States and in various cities abroad—a reflection of both the scope of the festival and the increasingly global appeal that the project has generated.

In selecting films for the festival, Human Rights Watch concentrates equally on artistic merit and human rights content. The festival encourages filmmakers around the world to address human rights subject matter in their work and presents films and videos from both new and established international human rights filmmakers. Each year, the festival's programming committee screens more than 600 films and videos to create a program that represents a wide number of countries and issues. Once a film is nominated for a place in the program, staff of the relevant division of Human Rights Watch also view it to confirm its accuracy in the portrayal of human rights concerns.

The Human Rights Watch International Film Festival was established in 1988, in part to mark the tenth anniversary of the founding of what has become Human Rights Watch. After a hiatus of three years, it was resumed in 1991 and has since been presented annually. The 1996 festival featured over forty films, twenty-nine of which were premieres from thirteen countries presented over a two-week period first in New York, as a collaborative venture with the Film Society of Lincoln Center, and then in Los Angeles with the Museum of Tolerance. A majority of the screenings were followed by discussions with the filmmakers and Human Rights Watch staff on the issues represented in each work. The festival included feature-length fiction and documentary films as well as works-in-progress and experimental and animated films.

Each year the festival is launched in New York with an opening night fundraising celebration featuring a film's U.S. premiere. In 1996 the festival's opening night centerpiece was the drama "Lone Star," by American writer-director John Sayles. The film won praise at the Cannes International Film Festival and from North American critics, for its treatment of racial intolerance, tensions along the U.S.-Mexico border, and police abuse.

In conjunction with the opening night, the festival annually awards a prize in the name of cinematographer and director Nestor Almendros, who was a cherished friend of the festival. The award, which includes a cash prize of $5,000, goes to a deserving new filmmaker in recognition of his or her contributions to human rights.

The 1996 recipient of the Nestor Almendros Award were filmmakers Mandy Jacobson and Karmen Jelincic whose outstanding work, "Calling the Ghosts: A Story about Rape, War and Women," chronicles the remarkable transformation of "two ordinary modern women" in Bosnia-Herzegovina, whose personal struggle for survival evolves into a larger fight for peace and justice after they were held in a concentration camp and raped and tortured by their neighbors. They determined to put rape into the international lexicon of war crimes. Their success can be judged by the fact that their torturers now stand indicted by the International War Crimes Tribunal. This very powerful, personal film also became the centerpiece of the festival's Women's Day Program—a day and night exclusively devoted to films and videos that address women's rights around the world.

In 1995, in honor of Irene Diamond, a longtime board member and supporter of Human Rights Watch, the festival launched a new award, the Irene Diamond Lifetime Achievement Award, which is presented annually to a director whose life's work illuminates an outstanding commitment to human rights and film. The 1996 award went to renowned Senegalese director Ousmane Sembene, in honor of his dedication to furthering the cause of human rights through film, and of his role in encouraging African independent filmmakers to produce daring, challenging human rights films.

Highlights of the 1996 festival included a retrospective of the work of acclaimed South Korean director Park Kwang-Su, whose latest film, "A Single Spark," won critical acclaim at the 1996 Berlin International Film Festival. Park, acknowledged as the leader of the "New Cinema" in South Korea, has consistently explored the points of tension in his homeland's history and society, never shying away from political and controversial themes.

The festival also featured a touring program of films and videos from Israeli and Palestinian filmmakers made since the historic signing of the 1993 peace accord. These personal works portray the complex and contradictory emotions, circumstances, and beliefs affecting all parties as the struggle to find peace unfolds. Other highlights of the festival included a series of films on the death penalty, chain gangs and political prisoners. Additionally, in this U.S. election year, the festival featured a series of works dealing with elections and democracy.

Throughout the festival's two-week run in New York, its high school project, in its fourth year, offered daytime screenings for students followed by interactive discussions among the students, their teachers, visiting filmmakers, and Human Rights Watch staff. In 1996 the program expanded to include collaborative screenings with the New York African Film Festival, highlighting human rights themes in new African cinema.

In an effort to reach a wider audience and satisfy the growing demand for these films, the festival established a "Global Showcase" touring program of films and videos, which appeared in eight U.S. cities: Seattle, Washington; San Francisco, California; St. Louis, Missouri; Durham, North Carolina; Columbia, South Carolina; Boston, Massachusetts; Martha's Vineyard, Massachusetts; Huntington, New York; Hartford, Connecticut. The "Global Showcase" also traveled to Buenos Aires and to Gent, Belgium.

In December, in collaboration with the Human Rights Watch office in Brazil, the festival appeared in both Rio de Janeiro and São Paolo exhibiting new films from the Americas dealing with human rights themes. This was the first Human Rights Watch International Film Festival held in Brazil.

In 1996, the festival also launched its first full-scale Human Rights Watch International Film Festival in Europe, opening in London on October 18. A new collaborative venture between the festival and the Institute of Contemporary Art (ICA) hosted a gala opening night with the European premiere of the award-winning documentary, "Mandela," produced by Jonathan Demme and Chris Blackwell, followed by a one-week festival of film and video screenings along with panel discussions with filmmakers from around the world and Human Rights Watch staff.

In 1992, Human Rights Watch created Film Watch, an association of the Film Festival and a group of American filmmakers, to monitor and protect the human rights of film makers who are threatened or censored or otherwise abused for their expression through film. In 1996, Film Watch took up the case of Kim Don-Won, a South Korean independent producer of documentary videos and films whose mission is to provide alternative media for educational purposes to the public. Kim Don-Won was arrested on June 14, 1996, and his tapes and editing equipment were confiscated from his office. No explanation was given by the government in this punitive action. Kim Don-Won was released several days later but, again, with no explanation by the government.

1996 PUBLICATIONS

To order any of the following titles, please call our Publications Department at (212) 986-1980 and ask for our publications catalog or visit our site on the World Wide Web at http://www.hrw.org.

Albania
Democracy Derailed: Violations in the May 26, 1996 Albanian Elections, 6/96, 11 pp.

Human Rights in Post-Communist Albania, 3/96, 168 pp.

Angola
Between War & Peace: Arms Trade & Human Rights Abuses since the Lusaka Protocol, 2/96, 44 pp.

Bangladesh
Political Violence on All Sides, 6/96, 23 pp.

Bolivia
Bolivia under Pressure: Human Rights Violations & Coca Eradication, 5/96, 32 pp.

Bosnia-Hercegovina
No Justice No Peace: The United Nations International Police Task Force's Role in Screening Local Law Enforcement, 9/96, 16 pp.

Update—Non-Compliance with the Dayton Accords: Ongoing Ethnically-Motivated Expulsions and Harassment in Bosnia, 8/96, 17 pp.

A Failure in the Making: Human Rights & the Dayton Agreement, 6/96, 37 pp.

Human Rights in Bosnia-Hercegovina Post Dayton, 3/96, 10 pp.

Northwestern Bosnia: Human Rights Abuses during a Cease-Fire & Peace Negotiations, 2/96, 40 pp.

Brazil
Fighting Violence with Violence: Human Rights Abuse & Criminality in Rio de Janeiro, 1/96, 29 pp.

Bulgaria
Children of Bulgaria: Police Violence & Arbitrary Confinement, 9/96, 160 pp.

Burma
The Rohingya Muslims: Ending a Cycle of Exodus?, 9/96, 37 pp.

China
Slamming the Door on Dissent: Wang Dan's Trial and the New "State Security" Era, 11/96, 15 pp.

The Cost of Putting Business First, 7/96, 33 pp.

Cutting Off the Serpent's Head: Tightening Control in Tibet, 3/96, 208 pp.

Chinese Orphanages: A Follow-Up, 3/96, 11 pp.

Death by Default: A Policy of Fatal Neglect in China's State Orphanages, 1/96, 408 pp.

Commonwealth of Independent States
Refugees & Internally Displaced Persons in Armenia, Azerbaijan, Georgia, the Russian Federation,& Tajikistan, 5/96, 33 pp.

Croatia
Impunity for Abuses Committed during "Operation Storm" and the Denial of the Right of Refugees to Return to the Krajina, 8/96, 43 pp.

Czech Republic
Roma in the Czech Republic: Foreigners in Their Own Land, 6/96, 39 pp.

General
All Too Familiar: Sexual Abuse of Women in U.S. State Prisons, 12/96, 360 pp.

Putting Human Rights Back into the Habitat Agenda, 6/96, 10 pp.

Silencing the Net: The Threat to Freedom of Expression On-line, 5/96, 24 pp.

Children in Combat, 1/96, 23 pp.

Guatemala
Return to Violence: Refugees, Civil Patrollers, & Impunity, 1/96, 31 pp.

Haiti
Thirst for Justice: A Decade of Impunity in Haiti, 9/96, 30 pp.

Hungary
Rights Denied: The Roma of Hungary, 7/96, 160 pp.

India
Police Abuse and Killings of Street Children in India, 11/96, 200 pp.

The Small Hands of Slavery: Bonded Child Labor in India, 9/96, 192 pp.

India's Secret Army in Kashmir: New Patterns of Abuse Emerge in the Conflict, 5/96, 49 pp.

Communal Violence & the Denial of Justice, 4/96, 28 pp.

Indonesia & East Timor
Tough International Response Needed to Widening Crackdown, 8/96, 28 pp.

Election Monitoring & Human Rights, 5/96, 11 pp.

Iran
Power Versus Choice: Human Rights & Parliamentary Elections in the Islamic Republic of Iran, 3/96, 19 pp.

Israel & Israeli-Occupied Territories
Israel's Closure of the West Bank and Gaza Strip, 7/96, 59 pp.

Civilian Pawns: Laws of War & the Use of Weapons on the Israel-Lebanon Border, 5/96, 152 pp.

Lebanon
Civilian Pawns: Laws of War & the Use of Weapons on the Israel-Lebanon Border, 5/96, 152 pp.

Macedonia
A Threat to "Stability": Human Rights Violations in Macedonia, 6/96, 120 pp.

Mexico
Labor Rights and NAFTA: A Case Study, 9/96, 30 pp.

No Guarantees: Sex Discrimination in Mexico's Maquiladora Sector, 8/96, 58 pp.

Torture & Other Abuses during the 1995 Crackdown on Alleged Zapatistas, 2/96, 19 pp.

Nigeria
"Permanent Transition": Current Violations of Human Rights in Nigeria, 9/96, 51 pp.

Peru
Presumption of Guilt: Human Rights Violations and the Faceless Courts in Peru, 8/96, 37 pp.

The Philippines
Human Rights & Forest Management in the 1990s, 4/96, 28 pp.

Russia
Report to the 1996 OSCE Review Conference, 11/96, 14 pp.

The Ingush-Ossetian Conflict in the Prigorodnyi Region, 4/96, 112 pp.

Caught in the Cross Fire: Civilians in Gudermes & Pervomayskoye, 3/96, 31 pp.

Rwanda
Shattered Lives: Sexual Violence during the Rwandan Genocide & its Aftermath, 9/96, 112 pp.

Sudan
Behind the Red Line: Political Repression in Sudan, 5/96, 368 pp.

Syria
The Silenced Kurds, 10/96, 63 pp.

Syria's Tadmor Prison: Dissent Still Hostage to a Legacy of Terror, 4/96, 26 pp.

Sweden
Swedish Asylum Policy in Global Human Rights Perspective, 9/96, 34 pp.

Tajikistan
Tajik Refugees in Northern Afghanistan, 5/96, 35 pp.

Tibet
Cutting Off the Serpent's Head: Tightening Control in Tibet, 3/96, 208 pp.

Turkey
Turkey's Failed Policy to Aid the Forcibly Displaced in the Southeast, 6/96, 14 pp.
    Violations of the Right of Petition to the European Commission of Human Rights, 4/96, 39 pp.

United States
Race and Drug Law Enforcement in the State of Georgia, 7/96, 21 pp.
    Modern Capital of Human Rights?: Abuses in the State of Georgia, 7/96, 208 pp.

Uzbekistan
Persistent Human Rights Violations & Prospects for Improvement, 5/96, 43 pp.

STAFF AND COMMITTEES

Human Rights Watch

Staff
Executive: Kenneth Roth, Executive Director; Jennifer Hyman, Executive Assistant.
Advocacy: Holly J. Burkhalter, Advocacy Director; Lotte Leicht, Brussels Office Director; Joanna Weschler, United Nations Representative; Lynette Munez, Christina Portillo, Associates.
Communications: Susan Osnos, Communications Director; Robert Kimzey, Publications Director; Jean-Paul Marthoz, European Press Director; Karen Sorensen, On-line Research Associate; Suzanne Guthrie, Publications Manager; Fitzroy Hepkins, Mail Manager; Lenny Thomas, Production Manager; Sobeira Genao, Publications Associate; Liz Reynoso, Communications Associate.
Development: Michele Alexander, Development Director; Diana Ayton-Shenker, Foundations Relations Director; Pamela Bruns, California Director; Rachel Weintraub, Special Events Director; James Holland, Individual Giving Coordinator; Marianne Law, Special Events Coordinator; Heather Cooper, Kristin Field, Keasha Dumas, Associates.
Finance and Administration: Barbara Guglielmo, Finance & Administration Director; Maria Pignataro Nielsen, Administrative Director; Walid Ayoub, Systems Administrator; Anderson Allen, Washington Office Manager; Urmi Shah, London Office Manager; Isabelle Tin-Aung, Brussels Office Manager; Iris Yang, Accountant; Bessie Skoures, Bookkeeper; Andrea Rodriguez, Receptionist/Office Assistant; Mia Roman, Receptionist/Office Assistant.
General Counsel: Dinah PoKempner, Acting General Counsel; Marti Weithman, Associate.
Program: Cynthia Brown, Program Director; Michael McClintock, Deputy Program Director; Jeri Laber, Senior Advisor; Jemera Rone, Counsel; Richard Dicker, Associate Counsel; Jamie Fellner, Associate Counsel; Joanne Mariner, Associate Counsel; Allyson Collins, Senior Researcher; Arvind Ganesan, Research Associate; Marcia Allina, Program Associate; Sahr MuhammedAlly, Associate.
International Film Festival: Bruni Burres, Director; Heather Harding, Associate Director.
1996 Fellowship Recipients: Gamal M. Abouali, Orville Schell Fellow; Julia A. Hall, W. Bradford Wiley Fellow; Mercedes Hernandez-Cancio, Sophie Silberberg Fellow; Kokkayi Issa, Leonard

H. Sandler Fellow.

Board of Directors
Robert L. Bernstein, Chair; Adrian W. DeWind, Vice Chair; Roland Algrant, Lisa Anderson, William Carmichael, Dorothy Cullman, Gina Despres, Irene Diamond, Edith Everett, Jonathan Fanton, James C. Goodale, Jack Greenberg, Vartan Gregorian, Alice H. Henkin, Stephen L. Kass, Marina Pinto Kaufman, Bruce Klatsky, Harold Hongju Koh, Alexander MacGregor, Josh Mailman, Samuel K. Murumba, Andrew Nathan, Jane Olson, Peter Osnos, Kathleen Peratis, Bruce Rabb, Sigrid Rausing, Anita Roddick, Orville Schell, Sid Sheinberg, Gary G. Sick, Malcolm Smith, Domna Stanton, Nahid Toubia, Maureen White, Rosalind C. Whitehead, Maya Wiley.

Human Rights Watch/Africa

Staff
Peter Takirambudde, Executive Director; Janet Fleischman, Washington Director; Suliman Ali Baldo, Senior Researcher; Alex Vines, Research Associate; Bronwen Manby, Binaifer Nowrojee, Counsels; Ariana Pearlroth, Juliet Wilson, Associates; Alison L. DesForges, Consultant.

Advisory Committee
William Carmichael, Chair; Roland Algrant; Robert L. Bernstein, Julius L. Chambers, Michael Clough, Roberta Cohen, Carol Corillon, Alison L. DesForges, Adrian W. DeWind, R. Harcourt Dodds, Aaron Etra, Thomas M. Franck, Gail M. Gerhart, Jack Greenberg, Arthur C. Helton, Alice H. Henkin, Robert Joffe, Jeh Johnson, Richard A. Joseph, Thomas Karis, Stephen L. Kass, John A. Marcum, Gay McDougall, Toni Morrison, Samuel K. Murumba, James C. N. Paul, Robert Preiskel, Norman Redlich, Randall Robinson, Sidney S. Rosdeitcher, Howard P. Venable, Claude E. Welch, Jr., Aristide R. Zolberg.

Human Rights Watch/Americas

Staff
José Miguel Vivanco, Executive Director; Anne Manuel, Deputy Director; Joel Solomon, Research Director; James Cavallaro, Brazil Office Director; Jennifer Bailey, Sebastian Brett, Sarah DeCosse, Robin Kirk, Research Associates; Steven Hernandez, Paul Paz y Miño, Associates.

Advisory Committee
Stephen L. Kass, Chair; Marina Pinto Kaufman, David E. Nachman, Vice Chairs; Roland Algrant, Peter D. Bell, Robert L. Bernstein, Albert Bildner, Reed Brody, Paul Chevigny, Roberto Cuéllar, Dorothy Cullman, Patricia Derian, Adrian W. DeWind, Tom J. Farer, Alejandro Garro, Wendy Gimbel, John S. Gitlitz, James Goldston, Ronald G. Hellman, Wade J. Henderson, Alice H. Henkin, Bianca Jagger, Margaret A. Lang, Robert S. Lawrence, MD, Jocelyn McCalla, Theodor Meron, John B. Oakes, Victor Penchaszadeh, Clara A. "Zazi" Pope, Bruce Rabb, Tina Rosenberg, Jean-Marie Simon, George Soros, Eric Stover, Rose Styron, Jorge Valls, Horacio Verbitsky, José Zalaquett.

Human Rights Watch/Asia

Staff
Sidney Jones, Executive Director; Mike Jendrzejczyk, Washington Director; Robin Munro, Hong Kong Office Director; Patricia Gossman, Senior Researcher; Zunetta Liddell, Research Associate; Jeannine Guthrie, NGO Liaison; Paul Lall, Olga Nousias, Associates; Milbert Shin, Mickey Spiegel, Joyce Wan, Consultants.

Advisory Committee
Andrew Nathan, Chair; Orville Schell, Vice Chair; Maureen Aung-Thwin, Edward J. Baker, Harry Barnes, Robert L. Bernstein, Julie Brill, Jerome Cohen, Adrian W. DeWind, Clarence Dias, Dolores A. Donovan, Adrienne Germain,

Merle Goldman, James C. Goodale,
Deborah M. Greenberg, Jack Greenberg,
Paul Hoffman, Sharon Hom, Rounaq
Jahan, Virginia Leary, Daniel Lev, Betty
Levin, Perry Link, Rt. Rev. Paul Moore,
Jr., Yuri Orlov, Victoria Riskin, Sheila
Rothman, Barnett Rubin, James Scott, Eric
Stover, Maya Wiley.

Human Rights Watch/Helsinki

Staff

Holly Cartner, Executive Director; Rachel
Denber, Moscow Office Director; John
MacLeod, Central Asia Office Director;
Fred Abrahams, Erika Dailey, Christopher
Panico, Diane Paul, Research Associates;
Alexander Petrov, Assistant Moscow
Office Director; Ivan Lupis, I. Maxine
Marcus, Research Assistants; Liudmila
Belova, Malcolm Hawkes, Emily Shaw,
Juliet Wilson, Associates.

Advisory Committee

Jonathan Fanton, Chair; Alice H. Henkin,
Vice Chair; M. Bernard Aidinoff, Roland
Algrant, Robert L. Bernstein, Charles
Biblowit, Martin Blumenthal, Roberta
Cohen, Lori Damrosch, Istvan Deak,
Adrian W. DeWind, Fr. Robert Drinan,
Stanley Engelstein, Ellen Futter, Willard
Gaylin. M.D., Michael Gellert, John
Glusman, Paul Goble, Jack Greenberg,
Rita E. Hauser, Robert James, Rhoda
Karpatkin, Stephen L. Kass, Bentley
Kassal, Marina Pinto Kaufman, Joanne
Landy, Margaret A. Lang, Leon Levy,
Wendy Luers, Theodor Meron, Deborah
Milenkovitch, Toni Morrison, John B.
Oakes, Herbert Okun, Jane Olson, Yuri
Orlov, Srdja Popovic, Bruce Rabb, Peter
Reddaway, Stuart Robinowitz, John G.
Ryden, Herman Schwartz, Stanley K.
Sheinbaum, Jerome J. Shestack, George
Soros, Susan Weber Soros, Michael
Sovern, Fritz Stern, Svetlana Stone, Rose
Styron, Liv Ullman, Gregory Wallance,
Rosalind C. Whitehead, William D. Zabel,
Warren Zimmermann.

Human Rights Watch/Middle East

Staff

Eric Goldstein, Acting Executive Director;
Virginia N. Sherry, Associate Director;
Joe Stork, Advocacy Director; Fatemeh
Ziai, Counsel; Shira Robinson, Awali
Samara, Associates; Elahé Hicks,
Consultant.

Advisory Committee

Gary G. Sick, Chair; Lisa Anderson, Bruce
Rabb, Vice Chairs; Shaul Bakhash, M.
Cherif Bassiouni, Hyman Bookbinder,
Paul Chevigny, Helena Cobban, Patricia
Derian, Stanley Engelstein, Edith Everett,
Mansour Farhang, Rita E. Hauser, Rev. J.
Bryan Hehir, Edy Kaufman, Marina Pinto
Kaufman, Samir Khalaf, Judith Kipper,
Pnina Lahav, Ann M. Lesch, Richard
Maass, Stephen P. Marks, Philip Mattar,
David K. Shipler, Sanford Solender,
Shibley Telhami, Andrew Whitley,
Napoleon B. Williams, Jr.

Human Rights Watch Academic Freedom Project

Staff

Marcia Allina, Program Associate.

Advisory Committee

Jonathan Fanton, President, New School
for Social Research; Hanna Holborn Gray,
University of Chicago; Vartan Gregorian,
President, Brown University; Charles
Young, Chancellor, University of
California at Los Angeles; Co-Chairs;
Johnetta Cole, President, Spellman
College; Joel Conarroe, President, John
Simon Guggenheim Memorial Founda-
tion; Lord Ralf Dahrendorf, Warden, St.
Antony's College, Oxford; Ariel Dorfman,
Research Professor, Duke University;
Thomas Ehrlich, Stanford University Law
School; James O. Freedman, President,
Dartmouth College; John Kenneth
Galbraith, Professor Emeritus, Harvard
University; Bernard Harleston, Professor,
Harvard Graduate School of Education;

Alice Stone Ilchman, President, Sarah Lawrence College; Stanley N. Katz, President, American Council of Learned Societies; Nannerl O. Keohane, President, Duke University; Paul LeClerc, President, The New York Public Library; Fang Lizhi, Professor, University of Arizona; Walter E. Massey, President, Morehouse College; Krzysztof Michalski, Professor, Institute for Human Sciences, Vienna; Joseph A. O'Hare, President, Fordham University; L. Jay Oliva, President, New York University; Yuri Orlov, Senior Scientist, Cornell University; Frank H. T. Rhodes, President Emeritus, Cornell University; Neil Rudenstine, President, Harvard University; George Rupp, President, Columbia University; Judith R. Shapiro, President, Barnard College; Michael Sovern, Columbia University Law School; Chang-Lin Tien, Chancellor, University of California at Berkeley.

Human Rights Watch Arms Project

Staff
Joost R. Hiltermann, Director; Stephen D. Goose, Program Director; Ernst Jan Hogendoorn, Research Assistant; Rebecca Bell, Associate; Zahabia Adamaly, William M. Arkin, Katherine L. Austin, Andrew Cooper, Ann Peters, Monica Schurtman, Frank Smyth, Consultants.

Advisory Committee
Ken Anderson, Nicole Ball, Frank Blackaby, Frederick C. Cuny, Ahmed H. Esa, Bill Green, Alastair Hay, Lao Mong Hay, Di Hua, Frederick J. Knecht, Edward J. Laurance, Vincent McGee, Janne E. Nolan, Andrew J. Pierre, David Rieff, Julian Perry Robinson, Kumar Rupesinghe, John Ryle, Mohamed M. Sahnoun, Gary G. Sick, Torsten N. Wiesel, Thomas Winship.

Human Rights Watch Children's Rights Project

Staff
Lois Whitman, Director; Yodon Thonden, Counsel; Lee Tucker, Consultant.

Advisory Committee
Jane Green Schaller, Chair; Goldie Alfasi-Siffert, Roland Algrant, Michelle India Baird, Phyllis W. Beck, James Bell, Albina du Boisrouvray, Rachel Brett, Nicole Burrowes, Bernadine Dohrn, Fr. Robert Drinan, Barbara Finberg, Sanford J. Fox, Lisa Hedley, Anita Howe-Waxman, Eugene Isenberg, Kela Leon, Alan Levine, Hadassah Brooks Morgan, Prexy Nesbitt, Elena Nightingale, Martha J. Olson, Marta Santos Pais, Susan Rappaport, Jack Rendler, Robert G. Schwartz, Mark I. Soler, Lisa Sullivan, William Taggart, William L. Taylor, Geraldine Van Bueren, Peter Volmink, James D. Weill.

Human Rights Watch Women's Rights Project

Staff
Dorothy Q. Thomas, Director; Regan E. Ralph, Washington Director; Samya Burney, LaShawn R. Jefferson, Research Associates; Kerry McArthur, Evelyn Miah, Associates; Robin Levi, Consultant; Jane Kim, Women's Law and Public Policy Fellow; Kulsum Wakabi, Leadership and Advocacy for Women in Africa Fellow.

Advisory Committee
Kathleen Peratis, Chair; Nahid Toubia, Vice Chair; Mahnaz Afkhami, Abdullahi An-Na'im, Helen Bernstein, Alice Brown, Charlotte Bunch, Rhonda Copelon, Lisa Crooms, Patricia Derian, Gina Despres, Joan Dunlop, Mallika Dutt, Martha Fineman, Claire Flom, Adrienne Germain, Leslie Glass, Lisa Hedley, Zhu Hong, Stephen Isaacs, Marina Pinto Kaufman, Gara LaMarche, Wangari Maathai, Joyce

Mends-Cole, Marysa Navarro-Aranguren, Donna Nevel, Susan Petersen, Celina Romany, Margaret Schuler, Domna Stanton.

Human Rights Watch California

Advisory Committee
Stanley K. Sheinbaum, Honorary, Chair; Mike Farrell, Jane Olson, Co-Chairs; Clara A. "Zazi" Pope, Vice Chair; Joan Willens

Beerman, Rabbi Leonard Beerman, Justin Connolly, Chiara Di Geronimo, Alan Gleitsman, Danny Glover, Paul Hoffman, Barry Kemp, Maggie Kemp, Li Lu, Lynda Palevsky, Tom Parker, Alison Dundes Renteln, Tracy Rice, Vicki Riskin, Cheri Rosche, Lawrence Rose, Pippa Scott, Sid Sheinberg, Bill Temko, Andrea Van de Kamp, Francis M. Wheat, Dianne Wittenberg, Stanley Wolpert.